P. HAMPSON.
15/MAY/1976

Dam Buster

J. D. Carrick has depicted here the actual attack on the Mohne Dam by Lancaster ED906/G
piloted by Flight Lieutenant D. J. M. Maltby. While the reflection of the spotlights on the
water indicated the correct height of a mere sixty feet, the cylindrical bomb, revolving backwards at 500 r.p.m., was released during this 220 m.p.h. run-in. Skipping along to the dam
wall, it rolled down the dam face to the base where its explosion set up a reaction that split
the dam. While Maltby approached the critical part of this operation, other Lancasters of
No. 617 Squadron circled around in an attempt to draw off the anti-aircraft fire.

LANCASTER—THE STORY OF A FAMOUS BOMBER

Compiled and Written by
BRUCE ROBERTSON

Tone Paintings by
W. F. HEPWORTH, *M.S.I.A.*

Based on Original Drawings by
J. D. CARRICK

Produced by
D. A. RUSSELL, *C.Eng., F.I.Mech.E.*

First Published 1964
Second Impression 1965
Third (Revised) Impression 1967
Fourth Impression 1974

ISBN 0 900435 10 0

Library of Congress Card No. 63-14330
(United States)

A HARLEYFORD PUBLICATION
Model and Allied Publications Ltd.,
13–35 Bridge Street, Hemel Hempstead, Hertfordshire, England

PRINTED IN ENGLAND BY
CLARKE, DOBLE & BRENDON LTD., PLYMOUTH, DEVON

Symbols of Victory

The R.A.F.'s most famous bomber of World War II, the Avro Lancaster, with the most famous of the fighters, the Supermarine Spitfire.

Foreword

THIS book has been designed in four parts—a narrative by chapters, data in a type-by-type review, briefs on squadrons and units and the individual history of each Lancaster recorded in a log by serial number. Since the Lancaster evolved from the Manchester and the development progressed to the Shackleton, details of types other than Lancasters are recorded where considered appropriate, particularly the Lincoln, which was originally a mark of Lancaster. The general arrangement drawings, spaced throughout the book, show each major step in the design. In the course of this progression several changes occurred in the official nomenclature. Role prefixes to mark numbers were introduced in 1942, and in 1948 the mark number form changed from Roman to Arabic figure presentation; later, the G.R. for General Reconnaissance was changed to M.R. for Maritime Reconnaissance. Thus, in an attempt to be accurate for each period there results a consistent inconsistency! Where possible I have used the serial number of the particular aircraft concerned, rather than the word Lancaster.

Merlin was a wizard — of over 1,000 horse-power. The common factor of Spitfire the famous fighter and Lancaster the famous bomber— the Rolls - Royce Merlin engine.

My grateful thanks are due to the 'Lancaster Syndicate', a group consisting of Brian Goulding, Ray Sturtivant, Michael Garbett, R. C. B. Ashworth and D. E. Monk, who have made a joint study of the Lancaster and who placed their extensive records and material at my disposal. Frank Cheesman and Michael J. F. Bowyer have been closely associated with this book, supplying information and making valuable suggestions. For the details of Lancaster aircrew members in training I drew on the personal experiences of Charles Clark. David Johnson briefed me on the service histories of Lancasters and Lincolns in Australia and Miss Jean Alexander outlined the chapter on Operation Paravane.

For access to official records I am indebted to L. A. Jackets, Esq., and his staff, particularly E. H. Turner, Esq., of the Air Historical Branch, Ministry of Defence. I am also indebted to various officials of the Ministry of Aviation and the Imperial War Museum.

To the hundreds of persons who have assisted in various ways I offer my sincere thanks and note especially Wing Commander G. W. Bennington, D.F.M.; Peter Corbell, Esq.; J. Clack, Esq., D.F.M.; E. Dean, Esq., A.M.C.T., Assistant Chief Engineer-Administrative, Avro Whitworth Division, Hawker Siddeley Group; M. J. Evans, Esq., Historical and Information Officer, Rolls-Royce Ltd.; Mrs. P. Fraser; P. C. Finucane, Esq.; Roger Freeman, Esq.; Bryan Gibbins for compilation work; S. Gover, Chief Aircraft Engineer, College of Aeronautics; John R. Gray, Esq., D.F.C., M.I.A.M.A., Public Relations Officer, Hawker Siddeley Aviation, Avro Whitworth Group; C. L. Hatton, Esq.; H. Hill, Esq.; J. R. Hitchcock, Esq., Technical Publications Manager, Boulton Paul Aircraft Ltd.; Harry Holmes, Esq.; Alexander Johnston, Esq.; Miss M. Patricia Key, Assistant Press Officer, Bristol Siddeley Engines Ltd.; Wing Commander R. V. Manning, R.C.A.F.; E. B. Morgan, Esq.; J. H. Orrell, Esq., O.B.E., Flight Superintendent, Hawker Siddeley Dynamics Ltd.; Ernest Stott, Chief Information Officer, Royal Aircraft Establishment; G. A. Thorne, Esq., D.S.O., D.F.C.; G. A. Whitehead, Esq., A.M.C.T., A.F.R.Ae.S., Deputy Chief Engineer, Avro Whitworth Division, Hawker Siddeley Group; Donald C. Wood, Esq.; Gerrie S. Zwanenburg, Esq.

London, July 1964.   BRUCE ROBERTSON.

ACKNOWLEDGMENTS FOR PHOTOGRAPHS

The publishers and author gratefully acknowledge the following sources, listed alphabetically, of photographs and certain drawings: *Air Britain*; Messrs. Air Service Training Ltd.; R. C. B. Ashworth, Esq.; Messrs. Austin Motors Ltd.; Messrs. Boulton Paul Ltd.; British Aircraft Corporation (Filton) Ltd. and Bristol Siddeley Engines Ltd.; Flight Lieutenant D. R. Bull, D.F.C.; *John Bull*; Canadian Department of Defence and National Aviation Museum, Ottawa; T. B. Cole, Esq.; Squadron Leader F. P. J. L. Danckwardt; G. F. Davis, Esq.; Ministry of Defence; Flight Sergeant Dobson; *Flight International*; *Flygslaben*; Fox Photos; Michael Garbett, Esq.; Bryan Gibbins, Esq.; Brian Goulding, Esq.; C. J. Hatton, Esq.; Hawker Siddeley Aviation Ltd., Avro Whitworth Division; F. Hartley, Esq.; Terry J. Hobbs, Esq.; C. Hollard, Esq.; Harry Holmes, Esq.; Imperial War Museum; David Johnson, Esq.; Messrs. Martin & Kelman; R. Meads, Esq.; E. Meos, Esq.; D. E. Monk, Esq.; Napier Aero Engines Ltd.; R. A. Neal, Esq.; Heinz J. Nowarra, Esq.; Messrs. Power Jets Ltd.; Royal Aircraft Establishment; T. B. O'Brien, Esq.; Messrs. Real Photographs Ltd.; Messrs. Rolls-Royce Ltd.; Roger Caratini, Esq.; Royal Australian Air Force; Messrs. Samson Clark; C. P. Smith, Esq.; Eric Tayler, Esq.; Messrs. Temple Press; F. Tutton, Esq.; Wing Commander P. Ward Hunt; Charles S. Waterfull, Esq.; Gerrie S. Zwanenburg, Esq.

About This Book

By **D. A. RUSSELL**, *C. Eng., F.I.Mech.E.*

Markings of war. 101 operations were made by NE181, which made its century on January 29th, 1945, when with No. 75 (New Zealand) Squadron. It was earmarked to fly to New Zealand for preservation, but was later destroyed.

IT was logical that *Lancaster—The Story of a Famous Bomber* should follow *Spitfire—The Story of a Famous Fighter*; thus are documented the two most famous aircraft types of the R.A.F. in World War II. Both aircraft had their beginnings pre-war and both continued in service post-war.

The Spitfire book, first published in 1960 and revised the following year, has set a style in aircraft type history books, and the same pattern has been followed with Lancaster—a narrative supported with detailed drawings, many photographs and technical detail in appendices. With Lancaster an additional and important step farther has been taken—the documentation of each and every Lancaster. With over 20,000 Spitfires built, it would not have been possible to record all within the confines of a Harleyford book; with over 7,000 Lancasters built this presented a formidable research and compilation task, but it has been achieved after much searching in official archives, perusing hundreds of personal log-books and by correspondence world-wide. This is believed to be the first time ever that such a compilation has been published for an aircraft type built in thousands.

One of the most interesting, and indeed controversial, of matters is the dam-busting Lancasters of No. 617 Squadron specially modified in the spring of 1943. Recently published drawings are claimed to be authentic and various authorities are quoted, but these are at variance with drawings shown here which are supported by actual photographic evidence (see pages 30, 31 and 129). These other drawings were said, in July this year, to have been made possible by a recent tracing of information. One of the authorities mentioned said that he understood that all drawings of the modification were destroyed on Ministry instructions for security reasons! THIS WAS NOT SO.

Markings of peace. From May 28th, 1947, a series of flight-refuelled flights were made from London Airport to Bermuda, 3,355 miles non-stop, by converted Lancasters taking in 1,700 gallons of fuel over the Atlantic.

The information on the special modification to the dam-busting Lancasters was released at 10.30 a.m. on October 18th, 1962. Ministry of Aviation sanction having been obtained, it was the prerogative of Messrs. A. V. Roe Ltd., whose property the drawings were, to release the information. The general arrangement drawing Z2352, titled 'Lancaster Type 464 Provisioning', dated March 1st, 1943, was produced and spread out in an office at Messrs. A. V. Roe's Chadderton works. The firm's security officer, a retired wing commander, in the presence of two senior staff members of the firm, struck out the words "MOST SECRET" on the drawing, appended his signature to this declassification and HANDED IT TO THE ONLY OTHER PERSON PRESENT—THE AUTHOR OF THIS BOOK. It was passed on immediately to Harleyford's draughtsmen.

At this time Messrs. A. V. Roe Ltd. had already supplied drawings for the draughtsmen to use in the preparation of the 1/144th scale tone paintings presented here. The markings on the aircraft drawings shown in the type-by-type review were recorded by M. J. F. Bowyer when touring East Anglian airfields at a time when cameras, except by official photographers, were forbidden.

LANCASTER—THE STORY OF A FAMOUS BOMBER appears when the number of Lancasters still flying can be counted on one hand. Their day is over, and now is the time to record their history, before memories fade and records are lost. For this book the past has been retraced, new facts have been brought to light and the hitherto unpublished information and many rare photographs are presented with all that was known to make complete the Lancaster story.

Lancaster — The Story of a Famous Bomber

CONTENTS

		Page
Painting, "Dam Buster" ... ... by J. D. Carrick		Frontispiece
Author's Preface ... ... by Bruce Robertson		3
About This Book ... ... by D. A. Russell, C.Eng., F.I.Mech.E.		4
Narrative (contained in chapters one to nineteen: see below)		7 to 108
Manchester/Lancaster/Lincoln Squadron Briefs		109 to 119
Manchester/Lancaster/Lincoln Unit Briefs		122 and 123
Type-by-Type Review : Manchester, Lancaster, Lincoln, Lancastrian, Shackleton		124 to 144
Manchester and Lancaster Log : A Brief on each and every Manchester and Lancaster by Serial Number		145 to 211
Glossary and Index		215 and 216

NARRATIVE

Chapter	Title	Page	Chapter	Title	Page
One	A Need is Specified	7	Ten	Battle of Berlin	50
Two	The Manchester	9	Eleven	They Flew Lancasters	58
Three	The Lancaster Enters Service	14	Twelve	Battle of France	63
Four	The First Lancaster Group	18	Thirteen	Operation Paravane	74
Five	Threefold Expansion	26	Fourteen	Producing to Perfection	79
Six	Special Operation	30	Fifteen	Instrument of Victory	82
Seven	Battle of the Ruhr	34	Sixteen	Variations on a Theme	90
Eight	A Matter Still in the Air	42	Seventeen	Post-war Prospects	95
Nine	Wings for Victory	45	Eighteen	From Lancaster to Lincoln	101
			Nineteen	Developments Civil and Military	106

DOUBLE-PAGE 1/144th SCALE THREE-VIEW TONE PAINTINGS

	Page		Page		Page		Page
Manchester I	24	Lancaster G.R.3 ...	72	Lincoln B.30	120	Shackleton M.R.1 ...	168
Lancaster I	40	Lancaster B.VII ...	88	Lancastrian III ...	136	Shackleton M.R.2 ...	184
Lancaster II	56	Lincoln B.I	104	York I	152	Shackleton M.R.3 ...	200

PICTORIAL FEATURES

	Page		Page		Page
Symbols of Victory	2	Target for Tonight	48	Lancaster Personalities	112
To Maintain a Lancaster in the Air	6	The Lancaster Could Take It	55	Lancaster Miscellany	212
		Aussie Emblems	62	Lincoln Miscellany	213
Dam Busters	33	Lancaster Build-up	78	Crew Haunts	214

TABLES

	Page		Page
Breakdown of Production : Manchester, Lancaster, Lincoln	94	Lancaster Squadrons at Bomber Command Peak Strength, August 1944	94

MAP

	Page
Lancaster Locations	71

DIAGRAMS

	Page		Page
Lancaster Cutaway Drawing	130	Lincoln Cutaway Drawing	131

To maintain a Lancaster in the air . . .

THE LANCASTER

Petrol bowser and crew.   *Mobile workshop and crew.*

Corporal mechanic, four aircraftmen (mechanics), engineer officer, fitter (armourer), three armourers, radio mechanic, two instrument repairers, three bomb handlers, fitter.

Bomb train with W.A.A.F. driver and bombing-up crew.

Flight maintenance crew: N.C.O. fitter, mechanic, N.C.O. fitter, five mechanics, electrical mechanic, instrument repairer, two radio mechanics.

Flying control officer, W.A.A.F. parachute packer, meteorological officer, pilot, navigator, air bomber, flight engineer, wireless operator/air gunner, two air gunners.

CHAPTER ONE

A Need is Specified

Roy Chadwick, Avro's chief designer and thereby responsible for the Lancaster, photographed (right) during a drawing office discussion. He remained with the firm from the 1914-1918 War until he was killed, together with the firm's chief test pilot, S.A. "Bill" Thorne, and two technicians, when the prototype Tudor 2 G-AGSU crashed at Woodford August 23rd, 1947.

Origin in this practical world is usually itself a result of requirement and in this respect it could be said that the Lancaster was evoked as much by Adolf Hitler as by any British subject.

An expansion of the Royal Air Force had commenced from mid-1934 when a striking force target of 500 bombers by March 1939 was set. Within a year, as a result of Sir John Simon and the then Mr. Anthony Eden visiting Germany and meeting Herr Hitler, the target figure was not only raised to 840 bombers, the time was reduced by two years. Before 1935 was out, the effect of the Abyssinian War and the attitude of Germany caused the target to rise to over 1,000 bombers by March 1939. This increased the whole tempo of production and while in actual orders it represented Battles, Blenheims, Hampdens, Whitleys and Wellingtons the seeds were sown for the heavier bombers to come.

Since the effectiveness of a bomber force was measured largely by the bomb load that could be lifted, numbers of aircraft were not a true guide to the value of a striking force. Specifications sponsored in May 1936 by Group Captain R. D. Oxland, Director of Operational Requirements at the Air Ministry, called for a four-engined bomber Specification B.12/36 and a twin-engined bomber P.13/36. Detailed data set out requirements relating to bomb loads, speeds, operational heights, all-round defence and buoyancy in the event of landing on water. Even at that early date, the carriage of a single 8,000 lb bomb was envisaged and a maximum of 12,000 lb in bomb load was written into the specification. Mine-laying was apparently not considered a task for a bomber at this time, but torpedoes were and the bomb bay had to be capable of accommodating two. A surprising requirement was for resting quarters for the crew. Initial production Manchesters actually had a pull-down sprung bed. These were soon removed—with a certain station

engineer staking a first claim for one of them!

The requirement met with some severe criticism by the finance branches of the Air Ministry. Quite apart from the cost of sponsoring prototypes and production, the fact that such weighty machines would involve costly works of hard standings and runways, and an increase in the size of airfields entailing the acquisition of new land, led to alternatives being suggested. A large hydro-pneumatic catapult had been designed in 1935 by P. Salmon of the Royal Aircraft Establishment to achieve frictionless take-off and its possibilities were considered. The Air Staff were not averse to experiments on these lines which showed promise of permitting take-off in any direction irrespective of wind. Thus into Specification P.13/36 was written an additional requirement, 'stressed for frictionless take-off'.

Several firms tendered designs to the 1936 bomber specifications and two prototypes of two types to B.12/36 were ordered in 1937 from Supermarine and Short Bros; the former, designed by R. J. Mitchell, were destroyed by bombing during construction in 1940 and the latter developed into the Short Stirling, which is another story. The P.13/36 prototype led to the Handley Page H.P.56 and the Avro 679. The Handley Page contender, due to anticipated shortages of the Rolls-Royce engines, was abandoned in favour of a four-engined aircraft and developed into the H.P.57 Halifax while the Avro 679 became the Manchester, forerunner of the Lancaster. Within weeks of ordering the prototypes, a production order was placed for two hundred to a new standard indicated in Specification 19/37. A wooden mock-up was built at Avro's Newton Heath factory; this was viewed by officials from Metropolitan-Vickers who were asked in 1938 to co-operate with Avro in its production.

The Manchester was large compared with its twin-engined contemporaries, and in concept, if not configuration, it was considered four-engined in that its two engines were actually double engines. It was to be powered by Vultures, a new Rolls-Royce engine which was in effect two Kestrels (the power unit of the famous Hawker Hart series) with a common crankcase. Mated, the two 12-cylinder 'V' engines became one 24-cylinder 'X' type.

To prove the engine before installation, Hawker Aircraft were asked early in 1939 to modify the prototype Hawker Henley, K5115, to take a Vulture in place of its Merlin for development flying and within months it was sent to Hucknall, the Rolls-Royce test and development airfield. Unfortunately the new engine proved particularly troublesome and another Henley, L3302, had to be sent.

Meanwhile, at Harwell, work started in 1938 on the installation of the catapult was going ahead. This too had its snags and in the fall of 1939 it was abandoned in favour of a new R.A.F. catapult development for frictionless take-off using a long truck with trolleys for mounting aircraft. The wheels fitted into cradles and the tail was held by struts, in the flying attitude.

The prototype Manchester, L7246, was test flown on July 25th, 1939, by Captain H. A. Brown. This 17-minute flight from Ringway was not very satisfactory. The Vultures were not giving the power calculated and with the high wing loading it made the aircraft difficult—perhaps dangerous—to fly. To provide more lift the wing was later extended by ten feet to give a ninety-foot span.

Although war had not then been declared, the tests were conducted in strict secrecy and no mention appeared in the Press. The aircraft was then known as the Avro P.13/36. Its ninth flight, on November 28th, 1939, was to the Aircraft and Armament Experimental Establishment at Boscombe Down for service evaluation. So powerful were the Vultures considered that precautions were taken to avoid injury by the wash of the propellers and red flags were staked out behind it. Then, because of reports of instability, it went on to the Royal Aircraft Establishment at Farnborough for aerodynamic tests. A central fin was added to the rear fuselage making the Manchester a 'three-tailed' aircraft and the

second prototype, which did not fly until May 26th, 1940, had this fitted. Later the shape was modified and although production aircraft initially had central fins these were later removed from many. The second aircraft, L7247, unlike the first, had armament installed, consisting of six .303 Browning guns; two each in nose, ventral and tail turrets. The ventral FN21A turret gave way in service to a dorsal position. The wings were increased in span and it was unfortunate that when the Manchester was given a full release to the Press general arrangement drawings of the original Manchester were handed out to the technical press.

Meanwhile L7246 was being tried on the catapult. A Handley Page Heyford was tried first and took the air in a seemingly effortless manner. The Manchester, however, at 37,000 lb, was three times the Heyford's weight. There was not a little difficulty in cradling it into the trolleys and considerable apprehension as the area was cleared for the first demonstration. There were sighs of relief as the monster, with its Vultures roaring, was literally hurled from Farnborough. But after having proved the feasibility of launching bombers thus, the project lapsed.

Production followed quickly on the prototype. L7276, the first production model, left for Boscombe Down on August 5th, 1940. The Battle of Britain was approaching its climax and the threat of invasion, following the collapse of France, imbued workers with a sense of urgency. Fighters, for the moment, were given overriding priority and in all factories engaged on war work the tempo of production increased. First there were long, wearing hours of overtime which was replaced, as labour became organised, with shifts so that work went on non-stop twenty-four hours a day.

However willing the workers were, there was little point in pushing an aircraft unless it was sound. Tests with the two prototypes were engendering a spate of modifications and it was October 25th before L7277, the second production aircraft, got away to Boscombe Down. Needs were pressing and that same month L7278 was sent to No. 27 Maintenance Unit at Shawbury, earmarked for No. 207 Squadron. The first Manchester had been delivered for service.

The first of the Manchesters, L7246 first flew from Ringway on July 24th, 1939, in the hands of Captain H. A. Brown. Due to instability on tests it was fitted with a third fin on the fuselage.

On test the modified first prototype Manchester force-landed near Boscombe Down and slithered along rows of cabbages, which were rammed into the fuselage. It was dismantled and taken to Newton Heath for repair.

No. 207 Squadron R.A.F. had a record of which they were justly proud. As No. 7 Squadron R.N.A.S. they had been one of the first units to fly the famous giants of the 1914-1918 War, the Handley Pages—types 0/100 and 0/400. When the Royal Naval Air Service and Royal Flying Corps amalgamated to form the Royal Air Force, they, as an R.N.A.S. squadron, had '200' added to their squadron number to become No. 207 Squadron, R.A.F. Apart from a short period, a mere eleven days in fact, they had been in existence since November 1916. With this tradition their personnel found it irksome that when war came they were a non-operational unit at Cranfield where they were later absorbed into No. 12 Operational Training Unit. However, on November 1st, 1940, No. 207 Squadron was re-formed as a separate entity at Waddington to fly the new, and still secret, twin-engined Manchester.

The original Manchester allotted to the squadron arrived at Waddington from Shawbury on November 10th, but it was preceded by L7279 which, in spite of a delay because of bad weather, had been quickly processed through No. 6 Maintenance Unit at Brize Norton. These two were extensively flown throughout November to complete 500 flying hours, during which time Rolls-Royce representatives supervised engine maintenance. Early the next month L7280 arrived and the build-up of the squadron commenced.

By the end of the year some twenty Manchesters had left the works, but they could not be regarded as satisfactory. They did not have Standard Beam Approach equipment which was planned for the 21st and subsequent aircraft, and other important modifications recommended as a result of A. & A.E.E. testing were not embodied. Following a visit by Sir Robert Renwick of the Ministry of Aircraft Production on December 9th, it was agreed that the squadron should be allotted aircraft after the first twenty. But, apart from the service snags, a major hitch in output occurred due to production being held up on high pressure couplings of which the producers were then the sole suppliers, and 600 of these were required for each Manchester. For a time they

were the limiting factor in production and No. 207 Squadron was forced to keep their early models.

After six early Manchesters had been intensively flown on Bomber Command's instructions, for which L7278, L7279, L7280, L7283, L7284 and L7286 were selected, another round of modifications started. Exhausts in the Vulture frequently burnt through and trouble with the rocker arms ensued. One aircraft, L7295, went to Rolls-Royce for flame damping tests; ironically it was fated to be burnt out.

Wing Commander N. C. Hyde at Waddington, anxious to get his squadron operational, kept four aircraft fully serviceable, while the others underwent modification to both engines and airframes. In early January, shortly before the squadron was declared operational—at least in part strength —they were visited by Their Majesties the King and Queen.

The existence of the Manchester was revealed to the Royal Air Force as a whole by an Air Ministry Order of January 9th, 1941. This information was restricted to the Service as it was policy not to reveal new aircraft types until they had flown over enemy territory. Six crews were ready and A. V. Roe had provided a working party at the station to keep abreast of the modifications, when an administrative snag arose over the congestion of aircraft at Waddington. When the squadron received its first operation order at short notice, on February 24th, nine of their Manchesters were dispersed out at Coleby Grange.

A *Hipper* Class cruiser was reported at Brest and together with thirty aircraft detailed from No. 3 Group, and 25 Hampdens of No. 5 Group, were six Manchesters. On this first Manchester operation, L7279, L7284, L7286, L7288 and L7294, with the C.O. in L7300, participated. They all returned safely, but Wg. Cdr. Hyde was forced to land at Boscombe Down through oil on the windscreen obscuring his view and L7284 crashed on landing back at Waddington due to failure of the hydraulic system, fortunately without injury to the crew. One important fact emerged from the de-briefing of this operation—that the bomb-aimers could

9

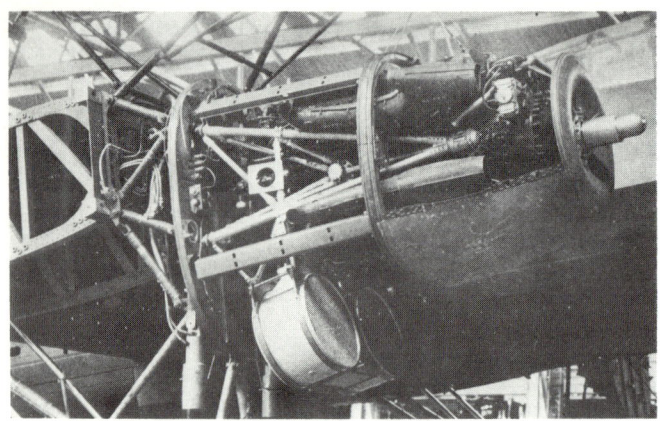

The Vulture engine of the Manchester. The Manchester was the victim of the consequences of placing an engine in service before it had been fully developed, but any recriminations must be tempered by an understanding of the tenor of the times—the year Britain declared war on Germany.

not observe the result of their aiming, and modification action was put in hand to incorporate a new perspex panel.

Two days later the squadron were detailed to join in an attack on Cologne, but due to trouble with the hydraulic system only five were serviceable and one of these came back shortly after take-off with its hydraulics unserviceable and another with low oil pressure only reached Flushing, where its bombs were dropped on the docks.

The trouble with the hydraulic system was that the oil was seeping out and affecting the operating of the under-carriages. The oil also seeped into the undercarriage micro-switches and by their malfunctioning the pilot was not receiving the assurance via his indicator lights that the wheels were safely locked up or down, even if they were.

Lockheed engineers were called in to advise on the hydraulics and Alan Kelsall of Pye Ltd. went to Manchester to consult with A. V. Roe on the vulnerability of the vital switches. As a result the actual press-button of the switches was integrated with an oilskin diaphragm sealed into the sides of the switch case—but how to test each one to prove that the inside, with the contact points, was in fact airtight without breaking the seal was a problem confronting the makers and raised by the Aeronautical Inspection Direc-torate. This was solved overnight with tubing, a bicycle pump and a rod of whalebone! It was argued that if air pumped into each switch could not escape then that switch was sound. A bicycle pump was mounted on a board con-nected through tubes to a suction pad while a junction went to a large glass 'U' tube filled with water. If pumping air through a hole drilled in the case raised the water (replaced by red ink to give a better indication) and it held steady, then the switch was airtight; if it did not the switch leaked and was rejected. As for the small hole—it was plugged with whalebone and sealed with resin. This solved the matter for the switches, but not the system. That was resolved by changing the couplings at the expense of pro-duction output.

This all took time. Only five aircraft were reported at readiness when orders were received for the squadron to participate in a raid on Hamburg on March 13th. L7319, the last of the five to set out, was delayed by a burst tyre.

This caused the squadon's first loss when, racing after the others, it was intercepted by a German intruder five miles from Waddington and shot down in flames. Only one crew member survived. Soon afterwards the unit moved to Coningsby airfield.

By that time the existence of the Manchester was generally known from a Press release of March 5th which stated: 'Manchester—bomber, Engines—two, Manufacturer —A. V. Roe.' No other details were given, but the American Press was full of hints. The Minister of Aircraft Production, Lord Beaverbrook, in a speech to the House of Lords on April 23rd, spoke rather sardonically of the American allusions—'The Manchester has a 90 foot span, speed of 325 m.p.h. and two engines. The Americans do not tell you what the engines are, but I will tell you they are Vultures.' Perhaps, with no bomb load, in a dive, with a following wind, the noble lord's figure of 325 m.p.h. could be fully justified!

No. 207 Squadron could not share Lord Beaverbrook's optimism. However, the die was cast. The Manchester was in production and committed to service. Not only were they coming from A. V. Roe's Manchester factory, but Messrs. Metropolitan Vickers, with whom an order had been placed in 1939, delivered R5768, their first Manchester, to Woodford for A. V. Roe to assemble and test. It flew on March 10th and later it joined No. 83 Squadron.

New squadrons had been forming with Manchesters. Second to receive this type was No. 97 (Straits Settlements) Squadron which, like No. 207, had been reinstated as an operational squadron after being absorbed in an O.T.U. The Straits Settlements, following a precedent in the First World War, had donated a large sum of money to finance a bomber squadron and at a time when most contributions were from donors enamoured with fighters in general and Spitfires in particular. The new squadron formed around a nucleus provided by No. 207 Squadron—at the very time they were making their first operational raids. However, they moved their aircraft from Waddington to Coningsby, which allowed No. 207 to bring its Manchesters back from dispersal at Coleby.

Most of the initial mechanical troubles with the Manchester appeared to have been solved by March 1941. Unfortunately, solving the series of relatively minor mechanical troubles did nothing to remedy the basic fault of lack of sufficient power. On one engine it quickly lost height and this, added to the fact that the engines them-selves were still giving trouble, made the Manchester a tricky machine to fly. At this time the new four-engined Stirling was the 'star' and the Manchester with its twin engines of doubtful worth came a very poor second.

One of the two original service Manchesters was lost through an engine failing on the night of March 21st. It had bombed Lorient and was nearing its airfield when the port engine seized up and caught fire. As the aircraft lost height rapidly the pilot ordered the crew to bale out while he tried to bring the machine down. Two of the crew were killed after jumping as the machine was already very low and as the pilot brought it into a field for a belly landing near Wymondham the port wing struck a tree, which caused the machine to slew round and crash, killing two more members of the crew and injuring another. A matter kept highly secret at the time was the fact that two U.S. naval officers went on this submarine base raid—at a time when America was still officially neutral.

Early next month No. 207 lost their Commanding Officer during an attack on Kiel shipyards. Fortunately he and his crew escaped with their lives as they were reported as prisoners-of-war.

As a result of the Wymondham crash and engine defects on other machines, a new fault was traced to engine bearings and all Manchesters were grounded on April 13th. While thus inoperative, modifications were put in hand to enable a 4,000 lb bomb to be carried, which involved new racks. The flying ban was lifted after a few days to permit test flying and was extended to include training flights, and then to limited operations. No. 97 Squadron commenced operations on April 8th when four of their aircraft took off to attack Kiel. Later in the month No. 207 flew L7379 with a 4,000 lb bomb and a few nights later, on May 3rd, L7377 and L7378 with a four thousand pounder apiece dropped them over Cologne.

On May 10th Berlin was reached by a single Manchester which dropped five 1,000 lb bombs, three 250 lb bombs—and a packet of leaflets! There were complaints of the Manchester's climbing ability with full load and during May a series of war-load tests were flown. June brought another grounding, on the 16th, to effect modifications to the engine cooling and cabin heating.

The Manchester squadrons were non-operational until June 22nd when, almost as if for a morale booster to let them bomb something, an attack was ordered—on Boulogne! It would seem as if the Manchester was an ill-fated machine in every way, for after L7314 of No. 207 Squadron had taken off, the Midland area controller informed all aircraft of an intruder in the area. A Beaufighter of No. 25 Squadron, closing in on an A.I. response, shot at an assumed twin-tailed Dornier and the Manchester fell at Wollaston, Northants, killing all seven of the crew. At about the same time a Defiant was attacking Manchester L7325 of No. 97 Squadron within three miles of Coningsby. The Manchester pilot, with great presence of mind, dived and ordered the colours of the night to be fired. At this the Defiant stopped firing, but the Manchester had already been damaged.

Apart from these distressing accidents a series of mishaps had occurred during an operation which, to use the phraseology of the time, should have been a 'piece of cake'. A billowing parachute inadvertently opened by a front gunner had caused one Manchester to turn back, and another landing at Biggin Hill with a blazing engine made it evident that all engine 'bugs' had not been eliminated.

Again the Manchesters were grounded, on June 30th, for engine overhauls, with the exception of a single machine allotted to each squadron with engines overhauled by Rolls-Royce and incorporating all the latest modifications. They were to be flown for 250 hours as soon as possible by intensive day flying and servicing at night. Like everything else with the Manchester, this did not go without incident. L7389 of No. 61 Squadron landed with its undercarriage up at Fowlmere and L7426 took over as the trials aircraft. No. 97's machine, L7427, had an engine seizure and lost height rapidly; the pilot managed to keep control and bring it down to a crash landing two miles east of Spalding without harm to the crew.

By flying the selected Manchesters fifteen hours a day with a three-shift crew the 250 hours were soon completed and the engines went back to Rolls-Royce for their verdict on the future of the Vulture.

Yet again came a spate of modifications and by then seven squadrons were concerned, Nos. 49, 50, 61, 83, 97, 106 and 207. To maintain operations some of these were partially re-equipped with other bomber types, chiefly Hampdens. Some of No. 207's personnel were switched to No. 408 (R.C.A.F.) Squadron and the squadron was later re-organised on a two flight basis with 'A' Flight operational and 'B' Flight training.

Operations with Manchesters were resumed on August 7th, after which two more faults showed up. The first, tail flutter, was tackled by an Avro test pilot who took a Manchester up at Waddington with full load and experienced the buffeting encountered with the aircraft climbing. By restricting further the rate of climb quoted in the Pilot's Handling Notes for the type, this was settled without grounding, if not remedied. The tail was again modified and the twin-fin configuration later familiar on the Lancaster was adopted. No. 97 Squadron received their first modified machine, L7489, on September 20th.

The second fault concerned propellers. Already handicapped by an unsatisfactory power/weight ratio through the vagaries of its engines, the Manchester was further bedevilled by erratic behaviour of the feathering

Second of the Manchester prototypes, L7247, the first with armament. Both prototypes ended their flying days as ground instructional airframes.

Manchester L7316 of No. 207 Squadron shot down near the Frisian Islands being examined by Nazi troops.

units of the propellers. The feathering of a propeller whether by mechanical fault or intent left the Manchester with insufficient power to remain airborne. L7375 came down with a feathered airscrew four miles north of Boston, near East Sibsey, while actually on an airscrew feathering exercise. But operations were still going on, in spite of mishaps in routine flying. When L7487 dropped into the North Sea, on the night of October 21st, drowning its crew eighteen miles off the Norfolk coast, it was linked both with the earlier bearing trouble and the more recent feathering troubles. Earlier that very day, R5783 had flopped into marshland at Frisking three miles south of Wainfleet with an engine that had failed when the machine was barely at a thousand feet. Before October was out, L7422 had landed in farmland and L7308 in a field bordering Woodhall Spa airfield. Both pilots had experienced loss of power, forcing them to make immediate landings, and in the latter case it was proved that both propellers had feathered. It was evident that the Manchester had yet another snag.

While attention turned to the propellers, deliveries were being made to O.T.Us. Plans were already in hand to limit production and produce a four-engined version as will be related. At the O.T.Us. the Manchester had little to commend itself to either pupils or instructors. No. 25 O.T.U. lost L7428 on the night of November 18th. Five days later another Manchester, L7300 of No. 207 Squadron, had a most spectacular crash. Turning into the wind to land, the aircraft suddenly yawed to starboard at an altitude of a

mere 200 feet. The pilot instantly opened up the engines to gain height. The Manchester shuddered violently with the pilot in only partial control. It skimmed over treetops and while the pilot fought his losing battle for power and altitude the tail struck the ground, causing the machine to slew round and then skid along the surface into a lake. Miraculously, all the occupants, nine in this case, escaped with their lives; albeit they were severely shaken—and so was their confidence in the Manchester.

Yet operations continued. At this time the Manchester was, numerically, the most important of the heavy bombers. The Wellingtons and Whitleys had been re-classified as medium bombers, leaving the Manchester, Halifax and Stirling in the heavy category. (The Lancaster had not then evolved to operational status.) Of 531 operational bombers in Bomber Command only 66 were 'heavies'—17 Halifaxes, 18 Stirlings and 31 Manchesters. Over a hundred Manchesters had left the two factories, but many were non-operational in training units and non-effective in maintenance units—and then there were the write-offs.

No. 97 Squadron, victims of the Manchester's failings, had to bear the gibes of a neighbouring Wellington squadron who referred to them unkindly as—The 97th of Foot! It was a joke of dubious taste in No. 207 Squadron that squadron reunions would be held in P.O.W. camps. The C.O. of this squadron arranged an emergency code, to be tapped out when a forced landing was imminent to provide statistics on losses as by 'Fighters', 'Flak' or 'Engine Failure'. There is record of reception of only one such message before crashing—and that was 'Engines'!

The appropriate experimental establishments were vitally concerned with the shortcomings of the Manchester, but they had little need to go to squadrons as their troubles came to their door-step, so to speak. L7320, attached to the Aircraft and Armament Experimental Establishment, was being tested with full bomb load on December 12th and unaccountably lost height. The pilot brought it down in Potts Field, Elstead, Surrey. Two days after Christmas, the engine revolutions of L7483 suddenly dropped as it was coming in to land at Martlesham Heath. To prevent a stall the pilot opened up intending to go round again. The speed increased but the Manchester continued to lose height and having hit the ground lightly the pilot cut the engines and went careering through the boundary fence.

There were a number of incidents of Manchesters overshooting. Probably pilots, well aware of its limitation

Manchester Railway!
A Manchester on the catapult rig at Farnborough in 1942. Another Manchester is visible near the hangars.

12

in power, preferred a fast landing with the possibility of overshooting, to the chances of a stall on the approach. The Royal Aircraft Establishment were sufficiently impressed to devise an arrester gear. This was tried out with a Manchester which was brought to rest from 72 m.p.h. in 460 yards. One hundred and twenty sets were ordered for various airfields in 1942 but, as with the catapult, the idea lapsed.

Whatever the shortcomings of the Manchester, there was little worry with morale. The crew of R5796, bent on causing the maximum destruction in Munster, on January 21st, 1942, soon located their target by the revealing horse-shoe shape of the Dortmund-Ems canal around the town. Six 1,000 lb bombs went down from 10,000 feet after a steady run in, after which the Manchester went down to 500 feet to machine-gun a train entering Bergstein Fort!

The famous bomber pilot Guy Gibson arriving to take over the Manchesters of No. 106 Squadron quotes Flt. Lt. P. J. Dunlop Mackenzie as saying ' These Manchesters. They're awful. The kite's all right, but it's the engine. They're fine when they keep turning but they don't often do so.' In a matter of days, Dunlop Mackenzie himself became a victim of the Manchesters when he crashed in Holland on March 25th in L7390. Gibson did achieve a record with Manchesters. The eight he detailed for mining on May 3rd was the greatest number of Manchesters ever sent out from one squadron on operations and two of these were the only Bomber Command aircraft lost that night.

In June 1942 the Manchester was withdrawn from operations, but there was no question of scrapping them. They were merely relegated and many found their way to

Manchester L7378 seen here in No. 207 Squadron service during February 1942, survived service in three squadrons and a heavy conversion unit, to finish its days as an instructional airframe.

No doubt there were many acts of heroism in Manchesters and the devotion to duty of one pilot was recognised by the posthumous award of the Victoria Cross, several months later. This happened on one of the last operations in which Manchesters participated, on the night of May 30th, 1942. Flying Officer L. T. Manser held L7301 unswervingly on its course at 7,000 feet over Mannheim as he made the bombing run in spite of intense and accurate anti-aircraft fire. Shrapnel repeatedly hit his machine and wounded the rear gunner as the pilot set course for home with his cabin swirling with smoke. He was forced down to a mere 1,000 feet and as he fought for height the port engine overheated and by the time he had climbed to 2,000 feet it burst into flames. It was ten minutes before the fire was brought under control, leaving a dud engine and a burnt wing.

Manser had no doubts about the trickiness in flying a Manchester on one engine. He knew his aircraft and this was his sixth operational flight with No. 50 Squadron. He appeared determined to stay with the aircraft and to fight to bring it back. Slowly it lost height and control difficulties increased. Manser ordered the crew to bale out and quickly one after the other Flg. Offs. Barnes and Horsley, Sgts. King, Mills, Naylor and Baveystock dropped out. Before leaving one of the N.C.O.s had handed Manser a parachute but he waved it away. As the others floated down, even before they reached the ground, Manser was dead. The Manchester had stalled, dived, hit the ground and burst into flames.

Conversion Units. These units had first started during 1941 in squadrons, where four aircraft formed an additional conversion flight. In October 1942 these flights were withdrawn from squadrons and integrated to form Conversion Units. Although the Manchester as a twin-engined aircraft was hardly suitable for pilot training, it did give crew members an excellent idea of the Lancaster's fuselage layout at a time when the latter type was not available in sufficient numbers to equip H.C.U.s. Later in 1943 the Manchesters' rather evil reputation kept them very much on the ground and a general redistribution took place.

There was one saving grace with this aircraft: the fact that its basic design was sound and that with sufficient power, as the Lancaster, it became the most effective bomber of the war. The verdict of history is not kind to the Manchester. It could hardly be otherwise. The official history, " The Strategic Air Offensive against Germany", makes no reference to the catalogue of mishaps recorded here, but reference is made to a 'brief and disastrous' operational career and there is a pronouncement—'that Bomber Command would have been ultimately stronger if the Manchester had never been produced'. This could be true and no doubt statistics present that view, but it is questioned whether or not the historians considered this issue: that had the Manchester never existed and failed, it is doubtful if the Lancaster would ever have evolved. There was no tabled Air Ministry requirement for the Lancaster, it resulted from the failure of the Manchester.

The first prototype Lancaster BT308 started life as a Manchester airframe, evident from the fin at the rear of the fuselage.

The Lancaster evolved from the Manchester; basically, it could be said to be a four-engined version of the latter. From the initial trials of the Manchester prototype, and even before that from engine tests, it was evident that the Vultures were not coming up to expectations. There were two projects for remedying the shortcomings: replacing the Vultures with two Napier Sabre or two Bristol Centaurus engines—tentatively allotted the designation Mk. II—or using four engines—provisionally the Manchester Mk. III. The second course was pursued first and as it proved successful the other project was abandoned.

A standard Manchester airframe was fitted with a new wing centre-section to take four Rolls-Royce Merlin engines, a type already proven in the Spitfire, Hurricane and Whitley. This machine, BT308, first flown on January 9th, 1941, was allotted to the A. & A.E.E. on February 28th and so successful was its debut that Manchester contracts with A. V. Roe and Metropolitan Vickers were amended to Lancasters to take effect after the 200th model of the former had left the production lines. Plans were for No. 5 Group to introduce the new bomber and the Group Commander, Air Vice-Marshal N. H. Bottomley, flew the prototype on February 1st.

After a second prototype, DG595, had flown on May 13th, 1941, production followed using the Manchester airframes under assembly. The first, L7527, flew on October 31st from Woodford and went to Boscombe Down for trials which were held up for a time when it landed with its wheels up. The second went in November to the Telecommunications Flying Unit at Hurn for the radio installation to be approved and it returned to A. V. Roe's airfield at Woodford on Christmas Eve. The third, L7529, was another machine for the A. & A.E.E. but the fourth, flying from Woodford on November 22nd, was the first ready for service.

Lancaster output from the Metropolitan-Vickers factory at Manchester commenced at this same period. The first went to Avro's Woodford factory for final assembly on January 5th, 1942, two followed the next month, three the next, five in April and so on in arithmetical progression as production in this second source of supply got under way. As early as June 12th, 1941, the Lancaster was announced to the Service as a 'variant of the Manchester I', but squadron deliveries did not commence until later.

No. 44 (Rhodesian) Squadron flew Hampdens which, in late 1941, were well past their prime. It was with great

satisfaction, therefore, that the squadron learnt that they would be the first to be equipped with the new Lancaster and the prototype, BT308, was demonstrated to them on September 15th, 1941. The squadron was an integral part of Bomber Command with Rhodesian aircrew and, at the time, 128 of the 490 ground crew were Rhodesians, under the command of Wg. Cdr. R. A. B. Learoyd, V.C., who was posted temporarily to Boscombe Down in December to familiarise himself with the new Lancaster.

On Christmas Eve 1941, their first Lancasters, L7537, L7538 and L7541, arrived at Waddington and, apart from the odd diversion to the experimental establishments, the whole of A. V. Roe's Lancaster output was earmarked to bring the squadron up to a strength of 24 aircraft. During the last days of 1941 the squadron was busy training with the Lancasters, the gunners were familiarising themselves with the turrets while armourer crews practised loading with the various combinations of stores. At the same time, their 22 Hampdens went to No. 420 (R.C.A.F.) Squadron.

The new Group Commander, Air Vice-Marshal J. C. Slessor, C.B., D.S.O., M.C., visited them early in the New Year and took a flip in L7536. He found the Rhodesians very pleased with their new acquisition. Inevitably they had the odd mishap and the first Lancaster accident report concerned Sqn. Ldr. Nettleton who later won the V.C. The cold weather bringing snow and ice had severely curtailed flying, but by sweeping a runway clear of snow limited training was possible. Nettleton had the tail wheel of his Lancaster broken off after hitting a mound of swept snow that had frozen hard. It was soon repaired. A rather more serious crash occurred on the night of January 24th to L7535 under test by the A. & A.E.E. Plt. Off. Maudslay could not obtain permission to land at Stanton Harcourt and tried Cheddington, which was still under construction. After touchdown, his aircraft struck a pile of concrete posts and swung round; the undercarriage collapsed and the aircraft slid backwards into mud. That was a major repair job, but fortunately no one was hurt.

At Waddington No. 44 were making friends with the local organisations and the Lincoln Air Training Corps boys were given the thrill of their young lives, a trip in Britain's latest bomber. The Rhodesians had a great respect for these keen youngsters. When six of their aircrew went to Lincoln to compete with the boys in an aircraft recognition contest, the boys beat them 23 points to 15½! The squadron also co-operated well with the local Home Guard, but unfortunately a scheme whereby 24 of these stalwarts were to be flown to Scampton in a Lancaster and set loose on the airfield defences fell through because of bad weather.

Operations were pending. The first order came on January 25th. It referred to the *Tirpitz*, then reported in a Norwegian fiord. They were warned for readiness to sow mines at the mouth of the fiord operating from Wick. Weather conditions intervened and the move was set back for an early start next morning if there was an improvement. However, this all fizzled out and it was not until a month later, on February 23rd, that the squadron was again called upon. Loaded with mines, their aircraft stood by all the next day and then they were stood down until March 1st brought another 'flap'! It was March 3rd before they really set off on their first operation. Air Vice-Marshal Slessor, knowing that 'it' was definitely on this time, came over to watch Nettleton take off in L7546 at 6.15 p.m., followed by L7547, L7566 and L7549 at three-minute intervals. Over Heligoland Bight they performed their gardening—the invariable operational term for 'laying mines in enemy water'. All returned safely. The Lancaster was operational.

In rather the same way that pilots new to operations were given 'Freshmen' operations, 'local' runs to, say, Paris to drop leaflets, so squadron introductions to operations in new types normally consisted of initial mining runs—but this of course, like leave, was subject to the exigencies of the Service!

An exigency came on March 8th—the *Tirpitz* again. After two days of standing by, eight Lancasters were ordered to Lossiemouth. This first gaggle of Lancasters (they did not aspire to a formation at this early stage) did not have a very friendly reception. An Allied convoy escort dotted the sky around them with ominous puffs of smoke. There was a view held by R.A.F. crews—entirely without foundation of course—that to the Navy if an aircraft had a single tail fin it was a Heinkel or Junkers and you fired, if it had twin tail fins, then it was a Dornier and you fired—and if it had three or more fins it was an unidentified enemy aircraft and you fired! However, the R.A.F. could not afford to be smug about this, for a Spitfire that very day had fired at one of the Lancasters, fortunately without causing serious damage.

With eight aircraft away at Lossiemouth, the balance of the squadron at Waddington were asked to join in a raid in Essen on March 10th with their remaining Lancasters.

This explains why only two Lancasters participated in the Essen raid that marked the first bombing operation by Lancasters. On this occasion, L7536 and L7566, piloted by Flg. Offs. Ball and Wilkins, set out with incendiaries and arrived back safely; L7536 had evidence of being hit by flak—the first Lancaster to be blooded—and L7566 landed at Docking.

The next, the second Lancaster bombing operation, was on March 13th when a single Lancaster joined 61 Wellingtons, 13 Hampdens, 10 Stirlings, 10 Manchesters and 9 Halifaxes in bombing Cologne. This lone Lancaster was L7548 flown by Sgt. Rhodes, who had a mishap on return. Signalling for the floodlight and receiving no response, he landed without the lights and overshot the airfield.

Lancasters from production up to L7569 had been allotted to No. 44 Squadron or experimental establishments, but further deliveries were earmarked for No. 97 Squadron, who received their first on January 14th. A month later they had 17 together with a single remaining Manchester and with these they moved to Woodhall Spa. L7578 at Bottesford on March 8th revealed that No. 207 were next in line for re-equipment.

On March 20th, the second Lancaster Squadron, No. 97, made their first operation with six aircraft out mining. R5482 flew along the coast of Ameland of the Frisian Islands and machine-gunned a hotel and a party of soldiers. They climbed into cloud when a crew member spotted a Messerschmitt Bf.109. All six crews eventually arrived back, but one Lancaster crashed near Boston, and another landing at Abingdon crashed owing to the soft state of the ground. Two others landed safely at Upper Heyford and one at Bicester. It must have alarmed the remaining members of the squadron, to whom it appeared at first that only one aircraft had returned from their first Lancaster operation—and a mining one at that!

The crash near Boston caused something of a stir and a temporary grounding following examination by experts. No. 5 Group ordered squadrons on March 20th to ground all Lancasters until the upper wing surfaces had been examined for buckling or any forcing of the flush riveting. A modification was also immediately effected to the wing tips. The circumstances of the crash are related elsewhere.

The King and Queen visited the Yeadon works of A. V. Roe on the same day that the Lancaster was grounded, a matter on which they were not apprised. King George VI

The first of the production Lancasters, L7527, resulted from a production-line change of Manchester airframes completed as Lancasters. After test this machine went to No. 1654 H.C.U. in November 1942 and was finally lost on operations in March 1944 from No. 15 Squadron.

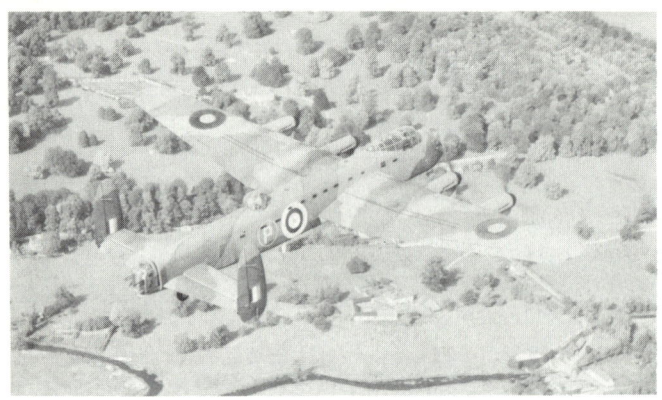

The second prototype Lancaster, DG595, demonstrates the efficiency of its camouflage. In June 1942 the aircraft was used in carbon monoxide contamination tests after gun-firing.

named R5489 'George' and Queen Elizabeth, now the Queen Mother, christened R5548 'Elizabeth'. They were flown to Nos. 44 and 97 Squadrons respectively.

Inevitably it had to come, and was to be repeated as long as the war lasted and the Lancaster was operational—the first casualties. These were suffered on the night of March 24th when R5493 failed to return from gardening. A No. 420 (R.C.A.F.) Squadron pilot reported that he had seen a four-engined bomber heavily engaged with A.A. fire over Lorient and the Royal Observer Corps reported flares out to sea. A search was made without result and Flt. Sgt. L. Warren-Smith, Sgts. R. A. Marston, C. E. W. Clifford, A. F. Murdoch, E. B. Cluff, J. Boyd, W. H. Flower and Flt. Sgt. J. McN. Davidson were reported missing. They were respectively the first and second pilot, first and second navigator, first and second wireless operator and mid-upper and rear gunners.

The crew composition of 'firsts' and 'seconds' reflects the fact that crews were still training on Lancasters, but a first and second pilot was normal up to then. However, in the spring of 1942 the second pilot was considered superfluous, but a new and important crew member was introduced, the flight engineer. From this time onwards, the normal crew stations were pilot, navigator, flight engineer,

The Lancaster's designer, Roy Chadwick, with the Avro test pilot, " Bill" Thorn, testing a Lancaster. On Manchester test-flying Thorn had made five forced landings!

two wireless operators/air gunners, and two air gunners.

On April 11th No. 44 Squadron was ordered to fly long distance flights in formation to obtain endurance data on the Lancaster. This was a blind as the squadron surmised when two days later they were told to prepare for eight machines to move to an advanced base. Similar instructions went to No. 97 Squadron and aircraft flying low in groups of three in 'vee' formation went round Selsey Bill, then up to Lanark, across to Falkirk and up to Inverness to a point just outside the town, where they feigned an attack, and then back to their bases. At the Air Ministry a spate of complaints were received from local authorities all over the country of 'pranks by the R.A.F. flying large four-engined aeroplanes low over the country'. A tactful letter was sent to all police districts.

In both squadrons, the crews realised that they were training for a special operation and speculated on the target. When they were told, they must have caught their breath. It was at Augsburg in southern Germany—the other side of the Danube: some 1,500 miles of flying over enemy territory was involved. There, in the *Maschinenfabrik Augsburg Nurnberg A.G.*, diesel engines for submarines and munitions were being turned out; their task was to destroy the factory.

On the morning of April 17th the operation orders were circulated. Briefing at No. 44 Squadron was at 11.00 hrs and the crews attending were ordered to take their tin hats—more correctly known as steel helmets—on this raid. The armourers received their instructions to load each of the aircraft concerned with four 1,000 lb G.P. bombs fused to give an eleven-second delay. Ground crews were topping up the tanks to maximum fuel—2,154 gallons. These figures were to be quoted significantly by crews for the next three years—'I hear they're filling up 2,154' portended a long run. For take-off the duty Aerodrome Control Pilot, Sgt. Knight, had to be aware of the timing of the raid and in the cookhouse the Duty Ration Detail, A. C. Shaw, preparing sandwiches and flasks, had to know how many and an idea of the duration. It would be dark when crews were due to return and the officer in charge of night flying, the duty flarepath assistants and floodlight operator, together with the duty electrician, Aircraftman Saunders, in case of any snags, had to be aware of the timings and the aircraft participating. It was a squadron matter.

The plan was for six aircraft each from Nos. 44 and 97 Squadrons, in groups of three, which by flying low to avoid being netted by the German radar stood a chance of getting through to this important target. As they prepared to take off just before 3 p.m. on April 17th, 30 Bostons raided French targets and hundreds of fighters swept the Pas de Calais, Cherbourg and Rouen areas to involve the German fighters in prolonged fighting so that the passage of the Lancasters would coincide with their refuelling and rearming. Unfortunately it had the effect of stirring up a hornets' nest and putting the *Luftwaffe* on the alert.

Eight Lancasters from each squadron warmed up and as all were serviceable the crews detailed as second reserve cut their engines and watched the others take off; over Selsey Bill the first reserves, noting that all was well, swung round to return, leaving twelve Lancasters flying low over the water. Leading, Sqn. Ldr. J. D. Nettleton took his formation down to a bare 50 feet over the waves as the

French coast hove into view. But this ruse failed for, just after crossing the Channel, No. 44's Lancasters were heavily engaged by fighters.

The Lancasters tightened formation, flying wingtip to wingtip to give mutual protection with their guns. Low as they were, skimming over villages and rising and falling to the contours of the countryside, the Messerschmitts were forced to attack from above with their cannon shells exploding on the ground to the consternation of French villagers. But many took effect—L7536, flown by Sgt. Rhodes alongside Nettleton, was first to go. Hit at that low height and travelling at 200 m.p.h., there was no chance of taking to parachutes. One by one, the whole of the No. 44's second 'Vee', R5506, L7548 and L7565 flown respectively by Flt. Lt. R. R. Sandford and two Warrant Officers both with D.F.M.s, H. V. Crum and J. F. Beckett, crashed and burst into flames.

Undeterred, Nettleton and Flg. Off. A. J. Garwell, another D.F.M. holder, carried on. With four down before Paris was skirted, there appeared little hope of any reaching the objective, but the German fighter controller was now foxed. They were getting beyond the range of the coastal fighters and there was no indication as to whether the Lancasters would strike north to the Ruhr or switch to Italy and there was no radar cover for central France. Nettleton led the way across France, skirted the Swiss border, flew low in the afternoon sun across southern Germany until he sighted the River Lech, which he followed to his target.

By then the sirens were sounding in this remote corner of Germany and the Augsburg factory was alerted. Coming over the brow of a hill on to the target the two Lancasters were met with heavy fire from quick-firing guns. The Lancasters couldn't miss at chimney-top height on a factory covering an area of 626 x 293 feet. Garwell went in and blasted the target, but was hit and set on fire. He landed in a field two miles west of the town, evidently heavily as the fuselage of R5510 broke at the mid-turret.

The six from No. 97 Squadron had taken a slightly different route and had avoided the fighters in France. A hail of fire greeted them as they appeared in view two miles from the factory. They swept in just as Nettleton had bombed. Visibility was good and they attacked as briefed from 400 feet in spite of the opposition. Sqn. Ldr. Sherwood, D.F.C., leading in L7573 was hit over the target and went down smoking to crash in a ball of flame north of the town. Warrant Officer Mycock had the port wing of R5513 on fire

Servicing a Merlin XX engine on R5493, a No. 44 Squadron aircraft and fated to be the first Lancaster to be lost on operations when it failed to return from a mining mission in March 1942.

over a mile from the target. He continued on to drop his bombs on the factory and became enveloped in flames and crashed. Flt. Lt. Deveral's Lancaster caught fire, but the wireless operator dealt with this while on the bombing run. It was close fighting; one rear-gunner spotted a German behind a machine gun on the roof and saw him collapse under his return fire.

As the survivors turned westward, the light failed and over France they had cover of darkness. Four returned from No. 97's six, but of No. 44 only Nettleton in R5508 returned. He had taken off at 3 p.m. and landed back at Squires Gate next morning just before 1 a.m. For this exploit he received the Victoria Cross.

The Prime Minister sent a message to C.-in-C. Bomber Command—"We must plainly regard the attack of the Lancasters on the U-boat engine factory at Augsburg as an outstanding achievement of the Royal Air Force. Undeterred by heavy losses at the outset the bombers pierced in broad daylight into the heart of Germany and struck a vital point with deadly precision.

"Pray convey the thanks of His Majesty's Government to the officers and men who accomplished this memorable feat of arms in which no life was lost in vain."

The public now knew of the Lancaster and the Germans, examining the smouldering remains of seven, knew that the British had a new four-engined bomber in service. Both were to hear much more about this bomber.

A No. 44 Squadron Lancaster showing the Frazer Nash FN64 mid-lower turret fitted to a number of early Mk. Is. R5556 is shown at the Air Fighting Development Unit, Duxford, in 1942 on fighter affiliation.

CHAPTER FOUR

The First Lancaster Group

Loading mines. A scene in late 1942 with Lancaster W4118 ZN.Y of No. 106 Squadron in the foreground and Manchester L7434 of the same squadron in the background. This squadron had been operating from Coningsby but had moved to Syerston on October 1st 1942 where this picture was taken, when runways being laid at the former restricted flying.

So far only Nos. 44 (Rhodesian) and 97 Squadrons, both in No. 5 Group, were operating with Lancasters. The policy was to make No. 5 Group a Lancaster Group and equip Nos. 44, 97, 207, 61, 83 and 106 Squadrons in that order, leaving temporarily Nos. 49 and 50 to try to make a go of the Manchester. No. 207 Squadron, who had borne the brunt of the Manchester's troubles, considered these troubles over when they received the Lancaster, but they were dogged with ill-luck. On March 28th, while familiarisation flying was being carried out locally, a pupil from Cranwell flying Miles Master DK973 sighted the bombers and decided to have fun with them. Singling out R5501, he dived into a mock attack—and collided! The Master spun in and burnt on impact while the Lancaster, diving straight ahead, struck the ground at Canwick Hill near Lincoln and also went up in flames. Two of the crew died in the crash.

Tests continued at the A. & A.E.E. and during the diving tests of the intensive flying development trials, R5539 crashed at Charlton, near Malmesbury, Wilts, killing Wg. Cdr. P. S. Salter, Sqn. Ldr. J. D. Harris and three other crew members. From an examination of the wreckage it appeared that some of the skin of the port mainplane had become detached and caused loss of control. A production modification was immediately effected.

One of the seemingly forgotten raids of the war, possibly because it was on a small scale and unsuccessful, was the first Lancaster attack on the *Tirpitz*. This German capital ship, together with two cruisers, was at Trondheim; the assemblage being the result of German fears, prompted by Hitler's fallacious intuition, that Britain intended to invade Norway. That Hitler should divert troops to Norway for that purpose suited British strategy very well, but the presence of German naval units in Norway was an acute embarrassment to Russian convoys. Lancasters were sent to see what they could do about it.

Detachments from Nos. 44 and 97 Squadrons were detailed for the job and on April 21st a special train steamed northwards to Scotland conveying ground crews, stores and spares. Two days later Lancasters flew up to Lossiemouth, their springboard for the operation which was mounted on

the evening of the 27th. 4,000 lb and four 500 lb bombs by each were carried, with little effect. Splashes within hundreds of yards were reported, but no hits. A ball of flame seen over the target was presumed to be L7572 of No. 97 Squadron which failed to return to Lossiemouth. A few days later the Lancaster detachments, together with Halifaxes from Nos. 10, 35 and 76 Squadrons, dispersed to their bases.

With every new aircraft type, ground crews were presented with a new maintenance routine and its associated problems. The appropriate manuals were often not available in the early stages of service and the Lancaster had been brought into service in less time from prototype to service stage than any other R.A.F. bomber. Since servicing manuals were based largely on service, they had only just become available, and in wartime there was no case for withholding a bomber from operations merely because its papers were not complete. But this did bring its problems.

The centre section of the wing leading edge on a Lancaster was hinged at the top of the front spar. This allowed easy access for inspection and maintenance of the cabin heater and other equipment. As the maintenance handbook subsequently pointed out, in bold letters, failure to screw down this component before engines were run would result in serious damage to the aircraft. There is a story behind this warning.

Squadron Leader T. H. Boylan was taking up L7531 on air test at Coningsby on April 23rd. This machine formerly of No. 44 Squadron was being used for conversion flights by No. 97 Squadron. It behaved normally until it gathered speed and then the leading edge suddenly flew off. The machine crashed just beyond a bomb dump! An investigation was held immediately and the rigger was placed under close arrest. Later he faced a Court Martial and the Flight Sergeant and another rigger were also charged. Then a similar accident happened within a month to L7581 of No. 44 Squadron. The leading edge flew back on its hinges just as the aircraft was about to become airborne; careering out of control it crashed into two of No. 420 Squadron's Hampdens, P2094 and X3149.

The first accident had been witnessed by Wing Commander Guy Gibson who had arrived at Coningsby to take over No. 106 Squadron which was scheduled for equipment with Lancasters, the first of which arrived on May 19th. He was particularly impressed by Sqn. Ldr. Boylan who, arriving at the Mess with a face blackened by dust and smoke from the Lancaster in which he'd crashed, coolly ordered a drink and took it with an unshaking hand.

Rostock had been the Command target for four nights in succession from April 23rd, with the Heinkel works some four miles out of the town as the specific target for No. 5 Group which included the Lancasters. Only a few aircraft operated the first night. The second night some sixty bombers, including No. 207 Squadron's Lancasters on their first operation, bombed the works with 4,000 lb bombs. After the final attack, photo-reconnaissance revealed considerable damage to the factory.

The target changed to Kiel on the 28th and then to the Gnôme-Rhône works at Gennevilliers the following night. The latter raid was the first in which No. 83 Squadron operated Lancasters; R5564 and R5621 joined in the Main Force raid, while R5566 went mining off Copenhagen. On May 2nd, nineteen Lancasters out mining was the largest number operated in a single night up to that time. During the preceding day R5504 had hit high tension cables near Cambridge—and returned to its base slightly damaged!

R5562 and R5846 dropping leaflets on the night of May 5th were the vanguard of No. 61 Squadron's Lancaster operations. After another two weeks' training they were out in strength in May and by the end of the month were on bombing operations over Germany.

Apart from the enemy, the hazards of wartime flying are illustrated by an incident on the night of May 20th, when the Gnôme-Rhône engine works in France were attacked. Six miles north of Grantham the pilot of Lancaster R5565 of No. 83 Squadron reported a violent shudder. Over the same location, the captain of a Manchester of No. 49 Squadron reported a similar occurrence. From an examination of the aircraft in daylight it was evident that their starboard wings had touched! Both were flying without navigational lights in accordance with orders.

Earlier that day a Lancaster had been used in an errand of mercy. Just after lunch, a Fleet Air Arm Hurricane flying over Wiltshire suddenly dived into the ground and burst into flames, half a mile from the A. & A.E.E. The crash crew, fire tender and ambulance raced from the Boscombe Down airfield and found that the pilot had run 300 yards with his clothing burning before collapsing, and was being tended to by a motorist. The injured man was rushed to the sick bay, but being badly burnt, the M.O. decided that it was vital he was rushed to the Burns Centre at Halton. Sqn. Ldr. Slee, testing a Lancaster, immediately offered it as an air ambulance and by taking the poles from a stretcher a hammock was rigged in the fuselage. An attendant nursing orderly was probably the first woman to fly in a Lancaster. At Halton autogyros and Tiger Moths were parked around the small field—it was unsuitable for anything larger—when the Lancaster came in on a low approach and by braking hard stopped just short of the hangars at the end, to deliver the patient.

Lancasters continued to operate in very limited numbers. For the Stuttgart raids, of which there were three on successive nights from May 4th, Lancaster squadrons were each sending three or four and when for the Warnemunde raid on the night of the 8th fourteen Lancasters set out, it was the largest number of the type to operate over enemy territory to date. But at the end of the month maximum effort was the call, for Operation Millennium—the first of the 1,000 bomber raids. The story of this operation, its planning and the calling upon O.T.U.s to provide crews and aircraft is not properly part of the Lancaster story, for although it was a maximum effort for Lancasters too, they represented only 6.5% of the force of 1,047 aircraft. However, they were well on the way to superseding the Manchester, for only 35 of the latter could be raised compared with 68 Lancasters. One Lancaster and four Manchesters were lost.

The first of the 1,000 bomber raids devastated 600 acres of Cologne. It was carried out with full moon giving excellent visibility, but for the next maximum effort, two nights later on Essen, there was much cloud and mist giving poor visibility with the result that bombs fell over a large area of the Ruhr Valley doing little damage. Some 59 Lancasters were sent and one was lost: No. 207 Squadron despatched a squadron record of fourteen, but four returned early with engine trouble.

No. 83 Squadron had been particularly lucky. They had an enviable record for accident-free operations, even with

Manchesters continued to complement Lancasters on operations for a period. This Manchester serialled L7515 bears the unit code letters of No. 207 Squadron and was to serve on with both Nos 49 and 106 Squadrons.

Manchesters. Unhappily this clean record was broken in June when Aircraftman Palmer was killed when the undercarriage of a Lancaster collapsed.

Six Lancasters with their crews and seventy airmen of No. 44 Squadron were loaned to Coastal Command on June 11th, 1942, for long range anti-U-boat escort and commenced operations next day. They were attached to No. 15 Group of the Command at Nutts Corner in Northern Ireland until July 6th. During that month in which 61 hours were flown, two attacks were made on U-boats, both on June 15th when an unidentified U-boat was attacked without result and in another attack the U-552 was claimed. The day before, R5858 had been ditched in the Atlantic when an engine caught fire. An outward bound convoy picked up the crew who were later reported safe—in Africa! At least one Lancaster was signalled by a U-boat whose commander evidently mistook it for a Focke-Wulf Fw200.

Emden was the target on June 19th, 20th and 23rd, but on the first of the three occasions the Force was divided between that town and Osnabruck. On the second raid R5860 of No. 207 Squadron came down in the North Sea after the failure of hydromatic feathering controls on all engines and with both starboard engines on fire. The crew ditched successfully and were all rescued with two members slightly injured. A Court of Inquiry was convened to look into the cause of this accident, but in the event it was anulled—the crew went missing on a later operation. Such were the vicissitudes of service in Bomber Command.

Bremen was the target area on the night of June 25/26th with the Focke-Wulf works as the specific target. This was the third of the mass attacks and the last in which Manchesters operated. Fifteen Manchesters to 83 Lancasters among the 1,006 aircraft despatched bore witness to the build-up of No. 5 Group squadrons with Lancasters and even Nos. 49 and 50 who had quite recently converted to Manchesters were getting Lancasters; in fact Wg. Cdr. Slee of the former had attempted to make the squadron's first Lancaster operational that night, but R5850's hydraulics failed.

By the 1,000 plus raids, Bomber Command may appear more powerful than was actually the case. The front line strength of the Command was actually *less* than the previous year, in fact by nearly 25%—878 to 670 being the precise figures for July 1941 and 1942 respectively. The thousand-bomber raids were achieved only by bringing in the operational training and conversion units; the depletion in numbers was due to squadrons diverted to Coastal Command,

the failure of the Manchester and the introduction of four-engined bombers which inevitably affected output from the factories during the changeover on the production lines.

The Bremen raid was particularly successful. A 4,000 lb bomb from one Lancaster hit the machine shop of the Focke-Wulf works and other buildings of the factory were gutted by fire. On June 27th and 29th the town was again attacked.

Apart from Bomber Command squadrons diverted to operation under Coastal Command, many operations by the former were in the cause of the Battle of the Atlantic. The Admiralty had advised that some twelve U-boat sections were being turned out monthly at Danzig. To bomb the port would entail a round trip of some 1,500 miles and since accuracy was important, lest Polish civilians be harmed, it was essentially a low level daylight job. Forty Lancasters from Nos. 83, 97, 106 and 207 Squadrons were detailed and they set out with the idea of bombing at dusk in order that they could return under cover of darkness. As it was, most crews arrived in pitch darkness and could not locate their target. To avoid harm to civilians most dropped their bombs on shipping—or rather at shipping. This raid, in which three Lancasters were lost, was not very effective and was followed a week later by another unusual attack when Lancasters went out singly in daylight, using cloud cover, with the object of causing sirens to be sounded over large areas and so cause disruption of work in munition factories.

Lancaster squadrons were soon back with Main Force raids on German towns: Duisburg on July 21st and again on the 23rd, then Hamburg and an evening raid on Flensburg, where Lancasters attacked the submarine-building works and wrecked a large workshop. In spite of this 64 Lancasters were out the very next night to supplement a raid on Saarbrucken. For the first time over a hundred Lancasters—104 to be exact of which two were lost—raided Dusseldorf on the last night in July. They represented 20% of the total force which attacked in moonlight in clear weather and caused considerable damage, in particular at the Schiess A.G. works, which were the largest machine-tool production unit in Germany.

August was a busy month for the Command. There were raids on three consecutive days, the 4th, 5th and 6th, the first two on Ruhr targets and the third on Duisburg. Towards the middle of the month, coupled with participation in Main Force raids was a 'gardening' task. Mines were laid in the Baltic to prevent the *Prinz Eugen* breaking out into the Atlantic. Due to the distances involved, No. 5

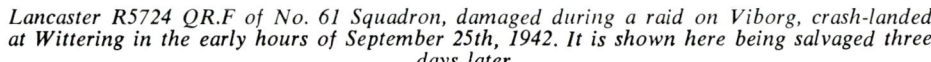

Lancaster R5724 QR.F of No. 61 Squadron, damaged during a raid on Viborg, crash-landed at Wittering in the early hours of September 25th, 1942. It is shown here being salvaged three days later.

No. 49 Squadron Lancasters at dispersal. The turrets of the Lancaster in the foreground have been covered over to protect them from the elements. This photo is believed to have been taken at Scampton.

Group Lancasters were given this task. They were averaging trips each of seven or more hours' duration on consecutive nights in the typical heavy low-cloud weather that still seems to plague the British in August.

During 1942 much of Bomber Command's effort was devoted to assisting the war at sea at this critical stage of the Battle of the Atlantic. In this Lancasters played an important part. As related, the first operation carried out by Lancasters was mining, an activity that increased on nights when the weather was unsuitable for operation over Germany. Apart from operations *for* naval or coastal requirements, several Bomber Command squadrons were switched to operating *under* Coastal Command. So far this only affected the brief detachment from No. 44 Squadron but in August a complete Lancaster squadron was placed under the operational control of Coastal Command.

No. 61 Squadron had an unlucky time in their brief attachment. They flew to St. Eval on August 3rd to commence operations on the Atlantic anti-submarine patrol. Three days later, Flt. Sgt. O. Haynes, spotting a French tunnyman, decided to give the crew a couple of bundles of leaflets for their edification. One bundle actually hit the mast! Evidently the French mistook these kindly intentions for R5511 was holed in a fuel tank and landed at Portreath with fuel for only seven minutes flying left.

An enemy supply tanker was sighted on the 19th, and reported by Flg. Off. A. L. Searby in R5661 to be outward bound from the north coast of Spain. Searby however did not return and of the seven Lancasters that went into the attack on this tanker two were shot down and another damaged before it was forced back. During the search for its whereabouts next day, revealed to be at La Pallice, another Lancaster was lost. On August 22nd the squadron returned to Bomber Command. Although four aircraft had been lost, on the credit side was the bombing and sinking of the U-boat U-751 by Sgt. P. C. Joslin in R5888 jointly with a Whitley of No. 502 Squadron.

The inaccuracy of bombing at this period and the controversy that led to No. 8 Group, the Pathfinder Force, being formed do not come directly into this story. Lancasters represented as yet less than a quarter of the Main Force. But when the Pathfinders formed on August 15th, 1942, it did embrace one Lancaster Squadron, No. 83, which then left Scampton for Wyton where, to quote one of the pilots concerned, 'the beer's good and the girls aren't bad'. It is something of a paradox, in view of the need for a target

marking group, that the last 'pathfinderless' raid was a great success with 135 acres of Mainz destroyed. That night 64 Lancasters were operational and represented over 20% of the Force.

While the main Force attacked Kassel on August 28th, twelve Lancasters of No. 106 Squadron set out on a mission of their own. A new anti-capital ship bomb had been produced and the time had come to use it on Gdynia where three major targets were assembled, the *Scharnhorst* and *Gneisenau*, and the new and only German aircraft carrier, the *Graf Zeppelin*, was being fitted out. No. 106 trained for this operation for several weeks to gain accuracy in planting the turnip-shaped capital-ship bomb on a range target. It is noteworthy that No. 106 were chosen for this task; their commander was Wing Commander Guy Gibson, who later achieved fame as leader of the 'Dam Busters'.

The operation was meticulously planned and participating was Squadron Leader Richardson, an acknowledged expert on bomb-sights who was making his first operational trip since 1918! The Lancasters needed full fuel load to return to base from their target 950 miles distant so that, together with the weight of the bombs, they took off at the unprecedented all-up weight of 67,000 lb. Hitherto 60,070 lb had been the maximum permissible. Unfortunately a haze over Gdynia reduced visibility to a mile and in spite of some Lancasters spending as long as an hour over the target none of the ships was hit.

To put every Lancaster into one operation over enemy territory in daylight seemed questionable to say the least. But this was put into effect and justified by results. In October 1942, No. 5 was still the only Group of Bomber Command with Lancasters except for the pathfinders who had been allotted No. 83 Squadron from No. 5 Group; in lieu the latter received No. 57 Squadron, with Wellingtons from No. 3 Group. By converting their new squadron to Lancasters in September, No. 5 Group could put a total of nine Lancaster squadrons in the air—Nos. 9, 44, 49, 50, 57, 61, 97, 106 and 207—and this they did on October 1st. Flying in magnificent procession across the English countryside, while fighters made mock attacks and wallowed in the slipstream of four hundred 1,000 h.p. Merlins, they fanned out over the Wash and re-converged to drop their bombs on Wainfleet Range. This, the complete Lancaster bombing force, was to be thrown into a daylight attack on the great Schneider armament works—the French equivalent of Krupps—located at Le Creusot near the Swiss frontier.

Aircrew entering a No. 103 Squadron Lancaster at Elsham Wolds (left) and a Lancaster of No. 83 Squadron (right). The latter squadron was the first Lancaster unit to serve the Pathfinder Force of No. 8 (Bomber) Group.

Secrecy was strictly observed, although the code-name Operation Robinson was rather allusive if the popular mispronunciation of Creusot is considered. Any inkling of the target by the enemy could cause crippling losses by fighters. By planning to fly low below the German radar cover and to arrive as the sun was setting, to have the advantage of daylight for bombing and the cover of dusk and then darkness on the return, the risks were reduced.

The weather on the morning of October 17th promised suitable and Operation Robinson was signalled. The crews were told their target for the first time and anyone who entered a No. 5 Group station that day was held there until after the bombers had left—such were the security arrangements. After take-off the bombers made for Upper Heyford from their various stations and formed up. Meanwhile, coastal Whitleys were sweeping the Channel to ensure that U-boats kept well down and that no E-boats or patrol vessels were about that might radio a warning. With Wing Commander L. C. Slee leading with his squadron, No. 49, the formation swept out to sea over Land's End, keeping under 1,000 feet. They flew south-westward over the Bay of Biscay and then turned in over the French coast and continued the next leg of the journey, low down for 300 miles.

It was exhilarating for the gunners as the scene immediately below flashed past. Chickens were seen to scatter and fly as the slipstream caught them. A team of oxen apparently stampeded, for one gunner caught a fleeting glimpse of neat furrows ending abruptly in a zig-zag pattern. Some of the French waved, but all who witnessed these flyers must have been apprehensive of the nationality and the business of these bombers, with jet-black undersurfaces and sides relieved only by dull red markings.

Mt. Blanc, snapped unofficially from Lancaster W4259 during a daylight raid on Milan in October 1942.

Once opposition was met—from a covey of partridges—and two or three Lancasters were damaged. For the pilots, it was tiring work looking out for obstructions and other Lancasters and the navigators were kept busy checking locations and times. The gunners gave valuable assistance as look-outs.

Forty-four miles from the objective the bombers fanned out and came into their target as practised at Wainfleet. At precisely the minute planned, 6.9 p.m., the first Lancaster bombed and within seven minutes all had dropped their bombs on this French arsenal which covered 287 acres, except for the Lancasters detailed to bomb the Henri Paul transformer and switching station at Montchanin. As the dusk gathered 93 Lancasters were spaced out over France, racing for the coast. At Command and Group Headquarters, and the bases, their return was waited with considerable apprehension. At the planned schedule time for the last Lancaster due back, 23 were overdue. But inevitably a few had strayed off-course or experienced engine trouble and at least one had an engine out of action through hitting birds; fifteen minutes later and only twelve blanks showed on the Command Board and gradually this figure diminished until only one aircraft was left. This was W4774 flown by Sqn. Ldr. W. D. Carr, which had been seen to crash near the target at Montchanin. Apart from that crew, one flight engineer was killed by the only German opposition met in the air—offered by three Arado seaplanes along the coast off Brest to a No. 207 Squadron Lancaster turning back with engine trouble. Two were shot down and the third made off after damaging the Lancaster.

The fuel installation in Lancasters was giving considerable trouble in the autumn of 1942 and restricted operations to a Lancaster strength of less than eighty at a time when the potential was around 175. These troubles adversely affected their operational height because the impellers of the pumps in the fuel tanks were becoming blocked; although they could be by-passed by stack-pipes, the pumps were necessary to maintain fuel pressure at heights of over 12,000 feet. Nevertheless a number of 'over-the-Alps' attacks were called for in late October. Genoa and Turin were attacked on the nights of the 22nd and 23rd followed by a daylight raid on Milan on the 24th in which some sixty Lancasters made their first daylight flight over the Alps. This time a fighter escort of Spitfires accompanied the force across the Channel to the Normandy coast, where the bombers split up and made their way individually to Italy. Some crews went down as low as 200 feet and observed cars that had run off the pavement in some panic. One crew reported that a searchlight was switched on!

Reports by No. 61 Squadron pilots were typical of the force as a whole: Plt. Off. A. E. Foster in W4236 identified the town by the racecourse and was able to aim at the station which was the specific target, Flt. Sgt. L. Ferguson in R5699 was foxed by the cloud and gave up after a 25 minute search and dropped his bombs on a town which he believed to be Vigevaro, Warrant Officer R. Lever in W4317 found breaks in the cloud and was able to get bombsights on to the new railway station, Sgt. P. L. Elliott in W4244 found 10/10th cloud but went below it and observed the town and marshalling yards, Sgt. J. B. Cockshott's Lancaster was attacked by a Fiat Cr42 which did not close in and he was left unmolested to bomb from 10,000 feet. A Macchi 202 shot at another bomber. Total losses were one Lancaster over the target and two which fell to German night-fighters on the way home in the evening.

Targets for Lancasters alternated between Germany and Italy in November. On the 6th Osnabruck was bombed in daylight and next night, as troops formed up for the North African landings, Lancasters were attacking Rommel's main supply base at Genoa. A particularly heavy attack was

inhabitants of Newark and district were able to hear for themselves the explosion of a 4,000 lb bomb. However, by this time even the Italians were experiencing 8,000 lb bombs, the first having been lifted over the Alps to Turin by Lancasters R5551 and R5573 of No. 106 Squadron on the night of November 28th, piloted by Wg. Cdr. Guy Gibson and Flt. Lt. W. N. Whamond respectively. Plt. Off. F. G. Healy had also set out with an 8,000 lb bomb, but as the aircraft's undercarriage would not retract its bomb had to be jettisoned into the sea.

The heaviest attack of December was on the 20th when Duisburg was the target. Unfortunately two Lancasters were lost at the outset. W4182 of No. 9 Squadron, climbing for height, hit W4259 of No. 44 Squadron in mid-air. They fell in Canwick Road, Bracebridge Heath. Next night Lancasters bombed Munich and then 1942 operations ended with gardening in enemy lakes.

The turn of 1942-43 saw the introduction of new radio aids. Oboe, which gave a sonic indication of when to bomb, was first used by Pathfinder Mosquitos that December and H2S, which gave a visual indication of the terrain below, was first used in January.

By 1943 No. 5 Group, comprising Nos. 9, 44, 49, 50, 57

The town of Mon Richard vibrating under the roar of Merlin engines as the entire operational Lancaster force of October 1942—94 Lancasters—flew low over France to bomb the Le Creusot works at dusk on October 17th, 1942.

launched on Turin on the 21st. That night a new Lancaster unit became operational, an Australian squadron, No. 467. They had received Halifaxes, but re-equipped with Lancasters within a few weeks. No. 467 completed the re-arming of No. 5 Group

Bad weather restricted operations as 1942 came to a close and Lancasters were only bombing on eight nights during December, but these included three runs to Italy, one in extremely bad weather. Preparing to bomb Turin with its contemporaries, Halifaxes, Stirlings and Wellingtons, on the 8th, one Lancaster's 4,000 pounder went off before take-off. While bombing up R5864 of No. 61 Squadron at Syerston, incendiary bombs fell from their racks, exploded and set fire to the Lancaster. The area was cleared and the

61, 97, 106, 207 and 467 (R.A.A.F.) Squadrons, was completely equipped with Lancasters while No. 1 Group was in the middle of its changeover from Wellingtons to Lancasters and by February Nos. 12, 100, 101, 103 and 460 (R.A.A.F.) Squadrons were up to the full establishment of 16 operational plus 2 reserve aircraft. No. 3 Group at this time was still operating Stirlings while No. 4 Group was completing its changeover from Wellingtons to Halifaxes and No. 6 (R.C.A.F.) Group formed the first day of 1943 was following suit. In the new No. 8 (P.F.F.) Group Nos. 83 and 156 Squadrons were so far the only squadrons with Lancasters. No. 2 Group for their day-bombing duties flew Bostons, Venturas and Mosquitos. Altogether, some 200 Lancasters were on the Command strength.

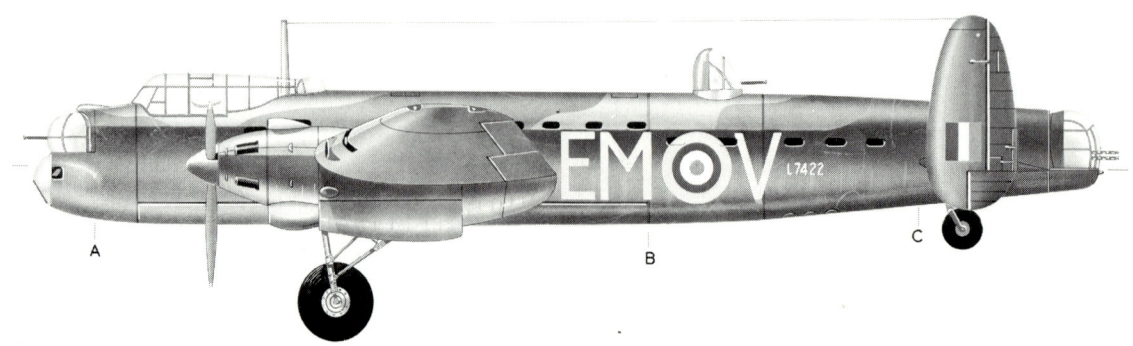

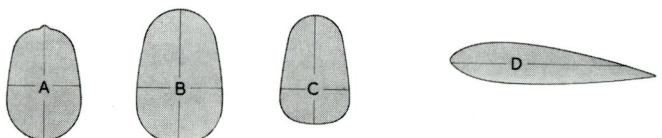

24

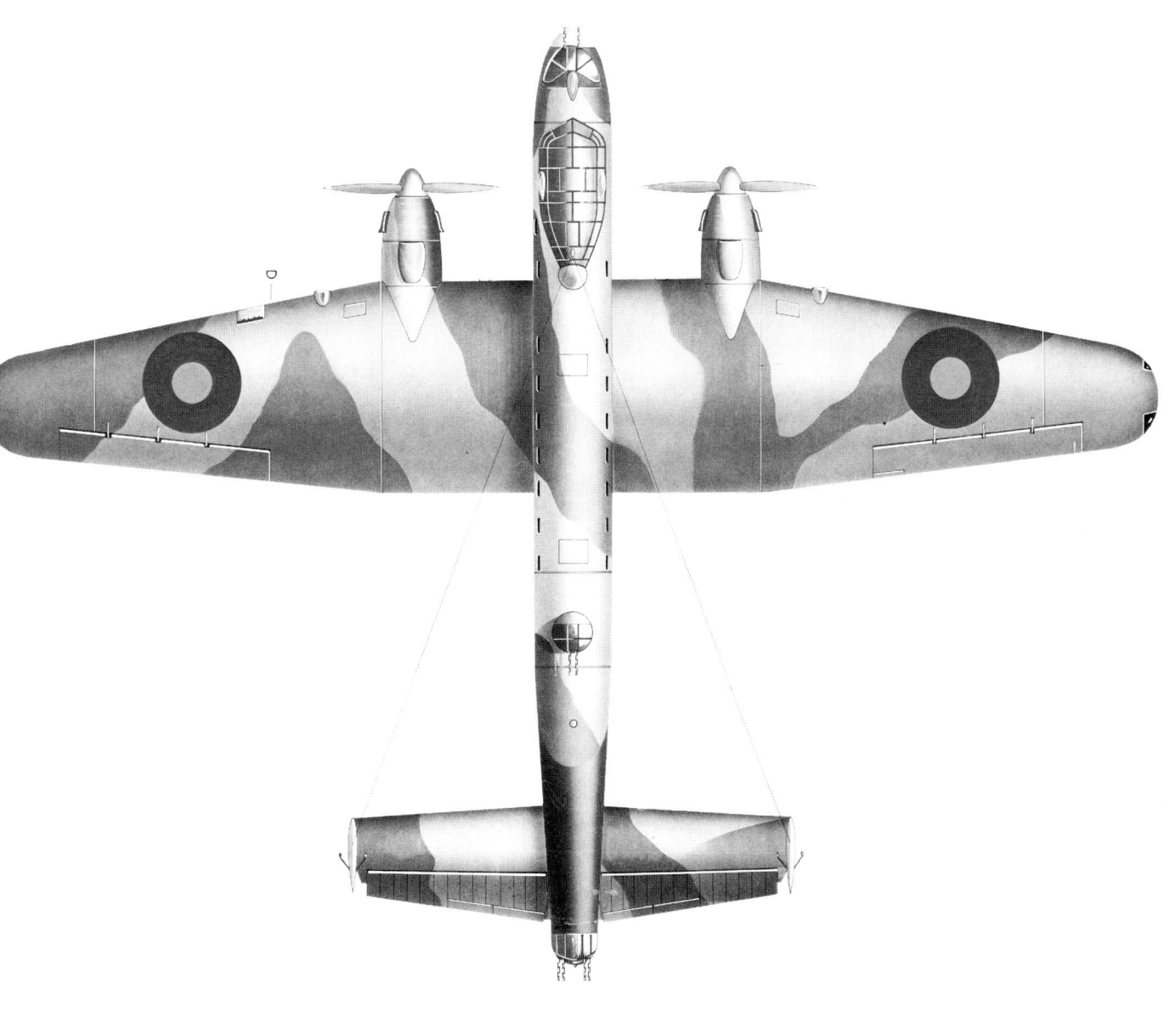

A No. 207 Squadron Manchester I, mid-1941. This version was temporarily designated IA to differentiate from the triple-finned version.

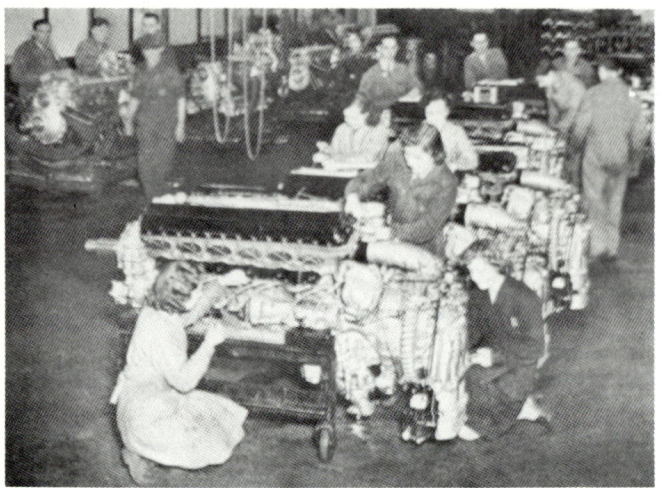

Lancasters were Mk. I or III according to the fitting of a British- or American-built Merlin engine respectively.

Four-engined bombers made heavy demands on engine supplies and the Rolls-Royce plants at Derby, Crewe and Glasgow, and Ford's at Trafford Park, could not supply Merlins quickly enough for the many types including Spitfires powered by this engine; the 18,000 per year rate by 1943 was not sufficient. Fortunately before the Lancaster evolved Lord Beaverbrook had suggested that Merlins be produced in America. Ford's plant was suggested, but apparently this was a matter on which the father and son, Henry and Edsel, had differing views and Packards stepped in. Drawings were already in America, having been despatched in a warship as soon as France fell so that even if England fell—there would always be a Merlin!

Packards went into production in a big way; first they cleared their car production lines—for three-quarters of a mile! Completely new tools had to be installed while the drawing staff worked from the 20,000 master drawings that had been deposited at Wright Field. The Americans found some difficulty, at first, in working to Rolls-Royce tolerances, but they amazed the parent firm by producing their first engine within a year.

Their first two-speed supercharged engines which delivered 1,420 b.h.p. at take-off and developed 1,460 h.p. at 10,500 feet were designated Merlin 28 in the R.A.F. and Packard V-1650-1 in the U.S.A.A.F. The Americans wanted the Merlin for their P-40 while the first British allocations were for Canadian-built Hurricanes, then Lancasters and next came Mosquitos. These engines differed from the British Merlin 22 on which they were based, by an American magneto, and because S.U. carburettors could not be produced in time in the States an American Bendix was initially used.

To satisfy Lancaster production requirements, both British and American Merlins were needed and, because of the slight differences between the two engines, a Lancaster became a Mk. I or III respectively, according to British or American engines. There were no external differences when the engines were cowled. Manufacturers were allotted specific quantities of one or the other, so that, in general, serial number batches are a guide to the initial engine installation, but some changes resulted through one or the other being temporarily in short supply because of shipping losses affecting American supplies or priority offsets for Mosquitos from British production. In service, engines were automatically changed after a set number of flying hours and a Lancaster I could become a Mk. III. There are recorded cases of Lancasters with American engines outboard and British Merlins inboard and vice versa. The ground crews were very impressed with the magnificent tool-sets supplied with the Packard Merlins.

A number of bombing aids were coming into use that were to make the 'heavies' far more effective weapons. Oboe, a radar navigation and blind bombing system, which, by signals from ground stations, guided the crew to the target—and indeed could release the bombs automatically—had first been used on December 20th and trials continued on Ruhr targets including Essen on January 9th and 13th. The equipment was fitted into Mosquitos of the Pathfinder Force.

For the first time since 1941, Berlin was attacked on January 16th, 1943. This was by an all-Lancaster force that, due to snow and haze, caused only scattered damage, but the cost was relatively light with only one aircraft missing, although 34 were damaged. This was followed up the next night and this time the defences, particularly the night-fighters, were fully alerted and 22 aircraft were lost, mostly shot down, and another thirty were damaged.

On the first of these Berlin raids, radial-engined Lancasters became operational for the first time. These were the Lancaster Mk. II, powered by four Bristol Hercules engines. As an insurance against delay in American supplies of Merlin engines or the bombing of Rolls-Royce plants in Britain, an order was given to A. V. Roe to build a radial-engined Lancaster utilising Bristol Hercules engines in a standard airframe. Designated Mk. II, DT810, the prototype, first flew on November 26th, 1941. After Pearl Harbour when it was thought America might become preoccupied with the war in the Pacific, production was pressed forward and Armstrong Whitworth, who were tailing off Whitley production, changed over to producing the Avro Lancaster with Hercules engines.

To pioneer this version in service, No. 61 Squadron was chosen to operate a flight at the turn of the year. DS607 was prepared for operations on the night of January 11th and actually set out, but Sgt. A. Meagher was forced to jettison his bombs in the sea and return as he could not climb above 18,400 feet. Wg. Cdr. R. M. Coad decided to take this same machine on the Berlin raid already mentioned, with the Alexander Platz railway station as his specific aiming point, but engine trouble over Germany forced him to bomb the 'last resort' target of Griefswald. Three other Mk. IIs had set out and two, DS608 and DS609, reached their target. Thus the Mk. II became operational and first bombed Germany on the night of January 16th.

Another radar device, H2S, was first used on January 30th and again Lancasters benefited but did not pioneer this aid, which was first fitted in Stirlings and Halifaxes. The electronic equipment of the heavies was becoming exceedingly complex and each created its own problems. An important item was the I.F.F.—Identification Friend or Foe—which emitted signals our own defences could receive and identify. This necessitated an aerial—one of the eight aerial systems in a Lancaster—slung from the tip of the fins to the I.F.F. instrument near the mid-turret. Damage to this or the aerial system often resulted in an unwelcome reception over Britain. W4175, returning in the early hours of February 3rd, had our own defences open up on it, causing further damage to that inflicted over Cologne. The I.F.F. system was highly secret and to prevent it falling into enemy hands two press-buttons at each of the pilot's, navigator's and wireless operator's positions could fire the detonators to destroy the equipment. In the event of a crash these automatically blew, but to safeguard the crew if it was a crash-landing in friendly territory there was a cut-out switch. The TR1335 transmitter/receiver was similarly secret and was also fitted with explosive charges.

There were raids in several different directions in early February. On the 3rd it was Hamburg, next night 198 aircraft set out for Turin with four Lancasters carrying 4,000 lb bombs destined for the naval base at Spezia. In between three attacks on Wilhelmshafen, 466 aircraft raided Lorient and on the 14th Milan had an all-Lancaster attack from which two of the 142 aircraft failed to return.

The Lancasters of No. 5 Group were busy at the turn of the month; 86 bombed St. Nazaire on the last day of February and 79 were over Berlin on the first of March. Three days later, eight Lancasters from No. 100 Squadron bombing U-boat pens at St. Nazaire were carrying out that squadon's first operation since its demise on the fall of Singapore. That night a lone ally died. The Yugoslavs were not in a position to form squadrons of their own within the R.A.F. until later, meanwhile a number served in various units; Flying Officer Kujundzic was with No. 103 Squadron. He had taken up a Lancaster for night flying practice on this particularly dark night—there was no moon—when flames shot from an engine and spread, threatening to engulf the fuselage. Kujundzic ordered the crew out and one by one they dropped into the dark night while he held W4333 steady until he was alone. Whether he tried after all to land the aircraft, or some further happening prevented him from baling out will not now be known. He was killed when it crashed at Yaxley near Peterborough.

The so-called Battle of the Ruhr opened on March 5th, 1943, with an attack, 412 strong, on Essen, which included 140 Lancasters led by 22 others from the Pathfinder Force, in the first large-scale Oboe attack. Preparations had been going on for some time for an all-out assault on the heart of the industrial valley and while Bomber Command raids were still spread to meet specific commitments the main weight of bombs was delivered to 'The Happy Valley' as it became known to crews.

The aim of Bomber Command was to eliminate the

The Lancasters' offensive and defensive capability. Lancasters at this time were taking up to 8,000lb. in total bomb load. The .303 Browning guns in the front and mid-upper turrets, two in each, and the four guns in the rear turret are shown (top to bottom).

Ruhr as an industrial district vital to the maintenance of the German war effort; in turn the German defences aimed at inflicting such crippling losses that raids would not be practicable. Hitherto, Germany had relied mainly on anti-aircraft gunfire—flak—but later in 1942 the Lichtenstein apparatus had been introduced in German night fighters and was comparable to the A.I. radar used with increasing effect over Britain by Beaufighters from May 1941. For this war of attrition the supply of Lancasters was essential and a three-fold expansion was ensured; there were now three marks of Lancaster in production, new contractors were to be brought into Lancaster production and new Lancaster squadrons were being formed. When the battle opened Lancaster squadrons included No. 5 Group, complete with Lancasters in Nos. 9, 44, 49, 50, 57, 61, 97, 108, 207 and 467 (R.A.A.F.) Squadrons, No. 1 Group 50% equipped with Lancasters, viz. Nos. 12, 100, 101, 103 and 460 (R.A.A.F.) Squadrons. In the Pathfinders, No. 8 Group, both Nos. 83 and 156 Squadrons had Lancasters. As part of the preparations for the battle it had been decided to replace all the Merlin 20 engines installed in operational Lancaster Is with Merlin 22s which were now in general supply. Crews noted that Lancasters in squadron service were better than those at Conversion Units—and this was one of the reasons why.

The accretion of ice on the wings affecting lift and control and ice forming on windscreens and windows affecting visibility were hazards, additional to the enemy. To ensure that the pilot's windscreen and bomb aimer's panel could be kept ice-free, glycol sprays were fitted; the nozzles for the main windscreen could be seen sticking up from the nose like antennæ. They were not included in the original airframe and Manchesters were not so fitted until late in their service, in fact not until a Manchester was lost because of this deficiency. Sgt. G. K. Carter returning from a cross-country training flight in a Manchester on the dark night of March 12th was coming in to land at Coningsby. But the Drem lighting on the airfield only showed weakly through the ice accretion on his windscreen. Unable to see clearly, he hit the ground heavily on one wheel and the machine bounced. Carter quickly opened up and went round again but found that one undercarriage leg would not lock down. Notifying Flying Control of his dilemma he was ordered to fly out towards the sea and abandon the aircraft. This was safely accomplished and at the cost of L7474 falling crewless at Winceby near Horncastle. The subsequent report on this crash led to all Manchesters being

brought to the Lancaster standard of de-icing equipment.

Bombing-up was a technique in itself. Depending on the target and the role a particular unit was to play, the load could vary from fourteen 250 or 500 lb bombs to a single 8,000 lb bomb. In general all Lancasters were fitted to carry up to the 4,000 lb bombs; most production Lancasters from early 1943 could carry 8,000 lb bombs. Lancasters carrying the later 12,000 lb and 22,000 lb giants were classified as 'Specials'.

The smaller bombs were of varying types, general purpose, armour piercing, semi armour piercing and of low, medium or high capacity. Low capacity bombs had a small charge to weight ratio and therefore penetrated before exploding while high capacity bombs with a relatively light casing would explode on contact. The type of bombs carried depended on the nature of the target. A typical load was $1 \times 4,000$ lb 'Cookie', 4×500 lb G.P. (General Purpose), $12 \times$ S.B.C. (small bomb containers either with 8×30 lb or 90×4 lb incendiaries).

Bombs were brought up from their dumps by special trolleys to the dispersed aircraft. The bombs were wheeled underneath after the bomb doors had been opened, fitted to carriers lowered from the bomb cells, and winched up after adjusting the fuse setting control link, in a special sequence to maintain a correct centre of gravity for the aircraft when they were released. Rigid checks were necessary to ensure that each bomb was securely held and locked in position.

The jaws of the bomb carriers for 4,000 and 8,000 lb bombs were locked by a small lever on the side of the bomb release. During the loading drill this was sometimes confused with the mechanical release—and down would drop the bomb! An electrical fault too could cause a premature release. Normally, in a straight drop from an aircraft on the ground neither the fuse action nor the impact would be sufficient to set the bomb off, but there are always exceptions to the rule.

Inevitably there were accidents and several airmen suffered crushed limbs in loading accidents and in a few cases there were explosions. The first big Lancaster bomb disaster had occurred on March 15th, 1943, at Scampton when a 4,000 lb bomb went up at 9.15 a.m. during bombing up and blew up three Lancasters of No. 50 Squadron and three of No. 57 Squadron. These six were complete write-offs and another five were badly damaged.

All Lancasters could now operate around 22,000 feet

and in this they had a distinct advantage, since attacks were concentrated with some ten aircraft attacking every minute; the advantage of height made them less prone to being hit by falling bombs, which was the fate of many aircraft.

No. 61 Squadron, having pioneered the Mk. II Lancaster, had their flight withdrawn and it was left to No. 115 Squadron to become the first Mk. II Lancaster squadron. This was the first squadron in No. 3 Group, predominantly a Stirling Group, to use the Lancaster and it was logical that they should go to the last squadron in the Group still operating Wellingtons. No. 1678 Heavy Conversion Flight was formed at East Wretham with early production Mk. IIs to facilitate conversion training and this enabled other squadrons quickly to reach operational status. Assigned the normal 'piece of cake' initial operations, four of their aircraft laid mines between La Rochelle and the Ile de Re five days later. The Lancaster II first operated in squadron strength over Berlin on March 29th. Piloting DS621 of the squadron was Flt. Lt. Bazalgette who later won a V.C. in a Lancaster. That night came the first Lancaster II loss, Plt. Off. H. J. Ross and his crew in DS625. Now the Germans knew that radial-engined Lancasters were in service.

Over Spezia on the night of April 13th, ED660 was fired upon by another Lancaster, fortunately without damage. It might have been a different matter if it had been a German night fighter with 20 or 30 mm. cannons, but Lancasters still had armament of the same calibre and much the same velocity as the defensive guns on bombers in the later stages of the 1914-1918 War. It is true that the rate of fire had increased, but defensive armament had not developed concurrently with other aspects and the Germans were in advance in this field. Air Marshal Harris had pressed for a new type of turret, manufactured by Rose Bros. of Gainsborough, but the firm lacked the production capacity. The intention was to introduce 20 mm. cannon in turrets and as early as 1941 engineers had visited No. 207 Squadron with a view to installing cannons in the Manchester. Now the Americans were on the scene with their Fortresses with .50 calibre machine-guns and it was planned to use these as an interim measure until cannon could be installed.

Imagine the discomforts of the air gunner, particularly in the rear turret. He sat out on a limb, alone. He had to be on the alert for up to eight hours at a stretch, when by Army standards a two-hour turn of sentry-duty is normally the maximum. There was no question of marching up and down to relieve his boredom, he was committed to his cramped quarters. He stared out into the night and faced all its dangers—collision with another aircraft, an enemy night-fighter, flak. He watched others go flaming down, he could feel his own machine being hit by flak and had to wait to hear what was going on 'up-front'. Enemy night fighters usually attacked from the rear, they could then maintain a speed relative to the bomber and fire into the fuselage or at the wings to ignite the fuel tanks, and put the engines out of action. A number of Lancasters that did eventually elude an attack in this way brought back a dead or wounded rear-gunner. As for the gunner shot at by the 'friendly' bomber mentioned earlier, he made his report and was told that it would be useless to pursue the matter. The 'tail-end Charlies' just had to grin and bear it.

One crew from the Spezia raid got back three days later. They had to ditch ED703 in the sea and take to their dinghy, which was stored in the mainplane and contained emergency rations. A Whitley on anti-submarine patrol later spotted them and dipped low and circled to reassure them. Sixty-three hours later Flg. Off. M. E. Chivers and his six sergeants were hauled aboard an R.A.F. rescue launch.

Stuttgart was raided, mainly by Lancasters, on April 15th and the following night the Skoda works at Pilsen was the intended target; unfortunately in the latter raid a mistake by the Pathfinders resulted in a large asylum being the focal point for the bombing. The Baltic port of Stettin, Duisburg and general Ruhr targets completed Lancaster operations for March. During May Lancasters attacked chiefly 'Battle of the Ruhr' targets, but one raid, by one squadron on their first operation, brought the Lancaster into even greater prominence as 'The Dam-busters'.

Certainly the Lancaster showed promise as *the* bomber of the R.A.F.; it served in three bombing groups, three different marks were in service, there was output from three different contractors, with others in the process of tooling up, plus many sub-contractors being organised.

A mixed Commonwealth and homeland crew, which included an Egyptian Government employee, a blacksmith and a pie wholesaler, of No. 57 Squadron (left) and a crew snapped on return from the Friedrichshafen raid via North Africa, hence the sun helmet!

CHAPTER SIX

Special Operation

A closely guarded secret, the details of which were only officially de-classified in 1962, was the famous dambusting bomb and the modification of the Lancaster to carry it. When the bombs were fitted ready for the raid the special Lancasters were dubbed the "Steamrollers of Scampton," the reason is apparent from the view. Revolving backwards rotated by power from the Lancaster's hydraulic system, the bomb was dropped to skip, roll to the base of the dam and explode, when the shock waves of the under-water explosion would cause the dam wall to crumble.

No account of the Lancaster would be complete without mention of one of the most famous raids of the war, the breaching of the Mohne and Eder Dams by No. 617 Squadron, which became known as the 'Dambusters'. On the other hand no account here could match that already given by the man most qualified to write it, the late Guy Gibson, whose book 'Enemy Coast Ahead' is a classic of war literature. Apart from this personal account, it was graphically related in Paul Brickhill's 'The Dam Busters'. Two accounts have appeared in official histories and it has also been written up in other works.

The approach here is a little different, the object being to ascertain the contribution by each individual Lancaster. There is a popular misconception that the object was to breach the Mohne and Eder dams; the aim was in fact to breach all the important ones in Western Germany, the Mohne, Eder, Sorpe, Ennepe, Lister and Schwelme. The first two were by far the most important and were successfully breached; this fact has tended to obscure the full aim of the operation. The object was not merely to achieve flood damage, but to disrupt an important industrial area by floods and deprive industries of their source of hydro-electric power. The Lancaster was chosen for this operation because it was the only bomber in service capable of lifting the special bomb that had been designed by Dr. Barnes Wallis for such an operation. Even so, specially modified Lancasters were required and a special squadron had to be formed because the Commander-in-Chief of Bomber Command had so little faith in Wallis's bomb that he would not withdraw a Lancaster squadron from operations to train for this venture. When finally he yielded to outside pressure, he sanctioned it on the understanding that his front-line squadrons would not be affected. Hence the formation of

No. 617 Squadron on March 21st, 1943. The No. 617 'number plate' created a precedent. It was the highest number as yet allotted to an R.A.F. squadron (except for balloon squadrons) and it followed on from the pre-war Auxiliary Air Force squadrons which had taken up Nos. 600-616 and were now normal service squadrons.

The special bombs resembled giant garden rollers and a requisite was that they had to spin away from the Lancasters. Their bulk necessitated fitting external pylons to the Lancasters to take the axle of the bomb. Avro's task was to supply the means of revolving it before release. A Ford V-8 engine installed in the fuselage was suggested, but because of the weight involved this was dropped in favour of using the normal hydraulic system. This system would not be needed to operate the bomb doors, which had to be completely removed to accommodate the bomb, and would not be necessary to revolve the mid-upper turret which was not fitted to compensate for the great weight of the missile. By a cut-out arrangement in the hydraulic system, after the undercarriage had been retracted in the normal way, the pressure was diverted to a hydraulic motor in the fuselage which, by means of a belt drive, revolved the bomb on its axis on the pylons to the required 500 r.p.m.

Prototype of the dam-busting Lancasters was ED765/G. The 'G' signified 'Guard'; this suffix to the number was usually applied when an aircraft had equipment of a higher security grading than the aircraft type and often applied to aircraft with special electronic equipment. Two more prototype conversions were followed by a firm order for another twenty. The first works instruction, signed by the Lancaster's designer, Roy Chadwick, was issued on March 8th. In just over two months the conversion programme was complete. Strict secrecy was observed and the project, known to the Service as 'DOWNWOOD,' was known in the Avro Works as 'Type 464 Provisioning'. Apart from the modifications mentioned, the air bomber's panel was changed and a Vickers 'K' gun was fitted on a ball mounting to fire downwards from the floor of the fuselage.

Until the 'specials' arrived, No. 617 trained hard on standard Lancasters. Practice low-flying was the order of the day—and night. The canopies of several Lancasters were screen-painted to give the impression of night-flying during day flights. A spate of complaints about low-flying was received. A local mayor quoted an instance of a motorist who felt compelled to duck as a Lancaster roared by. A No. 5 Group letter of apology, according to a member of that H.Q., stated in reply that pilots would in future be instructed to have a due regard for other road users!

The prototype of the specials, ED765/G (which appeared in Avro drawings as ED764/G), reached Farnborough on April 8th, 1943. While this was being tested, the drop tests were being conducted in the sea off Reculver, Kent, for which purpose ED817/G, the second prototype, was sent to Manston on April 20th. Third of the prototypes was ED825/G for A. & A.E.E. testing which reached No. 617 Squadron only a few hours before the famous raid, but it did not participate.

ED864/G, the first of the 'production specials', was delivered to No. 617 Squadron on April 18th. At intervals the remaining nineteen arrived until the last, ED937/G, reached Scampton only three days before the operation.

Loading the bomb appeared to the squadron armourers as a case of the mountain going to Mahomet, for instead of winding up the bomb to the aircraft, the aircraft was settled down on the bomb! A Coles crane lifted the tail of the aircraft up, while the bomb was trundled in from behind.

One of the twenty 'G' Lancasters was damaged five days before the operation and could not be made ready in time. Squadron Leader H. G. Maudsley carrying out an experimental drop of a 'special training mine' was too low and the spray damaged the underside of the aircraft. On return it was found that ED933/G was beyond unit repair on site and it was held for spares to maintain the others.

Thus, on the night of the operation, nineteen aircraft was the response to the call for maximum effort. The squadron had been briefed on May 15th and the force was divided into three waves: one of nine aircraft and two of five each. The first nine, with pilots' names, were as follows:

ED932/G AJ. G Wg. Cdr. Guy Gibson
ED925/G AJ. M Flt. Lt. J. V. Hopgood
ED909/G AJ. P Flt. Lt. H. B. Martin
ED887/G AJ. A Sqn. Ldr. H. M. Young
ED864/G AJ. B Flt. Lt. W. Astell
ED906/G AJ. J Flt. Lt. D. J. H. Maltby
ED937/G AJ. Z Sqn. Ldr. H. E. Maudsley
ED912/G AJ. N Plt. Off. L. G. Knight
ED929/G AJ. L Flt. Lt. D. J. Shannon

Taking off at 10-minute intervals on the evening of May 16th, they flew seawards in groups of three. They were briefed to attack the Mohne Dam first, then, if it was breached successfully, to go on to the Eder Dam. In both cases they were to fly at a mere sixty feet above the water at 220 m.p.h. to achieve accuracy on the run-in—and that at night over a lake bounded by hills! Should both dams be satisfactorily breached any aircraft with mines not dropped would be available to assist in the attack on the Sorpe. Gibson led into the attack first and bombed accurately, but did not breach the dam. He called up 'M' to attack next, but it was hit by cannon-fire on the run-in and the bomb hit the parapet of the dam and exploded. Hopgood climbed away with one engine on fire, but suddenly the aircraft dived and crashed in flames. Two of the crew members were later reported prisoners-of-war. Next came Martin in ED909 which was hit in a fuel tank and one aileron. His bomb fell some twenty yards short, but he circled round nearby to draw fire away from Sqn. Ldr. Young who came in next to make an accurate attack, but it took the next to attack, Maltby in ED906, to breach the dam. Flt. Lt. Astell would have been called in before Maltby but he could not be contacted. It transpired that on crossing over a canal he turned at right-angles along it, possibly to check his position, and came under fire from the defences near Gilze-Rijen airfield in Holland. Dutch witnesses said that the Lancaster's navigation lights were on and presumably this was to mislead the defences as to its identity, but to no avail for ED864/G was shot down. It crashed into a barrack block on the edge of the airfield and blew up.

With the dam gone and water rushing through the villages below, the remaining three were called on to the Eder dam. Special V.H.F. sets had been installed so that Gibson could control the first two waves. He used their individual aircraft letters: 'Z' was signalled to attack first and made a number of unsuccessful runs, as did the other three in turn. The exacting conditions of height and speed were the same, but the hills this time made a run-in even more hazardous. Of the three Lancasters with bombs left, 'Z' hit the parapet and was destroyed by the explosion, 'L' scored a direct hit and 'N' breached the dam. After this

Of the specially modified "dam busting" aircraft ED817 shown went to Manston on April 20th 1943 to drop a test bomb preparatory to the actual dams raid.

the general return signal was given to this wave, but Sqn. Ldr. Young, as Gibson's deputy, accompanied his commander back to view the Mohne before setting course for home. He did not get back. Caught by flak crossing the Dutch coast, his Lancaster was brought down. The crew were buried at Bergen aan Zee.

The second wave was second in plan, if not in sequence, for they took off first. This consisted of:

ED923/G AJ. T. Flt. Lt. J. C. McCarthy
ED934/G AJ. K Sgt. V. A. Byers
ED927/G AJ. E Flt. Lt. R. N. G. Barlow
ED936/G AJ. H Plt. Off. G. Rice
ED921/G AJ. W Flt. Lt. K. L. Munro

They were briefed to attack the Sorpe Dam at a speed of 180 m.p.h. from the lowest possible height. McCarthy, an American in the R.A.F., was a late starter due to compass trouble. His take-off twenty minutes late did not affect the plan as in this wave the aircraft were acting individually. He located his target, dropped the 'special store' which hit the parapet causing some crumbling. Byers and Barlow did not

the Sorpe Dam in view of the failure of the second wave. En route, his gunners could not resist the temptation of firing at a train that came clearly into their sights. Finding it difficult to locate his target as he flew low over the lake, Brown dropped some incendiaries on the wooded bank to provide a directional landmark. With this aid he bombed accurately, but the dam held. Anderson too was called to the Sorpe, but due to the mist he could not locate it and reluctantly headed for home with his bomb. Burpee, also detailed there, failed to return, having been shot down at Gilze Rigen, Holland, on the outward journey. Ottley was diverted to the Lister Dam. This was acknowledged by him on W/T but he neither returned nor reached his target. Presumably his Lancaster was the wreckage found by the Germans at Hamm that morning.

The survivors returning on the morning of May 17th were de-briefed, had a brief celebration and a short nap and then went off in coaches to a party at Woodhall Spa. Here were kindred spirits, another squadron in the mysterious 616 plus series, No. 619. It was presumed that this was

Left : Nets supported by floats were a precaution against attacks on dam walls adopted by the Germans, who had no idea of the technique employed by Barnes Wallis. Such floats are shown on the Mohne Dam. Right : the breach in the Eder Dam revealed by photo-reconnaissance after the famous raid.

turn up; Byers, hit by flak over Texel, crashed in the Waddensea, and Barlow, so it was thought from wreckage found in 1962, came down in Germany, not far from the Dutch border. Rice had hit the water in the Zuyder Zee, which had wrenched off the bomb and put two engines out of action; there was nothing he could do except nurse ED936 back home. That left Munro, and his ED921 was hit by light flak over Vlieland putting the intercommunication system out of action, so he too was forced to return.

The third wave was the mobile reserve, so to speak. It was under the direct control, by radio, of No. 5 Group Headquarters and not under Wg. Cdr. Gibson, who was in operational control of the first two waves. Reserves were:

ED886/G AJ. O Flt. Sgt. W. C. Townsend
ED918/G AJ. F Flt. Sgt. K. W. Brown
ED924/G AJ. Y Flt. Sgt. L. T. Anderson
ED910/G AJ. C Plt. Off. W. H. T. Ottley
ED865/G AJ. S Plt. Off. L. J. Burpee

Townsend was detailed for the Ennepe Dam. He located his target and made three runs before dropping his bomb accurately, but ineffectively, at 3.37 a.m. It was daylight as he re-crossed the Dutch coast. Brown was sent to

another special squadron, but in fact it was a normal squadron introduced as a result of No. 5 Group expansion. They had only just received their Lancasters, in fact their first two had come from No. 617 when they changed over to their 'specials'.

Leave of 7 days was given to aircrew who had participated in the raid on the dams and ground crews received an extra 48 hour pass. The squadron did not operate again for a month.

In the Ruhr, coal mines, power stations and factories as far as forty miles distant from the Mohne and Eder were flooded and communications were disrupted over a wide area. Hundreds of people were drowned and livestock losses, cattle and pigs, ran into thousands.

Surviving 'G' aircraft were remodelled to standard aircraft and reissued. Nearly a year later, the few remaining were withdrawn for storage at Metheringham. Gibson's aircraft ED932/G, which was AJ.G for the raid, became AJ.V later. In August 1946 it was withdrawn from storage at Lossiemouth for No. 61 Squadron but it crashed the following November and was returned to store. It was scrapped in 1947.

Top: Men from the Commonwealth on the Dams Raid—left to right—standing: Sgts. Oancia, Sutherland and O'Brien, Flt. Sgts. Brown, Weeks, Thrasher and Deering, Sgt. Radcliffe, Flt. Sgt. McLean, Flt. Lt. McCarthy, Flt. Sgt. McDonald; stooping: Sgt. Pigeon, Plt. Off. Taerum, Flg. Off. Walker, Sgt. Gowrie. Middle (left): Wg. Cdr. Gibson with his dog Nigger, and (right): A.C.M. Sir Arthur Harris and A.M. Sir Ralph Cochrane at the raid de-briefing. Bottom: H.M. King George VI talks to Flt. Lts. H. B. Martin (left) and J. McCarthy (right); Wg. Cdr. Gibson is in the right foreground in both cases.

CHAPTER SEVEN

Battle of the Ruhr

Return from Peenemunde. A No. 44 Squadron aircraft that sustained damage during the attack on the German experimental station near the island of Rügen during the early hours of August 18th, 1943, in which 597 bombers participated.

A new intensive programme of bombing commenced in an attempt to reduce the production capacity of the vast industrial areas of the Ruhr valley. This was Bomber Command's 'spring offensive' of 1943. Apart from all the hazards of the operations reported and recorded, there was for aircrew all the pre-operational anxiety and strain of the hundreds of raids planned but never executed. Some were even cancelled after take-off by a recall signal. Published records show that Wuppertal had an attack on May 29th, but there is little recorded until a Dusseldorf raid on June 6th and 130 acres of Bochum being destroyed the next night. In that dozen, seemingly inactive, days between May and June meteorological records will provide the reason for the lull—but consider the strain in one squadron alone during the period. On June 5th at No.115 Squadron, 14 crews had been briefed in the morning to attack Oberhausen that night. It was cancelled in mid-afternoon, except for Flt. Sgt. R. Peate and crew, who went off in DS634 to drop mines off the West Friesian Islands. Next morning the same crews were called to a quick briefing and told that it was to be the same target again except for Peate's crew, who were dismissed in view of their recent trip. At 6 p.m. all were stood down for the night. Again next morning they went in for a briefing, this time for Mulheim. New charts were produced and everything made ready for the night. This time it really appeared to be on. Crews dressed and went out to their aircraft. Just before take-off at 10 p.m. it was 'scrubbed'!

A new phase in the bomber offensive opened in June 1943, the 'shuttle service' raids. By the advances made in North Africa, airfields there came within range of aircraft based in Britain, allowing more distant targets to be attacked, and this was first exploited by Lancasters. Equipment for receiving the type was shipped to Blida and Maison Blanche in North Africa, to be installed by the full-moon period in mid-June. The Zeppelin factory at Friedrichshafen on the shores of Lake Constance, bombed by Avro 504s in 1914, was the victim selected for the attack by Avro 683s in 1943. No longer were Zeppelins being produced or housed there, but it was an important production centre for radar sets.

The attack was due on June 20th, only four days after the operation order, marked BELLICOSE, had been received. This gave little time for training in the tactical innovation specified—that of receiving instruction by radio telephone over the target by the leader, Group Captain L. C. Slee, D.S.O. This was introduced following Wg. Cdr. Gibson's successful use of V.H.F. on the dams raid. Sixty Lancasters set out, 56 from No.5 Group and the remainder from the Pathfinders. This time the Channel was crossed at maximum height and gradually they came down to between 2,000-3,000 feet and then up again as they crossed the Rhine. Circling the target the crews awaited instructions which, given by the deputy leader, Wg. Cdr. G. L. Gomm, D.S.O., ordered them to bomb from 5,000 feet higher than briefed because of the intense flak. The bombing was not very accurate and only about six crews scored hits in the target area, but these did cause considerable damage. Six aircraft were damaged by flak but not one was lost and night fighters put up by the Germans in the Florennes (Belgium) and Juvincourt (France) areas to catch the bombers on their return were cheated of their prey, as the bombers turned southward across the Mediterranean to North Africa. On these shuttle raids some 5,000 lb of bombs were carried by each aircraft and these were loaded up again at Blida or Maison Blanche to bomb Italy on the return journey.

Gp. Capt. Slee with one engine of ED702 knocked out of action by flak bombed late, having already handed over control to his deputy. In his aircraft, limping along to Blida, was Major Mullock, M.C., the No.5 Group flak liaison officer. He had flown with Gibson to Italy and he participated in raids over the Ruhr to observe the German defences. He was a man dedicated to the task of minimising losses by giving advice on eluding the German defences and could speak from experience.

Another bombing-up accident happened at 6 p.m. on the evening of July 3rd, 1943. Lancasters of No.460 (R.A.A.F.) Squadron at Binbrook were being prepared for take-off at dusk. Work on most had been completed and some crews were already having their evening meal. Suddenly, through an electrical fault—according to the findings of a subsequent Court of Inquiry—the entire bomb-load dropped from DV172. This comprised a 4,000 lb and several 500 lb H.E. bombs and clusters of 4lb incendiary bombs. Up went the incendiaries with the H.E.s roasting in the centre of the inferno. Two shocked maintenance crew members, jumping from the aircraft, gallantly attempted to roll the bombs away, realised that it was futile and ran. Even as they ran they were knocked flat by shock waves as the explosions occurred, but fortunately they escaped injury.

Not only did the Lancaster disintegrate, but burning incendiary bombs were scattered over a large area by the explosion. R5745, the nearest Lancaster, burst into flames and within two minutes up went its bomb load, scattering more incendiaries. The station's fire services roared into action and directed by the squadron C.O., Wing Commander C. E. Martin, D.F.C., dealt with incendiaries burning near aircraft first, then concentrated on other equipment such as starter trolleys which were blazing and finally on the remaining incendiaries scattered over the airfield. During this, ED774 was suddenly found to be on fire. Rushing up on a fire tender the C.O., together with Flight Sergeant A. E. Kan, who had been bowled over in the first explosion, tackled the blaze from inside the Lancaster with hand extinguishers. Among others damaged was W4783, the famous veteran now in Australia. That night crews were briefed to bomb the port and local areas of Cologne, following up a raid on that town made on June 26th. Of the 26 Lancasters originally bombed up at Binbrook 17 took off and happily all returned safely. Cologne was again attacked on July 8th but the next night the target changed to Gelsenkirchen.

After the series of raids on Germany, Italy's turn came again on July 12th. This was the heaviest attack made on Turin to date. An all-Lancaster force set out in the first of a new series intended to hasten the surrender of Italy now that Allied Forces were advancing up from the toe of Italy, and it followed almost immediately upon the deposing of Mussolini. It was in this raid that Squadron Leader Nettleton, V.C., the courageous leader of the Augsburg raid, failed to return. At the de-briefing the crew of ED953 had an unusual experience to relate. When returning at 21,000 feet, the mid-upper turret canopy suddenly broke. The aircraft whipped over on its back and dived steeply while pieces flew off the cowlings and the pilot's windscreen disappeared. In spite of this he regained control at 4,000 feet and the Lancaster reached base without a single casualty. The cause is unknown, but most probably it was a collision or a near miss.

To restrict supplies on the Italian electric railways a precision attack was ordered on power and transformer stations at San Pola D'Enza near Bologna and Aquata Scrivia near Genoa by No.617 Squadron. Because of the distances involved, the crews were briefed to carry on south and land at Blida. There was little opposition, but the target areas were cloaked in haze and accuracy was not possible. In North Africa the weather proved even more tiresome than in the U.K. and the squadron had an enforced sojourn for ten days. They flew back via Leghorn, where bombs were dropped through the persistent haze into the harbour below. Back at Scampton the crews unloaded the Lancasters. In spite of the mists they could hardly regard it as a fruitless trip as they struggled towards the mess with crates of figs, dates, oranges, bottles of red wine and Benedictine. At least one was wearing a fez!

Lancasters were now flying westwards for the first time. The United States Army Air Force was interested in this bomber. When Sqn. Ldr. Nettleton and his crew had been sent to America on a visit shortly after the Augsburg raid, Bomber Command did not think that the prestige to be gained by 'showing the flag' in a Lancaster would balance the weight of bombs it could have dropped on Germany during its sojourn. However, political pressure was now brought to bear and the Command assigned Warrant Officer N. R. Ross to collect EE182, a No.103 Squadron aircraft with two operations chalked up, from Elsham Wolds. It was fitted with two 400 gallon long-range tanks in the bomb bay, giving a loaded weight of 63,000 lb with its total of 2,954 gallons of fuel. In early July 1943 it left Prestwick for Wright Field. Soon afterwards ED605 was prepared for a visit to Canada.

After an assault on the relatively close target of Aachen, on July 13th, Bomber Command prepared a holocaust for Hamburg and the code-word GOMORRAH was apt, in that it proved prophetic, but the presumption of the divine prerogative would appear to have been chosen by a staff officer more in caricature than character. In this concentrated attack which opened the Battle of Hamburg, on the night of July 24th, Lancasters were predominant, there being 347 to 246 Halifaxes, 125 Stirlings and 73 Wellingtons. In $2\frac{1}{2}$ hours they delivered 2,296 tons of bombs which included a large percentage of incendiaries and these

No. 9 Squadron crews. Left: Flt. Lt. Wakeford (on the steps) is about to begin his 50th operation, on this occasion the Friedrichshafen attack of June 20th. Right: Another crew of the squadron photographed on the same occasion.

Veteran W4236, June 1943. The Skipper, Plt. Off. Eager, points out the score. The aircrew, left to right, standing, are Flt. Lt. Hewish (Heston), Plt. Off. W. H. Eager (Winnipeg), Sgts. Stone (Pontypridd), Vanner (Romford), Petts (Ripley), Sharrard (Toronto) and Lawrence (Barnsley).

saturated the resources of the fire services. Police and A.R.P. headquarters were burnt and next morning, while a heavy pall of smoke hung over the city, American Fortresses carried out a daylight attack. Next night, Essen was planned as 'Sodom' with over two thousand tons of bombs dropped, with extensive damage to the Krupps works—as much as all previous raids put together—at the cost of 26 bombers.

Without a night's rest, crews were back over Hamburg, concentrating this time mainly on different districts of the town. Fires were still out of control from the earlier raid and the new attack created a lake of fire in the centre of the dock area which caused an enormous suction, uprooting trees and drawing many hapless citizens to their doom. Driven to shelter by flames and bombs they were suffocated in them by fumes and then cremated. Such was the unhappy fate of the citizens of this ancient Hanseatic town.

But the *coup de grace* had yet to be delivered in the C.-in-C.'s estimation. His original directions had been based on an estimate of 10,000 tons of bombs to destroy this second largest town in the *Reich*. Possibly this tonnage would have been reached if the weather had been suitable on the night of August 2nd/3rd. As it was cumulo-nimbus

One of the famous personalities involved in flying Lancasters—Wing Commander Guy Gibson, V.C. (right).

cloud caused them to fly up to 20,000 feet. That put the Stirlings and Halifaxes at a disadvantage. Not so the Lancasters, which, in theory, could fly above that height. So in cloud and storm, 329 Lancasters among the 740 bombers took another 1,426 tons to the city to drop in the smouldering ruins that covered thousands of acres.

Altogether, 8,621 tons of bombs were dropped on Hamburg of which half were incendiaries. A town with 3,000 industrial establishments, including the Blohm & Voss shipyards, had been destroyed at a cost of 87 bombers. Five days later came an all-Lancaster attack on Italy with Milan, Turin and Genoa as targets.

It was at this stage that 'Window', a simple but efficient means of reducing the effectiveness of German radar, was used. Metallised strips of paper were dropped in quantities from despatching chutes hastily installed—though not hastily introduced. Bomber Command had been pressing to use 'Window' but it had been withheld lest its effects rebounded to German advantage in attacks on this country. At first the enemy night fighter controllers were completely foxed and their fighters were despatched in force to deal with a presumed stream of bombers that were simulated by a single decoy aircraft dropping these strips.

A temporary grounding of the Mk. II was ordered in late July. This followed an incident on the 24th when 2/Lt. S. Gaunt, U.S.A.A.F., taking off in DS679, saw that his port outer engine was on fire. Immediately he cut the fuel and brought the appropriate Graviner extinguisher, mounted in the engine nacelle, into action and landed on three engines. An investigation showed short circuiting of wiring in the fuel pressure warning system and an examination of other No.426 (Canadian) Squadron Lancasters showed that the possibility of shorting was not an isolated case. This was reported immediately to Air Ministry, who ordered the grounding of all Lancaster II units, until a safe re-wiring had been effected. Subsequently this was documented in an official Lancaster modification—one of 800 issued so far involving such items as an improved navigator's table, provision for carrying an extra 2,000 rounds of .303 ammunition, introduction of the Mk. XIV bombsight in general and the stabilised auto-bombsight (S.A.B.S.) for No.617 Squadron.

The loss of forty aircraft, at least 17 of them Lancasters, is a heavy price, but if ever an operation was vitally necessary, it was the raid on the German experimental establishment at Peenemunde where the Germans were preparing their 'V' weapons. Hitler had already hinted at new weapons as a palliative for his people and intelligence had pinpointed Peenemunde as the research centre. Crews practised for the operation along the East Coast, and Operation HYDRA was put into effect on the night of August 17th. Group Captain J. H. Searby, commanding No.83 Squadron, directed operations from his Lancaster, which circled round and round while he watched target markings and then broadcast to the 597 aircraft approaching that the markers were accurately placed. He exhorted the main force to bomb on them with similar accuracy. During the final stages, German night fighters had concentrated and this accounted for the heavy losses.

Five days later Lancasters joined in attacks on chemical works at Leverkusen, Dusseldorf and various Rhineland targets. On August 23rd it was Berlin, where 1,700 tons were dropped in fifty minutes. Encounters with German night fighters were becoming more frequent and there were 31 combats that night. In fact the value of the air-gunners as such was being debated. Halifaxes had sacrificed gun positions originally fitted, for an increase in performance, but there is no doubt whatsoever that air-gunners were invaluable as lookouts and in the Berlin raid they proved most necessary in their primary function, for Lancaster losses were 5.4% compared with a corresponding 8.8% and 12.9% for Halifaxes and Stirlings respectively.

extinguisher into the flames without success. As the English coast hove in sight the port inner engine stopped and an emergency landing was requested at the first airfield. With the port-wing framework red-hot the Lancaster landed, and the station fire-fighting personnel soon had the fire out. Another five minutes flying and the metal would have been completely burnt through.

The gunner of another Lancaster that night claimed that they were attacked by six Bf109s right over Berlin itself. Cunningly the enemy fighters attacked in pairs, and while the gunners might well have been mistaken in their recognition and in the numbers, there was no doubting the intensity of the attack by the riddled appearance of JA868 back at its base.

In this raid, Group Captain H. I. Edwards, Australia's first air V.C. of the war, participated. In the rear turret of his Lancaster was Flying Officer R. C. Dunstan, a one-legged air gunner who used to take crutches with him in the air. He had lost a leg in action in the Army.

After joint participation in main force attacks on Nuremberg, Rheydt and Munchen-Gladbach and Berlin again on the nights of August 27th, 30th and 31st respectively, the first of September's raids was an all-Lancaster attack on Berlin made in good weather from 21,000 feet during the last hour of the 3rd. In the course of this raid, incidentally, the B.B.C. actually made a recording in a Lancaster over Berlin. Unfortunately, 22 aircraft were lost.

Mannheim was the target for No.5 Group aircraft on the 5th and next night came a 30 minute Lancaster attack on Munich. During the latter raid, a pilot passed out

The first Canadian-built Lancaster, KB700. Designated the Mk. X, it was the forerunner of 430 built by Victory Aircraft. KB700 was burnt-out after hitting a grass-cutter when it overshot landing at Middleton St. George. Fortunately the crew made a safe escape.

An hour's flying time from the target ED802 was intercepted by a Junkers Ju88. The rear gunner, Sgt. R. Middleton from Leeds, and the Ju88's gunner opened fire simultaneously. A red glow appeared in the cockpit of the Junkers and it disappeared below, but its fire had taken effect. The starboard fuel tank of the Lancaster, then more than half full, was set on fire. The skipper, Plt. Off. J. McIntosh, a veteran of the earlier Berlin raids, took the only sensible course open; jettisoning his bombs, he turned for home and dived in an effort to blow the flames out. Three times he dived the Lancaster, but each time flames spurted when the Lancaster levelled out. Fortunately all four engines were still working and McIntosh gave them full throttle to cut time to the coast. The flight engineer hacked at the fuselage in order to make a hole to get an

at 23,500 feet from lack of oxygen and ED749 plunged down. The navigator and flight engineer wrestled for control in the up-ended Lancaster and succeeded in pulling it out at 8,000 feet. At this lower altitude the pilot recovered and took over control. It was then that the bomb-aimer was found to be missing and it was not known if he baled out or was thrown out. After landing it was found that, in the terrific strain of the pull-out, cowlings had been wrenched from the outer engines, the astro-dome cracked, a canopy panel was missing, the starboard fin and port elevator were damaged, and aileron fabric had torn, but the structure had held.

The new blind bombing and navigation aid H2S was coming into increasing use. This apparatus was self-contained and did not rely on transmissions from ground

Named " Ruhr Express," the first Canadian-built Lancaster went on operations. The crew's mascot " Bambi" is being taken aboard.

stations. It necessitated a large housing which was slung beneath the fuselage. During the month of September No.12 Squadron was stood down to train with the new apparatus, but not until two months later was the more effective Mk. III H2S introduced, which became standard.

The most concentrated attack delivered to date fell on Hanover later in the month to be followed by another attack a few days later. No.619 Squadron was alarmed that only one of its twelve aircraft returned from the raid that night, but signals in the early hours came from Stradishall reporting six landed safely and the remainder were safe but scattered at Feltwell, Chedburgh, Great Sampford, Framlingham and Wratting Common. During a raid on Bochum on September 29th a crewless Lancaster of No.83 Squadron flew eighty miles. JB187 had gone into a dive from which recovery took the combined efforts of the pilot with his feet on the instrument panel and the navigator and flight engineer. The machine was still nose-heavy so it was headed for home. Once over the U.K. the pilot ordered the crew to bale out and to keep it steady for his own exit he jammed a bag between the control column and the instrument panel. It then flew on an approximately straight course for 80 miles before striking the ground.

Early in October 1943 a force of No. 5 Group's Lancasters bombed as far afield as Munich but this failed because of inaccurate marking. Raids followed on Kassel, Frankfurt, Offenbach, Lugwigshafen, Stuttgart and Friedrichshafen. Lancasters were now joining in from No. 6 (R.C.A.F.) Group. These were Mk. IIs operated by Nos.408 and 426 Squadrons. The former had only changed over to Halifaxes a few weeks previous when the decision was made to re-equip again with Lancasters. Conversion training was carried out in typically wet English summer weather that delayed their first operation. During this period, on September 15th, the squadron was visited by KB700, a Mk. X, the first Canadian-built Lancaster.

Canadian industry had been seeking the opportunity to make a really worthwhile contribution to the war effort. At first it was arranged that the Stirling would be built, but this was hurriedly changed to the Lancaster, using American-built Merlins. Victory Aircraft was formed and the first to leave the lines, KB700, was christened 'Ruhr Express' by Mrs. C. G. Power, wife of Canada's Minister of National Defence for Air. Handed over from the factory on August 6th, it hopped the Atlantic in 9 hours 30 mins.

That the Canadian Lancasters were Mk. X did not mean that Mks. I–IX existed. The policy was to reserve up to Mk. IX for British built versions and use from Mk. X upward for Canadian versions. Broadly, the Canadian X corresponded to the British III with main differences as detailed in the Type-by-type Review at the end of the narrative. Canadian production was not then geared for large scale deliveries and the Mk. X did not enter service straight away. The policy with No. 6 (R.C.A.F.) Group was to standardise on Halifaxes, but to utilise the Lancaster II which had its Hercules engines as a common factor with the Halifaxes, and then to re-equip with Lancaster Xs when Canadian production permitted.

No.408 (R.C.A.F.) Squadron, after several frustrating delays, became operational with Lancasters on October 7th. Sixteen aircraft took off and fourteen returned; all the crews were safe but there was a tragic third party accident. DS724, in difficulties over Hutton-le-Hole, Yorks, some eighteen miles east of Thirsk, was abandoned by its crew, who took to their parachutes. Their bomber fell at Manor Farm, Stainton, where a fifty-one-year-old farmer, George Strickland, was killed when the 4,000 lb bomb exploded.

A Lancaster could fly on two engines and more than once was forced to do so. During the Hanover raid on October 18th EE137 was hit as Warrant Officer J. E. Thomas steadied up for the run-in, with the bomb doors already open. For minutes there was a fusillade of flak and the mid-upper gunner, Sgt. A. D. Collins, was wounded. Then a lull portended the presence of night-fighters and a

A W.A.A.F. member cleaning sparking plugs at Syerston in 1943—there were 96 plugs to each Lancaster.

Me210 closed in firing short bursts which set the port inner engine on fire and started a fire in the fuselage. Collins, with flak shrapnel embedded in his back, stamped the flames in the fuselage out, although this meant leaving his oxygen supply post.

However, the night-fighter had been eluded in the evasive turns the pilot had made. Over the French coast, at a lower height, it was a target for light Ack-Ack fire and was hit again. Over the English coast the port outer engine stopped, yet Thomas brought it down safely to his base on two engines.

It might well seem like going one better purely for the sake of effect to recount how a Lancaster returned home

Maintenance on a Lancaster at dispersal, Syerston, May 11th, 1943. Apart from repairs and major overhauls there were 400 routine inspection operations to be carried out by ground crews between operations.

when circling with a flaming engine, he replied that a few more minutes waiting for a clear wouldn't matter as he'd already been alight for hours! When he did land he stayed with the fire crew until the flames were extinguished.

Raiding Kassel presented a number of hazards to Lancaster crews two days later. DV193 was holed in a number of places in quick succession and before the crew —including three Australians, a New Zealander and a Canadian—had recovered from this they were shot up by a fighter. By throwing the Lancaster in a dive, the pilot, Flt. Lt. Eric Greenacre, managed to elude the fighter and bring his crew, including a wounded gunner, back to his base. Mention of this Commonwealth crew is appropriate

on one engine. But such a case is fully documented with a squadron commander at the controls and a veteran crew whose operations totalled 300. The Lancaster concerned was ED700, a Mk. III, and its engines were Merlin 28s Nos. A2867, A2762, A3870 and A2520 from port to starboard respectively. It was intercepted by a Junkers Ju88 when nearing home after attacking Hanover. Some sixty rounds of cannon shell hit the aircraft, the majority of which passed straight through but several hit vital spots. The trimming controls and airscrew pitch controls were damaged and hydraulic control pipes severed. Only one engine remained steady and the revolutions of that could not be altered owing to control damage. Of the other three engines, two stopped altogether and the propeller of the third raced like a Catherine wheel, shedding sparks.

Wg. Cdr. P. Burnett, D.F.C., actually nursed his machine to its base, but landing was thwarted by another Lancaster crashing on the main runway and only a subsidiary runway, across wind, was available. The undercarriage responded to the emergency system and a landing was effected without mishap. Within four days ED700 was reported serviceable, but three new engines and two new turrets had to be installed as well as the replacement of piping and minor components.

Seventeen Lancasters were lost in a maximum range raid to Liepzig on October 20th and many crews that returned had much to tell at de-briefing; the crew of ED370 reported three separate engagements with night fighters. ED366 was absolutely riddled with flak, but none of the crew were touched. JB362's crew reported being hit by incendiaries from an aircraft above; several gunners made claims for enemy fighters shot down, chiefly reporting Ju88s. But for sheer coolness, Warrant Officer White took the cake that night. When asked if he wanted an emergency landing

in that, apart from mixed crews, R.C.A.F. and R.A.A.F Squadrons of Lancasters participated in this raid.

There had been frequent reports of incendiary bombs falling on to bombers below. Some twenty-five cases were recorded during 1943. Also, there were occasions on which Lancasters fired at friendly aircraft; but a singularly distressing accident to a No.166 Squadron crew happened during the Kassel raid, of one crew member killing another. The mid-upper gunner of DV220, traversing his turret as he followed the course of an enemy fighter, shot into the rear-turret and killed the rear-gunner. In theory this was impossible due to an interrupter gear, but for some reason, possibly through enemy action, it did not function.

It was in 38 Lancasters of the Canadian squadrons and No.115 Squadron of No. 3 Group that the G-H blind bombing radar device was first tried out in an attack on Dusseldorf on the night of November 3rd when 2,000 tons of bombs were dropped in 27 minutes. LM360 of No.61 Squadron was shot up by an Bf110 on the way to this target and the pilot, Flt. Lt. William Reid, was wounded in the head, shoulder and hands; but finding his crew unhurt he decided to press on. Another attack was made by a Fw190, which apart from further damaging the Lancaster killed Flt. Sgt. J. S. Jefferies and mortally wounded the wireless operator, Sgt. J. W. Norris. Reid, wounded yet again, still kept on to the target 50 minutes' flying time away. With his navigator dead and instruments smashed he steered by the Pole Star and the moon to bring his Lancaster down at Shipdham. Reid was awarded the Victoria Cross for his gallant flight and his Lancaster continued in service until it was stalled and crashed at Fiskerton.

The emphasis in operations was now shifting from the Ruhr to the German capital, and in this new phase Lancasters played the prime rôle.

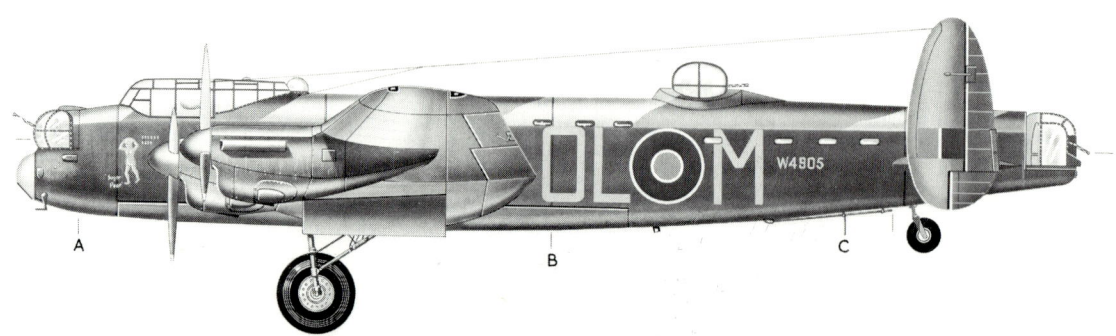

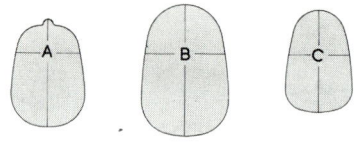

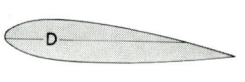

'Sugar Plum' of No. 83 (Pathfinder) Squadron at Wyton, July 17th, 1943, and the
high-speed Lancaster mailplane project.

CHAPTER EIGHT

A matter still in the air

After flying ND458 on its 121st operation, the pilot congratulates the ground crew who had serviced it since arrival at No. 100 Squadron, viz. Sgt. W. Hearne (West Wickham), Cpl. R. T. Withey (Henley) and L.A.C.s J. E. Robinson (Solihull), J. Hale (Tottenham) and J. Cowls (Penzance).

There were two words, ugly in their implication, that were rarely used officially because of their damaging effect on morale. These words were Structural Failure and Sabotage; both were mentioned in connection with Lancasters. Structural failure may appear to reflect on the manufacturers, but it should be appreciated that the very best of cars, driven excessively fast around a very sharp corner, will inevitably overturn. The best have their limits.

One Lancaster was driven to the limit in the early morning of March 20th, 1942. The pilot, lost in cloud returning from No.97 Squadron's first operation with Lancasters, took his aircraft down through the gloom to observe his position. Unaware that the cloud base was so low, he broke out at a mere 200 feet in a shallow dive and he had literally to yank the control column to lift the nose clear of a row of houses at Boston. Perhaps some of the occupants are still there, if so it is an incident that they are unlikely to forget. A roaring four-engined monster skimming the roof-tops leaves an indelible impression. As for the crew, they must have been petrified as the starboard wing hit a roof and the wingtip broke away while the port wingtip, for no apparent reason, but as if in sympathy, stuck upright at 90 degrees to the plane! Fortunately L7570 remained airborne and the pilot kept cool. Although finding control difficult, he brought the Lancaster down near the beach at Freiston near Boston and all the crew walked away. The missing wingtip they could understand but the upturned one baffled them. They had only hit one house. Technicians from Farnborough who later examined the wreckage showed that in the circumstances it was a happy chance, for it showed just what would go first when a Lancaster was jerked out of a dive. Modification action was taken to strengthen the wingtips.

Experts from A. V. Roe's were immediately called to No. 5 Group Headquarters where a conference was held. That night, in the lounge of the George at Grantham, after closing time, the carpet was rolled back and on the floor Harold Rogerson of Avro's chalked out the changes necessary to strengthen the tips. This modification was first tested exactly ten days after the accident on R5508—the machine in which Nettleton won his V.C.

Sabotage on Lancasters was first mooted in mid-November 1942 after W4324 of No.101 Squadron had crashed in Wales. There had been an explosion in the air, the tail had blown off and the fuselage dived in flames into the ground beside a cross-roads. Sabotage was the only solution that appeared to make sense.

Suspected sabotage at Waddington revived memories. A Lancaster from No.50 Squadron, ED486, took off with a full load of bombs including incendiaries, and disappeared into the clouds. Shortly afterwards it reappeared in a dive and crashed. Indications that it exploded and crashed—instead of the expected sequence of crashed and exploded—gave rise to rumours of sabotage. In spite of the strictures on security it was almost inevitable that the locals at Waddington would sense the aura of mystery surrounding this crash; in any case several local men worked on the airfield. The reaction was surprising—the older inhabitants put it down to the saboteur!

Apparently sabotage at Waddington was not new; it had happened in the 1914-1918 War when No. 48 Training Depot Station had been located there. A series of mysterious accidents had occurred, and investigations were made following the crash of B.E.2E A1350 in which it appeared that someone had tampered with a wing spar. Then a D.H.6 suddenly nose-dived into the ground and it appeared that the control column had been damaged before take-off. The controls of a D.H.4 suddenly jammed; the pilot survived but the machine was so damaged that the cause could not be found. Security was tightened and no more crashes could be attributed to sabotage, but the culprit was never found. Rumour had it that two mechanics were caught at night sawing partly through a control column and that they were shot in Lincoln Castle! Now there were rumours again at Waddington, but if a saboteur there was, this undertalk evidently frightened him off. In any case, there was no direct evidence—but was it structural failure?

Seemingly an obvious weakness, but necessary to the design, were the twin fins at the ends of the tailplane. They were stressed for all normal bomber flying but what was not envisaged in design was the violent evasive manoeuvres to shake off enemy fighters. The approved drill for evasive action was actually a corkscrew motion. On February 7th, 1943, during fighter affiliation exercises by ED442, a Mk. III of No. 50 Squadron, the starboard fin collapsed inward as the Lancaster was deliberately side-slipped. The pilot brought off a forced landing without casualty. Not so the pilot of Mk. I R5676 of No. 1660 H.C.U. at Scampton that same month, who was allowed no time, for as he levelled out from a turn, pieces were seen to break off from the aircraft and it spun into the ground taking all its crew. The port and starboard fins had evidently become detached for they fell several thousand yards from the main wreckage. Again that month, this time with a No.103 Squadron aircraft, W4857, the port fin collapsed during evasion exercises and tore the port elevator away. The pilot ordered the eight occupants to bale out and he himself tried to fly the aircraft back to base, but as he approached Elsham Wolds the other fin and elevator broke away and he was killed in the resultant crash. Modifications to the fin were already under way and the last documented accident due to the failure of that component was on June 6th, 1943, to ED569 of No.207 Squadron which landed successfully. Following this, however, came a spate of mysterious accidents for which investigations were carried out on suspected structural failures, but which could well have been sabotage.

On the night of July 7th ED548 of No.12 Squadron was flying on a practice cross-country flight at some 8,000 feet. It was somewhat off-course, but this could have had little effect on what happened—according to observers on the banks of the Firth of Forth, an explosion and a wind-searing sound as the aircraft plunged into the water. Salvage was impossible, but some parts were found on land some three miles away. The weather was bad, with clouds and icing, but that did not account for the explosion.

For no apparent reason DS665 of No.115 Squadron blew up. The pilot, on his first operational flight, and all the crew perished. The wreckage was strewn over two miles near Maidstone. Workmanship did come under suspicion as eight days later a port outer engine fell out of a Lancaster of No.1654 H.C.U. as it made a fair landing at Wigsley. This was traced to faulty welding, but since the machine concerned was R5483, very much a veteran by that time, it was not representative of that early production batch in which crews had unbounded confidence.

From then on, a Lancaster crashed in mysterious circumstances every few weeks. Sabotage was mooted. On operational units security was strict, but on operational training units it was often possible to walk on to the airfields unchallenged. It was not that security was lax but that personnel just could not be spared to patrol airfield perimeters which in some cases were several miles in extent.

One after another, with frightening frequency, Lancasters dropped from the sky. On the night of September 3rd fate, or some malignant force, struck at R5492 of No.1661 H.C.U. It was over Exeter on night-flying exercises while the local defences practised. Caught in the blinding beams of five or six searchlights it dived and twisted. The moving fingers of light followed it as it turned, keeping within its specified 12,000-16,000 feet altitude. Then, suddenly it plunged. It was followed down by the lights for several thousand feet but its descent, increasing to terminal velocity, was quickly lost to them. None of its occupants had time to leave although an escape hatch was found a mile from the wreckage. The reports from the A.A.

Veterans. Top to bottom: The unofficial motto of Bomber Command, PRESS ON REGARDLESS; a presentation bomb being prepared for delivery; DANTE'S DAUGHTER, ED731, on which an American pilot completed a tour of operations and partner to ND458 opposite, ND644 of No. 100 Squadron.

43

observers were collated and pieces of wreckage were gathered by the experts from the Royal Aircraft Establishment. However, on an analysis of the facts, one rather startling fact emerged, that the Lancaster had flown well over 600 flying hours at a time when over 500 hours was the exception with four-engined bombers.

The possibility of fatigue was explored, but it did not explain another Lancaster accident that month, when W4904 from No.1667 H.C.U., Faldingworth, on a bombing practice flight, thumped into the ground. A man near the scene of the crash had heard the drone of a high flying aircraft suddenly change to the whine of a fast diving machine, followed by a succession of thuds as pieces fell in a two-mile trail. Again pieces were collected for Farnborough. That Lancaster had only been flown for 162 hours.

Six days later came the same tragic sequence of events with all the crew killed. This time it was ED583 of No.100 Squadron, which was being flown on a height test by an American pilot with over 200 flying hours on Lancasters. Ground witnesses heard a cracking sound in the sky and a rain of wreckage fell over an area seven miles in circumference. The wreckage was taken to No. 58 M.U. for the inspection by experts who had to decide on the cause. There was no doubt of structural failure to the wingtips and in other cases the fins were shown to have broken inwards. However, the problem was—did these failures cause the accident, or did they occur in a sudden dive following the primary cause?

During the next few weeks L7575, ED812 and DS653, all from H.C.U.s, dived to earth and crashed before a single occupant could escape. In the case of ED812 from No. 1660 H.C.U. a definite explosion had been heard above the clouds. Sabotage was never far from the minds of the authorities, but there was some controversy. It was argued that the accidents were too widespread for saboteurs. This was countered by the argument that saboteurs would try to avoid repetitive crashes at one location, which would bring suspicion too close. Another question nagged at those investigating the accidents—if these unaccountable accidents happened over our own territory, how many more aircraft, reported as missing from operations presumed by enemy action, may have crashed in similar circumstances?

At the end of 1943 all evidence on Lancaster accidents

was collated and the Chief Inspector of Accidents, Air Commodore Vernon Brown, issued recommendations. There were three major points: instruction to units on the diving characteristics of the Lancaster, the incorporation of all recommended modifications at factories producing the aircraft and the retrospective modification of all in service—and further investigation. A side issue was a recommendation to enforce the use of flying harness. This was perhaps surprising as in practically all cases the crews had no time to jump, let alone get out of a harness, and also in all cases the impact was too great for any chance of survival, harness or no harness.

During 1944 two Lancasters, LM619 and PB749, lost their ailerons in high speed dives and investigations switched to possible jamming of the elevator trimming tabs and also to the distortion of the elevator covering. Further modifications were put in hand and although mysterious accidents did not cease they were not repetitive. In retrospect, 1943 stood out as a dark year for Lancaster mishaps and it may be possible that saboteurs were at work and the mysterious accidents were, to use a legal phrase, the work of a person or persons unknown.

A saboteur was actually caught, but it was something of an anti-climax. At the Vickers Armstrongs Castle Bromwich factory in June 1944, wires in a Lancaster were found to have been cut. A watch was kept, but two other instances occurred before the offender was caught. Military intelligence and a criminologist from the Special Branch at Scotland Yard were called in and traced it to the hand of a disgruntled workman. There was no connection with the spate of accidents to service Lancasters the previous year. These have never been properly explained and perhaps never will be. Modifications continued to be made from the strengthening of the formers to the storage of an additional fireman's axe.

Some of the accidents may well have been caused by seemingly trivial things such as loose equipment. It had been common practice to stow articles on the platform under the transmitting/receiving set until it was realised that they could foul certain grease nipples and so cause controls to jam. One defect was traced to water entering an oil cap on the elevator tab jacks and freezing, so jamming that control. Perhaps the aircraft were mishandled or perhaps . . . This matter can only be left in the air.

Fire and water. An H.C.U. Lancaster that crashed on landing and burst into flames (top) and a Lancaster "ditched" in a river. In both cases the crews are believed to have escaped unhurt.

61 SQUADRON, SEPTEMBER/5-6/1943
B III DV232 QR-K. LANDING AT
SYERSTON, STALLED TO PORT, FLYI...
AT ZERO FEET SHE TOOK A ST...
TURN AND 'BELLY-FLOPPED' INTO THE
TRENT, ¼ MILE NORTH OF EAST ST...

CHAPTER NINE

Wings for Victory

A Lancaster in Trafalgar Square! L7580 of No. 207 Squadron displayed for London's "Wings for Victory Week" for which the target was £150,000,000 in War Savings. The sum, bottom left, represents the total when the photograph was taken. A Services team can be seen giving a physical training exhibition.

Lancasters played an important part in War Savings Campaigns. In the same way that the Spitfire had been symbolic of defence in 1940, and large sums had been donated to purchase more, so later did the Lancaster become symbolic of victory in the series of 'Win the War' Savings Campaigns. Committees in various towns throughout the country organised 'Wings for Victory Weeks' and for these a Lancaster became an indispensable adjunct to the occasion. A Lancaster was assembled in Trafalgar Square for London's 'Wings for Victory Week' and following Edinburgh's week, Air Vice-Marshal Smart, in announcing the sum raised of £13,250,000, stated that it represented 330 Lancasters.

For Manchester's 'Wings for Victory Week' in March 1943, a locally produced Lancaster, ED749, together with a damaged fuselage of one from service, was exhibited in Piccadilly. Appropriately, Lancaster had a Lancaster, ED999, for their week.

It is true to say that the Lancaster received acclaim out of proportion compared with its worthy contemporary, the Handley Page Halifax, but ever since the daring daylight raid of April 17th, 1942, on Augsburg it had been in the public eye and the most famous attack of the war, that of breaching the Mohne and Eder Dams, was carried out exclusively by Lancasters.

An Australian savings group suggested that an actual Lancaster be sent out to the Commonwealth to stimulate their savings. This met with a rebuff in certain quarters, where it was argued that the war effort would best be served by keeping every Lancaster within striking distance of Germany. On the other hand, not only would it boost savings, but also morale at a time when the Japs were on Australia's doorstep.

Canada, the Australians said, already had a Lancaster. This was true. R5727 was flown to Montreal on August 25th, 1942, for the dual purpose of stimulating labour recruitment and as a pattern aircraft for Canadian production. Incorporating all modifications to date and fully armed except for bomb load, it had set out carrying special freight at an all-up weight of 60,000 lb, flown by a Ferry Command crew captained by a well-known pre-war

American pilot, Captain Clyde Pangborn from Wennatchee, Washington. Another American, Captain Newton Collins, of Laurel, Missouri, was co-pilot on the transatlantic run to Dorval.

To fly 3,000 miles to Canada was one thing, to fly half-way round the world to Australia was another. A Lancaster could fly down to North Africa and across the Middle East to India, but from there to Australia all staging posts were in the hands of the Japanese. The only way was across two oceans, the Atlantic and Pacific.

A new Lancaster III was allotted from Avro's on May 11th, 1943, via No. 39 M.U. for kitting up with spares to be carried. The crew selected were all Australians due for a rest from operations. They were:

Captain	Flt. Lt. P. S. Isaacson, D.F.C., D.F.M., of Melbourne
Navigator	Flt. Lt. R. S. McF. Nielson, D.F.M., of Wollongong
Bomb Aimer	Flt. Lt. A. V. Richie, D.F.M., of Linfield
Flt. Engineer	Plt. Off. D. Delaney, of Sydney
Second Pilot	Flt. Off. E. M. Copley, D.F.M., of Perth
Air Gunner	Flt. Sgt. J. Grose, of Leabrook
Air Gunner	Flt. Sgt. A. F. Page, of Hobart
Fitter	Cpl. C. Spencer, of Alphington

In addition to the crew there were two passengers: Lord Burghley, British Controller of Repair and Overseas Supply, and Group Captain C. V. Wincott, R.A.F., of the British Air Mission to Washington.

At Prestwick all was made ready to start the first lap. ED930 'Q for Queenie' took off on May 22nd, but after a few hours the weather clamped down and the captain was ordered by radio to return. Soon the weather cleared and Queenie hopped from Prestwick to Dorval in 15 hours 10 minutes. Then on across Canada and down through the U.S.A. and then out to sea across the Pacific. Australia was reached on June 4th after 72 hours 12 minutes in the air. The flight achieved a Pacific crossing record that remained unbeaten for a year until the famous R.A.F. Liberator 'Commando' AL504, used by Winston Churchill, arrived.

It was planned that New Zealand rallies would be served first and after overhaul at No. 1 Aircraft Depot

R.A.A.F. Laverton, Queenie left five days after its arrival for New Zealand in connection with that Dominion's Second Victory Loan Campaign.

At 4 p.m. on June 11th the inhabitants of Ohakea welcomed Queenie, which had flown via Melbourne at an average speed of 191 m.p.h. at 10,000 feet. Next morning, punctually at nine, it took off and flew north to Taumarunui; then changing direction landed at both Blenheim and Wigram. Flight schedules were constantly reaching the captain, with instructions where leaflets should be dropped, and the navigator and gunners had a busy time throwing them overboard. The last port of call before return to Australia was Whenuapui. Attempting to take off on the morning of the 16th, after heavy rain, the aircraft skidded off the runway. The captain cut the engines immediately but the fuselage and undercarriage had to be checked for strain before it continued on its way.

Back at the Laverton Depot four days later it received its R.A.A.F. number, A66-1, in place of its R.A.F. service number ED930, but it was universally referred to as Queenie. In October it flew to Tasmania, calling at Westum and Hobart and flying over west coast towns. Next, a New South Wales tour was scheduled, but at No. 1 Bombing and Gunnery School, Evans Head, New South Wales, Queenie landed in a swamp on October 26th and a fitting party of ten, unfamiliar with the type, repaired it on site. It was flown out after temporary repairs to No. 3 Aircraft Depot, Amberley, and went on to Laverton, where its standard R.A.F. finish was replaced by natural metal finish with S.E.A.C. type roundels. It was placed on display at Mylands Aerodrome four miles from Perth, then flown over a series of western coast towns and at Brisbane it was joined by Spitfires of Nos.548 and 549 Squadrons for formation flying over the city.

Queenie was covered in autographs. On one fourteen day tour of 10,500 miles no less than 71 take-offs and landings were logged and a host of people passed through her fuselage. Various towns were 'beaten-up' and bombed with tour pamphlets. To impose a necessary control on all who wanted to look-over the machine, it was arranged that bond purchasers of £10 or over could inspect the inside and purchasers of £100 or over would be given a flip.

A typical visit was that to Rockhampton on April 23rd, 1944. After circling the town several times Queenie landed at 11.30 a.m. The crew received a civic welcome and the captain described a typical operation in which he had participated. To guard the aircraft, the local Air Training Corps Squadron, No.60, turned up in full strength. During the day 381 applications for investments were made totalling £17,480. The following morning Queenie was off to the next rally.

After a series of tours this much-travelled Lancaster was allotted to No. 1 Aircraft Performance Unit at Laverton for trials with special signals equipment. When plans were made to produce the Lancaster in Australia, Queenie was allotted to the Australian Department for Aircraft Production as pattern aircraft in late October 1944 but was released for a period to permit a second Loan tour. It was back with the Department in November but by that time another Lancaster had arrived in Australia. Perhaps it had been a mistake to have sent Queenie straight from the works without the glamour then associated with operations. But when 'G for George' was sent this aspect was certainly not overlooked; this was truly a veteran Lancaster.

The 100th operation is marked on ED588 after attacking the V.1 base at St. Leu, July 4th, 1944. It was the third Lancaster at Skellingthorpe to reach its century.

W4783 was delivered to No.460 (R.A.A.F.) Squadron on October 27th, 1942, where it became 'G for George'. It went on the first of its ninety operations on the night of December 5/6th, 1942, to Mannheim. During its sixteen months of operations, it was flown by 29 different pilots and taking into account the various crews, some 200 different men, mostly Australians, flew in this Lancaster during its 664 flying hours with the squadron. Several crews completed their tours on this machine. Its first pilot was Flight Sergeant J. A. Saint Smith and alongside the bomb insignia to signify each bombing sortie appeared a Leslie Charteris 'Saint' insignia. On the night of January 13/17th George operated against Berlin taking a war correspondent as passenger, and returned with 13 flak holes for him to write about!

George first operated from Breighton, until June 4th, 1943 when the squadron moved by air to Binbrook. The ground crews and equipment were moved in Horsa gliders while the aircrews flew in their Lancasters.

Some unusual incidents occurred on the night of October 22/23 in an electrical storm on the way both to and from the target—Kassel. Balls of fire, other than German pyrotechnics, were observed and blue flames of St. Elmo's fire appeared to dance on the propellers. Worst of all, a lump of ice hurtled through the perspex side window and struck the flight engineer on the head, causing minor injuries.

In the air George was damaged over twenty times by enemy action and once by accident when on the last day of August 1943, over Munchen Gladbach, an incendiary dropped from another bomber went through the tailplane. It was also damaged in No.460 Squadron's Lancaster catastrophe already related. On April 22nd, 1944, after its 90th and last operation the previous day, it was officially retired from operations.

This was the aircraft that was presented to Australia in mid-1944 for display in the War Museum at Canberra. It was extensively overhauled for its flight and the unit letters AR-G disappeared but the bomb silhouettes remained together with a small 'G' on the nose.

W4783 is visited by Mr. Curtin, the Australian Prime Minister, when it was serving in No. 460 Squadron, with which it went on 90 operational flights.

Photographed circa February 1943, the days of this Lancaster, like so many, were numbered. On the night of March 1st/2nd it was shot down over Holland.

The crew was:

Captain	Flt. Lt. E. A. Hudson, D.F.C. & Bar, of Rockhampton
Second Pilot	Flg. Off. E. P. Smith, D.F.C., of Newcastle
Navigator	Flg. Off. W. C. Gordon, D.F.C., of Raleigh
Bomb Aimer	Flg. Off. T. V. McCarthy, D.F.C. & Bar, of Brisbane
W.Op./Air Gunner	Flg. Off. G. H. Tindall, D.F.M., of Cremorne
W.Op./Air Gunner	Flg. Off. Young, D.F.M., of Matraville
Fitter	Flt. Sgt. H. Tickle, of Adelaide
Fitter	Sgt. K. A. Ower, of Telamon

George left Prestwick on October 11th, 1944. A message before take-off was received from H.R.H. The Duke of Gloucester, the Governor General Designate of Australia, who sent a good-will message wishing them a safe voyage and hoping that George would be joined by many Australian-built Lancasters.

George finally reached Australia at 11.32 a.m. on November 8th when it landed at R.A.A.F. Station Amberley, to the west of Brisbane.

The aircraft was required for a tour in the south, but a request by Mr. S. G. Hudson of Rockhampton was first granted and after taking off on the 10th and circling Brisbane, George landed at Rockhampton at 3 p.m. after twice circling that town. The crowd cheered as the aircraft's captain stepped out to be greeted by his father and family from whom he had been parted for over four years. The crew were fêted and George was put on show. It was still touring in April 1945 when it visited Rockhampton again in company with Beaufort A9-580 in connection with the Third Victory Loan.

By July 1945 George had become surplus and was parked out in the open, but when the Netherlands East Indies aircraft moved from Canberra in late August 1945 and made space available, it was stored at Station Headquarters earmarked for the Australian War Museum. Meanwhile the original Queenie was at No. 7 O.T.U. East Sale for synthetic training pending the introduction of Lincolns. In February, 1946, it was transferred to Tocumwal, New South Wales and the following November was converted to instructional airframe No. 1. Queenie was broken up in mid-1948, leaving George the sole Lancaster survivor in Australia—until recently.

From left to right, downwards : Preparations for a raid. A bowser crew fill the tanks, then the armourers fit the guns that had been removed while the aircraft was at dispersal. A test flight is made to check that everything is in flying trim. H.E. bombs are dispatched from the dump and a load of incendiary bombs is shown on trolleys. Three views are shown of aircrew briefing at which an American major of the U.S.A.A.F. is in attendance. The final view shows the crews discussing the target immediately after the briefing.

From left to right, downwards: Crews draw their flight rations, before a tender takes them to dispersal. Entering the aircraft, cockpit and crew drill is carried out. Lined up ready at dispersal, they await the signal to start; headed into the wind, they take off with a send-off from their station's W.A.A.F.s. Fore and aft—rear gunner's view and air bomber's position—the latter has his hand on the release button. On return there is de-briefing and a meal. Later, photo-flash pictures taken automatically may be displayed for showing results.

Sir Arthur Harris in a minute to Mr. Churchill wrote of wrecking Berlin from end to end if the United States Army Air Force and the Royal Air Force jointly attacked the German capital and that for a price of between 400 to 500 bombers it would cost Germany the war. The U.S.A.A.F. at that stage were not ready for such long day flights—well over 1,000 miles for the round trip—over enemy territory. Harris apparently decided to go it alone, for the R.A.F. delivered sixteen major operations against Berlin between November 15th, 1943, and March 24th, 1944, and this became known, retrospectively, as the Battle of Berlin.

For attacks on the long distance targets, Lancasters predominated: in the 9,111 sorties against the German capital 7,256 were by Lancasters, 1,643 by Halifaxes, 162 by Mosquitos and 50 by Stirlings. Some 2,300 tons of bombs were dropped effectively on Berlin on November 22nd by the aid of the new Mk. III H2S. The Tempelhof Lake, an important location, showed up well on the instrument which, this time, Lancasters were pioneering. This apparatus, which worked on a 3 cm wavelength instead of the 10 cm of earlier models, was first instituted in ED350 and tested on June 23rd in the presence of Gp. Capt. D. Saward, O.B.E., of H.Q. Bomber Command and Colonel Ed. Grey of the U.S. Eighth Air Force. The first production H2S Mk. III sets were fitted in JB352 and JB355 by the Special Installation Unit at Defford, the airfield for the Telecommunications Research Establishment, in September and on November 15th they were rushed to No.83 Squadron and four nights later operated in 'The Battle of Berlin', the Command's main theme for the closing months of 1943.

A heavy raid was planned for November 26th for which the 'maximum effort' call was again made. One squadron, No.103, sent 30 aircraft out that night at a time when 24 was normally the maximum squadron establishment with six reserve aircraft. The attack was deemed most satisfactory, but there were setbacks both before and after. At Wyton JA686 blew up just before 5 p.m. while an armourer crew were working on it. An electrical failure caused the photo flash to explode and up went its fuel tanks and bombs. Four airmen and four civilians were killed and a total of twelve men were injured. Then coming back the airfields were congested and one captain could not obtain permission to land although his fuel was dangerously low. When down to the last few gallons he did the only sensible thing—ordered his crew to bale out and, having pointed EE111 out to sea, followed them. All the crew landed safely and the Lancaster was found next morning in the Humber.

En route to the target, DV365 was intercepted by a fighter over Belgium. The Canadian rear gunner was wounded in the groin and Sgt. C. Cushing in the mid-upper turret was hit above the eye by flying metal when a cannon shell exploded against his turret. Damage to the aircraft included holing both starboard propellers and damaging navigational instruments, including the compass. Flt. Sgt. Fennell decided to drop his bombs in the direction of the nearest military objective marked on his maps, a German aerodrome, and return home steering westward by the North Star. But no sooner had the aircraft risen with the release of the bombs than an Fw190 fired from behind. A cannon shell exploded between the flight engineer and the navigator. As the cockpit filled with smoke, the nose suddenly dropped and the Lancaster dived. Fennell ordered the crew to bale out. Wrestling with the controls as 350 m.p.h. registered on the air speed indicator, he thought, understandably, that the aircraft was doomed. Knowing some of his crew members to be wounded he remained at his post, miraculously regained control and cancelled the order to abandon.

Taking stock, Fennell found that now both his

Australian wireless operator, Flt. Sgt. D. B. Harvey, and the Irish navigator, Sgt. J. Smythe, had head wounds, but their troubles were by no means over for further and persistent attacks were made by a fighter. The rear gunner, in spite of his painful wound, kept up instructions to the pilot to 'corkscrew'. Finding difficulty in locating their position without instruments they came down warily to 3,000 feet, where they sighted the lights of an airfield. Descending further to 2,000 feet to try to effect recognition, they were met with intensive fire from light flak. They struck out towards the west and came down thankfully at an airfield in the south of England.

Berlin was again attacked in great strength on December 2nd. No.460 (R.A.A.F.) Squadron lost five Lancasters that night including one with two war correspondents, Nordhal Greig, a Norwegian, and N. Stockton, of Australian Associated Press. Next night, Leipzig was raided at 4 a.m., and Lancasters and Halifaxes were landing well after dawn. Berlin's next ordeal was an all-Lancaster attack during a night of bad visibility that defied Wg. Cdr. Cheshire's attempts in DV380 to satisfactorily mark the target. One Pathfinder Squadron, No.405 (R.C.A.F.), found the target for certain, but could not find their way back; three of their Lancasters crashed in England and of these Warrant Officer S. H. Nutting, D.F.M., a rear gunner on his 45th operation, was the sole survivor. Twelve Lancasters were wrecked in Britain that night.

December brought raids on the mysterious 'Ski-sites', noted in France by photographic reconnaissance, and which were connected with the secret weapons being forged at Peenemunde. Not until later was the nature of the German 'V' weapons known.

The Battle of Berlin continued throughout the winter and returning crews in the early hours of December 17th found a treacherous low-lying fog over East Anglia. No.97 Squadron alone lost, apart from a crew near the target, twenty-eight aircrew members in crashes. Of the 21 that set out only eight landed back safely at Bourne. JB171 crashed in the middle of the airfield, killing all its crew. On the edge of the airfield, JB119 burnt with three of its crew dead and the wreckage of JB176 lay a short distance away. Four of their aircraft came down at Graveley, one of which crash landed and only the mid-upper gunner survived. JB351 and JB482 circled round, but failed to see adequately the landing lights through the fog. Their crews took the wisest course and baled out, landing safely near Ely and Wyton respectively, but what happened to the latter Lancaster is still not known; most probably it went out to sea. Luck does at least seem to have been with one other Lancaster. Hit by incendiaries from another aircraft over Berlin, it limped back. With two engines out of action a signal was sent to the effect that it was ditching off the coast of Denmark. After a short interval, the message was cancelled and JA908 came safely across the North Sea on two engines to land at Downham Market.

On the first night of the New Year Lancasters took off around 7 p.m. to deposit 1,000 tons of bombs on the German capital. The wintry weather then took a hand, restricting operations, but Stettin was attacked four nights later before runways became snowbound and airfields cut off by blocked roads. Since Lancasters stood a better chance of getting above the cloud, it was an all-Lancaster force, 680 in total, that took 2,000 tons to Berlin on January 14th and on the 20th the town had the heaviest pounding to date. The next night, when Magdeburg was attacked, there were heavy losses of both Lancasters and Halifaxes. Berlin was attacked again before the end of the month and on the last occasion H2S was used with good effect. This proved the operational value of the apparatus and production and installation into aircraft was speeded. Attacks continued on the V.1 installations on the French coast and No. 5 Group received instructions to attack a number of French factories used in the German war effort. Berlin, if the main theme, was by no means the only activity.

The main types of bombs dropped by Lancasters with their weight in pounds excluding the 12,000lb. "Tall-boy" and 22,000lb. "Grand Slam" special stores. The small, shaped bombs are of low capacity designed to penetrate before exploding, while the sectionalized tubular bombs were of high capacity with light casings to facilitate explosion on impact and cause damage by blast. The 8,000lb. bomb was also in general use and can be visualised, since two sections of a standard 12,000lb. bomb comprised an 8,000lb. unit.

While some aircrew managed to complete two tours of operations others succumbed at the outset. Such was the case of the young pilot of ND563, Plt. Off. E. J. Murray, who was killed even before he became airborne on his first operation. His Lancaster of No.630 Squadron swung on take-off at East Kirkby, bumped across a road causing the undercarriage to collapse and then up went the 4,000 pounder. Taking off with full bomb and maximum fuel load gave a narrow safety margin. That same night as ND498 was taking off from Fiskerton for the attack that developed over Stuttgart at 2.30 a.m. on February 21st, a tyre burst. It slewed completely round, the undercarriage crumpled and collapsed. The crew were hauled out uninjured and the crash was isolated—which was just as well as its 4,000 lb bomb exploded later. As a result of the two explosions, glass was shattered over a wide area including the towns of Boston and Skegness. There were no civilian casualties but six aircrew were killed at East Kirkby.

Returning from Stuttgart that night ED749 was rammed by an enemy fighter. When still 200 miles from the nearest friendly coast a violent shock rocked the airframe and the bomber lurched and went down out of control. The pilot ordered the crew to stand by to bale out, but at 4,000 feet

Fog, mist or low cloud could call a halt to the bomber offensive but snow or mud rarely affected operations. These 1943/44 winter scenes are of No. 467 (top) and 50 Squadron (bottom) Lancasters.

control was regained. When checking on the crew the wireless-operator found the mid-upper gunner wounded in his turret, which had been crushed in, and the rear gunner was jammed in his turret but not badly hurt. The pilot carried on to Ford and landed safely. Reconstructing what had happened, it appeared that an enemy fighter had cut across their line of flight, turning in fast from port while the mid-upper gunner was rotating to starboard, so that there was no warning. It had bent the starboard fin and rudder outwards, carried the aerials away and torn a hole six feet long in the wing as well as crushing the turret. As evidence, pieces of the fighter were embedded in the top of the fuselage.

Schweinfurt was the target two days later and after the lapse of a similar period it was Augsburg's time to suffer. On March 6th came the first of the softening-up attacks as a prelude to D-Day. Air Marshal Harris had argued that his force was specifically designed for an assault on industrial targets at night; they had neither the armour nor armament suited to day operations and lacked the necessary training in formation flying. Any let-up in the bombing of Germany might give the Nazis a breathing space for industrial recovery; then there was the question of harming civilians in occupied territory. On the other hand much pressure was being put on Bomber Command to disrupt communications in France and the Low Countries and in the event it was something of a compromise.

To the crews this presented a far more personal problem. Thirty operational sorties, usually noted down in the log book in red, fulfilled a tour; but now there were sorties and sorties. Le Mans on March 7th was a short trip, bombing a factory at St. Etienne-la-Recamerie on the 10th or taking part in the extensive mining operations the next night was not to be compared with participating in the all-Lancaster attack on Stuttgart on the 15th when 3,000 tons were dropped in an hour.

A case was presented for using operational hours instead of 'trips' and this argument was strengthened by raids that followed, the Michelin factory at Clermont Ferrand and then two attacks on Frankfurt. The railway yards at Laon on March 23rd were followed next night by a Berlin attack after which the B.B.C. calmly announced " 73 of our bombers are missing ".

Missing did not include other Lancasters like ND572 that night, which had been considerably damaged by an encounter with an Fw190; the turrets were out of action, there was a five foot diameter hole in the mainplane, flaps were shot away and the tanks holed, both rudders were shattered and instruments smashed and the inter-communication system was disrupted. The pilot had the utmost difficulty in maintaining control, let alone in landing without flaps and instruments. He touched down at 160 m.p.h., swung off the runway and collided with another aircraft. Apart from the rear-gunner, who had been killed in action, the crew were uninjured but yet another Lancaster was written off. Another crew that night, returning in ME381 with two seriously injured gunners, reported a fight with a four-engined enemy aircraft, a Focke-Wulf Condor. With two gunners wounded it fell to the wireless operator, Sgt. K. T. C. Williams, to direct the pilot, Flt. Lt. R. W. Picton, from the astrodome.

This was a bad period for losses. Ninety-six crews were

lost in an attack on Nuremburg. First the enemy guessed the target correctly and then tell-tale vapour trails gave their fighters a lead. Added to this there were severe icing conditions, causing several crashes.

Lille, Villeneuve and St. Georges, all railway centres, were targets for April 9th. As the bombers took off in the gathering dusk, those watching at Binbrook were held spellbound by the behaviour of ME727 of No. 460 (R.A.A.F.) Squadron. This was virtually a brand new machine, the crew had been diverted to it after their own had been found to be unserviceable. This would have been its first operation. As it left the ground it turned to the left with its port wing down and went round and round in a circle. Five times the Lancaster circled at a few hundred feet with the turns getting steeper each time. It was obviously out of control and doomed at that low height. Finally, on its sixth turn, it side-slipped into a wood just over a mile away. There were no survivors.

It has already been pointed out that apart from actual

9,805 Lancaster delivery flights; that this is more than the number of Lancasters built is due to re-deliveries after repair or modifications.

Apart from Commonwealth squadrons, the Poles were the only ally to have a Lancaster squadron. No. 300 (Polish) Squadron was the first of the Polish squadrons of the R.A.F. and had been in existence since July 1940 when it formed with Fairey Battles. It was still bombing with Wellingtons in early 1944, but from late December 1943 crews had been going to No. 1662 H.C.U. at Blyton to prepare for Lancasters, and by April 18th, 1944, they were joining in the general disruption of transport in France by bombing a railway junction at Rouen, while 200 of No. 5 Group's Lancasters attacked marshalling yards at Juvisy near Paris.

The following night No. 5 Group's Lancasters bombed the railway yards at La Chapelle outside the Gare du Nord which No. 617 Squadron marked for them, while No. 3 Group were bombing Cologne. Brunswick was the target for 265 Lancasters from No. 5 Group and 135 from No. 1

Christmas 1943. The Lancasters of No. 463 (R.A.A.F.) Squadron at Waddington snapped in seasonal conditions, shortly after the Squadron's formation under Wg. Cdr. R. Kingsford-Smith from "C" Flight of No. 467 (R.A.A.F.) Squadron on November 25th. The Bomber Command Film Unit was attached to this squadron and participated in many operations.

operations there was the strain of operations planned and cancelled, but even when squadrons were stood down routine training continued. There were lectures on a variety of subjects such as evasion in the event of landing unrecognised in enemy territory, ditching training in the static pond, gun tests, clay-pigeon shooting and a host of other duties. Lancasters were flying on training exercises, practising new techniques, liaison exercises with the military, or as in No. 619 Squadron on April 9th, one Lancaster had to be reserved for the local Air Training Corps Squadron to inspect, and the boys looked over LM484 while the crew explained the equipment to these keen youngsters.

One veteran squadron leader, with a home posting after four years in the Middle East, was visibly shaken to find women on R.A.F. stations. " I've just seen a woman corporal", he was heard to mutter in the Mess, as if this went beyond the bounds of reason, but next day he was really staggered. A new Lancaster was delivered and he goggled in amazement as tresses fell when the Air Transport Auxiliary pilot removed *her* helmet. She was followed by the 'crew', a single sixteen-year-old cadet who acted as flight engineer. The A.T.A. during the war years made

Group on the night of April 22nd. Unfortunately some of the target markers dropped some three miles out; this was realised by the master bomber, Wg. Cdr. Cheshire, who made great efforts to overcome jamming by the Germans and contact the bombers. This exploit was one of those mentioned in this officer's citation for his well-deserved Victoria Cross.

Warrant Officer N. C. Jackson must have been elated yet apprehensive on April 26th, 1944. He had received a telegram announcing the birth of his son—but that night he was on operations, his last operation of his tour before leave and a rest. The target was Schweinfurt and it must have been with considerable relief that he felt the Lancaster lift as the bombs were dropped and it climbed out of the target area, while the pilot set course for home. But before they were clear cannon shells from a fighter ripped into the Lancaster, throwing Jackson to the floor with splinters in his right leg and shoulder and setting fire to one of the fuel tanks in the wing. Considering this a matter in his province as flight engineer, he told the pilot he would attempt to put out the fire and with a hand extinguisher tucked into his lifejacket, he clipped on a parachute, jettisoned the emergency exit in the top of the fuselage, and climbed out.

One of the few actual action shots of Lancasters, taken during a day raid. The bombs dropping appear to be 1000 lb. G.P. bombs. Below, the effect of bombing on Frankfurt 1945, viewed from aircraft taking ground crews to examine the damage to German towns.

The effect of a 200 m.p.h. slipstream is in itself an agony. As he forced himself out his parachute spilled into the fuselage and other crew members grabbed at the lines to play them out as Jackson progressed—but he slipped and falling from the fuselage on to the wing grabbed an air intake to secure a hold; the fire extinguisher slipped into the void below. The fire by then had spread and flames licked at Jackson, burning his clothing, face and hands and parts of the parachute. It was clear that the Lancaster was doomed and the pilot gave orders to abandon. Four of the crew made safe descents. Jackson with a smouldering parachute landed heavily and broke his ankle. Burnt so badly that the right eyelid had stuck shut, he crawled to a village, where the Germans picked him up. He was ten months in hospital before going to a prisoner-of-war camp. After the war, when his deeds became known, the award of the Victoria Cross was announced on October 20th, 1945. His Lancaster was one of the 23 aircraft lost that night.

Lancasters were at this time bombing a series of special targets. They went twice to St. Médard-en-Jalles near Bordeaux as the first attack set light to woods near the target and made so much smoke that accurate aiming was impossible. A *Luftwaffe* depot at Kjeller near Oslo had a visitation and an ammunition dump at Maintenau was attacked and blew up with a flash that was seen a hundred miles away. Unfortunately the weather that night caused seven accidents to bombers on their return. Aircraft factories, munition works, railway yards and coastal batteries all featured in crew briefings. On the night of May 7th seven Lancasters, with a large '60' marking instead of the usual code letters, were making the first operation of No.582 Squadron, an addition to the Pathfinder Force.

The battle of wits behind the scenes by the respective intelligence organisations affected Lancasters not a little. The Germans were meticulous in correlating all possible data from the machines and their crews when shot down. A printed form was produced listing all the items of equipment likely to be carried in British aircraft, quoting them by their Air Ministry reference numbers, with a space to fill in the works serial numbers! At 2 a.m. on the morning of April 28th a Lancaster was hit by fire from a German night fighter and exploded in the air. The wreckage fell just over a mile south of Diest in Belgium. Within seven days a report was submitted on Form T.Nr.2759 to the local commander in Brussels down to such detail as: Control unit Type 218 Ref. Nr. 10LB/264 Ser Nr. 1325.

On their standard proforma the Lancaster's usual T1154 transmitter, R1155 receiver and TR9F transmitter/ receiver were printed with adjacent spaces for the serial numbers of the instruments to be written in. The Germans had a phonetic alphabet of their own and ED768, for example, which crashed at Gravenwezel in Holland, was reported as Emil Dora 768.

The Battle of Berlin ended in March. If not decisive in this battle the Lancaster had been the chief weapon. Now the stage was set for the Army to invade the Continent and the battle for France commenced. To this it could be said that the Lancaster had contributed since 1942 by attacks on German industries and these continued, but in a tactical role it could also give direct support to local operations of the field forces.

Many a Lancaster returned damaged from operations. The top two views are of the same No. 50 Squadron Lancaster. The tail gunner's position was an unenviable one, as following views show, including ME703's return from Mailly-le-Camp, shown opposite a Lancaster with a shell-hole through the wing. Bottom views are of a night-fighter and A.A. shrapnel damage.

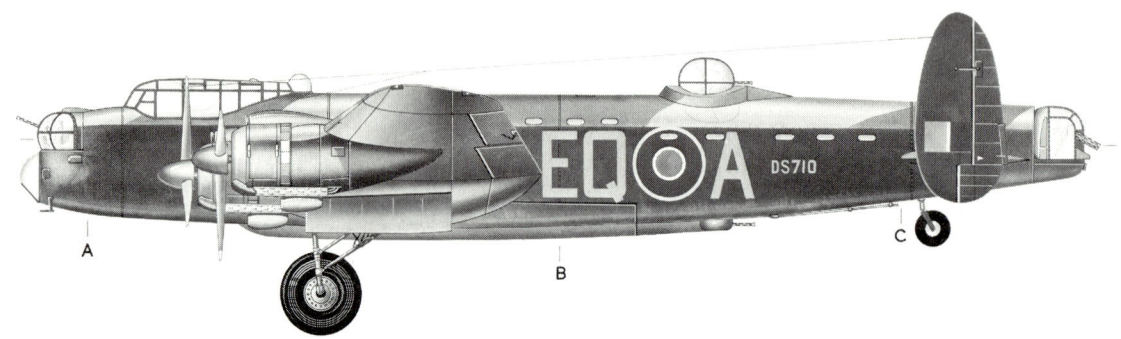

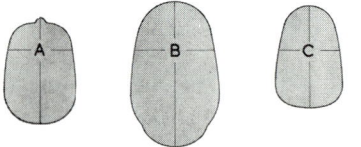

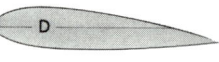

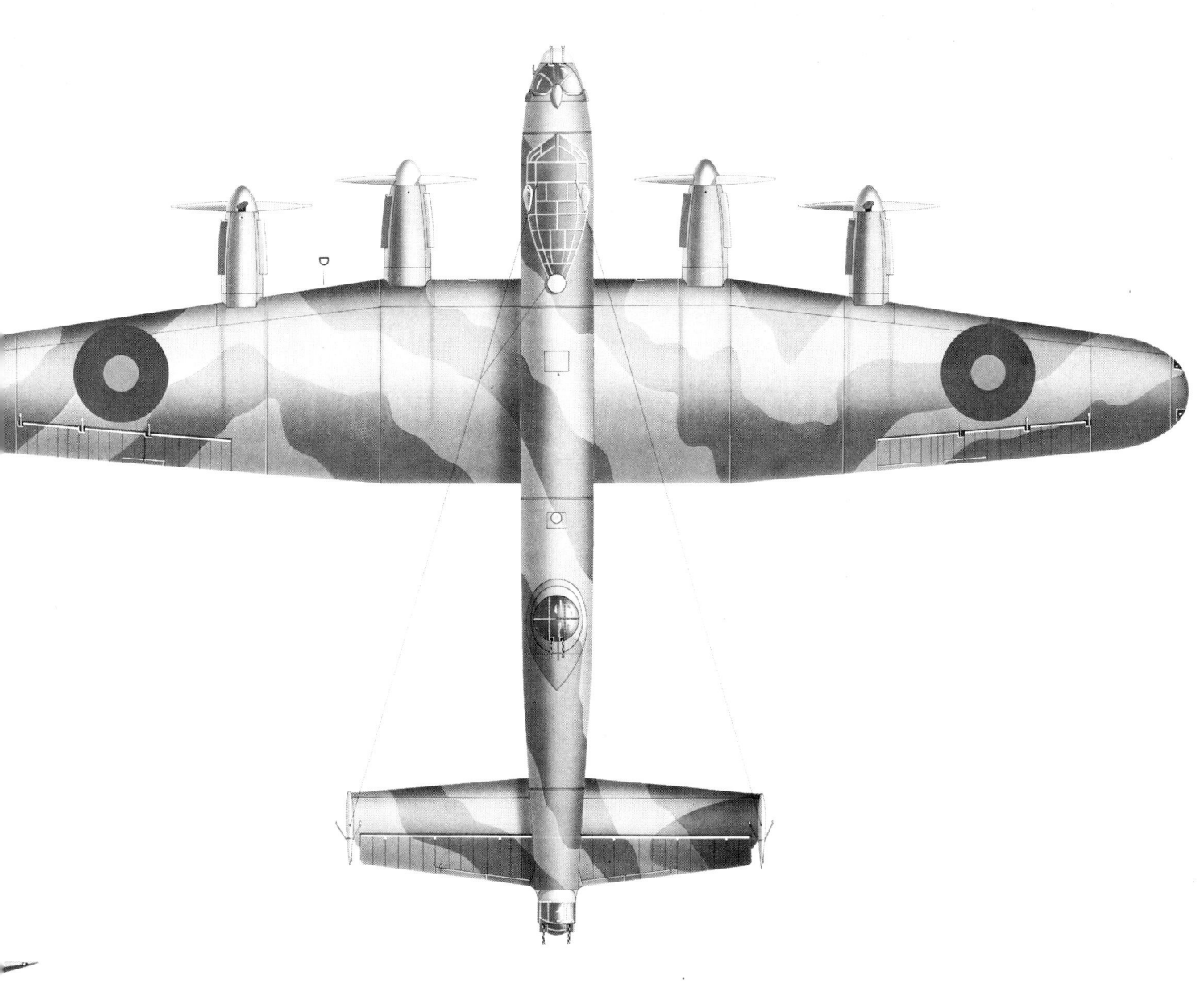

**A Lancaster II of No. 408 (Royal Canadian Air Force) Squadron at Linton-on-Ouse
in late 1943.**

Training aircraft types at the Empire Air Armament School, 1944. Arrayed in front of Lancaster PB136 and the Wellington are, left to right: Master, Martinet, Anson, Magister, Proctor, Moth Minor, Hurricane and Spitfire.

A Lancaster crew consisted normally of a pilot, navigator, flight engineer, air bomber, wireless operator/air gunner and two air gunners. From the tradition (not respected by 'back-seat drivers') that the man at the wheel is the man in charge, the pilot became the 'captain' or 'skipper' irrespective of rank. In him was vested the full responsibility for taking off, flying to the target and returning. The navigator was responsible for calculating the safe and accurate navigation of the aircraft; he rarely had occasion to look out on night raids, but had to be throughly conversant with all aids to navigation and was more of a 'calculator' than an observer. The air bomber was 'the eyes of the navigator' and the map-reader. He, too, had some navigational aids but his task was more visual. The decision of the exact moment of bomb release was his task and the pilot worked under his direction when on the bombing run. In an emergency the air bomber had to man the front turret. Apart from his normal duty of receiving and transmitting radio messages, the wireless operator had to be competent to obtain radio fixes and was responsible for the recognition signals. When instruments were installed to give warning of the approach of enemy fighters these too came under his jurisdiction. The air gunner's job is self-explanatory; a high standard of marksmanship and aircraft recognition was essential and in an attack by fighters he advised the pilot on evasive manoeuvres.

The pilots, navigators, air bombers, wireless operators and air gunners met first at an Operational Training Unit. After months of intensive training and no doubt frustrations, the various aircrew categories came together there to sort themselves out into fighting groups of flying men. For better or for worse, a crew was to be formed to work together, fly together, and as a combined unit convey the battle to the enemy. This was probably the most important point in the careers of bomber crews but, to be successful, it had to be approached informally. A course at No. 28 O.T.U., Castle Donington, early in 1944, provides a typical example.

The mixed bag of aircrew—pilots, navigators, air bombers, wireless operators, mid-upper and rear gunners— were brought into the large briefing room at nearby Wymeswold. There was considerable excitement, and the men at first grouped themselves broadly in their particular categories—after all, they were the groups in which they had arrived, having in many cases trained together. Here and there, the odd attachment had formed tentatively between different categories. The wings they wore were a general guide to their duties, full wings for pilots and single wings for others with indicative letters. Some air bombers would have gained their wings as observers—the single-winged 'O'—but with the changing demands of the Service, some of them may have been reclassified as straight navigators or as navigators-B, for bomb-aiming. From late 1943 the wireless operators were distinguised by a winged 'S' for signals.

The Station Commander gave his welcoming speech, and explained the idea—" Move around, chaps, and sort yourselves out. If anyone has any difficulty in fixing up with a crew, let us know. When you have settled your crews, the captains will report the names of their members."

Eyes met other eyes, a little self-consciously. Just how did you recognise the chap you wanted to be your pilot, or navigate you to the target and back again—or keep a sharp lookout at the back with a ready trigger finger? How did you know if you could rely on someone? How would you get on with that chap over there—or that chap with the big moustache?

The mutual selection went on. A pilot would go up to a navigator and say, diffidently, "Fixed up, yet?" The navigator would glance at the pilot. Looks O.K., he'd think. "No!" A few more words . . . and a crew had begun to form. Some pilots would know a pair of gunners—they might know a wireless operator. A navigator would perhaps know an air bomber. Within half-an-hour Bomber Command had found itself some new Lancaster crews— although the men would not meet their Lancaster for some time yet. The O.T.U. courses at first had regular intakes with a length of eight weeks in summer and twelve in winter, but this had changed to varying the intakes and maintaining a set ten-week course. This normally gave crews 80 flying hours. Some thirty-odd crews were reaching the twenty-two bomber O.T.U.s every month at this time and more were bound for Lancasters than any other aircraft type.

At the first opportunity, the newly formed teams would fix up their quarters, together if possible where rank did not make it impracticable. Sergeant was the lowest flying rank and it was therefore a matter of Warrant Officers' and Sergeants' Mess or the Officers' Mess. The first beer-up would be called for that same evening.

As the days went by, and the members of the crew got to know each other better, so they began to work together as a team. Wellingtons were the aircraft, and as the course progressed the time of action seemed nearer. The real thing was just around the corner, even if the most exciting thought on this course was the special Bullseye flight—near to the enemy coast, dropping window, to take the enemy's attention away from the real bomber stream.

All the crew had arrived at O.T.U. as trained men with wings, but were still 'sprog' crewmen. Now they were given an aircraft to share and look after, and to learn more of their job of war. They were a crew. And when off duty they visited the nearby towns and villages it was with a proud sense of family. They were getting into the real war soon—together. Ideally, they should have flown Lancasters there and then; the fact that they did not is due to Bomber Command policy, that until Lancasters were available in quantity, every available one should be in squadron service. However, for the gunners, air bomber and navigator, the 'Wimpy' provided a good training medium.

The next stage was familiarisation with four-engined aircraft, but the units concerned were not always ready to accept pupils and Battle Schools, later renamed Aircrew Schools, provided a course to improve physical fitness and imbue some general military training. There were lectures on discipline, administration and exercises to assist evasion in the event of being forced down uninjured in enemy territory. More directly to the point there was synthetic training for the various categories of aircrew. So far, they were in crews of six. The seventh member, the flight engineer, was collected at the next stage, the Heavy Conversion Unit, where he had already been flying for several weeks. The flight engineer was the aircrew's official link with the ground crew; he supervised their work and in the air was responsible for the operation of the engine controls such as cooling, and noting fuel consumption and temperatures. In mid-1944 they were trained to take control in an emergency, sufficiently to bring the aircraft back over this country for a bale-out.

At H.C.U.s too, ideally there should have been the type that they would fly on operations, but the 32 aircraft that made up the establishment of a normal H.C.U. were mainly Halifaxes supplemented by Stirlings. The course was normally five weeks but could be extended by two weeks for crews that had not been to an Aircrew School. For the first week it was usually ground training, then followed day flying and finally night flying to complete a total of about 40 hours in the air.

Since it was essential that Lancaster crews had some actual Lancaster experience before reaching squadrons, the Command were forced to spare a few Lancasters for training by a Lancaster element at the H.C.U. which constituted the final stage in training at these units. Later the Lancaster elements were formed into separate units as Lancaster Finishing Schools, on the basis of one to each Bomber Group using the type. Thus, there was a No. 1, a No. 3, a No. 5 and, later, a No. 6 L.F.S. However, when later in 1944 the supply position became more satisfactory, the finishing schools were disbanded and the Lancasters went to H.C.U.s.

With a few exceptions, neither H.C.U.s nor L.F.S.s received Lancasters direct from production. Squadrons were allocated aircraft from production and the training units received them from Maintenance Units following repairs after damage on operations or by crashing. Thus, even if the crews were 'sprogs' their Lancasters at this stage were veterans. EE139 'The Phantom of the Ruhr' served successively in Nos. 1656 and 1660 H.C.U.s. There were conversion sets for fitting Lancasters with dual control and normally two or three at training units were so fitted.

When crews reached a Lancaster squadron, they had received at least twelve hours' flying in the type and normally another twelve hours would be arranged before they were called upon to operate. The 'new boy' atmosphere was overcome by the fact that crews entered a squadron as a team. They would be allocated their machine, which might be anything from a '100 op' veteran on which a crew had just completed their tour to a factory-new aircraft just brought in by an A.T.A. ferry pilot. On the other hand, in some squadrons a particular aircraft was not allocated to a crew until later.

At this time, before centralised servicing, each Lancaster had its own ground crew. There was a close feeling between the two crews. 'Their' aircraft belonged to the mechanics as much as to the men who flew in her. Both crews knew their 'Lanc' inside-out. She was fussed over and treated with every care. It was a matter of pride that when required she would start up at once and that she would be serviceable at all times. The aircrew knew she would take them there and back efficiently and safely, because of the care of those who looked after her on the ground—unless by some quite faint chance the enemy might interfere! Most of the time things went smoothly and the crashes and losses recorded throughout Bomber Command here must not be taken as typical occurrences in each and every squadron. For a three-month period, mid-September to mid-December 1944, No. 100 Squadron performed 800

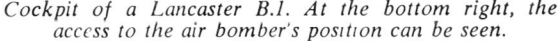

Cockpit of a Lancaster B.1. At the bottom right, the access to the air bomber's position can be seen.

Dark green 4,000 lb. H.C. bomb bodies, each nearly seven feet long, being taken to dispersal by W.A.A.F. drivers.

sorties without a single loss. Nevertheless, Bomber Command suffered more casualties than any other Command and some nights over 500 trained aircrew were lost.

For the first operation crews usually had an easy target if it could be arranged, but often they had to plunge straight into a full-scale operation. A new crew arriving at North Killingholme in April 1944 had LM455 allotted for their first operation on May 1st against the Société Berliet Motor Vehicle Works at Lyons. To their surprise they found that the squadron commander, Wg. Cdr. J. S. Bennett, D.F.C., was joining them. Usually Squadron Leader was the highest rank regularly detailed for operations, although many squadron commanders (normally at Group Captain level for the Pathfinders and Wing Commander level for Main Force squadrons) operated. In No. 100 Squadron aircraft during early 1945, not only their commander, Wg. Cdr. R. V. L. Pattison, operated, but the station commander, Gp. Capt. R. A. C. Carter, took a trip to Essen and in March 1944 the 48-year-old Air Commodore A. M. Wray, D.S.O., M.C., D.F.C. & Bar, A.F.C., a veteran of the 1914-1918 war, took ND456 to Stuttgart and back with a 'sprog' crew.

Normally crews had to go it alone. They would file expectantly into the briefing room, after the flying meal (always eggs and usually bacon and beans with them). The target would go up on a large map at the far end of the room, the route depicted by red tape fastened round pins at the turning points. Mock groans or cries of 'whizzo' would indicate immediately whether it was a deep penetration or a Ruhr run. The Ruhr was likely to be the heaviest defended, but it was a short uncomplicated journey. On a long trip there were more chances of trouble, particularly with night fighters. Besides, a long trip took so much time!

At briefing the reason for the operation was given. The significance of such targets at St. Vith meant little until it was explained that it was a German detraining area for armoured units.

The briefing over—with call signs, weather, target and force details, and flight plans made—the gear was collected and the crews piled into the buses with 'chutes and nav. bags, etc., for the trip to the dispersed aircraft. This, one aircrew member wrote, was the most exciting time. All the glamour of the whole business would be present at that moment. Cheery calls of " Have a good trip! " were almost a ritual. The stubbing out of cigarettes would remind them how welcome was the first fag on return—if . . . There was of course the 'over the top' atmosphere. Then the start up. One by one, the four Rolls-Royce Merlins would roar into life, be warmed up and the 'revs' tested; equipment would be checked, everything prepared. They would await their signals, first to taxi out and then to take off.

Perhaps the most apprehensive time was the take-off, especially with heavy loads of fuel and bombs. As the Lancaster swept down the runway there would be a mental urge to will the speed to build up fast at this critical time. Possibly they were haunted by the warnings of what happened if engines failed on take-off—a pile-up at the end of the runway. Loss of power on just one engine, or a burst tyre, could cause a loaded bomber to swing off the runway. In any case there was a tendency for the Merlin-engined Lancasters to swing to port and for the Hercules-engined ones to swing to starboard. At Kirmington in the late evening of April 10th, 1944, 22 Lancasters of No. 166 Squadron were lined up for take-off to bomb Aulnoye. As the fifth one, EE200, roared along the runway, a wing dipped. Careering to the side, it lurched from the runway. Strained by the momentum of the heavy bomb load, the undercarriage collapsed and the fuselage ploughed along the ground for a few yards before coming to rest. The crew, uninjured, jumped out only just in time as it burst into flames. With all four tanks blazing the fire crew, who had raced up in their tender, realised that it was hopeless. Since the crew were safe, they withdrew to await the explosion, which so damaged the runway that it was unserviceable and the remaining seventeen of the squadron's aircraft could not take off.

Assuming a safe take-off, aircraft would begin to climb to a given height over their base and they would then set course on the first leg, still climbing. More checks, and as the coastline appeared the 'can' would be passed—just as well to be comfortable! Over the Channel there were more checks and guns were tested. Alternatively, of course, there might be instructions to cross the Channel and climb later; this depended on tactics and the weather.

Once over enemy territory there might be some searchlights and flak at the coast. Later, of course, as the tide of battle swept north-westwards, there was activity on the battle front to be observed. There was now very little talk on the intercom system in case someone needed to pass an urgent message. Rarely were crews briefed to fly direct. They flew in a stream in a direction designed to mislead the defences. Somewhere over enemy territory they would turn on to the final leg for the target. Soon groups of searchlights would appear ahead intermingling with the flashes of flak in the sky. Red and green target indicators could be seen going down as the Pathfinders did their job.

It all came nearer and then the turn for the target run. Perhaps instructions would be heard from the master bomber about aiming points. Bumping began from the blast of shell explosions. Occasionally there was a 'ping' as a piece of shrapnel rapped or penetrated the aircraft. Searchlights swept the sky trying to pick out individual aircraft; the pilot was ready to twist away, should his Lancaster be thus coned to provide a target for the guns.

Close to the target they would see the markers, but if they were on a late wave, smoke and fire might have built up and made observation difficult. As the bombs and incendiaries went down from aircraft nearby, there were glimpses of Lancasters ahead and around—comforting, solid, familiar shapes silhouetted against the flames and glare. The air bomber directed the run in. The bomb doors opened. The flying then had to be smooth, accurate and undeterred by what was going on around. Left, left . . . steady . . . left, left . . . the aiming of the Lancaster as a bombing vehicle lined up on the marker. Down below, it was bright like a firework display. Smoke billowed, fires glowed as incendiary bombs took hold, flashes of light from flak dotted the blackness, the markers brilliant in the sky provided the right aiming point, and the noise was sensed rather than heard in the concentration of activity. Bombs gone! The bomb doors were shut and a turn was made on a homeward course. Only on day raids did crews have the satisfaction of seeing what their bombs were doing, although their camera would have recorded this for them. False target markers and dummy fires could be seen from German attempts to divert some of the attack.

Some gunners did a complete tour without once firing their guns other than for testing or practice, others had several encounters. A quick exchange of tracer and suddenly a red glow from the aircraft attacked was sometimes observed. A lookout was maintained for night fighters trying to get some kills as the stream went home, now that they knew where the bombers were. Usually the return trip was quiet, and the Merlins sang strongly, even if the exhausts did seem to be too much of a give-away to the enemy.

Another turning point and the coast was crossed. They were really on the way home then, still in a stream, yet apart from over the target, rarely was another machine sighted. Once out of that flow of aircraft the searchlights and guns would give them their undivided attention. Then they had to act quickly, the pilot diving and twisting while others threw out 'Window' to foil the enemy radar.

The loss of protection in the stream was felt on 'gardening' trips to place mines around the enemy coast. Normally only four to six aircraft would go on one route. It meant long trips over the sea and, if detected by enemy radar, several night fighters might well be vectored to deal with these few bombers. By 1944 most wireless operators had a radar surveillance of the tail area by 'Monica' but this would only give a few seconds' warning of a fighter homing on to them. Then it was a case of diving and corkscrewing and wondering if a burst of cannon fire was going to rip the aircraft asunder.

Towards the end of the run home, the uptilted beam of the searchlight over base was often a welcoming sign. Sometimes, however, there might be fog, which would mean a diversion to an airfield with FIDO—the fog dispersal equipment skirting the runway which shot tongues of flame into the sky. It was somewhat bumpy and frightening going in over the flames, but there was nothing as lonely as being up above thick blankets of fog at night when the fuel supply was running low.

FIDO was a great boon, albeit very expensive. The letters stood for Fog Investigation and Disperals Operation, and Lancasters were used in early experiments as the initial trials were at Graveley and Lakenheath. In all fifteen airfields were so equipped, including Fiskerton, Carnaby and Woodbridge. When the first full-scale trial commenced at Fiskerton some of the local inhabitants, thinking a terrible catastrophe had taken place, phoned for help. Units of the Lincoln Fire Brigade rushed towards the flaming airfield—just as they reached there, the flames, to their astonishment, suddenly went out! They were cheered by the station personnel who were out witnessing the spectacle and were royally entertained in the Officers' and Sergeants' Messes. It was not altogether a wasted journey.

Back at base, as the wheels touched down, there was a real feeling of having 'come home'. Sometimes a bomb might be hung up, perhaps even lodged on the bay doors, which meant a careful taxi to dispersal where the armourers would take on the ticklish task of winding open the bomb bay and carefully lowering the bomb.

Usually there was a cheerful greeting from the ground crew, who wanted to know details of the trip. Then the bus collected the crew for de-briefing and interrogation—plus piping hot coffee with rum dispensed by a charming W.A.A.F. in the warm, brightly lit briefing room.

The Station Commander would hear the crews' reports, and then the intelligence officer would note details while crews lolled comfortably in chairs smoking and sipping their rum-laced coffee. A wonderful relaxation after a long period of sustained excitement. But there would also be the pangs of sorrow when they checked on who hadn't got back. . . . It was war.

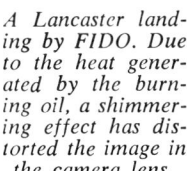

A Lancaster landing by FIDO. Due to the heat generated by the burning oil, a shimmering effect has distorted the image in the camera lens.

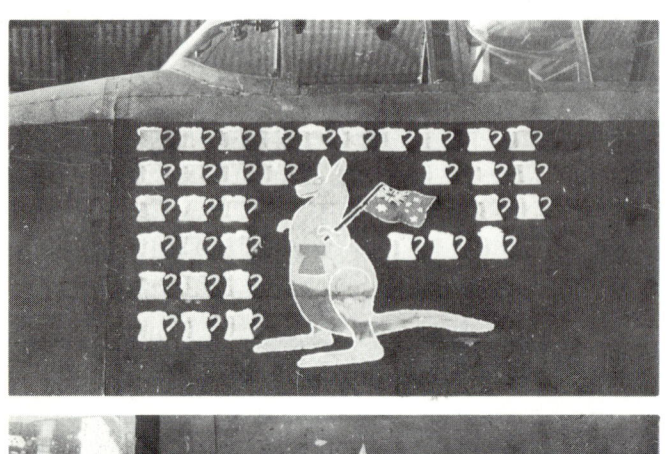

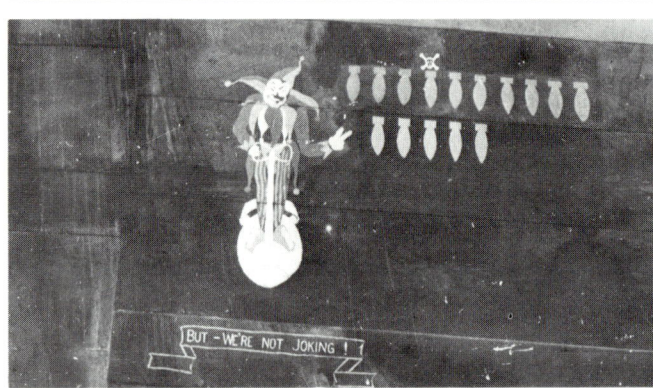

Emblems on Lancasters manned by Australians: a foaming tankard for each "op"; code letter changed from "U" to "M" on Jose; Plt. Off. D. J. Sullivan flew with Olive Oyl of Popeye fame; the new "U" for Uncle; Sqn. Ldr. E. K. Sinclair's joker; a devil that, by the cone symbols, operated over Italy; Disney characters with a bone for each operation by Pluto.

Prestwick became a transatlantic terminal during the war. Here, mingling with other types recently arrived via Canada, are Lancaster B.Xs destined for No. 6 Group, Bomber Command, after processing through maintenance units. They can be seen in the foreground (two), at the left (group of three), top right (one), and there is one in the centre of the picture.
The white aircraft are Liberators bound for Coastal Command. Other aircraft that can be discerned are Dakotas and Mitchells.

In April 1944 the switch in No. 6 Group from Halifaxes to Lancasters started in earnest. It was natural that this Canadian Group would wish to fly the Canadian-built models and No. 419 Squadron was the first to become operational with this Lancaster, the Mk. X, on April 24th, but this was a token initiation; April 27th when the squadron sent 8 Lancasters and 5 Halifaxes to disrupt the marshalling yards at Mantzen was its first effective operation.

Crews of No. 419 Squadron found that the tail-warning 'Monica' sets worked far more satisfactorily in their Lancasters than their earlier Halifaxes and 'Boozer', a new warning equipment, was fitted for squadron trials in KB700, 'Ruhr Express', the first of the Canadian-built Lancasters.

By May 1944 Bomber Command had a daily average operational strength of 1,100 aircraft of which 616 were Lancasters, 354 Halifaxes, 58 Stirlings and 72 Mosquitos and some 300-400 were operating nightly, weather permitting. The Mediterranean Allied Air Forces Command at this time were asked to consider the implications of accommodating temporarily 150 Lancasters for operations against distant targets, but the occasion did not arise and the bombing became even more 'local' as 'D-Day' drew nearer. Although the distances were shorter and less flak was encountered, a new challenge faced crews. German night fighters now had the *Naxos* radar device which enabled them to home on to H2S transmissions at a distance of 32 miles. From operations over a French target, Mailly-le-Camp, forty-two of the 362 Lancasters despatched failed to return. To add to the confusion that night, the operating wavelength clashed with a civil broadcasting station and one crew reported that they operated to the strains of 'Deep in the heart of Texas'! However, electronic counter-measures prevented crippling losses and roving Mosquito intruders did much to help.

In early May the Base Commander at Elsham Wolds,

Air Commodore Ivelaw-Chapman, joined Flt. Lt. J. M. Shearer and an N.C.O. crew in ND783 for an attack on Aubigne Racan. He did not return until after the war and was the highest ranking officer to be lost on an operation in a Lancaster. He is now Air Chief Marshal Sir Ronald Ivelaw-Chapman, G.C.B., K.B.E., D.F.C., A.F.C., and is retired from the R.A.F.

Lancasters and Halifaxes pounded Louvain and Boulogne on May 5th and among those operating was R5868, the Lancaster that now adorns the entrance to R.A.F. Scampton. It was on its hundredth operation. It was one of the early proven batch of Lancasters and to investigate some adverse reports on new aircraft the A. & A.E.E. carried out a check on ten Lancasters from production by the various contractors. The findings were not conclusive. Apart from this establishment's own quest to introduce heavier armament, Wg. Cdr. Connolly of No. 550 Squadron fostered experiments with one of his own Lancasters by mounting a .5 gun in a ventrally-positioned turret. Efforts were being made to improve the mounting and overcome the effect of slipstream when Connolly was lost on operations.

Round figure statistics may give some idea of the magnitude of operations, such as 700 Lancasters sent to drop 2,000 tons on Duisberg on May 21st from which 30 failed to return, but cannot give the hundred and one incidents attendant on each operation; nor is there room here to mention more than the odd example. Over Aachen three days later the crew of ND915 saw an enemy aircraft with a searchlight mounted in the nose trying to illuminate their aircraft, on which it had presumably been homed by radar. This had the effect of revealing its presence and it fell to the Lancaster's guns.

Recalled in the early hours of June 1st, ME794 landed

A "Tallboy" being winched up to a Lancaster B.III, unofficially named "Honor," in October 1944.

at Westcott. Coming in at 130 m.p.h. with a 13,000 lb bomb load, it rumbled across the road, jumped a ditch and landed heavily, causing the undercarriage to collapse, then slithered to a stop, whereupon it burst into flames and in a matter of minutes up went the bombs, taking with them Wellington LN743 of No. 11 O.T.U.

Throughout May and June intensive operations were carried out. An impression has been given that operations mounted as D-Day approached. Such tactics would have given an inkling of the climax. In any case it was known as D-Day because it was not a pre-set date. The operation orders, marked OVERLORD, had in fact been issued to some units some weeks ahead. The date had to be set a day in advance to permit the all-important D Minus 1 preliminaries which included, of course, the embarkation. In these preparations Lancasters had a most important part to play and in the early hours of June 5th the squadrons concerned were notified that D-Day was on the morrow. That evening they set out on their various missions.

Hitherto, it had been necessary to attack coastal batteries the length of Hitler's Atlantic Wall so that the vital batteries were silenced without revealing where the Allies would land. Now concentrated attacks could be made solely on batteries on the Normandy coast and Lancasters joined in these attacks.

The Lancasters of No. 617 Squadron had an important and exacting task. Once again they were flying special aircraft in that new automatic pilots had been fitted by A. V. Roe engineers. That night they operated with twelve crew members. In addition to the normal crew there were co-pilots and co-navigators and three 'Window' dispatchers. The squadron commander, Wg. Cdr. Cheshire, put himself down as co-pilot in LM492. By dropping 'Window' while they followed a set course meticulously, rather like soldiers counter-marching, but advancing laterally at some 10 knots

towards French channel ports, they succeeded in building a picture on enemy radar of a large convoy. The crews were rewarded by the sight of flashes from enemy batteries firing at non-existent ships, while much farther south the Allied Expeditionary Force approached Normandy. Other Lancasters were out jamming enemy radar and, just for realistic effect, made deliberately unsuccessful attempts to jam it in the 'special convoy' areas.

Bomber Command did not come under the Allied Expeditionary Air Forces Command and they did not, therefore, have the conspicuous black and white identification stripes marked around wings and fuselage. Nevertheless they operated over the beachhead and on D-Day Lancasters bombed road and rail bridges close to Caen, where our paratroops were attempting to withhold German reinforcements from the bridgehead, and road and rail centres such as Vire. In not a few pilots' reports that day appeared the observation—'tremendous activity in the Channel'.

Most of the Lancasters' operations for the next few weeks were concerned with preventing German reinforcements reaching the battle area. To this end, 'Tallboy' was first used. This was a 12,000 lb penetration bomb, a scaled down version of a larger bomb, 'Grand Slam', mooted but not so far produced. A 12,000 lb bomb was not a new innovation as No. 617 Squadron had used them in 1943, but this bomb specially designed by Dr. Barnes Wallis to penetrate was a new weapon.

To prevent German armour reaching the front, it was decided to block the Saumur tunnel on the main railway running south-west to Normandy. Using H2S as a navigational aid four Lancasters of No. 83 Squadron marked the target with sticks of flares. Eighteen of No. 617's Lancasters carrying 'Tallboys' then arrived and made several runs before bombing. McCarthy, the American mentioned earlier, now a Squadron Leader, scored a direct hit on a marker. One of the Lancasters, with its bomb-bay cut away to accommodate the 'Tallboy', was ED909—Flt. Lt. Martin's aircraft on the famous 'Dams Raid' over a year previously.

A Canadian Lancaster, KB726, raked by cannon fire from a Junkers Ju88 on its way to bomb Cambrai on the night of June 12th was doomed. This was obvious to the pilot, Flg. Off. Art Debreyne, who gave the order to abandon the aircraft, but for the rear-gunner, Flg. Off. G. P. Brophy, this was easier said than done—he was trapped in his turret.

The ground crew of R5868, seen when at Scampton opposite. This Lancaster went to the R.A.F. Museum, Hendon, 1972.

The mid-upper gunner, Plt. Off. A. C. Mynarski, realising Brophy's plight, stayed in the blazing aircraft to try to drag him out, but in spite of his strenuous efforts he failed. Brophy motioned for him to leave and save himself, as the aircraft was by then perilously close to the ground. Only when he realised it was not humanly possible to free his comrade did he go; as he reached the escape hatch he drew himself up and saluted the gunner whom he thought fated to die. Fate twisted the course of events. Mynarski escaped from the aircraft only to die of his terrible burns; Brophy remained trapped in the Lancaster and when the crash came his turret broke away from the airframe and flung him clear. He survived to testify to the heroism of Mynarski, which was recognised by the posthumous award of a Victoria Cross.

For the first time since 1942, Lancasters operated in strength in daylight on June 14th. Escorted by Spitfires of No. 11 Group, 234 attacked enemy naval vessels harbouring in Le Havre and Boulogne. Attacking independently in the evening, No. 617 Squadron dropped 'Tallboys' on the E-boat pens at Le Havre which had been marked by Wg. Cdr. Cheshire during a low run in a Mosquito. Several direct hits were obtained. The main force attacks continued on these targets the following night and next day.

The strategic bombing was now directed against oil installations as it was evident that the diminishing power of the *Luftwaffe* was due in no small way to fuel supply difficulties. At the same time, the Command was committed to a series of operations against the V-weapon sites quite apart from assistance to the Army.

Daylight attacks were becoming more frequent. These raids were very different from night work and were considered more exhilarating as everything that was going on, provided cloud permitted, could be seen. On these occasions it was also comforting to see the vapour trails of Spitfires or American fighters high above, taking care of any enemy fighter that might interfere, and often close cover was provided as well. Wg. Cdr. J. M. Maling, A.F.C., had addressed his squadron, No. 619, on the prospects of increasing operations in daylight on June 21st; but if increased

A No. 149 Squadron Lancaster fitted with H2S, shown here at Methwold with bomb-bay doors agape.

losses were anticipated it could hardly be worse than the raid that night when the squadron lost six of the sixteen Lancasters they dispatched. Nos. 44 and 49 Squadrons lost the same number each, and from East Kirkby base no less than 17 crews were missing from operations over Wesselring.

Low level bombing at night was now demanded as our armies pushed hard on the heels of the retreating Germans. Here the bombing line had to be clearly defined, and 'spot on' accuracy was demanded to avoid attacking our own troop positions. It also gave the gunners a chance to fire *down* to the ground for a change.

Occasionally a Lancaster turned night fighter. The crew of Lancaster LL677 observed another Lancaster being attacked by an Me410. The pilot decided to assist. Closing in, his gunner opened fire and as the Me410 turned to meet the new threat it provided a target for the guns from both Lancasters. It fell away in flames.

For a time the military situation dictated most Lancaster operations and took precedence over the strategic bombing of German industry. This caused a great strain on crews, who were briefed, told the pros and cons, and were left to wait while a final decision was made. The weather at target might be unsuitable or heavy fog at base on return might be expected; the military situation might be in a state of flux due to a counter attack by the enemy—it was all a matter of waiting.

Many Lancaster crews will have memories of some of those waiting periods at dispersal that summer, when the weather was kinder than usual. Sitting on the grass in the late evening sunshine, listening to the birds . . . and waiting. The dispersal hut—the domain of the ground crew—was 'open house' for the aircrews. When all checks had been satisfied, and it meant hanging on for the word to go, tea would be brewed—or the tea van would call round, and cards might be brought out. Sometimes a tin might be used as a target for stones—just as if on the seashore—to while away the time.

During daylight trips in June, V-1 'doodle-bugs' were often reported by crews and for a time intelligence officers were keenly interested in reports on the flight characteristics and speeds of these pilotless aircraft.

In the early hours of June 30th, LL942 blew up at Mepal and four other Lancasters, all of No. 75 Squadron, were put out of action. A call came that day for roads leading to Villers Bocage to be bombed to prevent Panzer

R5868, the famous "Sugar," preserved at Scampton, being viewed by Brian Goulding, who headed a Lancaster study group after the war.

units moving up. During this operation ND917 had engine trouble and landed on one of the beach-head fighter strips. As far as can be ascertained, this was the first Lancaster to land in liberated territory. A week later LL907 made a belly-landing behind the Allied lines and was repaired.

During July a number of heavy attacks were directed, at the request of the 21st Army Group, against Caen. Lancasters and Halifaxes dropped 2,350 tons in forty minutes on the evening of the 7th and in the early morning of the 18th their bombing preceded a ground attack. On the 30th targets around Caen and St. Lo were still being attacked. The *News Chronicle* reporter, Ronald Walker, witnessed this raid in LM235 of No. 622 Squadron.

As in earlier years, so in 1944, August came in wet and cloudy and out of 719 Bomber Command aircraft detailed to bomb various sites and a depot in the Forest of Nieppe on the first of the month only 74 reported finding their targets. Four days later the success of a raid on Troissy St. Maximin hung in the balance after the master bomber's aircraft was set on fire by a night-fighter and his deputy was shot down. Nevertheless, the master bomber, Sqn. Ldr. I. W. Bazalgette, D.F.C., of No. 635 Squadron, both marked and bombed with ND811 on fire. Ordering his crew to jump, he remained himself to give a chance of life to his wounded air bomber and a gunner, but the aircraft exploded on impact near the French village of Senantes. A year later the posthumous award of the V.C. to Sqn. Ldr. Bazalgette was announced.

Flt. Lt. Overgaauw, one of several Dutch pilots flying Lancasters with the R.A.F., left Spilsby on August 15th to attack Deelen airfield with eleven 1,000 lb and four 500 lb bombs. This would have been his 33rd operation, but a direct hit on the bomb-bay caused his No. 207 Squadron Lancaster to explode in mid-air and he fell within a few miles of his home-town in Holland.

Eight 'Tallboys' were dropped in daylight on U-boat pens at Ymuiden on August 24th, scoring two direct hits. Raids followed next day on V-1 sites and at night 190 Lancasters had a rather aimless flight over Darmstadt as a result of the master bomber's aircraft having an electrical failure and his two deputies being shot down. Kiel and Königsberg were the victims the very next night. Returning in the early morning ND632 of No. 103 Squadron had been hit by friendly fire and, with one engine out of action, came in to an emergency landing at Ford, where patches of mist were swirling over the airfield. The pilot apparently could not see the runway and attempted to circle round but hit the ground and skimmed along, crashing into the aircraft of the Fighter Interception Unit. Mosquito HK419 was completely wrecked and Beaufighter MM857, hit in passing, was damaged. When the Lancaster finally came to rest, it burst into flames that consumed Beaufighter R2243 and Mosquito MM564 parked nearby.

No. 3 Group could claim a battleship on the night of August 28th when they attacked Brest, but there was little elation over the sinking of the French *Clemenceau*. Three ships were sunk and some 34,000 people were rendered homeless in Stettin the following night. No. 300 (Polish) Squadron participated; the Poles, with their intense hatred of the enemy, were known for their tactics of 'press on regardless'. This would appear to have been the case that night, for one Pole wrote in his log book that there was considerable flak over Denmark—and Sweden!

Coming back from Stettin, Plt. Off. D. C. Balfour, an Australian, claimed the destruction of a Ju88 without the Lancaster having fired its guns. Five minutes after leaving the target the mid-upper gunner reported a Ju88 immediately below, intent on tailing a Lancaster ahead. Balfour pulled up to avoid a collision, but wings touched and the fighter dived straight down. The rear gunner observed it burning on the ground. Back at the station the port wing was examined and the top surface was found to be holed and the wing itself dented.

A veteran Lancaster, ED905, on its 83rd operation was made a sitting target when an electrical fault caused all the navigational lights to go on. An approach was made by a Ju88 but the gunners, aware of their predicament, were extra-alert. Their third burst of fire caused it to turn over and plunge in flames. One veteran, however, failed to return that night. This was ED588 VN.G, the third Lancaster to reach 100 operations and the first to reach a century in one squadron—No. 50 in this case. Its century had been reached on July 4th when the V-1 base at St. Leu d'Esserent was attacked. Its final operation, with the 27th crew to fly in it, brought its total to 116. Probably it was one of the fifteen lost to fighters that night.

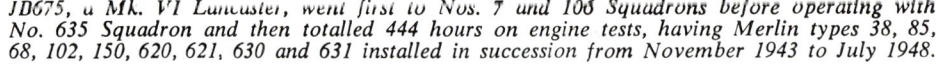

JD675, a Mk. VI Lancaster, went first to Nos. 7 and 106 Squadrons before operating with No. 635 Squadron and then totalled 444 hours on engine tests, having Merlin types 38, 85, 68, 102, 150, 620, 621, 630 and 631 installed in succession from November 1943 to July 1948.

The Mk. VI was intended to increase Lancaster performance by using more powerful versions of the Merlin engine for which DV170 and DV199 were prototype conversions. DV170 (depicted) had Merlin 65, 85, 38, 68, 100, 102 and 621 engines successively installed, while DV199 was used for general Merlin 100 series development. Not until 1947, by which time both had flown over 300 hours on engine testing, were they dismantled and sent to No. 58 M.U. Newton for scrapping.

Six hundred Lancasters and Halifaxes pounded V-1 sites in daylight on the last day of August. On September 2nd, 67 Lancasters of No. 5 Group attacked in daylight two ships in Brest harbour. Next day airfields in Holland were the main targets for the heavies and in the evening of the following day 1,000 tons of bombs were dropped to soften up the stubborn resistance of the German troops holding out at Le Havre. On this last occasion another Lancaster, EE139 BQ.B, reached its century. It had started life with a squadron that had a record for the longevity of its Lancasters, No. 100, with which it carried out forty operations. Surprisingly, it sustained little damage from enemy action in the air in spite of visiting Berlin eleven times and raiding Stettin and Kiel as well as trips to Italy. On the other hand, it was damaged on the ground by a German night intruder as it was being marshalled into dispersal. The airman guiding it in dropped his torch and jumped away just in time, as two bursts of fire tore through its fuselage. Repaired, it was kept in excellent condition by its No. 550 Squadron ground crew, who were mainly Scotsmen; in charge was Sgt. Cuthbertson, from Kilmarnock, and the fitter and rigger were L.A.C.s R. Tayler, from Dollar, and J. Birney, a Glaswegian, respectively. The aircrew had changed several times, but on the Le Havre trip Flg. Off. J. C. Hutcheson, a chemist from Troon, piloted.

At Upwood a Lancaster had returned from a raid on September 9th with one of its bombs which had failed to drop. The ground crew gingerly removed it and noticed that it had been scored by shrapnel. It was moved a short distance away to await examination. Shortly afterwards there was a violent explosion and Lancaster ND978, last seen in the vicinity of the bomb, disappeared! Two others, NE119 and ND618, were damaged, but fortunately no one was hurt.

Several heavy attacks were made on Le Havre. On one occasion all returned except a P.F.F. Lancaster which crashed on the target. On September 11th, three separate, simultaneous attacks were launched in daylight against oil targets in the Ruhr. Twenty Spitfire, three Tempest and three Mustang squadrons provided escorts to the Nos. 3 4, 5 and 6 Group forces which each included Lancasters. It was followed up by a night raid by 240 No. 5 Group Lancasters on Darmstadt from which twelve did not return.

Lancasters, apart from DV171 filming the assault on September 17th, were not directly concerned in the Arnhem landings like Halifaxes and Stirlings. Had they been less satisfactory in their primary role it is probable that some may have been converted for troop carrying or glider towing. Provision for glider towing equipment was actually made in late 1942 following the first Lancaster glider tug flight on April 15th that year by P. J. Field-Richards flying R5517. In December 1943 a glider-tow signalling tail lamp was incorporated in Lancasters, but apart from experimental tows at the Airborne Forces Experimental Establishment, Ringway, which included R5606 taking a Hamilcar into the air, no operational towing was carried out. They did support the Arnhem operations by joining in the bombing of airfields and they deposited 700 tons of bombs on gun batteries at Walcheren.

In the afternoon of September 17th, No. 3 Group Lancasters attacked Boulogne. Precision bombing was necessary in view of the proximity of the Allied lines, a mere 200 yards. To ensure accuracy PB430 came down to 3,000 feet, at which range the flak was intense and accurate. With two engines shot out of action, it was lucky to make the Channel coming back, and as it was it hit an obstruction on landing, injuring four of the crew.

With all the bombing that Lancasters had done, changing to some extent the face of the earth, it was a single Lancaster that caused a change to a map. At Eastmoor, where No. 419 (R.C.A.F.) Squadron was stationed, the airfield was bounded by a ditch. There was hardly a bomber station that did not experience overshoots at some time or another. Sometimes it was crashing into a boundary fence,

Power unit of the Lancaster B.II—Bristol Hercules.

or merely running over into a farmer's land, but at Eastmoor where the runway sloped downward, aircraft overshooting usually got caught in the ditch at the end. One after another aircraft were caught in the notorious ditch, but not until the unlucky thirteenth time was effective action taken. KB735 was the 13th; it had been unable to reach Bremerhaven on the night of September 18th and it returned with its bombs to Eastmoor. Thundering down the sloping runway, carried forward by the momentum of its bomb load, it swept over the end of the runway. The ditch did not stop it, it merely wiped off its undercarriage and it came to a stop, completely wrecked, with the crew very much shaken up. Fortunately the bombs did not explode—but the A.O.C. nearly did when yet another of his aircraft was reported ditched! Within a week there was an A.M.W.D. hut on the perimeter and workmen were busy filling in the ditch.

From a night raid on Munchen-Gladbach and Rheydt, five aircraft were lost. One of these, a Mosquito, was flown by the master bomber for the Rheydt attack; he was Wg. Cdr. Guy Gibson. A few nights later No. 5 Group succeeded in a task that Gibson had once attempted, the breaching of the Dortmund-Ems Canal.

Day and night Lancasters were out. On October 3rd they attacked the sea wall at West Kapelle on Walcheren and the wall was again attacked four days later, while 14 from Nos. 9 and 617 Squadrons, covered by three squadrons of Mustangs, set out to breach the Kembs Dam to prevent the Germans controlling the level of the Rhine and perhaps causing floods during our assault. A few days later No. 619 among other squadrons was sent to widen the breach in the West Kapelle wall.

G.-H., a new blind bombing device, was coming into favour and it was agreed in July 1944 that this should be introduced into No. 3 Group, by which time it was an all-Lancaster group. By the target date of October 2nd, only 61 of its 234 Lancasters had been equipped, but for the day raid on Bonn, carried out on the 18th, Lancasters equipped with G.-H., marked with two yellow strips on their fins, led 'vees' of three which followed their leaders and dropped their bombs simultaneously.

Of all the airfields in Britain, none saw so many tragedies and acts of heroic endeavour as the personnel of the general diversion airfields, Carnaby for the Yorkshire/Lincolnshire area, Woodbridge for East Anglia, and Manston in the south-east. Woodbridge, a large airfield by Sutton Heath, was perhaps the most active diversion station for aircraft operating over the Continent. Daily, crippled aircraft landed—or crash-landed—on this field with special fire, ambulance and rescue equipment. Not a few Lancasters were written off after staggering to Woodbridge, some on three engines, perhaps on two, or even—as in one recorded case—on one. Returning from operations in the south, Woodbridge was nearer than the bomber stations grouped up in Lincolnshire and Yorkshire and many bombers with wounded crew landed first at Woodbridge. On October 23rd ME787 arrived in with only the pilot in the aircraft, the crew having been scattered over two countries. Hit over Walcheren by flak, a fire had started in the bomb bay. The pilot ordered the bombs to be jettisoned and the crew to

Much of Bomber Command's effort was directed to assist in the Battle of the Atlantic and the first daylight raid by Lancasters to Augsburg was in this connection. Main U-boat bases were at Bordeaux, Brest, La Pallace, St. Nazaire and Lorient, of which the last-named alone received 4,500 tons of bombs. Shown here is the destruction at the Hamburg U-boat construction yards.

Return from Stettin in WS.J of No. 9 Squadron, a Lancaster that did over a hundred operations, photographed at Bardney early in January 1944. Bomber Command statistics show that proportionally there were fewer casualties on operations with Lancasters than their contemporary Halifax and Stirling bombers, but the crew survival rate of bombers missing was unfavourable to the Lancaster in comparison with its contemporaries.

abandon the aircraft—but only four took to their parachutes. Presumably the navigator and flight engineer 'up front' requested permission to hold on, as they were not then affected by the fire. By the time the coast was reached, they were only too pleased to take to their 'chutes and they landed in England shocked and burnt. Sqn. Ldr. Purnell of No. 619 Squadron, however, stuck to his machine until he could bring it down at Woodbridge.

A few days earlier a No. 635 Squadron aircraft, piloted by Flt. Lt. G. A. Thorne, had just failed to reach Woodbridge. With part of the tail shot away over Gelsenkirchen and only two engines in operation an S.O.S. had been sent out to report a ditching position, but the two Merlins remaining active kept the aircraft above the water. The signal was cancelled and course was set for Woodbridge. At a mere 500 feet the coast was crossed and ND453 started to lose height. Near Ipswich, it was touch and go if it would pass above H.T. cables and then a third engine packed up, causing the machine to yaw. The pilot, then within six miles of Woodbridge, realised he would not quite make it. Switching off the last engine to glide in evenly, he came down in a gentle dive towards a field to make a belly-landing. The machine burst into flames and all except the wireless operator got clear. Presumably someone dragged the pilot out, for he regained consciousness lying on a hayrick. By his side was a tray of tea with a spotless white traycloth and silverware brought out by a farmer's wife!

No. 635 was the only squadron to operate regularly with the Mk. VI Lancaster which had the more powerful Merlin 85/87 series engines, each developing 1,635 h.p. They made their operational debut on the night of August 8th, 1944, when three bombed Bremen. With front and mid-upper turrets removed and fitted with tail-warning devices, they were something of an interim Lincoln, with the power, if not the proportions, of the latter, which was then at the prototype stage as the Lancaster B.IV; for this reason the Mk. VI conversions were limited to eight. Squadron reports on these aircraft varied considerably. Of the four used, JB713 F2.Z was lost raiding Ghent on August 18th, which left JB675 F2.U, ND673 F2.V and ND418 F2.Q for comparative tests

with the Mk. Is and IIIs of the squadron. The engines were said to be hard on the plugs and synchronisation was impossible, but their extra power was much appreciated. They were withdrawn from the squadrons during October after having made about 20 operational sorties.

There were extensive operations throughout October, particularly on the 28th when 700 Lancasters and Halifaxes bombed Cologne at noon, 300 Lancasters bombed batteries at Walcheren and at night Bergen was raided. That day brought ED860 to the end of its career. It was so severely damaged when it swung off the runway at Skellingthorpe that it was struck off charge after having completed 130 operations.

On the first day of November as the heavies were setting out for the Ruhr, PD290 of No. 207 Squadron swung on take-off at Spilsby. It crashed into Halifax III NP954 and set it on fire, which in turn touched the bombs off, which wrecked two other Halifaxes, MZ424 and MZ824, of No. 419 (R.C.A.F.) Squadron, that had been diverted to Spilsby in the early hours of the morning.

No. 106 Squadron were displaying special interest in JB663 ZN.A, which had been with the squadron since the 18th of the previous November. It bore ninety-odd bomb silhouettes on its fuselage, each denoting a sortie. Such was the tempo of operations that it had flown thirty sorties in 56 days. The station commander as well as the squadron commander had been on 'ops' in it, as had a B.B.C. correspondent. It survived to make its century, on November 4th, by a raid on the Ladbergen Canal. Next day a huge yellow bomb was painted alongside the 99 small bomb silhouettes.

The importance electronics were assuming is evident from the increasing work of the Telecommunications Research Establishment, which was later named, more appropriately, the Royal Radar Establishment. The flying test work was carried out by the Telecommunications Flying Unit at Defford, through which over a dozen Lancasters passed at the end of 1944 each with its own special equipment. Six were there in connection with H2S. ED350 had H2S Mk. III, JA845 had H2S Mk. IV, another was on blind bombing trials with H2S Mk. V which was planned for the

Lincoln, then still known as the Lancaster Mk. IV, ND823 and PA976 were on development trials of H2S Mk. VI after the prototype installation had been made in another Lancaster, while JB544 had an experimental installation of an H2S Mk. VII. Apart from these more or less standard H2S versions, there was a special six-foot aerial array for high and low level systems on JB558 in which Bomber Command were most interested. Coastal Command had a project with PA976 utilising a similar set with a high definition 'X'-band which it was hoped would be sensitive enough to pick up the *schnorkel* device the Germans had introduced on their U-boats to enable them to stay submerged for much longer periods.

Armament was the concern of the A. & A.E.E. but the projected remotely controlled gun-turrets were planned in connection with 'Monica'—an electronic device to give early warning of an approaching enemy fighter. For this reason ND712 was at the T.F.U. at the time and JB705 was carrying out flying tests to judge the interference 'Window' would cause on A.G.L.T. (Automatic Gun-laying Turrets) Mk. I. An improved A.G.L.T. Mk. III was fitted in LL736 and LL737. Later, at the very end of 1944, Canadian built KB805 arrived for flight testing with American A.G.L.T. installed. There were two other Lancasters at Defford during late 1944: EE187 was used on experimental work for four years, including radio counter-measure experiments, and PB151 was an early starter in the field of electronic computing with navigational and bombing data programmed.

The Rose turret was being pressed forward and one of the first Lancasters with this two .5 gun turret went to No. 150 Squadron. This squadron had re-formed on November 1st, 1944. Wg. Cdr. G. G. Avis, D.F.C., was appointed to command and, viewing the stores from the unit's earlier existence, took over the original squadron crest, a grand piano, two billiard tables and some pewter jugs, together with five Lancaster Mk. Is that arrived that day! It was a start. Actually one of their Lancasters was operational before the personnel, having been borrowed by No. 576 on November 6th for operations. Four days later No. 150 was operational with an attack on Houiz Benzin in the Dortmund area.

'Lucero', a new landing aid which consisted of an airborne receiver indicating the aircraft's position relative to the datum line of the runway, was being tried out operationally on No. 12 Squadron's Lancasters at Wickenby. It did not prove satisfactory but the principle was adapted for equipment which is in use today.

Some unwonted excitement occurred at Scampton on November 29th as NG185 of No. 153 Squadron taxied to join a No. 3 Group day raid on Dortmund. The wireless operator was attempting to load a Very pistol which, as it happened, was already loaded. The cartridge went off inside the aircraft. Seeing a blinding flash followed by smoke, the pilot, imagining fuel tanks on fire, ordered the crew to get out and he himself fell out of the nose exit and had to be carried away. Meanwhile the navigator had stamped on the cartridge and put out the flare.

Another dam raid was scheduled for December 2nd, with No. 5 Group Squadrons dropping 'Tallboys' aided by No. 1 Group with more conventional bombs; in fact 1,000 lb ANM bombs supplied by America under Lend/Lease. This operation was made in support of American troops on high ground, by flooding the Germans out of their positions. It proved a difficult target and it was scheduled again the next day, when the crews were again frustrated and landed in heavy rain with their bombs still aboard. They were briefed yet again but this dam raid was finally cancelled.

Bomber operations continued day and night against industrial towns, communications, airfields and in support of troops. No. 3 Group Lancasters, together with Halifaxes, bombed troops and armour in the German detraining centre at St. Vith. Ten minutes' flying time from the Belgian lines, PB237 was hit by three bursts of flak and set on fire. The crew, with the exception of the rear gunner, who was killed, fought the fire for 65 minutes. All the extinguishers and even the contents of the thermos flasks were used up—as well as parachutes to damp down the flames. The whole of the rear fuselage was buckled by the flames and the rear and mid-upper turrets were burnt out. Exploding ammunition had further damaged the aircraft and control was difficult, but it held together for an emergency landing behind our lines in France.

Both the 'Oboe' leader, Sqn. Ldr. R. A. M. Palmer of No. 109 Squadron flying a No. 582 Squadron Lancaster and crew, and his deputy Flt. Lt. Carpenter in a Mosquito were lost raiding Cologne two days before Christmas. The heroic last hours of the leader were recognised later by the award of a Victoria Cross.

Lancasters were out with 12,000 lb bombs on December 29th, bound for E-boat and R-boat pens at Rotterdam. At night there were raids on railways at Troisdorf and on synthetic oil plants at Scholven-Buer. During bombing up for the night raid came an explosion which caused a distinct tremor at Cambridge. PD325 had blown up at Waterbeach, killing nine and injuring four people, completely wrecking another Lancaster and damaging two others. The year ended with No. 3 Group, led by No. 8 Group Lancasters, attacking railways at Solingen and No. 5 Group Lancasters searching for ship targets in Oslo Fjord.

Sgt. Zammitt of New York returning from his ninth operation, an attack on Stettin on January 1st, 1944.

LANCASTER LOCATION MAP

I. COLEBY GRANGE	9. FELTWELL	17. BOURN
2. METHERINGHAM	10. WITCHFORD	18. GRANSDEN LODGE
3. WINTHORPE	11. WATERBEACH	19. MELBOURN
4. FULBECK	12. OAKINGTON	20. WRATTING COMMON
5. BALDERTON	13. WARBOYS	21. EXNING (NO.3)
6. SYERSTON	14. WYTON (NO.8)	22. NEWMARKET
7. BOTTESFORD	15. HUNTINGDON (NO.2)	
8. METHWOLD	16. GRAVELEY	

ACKLINGTON

NEWCASTLE

NORTH SEA

MIDDLETON ST. GEORGE
SKIPTON-ON-SWALE
TOPCLIFFE

CROFT

LEEMING

WOMBLETON

LINTON-UPON-OUSE
ALLERTON (RCAF)(NO.6)
YORK (NO.4)

THOLTHORPE
EAST MOOR

CARNABY

DRIFFIELD

YORK

SQUIRES GATE

YEADON

BREIGHTON

KILLINGHOLME
KIRMINGTON
GRIMSBY
BINBROOK
LUDFORD MAGNA
KELSTERN
FALDINGWORTH
WICKENBY

ELSHAM WOLDS
SANDTOFT
LINDHOLME
FINNINGLEY

MANCHESTER

CHADDERTON

TRAFFORD PARK
RINGWAY
WOODFORD

CHESTER

(NO.1)
BAWTREY

BLYTON

LINCOLN

HEMSWELL
INGHAM
SCAMPTON
DUNHOLME LODGE
WADDINGTON
SWINDERBY

STRUBBY
FISKERTON
BARDNEY
SKELLINGTHORPE
SPILSBY
EAST KIRKBY
WOODHALL SPA
CONINGSBY

LITTLE SNORING
OULTON

HUCKNALL

3
6 5 4
7

GRANTHAM (NO.5)

DOCKING
FOULSHAM

LANGAR

FOLKINGHAM

WYMESWOLD

SHIPDHAM

CASTLE BROMWICH

COTTESMORE
WOOLFOX LODGE

NORTH LUFFENHAM

DOWNHAM MARKET

BIRMINGHAM

BITTESWELL

UPWOOD

MEPAL

8
9

EAST WRETHAM

LONGBRIDGE

BAGINTON

GRAFTON UNDERWOOD

LITTLE STAUGHTON
TEMPSFORD

13
15 14
16
12 11
17
18
21
22
20

MILDENHALL
TUDDENHAM

CHEDBURGH
STRADISHALL

10

19

BASSINGBOURN

WOODBRIDGE
MARTLESHAM HEATH

DEFFORD

SILVERSTONE

CRANFIELD

UPPER HEYFORD

WESTCOTT

HALTON

STANTON HARCOURT
ABINGDON

HIGH WYCOMBE

LONDON

MANSTON

- ▮ H.Q. BOMBER COMMAND
- ▲ BOMBER COMMAND GROUP H.Q'.s.
- ● OPERATIONAL LANCASTER STATIONS
- X STATIONS WITH ASSOCIATION WITH 'LANCASTER STORY.'
- ■ FACTORIES BUILDING LANCASTERS

● CITIES

BOSCOMBE DOWN

SOUTHAMPTON

TARRANT RUSHTON

71

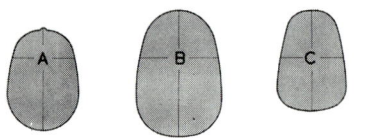

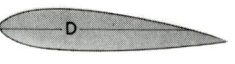

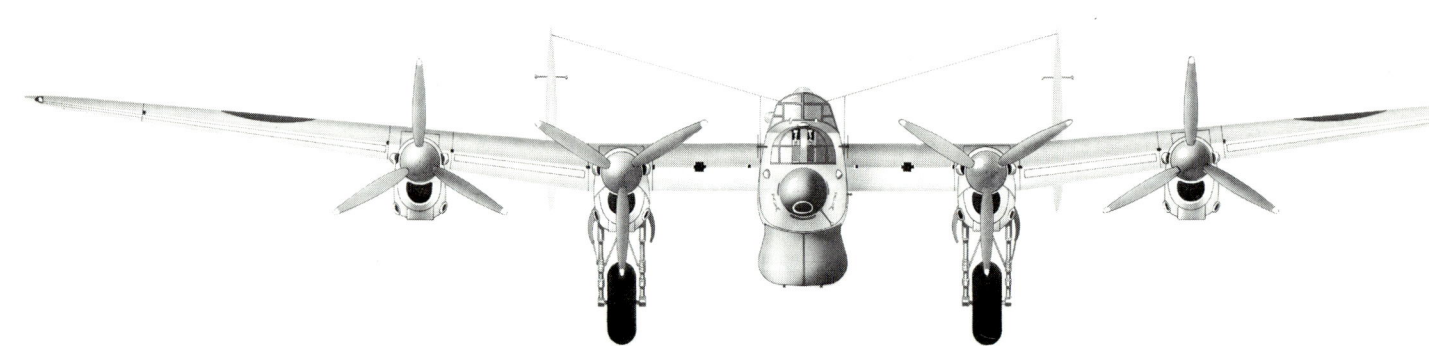

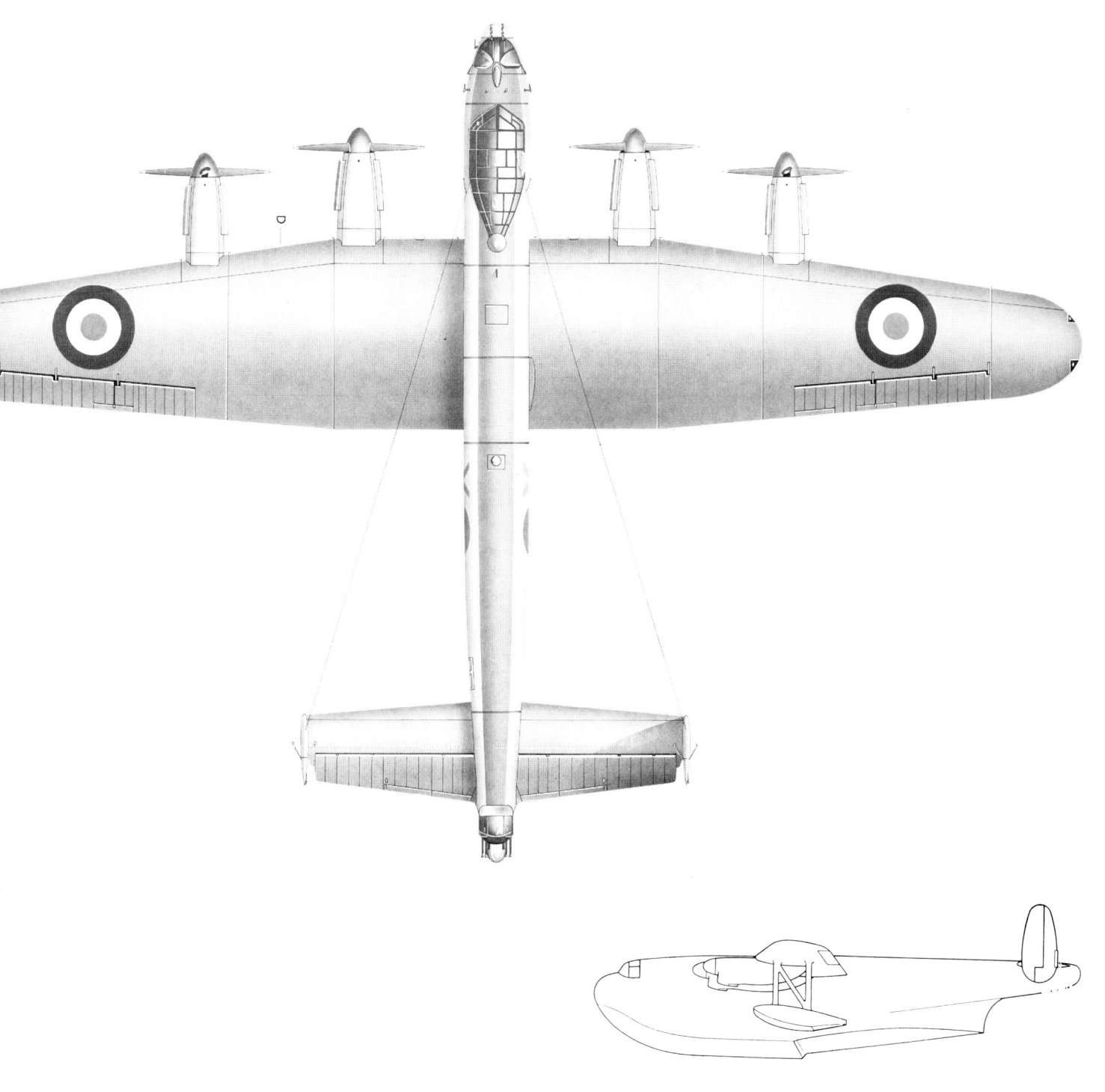

A Lancaster G.R.3 with airborne lifeboat and the projected Avro 685A York G.R.
flying boat utilizing a Lancaster wing.

No. 617 Squadron was used in many operations and operated non-standard Lancasters at times. This B.III of theirs, JA894, ex-EA.C of No. 149 Squadron, has an enlarged bomb bay similar to Mk. II standard, which was fitted to a number of Mks. I and III. This aircraft was lost in a mid-air collision with an Oxford.

The Royal Air Force has operated from Russian soil no less than six times: during 1918-1919 in both North and South Russia; in 1941, the Russian Wing, made up of Hurricane Squadrons Nos. 81 and 134, was formed and sent to Murmansk to help fight the invading Germans; in 1942, a Coastal Command force was sent to North Russia to help protect Convoy PQ 18 in September; three P.R.U. Spitfires supported by a Catalina from Coastal Command were based there in September 1943 when they were making reconnaissance flights for the midget submarine attack on the *Tirpitz* and again in March 1944, prior to the combined Naval/Fleet Air Arm attack; and, lastly, in September 1944, two Bomber Command Lancaster Squadrons went there to bomb the *Tirpitz*. In all six cases, the bases used included airfields in the Murmansk and Arkhangel'sk regions.

The *Tirpitz*, a sister ship of the *Bismark*, was a 45,000 ton battleship launched at Wilhemshaven on April 1st, 1939. Although she had not taken part in any major action—her main armament was in fact only once fired in anger—she was a constant threat to the Russian convoys as long as she remained in Norwegian waters.

In January 1942, Convoy PQ 9 had to be postponed because of the *Tirpitz's* presence in northern waters; and in July her presence was again sufficient to cause the First Lord of the Admiralty to order Convoy PQ 17 to scatter and, as a result, 21 of the 24 Allied merchant ships in the convoy were claimed by U-boats and the *Luftwaffe*. Further convoys had to be temporarily postponed.

The Commander-in-Chief of the Home Fleet is said to have considered the sinking of the *Tirpitz* to be of incomparably greater importance to the conduct of the war than the safety of any convoy. From early 1942 until late in 1944, the *Tirpitz* had kept major units of the Royal Navy tied down in northern waters, when they might have been usefully employed elsewhere—particularly in the Far East.

The *Tirpitz* was attacked—unsuccessfully—for the first

time at Wilhelmshaven in 1941, several months before her completion. From the time of her arrival at Trondheim in January 1942, until her eventual destruction in November 1944, fifteen separate Bomber Command and Fleet Air Arm attacks were made upon her involving 754 offensive sorties and resulting in the loss of 32 aircraft. Soviet aircraft, too, made a night attack in February 1943, but only four of them found the target and no damage was inflicted.

There were many difficulties in attacking the *Tirpitz* at her anchorage in Kaa Fjord—either from the sea or from the air In July 1942, a Russian submarine had attacked her and she was in dock for six months as a result; in September 1943 two Royal Navy midget submarines succeeded in reaching the *Tirpitz* and attacking her in the fjord, as a result of which she was removed to Alten Fjord for repairs. By March 1944, it was assumed that she was ready to put to sea again, and in April the Fleet Air Arm's new carrier-borne torpedo-bomber, the Fairey Barracuda, was used against the German battleship—fourteen bombs hit her, but by the late summer of 1944 she was again judged to be ready to put to sea.

At Alten Fjord the *Tirpitz* was protected by a torpedo boom, the natural dense cloud which frequently prevailed over the Norwegian fjords as well as a very effective smoke screen, shore-based anti-aircraft artillery in addition to the *Tirpitz's* own weapons, and *Luftwaffe* fighters which were stationed reasonably near.

Although taken by surprise by the Fleet Air Arm when they attacked in April 1944, when in July they returned to bomb again the Germans were alerted as soon as the Barracudas and their escorts crossed the coast, and the *Tirpitz* was quickly enveloped in her smoke-screen. After this unsuccessful raid, Vice-Admiral Sir Henry Moore, who had commanded the operation, became convinced that the Barracuda was too slow for such attacks. Previously, he had expressed the opinion that the *Tirpitz* could not be sunk with the bombs then available to the F.A.A.—even the 1,600 lb A.P. bombs which struck her in April had failed to pierce her main armour. The alternative use of the much faster Mosquito was discussed, but they were all at the time under General Eisenhower's supreme command and he did not think their temporary removal from tactical operations in France justifiable.

Towards the end of August, however, the importance of the *Tirpitz's* destruction was discussed by the Joint Planning Staff and it was decided that shore-based bombers should be used.

To penetrate the two layers of horizontal armour, 2 ins. and 3.2 ins. thick respectively, on this ship, 'Tallboys' were used backed up by the anti-shipping bomb known as 'Johnny Walker'—this bomb rose and fell upon entering the water until, it was hoped, it rose up against the unarmoured bottom of a ship. As it only weighed 400-500 lb, a Lancaster could carry a number of these bombs.

In late August Bomber Command was asked to look into the prospects of sinking the *Tirpitz*. Now that she was at Alten Fjord, however, she was just beyond the range of the Lancaster, which was the only aircraft able to carry 'Tallboy.' Just to prove it, three Lancasters were loaded up with fuel and bombs, and sent flying round Britain a distance equivalent to that they would be required to fly to the *Tirpitz*; another, with a half load of petrol, simulated the return flight. When the sums were done, the answer was the same—the distance was just too much. And so No. 30 Mission in Moscow was asked to send particulars of Russian airfields where the Lancasters might land after making their attack. The airfield eventually chosen was Yagodnik, on an island on the River Dvina, about twenty miles south of Arkhangel'sk; the runways were only grass, but because the soil was very sandy they never became waterlogged.

Operation PARAVANE was issued on September 7th. Next day, in the course of which the Station Commander at Woodhall Spa had the temerity to conduct an inspection of senior N.C.O.s' bunks, the No. 5 Group A.O.C., Air Vice-Marshal The Hon. R. A. Cochrane, briefed 19 crews from No. 617 Squadron, and 17 from No. 9 Squadron that had been called over from Bardney.

The force commanded by Gp. Capt. C. C. McMullen, A.F.C., was composed of 38 Lancaster I/IIIs from Nos. 9 and 617 Squadrons, a P.R.U. Mosquito, two Liberators from No. 511 Squadron, and LM587, a specially equipped Lancaster from No. 463 Squadron with, in addition to its crew, two officers of the Film Production Unit, Guy Byams of the B.B.C. and W. E. West of the Press Association.

When on the 11th the Group Meteorological Officer advised that weather conditions over Norway were deteriorating and good weather breaks were becoming rarer and briefer, the decision was taken to fly straight to Yagodnik and bomb the *Tirpitz* from there.

On the evening of September 11th the PARAVANE force, 42 strong, took off from Bardney. A refuelling stop was made at Lossiemouth, and then non-stop to Russia. With bombs and fuel the Lancasters were about a ton overweight. The Liberators carried the ground crews, spares, such as a Merlin engine, Lancaster undercarriage legs and wheels, radio parts and tinned food.

The flight to Yagodnik proved to be the most eventful

Close-up of the intricate gear to hold bombs firmly in place, yet permit release at the critical moment.

part of the trip. One of the Lancasters had to return to base shortly after take-off when it was discovered that its 'Tallboy' had come adrift and had to be jettisoned. The others flew into cloud over Russia—and visibility was down to about 600 yards at times. The only available maps were totally inadequate for map reading under the conditions, none of the wireless operators was able to raise the Yagodnik radio beacon because the call-sign 'SVP' had been wrongly transliterated from the Russian, and most of the aircraft ran short of fuel.

When the Force Commander counted his Lancasters at Yagodnik, shortly after his own arrival, there were only twenty-four. However, all were accounted for next day. Five were with the Liberators on the wrong aerodrome at Kegostrov, opposite Arkhangel'sk, one having made a belly-landing; the remainder were scattered over the Russian countryside. Russian parachutists were dropped beside the stranded aircraft and Wing Commander Tait was flown in a Po-2 biplane to a field where two of the Lancasters had

A two-sectioned 8,000 lb. Amatex-filled high-capacity bomb. Nose and tail sections were fitted before final bombing up.

Wg. Cdr. Tait and crew by EE146, a Lancaster which participated in the first and last attacks on the Tirpitz.

force-landed. Both were successfully flown out; the first barely cleared the trees which surrounded the field, and the second with the throttles pushed through the gate brushed a path through tree-tops. At Yagodnik it was found to have a smashed nose and bits of tree were jammed in the radiators, causing one Merlin to stop through over-heating.

Two No. 617 Lancasters, EE131 and ME559, and four belonging to No. 9 Squadron had to be abandoned in the marshes where they had landed. It would be interesting to know how effective Russian salvage teams were after the PARAVANE Force left Russia. The Lancasters operated by these two squadrons were specially equipped with some of our latest radar aids, which had not been supplied so far to Russia under Lend-Lease, including the stabilised automatic bomb-sight Mark IIA (SABS) used by 617 Squadron and the Mark XIV bomb-sight used by No. 9 Squadron. One other Lancaster, NF920, had been damaged by flak over Finland, but this aircraft was repaired at Yagodnik.

The ground crews were kept hard at it during the next 48 hours. They carried out an engine change—without any equipment to remove it from the Liberator's hold other than a ramp made from tree trunks—they made minor adjustments to sixteen aircraft and transferred a 'Johnny Walker' bomb-load to ME555 from the damaged NF920. Refuelling alone took 18 hours as there were only a few 1,500 litre (less than 350 gallons) bowsers available.

Left to right, Flg. Off. Harvey, Sqn. Ldr. Williams, Flt. Sgt. Watts, Wg. Cdr. Bazin of No. 9 Squadron during operation Paravane.

By September 14th, twenty-six Lancasters were serviceable and ready for use. The weather seemed unsatisfactory, but the P.R.U. Mosquito took off at 02.10 hours to inspect conditions over the target area. When it returned at 06.45 hours, the pilot confirmed the poor forecast and the attack was cancelled.

The Soviet commander, Col. Loginov, Chief of Staff to the Commander of the Air Forces and post-war chief of *Aeroflot*, arranged an official lunch and in the afternoon there was a football match between the R.A.F. and a 'local' Russian team.

The Mosquito returned at 05.45 hours on the 15th with a favourable weather report and at 06.30 hours the first Lancaster took off, and the whole of the bomber element was airborne within 23 minutes. It was divided into two sections consisting of 21 Lancasters armed with 'Tallboys' and 6 with 'Johnny Walkers' and the photographic Lancaster. The plan was for the 'Tallboy' Lancasters to attack in sections of five at 14,000-18,000 ft., and the 'Johnny Walker' Lancasters to run in at 10,000-12,000 ft. In order to achieve surprise, they were to fly to the Finnish border at 1,000 ft., then to climb above bombing height so that they might dive to this height when sixty miles from the target. Three No. 9 Squadron aircraft were to act as wind finders at 16,000 ft., then fall in behind the rest when the dive began. The attack would be from the south.

In spite of being a little off course, surprise was achieved and the weather over the target was good. About six 'Tallboys' were seen to drop between the *Tirpitz* and her torpedo boom during the first minute of the attack before the smoke-screen obscured the ship—the remaining Lancasters had to aim their bombs at the ship's gun flashes. The film Lancaster flew straight back to Waddington—but owing to the smoke the films showed little on which to judge the success of the operation.

Seventeen 'Tallboys' were dropped, four were brought back to Yagodnik—two had failed to release and two bomb-aimers had been unable to see the target. There had been no fighter opposition, but two aircraft were damaged by flak. PB416, a No. 617 Lancaster captained by Flg. Off. F. Levy, failed to return—it was thought that it flew into the mountains over Norway.

The Mosquito made several more reconnaissance flights to try to get photographs: on the 15th, the 16th when it sustained slight damage from flak, the 20th and 24th.

The majority of the Lancasters returned to England on the 16th and four days later the last, NF920 which had been under repair, returned home. The Mosquito flew back on the 26th, and last of all the two Liberators returned to Bardney on the night of the 27th/28th. The crashed Lancasters were, according to enquiries recently made in Russia, broken up.

It was not until the 20th that the Mosquito brought back a photograph of the *Tirpitz* showing that she had, indeed, been hit, but was still afloat. The Russians were somewhat disappointed by the apparent failure to sink the *Tirpitz*—she had, however, been severely damaged and, according to German estimates, it would have taken at least nine months work in a German port to effect repairs.

The Russians had welcomed the PARAVANE Force with a banner inscribed 'Welcome to the Glorious Flyers of the Royal Air Force'; 196 officers and senior N.C.O.s had been accommodated in an old river-boat on the Dvina, and 125 junior N.C.O.s and airmen had been put up in the Russians' own underground huts. Film shows and lectures were laid on, also a concert by the 'camp band and choir'. Cutlery and napkins came from an Arkhangel'sk hotel.

The *Tirpitz* was moved to Haak Island, four miles west of Tromsö, on October 15th with increased defences as a floating battery for the defence of Norway, but this new role was not known in Britain; it was decided to attack again.

She was now within range of bombers operating from England and the same two squadrons were warned to stand by. On the 22nd No. 617's aircrews were ordered off on a route march! It caused almost as much stir as the senior N.C.O.s' bunk inspection. But the event of the month was the announcement of the new pay code on the 27th. The instructions next day to fly to Lossiemouth to bomb the *Tirpitz* came as something of an anti-climax.

An extra 252 gallons of fuel was carried in a Mosquito drop tank and a Wellington overload tank was installed in the fuselage of the Lancasters which already had their mid-

not, they were to land in Russia. In the event, none did, although NF920, hit over the target, force-landed in Sweden. Thirty-two 'Tallboys' were dropped, but the *Tirpitz* still remained afloat.

There were some repercussions when the weekly state returns of aircraft and mark numbers showed machines previously listed as Mk. III now as Mk. I. Meanwhile, early in November, the 'Paravanes' were warned again and they flew to Lossiemouth, but the weather proved unfavourable so they flew back next day.

The end finally came around 9.52 a.m. on November 12th. Thirty-eight Lancasters carrying 'Tallboy' bombs took off with the filming Lancaster at about 03.00 hours. There was no cloud, no smoke-screen, and no fighter opposition. Twenty-eight 'Tallboys' were dropped, at least two of which scored direct hits. When photographed by a Mosquito about two hours after the attack, the *Tirpitz* was lying capsized in shallow water. LM448 failed to return to base, but managed to force-land in Sweden.

At Woodhall Spa No. 617's crews were welcomed back by the ground staff and the band of the Border Regiment. Two days later came their reward—a 48 hour pass for all.

Keel uppermost lies the Tirpitz, victim of Nos. 9 and 617 Squadrons' Lancasters. The Germans were unable to make holes in the hull in time to rescue the hundreds trapped inside.

upper turrets removed. However, with this petrol load of 2,406 gallons and the 'Tallboys' it was doubtful if take-off could be safely accomplished. The acting Engineer Officer of No. 5 Group, Sqn. Ldr. P. C. (Paddy) Finucane, took the initiative by ordering that all surplus Merlin 24 engines in the group be made available to the two 'Paravane' squadrons. Of the various Merlins installed in Mk. I and III Lancasters, this version gave the best performance at take-off and the Lancasters of Nos. 9 and 617 Squadrons, previously Mk. I and III, now became Mk. Is throughout with Merlin 24s.

A new filming Lancaster had to be found. The Lancaster element of the Film Production Unit operated under No. 463 Squadron; they had used that unit's distinguishing letters JO, with the individual letter 'O' and 'L' on their Lancasters DV171 and LM587, which had both been lost in September. PD329 was then hastily converted by installing a cine-camera in the front turret and arranging a large detachable panel in the fuselage side which gave the cameraman a wide field of view, but necessitated the wearing of safety straps to prevent him falling out. It was made ready in time and flew with two camera operators in addition to a crew of seven.

Take-off of the force was successfully accomplished. The crews were instructed to return to Lossiemouth if they had 900 gallons or more fuel remaining after the attack—if

The *coup de grace* was given to the *Tirpitz* after two direct hits, one on a turret and the other on the catapult. It is not possible to say which individual crew and Lancaster were responsible but if any one Lancaster be mentioned, then a veteran aircraft, 'D' of No. 617 Squadron—EE146—deserves record as Wg. Cdr. Tait's aircraft on the original PARAVANE operation to Russia as well as in the final attack. It was in this same machine that Tait set out to breach the Urft Dam with 'Tallboys' when the squadron reverted to their original role on December 8th. This time they were accompanied by nearly 200 other Lancasters of No. 5 Group. There was, however, dense low cloud that morning and after orbiting the dam six times with only an occasional glimpse of the lake, No. 617 returned with their 'Tallboys'. Three days later 233 Lancasters set out in the afternoon for the same target, attacked it and returned just before 6 p.m. in time for No. 617's crews to get ready for a far more satisfactory operation—the squadron dance held in Boston. The Urft Dam was still not breached and only a small amount of water seeped away.

No. 617 Squadron went back to 'routine' work; U-boat and E-boat pens at Ijmuiden were next to receive their 'Tallboys'. Altogether, with No. 9 Squadron and a few special Lancasters in other squadrons, 854 'Tallboys' were dropped in operations by Lancasters.

The Lancaster fuselage was produced in four sections to facilitate road transport, which was of considerable importance here, where sections, built mainly at A. V. Roe's Chadderton plant, were brought nearly twenty miles to Woodford for assembly as seen here. Metropolitan-Vickers, too, delivered to Woodford for assembly from where Lancasters were test-flown.

The basis of any Lancaster, the centre section, to which nose sections, top left, will be fitted. This is a scene at the Longbridge works of Austin Motors, then known as Austin Aero Ltd. Their peak production was reached in June 1945, when thirty-five Lancaster Mk. VIIs were delivered.

The Lancaster was probably the most important of the instruments of victory. The Commander-in-Chief of Bomber Command, Sir Arthur Harris, has this to say of the Lancaster—" Its efficiency was almost incredible, both in performance and in the way in which it could be saddled with ever increasing loads without breaking the camel's back. It is astonishing that so small an aircraft as the Lancaster could take the 22,000 pound 'Grand Slam' bomb, a weapon which no other aircraft in the world could or yet can carry. The Lancaster far surpassed all the other types of heavy bombers. Not only could it take heavier bomb loads, not only was it easier to handle and not only were there fewer accidents with this than with other types; throughout the war the casualty rate of Lancasters was also consistently below that of other types."

The Lancaster evolved from the Avro design team headed by Roy Chadwick, F.R.Ae.S., and was further developed by his team, and by S. D. Davies, B.Sc., A.F.R.Ae.S., in the experimental shops.

A Lancaster consisted of some 55,000 separate parts including such composite items as engines and turrets as one and excluding nuts, bolts and rivets. To produce one, some 500,000 manufacturing operations were involved, and a total of 7,374 were built, excluding prototypes. This involved an immense organisation, the output of several factories and a large labour force. Firms producing Lancasters were formed into the Lancaster Group.

As related, both A. V. Roe and Metropolitan Vickers were producing Lancasters in 1941 and were joined that same year by Armstrong Whitworth Aircraft, who produced their first Lancaster in September the following year. Short & Harland and Vickers Armstrongs were co-opted in 1943, but since machine tools were a limiting factor only Vickers Armstrongs achieved production of the type and the Short & Harland order for 200 was cancelled. Fairey Aviation were also affiliated to the Group, but due to changing requirements they did not commence production; Austin Motors, however, the last of the large firms co-opted, produced a number in time for operations.

The magnitude of the task of production can perhaps best be realised by popular statistics. It took nearly ten tons of light aluminium alloy to make each Lancaster and a six month production at peak would require sufficient light alloy sheet to cover a roadway 31 feet wide and stretching between the Manchester factory of A. V. Roe and London.

The parent firm, A. V. Roe, had several factories. A Lancaster was designed to break down conveniently into smaller units. The fuselage of light alloy stressed skin monocoque broke up into five sections to permit ground transport and the whole aircraft could be subdivided into 31 main components to facilitate dispersed production. Avro's main factory was at Chadderton, on the outskirts of Manchester. There, main components were built and transported eighteen miles to Woodford, where Lancasters were erected in the large, relatively new, sheds and were then wheeled out and test flown. Traces of the original wartime camouflage paint can still be seen on buildings there. A number of aircraft, especially prototypes, were flown from Ringway, now the municipal airport of Manchester. Another large factory with its own flight testing facilities was at Yeadon, near Leeds, while at Newton Heath mainplanes and other sections were produced.

The staff of Avro rose from 23,500 in 1941 to 40,000 in 1943, at which figure it remained fairly constant until the end of the war. However, it should be realised that in this period of Lancaster production the firm also produced 5,330 Ansons, 141 Lincolns, 46 Lancastrians and 76 Yorks. A number of satellite factories were operated by taking over mills in the district such as the Ivy Works and Laurel Works, and the Empire Works is still part of their present-day organisation. There were plants in Wythenshawe and Ashton and a depot of the United Co-operative Dairies was taken over as a stores. In these days of campaigning for shorter hours it is revealing to recall that the *average* working week was 66.75 hours and 44% of the employees were women.

It was the responsibility of the parent firm to provide the Group with drawings and modification details to ensure

100% interchangeability of all parts—an important factor in repair. Group meetings under the chairmanship of Mr. C. E. Fielding, Avro's Assistant General Manager, were held monthly at first and later every two months. Mr. J. A. R. Kay, Chief Superintendent at Avro's, acted as Secretary to the Group. Under Sir Roy Dobson the Managing Director and Mr. J. Green the General Works Manager, the Avro factories reached their peak production in August 1944 when 155 Lancasters were delivered that month. Their test flying was under Captain H. A. ('Sam') Brown and later under Bill Thorne.

Metropolitan Vickers worked closely with A. V. Roe and were the only company other than the parent firm to produce the Manchester, which necessitated a new factory at Trafford Park, some distance from the main plant, and known as the Mosley Road Works. The first sod was cut in April 1939 and in October, although still in building, the machine shop had commenced limited production. Some 26,000 jigs and tools had to be produced before production of the Manchester could get under way and it was a year before the first was ready for assembly.

On Friday, December 20th, the first Manchester was assembled for inspection and was still in the shops on Sunday when Manchester was heavily raided. The main factory was extensively damaged but so far the aircraft factory had only been slightly damaged; but next night the raiders returned, and this time both the main and the aircraft factories had several fires started by incendiary bombs. Perhaps the greatest damage was done by a single 1,000 lb high explosive bomb which fell in the centre of the new

A repair line of Lancaster nose-sections at Bracebridge Heath. In the foreground is the nose of JB351.

aircraft factory and destroyed the first Manchester together with a number of fuselages nearing completion.

In spite of prompt factory repair action, for which a train to house and feed repair workers and provide heating was run alongside, production was set back six months. Then the changeover to the Lancaster involved the production of another 2,000 jigs and tools. Completed aircraft were transported in sections to Woodford for assembly in the Avro factory. Highlights of 'Metro-Vickers' production were the completion of their 1,000th Lancaster, named 'Margaret', after Miss Margaret Barber, one of the workers chosen by ballot, and the visit of the crew of 'S' for Sugar, the veteran R5868, on May 31st, 1944, which was billed in the factory as—'You Build Them—They Fly Them'. The General and Works Managers during their peak production of 45 a month in August were Messrs. T. Fraser and A. J. Leslie respectively. As well as constructing Messier undercarriages for Halifaxes, Metropolitan Vickers made numbers of Dowty undercarriages for Lancasters.

Armstrong Whitworth Aircraft produced the Lancaster from two plants, Baginton at first, joined later by Bitteswell. Their peak production, under the administration of Messrs. H. M. Woodhams, P. G. Crabbe and W. S. D. Lockwood, was reached in October 1944 when 75 Lancasters were completed.

Vickers Armstrongs came later on to the scene, as they had been preoccupied with that successful but out-dated twin-engined bomber the Wellington. This famous organisation's first Lancaster came from the Castle Bromwich works which, designed originally for bomber production, was producing Spitfires. Lancaster production was concurrent with this famed fighter and the first left the works in October 1943. It was tested on the 22nd by a well-known pre-war pilot, Alex Henshaw, who was test-flying Spitfires. It is interesting to recall that the Avro test pilot, J. H. ('Jimmy') Orrell, conducting a comparative test on November 6th, found the controls too light for his liking and jokingly pointed out that it was not a Spitfire! Peak production, under Mr. W. A. Dixon the Resident Director, was 25 Lancasters in December 1944.

The Vickers factory at Chester received orders to tail off Wellington production early in 1943 when orders for 500 Lancasters were placed. Large sub-contracting was organised by Mr. Lefevre for final assembly at Chester under the supervision of Mr. B. A. Duncan. The peak output at this plant was in March 1945 with 36 Lancasters delivered.

Unserviceable equipment, light damage such as being holed by flak, damaged wingtips and fins could be repaired under R.A.F. ground servicing arrangements, if not on site, in station workshops. It was a matter of pride with bomber squadrons to achieve 100% serviceability. If an aircraft was grounded awaiting spares not available locally, a telegram (signal in service jargon) starting with the letters AOG for 'Aircraft on Ground' would be sent to the works for an immediate despatch of the appropriate part.

When extensive damage was sustained with strain evident or suspected, the Lancaster was 'sent back to works'. This implied back to the constructor but in effect it was to a special organisation set up by A. V. Roe under the direction of Mr. C. L. Hatton, now the Superintendent of their Woodford factory.

Crashed Lancasters were brought in by road to Bracebridge Heath and the main sections were allotted to contractors in Northampton and Loughborough and to the L.M.S. Railway Workshops at Derby. Although records give 7,377 Lancasters built, parts for an estimated 622 were built additionally to maintain the Lancasters in service. Orders for spares were a routine requirement from the parent firm. The most vulnerable part of a Lancaster was found to be the bomb doors and more of these were built than any other component. Being fitted beneath the fuselage they were invariably damaged in a belly landing and they were constantly being peppered by shrapnel in action; not

the centre-section was not as vulnerable as other parts and a number of these were gratefully absorbed by Austin Motors at Birmingham where Messrs. F. V. Smith and G. A. Durant were organising Lancaster production in early 1944.

Both repair and production plants had to deliver aircraft to the latest standard, which changed almost daily as new modifications were introduced. Some changes like the introduction of arrester gear and glider towing equipment were cancelled before they were fully effective, but repositioning of equipment and strengthening of parts resulted in the issue of 800 modification leaflets by early 1944. Special equipment was sometimes fitted under R.A.F. arrangements, but H2S became a standard production fitting from LM522 onwards in March 1944.

Each group had individual requirements. No. 8 (Pathfinder) Group required the astro-hatch to be raised and there was no provision for the carriage of bombs in excess of 4,000 lb in their Lancasters. No. 3 Group required all their Lancasters to be capable of carrying 8,000 lb. No. 1 Group was keen on underturrets and No. 5 Group included the two squadrons with Lancaster (Specials), Nos. 9 & 617 Squadrons. No. 6 Group required the Mk. Xs.

A. V. Roe had two main assembly plants and aerodromes for Lancasters, at Woodford and Yeadon; the last Lancaster to be produced at the latter is here seen taking off for service. In all 695 Lancasters were produced at the Yeadon factory.

a few were damaged by being only partially open when bombs were released.

After being farmed out to the various plants, the Lancaster fuselage sections, wings and tailplanes were brought together at Langar for re-assembly. Although a record of the original airframe from which they had come was kept, it was rarely possible to re-assemble the same parts together and to facilitate the return of repaired machines to service components were assembled as available. The aircraft's log book was forwarded to Langar after receipt of the wreck at Bracebridge; thus it was possible that the only part of a Lancaster leaving repair that could be guaranteed as of the original aircraft was the log book! Altogether 3,816 were returned to service through this organisation. In a few cases a special request for the same airframe complete to be returned was arranged.

Since a number of the Lancasters going to Bracebridge would have certain sections beyond repair, only three Lancasters could be expected for any four accepted. On the other hand a surplus of certain sections would accrue, e.g.

The requirements of the British Purchasing Commission in America for the United States to build Lancasters did not meet with success and they turned to the National Steel Corporation of Canada, who formed, under governmental control, Victory Aircraft Limited to produce the Lancaster for the R.A.F. Under the original agreement, 218 B-26 Marauders destined for the R.A.F. were to be handed over to the Royal Canadian Air Force. By the time the first Lancaster was produced it had been decided that the Canadian Squadrons in No. 6 Group of Bomber Command would use this version and, apart from aircraft used for development, the total wartime production was flown to Britain for Canadian squadrons.

On August 7th, 1944, the hundredth Canadian-built Lancaster, KB799, left the works with a ceremony, being named 'The Moose' by Mrs. Ross, wife of Air Commodore A. D. Ross, who had commanded a station of Canadians in Britain. By the end of the war a Lancaster a day was leaving the Victory plant and 10,000 Canadians were involved in Lancaster production.

*A "Grand Slam"
bomb, the largest
carried by any air-
craft during the
war, at the moment
of release from a
B.1 (Special) Lan-
caster. Thirty-
three Lancasters
were converted to
carry "Grand
Slams," PB592,
PB995-998 and
PD112-139, details
of which appear in
the Lancaster Log.
They were declared
obsolete in late
November 1948.*

On the first day of the new year, 1945, the time was considered ripe for another raid on the important German waterway the Dortmund-Ems canal. Such was its value to the enemy that loaded barges were held in readiness to drop ballast into any breaches. Therefore, once the water had run out in a section, there was little point in further bombing until it was repaired and the water up to its normal level again, so that any new breach would be widened by the outward flow of water. The time had now come.

Nine No. 5 Group squadrons were despatched in day-light to breach this canal at Ladbergen, a section vulnerable with aqueducts and therefore heavily defended. This attack was so successful that the original course of the canal was difficult to trace from the photographs subsequently taken. No. 9 Squadron in particular suffered severe losses on this operation. Two of their Lancasters crashed on take-off; in NG252 only the bomb aimer, Plt. Off. Flynn, survived, but in PD368 the crew walked away except for the flight engineer, Sgt. Davis, who was injured. Of those which got safely airborne, two failed to return. In PD377, hit by flak, both mid-upper and rear turrets were blazing with their gunners lying unconscious as ammunition exploded around them. The wireless operator, Flt. Sgt. G. Thompson, went to the rescue of the gunners and was severely burned as he dragged them to safety. Then with his bare hands he beat out the flames from their clothing and while making his way to the captain to report he received icy blasts that gave him frost-bite. Such was his pitiful condition that the pilot did not recognise him. Three-quarters of an hour later the Lancaster made a crash landing and three weeks afterwards Thompson died of his injuries. He was posthumously awarded the Victoria Cross.

No. 101 Squadron was no ordinary squadron. True, they operated as a normal No. 1 Group squadron, but they had an additional duty which entailed an eighth crew member and special broadcasting equipment. They were involved in radio counter measures—not the straightforward jamming of enemy transmission, but the broadcasts of false information to German fighters by imitating their controller.

The additional crew member had to be able to speak German fluently—in fact some were Germans who had been expelled by the Nazis before the war.

At the turn of the year two Lancasters were much in the minds of No. 101 Squadron, DV245 'S for Sugar' and DV302 'H for Howe'. Both had done well over ninety operations and there was great rivalry between their respective ground crews. There had been Lancasters with hundred-up operations before, but to have two in the same squadron vying with each other was a novelty. Ground crews, being more permanently associated with their aircraft, were more excited than the aircrews, who were posted away after their operational tour. 'Sugar' made its century on returning from a raid on Hanover on January 5th and this was 'Howe's' 98th—actually 'Howe' had operated more than 100 times, but abortive operations where bombs were jettisoned were not counted for a qualifying bomb symbol on the nose. By operating three nights in succession 'Howe' reached its century on the 7th, but not until the 16th were operations again carried out by the squadron, and that night both participated. By February 1st 'Sugar' had been on

To take the 22,000 lb. "Grand Slam" the Lancasters were specially modified, with front and mid turrets removed to reduce the all-up weight.

104 operations and 'Howe' 103. Next night 'Howe's' trip was abortive, but the following night 'Sugar' returned having failed to reach Bottrop, the target, so it still only led by one. They both went out on the 7th, but to the dismay of 'Howe's' ground crew it was unserviceable on the 13th and 'Sugar' then led by two. Both were over Chemnitz on the 14th, Dortmund on the 20th and Duisburg on the 21st.

It was subsequently established that the attack on Pforzheim on February 23rd was one of the most concentrated and successful of the war. Both 'Sugar' and 'Howe' operated and while comparative newcomers to the squadron, PB457 and RA523, succumbed to the defences, both the veterans returned, although 'Sugar's' crew did have a tussle with a twin-engined jet fighter that was seen to explode after three bursts of fire from their guns.

The master bomber that night was Captain 'Ted' Swales with an experienced crew. For one member, now Wg. Cdr. G. W. Bennington, D.F.M., it was his 35th operation with Swales. Their flight across occupied France and Western Germany was without incident except for the inevitable flak, but as they lost height to 8,000 feet on their final run in, evidence of night fighter activity came up on the detecting equipment. As they orbited Pforzheim, they were attacked without warning by a Messerschmitt. The first burst of incendiary shells thudded into the starboard wing, setting fire to the inboard engine and holing one of the fuel tanks.

The engine was quickly feathered and the fire extinguishers were brought into action; the remaining three Merlins were opened up to regain height and the crew resumed their task of broadcasting instructions to the heavy force of bombers then arriving in strength. But the fighter returned to the attack, this time from the port side. Again it scored hits and this time the port inboard engine stopped. More precious height was lost and the two remaining engines could do no more than maintain height at about 4,000 feet. Swales quickly brought the Lancaster under control and went on the air for the third time to continue directing the attack.

At last, satisfied that his task was completed, the pilot turned the nose of the crippled bomber for home leaving behind a night sky illuminated by an inferno. By skilful use of the thin layers of cloud, Swales managed to bring the aircraft over friendly territory, but when stratus gave way to cumulus cloud the turbulent air conditions made control of the Lancaster almost impossible. The two engines had long since reached the overheated stage and were in danger of seizing up at any moment, and when rudder trouble developed, defeat was finally acknowledged and the order was given to abandon the aircraft. Some six and a half hours after becoming airborne, the last man slipped through the escape hatch. Hardly had he done so when the sky was lit up as the bomber nosed into some high tension electric cables.

At dawn the following morning, on the outskirts of Valenciennes, the crew found the body of Ted Swales among the wreckage of PB538. His hands still held the spectacle of the control column, while yards away a foot rested on the rudder bar. Later his gallant action was acknowledged by the posthumous award of the Victoria Cross.

Although the power of the *Luftwaffe* was waning, there

Victim of the first " Grand Slam " dropped on operations, the viaduct at Bielefeld, March 14th, 1944.

were three occasions in 1945 when a concentration of German aircraft took the Allies by surprise. The first time Lancasters were only affected incidentally. On the first day of the year, during the so-called 'Rundstedt Offensive' or 'Battle of the Bulge', a mass ground strafing attack by some 800 aircraft was carried out. At least one Lancaster, having made a forced landing on a Belgian airfield, was among the 144 aircraft completely destroyed.

The second surprise came at the end of February when a number of No. 6 Group's Lancasters and Halifaxes approaching Hanover were attacked at about 18,000 feet by 30 to 40 Messerschmitt Me262s. For the first time in many cases, flight engineers took over the front turrets. Several crews claimed Me262s shot down, but eight bombers were lost.

The third of the German surprises came in the early hours of March 4th when large scale intruder operations were carried out. Halifax squadrons were the hardest hit, but numbers of Lancasters, returning from a raid on Ladbergen and mining operations, were also caught out. Landing was suspended at East Anglian, Lincolnshire and Yorkshire airfields while aircraft, waiting to land, orbited in the darkness. In spite of plans for just such a contingency, there was a delay in giving the operational code-word 'Scram' to effect dispersal. For some thirty minutes the aircraft were subjected to the hazards of collision and fire from the home defences, which were very 'trigger-happy' that night, not to mention the intruders. When 'Scram' was finally broadcast, crews were directed to Midland airfields, chiefly Bitteswell where, incidentally, part of Armstrong Whitworth's Lancaster output was tested.

One of No. 44 Squadron's aircraft was lost that night with all its crew when an intruder shot it down over Brocklesby Park, Lincolnshire. Another of their crews, in PB380, had a problem unconnected with the major event of the night. A mine that had failed to release over the sea dropped in the bomb bay as the aircraft orbited base. They were forced to go back over the sea to open the bomb doors and deposit their deadly load unprimed into the dark waters. At Waddington an intruder machine-gunning the station

hit the incendiary bomb dump and created a conflagration. For a time it was thought that some 4,000 lb 'Cookies' were near the dump and the station fire-fighters were recalled and all personnel were ordered to take shelter. Fortunately these fears proved unfounded, but a worse misfortune for the Australians there was the loss that night of No. 467 (R.A.A.F.) Squadron's Commanding Officer.

During the first three weeks of March both the No. 101 Squadron veterans operated regularly until the 23rd when 'Sugar' did not return from its 121st operation, an attack on Bremen. The competition had ended. By the official squadron record, however, 'Sugar' continued regularly on operations, but presumably the clerk concerned, so used to typing out ' "S" DV245', could not take in the change to ' "S" NX572'.

'Grand Slam' can be said to be the ultimate in conventional bombs used operationally. This ten-ton monster— 22,000 lb to be more exact—was designed as an earthquake bomb to cause an earth tremor, not to blow a surface crater or effect blast. Dropped from 40,000 feet it could penetrate a hundred feet before the 6-7 tons of explosive rocked any structure in the vicinity. Plans for producing such a bomb had in fact been made when 'Tallboy' (its 12,000 lb minor) was mooted, but at that time no worthwhile target was within striking distance with the limited weight of fuel that could be carried with such a load. After D-Day the need for 'Grand Slam' became apparent and it was rushed into production.

Lancaster PB529/G was earmarked in October 1944 for modification to carry 'Grand Slam' and was ready for trials on the following February 1st. While this aircraft pioneered the carriage and release mechanism, PB995 was fitted with a weighted mock-up 'Grand Slam' for performance trials. The former aircraft did a number of casing drops, followed on March 13th by the first live drop on Ashley Walk range. Meanwhile, two lorries with tarpaulins covering boiler-like objects had arrived at Woodhall Spa for No. 617 Squadron destined to use these 'Special Stores' on the Bielefeld Viaduct.

This important viaduct carrying the main line from Hamm to Hanover had defied a series of attacks, including an attack with 'Tallboys' by the R.A.F. and the U.S. Eighth Air Force, who had, however, damaged some spans and a pier with 1,000 and 500 lb bombs. Quickly, the Germans had re-laid the track by placing girders over the broken spans. No. 617 Squadron set out fifteen strong on the early afternoon of March 14th; fourteen carried 'Tallboys' and

PD112 with Sqn. Ldr. C. C. Calder and four crew members carried the first of the 41 'Grand Slams' that No. 617 Squadron were to drop during the war. It was not possible to estimate the damage caused by the individual bombs, but the 'Grand Slam', dropped within thirty yards of the bridge, was near enough to take effect, and the net result was the destruction of 100 yards of the viaduct. A subsequent report of the raid assumed that only a 'Grand Slam' could have achieved this—to which might well have been added that only a Lancaster could lift it.

Another Ruhr approach bridge, the Arnsberg Viaduct, was No. 617's target next day. Both Sqn. Ldrs. C. C. Calder and J. V. Cockshott in PB996 and PD114 respectively carried 'Grand Slams'; the former was obliged to return and landed with the store, but Cockshott glimpsing the columns through the haze let his go. Reconnaissance revealed that the railway over the bridge was still functioning—but only until the 19th when No. 617 set out again and that time demolished the viaduct.

Meanwhile, day and night attacks had been going on and a sudden resurgence of the *Luftwaffe's* night flying strength caused a force of 231 No. 1 Group and 46 Pathfinder Lancasters to be depleted by 24 during attacks on Nuremberg and Wurzburg during the night of March 16th. Among the losses was ND644, a veteran of well over a hundred operations. For weeks this aircraft had vied with ND458 for the operational record in No. 100 Squadron and they had recently been level at 111 operations each.

German jet fighters were now being met with increasing frequency. LM672 was attacked by Me262s over Bremen and one was seen to turn over on its back and dive after the Lancaster had returned fire. ME497 of the same squadron, No. 100, had an inconclusive bout with a similar type of fighter. About this time the Germans claimed that a Lancaster was destroyed by upward-firing rockets from an Me163B.

Take-off was an anxious time for all concerned on an operational bomber station and a crash on the runway could hold up operations for the night. At Croft on March 22nd a No. 434 Squadron aircraft swung off the runway, settled down on its belly and burst into flames as the crew scampered to safety. Eight of No. 431 Squadron's aircraft had already taken off but the remainder of the Lancasters and all No. 434 Squadron's lined up for take-off were hurriedly taxied away as the burning aircraft had a 4,000 lb 'Cookie' aboard. The airfield was cleared except for the fire-fighters and since the burning Lancaster was doomed they were held back—which was just as well, as it blew up later.

While the 21st Army Group massed for the Rhine crossings at dawn, 77 Lancasters attacked the little town of Wesel at 3.30 p.m. the previous day, following it up with another attack 90 minutes before midnight as the 1st Commando Brigade followed by the 51st Highland Division closed in. Wesel was taken with only 36 army casualties and Field Marshal Montgomery said, "The bombing of Wesel last night was a masterpiece and a decisive factor in making possible our entry into that town before midnight."

To those who heard the wartime B.B.C. news bulletins, the recurring name of Hamm will no doubt surely be remembered; on March 20th the marshalling yards there received both morning and afternoon raids.

An immediate D.S.O. was awarded as a consequence of a lone, unescorted flight across Germany by a Lancaster on March 25th, although the citation referred to an earlier incident equally gallant—mistakes were not for promulgation! PB913 had been prepared as master marker aircraft for a raid on Osnabruck and the airfield controller scheduled it to take off first. However, the flight engineer, checking the aircraft, was not satisfied as the fuel gauges showed nil. The pilot, anxious to go, checked the Form 700 with the ground crew and, noting that the aircraft was documented as fully serviceable, suggested that the fuel gauges had merely stuck. Just as the pilot was about to taxi out the flight engineer, who had tapped the gauges in vain, reported that he would not be satisfied until the fuel had been checked. The engines were cut and the ground crew ordered to dipstick the tanks as a fuel check. They were found to be almost empty!

The pilot, Sqn. Ldr. G. A. Thorne, ordering the crew to follow, raced for the spare aircraft and hurriedly checked it over—but it was not fitted with V.H.F. for the master bomber to instruct crews! Racing back to their original machine, they taxied round to a bowser and ordered an immediate fill-up. To put 2,154 gallons into a Lancaster takes twenty minutes or so. Meanwhile, the rest of the squadron had taken off, leaving the master bomber behind. Rarely did aircraft fly direct to their target, but, as in this case, went south first to complete the first leg of the journey in safety behind the Allied Lines, to shorten the actual time over enemy territory.

Thorne asked the navigator the chances of getting there on time if they cut across the heart of Germany. They were

50/50. At maximum speed they sped in a direct line to Osnabruck without opposition except for intensive flak as they crossed the Dortmund—Ems canal which, now such a regular target, was heavily defended. As Osnabruck approached below, so the main force hove in sight. No sooner had they marked than bombs were dropping.

April followed much the same pattern as March. By now over a thousand Lancasters were in front line service and it was without question the predominant aircraft in Bomber Command; actual strength figures being 1,088 Lancasters, 349 Halifaxes and 170 Mosquitos. On the 10th, No. 460 (R.A.A.F.) Squadron celebrated their 5,000th Lancaster sortie and the squadron statistician estimated their Lancasters had dropped 24,000 tons of bombs and travelled some 4,000,000 miles. Oil installations figured often as Lancaster targets and at a time when petrol to civilians was meticulously rationed it is worthy of note that one Lancaster, ED888 which did 139 sorties, consumed an estimated 194,000 gallons of fuel. As a result of attacks on the Auguste Viktoria benzol plant and a similar plant at Bruchstrasse, the effectiveness of the enemy fighter force was considerably reduced. Mining was still being continued; No. 75 (New Zealand) Squadron, for example, attacked the oil targets mentioned and also 'gardened' off Kiel on the night of April 9th.

Fifty non-standard Lancasters came on to the scene early in 1945. In spite of plans for introducing a turret with 20 mm. cannons, and an interim measure of using Martin turrets with .50 calibre machine-guns, the .303 guns remained standard. The first Lancasters due from Austin Motors were planned to have the Martin turrets, but rather than hold production up until these arrived the first fifty were completed as Mk. Is—with a difference. The Martin turret was planned for positioning over the bomb bay and these fifty had Frazer Nash turrets in this position.

They were first issued to No. 427 (R.C.A.F.) Squadron, who were converting from Halifax IIIs at this time; being new to Lancasters they were in no position to make comparisons, but the remainder were distributed as replacements where required. No. 189 Squadron had two, of which the first went missing with a second-tour crew, leaving a single B.1 (non-standard). The air bomber on the latter aircraft, Sgt. G. Fraser, now a London civil servant, reported that these aircraft were not liked as the turret was difficult to enter and awkward for the crew to by-pass.

The last of the wartime Lancaster bomb accidents

Food for the starving Dutch dropping from the bomb bays of Lancasters in late April 1945.

happened at 5.45 p.m. on April 17th as machines were being bombed up. A night raid on railways at Cham near the Czech border was scheduled. At East Kirkby the Lancasters of Nos. 57 and 630 Squadrons were being attended by ground crews when two 1,000 lb M.C. bombs for PB360 went up, causing sympathetic explosions. The airfield appeared to be a shambles and ambulances had to be called from other stations. Three airmen were killed and fourteen injured and there were two civilian casualties, one of which was fatal. Next morning the station engineer officer, after a survey in daylight of wrecked and toppled Lancasters, reported five completely written off and fourteen with varying degrees of damage.

Next night, DV302, the famous 'Howe' of No. 101 Squadron, returned from its 121st and last operation of the war, thus just beating by one its late rival 'Sugar'. Then came the final raids of the war.

Escorted by P-51 Mustangs of the U.S. Eighth Air Force, a day raid was made on Hitler's chalet and the S.S. barracks at Berchtesgaden on April 25th. For once, the B.B.C. was permitted to announce the raid while it was in progress. Owing to mist and mountains obscuring the target and making aiming difficult only 53 bombers attacked their primary target, which was left in ruins. Plt. Off. L. Knight on his first operation and his crew were about to be reported as missing from this operation when, two hours overdue, PA229 landed safely back at Kelstern with two engines out of action. There had not been such an incident in No. 625 Squadron since February 8th when PD376 had returned from Politz with part of a Halifax tailplane wrapped around its own tail, following a collision over the Danish coast on the return.

Following the day raid on the so-called 'Hitler's Hideout' came a night raid in which 119 Lancasters from No. 5 Group joined in the last Lancaster raid of the war, directed by Wg. Cdr. Maurice A. Smith, D.F.C. (the present Editor of Flight International), as the master bomber, on U-boat fuel storage tanks at Vallo in Oslo Fjord. Operation orders for attacks on Heligoland on the 26th and 27th were each cancelled in turn.

No. 115 was the first squadron to be involved in the famous food dropping operation at the end of the European war. As early as February 24th, HK696 had been on detachment from its base at Witchford to Netheravon for experiments in dropping provisions. In early April tests were made at Witchford for loading containers in the two types of bomb bays with which Lancasters were fitted. By the 6th practice drops were made, and next day Major R. P. Martin gave a demonstration drop from HK798 to officers of Bomber Command Headquarters assembled at nearby Lacey Green.

At the end of April operation MANNA was signalled. Negotiations had been going on with the Germans for some weeks on the plight of the Dutch. The Dutch railwaymen had struck in protest against German demands and as a result there was no distribution of food whatsoever. This, following years on meagre rations, was endangering the health of the whole nation. Townsfolk went foraging in the country, thousands camped in fields in search of food. Children cried with hunger and adults were haunted by what the future would bring. Fortunately it brought their salvation, chiefly through the medium of Lancasters.

Slung panniers were fitted into the Lancaster bays, which could take five, each with some 70 sacks. They contained flour, yeast, powdered egg, dried milk, peas, beans, tins of meat and bacon, tea, sugar, pepper and special vitamin chocolate. Orders to each squadron were to drop the panniers in their allotted area, which they would find marked from liaison with the various Dutch municipal authorities, made possible by their underground movement.

Only the bedridden appeared not to be out when the bombers came over to drop their loads. There was a sea of hands waving handkerchiefs and flags to greet the machines while the authorities kept the dropping areas clear. Some German gunners standing by their anti-aircraft guns waved solemnly in acquiescence. There were, however, a few incidents and No. 186 Squadron bore the brunt of the relatively few mishaps. They were briefed to drop five large panniers each on Waalhaven aerodrome, near Rotterdam. Flt. Sgt. K. W. Jarvis got three packages down, by which time crowds had swarmed across the field and he could not risk dropping the others. Plt. Off. B. A. Rose could not get all his packages away because the bomb doors had been damaged by small arms fire. Back over Stradishall he also found difficulty in lowering the undercarriage. While 'jinking' his aircraft to jolt the wheels down, a package fell, strewing tea, sugar and tins over the countryside to the north of Stradishall. This caused something of a race between villagers and the official R.A.F. recovery party! Finally Rose flew over to Woodbridge and brought NF995 safely down on their long runway. Next day one of this squadron's aircraft was hit by two bags from an aircraft above, fortunately without causing damage.

The drops continued for several days. Crews reported that on a number of houses messages had been whitewashed —'Thanks R.A.F.' and 'Good Luck Tommy'. Many crews made a personal contribution. They gave their own sweet rations and their aircrew issue, wrapped up and tied by string to handkerchiefs or pieces of linen to make a parachute; they flung them from the windows with notes *Ver Het Kinde*—For The Children. While the pannier contents were for official distribution, these sweets were a free for all. One

Flt. Sgt. Beesley of Handsworth, Birmingham, was flown back from a prison camp in an aircraft that had replaced his in the squadron when he was shot down over a year previous. The press took the licence of reporting it as the very same aircraft, which the serial number belies. This photo was taken on V-E Day.

squadron saw stones marked out 'TABAC' and, pinpointing it on their charts, reported it at their station; a whip round of the cigarette ration was organised and it was dropped there next day.

One unfortunate incident was that a target indicator in the Rotterdam area fell by a house and set it on fire. One pannier dropped in a lake, but later crews reported rowing boats going out to salvage the contents. During the operation PD287, after dropping 284 sacks, got into trouble over the North Sea on the return journey. A short in a microphone heater caused a fire in the rear turret and exploded rounds of ammunition. The pilot was able to land at Oulton without injury to any of the crew. Altogether 6,684 tons of food were dropped in 3,156 sorties by Lancasters and 145 flown in Mosquitos.

The last operational order of the war for offensive action by Lancasters was issued on the morning of May 3rd. No. 427 Squadron were instructed to detail nine aircraft to lay mines in the Kattegat that night. At 10.30 p.m. the Lancasters started; eight had taken off when a general order suspending all operations was received. They were contacted by radio, recalled, and they landed with their mines.

Two French Resistance girls who had helped shot-down crews feted at Waterbeach by a No. 514 Squadron crew

No. 424 Squadron already had eight aircraft airborne when the recall was received, with instructions to fly locally for four hours to lessen their fuel and so reduce their load for landing.

While Operation MANNA was being effected, EXODUS Operation Order No. 1 was issued on May 2nd. Two days later Lancasters were landing at Brussels and Juvincourt to repatriate prisoners-of-war from Germany. Westcott was the main reception base and there were many touching scenes as soldiers, sailors and airmen jumped out of the Lancasters on to British soil for the first time for several years in some cases. Every effort was made to provide a welcome and military bands played the Lancasters in. At one reception station the response was measured in the rate of rations consumed in one day—15,000 cups of tea and ½ ton of cakes.

EXODUS went on during V-E Day, celebrated on May 8th. Most Lancaster units not on repatriation duty were stood down. At Middleton St. George, a Canadian Lancaster station, a pipe-band marched round followed, according to an eye-witness, 'by the station personnel in various stages of intoxication'. Informality was the order of the day at that station and anyone rash enough to be properly dressed had his tie clipped off! As the celebrations reached their climax, the clippings included the starboard growths of some of the luxuriant moustaches sported by certain of the aircrew, which made the victims feel—and look—very much out of trim next morning.

Next day came stark tragedy as the repatriation continued. RF230, loaded with 25 passengers and a crew of six, reported soon after take-off from Juvincourt that an emergency landing was necessary. It would appear that the passengers were warned to take up station at the rear and this upset the flying trim and the pilot lost control, for the aircraft dived to earth near Roye-Ami. All the occupants were killed. Apart from that tragedy, 74,000 ex-P.O.W.s were brought safely home in Lancasters up to May 28th when the final evacuation was carried out. At last the Lancaster was fulfilling its bomber/transport role.

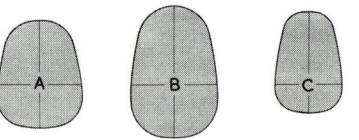

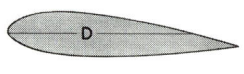

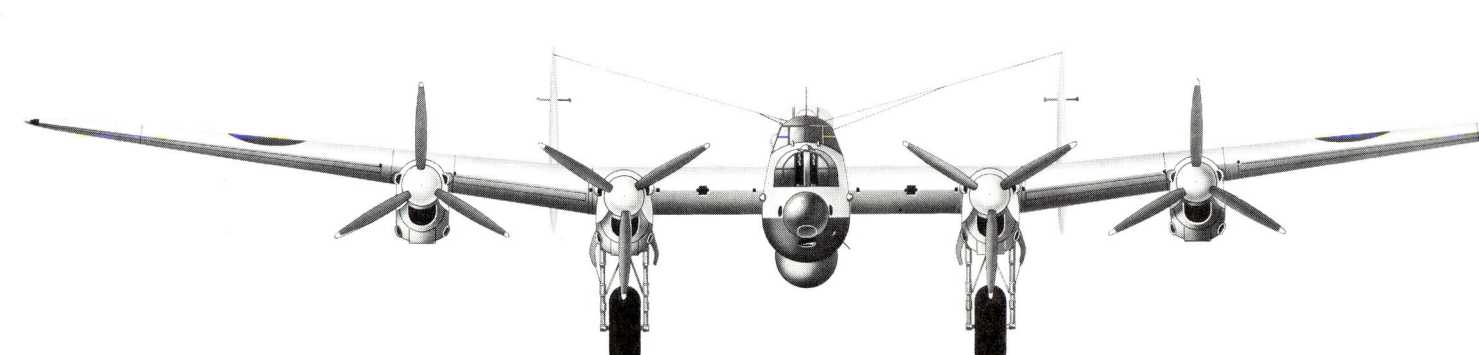

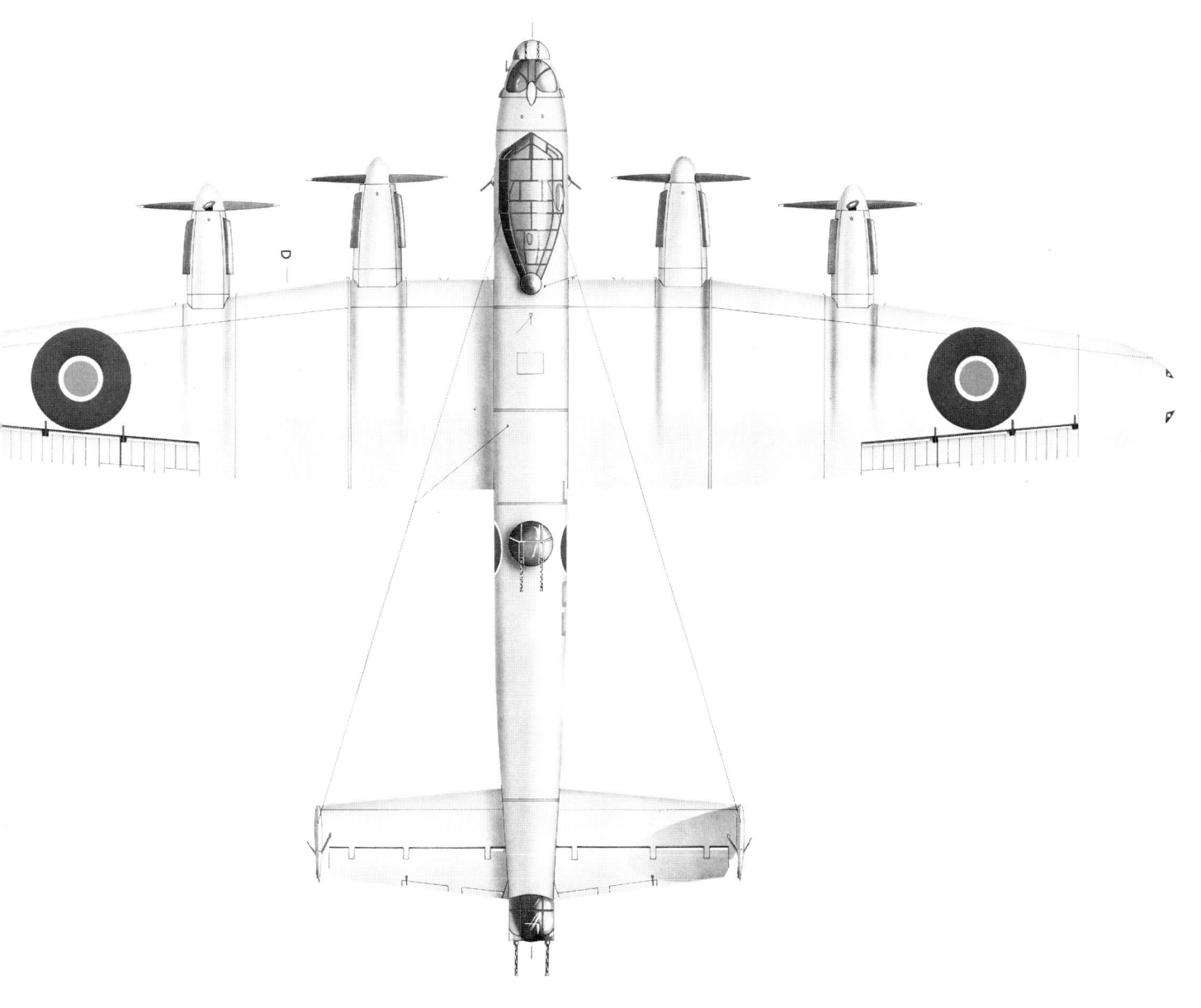

**EP·E, a Lancaster B.VII built by Austin Motors, of No. 104 Squadron at Shallufa
early in 1947.**

CHAPTER SIXTEEN

Variations on a Theme

Troops and nursing sisters giving the "V" on V-E Day itself after the men, ex-prisoners-of-war in Germany, had been flown back to England in this Lancaster from No. 83 Squadron. After this duty on Operation Exodus, Lancasters went farther afield to repatriate troops, particularly the "Desert Rats," from Italy.

With the war in Europe over, all Lancaster squadrons, committed to serve in the Far East or not, had several tasks in hand. The first was the disposal of bombs. Low capacity bombs could be returned to dumps but high capacity H.E. bombs and incendiaries deteriorated rapidly in store and had to be disposed. The obvious way was bombing up the Lancasters and dropping them in the sea and areas of the Irish and North Seas were defined. Another task was Operation DODGE, the repatriation of Eighth Army personnel. Home had seemed very far away for the 'Desert Rats' who had fought through the North African Campaign and driven the Germans back into Italy, but home was reached in seven hours by Lancasters. Using the airfield at Bari, Lancasters flew across France to Britain taking 24 men at a time with their kit-bags stowed in the bomb bays. Many of the crews kept them briefed with items of interest below, such as battered Caen or the Normandy beaches, but their chief question was—' How long before we sight England?' As with EXODUS, there were again many scenes as the men alighted; one corporal knelt and picked up a handful of soil, his eyes brimming with tears as he sifted it through his fingers. By operations POST MORTEM and SPASM, crews and specialists viewed and assessed the damage caused by bombing to the Ruhr and on Berlin; also enemy radar was manned and mock raids were conducted to assess the efficiency of German radar.

Some uncommitted squadrons already had orders to reduce establishment. An officer of No. 630 Squadron was detailed to deliver his Lancaster to Down Ampney. Landing and taxiing along to a row of derelict Lancasters, he looked around to report delivery, but could find only a civilian in a watch hut. Brought up in the service tradition of rigid accounting, whereby even the navigators signed for their instruments and carried them around in a bag, he was not a little surprised to hear the watchman say: 'Just leave it there like the others.' It dawned upon him then that Lancasters, after being in continuous demand for four years, were now redundant. True, it was still in production,

but to have called a halt to all production would have meant throwing thousands of workers into Labour Exchanges at a time when service demobilisation had commenced.

Britain was anxious that as soon as Germany had been defeated she would take her place alongside the American Forces in the defeat of Japan. The Army was fighting in Burma, the Royal Navy was reinforcing their Pacific Fleet and the R.A.F. could best contribute by joining with American aircraft in bombarding Japan. Meanwhile, in the background, very much in secret, *the* bomb was being developed.

The Americans were using the B-17 Fortress and B-29 Superfortress in their massive air offensive. The former was well known to the R.A.F., who were not impressed with it because of its relatively small bomb-load; they had little knowledge of the capabilities of the B-29, so an R.A.F. team, headed by Group Captain Waghorn, went to Washington in February 1944 to inspect and handle the Superfortress. However, it was decided to go ahead with a British design and use the new Lincoln in the Pacific with the

Installed in late-production Lancasters, the F.N.82 tail turret and cupola, armed with two .5 Browning machine-guns fitted with flash eliminators, weighed 411 lb. It could turn through 170 degrees and the guns could be depressed or elevated 45 degrees.

Lancaster as interim equipment. This would entail tropicalising the Lancaster and the R.A.E. studied the implications.

To increase the range of a standard Lancaster, which carried 2,154 gallons in six self-sealing tanks located in the wings, large saddle tanks on top of the fuselage were fitted by A. V. Roe to HK541 and SW244. Handling characteristics proved to be poor and what kind of reception such a version would have had in the service can scarcely be imagined—it could hardly have inspired confidence to crews to be aware of hundreds of gallons of highly inflammable fuel immediately above their heads.

While the A. & A.E.E. used Lancaster LM730 in December 1944 for flight refuelling coupling designs, the specialists were called in by the Air Staff. Flight Refuelling Ltd. had years of pre-war experience in air refuelling and were held in such high esteem internationally that the U.S.A. had asked them to experiment with a B-24 Liberator tanker to refuel a B-17 Fortress. They were now asked by the Air Ministry to prepare to convert 600 Lancasters to tankers and to modify 600 Lincolns to receive fuel by aerial pipeline, but before work commenced plans changed from mounting the Force in Burma with

mention of this went to the Hamilton Company in the U.S.A., who had kept Lancasters well supplied with three-bladed propellers. Lincolns began to emerge from the Avro and A.W.A. factories in the spring of 1945 but extensive trials were necessary before they could be ready made for service. The Force was therefore committed to the Lancaster with Lincoln replacement as a long-term plan, not an initial step as first envisaged.

Navigation was going to be of prime importance over the vast stretches of the Pacific and the Central Navigation School had earlier been asked to study the difficulties involved. This had coincided with a project the staff were contemplating and, in fact, facilitated it. The school had recently changed its name to the Empire Air Navigation School and a tour was projected embracing Canada, Australia and New Zealand. As early as 1942 a Wellington from the school toured North African units demonstrating navigational techniques and in the summer of 1944 a Stirling, equipped with the latest navigational equipment, toured Canada. Now an Empire tour was projected and sanctioned on the undertaking that while the useful task of disseminating information on the latest navigational

Two Lancasters were modified to have saddle tanks of 1,200 gallons capacity and were flown to India for trials, where they were attached to No. 1577 Flight. On return they were stored at Hullavington and eventually scrapped.

depots in India to operating from Pacific Islands integral with American Forces.

Planning was made difficult by conflicting priorities. The Air Staff were pressing for the Lincoln, or Lancaster IV as it was then known. Powered with two-stage Merlin engines it had a better all-round performance and refinements in armament and equipment. By June 1944 the monthly output of Lancasters was about 260 with 400 Lancasters/Lincolns a month scheduled for early 1945. It was logical that the Lincoln, utilising so many basic Lancaster components, would be made by contractors producing Lancasters, but the changeover in the factories would, inevitably, set back Lancaster production. The repercussions of this were widespread. If Lincoln production was set back by three months in 1945 then the additional Lancasters produced in lieu would entail 4,800 additional single-stage Merlins at a time when these were in demand for a dozen different aircraft types. However, the airframe manufacturers were reluctant to change over in view of standing demands for Lancasters which could be fulfilled more easily, so Lincoln production slipped back still further.

Production of the new Bristol B.17 turret armed with twin 20mm. cannon was also delayed. A change to four-bladed British propellers was mooted, but for a time no

aids would ostensibly be the only task of the tour, data would be collected on operating a Lancaster in changing conditions and a study could be made of navigational difficulties and American methods in the Pacific theatre. A further task was the collection of data for air transport routes. On the aspect of operations in the tropics, W4963 had been examined by the A. & A.E.E. in February 1944 upon its return from the Middle East.

A standard B.I Lancaster, PD328, was modified for the purpose. This involved little more than removing the mid-upper turret and fitting out the aircraft with the latest navigational equipment. When PD328 left for Prestwick on October 21st, 1944, there was no deliberate intention of making a round-the-world flight and it was not then known by the name under which it was later acclaimed—*Aries*.

With a crew of ten—six officers, three airmen (fitter, rigger and electrician) and a civilian specialist on navigational instruments from the Ministry of Aircraft Production—the Lancaster arrived in New Zealand on November 1st via Reykjavik, Montreal, Washington, Honolulu and Samoa. There were no untoward incidents except on the first leg when icing up of pitot tubes affected instruments. In contrast, when it left North West Cape, Australia, after touring and lecturing at 24 units in New Zealand, New

Guinea and Australia, it was 120 degrees in the shade. Fortunately there was no engine overheating and the return via Masirah, Cairo and Malta was uneventful until nearing London, where fog blanketed Northolt. The Lancaster was diverted to another airfield, where touchdown was made just 72 hours after leaving Australia.

This first operation of *Aries* augured well for the force. There had been no maintenance difficulties in spite of operations in extremes of temperature.

The British Element of the American Strategic Force was officially set up as the Very Long Range Bomber Force in late 1944 and a planning staff nucleus was functioning before the end of the year. Planning was for three groups of ten heavy bomber squadrons of sixteen aircraft each with six long range fighter squadrons for escort. This concept changed within weeks following a suggestion from the Americans that the British force be concentrated in the manner of their Twentieth Air Force based on five great airfields in the Marianas.

Training for the Far East started in earnest. The code name 'Tiger' was allotted to the project and the units earmarked for this venture became 'Tiger Force'. Exercises entailing long-leg round-Britain flights became the order

A new standard of finish for Bomber Command aircraft was introduced post-war which had its origins in the requirement for Tiger Force. The aircraft depicted are of No. 35 Squadron preparatory to an American tour.

of the day to gain proficiency in navigation and give experience in long range sorties. There was also low and high level bombing practice and fighter affiliation. Rumours went round the squadrons that they were to operate from Okinawa.

Tiger Force was not the only operation projected for Lancasters. It was considered that it might be practicable to use them in a close support role in Burma, bombing from low level. No. 7 Squadron was selected for trials in this country and operated under the V.C.P. (Visual Control Post) System. Targets were reported and crews scrambled like fighter pilots for the aircraft. The record was a scramble of nine Lancasters in 107 seconds from report to the last becoming airborne.

Plans changed once more as the Americans island-hopped nearer to Japan. Tiger Force was to be concentrated on a single island and the whole constitution of the force was changed. It was re-organised into two groups each of ten squadrons of twenty aircraft each. Fighter support was increased to six squadrons and a squadron of Mosquitos for photographic reconnaissance and meteorological reporting was added, together with a squadron for air-sea rescue work. This was to be completely self supporting and was to provide its own airfield construction facilities. Hadrian gliders for transporting materials were offset from the

United States Army Air Force and Lincolns were fitted with glider intercommunicating equipment.

Tropical operation and glider training had already been tried with success. Lancaster Is JA903 and JA904 arrived in India on October 5th, 1943, and not until November the following year were they recalled to the U.K. The first glider tow was accomplished at Mauripur on May 19th, 1944, when JA903 took up Horsa I LH237, which had been erected by personnel from No. 7 School of Technical Training. Next month, Hamilcar HH974 was successfully towed and Horsa I LH137 was taken up to 10,000 feet on tow. While the effects of the tropics on JA903 were examined back in England in November 1944, JA904 was held up for spares until January 1945 before the return flight could be attempted. During their service in India they had been operated by No. 1577 (Special Duties) Flight which later received both HK541 and SW244, mentioned earlier, for trials. From an examination of all these Lancasters and the reports of their crews a tropicalisation scheme known as F.E. (for Far East) standard was worked out.

Lancaster B.Is coming off delivery from Vickers Armstrong and Armstrong Whitworth were earmarked for tropicalisation to Far East standard. These were later designated B.Mk.I (F.E.). They were initially stored at No. 38 Maintenance Unit, Llandow, and flown as required to Short Bros. and Harland at Belfast for conversion to the new standard and from there were sent to squadrons of Tiger Force. Among these were Nos. 9 and 617, which were planned to drop 'Grand Slams' and 'Tallboys' on Japanese targets.

While flight refuelling experiments were still being conducted, they were not pressed for Tiger Force. The production of the required installation would set back Lincoln production still further and delay development of the Lancasters. It was finally agreed that the force standard for Lancasters would be initially Mks. I, III and VII with mid-upper turrets removed to compensate for an extra 400 gallon fuel tank installed in the bomb bay. Additionally, there were many minor changes such as the installation of SCR-522 (U.S. Signal Corps Receiver Type 522) in place of a British model.

In June the Canadian squadrons started to fly back to their homeland, a movement that entailed overflying the Atlantic, via St. Mawgan and the Azores, by large numbers of Mk. X Lancasters. At Greenwood, an assembly base was being prepared for Canadian squadrons bound for the Pacific. No. 428 was one of the squadrons that flew back in

Aries *was a Lancaster, not a Lancastrian as its appearance might suggest. It is marked here in South-east Asian Command markings for its flight across the Pacific.*

June, that is except for KB764 which was ditched soon after leaving Lagens in the Azores. It was planned that Tiger Force would follow this route when they set out for Okinawa.

It had been on April 9th that KB999, the 300th Lancaster built in Canada, arrived at No. 20 Maintenance Unit, Aston Down, for service preparation which was completed in six days. But within two months, after receipt of another twenty or so, the flow started in the opposite direction. While the Canadian-built Lancasters streamed back to North America, a lone British-built one, of No. 15 Squadron, piloted by Wing Commander C. C. Calder, D.S.O. and Bar, D.F.C., flew on July 24th to South America carrying Sir Arthur Harris, who was attending celebrations in honour of the homecoming of the Brazilian Expeditionary Force from Italy.

Several small projects involving Lancasters were brought to an abrupt halt when the war in the Pacific ended. In April 1945 the R.A.A.F. proposed a Research and Development Flight of Lancasters, to gain experience in heavy bomber operations and radar performance under tropical conditions. Four Mk. IIIs, PB974 and PB992-994, were prepared with H2S Mk. IIIA and A.G.L.T. for a nine month loan to Australia. In September this project was cancelled and the Lancasters returned to No. 5 M.U., Kemble.

Lancasters were required in India for several projects. As early as June 1943 it had been proposed that two Halifaxes and three Lancasters be attached for trials with No. 159 Squadron. The Controller of Communication Equipment and Ordnance, India, also requested two Lancasters for radar trials and NN749 and PB847 were allotted. In August, within days of the Japanese collapse, all these projects were cancelled.

Even the Royal Navy had a request for Lancasters. No. 734 Squadron which acted for the School of Engine Handling was at R.N.A.S. Worthy Down with Whitleys fitted out with fuel flowmeters and other instruments as flying classrooms. Plans were made for the squadron to move to Peplow and re-equip with Fortresses and Lancasters. This, too, was cancelled.

Had the atomic bombs not been dropped upon Hiroshima and Nagasaki and so ended World War II, Tiger Force would have moved to its Pacific bases. November 14th was the actual date planned for ground crews to be on site, with the first aircraft planned to arrive seven days later. As it was all movement was suspended when the Japanese surrender was received and the force disbanded in October before any squadron had left the country and before the Lancaster's successor, the Lincoln, entered service. From March 1942 when the Lancaster first commenced operations to the end of the war, Lancasters in the course of operations delivered a total of 608,613 tons of H.E. bombs, dropped 51,513,106 incendiary bombs and laid 12,733 mines in a total of 156,308 sorties which consumed some 228,000,000 gallons of fuel.

No. 57 Squadron at East Kirkby was first to receive the Lincoln. It was notified of the allocation of three on August 22nd and next day RE285 arrived followed by RE286 and RE287 four days later. The Lancaster was being superseded.

Hostilities over, the public queue for a view of the outstanding bomber of the war. The new finish permitted the pre-war practice of marking the serial number beneath the wings, but it was 1947 before the roundel changed to its present form.

LANCASTER SQUADRONS AT BOMBER COMMAND PEAK STRENGTH AUGUST 1st, 1944

Sqn. No.	Sqn. Code	Mk.	Group	Location
7	MG	I/III	8	Oakington, Cambridgeshire
9	WS	I/III	5	Bardney, Lincolnshire
12	PH	I/III	1	Wickenby, Lincolnshire
15	LS	I/III	3	Mildenhall, Suffolk
35	TL	I/III	8	Graveley, Huntingdonshire
44	KM	I/III	5	Dunholme Lodge, Lincs
49	EA	I/III	5	Fiskerton, Lincolnshire
50	VN	I/III	5	Skellingthorpe, Lincolnshire
57	DX/QT	I/III	5	East Kirkby, Spilsby, Lincs
61	QR	I/III	5	Skellingthorpe, Lincolnshire
75	AA/JN	I/III	3	Mepal, Cambridgeshire
83	OL	I/III	5	Coningsby, Lincolnshire
90	WP	I/III	3	Tuddenham, Suffolk
97	OF/ZT	I/III	5	Coningsby, Lincolnshire
100	HW/FZ	I/III	1	Grimsby, Lincolnshire
101	SR	I/III	1	Ludford Magna, Lincs
103	PM	I/III	1	Elsham Wolds, Barnetby, Lincolnshire
106	ZN	I/III	5	Metheringham, Lincolnshire
115	KO/IL	I/III	3	Witchford, Isle of Ely, Cambridgeshire
156	GT	I/III	8	Upwood, Huntingdonshire
166	AS	I/III	1	Kirmington, Lindsey Lincs
207	EM	I/III	5	Spilsby, Lincolnshire
218	HA	I/III	3	Woolfox Lodge, Oakham, Rutland
300	*BH	I/III	1	Faldingworth, Lincolnshire
405	†LQ	I/III	8	Gransden Lodge, Sandy, Bedfordshire
408	†EQ	II	6	Linton-on-Ouse, Yorkshire
419	†VR	X	6	Middleton-St.-George, Co. Durham
428	†NA	X	6	Middleton-St.-George, Co Durham
460	AR	I/III	1	Binbrook, Lincolnshire
463	‡JO	I/III	5	Waddington, Lincolnshire
467	‡PO	I/III	5	Waddington, Lincolnshire
514	J1/A2	I/III	3	Waterbeach, Cambs
550	BQ	I/III	1	North Killingholme, Lincs
576	UL	I/III	1	Elsham Wolds, Barnetby, Lincolnshire
582	GO	I/III	8	Little Slaughton, St. Neots, Huntingdonshire
617	KC/YZ	I/III	5	Woodhall Spa, Lincolnshire
619	PG	I/III	5	Dunholme Lodge, Lincs
622	GI	I/III	3	Mildenhall, Suffolk
625	CF	I/III	1	Kelstern, Louth, Lincs
626	UM	I/III	1	Wickenby, Lincolnshire
630	LE	I/III	5	East Kirkby, Spilsby, Lincs
635	F2	I/III	8	Downham Market, Norfolk

* Polish   † R.C.A.F.   ‡ R.A.A.F.

BREAKDOWN OF PRODUCTION

MANCHESTER

	Proto-types	Mk. I/IA	Serial Prefix
A. V. Roe & Co. Ltd.	2	157	L
Metropolitan Vickers Ltd.	–	43	R
Total ..	2 Prototypes	200 Production	

LANCASTER

	Proto-type	Mk. I	Mk. II	Mk. III	Mk. VII	Mk. X	Firms' Totals
A. V. Roe & Co. Ltd. (Manchester Area)	3	835	–	2140	–	–	2978
A. V. Roe & Co. Ltd. (Yeadon) ..	–	53	–	642			695
Armstrong Whitworth Aircraft	–	911	300	118	–	–	1329
Austin Motors ..	–	150	–	–	180	–	330
Metropolitan Vickers	–	941	–	139	–	–	1080
Vickers-Armstrong (Castle Bromwich)	–	300	–	–	–	–	300
Vickers-Armstrong (Chester)	–	235	–	–	–	–	235
Victory Aircraft, Canada	–	–	–	–	–	430	430
Total by Marks	3	3425	300	3039	180	430	
Grand total of all Marks including prototypes						..	**7377**

This Schedule is of Lancasters on delivery. There were some conversions in service of Mk. Is to Mk. IIIs and vice versa and these are, in each case, recorded in the Lancaster Log under the appropriate serial number. Mks. IV and V were renamed Lincoln Mks. I and II respectively and Mk. VI Lancasters were conversions from Mk. I/III Lancasters. Mks. VIII and IX were not allotted.

LINCOLN

	Proto-types	Mk. I	Mk. II	Firms' Totals
A. V. Roe & Co. Ltd. ..	3	52	116	171
Metropolitan Vickers ...	–	28	52	80
Armstrong Whitworth Aircraft	–	2	279	281
Total by Marks	3	82	447	
Grand Total for R.A.F.				532*

* In addition 18 B.2s built for the Argentine Air Force.

	Mk. XV	Mk. 30	Mk. 31	Total
Victory Aircraft, Canada ...	1	–	–	1
Beaufort Division, Australian Dept. of Aircraft Production	–	54	*19	73
Total by Marks ...	1	54	19	
Total Commonwealth Production				74*

* First five assembled from components supplied from the U.K. (uncompleted airframes not included).

Grand total of all Lincolns built **624**

Lancasters over America. Two of the sixteen Lancasters of No. 35 Squadron which participated in U.S. Army Air Force Day celebrations at Los Angeles on August 1st, 1946, as a token of the war-winning alliance of the U.S.A.A.F. and the R.A.F.

Operations at an end did not mean that development of the Lancaster was at an end. It was obvious that, due to delays in Lincoln production, Lancasters would be the interim mainstay of the post-war Bomber Command. There was a particular need for Lancasters to be sent overseas to replace Liberators which, supplied under Lend/Lease, were due to be forfeited now that hostilities were over. At home Lincoln re-equipment was slow and the Lancaster remained a first-line bomber until the end of 1949. Since its successor, the Lincoln, was an improved Lancaster, development work on the latter would be applicable to both. Lancasters continued to be used in automatic gun-laying trials and H2S improvement. Lancasters of No. 15 Squadron joined with American B-29 Superfortresses in test bombing of German U-boat pens at Farge, where the results were assessed.

Undoubtedly the most famous of the Lancasters in the immediate post-war years was *Aries* of the Empire Air Navigational School at Shawbury. This Lancaster, PD328, was introduced in Chapter Sixteen. During the early months of 1945 flights were made to North America, South Africa and Palestine. Up to May *Aries* had not differed externally from other Lancasters except for an astro-dome in place of a mid-turret, but at Waddington in April 1945 a transformation took place, to modify the aircraft for flights to the North Geographic and Magnetic Poles. The fore and after turrets were replaced by fairings, extra tankage was placed in the bomb bay and a Lincoln type undercarriage was fitted. A silver polished skin replaced the original camouflage and special recording and navigational equipment was installed. After taking off from Shawbury on May 10th some 17,000 miles were flown in the Arctic regions alone. On return, *Aries* set out for Canada on June 7th and flew non-stop to the Canadian Central Navigation School at Rivers and broke the east-west crossing record. Later the England-to-the-Cape, London-Karachi and London-Darwin records were broken.

In the same way that the E.A.N.S. had a Lancaster equipped with the latest navigational equipment, so the

Empire Air Armament School equipped a Lancaster with the latest armament for Empire tours. Named *Thor* in place of its undignified call sign ' White Pants Nan ' it toured Australia, New Zealand, India and S.E. Asia, covering over 25,000 miles in under 50 days.

While *Thor* was being given a send-off from Manby for a tour of Australia on March 25th, 1946, two Australian officers on the station, wearing false moustaches and theatrically robed, tip-toed to the aircraft with a large trunk. They were sternly ordered away by the aircraft's captain, Wg. Cdr. M. H. d'L Everest, and dejectedly they returned. However, their act was sufficiently convincing for one paper to report it as a serious attempt to stowaway on the aircraft!

There have been cases of pilots in Tiger Moths and similar light aircraft landing to ask the way, but there is only one case on record of a Lancaster pilot doing this and that was in the summer of 1946. No official record of the incident can be traced—perhaps the crew wanted it that way! However, the *North-Western Evening Mail* reported this incident on July 10th. Apparently a Lancaster lost over the Barrow-in-Furness area flew low along the coast, trying to pick up its position. Seeing the stretch of Duddon Sands, which recent high tides had left without their usual ridges, the pilot brought the Lancaster down and a crew member jumped out and walked across to a Millom fisherman, Mr. Ernie Williams, and calmly asked his position. That settled, he walked back and the machine took off and flew away.

Hitherto, during the war, only the odd Lancaster had visited the U.S.A. On July 9th, 1946, a complete squadron set out from Graveley on a goodwill tour, the B.I (F.E.) Lancasters of No. 35 Squadron. Fitted with H2S and F.N.82 rear turrets and finished in white except for black undersurfaces, they flew out via the Azores to Mitchel Field accompanied by a York. San Antonio, Kelly and Andrews Fields were among the American aerodromes visited. At Long Beach on August 1st, they participated in the Air Force Day celebrations. The Americans showed great interest in the British bombers, but the highlight of

From dropping bombs to dropping succour. RF310, one of the first Lancaster A.S.R. IIIs, shown here in December 1945, went out to Burma with No. 1348 Flight and crashed taking off from Pegu, March 4th, 1946.

the show was a demonstration by a P-80 Shooting Star. Several of the aircrew there were asked if Britain had jet aircraft yet! One flight sergeant, on being asked this, directed the questioner to a nearby officer and intimated that he might know—it so happened that Frank Whittle, on a lecture tour of the U.S.A., was standing nearby!

While these few Lancasters were in the news, the policy for their post-war deployment was not publicised. To meet the immediate need of Liberator replacement overseas, Lancasters tropicalised for Tiger Force were considered the most suitable, but several changes had first to be effected. Mid-upper turrets removed to reduce weight were re-fitted, British wireless equipment was substituted and the auxiliary fuel tanks were removed, except for those bound east of Suez, but all the fittings for the auxiliary tanks were retained. In general it was the policy to allocate all Lancasters to Far East (F.E.) standard to Middle East and Far East stations and equip Bomber Command at home with standard Lancasters, with one notable exception—No. 35 Squadron which had F.E. aircraft based in Britain. First estimate for the post-war force was 446 Lancasters, but this was axed to 270.

Nos. 9 and 617 Squadrons, so closely associated on operations during the war, were both sent to India in early 1946 to replace No. 159 and 355 Squadrons whose Liberators were being surrendered under the Lend/Lease agreement. These were called upon by the Indian Government for two greatly differing roles. One was participation in a fly past during Victory Week celebrations in Delhi, where the 100 R.A.F. and R.I.A.F. aircraft taking part made the

greatest air display ever seen in India. The other duty was as standby for emergencies during the revolt of certain Royal Indian Navy units. Both squadrons were brought back to Britain later in the year.

By mid-1946 the peacetime routine of summer exercises was being followed. Nearly a hundred Lancasters from Nos. 1 and 3 Groups participated in an attack on Heligoland. Four Lancasters marked the target area with green target indicators and flares, then came a further seven as ' backers-up ' while Mosquitos went in low to check. A master bomber then directed the main force of some 60-70 which dropped ' Window ' to confuse the defences, which were also being exercised.

At the end of 1946 another Bomber Command squadron, No. 7, re-equipped with B.I. (F.E.) Lancasters fitted with H2S Mk. IIIG, Mk. XIV bombsights, Gee and Rebecca for a far eastern visit. In January 1947 they flew out to Singapore on Operation ' RED LION ' and actually conducted live-bombing in Perak as a practice, some fifteen months before the Malayan emergency. They returned to Upwood early in March 1947 and were for a time earmarked by Bomber Command for mining trials.

Because of the wartime policy of using American Lend/Lease Hudsons, Liberators and Fortresses in Coastal Command, Britain was left without suitable maritime aircraft in the immediate post-war years when the American material was surrendered. Late in 1945 a large number of late production B.III Lancasters were sent to Cunliffe Owen for conversion to air-sea rescue duties, with provision of the carriage of an airborne lifeboat. It had been planned to equip Nos. 179 and 279 Squadrons with A.S.R.

A Lancaster in Fighter Command. NX739, used for official photography and maintained by Silver City Airways, came under the administration of Fighter Command. It is shown here with the Folland Midge.

Lancasters for operations in the Far East, but while the conversion of Lancasters proceeded only a few were deployed, the majority going into store. One flight, however, formed for delivery to No. 279 Squadron flew out to Pegu in Burma, where they were based for several months.

It was something of a paradox that one of the first of the rescue jobs for an air/sea rescue Lancaster should be in a country without a seaboard—Switzerland. A United States Dakota had crashed in the Swiss Alps on November 19th, 1946. Three days later the aircraft was located by Flt. Lt. D. G. Head in a No. 7 Squadron Lancaster which dropped Lindholme gear and blankets. Later the Dakota's crew, saved by the cushioning effect of landing in deep snow, were rescued by Storches of the Swiss Air Force.

The R.A.F., pressing for a maritime version of the Lincoln, were forced, for immediate needs, to deploy their A.S.R.III Lancasters in their general reconnaissance squadrons during 1947. For this work, a number of modifications were effected such as the fitting of A.S.V. radar and removal of the dorsal turret and arrangements were made in 1949 to process the A.S.R. aircraft through Armstrong Whitworth Aircraft to be prepared to a new maritime reconnaissance standard known then as G.R. for General Reconnaissance.

With the quantity of coastal Lancasters set and some reserves earmarked in M.U.s, there still remained a vast surplus of hundreds of B.I/IIIs and from late 1946 these were consigned to scrap in quantity. Tenders were sent out and the peak month for the sale of Lancasters as scrap was reached in May 1947. Of those serviceable a number,

together with several Lincolns, were damaged in the great gale of March 16th, 1947, when gusts of up to 100 m.p.h. were recorded.

A. V. Roe bought back numbers of Lancasters to meet various requirements. The Argentine ordered fifteen in late 1947. These were prepared at Langar and flown to the Argentine from Dunsfold or London Airport by British South American Airways and Skyways crews, at intervals from May 1948 to January 1949.

Lancasters had a part to play in Britain's unhappy burden of the Palestinian Mandate which ended on May 15th, 1948. Until that time it was Britain's problem to maintain impartially the *status quo*. Jewish immigration was strictly controlled and it became necessary to operate a form of naval blockade to prevent illegal entry by the thousands of Jews clamouring for residence in the new land of promise. To assist in this control Lancasters of both Nos. 37 and 38 Squadrons were sent to Ein Shemer in Palestine during the spring of 1947. Towards the end of the year a series of attempts were made to beat the blockade. The steamer *Elia* was spotted by a Lancaster crew on November 15th and the destroyer H.M.S. *Venus* was directed to intercept and nearly 800 Jews were disembarked.

The patrols were long and arduous. The approach to the Palestinian shore would often be made under cover of darkness. In the early morning of December 22nd Flt. Lt. K. Ruskell, D.F.C., flying a No. 37 Squadron Lancaster, spotted a small two-mast vessel of about 200 tons. Flying low to take photographs and survey the ship, he observed only two men—both at the wheel-house—but there were tell-tale brown stains that suggested that much sewage

7—LB

The last Lancaster in Coastal Command, RF325, piloted by Wg. Cdr. E. J. Brookes, D.F.C., leaving the School of Maritime Reconnaissance, St. Mawgan, on October 15th, 1956, for Wroughton, where it was broken up.

was being deposited. This was reported, the ship was intercepted and was found to be carrying 850 illegal immigrants. Later some Lancasters of both Nos. 37 and 38 Squadrons together with Lincolns from No. 617 Squadron and other aircraft were placed at the disposal of the ill-fated Count Folke Bernadotte, the United Nations mediator; but as it was, the first British aircraft to bear United Nations markings were Austers. Later in 1948 the two Lancaster squadrons were withdrawn to Malta. It was a Lancaster from each, on October 18th, 1949, that provided an air escort as a salutation to H.M.S. *Amethyst* as it headed for the Grand Harbour, a port of call on its way home after its famous Yangtse River dash.

The year the Atlantic Treaty was signed, 1949, was too early for N.A.T.O. exercises to be effected, but Western Union was already in being with France and the Low Countries, and the U.S.A.F. joined in these exercises. Exercise 'Tool' included Lincolns and Lancasters of Nos. 1 and 3 Groups of Bomber Command, which together with B-29s of the Third Air Division, U.S.A.F., equipped the attacking force. London, Birmingham, Liverpool, Sheffield and Coventry and other targets were 'attacked' after marking by synthetic markers—on the ground.

Under Western Union agreements in early 1948, it was planned to re-equip the French Naval Air Arm, *Aeronavale*, with ex-R.A.F. Lancasters modified for maritime reconnaissance. Both Mk. I and VII Lancasters, as available, were modified in the Avro plants at Woodford and Langar. Since the mid-upper turrets were completely removed and faired over, the common standard could be said to be Mk. I (modified).

These Lancasters were overhauled thoroughly to a degree which might well be called rebuilding. Additional fuel tanks were fitted into the bomb bays, provision was made for A.S.V. equipment to be fitted by the French and lugs were fitted for the carriage of airborne lifeboats. The aircraft were to have been finished in American 'midnite blue', but this colour was thought to be too sombre and a lighter shade resulted in an attractive royal blue. The first of 54, WU-01, was delivered to the chief test pilot of the *Escadrille de Réception et Convoyage*, Capitane de Corvette Aragnole at Woodford in January 1952. It was flown to the French Naval Air Station of Les Mureaux in Metropolitan France, but the majority of the deliveries were to North Africa.

A further five were ordered in 1952 for the *Secrétariat Général a l'Aviation Civile et Commerciale*. These were also up to A.S.R. standard and finish, but with the Cross of Lorraine superimposed on the French roundel and numbered in the FCL.01 to 05 series (French Civil Lancaster) as apart from the Western Union series. They were despatched to France between January 1st and April 30th, 1954.

In Canada the political situation led to numbers of Lancasters in storage being converted for various roles as detailed under Mk. X in the Type-by-Type Review towards the end of this book. Apart from defence considerations, Lancasters did valuable mapping, rescue and civil work; one job for the Canadian Department of Mines and Resources was caribou counting in the North-West Territory to estimate the distribution of these animals, on which the economy of the inhabitants depended in certain areas.

At 3.30 p.m. on March 28th, 1953, an R.C.A.F. Lancaster landed unexpectedly at the U.S. Naval Air Station at Glenview. Having encountered bad weather over Ottawa,

The first of fifteen Lancasters, B-031—045, supplied to the Argentine Air Force being weighed at Langar. These Lancasters were delivered to Buenos Aires by B.S.A.A.C. and Skyways crews from May 1948 to January 1949.

it inadvertently crossed into United States territory over Buffalo and flew from there to Chicago undetected by American radar. The U.S. military authorities were quite understanding over this 'violation', but not a little concerned by an apparent weakness in their detection equipment.

Late at night on August 22nd, 1953, a message was received at Churchill from a Lancaster about a hundred miles to the north, asking for a guide in. The aircraft was in serious trouble from electrical storms and the altimeter and signalling equipment, except for an emergency Morse tapper, were out of action. Nothing more was heard from it and since there was no knowledge of its heading, and when last heard it still had sufficient fuel for four hours cruising, the possible search area was a matter of 2,000,000 square miles! A large-scale search was put into effect which involved over a dozen Lancasters.

That the Lancaster crew were still alive was a miracle. It had finally been forced down when an engine had failed. Hitting an incline, it burst into flames, severely burning two of the crew, Flg. Off. A. R. Gossel and L.A.C. F. M. De Baie, but it slithered into a lake and came to rest on the only sandbar in that expanse of water. Thereby not only was the fire extinguished but the wreck provided shelter for the night. Unfortunately the area was under fog and not for two days could a search be carried out in this area. The crew beached a dinghy, and with this and parachutes made a tent. Two days later, in bright sunlight, the crew attracted the attention of a Dakota flying over, by means of flashes from a hand mirror. The complete crew were flown out by an Otter floatplane soon afterwards.

A Lancaster in Fighter Command is something of a paradox, but TW669 on air photography duty was once attached to that Command's Communication Flight. Later it operated under civil contract. It was replaced by NX739, a Mk. VII withdrawn from long-term storage, and became a familiar sight at Blackbushe until mid-January 1957 when it was delivered to a breaker's yard at Swindon and its place taken by Lincoln RF332.

Lancasters were withdrawn slowly from R.A.F. service. The last in front-line service were those of Nos. 37 and 38 Squadrons in Malta. The last to leave, RF273 returned to England early in 1954. By that time the last Lancaster in Bomber Command, PA427, had left; this was a P.R.I. of No. 82 Squadron which had completed a six-year survey of colonial territories in Africa covering over a million square miles. As maritime reconnaissance trainers they remained in Coastal Command until October 1956, when RF325 was at last retired from the School of Maritime Reconnaissance at St. Mawgan. One of the crew members, Frank Yeoman, has been concerned with the production of this book.

Now came a rush to depict the Lancaster in film before the opportunity would be lost. However distinguished the stars of the film 'The Dam Busters', the real stars were the Lancasters. For this four were collected at Hemswell. The leading part of Wg. Cdr. Gibson's own ED932/G was played by NX679 wearing this false identity on one side only. Using Mk. VIIs did not matter as their turrets, farther forward than earlier Lancasters, had in any case to be removed to be like the original 'Specials'; bomb doors were cut away to achieve realism. Supporting roles

Postwar Lancasters. Top to bottom: French Navy service for ex-B.VII RT693 modified for search and rescue work, B.I(F.E.) TW911 as Python turbo-prop engine test-bed, B.I(F.E.) PA424 exhibition aircraft, P.R.1 PA475 of No. 82 Squadron on survey work, B.II LL735 as Metrovick jet engine test-bed and G.R.3 RE181.

were played by NX673 and RT686 as other aircraft of No. 617 Squadron while NX782 was marked as ZN.G of No. 106 Squadron to represent an aircraft flown by Guy Gibson prior to service in No. 617 Squadron. The details of the special bomb and the precise nature of the modification to the Lancasters were then still secret and could not be fully revealed. It was said, too, that all drawings had been destroyed on official instructions as a security precaution. However, there seemed little objection to the bomb-bays being cut away in characteristic fashion as this was already revealed on the Mk. 1 (Special) designed to carry the 'Grand Slam' bomb. It was also known then that the bomb was cylindrical, so that superficially the Lancasters looked correct.

Within the framework of R. C. Sherriff's screenplay, the Associated British Picture Corporation aimed at ensuring that the film was as authentic as possible. Group Captain J. C. Whitworth, who was Station Commander at Scampton at the time of the raid, was present during the filming.

Lancasters featured in the film 'Appointment in London', where Dirk Bogarde was a 'Winco', Ian Hunter a 'Groupie', and Bryan Forbes, Bill Kerr and William Sylvester formed part of the crew of 'V for Victor'. Flying sequences were taken at Upwood and among the four Lancasters used was NX782, which also featured in the Dam Busters. In the film of Nevil Shute's novel 'No Highway', NX636 had its nose blacked over.

The French Navy used their Western Union Lancasters to equip *Flottiles 24F* and *25F* and they also formed part of the equipment of *Escadrilles de Servitude 9S, 10S, 55S* and *56S*. Three were until recently based at Noumea, where they shared maritime reconnaissance duties with four Privateers. Operated by *Escadrille de Servitude 9S*, they were coded 9S1(WU-16), 9S2(WU-27) and 9S3(WU-43) and were finished in gleaming tropical white. Since the Australasian outposts of the French Empire did not, understandably, have facilities for major overhauls, they flew periodically to Bankstown, New South Wales, for servicing by Fairey Aviation.

As related earlier, the Australians have a Lancaster in their War Museum at Canberra, but the R.A.A.F. Association also required one for a war memorial and had tried unsuccessfully to obtain one from Britain and Canada. However, the secretary of the Perth branch of the association, locating WU-16 staging through Sydney's Kingsford Smith Airport, started negotiations with the French authorities. The French were very understanding and willing to donate the airframe provided spares which included the four engines, radar installations and certain instruments, were returned! After further talks it was agreed that WU-16 could be handed over complete if the return air fare for the five French crew members and the cost of the fuel were guaranteed—a matter of £A600. Another, WU-15 (ex-NX611) acquired by the Historic Aircraft Preservation Society, was flown to Biggin Hill in England.

In Canada, a Lancaster is preserved as a memorial—mounted in flying attitude on a pedestal at McCall Field, Calgary. The Calgary Air Cadets, who maintain this memorial, provided a guard of honour at the dedication ceremony when Alderman Clarence Mack accepted the Lancaster on behalf of the City of Calgary. During the ceremony, a Tiger Moth, a Harvard and an Anson, contemporaries of the Lancaster, flew over. At the time of writing —mid 1964—the Lancaster has just been retired from service in Canada from No. 408 Squadron and No. 107 Rescue Unit. On rescue duties, one of the three Lancasters used has maintained a 24-hour standby for 365 days a year.

Although the Royal Air Force has long since discarded the Lancaster and has R5868 purely as a memorial, one Lancaster still flies on a quest for the future. This is PA474, operated at the time of writing by Handley Page in connection with their H.P.117 all-wing laminarised aircraft. A section of the wing mounted on PA474, with two pumps sucking air through numbers of spanwise slits in the wing surface, commenced flight tests at Cranfield on October 2nd, 1962.

Thus an aircraft well past its prime, if not quite of the past, plays its part towards a new era in aeronautics.

The Handley Page laminarised wing, resulting from some twelve years of research, was first tested on this Lancaster from the College of Aeronautics, Cranfield, in 1962. As the last Lancaster flying in Britain, it is to be preserved and its duties taken over by a Lincoln.

version and later G.R.IIIs until replaced by Neptunes in 1952.

No.214 Squadron R.A.F.

Lancasters arrived at Fayid in March 1946 to replace the Liberators of this squadron which re-formed at Upwood on November 4th 1946 with six B.I.(F.E.) Lancasters. Lincolns replaced the Lancasters in March 1950.

No.218 Squadron R.A.F.   No.3 Group   Coded HA

' B ' Flight converted from Stirlings to Lancaster I/IIIs at Woolfox Lodge in late July 1944 and moved to Meth-

Wg. Cdr. W. J. Smith commanding No. 218 Squadron (centre) beside a day-raid ' Vic-leader' denoted by the fin stripes.

wold, followed in early August by 'A' Flight also converting. On December 5th 1944 the squadron moved to Chedburgh and was upgraded to a 3-flight squadron. From June 1944 to April 1945 it dropped 8,268 tons of bombs over enemy territory.

No.224 Squadron R.A.F.   No.19 Group   Coded XB

The first Lancaster A.S.R.IIIs to replace this squadron's Liberators arrived at St. Eval on October 22nd 1946. However, in December the following year the squadron was run down and disbanded. It re-formed later with Halifaxes stationed at Gibraltar and Aldergrove.

No.227 Squadron R.A.F.   No.5 Group   Coded 9J

No.227 re-formed October 7th 1944 with 'A' Flight constituted from aircraft and crews supplied by No.9 Squadron at Bardney and ' B ' Flight from an off-shoot of No.619 Squadron at Strubby. Initially 'A' Flight operated from Bardney when three of their Lancasters attacked gun positions at Flushing on October 11th, but a week later the two flights joined together at Balderton with B.I/B.III Lancasters. A move was made to Strubby on April 6th 1945, and on the following June 7th to Graveley, where the squadron disbanded on September 5th 1945.

No.300 (Polish) Squadron R.A.F.   No.1 Group   Coded BH

After the arrival of the first Lancaster on March 4th 1944, the Wellingtons of this squadron were replaced by B.I/B.III Lancasters in April at Faldingworth, where the squadron was disbanded in October 11th 1946.

No.404 Squadron R.C.A.F.   Coded AF

Lancaster 10MR were received from April 30th 1951 on re-forming at Greenwood, Canada, and were operated until September 1955.

A Beaufighter and Mosquito squadron during the war, No. 404 R.C.A.F. Squadron received Lancaster 10-MRs at Greenwood, Canada, in 1951.

No.405 Squadron R.C.A.F.   Nos. 8 and 6 Groups   Coded LQ later AG

The Halifax IIs of this squadron were replaced by Lancaster I/IIIs August to October 1943 at Gransden Lodge, from where the squadron continued on pathfinding duties until May 25th 1945 when they moved to Linton-on-Ouse and joined No.6 (Canadian) Group and also changed over

The first Canadian-built Lancaster, KB700, a B.X, with No. 405 (Vancouver) Squadron, R.C.A.F., on Pathfinding duties.

from Lancaster IIIs to Xs. On June 16th the squadron flew back to Canada and was disbanded in September. Re-formed on March 31st 1951 at Greenwood it operated Lancaster 10MRs until November 1955.

No.407 Squadron R.C.A.F.   Coded RX

Re-formed with Lancaster 10MR/MP at Comox, B.C., on July 1st 1952. The last Lancaster in the squadron, FM219, left on May 12th 1959.

No.408 Squadron R.C.A.F.   No.6 Group   Coded EQ/AK/MN

It was the intention to replace the Hampdens of No.408 with Manchesters in early 1942 and one was allotted and then withdrawn to be replaced by Halifaxes. In turn, Lancasters arrived in August 1943 at the squadron's base at Linton-on-Ouse and first operated on the night of October 7th/8th. After using these for a year, the squadron re-equipped with Halifax VIIs in August 1944, but in May 1945, shortly before returning to Canada, a change was again made to Lancasters, this time Mk.Xs. Post-war the squadron operated from Rockcliffe with Lancaster 10Ps as their main equipment, including a few 10MP and 10AR versions, until 1964.

No.419 Squadron R.C.A.F.   No.6 Group   Coded VR

Lancaster Xs replaced the Halifaxes of No.419 at Middleton St. George in April 1944 and first operated that month on the night of 27th/28th. Early in June 1945 the squadron flew back to Canada.

No.420 Squadron R.C.A.F.   No.6 Group   Coded PT

Lancaster Xs replaced Halifaxes at Tholthorpe in May 1945 just too late for operations. Twenty left England June 12th-13th 1945 for Canada and the squadron disbanded at Debert in September.

NG347, a Lancaster B.1 which served only in No. 424 (Tiger) Squadron, R.C.A.F., photographed in 1945.

No.424 Squadron R.C.A.F.   Nos.6 and 1 Groups   Coded QB

On January 4th 1945, 'A' Flight of Halifaxes were stood down at Skipton-on-Swale for conversion to Lancaster I/IIIs, which first operated on February 1st when eight raided Ludwigshafen; by that time, 'B' Flight was being similarly converted. In August 1945 it was transferred to the control of No.1 Group prior to disbandment on October 15th.

No.425 Squadron R.C.A.F.   No.6 Group   Coded KW

The first Lancaster X for this Halifax squadron was received at Tholthorpe on May 1st 1945, in preparation for the return to Canada which was effected in mid-June.

No.426 Squadron R.C.A.F.   No.6 Group   Coded KW

The Wellingtons of this squadron were replaced by Lancaster IIs in June 1943 and first operated on August 17th when nine joined in the famous Peenemunde raid, in which one, with the C.O., Wg. Cdr. L. Crooks, was lost. Halifaxes replaced the Lancaster IIs during April and May 1944; with the latter, 605 sorties were made in 57 raids for a loss of 32.

No.427 Squadron R.C.A.F.   Nos.6 and 1 Groups   Coded ZL

Halifax IIIs of this squadron were replaced by Lancaster I/IIIs from March 15th 1945 at Leeming Bar. While other Canadian squadrons were scheduled to move back to Canada in preparation for operations in the Far East, No.427 was retained in the U.K. and transferred to No.1 Group in late August 1945. It disbanded on May 31st 1946.

No.428 Squadron R.C.A.F.   No.6 Group   Coded NA

In June/July 1944 at Middleton St. George the Halifaxes of No.428 were replaced by Lancaster Xs, which operated from the night of June 14th 1944. The squadron, on May 31st 1945, was the first of the Canadian squadrons to set out to fly back home.

No.429 Squadron R.C.A.F.   Nos.6 and 1 Groups   Coded AL

At Leeming during March 1945 this squadron's Halifaxes were replaced by Mk.I/III Lancasters and first operated in daylight on the last day of that month to Hamburg. In August the squadron came under No.1 Group; Mk.I/III Lancasters were still used except for a single Mk.VII, September to November. During May 1946 the Lancasters were ferried away to MUs, the last leaving on June 1st, the day after the squadron officially disbanded.

No.431 Squadron R.C.A.F.   No.6 Group   Coded SE

The first ten Lancaster Xs for this Halifax squadron arrived at Croft on October 10th 1944 and were allotted to 'B' Flight. First Lancaster operations were conducted on November 1st when ten set out to bomb Oberhausen. The aircraft left for Canada on May 31st 1945.

No.432 Squadron R.C.A.F.   No.6 Group   Coded QO

The last Wellington squadron in No.6 Group, No.432 received Lancaster IIs at East Moor on October 25th 1943, and first operated with them on November 26th when ten set out for Berlin. They were used until replaced by Halifax IIIs, January 31st 1944.

No.433 Squadron R.C.A.F. Nos.6 and 2 Groups   Coded BM

Conversion from Halifaxes to Lancaster I/IIIs commenced in January 1945 at Skipton-on-Swale, under Wg. Cdr. G. A. Tambling, 'A' Flight being converted first. Their first Lancaster operation was on January 29th; later in the year, on October 15th, the squadron was disbanded.

No.434 Squadron R.C.A.F.   No.6 Group   Coded IP/WL

The first Lancaster Xs for this Halifax squadron arrived at Croft on December 7th 1944 and operated on Christmas Eve. In addition to Mk.Xs the squadron operated about six Mk.Is, February to March 1945. The Mk.Xs were flown back to Canada in June, where the squadron disbanded, at Dartmouth, on September 15th 1945.

No.460 Squadron R.A.A.F.   No.1 Group   Coded UV/AR

The Halifaxes of this squadron received in July 1942 were replaced by Lancaster Is at Breighton in the October and first operated on the 21st of the following month. Subsequent replacement Lancasters were either Mk.I or III. Moves were to Binbrook May 14th 1943 (when the code changed from UV to AR) and to East Kirkby July 28th 1945. Their last Lancaster flight was carried out by RF191 to photograph the Australian War Memorial in France on October 2nd, before the squadron disbanded on the 25th.

No.463 Squadron R.A.A.F.   No.5 Group   Coded JO

No.463 formed from a Flight of No.467 Squadron at Waddington on November 25th 1943 and operated next night with six aircraft over Berlin. July 14th 1945 the squadron moved to Skellingthorpe; Lancaster I/IIIs were flown until September 14th 1945, and it disbanded on the 28th.

No.467 Squadron R.A.A.F.   No.5 Group   Coded PO

Formed at Scampton on November 7th 1942, No.467 moved to Bottesford on the 24th and first operated with B.I/III Lancasters January 2nd 1943. The C.O. was lost in LM342 and two nights later, on August 17th 1943, the acting C.O., Sqn. Ldr. A. S. Raphael, failed to return. A move to Waddington was made on November 13th 1943 and to Metheringham on January 15th 1945. The squadron disbanded September 30th 1945.

No.514 Squadron R.A.F.   No.3 Group   Coded JI/A2

Formed at Foulsham in September 1943 with crews from No.1678 H.C. Flt., the first of their 16 (+ 4 reserve) Lancaster IIs, DS735, arrived on September 11th. The

A Lancaster of No. 619 Squadron above the clouds.

squadron moved to Waterbeach on November 23rd and in the following July exchanged the Mk.IIs for Mk.IIIs, but later some Mk.Is were used. The squadron disbanded at Waterbeach on August 27th 1945.

No.550 Squadron R.A.F.   No.1 Group   Coded BQ
Formed at Grimsby November 25th 1943 from ' C ' Flight No.100 Squadron and operated next night. Moved to North Killingholme January 4th 1944 where it was disbanded October 31st 1945.

No.576 Squadron R.A.F.   No.1 Group   Coded UL
Formed under Wg. Cdr. G. T. B. Clayton, D.F.C., at Elsham Wolds, with 'A' and ' B ' Flights from Nos.103 and 101 Squadrons respectively, on November 25th 1943 and first operated on December 2nd with its standard equipment of Lancaster I/IIIs. The squadron moved to Fiskerton on October 31st 1944 and was disbanded there on September 13th 1945.

No.582 Squadron R.A.F.   No.8 Group   Coded 60
This Pathfinder squadron was formed at Little Staughton on April 1st 1944, by 'A' and ' B ' Flights constituted from Nos.156 and 7 Squadrons respectively. Initially Lancaster I/IIIs were used, but by April 1945 Mk.IIIs of the PB-serialled batch were exclusively used. Ten of their aircraft ferried to Mepal on the following September 10th foretold disbandment which took place seven days later.

A Lincoln B.2 of the " Dambusters " No. 617. This squadron's Lincolns won the Laurence Minot bombing trophy in 1950.

No.617 Squadron R.A.F.   No.5 Group   Coded AJ later KC/YZ
Specially formed at Scampton on March 31st 1943 for breaking the Ruhr dams. Standard B.I/III Lancasters were temporarily replaced in April and May by specially modified Lancasters. The squadron moved to Coningsby in August 1943 and to Woodhall Spa in January 1944. See chapters six and eighteen for further details. Earmarked for Tiger Force, the squadron equipped with B.I(Special) Lancasters and moved to Waddington on June 18th 1945. Together with No.9 Squadron it was in India January to

May 1946. Returning to the U.K. it was reorganised from an 'A' and ' B ' Flight basis to a single flying flight. At this time, ED909, one of the original dam-busters, was still with the squadron as a standard B.III. Their first Lincoln, expected in August 1945, was RE376, which arrived August 16th 1946. The next August their Lincoln B.2s flew to the U.S.A. and were demonstrated at Bolling Field and Andrews Field among other stations.

No.619 Squadron R.A.F.   No.5 Group   Coded PG
Formed under Wg. Cdr. I. J. McGhie at Woodhall Spa April 18th 1943 from three crews of No.97 Squadron left there when the latter transferred to No.8 Group. The squadron was gradually built up from one B.I and one B.III Lancasters ex-No.617 Squadron until June 11th when twelve Lancasters set out on the unit's first operation to Dusseldorf. There were a series of moves for this squadron in 1944 as follows: Coningsby (January 10th), Dunholme Lodge (April 18th), Strubby (September 28th). Lancaster B.I/IIIs were operated throughout until disbanded September 5th 1945 at Skellingthorpe.

No.622 Squadron R.A.F.   No.3 Group   Coded GI
Lancaster B.IIIs replaced the squadron's Stirling B.IIIs at Mildenhall in June 1944 and operated for the first time on July 2nd with an attack on Beauvoir. The squadron was disbanded on August 15th 1945.

No.625 Squadron R.A.F.   No.1 Group   Coded CF
The squadron formed nominally at Kelstern on October 1st 1943, but Lancaster B.I/III aircraft were not received until a fortnight later with the transfer of ' C ' Flight, No.100 Squadron. Their first Lancaster, JB122, was received on October 13th and five nights later the squadron was operational. ' A ' and ' B ' Flights moved to Scampton on April 6th 1945, but ' C ' Flight, which by then had been built up, went to Fiskerton, disbanded October 7th 1945.

No.626 Squadron R.A.F.   No.1 Group   Coded UM
Formed under Wg. Cdr. P. Haynes at Wickenby November 7th 1943 by ' C ' Flight of No.12 Squadron becoming their 'A' Flight. Their first operation was on November 10th 1943; they disbanded at Wickenby, October 26th 1945.

No.630 Squadron R.A.F.   No.5 Group   Coded LE
Formed from ' B ' Flight No.57 Squadron at East Kirkby on November 15th 1943, when eleven Lancaster Mk.IIIs were allotted. Their first operation was to Berlin the night of November 18th. The squadron disbanded on July 18th 1945; a Lancaster B.I/III unit throughout its existence, 2,147 sorties were made for a cost of 64 Lancasters missing and 6 crashed.

No.635 Squadron R.A.F.   No.8 Group   Coded F2
Formed March 20th 1944 at Graveley from ' C ' Flight No.97 Squadron at Benson and a flight from Graveley under Wg. Cdr. A. G. S. Cousens, D.S.O., D.F.C., M.C. (Czech). The first operation was on March 22nd against Frankfurt. Lancaster B.I/B.IIIs were used and, additionally in the autumn of 1944, four Mk.VIs. The squadron disbanded at Downham Market, September 1st 1945.

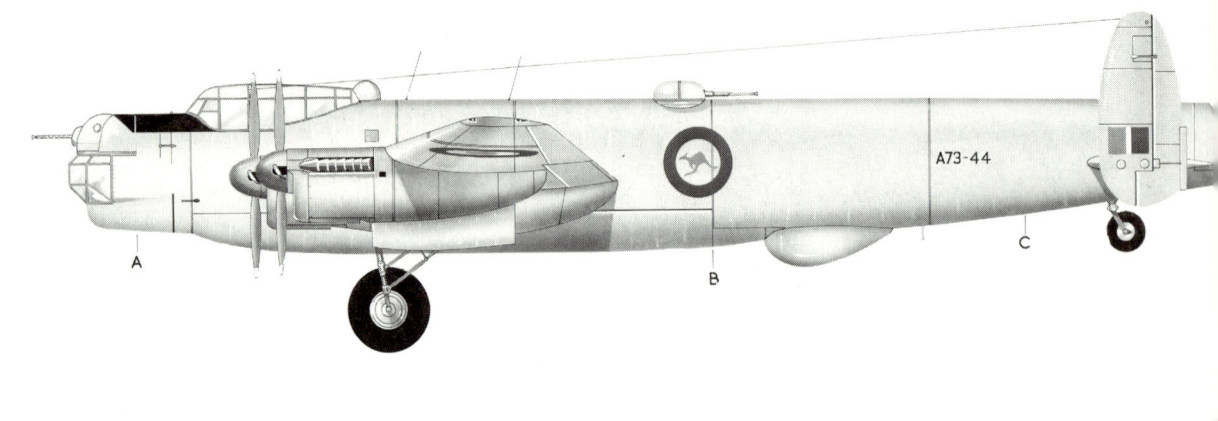

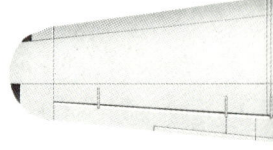

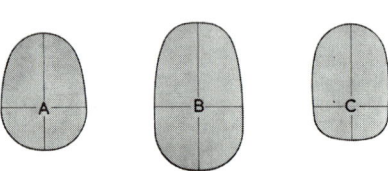

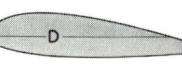

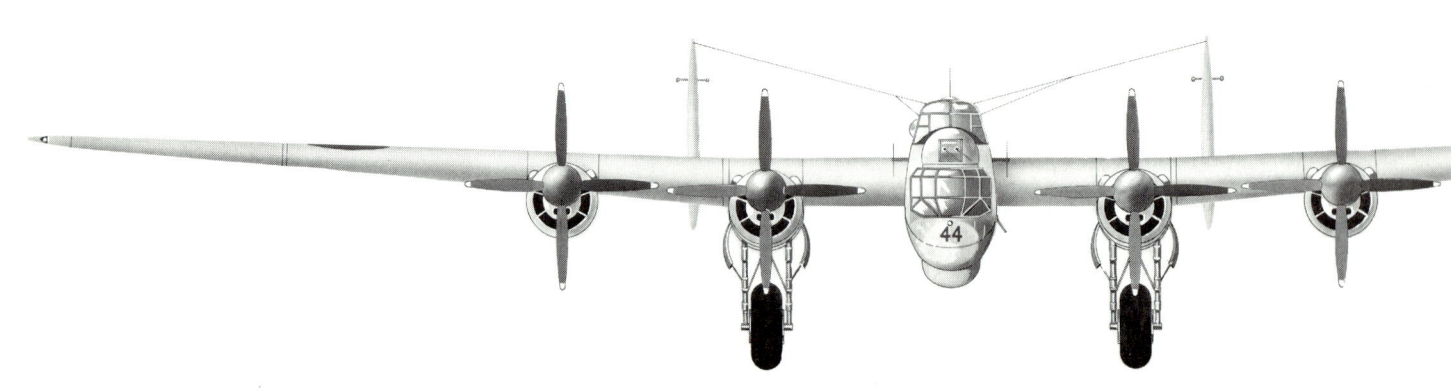

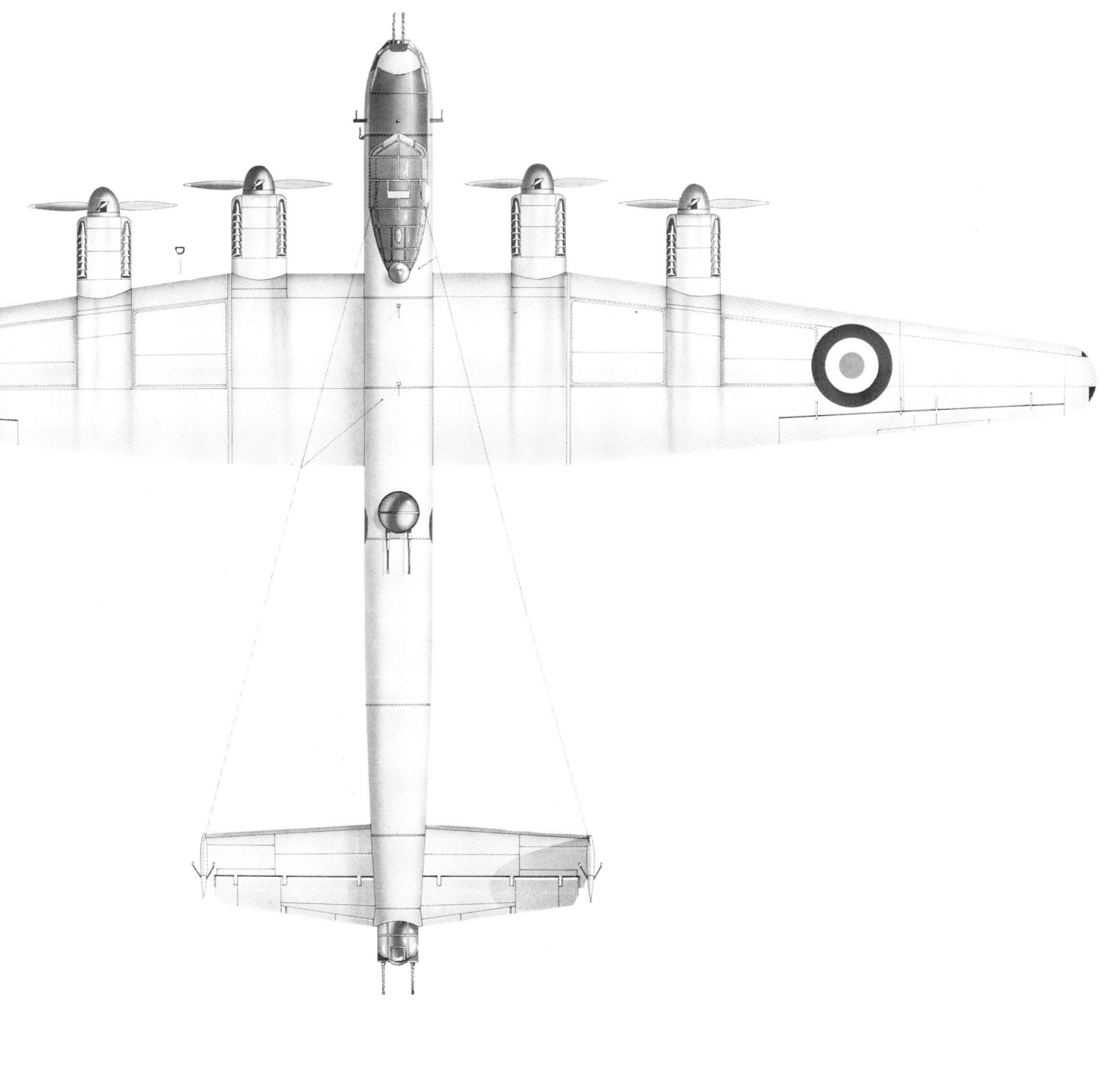

An Australian-built Lincoln B.30 which, with the fitting of Merlin 102 engines,
became a B.30a.

MANCHESTER/LANCASTER/LINCOLN
UNIT BRIEFS

Heavy Conversion Units

The backgrounds to Heavy Conversion Units and Lancaster Finishing Schools are given in chapter eleven. In these units, as in most squadrons, Mk. I and III Lancasters were mixed but the quantity of each was subject to technical considerations. The American-built Merlins were found to overheat quicker than the British-built Merlins; thus for the successive take-offs and landings which formed an important part of H.C.U. training Mk. Is were preferred, with just sufficient Mk. IIIs to allow crews to become familiar with them.

No. 1651 H.C.U., R.A.F.   No. 7 Group   Coded BS/QQ

Lancasters replaced the Stirlings of this H.C.U. at Woolfox Lodge in December 1944. Early in 1945 it reached a strength of 32 Lancaster I/IIIs, 4 fighters and an Oxford, but by March it was reduced to an establishment of 13 Lancasters. On the night of March 3rd/4th one of the Lancasters, QQ.K, was shot down by an intruder. This H.C.U. closed on June 13th, 1945.

No. 1653 H.C.U., R.A.F.   Nos. 1 and 7 Groups   Coded A3/H4/M9

Formed at Lindholme with Manchesters, Lancasters and Halifaxes from the Conversion Flights of Nos. 103 and 460 Squadrons on October 10th, 1942, No. 1653 H.C.U. moved to Colerne at the end of the year, where its Lancasters were given up. Lancasters were used in the unit at North Luffenham from January 1945 to December 1946 and at Lindholme from December 1946 until April 1948 when it became 230 O.C.U., by which time B.I(F.E.), as well as standard B.I/B.IIIs, were used. Moving to Scampton in 1949, where it eventually disbanded, the equipment changed to Lincoln B.2s.

No. 1654 H.C.U., R.A.F.   Nos 5 and 6 Groups   Coded UG/JF

Manchesters were used for conversion training at Swinderby from May 19th, 1942, and the unit continued with them at Wigsley from June 1942 where shortly afterwards some Lancasters were received. Some of the unit's Manchesters were damaged by an attack by two Junkers Ju88s in the evening of July 3rd 1942. Manchesters were withdrawn in July 1943 and Stirlings were delivered from November 28th 1943, but at the end of 1945 it re-equipped with Lancaster I/IIIs for a short period before disbandment.

No. 1656 H.C.U., R.A.F.   No. 1 Group   Coded EK/BL

The authorised establishment of 12 Lancasters and 20 Halifaxes of this H.C.U., which formed at Lindholme in November 1942, was more than met in February 1943 by 15 Lancasters, 6 Manchesters and 23 Halifaxes, but their Lancaster element moved later in the year to No. 1 L.F.S.

No. 1660 H.C.U., R.A.F. Nos 5 and 7 Groups Coded YW/TV

Formed at Swinderby October 20th 1942 with Nos. 61, 97 and 106 Squadron Conversion Flights, under Wg. Cdr. R. J. Oxley, D.S.O., D.F.C., with Manchesters, Lancasters and Halifaxes. Lancasters on occasions operated with the Main Force and four went to Berlin on the night of January 16/17th 1943. Manchesters were withdrawn and

Lancaster ED413 of No. 1651 H.C.U.

Lancasters were replaced by Stirlings in 1943. In late 1944 it became an all-Lancaster unit with Mk. Is and IIIs.

No. 1661 H.C.U., R.A.F.   Nos. 1, 5 and 7 Groups   Coded KB/GP

Formed by Sqn. Ldr. Nettleton, V.C., with Manchesters and Lancasters from No. 44 Squadron's Conversion Flight with "A" and "B" Flights at Waddington and "C" Flight at Scampton. By January 1st 1943 all three flights were based at Winthorpe and next month the establishment of aircraft changed from 12 Lancasters, 20 Halifaxes to 14 of each, but early in 1944 it re-equipped with Stirling IIIs which in turn gave way to Lancasters in December that year.

No. 1662 H.C.U., R.A.F.   No. 1 Group   Coded KF/PE

Formed at Blyton February 1st, 1943, with establishment for 12 Lancasters and 20 Halifaxes or Manchesters which changed to 16 Lancasters ("A" Flt) and 16 Halifaxes ("B" and "C" Flts). Later the Lancaster element helped to form No. 1 L.F.S.

No. 1666 H.C.U., R.C.A.F.   Nos. 6 and 7 Groups   Coded ND/QY

Formed at Dalton June 2nd 1943, this Halifax H.C.U. turned over to Lancasters and shortly before closing had, in March 1945, at Wombleton, a strength of 26 Lancaster I/IIIs, 3 Lancaster Xs, 2 Spitfire Vs and a Hurricane I.

No. 1667 H.C.U., R.A.F. Nos 1 and 7 Groups Coded GG/KR

Formed at Lindholme July 31st 1943 with 16 Lancasters and 11 Halifaxes, No. 1667 H.C.U. moved next month to Faldingworth, from where the Lancaster element went to No. 1 L.F.S. in November. Later Lancasters returned and 28 Mk. I/IIIs were on strength when it was based at Sandtoft in 1945.

No. 1668 H.C.U., R.A.F.   Nos 5 and 7 Groups   Coded J9, CE, 2K

Formed at Balderton, then a satellite of Syerston, on August 15th 1943, with an establishment for 16 Lancasters I/II and 16 Halifax II/IV which could not be met, so that some Manchesters were taken in charge. In November, when the Halifaxes were changed to Stirlings, the unit moved to Syerston, from where the Lancaster element left to form 5 L.F.S. Early in 1945 Lancasters were again introduced and by March 1945, at Bottesford, 19 of the 32 aircraft on establishment were Lancaster I/IIIs. Later in the year a move was made to Cottesmore.

No. 1678 H.C. Flight   No. 3 Group

Formed at East Wretham on May 18th 1943 with 4 Lancaster IIs of the Lancaster Flight of No. 1657 (Stirling)

H.C.U. with establishment for 8 Lancaster IIs. Disbanded after a short existence.

No. 1679 H.C. Flight   No. 3 Group   Coded SW
Lancaster IIs were used for a short period at Waterbeach after formation at Foulsham in October 1943.

Finishing Schools
No. 1 L.F.S.   No. 1 Group
Formed in November 1943 by combining the Lancaster elements of Nos. 1656, 1662 and 1667 H.C.U.s with flights dispersed as follows : "A" Flt. Lindholme, " B " Flt. Blyton and " C " Flt. Faldingworth. The unit H.Q. was at Lindholme but this moved later, with " C " Flight, to Hemswell.

No. 3 L.F.S.   No. 3 Group   Coded A5
Course No. 1 commenced at Feltwell with 4 Lancasters on December 19th 1943. The school subsequently expanded into three flights and was disbanded January 31st, 1945.

No. 5 L.F.S.   No. 5 Group   Coded CE/RC
Formed at Syerston from 1668 H.C.U. and disbanded there March 31st 1945.

No. 6 L.F.S.   No. 6 Group
Formed for conversion of Canadian squadron pilots to Lancasters at Ossington in December 1944.

Miscellaneous Units
No. 2 (Maritime) Operational Training Unit, R.C.A.F.
The first course at the Maritime O.T.U. commenced in December 1949 at Greenwood with Lancasters. In November 1953 the unit moved to Summerside, where Neptunes gradually replaced the Lancaster 10-MPs from March 30th 1955, when the first arrived.

No. 1323 (A.G.L.T.) Flight
Formed late in the war with Lancaster Is to develop automatic gun-laying. It operated from Warboys in conjunction with the Hurricanes and Spitfires of No. 1696 Bomber Defence Training Flight. Lancaster crew composition varied considerably in this unit and radar mechanics flew on duty as crew members. The flight disbanded September 30th 1945, two months after changing over from Mk. I to Mk. III Lancasters.

No. 1577 (Special Duties) Flight
Formed for heavy bomber trials in India with two Lancaster III and two Halifax V bombers on August 9th

W4113 of No. 1661 H.C.U. On some special occasions H.C.U. aircraft were detailed for Main Force operations.

1943. The Lancasters flew out from Llandow via Cairo, which was reached on October 1st. The flight was stationed initially at Salbani and moved to Chakeri on March 5th 1944, and to Manipur two months later. Glider training and bombing trials were conducted from Manipur until the end of the year when the Lancasters were replaced by additional Halifaxes. In 1945 both of the two saddle-tank Lancasters were attached for short periods.

Torpedo Development Unit
The T.D.U. had Manchesters and Lancasters attached from August 1942. The name of the unit was not particularly apt for its overall function, for which two flights were established, one for torpedo development and the other for special bombs and mines; it was the latter flight to which Lancasters were attached. The name changed to Aircraft Torpedo Development Unit in September 1943. Post-war several Lincolns were attached from time to time, including RE281 in April 1951.

Bomber Development Unit
Formed at Gransden Lodge in July 1942 the B.D.U. had a succession of Manchesters and Lancasters on strength particularly from the T.F.U. for development trials. This unit moved successively to Feltwell (April 1943), Newmarket (September 1943) and Lindholme (October 1945). Late in the war there were nine Lancasters on charge to one each of other bomber and miscellaneous types. During 1946 this unit was integrated with the Central Bomber Establishment at Marham.

Bomber Command Instructional School   Coded WB/IP
Formed at Finningley on December 5th, 1944, by absorbing the Night Bomber Tactical School, the Bombing Analysis School and other units. The initial establishment was 22 Wellington III/X, 10 Lancaster I/III and 5 Halifax, but the Lancaster element increased until 1946 when they were partially replaced by Lincolns, RA649, RE283, RF481 and RF504 being among the first. For flight affiliation work several fighters were held on strength.

Telecommunications Flying Unit
From the establishment of a Special Installation Unit at the T.F.U. Defford, a succession of Lancasters were processed through this unit and much experimental work was carried out on Lancasters as detailed in chapter twelve. Post-war a number of Lancasters were used in various experiments, including PB532 in early 1949 which had a Lancastrian type nose, with Rebecca aerials, and was used for cloud collision warning development. Lincoln B.2s used post-war for experiments included RF560 which unfortunately crashed in 1948, killing the crew; RF533 with H2S Mk. VIII and SX930 with H2S Mk. VIA and also Pye Beacon equipment in 1949.

G-H Training Flight   No. 3 Group
This Flight was formed at Feltwell with eight Mk. I/III Lancasters, fitted with FN121 turrets and G-H equipment, on December 29th 1944, and functioned until the spring of 1945 when H.C.U.s took over G-H training.

School of Maritime Reconnaissance
See chapter sixteen

TYPE-BY-TYPE REVIEW

To avoid repetition of details mentioned in other parts of the book, references are made as appropriate.

Avro Type 679 to A.M. Spec. P.13/36

Avro's original tender submitted in January 1937 to A.M. Specification P.13/36, as the Avro 679, had the basic configuration of the eventual prototype Manchester except that the fins and rudders were planned to be inset from the tailplane tips. With a span of only 72 feet, giving a wing area of 930 sq. ft., it was estimated to carry 8,000 lb. of bombs 2,000 miles at 289 m.p.h. with a maximum speed of 330 m.p.h.

The first prototype Manchester, which was not armed.

Manchester Prototypes

The origin of the Manchester in Air Ministry Specification P.13/36 is described in chapters one and two. The first prototype, L7246, was first flown on or about July 24th, 1939, by Captain H. A. Brown and was delivered to Farnborough on August 24th, 1940. After trials at Boscombe Down it was fitted with a shark-type stabilising fin which was subsequently modified. During trials, on December 12th, 1939, it crashed shortly after take-off into a field of cabbages, which, as the fuselage slithered along the ground, were jammed into the fuselage.

L7247, the second prototype Manchester.

The second prototype, L7247, first flew on May 26th, 1940. It was delivered with a shark type fin which was later modified to the original production standard triple-fin configuration, had all-metal ailerons and elevator for which fabric-covered ones were later substituted and had servo elevator balance tabs replaced subsequently by conventional elevator tabs. The wing span was increased by fitting new wing tips. Further details as in chapter one.

The second prototype Manchester with central " shark fin."

Detail Data

Power Units: 2 x 1760 h.p. Rolls-Royce Vulture engines.

Crew: Test staff only.

Armament: L7246 did not have armament fitted, all planned turret positions being faired over. L7247 had 2 x .303 machine-guns in nose, tail and ventral turrets and provision for the carriage of 8 x 1,000 lb. bombs.

Dimensions: Span 82 ft. 2 in. (L7247 was later modified to B.1 standard wing-span.)

Length: 68 ft. 4½ in., Wing Area 1,058 to 1,131 sq. ft. according to span.

Weights: Gross 45,000 lb., Empty 25,959 lb.

Performance: As per Mk. I.

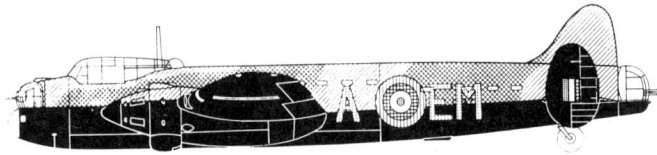

Manchester I L7278 in bomber finish standard for 1940.

Manchester I/IA

Service details as per chapter two; individual details of the 200 produced as per Serial Range L7276-7526, R5768-5841 of the Manchester/Lancaster Log. First 20 Mk. I had 28 ft. tailplane with small type fin and rudders and central fin; 21st and subsequent machines Mk. IA with 33 ft. tailplane with larger fins and rudders and centre fin deleted. It was declared obsolete in August 1944.

Manchester I in standard bomber finish, July 1941.

Detail Data

Power Units: 2 x 1,760 h.p. Rolls-Royce Vulture engines.

Crew: 7. First and second pilot, navigator, wireless operator and three air gunners, but composition varied with wireless operator/air gunner or air bombers replacing the appropriate category.

Armament: 2 x .303 in. Browning machine-guns in nose F.N.5, ventral F.N.21A and tail F.N.20 turrets initially, but ventral turret later replaced by F.N.7 'Botha-type' dorsal turret. Provision initially for carriage of 8 x 1,000 lb. bombs modified later to take up to 4,000 lb. bombs.

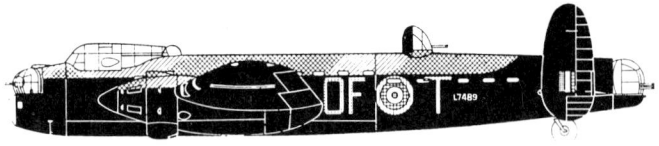

Manchester IA in standard bomber finish, September 1941.

Dimensions and data: Span 90 ft. 1 in., Length 68 ft. 10 in., Height 19 ft. 6 in.; Tailplane span 28 ft. initially, 33 ft. finally; Wing Area 1,131 sq. ft., Wing Loading 54 lb./sq. ft., Power/weight ratio 15.1 lb./h.p.

Weights: Fully loaded 56,000 lb., Tare 29,432 lb., Maximum bomb load 10,350 lb.

Performance: Maximum speed 265 m.p.h. at 17,000 ft. with 8,100 lb. load as documented, but with full load rarely went higher than 14,000 ft. Cruising speed 185 m.p.h. at 15,000 ft. Range of 1,630 miles with 8,000 lb. bomb load and 1,160 gallons of fuel or 1,200 miles with 10,350 lb. bomb load and fuel reduced to 882 galls. Service ceiling 19,200 ft. Take-off run 1,300 yds. to 50 feet.

Manchester II

Owing to the unsatisfactory performance of the Vulture-engined Manchester I, consideration was given to re-powering the airframes with Napier Sabre or Bristol Centaurus engines for which Mk. II was provisionally used. One Manchester airframe was sent to Napier's at Luton for Sabres to be installed, but with the satisfactory performance of the prototype Lancaster, provisionally Manchester Mk. III, it was used only as an engine test stand for Napier engines, including the Sabre.

Manchester III

Provisional designation for 4-engined Manchester, later named Lancaster.

Lancaster first prototype BT308 with central fin.

Avro Type 683 Lancaster Prototypes

The first prototype Lancaster, BT308, was a standard Manchester airframe fitted with four Merlin X engines in a modified wing, with increased rib spacing to give a span of 100 feet. A dorsal turret was not fitted. Performance was approximately as the figures given below for the Mk. I, except in respect of endurance as the total capacity was only 1,700 galls. held in four wing tanks.

After first flight and initial test (see page 14) it went successively to Nos. 44, 97 and 207 Squadrons on September 9th, 1941, January 10th and 21st, 1942, respectively. It was then used by Rolls-Royce at Hucknall for flame damping development from February 28th, 1941, to April 23rd, 1942, when it went to Ringway. Later, it was sent to Armstrong Whitworth Aircraft, who fitted a Metrovick F.2/1 jet engine in the tail for flying trials.

Lancaster second prototype DG595 in August 1941.

Unlike BT308 the second prototype DG595 had a dorsal turret, no centre fin and was powered by Merlin XX

engines. Following its first flight on May 13th, 1941, it went to the A. & A.E.E. for trials. During the following September and in March 1942 it was back at Avro's factory for repair and modification. Early in 1943 it went to the R.A.E to be used in ballistic trials. On June 20th it was damaged by clay and stones thrown up by an inert bomb dropped from 100 feet at 230 m.p.h. on Ashley Walk, Hants. Repaired, it ended its service at the Torpedo Development Unit.

Lancaster Mk. I (B.I. from 1942)

The policy change from Manchester to Lancaster production and the development of the Lancaster Mk. I is detailed in chapter three. The basic B.I was declared obsolete for all R.A.F. purposes in May 1948.

Detail Data

Power Units and Airscrews: 4 x Rolls-Royce Merlin XX, 22 or 24 engines each fitted with three-bladed De Havilland D.H.5/40 constant speed, variable pitch airscrews as per original provisioning plans, but three-bladed Hamilton A5/138 variable pitch, hydromatic airscrews were interchangeable.

Crew: 7. Duties detailed at start of chapter eleven.

Armament: Standard initial armament in hydraulically operated turrets as follows: F.N.5 nose, F.N.50 mid-upper each with 2 x .303 Browning machine-guns and F.N.20 tail with 4 x .303 Browning machine-guns. An F.N.64 ventral turret with 1 x .303 Browning machine-gun was standard in early production models. In late 1944 Nos. 1 and 5 Groups dispensed with all under protection, but No. 3 Group, which had fittings for 8,000 lb. bombs on their Lancasters and therefore no H2S bulge underneath, continued to retain the F.N.64 turret. An F.N.79 or F.N.150 mid-upper turret was first introduced on W4115 in January 1943 and was used as an alternative to the F.N.50 until June 1946 when it was declared obsolete. In late production models an F.N.82 turret with 2 x .5 Browning machine-guns or an F.N.121 with 4 x .303 Browning Mk. II machine-guns was fitted in lieu of the F.N.20 tail turret.

Lancaster I, on which Sqn. Ldr. Nettleton won his V.C.

Mainplane Dimensions: Aerofoil Section N.A.C.A. 23018 at root, Span 102 ft. 0 in., Chord at root 16 ft. 0 in., Area (complete with ailerons) 1,297 sq. ft., Wing loading 50 lb. sq. ft., Dihedral 7 deg. 0 min. to datum, Incidence 4 deg. 0 min., Aileron span 17 ft. 3½ in. each, Aileron area (including tabs) 85.5 sq. ft., Aileron chord (mean) 2 ft. 6 in., Aileron movement 16 deg. up and down, Trimming tab movement 19 deg. 0 min. up and down, Flap movement 56 deg. 30 min. down; distance between engine centres, 23 ft. 9 in. inboard, 50 ft. 3 in. outboard.

Fuselage Dimensions: Overall length 69 ft. 6 in. tail up, 68 ft. 10 in. tail down; Height 20 ft. 6 in. to top of fin with tail up, 20 ft. 4 in. to top of whip aerial with tail down.

Track 23 ft. 9 in., Ground clearance (minimum with H2S fitted) 1 ft. 3 in., Length of bomb compartment 33 ft.

Tail Section Dimensions: Span 33 ft. 0 in., Chord (mean including elevators) 7 ft. 0 in., Incidence 2 deg. 30 min., Area (including elevators and tabs) 237 sq. ft., Elevator area 82 ft. 6 sq. ft., Elevator movement 28 deg. up, 14½ deg. down, Trimming tab movement 6 deg. up and down, Rudder area (including tabs) 41.2 sq. ft., Rudder movement 22 deg. port and starboard.

Weights: All-up 65,000 lb., Tare 37,000 lb., Maximum bomb load 22,000 lb. Military load other than bombs including crew 4,056 lb., Fuel (2,154 galls.) 15,509 lb., Oil (150 gall.) 1,350 lb., Limitations 60,000/50,000 lb. take-off/landing as designed, 68,000/58,000 lb. permissible for straight flying from February 1945 and 72,000/60,000 lb. permitted in tropics from October 1945. Performance: Maximum speed 275 m.p.h. with full load at 15,000 ft., 245 m.p.h. at sea level, Cruising speed 200 m.p.h. at 15,000 ft., Rate of climb 250 ft./min.; Range 2,530 miles with 7,000 lb. load, 1,730 miles with 12,000 lb. load, 1,550 with 22,000 lb. load; Maximum permissible diving speed 360 m.p.h.; Stalling speed at 50,000 lb. weight 110 m.p.h. undercarriage and flaps up, 92 m.p.h. undercarriage and flaps down, Service ceiling 19,000 ft., Take-off run with full load 1,200-1,500 yds. according to boost.

Fuel capacity: Standard 100 octane fuel, 2 x 580, 2 x 383 and 2 x 114 gall. tanks in wings making a total capacity of 2,154 gall.; overload tanks, one or two of 400 gall. each, could be installed in the bomb bay; on the first six aircraft, L7527-7532, the total capacity was limited to 1,710 gall. in four wing tanks as per the first prototype. Oil 150 galls.

Non-standard Lancaster B.I (Spec.) carrying "Tallboy" bomb.

Construction: Fuselage of light alloy with transverse formers and longitudinal stringers, built in sections. Wing of two-spar type with outer planes attached to a centre section.

Standard Equipment: First Aid Kit, Elsan lavatory,

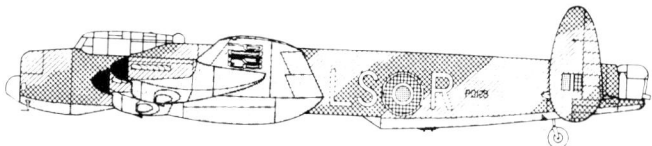

Standard Lancaster B.I (Spec.), Mildenhall, December 5th, 1945.

Balloon Barrage Cable Cutters, Window De-icing, F.24 camera in bomb aimer's compartment, inflatable dinghy stowed in starboard trailing edge of mainplane, Graviner fire extinguishers. Oxygen equipment distributed to crew compartments, etc.

Non-Standard Mk. Is: JB127 ex-Mk. III had paddle-blade propellers fitted in November 1944 and NF910 was experimentally fitted with four-blade propellers. NG408 fitted with large H2S housing, February 1945. PP752 10-ton bomb tests and tests of Dunlop Compacta tyres. PP755 had power-controlled elevators for Brabazon development. PP779 had Merlin T24/2 engines fitted outboard in the course of 350 flying hours on Merlin engine development.

Lancaster P.R.1
Modification of B.1 for No.82 Squadron. See page 114.

Lancaster B.1 (Special)
Lancasters modified (Lancaster Modification No. 1693) to carry loads in excess of 12,000 were officially classified as B.1 (Spec.) in early 1945. Their development and service is covered in chapter fifteen and under PB592, PB995-998, PD112-139 of the Log. With a tare weight of 35,457 lb. and loaded to 72,000 lb., i.e. an amount equivalent to its own weight, this version could fly 1,550 miles at 15,000 ft. at 200 m.p.h. Fuel was normally limited to 1,675 galls. This version was declared obsolete in November 1948.

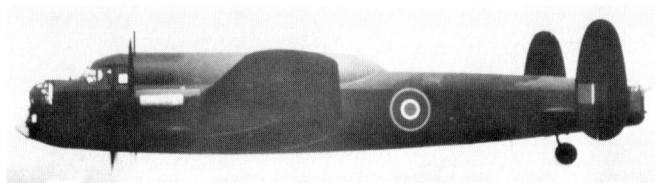

One of two saddle-tank Lancasters built.

Saddle-tank Lancaster
As an experiment in long-range operations from Far Eastern bases, two Lancaster Is were modified to carry large saddle-tanks of 1,200 galls. The first, HK541, was a standard service aircraft in for repair. After modification by A. V. Roe it went to Hucknall where Rolls-Royce engineers changed its Merlin 22 engines for Merlin 24s and passed it to Boscombe Down for testing. With a worthwhile bomb-load an all-up weight of 72,000 lb. was planned, which was thought to present some difficulties in operating from tropical bases. As a result Sqn. Ldr. H. G. Hazeldon, D.F.C., flew HK541 out to India for trials. It arrived on May 8th at Mauripur. However, the airfield there was not suitable for full trials and it was from Jodhpur on the 24th that HK541 first took the air at 72,000 lb. including 1,000 lb. and 500 lb. bombs which were jettisoned in the sea. Endurance flights of up to eleven hours were flown before return to the U.K. on June 12th.

The second, SW244, was modified directly after leaving the Woodford shop on November 24th, 1944. It arrived at Boscombe Down on April 22nd for tests and flew out to Mauripur in August and on to Perth, Australia, via Ceylon and the Coco Islands in November.

Lancaster B.I (F.E.) at Mildenhall in September 1947.

Lancaster B.1 (F.E.)
Lancaster B.1s of Bomber Command tropicalised for

Tiger Force as detailed in chapter sixteen were designated B.1(F.E.). This standard preparation included changes in radio equipment that were not effected until post-war when the Lancasters were withdrawn from service at the rate of eight a month for the fitting of Rebecca Mk. II, Loran Mk. I, GEE and H2S Mk. IIIG at No. 32 M.U. and reissued to service units.

Close-up of Python installation in Lancaster TW911.

Python Lancaster

The last of the B.1(F.E.) Lancasters to be completely built by Armstrong Whitworth Aircraft, TW911, was used as a test-bed for the Armstrong-Siddeley Python turbo-prop engine after a mock-up had been made in RE137. This engine had a fourteen-stage axial-flow compressor with a two-stage turbine driving two four-blade contra-rotating airscrews. Weighing 3,150 lb. apiece, a Python was substituted for the outer port and starboard Merlin 24s, and the wing trailing edge was extended a few inches. A 400 gallon fuel tank was fitted in the bomb-bay to meet the Python's consumption of 365 galls./hr.

Test-rig on Dart engine installed in Lancaster NG465.

Dart Lancaster

NG465, which arrived at Hucknall from Rolls-Royce on August 9th 1946, was, on October 10th 1947, the first aircraft to fly with a Dart engine. Dart No. 5 initially installed in the nose was replaced by No. 15 in November 1949, and then No. 3 the same month which in turn was replaced by No. 30 in January 1953. During the course of these tests an artificial icing rig was mounted for which two 100-gallon water tanks were mounted in the fuselage. After precisely 800 hours on engine development flying, NG465 was written off in a forced landing on a golf course near Mansfield.

Lancaster I (Western Union)

Of the 54 Lancasters supplied to the French Naval Air Arm, *Aeronavale*, under Western Union arrangements (details in chapter 17) 32 were converted from Mk. I to full A.S.R. standard. The aircraft concerned are detailed in the Lancaster Log in the PA, RA, SW and TW series.

Lancaster I (Egyptian)

Nine Lancaster B.Is were overhauled by A. V. Roe during the period November 1948 to August 1950 for the (then) Royal Egyptian Air Force, deliveries being effected from mid to late 1950. They were finished to R.A.F. standard except for radar. The aircraft concerned, PA476, PA441, SW308, TW893, PA435, PA391, TW890, SW313, TW656, were provisionally registered G-11-60 to 68 prior to becoming Nos. 1801 to 1809 of the R.E.A.F.

Lancaster awaiting delivery to Royal Egyptian Air Force.

Swedish Lancaster

RA805, held by A. V. Roe as a spare aircraft for the Argentine, was refurbished at Langar. Dual control and Avro-type rudders were fitted and the front turret was faired in a manner similar to the B.I (Special). It was flown to Air Service Training, minus its bomb doors, by the A. V. Roe test pilot Peter Field-Richards on June 22nd 1950 for the fitting of the Swedish Dovern axial flow jet engine fitted with afterburners. Flown to Malmslatt by Flight-Lieutenant T. R. Fowler, it was operated as a test-bed by *Kungl Flygfor Naltningon* of Stockholm.

Swedish Lancaster 80001 as Dovern test bed.

Civil Lancaster Mk. I

A number of Lancasters were converted for civilian use; for details see chapter nineteen, and the following in the Log: DV379, HK557, LL809 and PP series.

DV379, the first Lancaster on the British civil register.

Lancaster II Prototypes

The need for a radial-engined Lancaster is explained in chapter five. Two prototypes were ordered but only one, DT810, was completed. Following its first flight on December 21st, 1941, and initial tests with Bristol Hercules

VI radial engines it was used in September 1942 for fuel system tests with high pressurised vapour fuel and in the following month on flame damping tests. It was with the R.A.E. and A. V. Roe until 1944 when struck off charge.

Lancaster B.II

The 300 Lancaster B.IIs built were produced exclusively by Armstrong Whitworth Aircraft at Baginton from September 1942. This mark was pioneered in service by a flight of No. 61 Squadron, but No. 115 Squadron became the first full squadron to equip with this version as detailed in chapter five. Apart from service in No. 514 Squadron, it was used chiefly in the Canadian squadrons of No. 6 Group, Nos. 408, 426 and 432 where, having the same radial engines as their Halifaxes, it was suitable as in interim aircraft between Wellingtons and Halifaxes. Service details given in DS and LL serials in the Log.

A plan to have specially armoured Mk. IIs for day raids was mooted in 1942 but was not put into effect.

Proto Lancaster II DT810, December 1941.

Detail Data

Power Units and Airscrews: 4 x 1,735 h.p. Bristol Hercules VI or XVI 14-cylinder air-cooled radial engines driving Rotol R.E.C. electric, fully feathering airscrews. These were left-hand tractor airscrews as apart from right-hand rotation on all other Lancasters.

DT810 fitted with bulged bomb doors.

Crew: 7. As Mk. I except that F.N.64 turret was a standard fitting in ventral position and on certain raids when crews were briefed for low-level approach an eighth crew member was carried to operate this gun.

Frontal aspect of production Lancaster II.

The first radial-engined Lancaster, prototype Mk. II.

Armament: As Mk. I except that F.N.64 ventral turret was standard and that enlarged bomb doors for the carriage of 8,000 lb. bombs was standard. Plans in February 1944 were for the F.N.64 to be replaced by a turret with .5 guns, but as only 102 of this Mark were left in service at that time it was not affected. LL780 had special barbettes fitted experimentally.

Dimensions: As Mk. I except that as H2S never became standard, but F.N.64 ventral turrets did, fuselage clearance was 3 ft. 10½in. Weights: All-up 63,000 lb., Tare 36,449 lb.,

DS602, second production Lancaster II in October 1942.

Maximum bomb load 23,095 lb., Military load other than bombs including crew 3,870 lb., Fuel and oil as Mk. I, Limitations take-off/landing 63,000/56,000 lb.

Performance: Maximum speed 270 m.p.h. with full load at 16,000 ft. Other details as per Mk. I.

Standard Equipment: As Mk. I but G-H radar introduced as standard in 1943.

Lancaster II early production with normal bomb-bay doors.

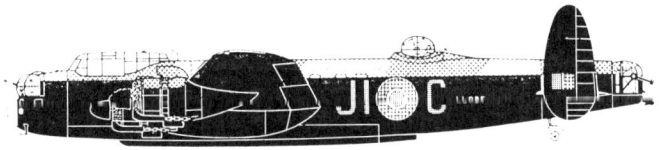

Lancaster II standard with bulged bomb-bay doors.

Non-standard Mk. IIs: DS602 used in carburettor tests May 1944 with Hobson 132MC/ME/MF carburettors; DS611 used in ballistic trials; DS708 evaluated servo-spring control tabs for the Bristol Brabazon; LL737/G armament trials with A.G.L.T.

Lancaster II universal test-bed, with jet engine in tail.

Lancaster II Universal Test Bed

LL735/G was extensively used as a test bed for jet engines and was successively on the charge of R.A.E. Farnborough, Power Jets Ltd., the National Gas Turbine Establishment, Metropolitan-Vickers and Armstrong Whitworth Aircraft at Bitteswell. During this time it had a Metrovick F2/1 installed in the tail in 1943 which was replaced by an F2/4 in 1945; an F2/4 was tested in the bomb bay in 1949.

Lancaster III Prototypes

Although W4114, by virtue of its Packard-built Merlins installed in place of its original Merlin 22s, was the official Mk. III prototype it was not the first Lancaster to fly with American-built Merlins. R5849, which had flown nearly 236 hours in British Merlin XX development, had American Merlin 28s fitted on August 15th, 1942, for intensive development work which led to W4114 being so fitted for A. & A.E.E. trials.

Lancaster III trials prototype with American-built Merlins.

Lancaster B.III

Detail Data

Power Units and Airscrews: 4 x Rolls-Royce (Packard-built) Merlin 28, 38 or 224 engines each driving three-bladed Hamilton A5/138 or A5/148 variable pitch, hydromatic airscrews, the former of which was interchangeable with D.H.5/40 airscrews.

Crew: 7. As Mk. I.

Standard B.III Lancaster recorded at Bourn, August 27th, 1943.

Lancaster B.III with G-H, as yellow bars denote, 1945.

Lancaster B.III with A.G.L.T. in rear turret, May 1945.

Armament: As Mk. I. A few had F.N.64 ventral turrets, but these were removed from January 1944. DV273 was fitted at Ringway with one .5 machine-gun for under defence and it was planned to introduce this additional

armament into Lancasters of Nos. 101, 467 and 207 Squadrons from October 1943, but the project was dropped. JB456 had a Martin mid-upper turret fitted in March 1944 and a Rose No. 2 Mk. I rear turret the following September; in early 1945 it was further modified with Bristol B.17 mid-upper and F.N.82 rear turret and a B.32 under-defence bed with 2 x .5 machine-guns. NG794/G had an F.N.150 mid-upper turret installed for test in February 1945 together with an F.N.121 rear turret with A.G.L.T., but LM730 in November 1944 appears to be first to have an F.N.121 with A.G.L.T. fitted. Later, F.N.82 or F.N.121 turrets were fitted post-war.

Dimensions, Weights, Fuel Capacity, Construction and Equipment as per Mk. I.

Non-Standard B.IIIs: LM426 flew nearly 700 hours on Merlin 38 and T24/2 engine development from December 1943 to August 1945 and ND340 flew 718 hours for Rolls-Royce from May 1945 to November 1948 on engine development, including liquid injection and power restoration tests; it arrived at Hucknall with Merlin 38 and 28s and was fitted with T.24 and T.24/2 Merlins, thereby becoming virtually a Mk. I.

"Dambusting Lancasters"

Lancaster B.IIIs specially converted for the attack on the Ruhr Dams in May 1943 are dealt with in chapter six.

Lancaster B.III "Dambuster Lancasters," May 1943.

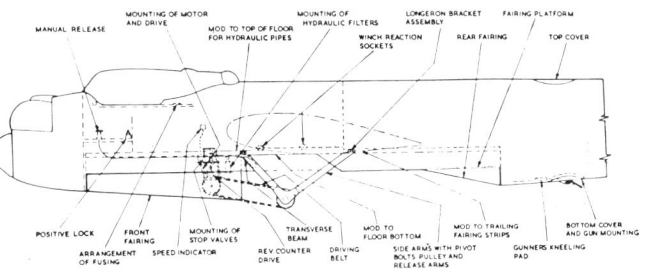

Official "Type 464 Provisioning" drawing for Dambuster modification.

Gust Alleviation Research Lancaster

A Lancaster III was chosen by Boulton Paul Aircraft in 1950 for studying gust alleviation. This involved fitting an electro-magnetic transducer in the nose of ME540 to

Boulton Paul's gust alleviation research Lancaster.

detect gust pressures and, by means of a Boulton Paul electro-hydraulic power unit, impose corrections to the ailerons. This quest was not only in the interests of passenger comfort in the future, but to reduce strain on wings and limit fatigue to prolong airframe life.

LANCASTER Sectional Drawing

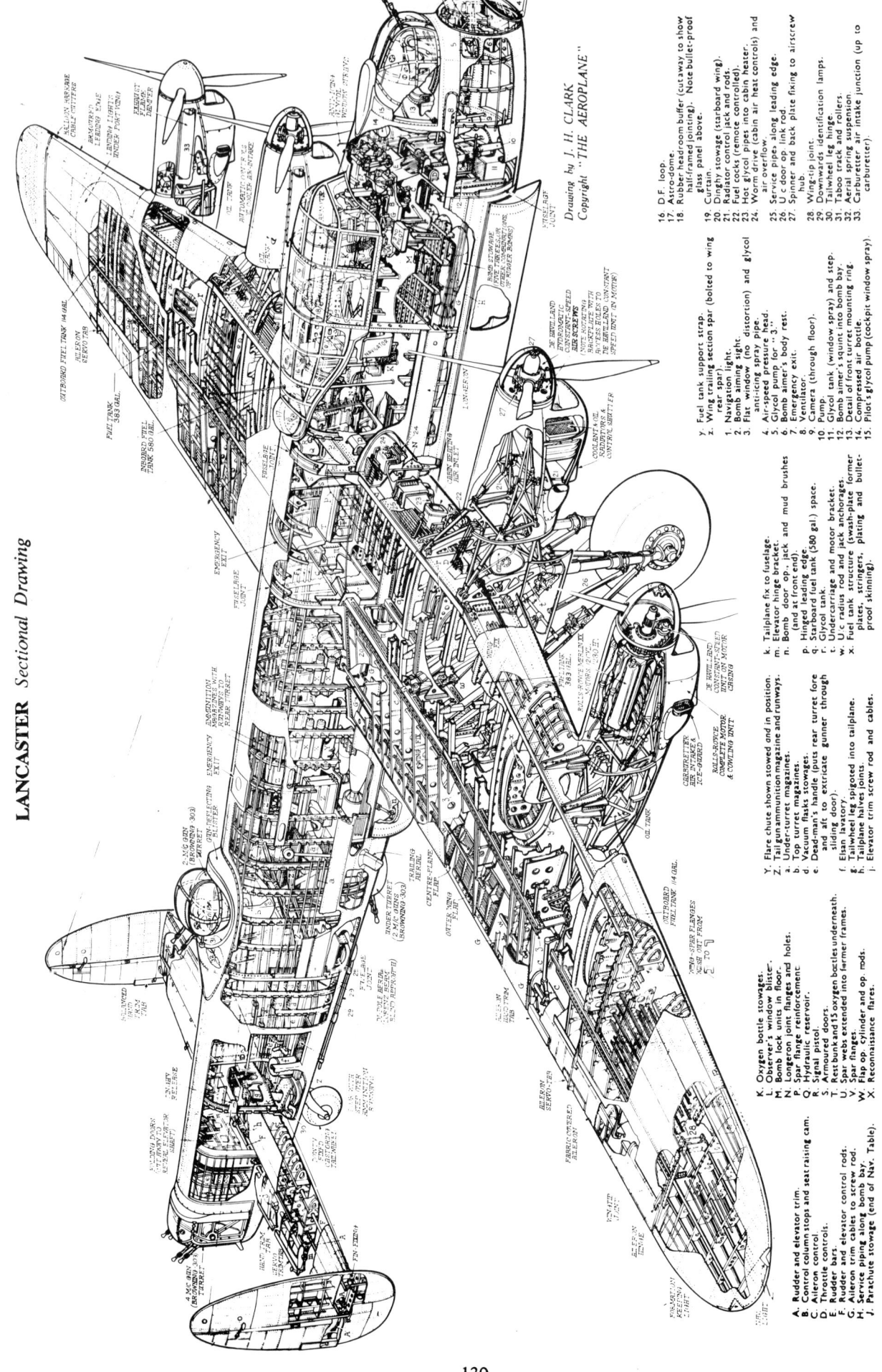

Drawing by J. H. CLARK
Copyright "THE AEROPLANE"

A. Rudder and elevator trim.
B. Control column stops and seat raising cam.
C. Aileron control.
D. Throttle controls.
E. Rudder bars.
F. Rudder and elevator control rods.
G. Aileron trim cables to screw cord.
H. Service piping along bomb bay.
J. Parachute stowage (end of Nav. Table).

K. Oxygen bottle stowages.
L. Observer's window blister.
M. Bomb lock units in floor.
N. Longeron joint flanges and holes.
Q. Spar flange reinforcement.
Q. Hydraulic reservoir.
R. Signal pistol.
S. Armoured doors.
T. Rest bunk and 15 oxygen bottles underneath.
U. Spar webs extended into former frames.
V. Spar flanges.
W. Flap op. cylinder and op. mods.
X. Reconnaissance flares.

Y. Flare chute shown stowed and in position.
Z. Tail gun ammunition magazine and runways.
a. Under-turret magazines.
b. Top turret magazines.
c. Vacuum flasks stowages.
d. Dead-man's handle (puts rear turret fore and aft to extricate gunner through sliding door).
e. Elsan lavatory.
f. Tailwheel leg spigoted into tailplane.
g. Tailplane halves joints.
h. Elevator trim screw rod and cables.

k. Tailplane fix to fuselage.
m. Elevator hinge bracket.
n. Bomb door op., jack and mud brushes (and at front end).
p. Hinged leading edge.
q. Starboard fuel tank (580 gal.) space.
r. Glycol tank.
t. Undercarriage and motor bracket.
w. U.c door and jack anchorages.
w. U.c radius rod and jack mounting ring.
x. Fuel tank structure (wash-plate former plates, stringers, plating and bullet-proof skinning).

y. Fuel tank support strap.
z. Wing trailing section spar (bolted to wing rear spar).

1. Navigation light.
2. Bomb aiming sight.
3. Flat window (no distortion) and glycol anti-icing spray pipe.
4. Air-speed pressure head.
5. Glycol pump for " 3."
6. Bomb aimer's body rest.
7. Emergency exit.
8. Ventilator.
9. Camera (through floor).
10. Pump.
11. Glycol tank (window spray) and step.
12. Bomb aimer's squint into bomb bay.
13. Detail of front turret mounting ring.
14. Compressed air bottle.
15. Pilot's glycol pump (cockpit window spray).

16. D.F. loop.
17. Astro-dome.
18. Rubber headroom buffer (cutaway to show half-framed jointing). Note bullet-proof glass panel above.
19. Curtain.
20. Dinghy stowage (starboard wing).
21. Radiator control jack and rods.
22. Fuel cocks (remote controlled).
23. Hot glycol pipes into cabin heater.
24. Worm drive (cabin air heat controls) and air overflow.
25. Service pipes, along leading edge.
26. U.c door op. link rod.
27. Spinner and back plate fixing to airscrew hub.
28. Wing-tip joint.
29. Downwards identification lamps.
30. Tailwheel leg hinge.
31. Taboo track and rollers.
32. Aerial spring suspension.
33. Carburetter air intake junction (up to carburetter).

130

LINCOLN *Sectional Drawing*

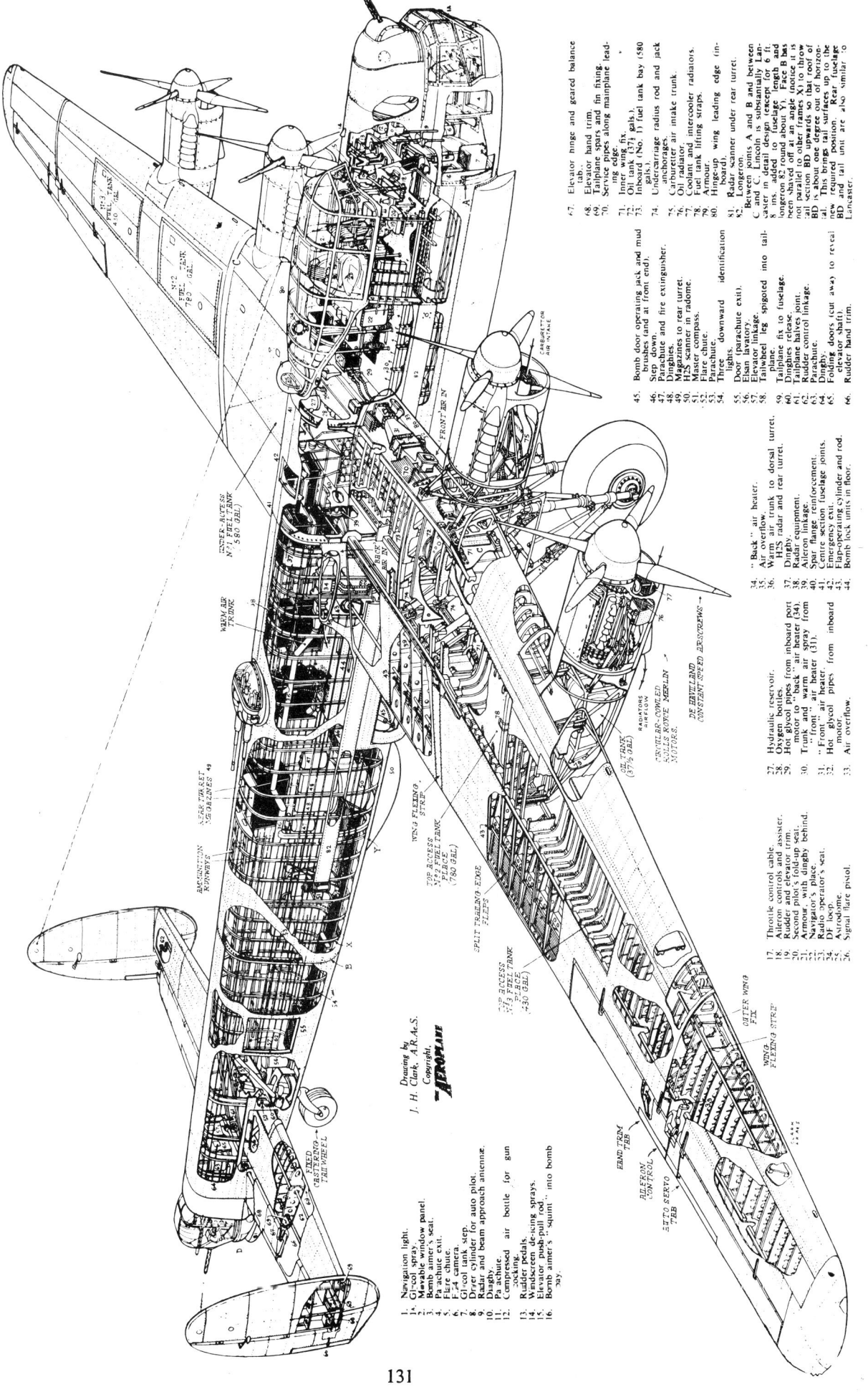

Drawing by
J. H. Clark, A.R.Ae.S.
Copyright.
Aeroplane

1. Navigation light.
2. Gl-col spray.
3. Movable window panel.
4. Bomb aimer's seat.
5. Pa achute exit.
6. Flare chute.
7. F24 camera.
8. Gl-col tank step.
9. Dryer cylinder for auto pilot.
10. Radar and beam approach antennæ.
11. Dinghy.
12. Compressed air bottle for gun cocking.
13. Rudder pedals.
14. Windscreen de-icing sprays.
15. Elevator push-pull rod.
16. Bomb aimer's "squint" into bomb bay.

17. Throttle control cable.
18. Aileron controls and assister.
19. Rudder and elevator trim.
20. Second pilot's fold-up seat.
21. Armour behind dinghy behind.
22. Navigator's place.
23. Radio operator's seat.
24. DF loop.
25. Astrodome.
26. Signal flare pistol.

27. Hydraulic reservoir.
28. Oxygen bottles.
29. Hot glycol pipes from inboard port motor to "back" air heater (34).
30. Trunk and "warm" air spray from "Front" air heater (31).
31. "Front" air heater.
32. Hot glycol pipes from inboard motor.
33. Air overflow.

34. "Back" air heater.
35. Air overflow.
36. Warm air trunk to dorsal turret.
37. Dinghy.
38. Radar equipment.
39. Aileron linkage.
40. Spar flange reinforcement.
41. Centre section fuselage joints.
42. Emergency exit.
43. Flap-operating cylinder and rod.
44. Bomb lock units in floor.

45. Bomb door operating jack and mud brushes (and at front end).
46. Step down.
47. Parachute and fire extinguisher.
48. Dinghies.
49. Magazines to rear turret.
50. H2S scanner in radome.
51. Master compass.
52. Flare chute.
53. Parachute.
54. Three downward identification lights.
55. Door (parachute exit).
56. Elsan lavatory.
57. Elevator linkage.
58. Tailwheel leg spigoted into tailplane.
59. Tailplane fix to fuselage.
60. Dinghies release.
61. Tailplane halves joint.
62. Rudder control linkage.
63. Parachute.
64. Dinghy.
65. Folding doors (cut away) to reveal elevator shaft.
66. Rudder hand trim.

67. Elevator hinge and geared balance tab.
68. Elevator hand trim.
69. Tailplane spars and fin fixing.
70. Service pipes along mainplane leading edge.
71. Inner wing fix.
72. Oil tank (171 gals.).
73. Inboard (No.1) fuel tank bay (580 gals.).
74. Undercarriage radius rod and jack anchorages.
75. Carburettor air intake trunk.
76. Coolant and intercooler radiators.
77. Oil radiator.
78. Armour.
79. Fuel tank lifting straps.
80. Hinge-up wing leading edge (inboard).
81. Radar scanner under rear turret.
82. Longeron.

Between joints A and B and between C and C, Lincoln is substantially Lancaster in detail design (except for 6 ft. 8 ins. added to fuselage length and longeron 82 round about Y). Face B has been shaved off at an angle (notice it is not parallel to other frames X) to throw section BD upwards so that roof of BD is about one degree out of horizontal. This brings tail surfaces up to the new required position. Rear fuselage BD and tail unit are also similar to Lancaster.

Mamba/Adder/Viper Lancaster

The Armstrong Siddeley Mamba, planned for the Avro Athena, Boulton Paul Balliol and Short Seamew, was first flown in the nose of Mk. VI Lancaster ND784 (originally a Mk. III) specially modified by Air Service Training, Hamble.

A second test-bed, SW342, was modified by Armstrong Siddeley at their Bitteswell Flight Test Department. Installed in the nose, the Mamba, with cropped propeller blades, was subjected to a water spray from a rig to provide a check on its proneness to icing; remotely controlled cameras were used to record the ice build-up on the spinner and on the inlet guide vanes. At this stage it was known as the " Mamba Anti-Icing Lancaster." Later it was modified to take an Adder in the tail and subsequently a Viper with reheat.

Mamba de-icing test-rig installed at Bitteswell.

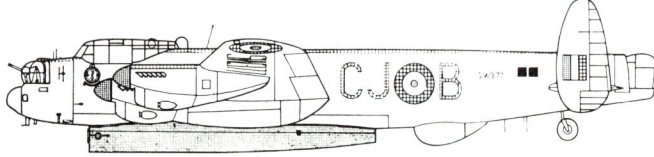

Lancaster A.S.R.III with lifeboat, St. Eval, 1947.

Lancaster A.S.R.3

From late 1945 a number of Lancasters were converted for air-sea rescue duties as a replacement for the Warwick. Details appear in chapter seventeen. Conversion was carried out by Cunliffe-Owen at Eastleigh and Merlin 224s were the standard power unit. They were adapted to carry airborne lifeboats, and in September 1946 the Lifeboat Airborne Mk. IIA was introduced to supersede the Mk. II used on Warwicks. The type was declared obsolete in August 1950.

Close-up of lifeboat fitted to A.S.R./G.R.III Lancaster.

Lancaster G.R.3

A.S.R.3 Lancasters converted for maritime reconnaissance became G.R.3 as detailed in chapter seventeen.

Lancaster IV/V

The Lancaster IV and V became the Lincoln I and II respectively.

Lancaster B.VI

To increase Lancaster performance, Merlin 85 or 87 engines, both of 1,635 h.p., were proposed and two Mk. III airframes with Merlin 28s, DV170 and DV199, were sent to the Rolls-Royce testing airfield at Hucknall in June and July of 1943 respectively for conversion. Both were retained for extensive test work.

DV199, prototype Lancaster VI operated by Rolls-Royce.

Plans were put in hand to modify a number of Lancaster IIIs to this standard, of which JB675 was the first. In turn, at intervals from November 1943 to March 1944, JB713, ND418, ND479, ND558 and ND673 were modified in that order. ND479 crashed on stick force tests but others went into service (see chapter twelve). In general they were fitted with the latest H2S and a large number of radar jamming devices, together with large bales of window. Thus equipped, with target indicators and a few bombs, they could fool the German defences into anticipating a heavy raid as a diversion.

Lancaster B.VI in squadron service.

JB675 had a particularly long life and was generally regarded as the prototype Mk. VI after its engineering appraisal at the A. & A.E.E. in April 1944. Early in 1945 it went to Hucknall, where its Merlin 85 engines were changed successively to Merlin 68, 102, 150, 620, 621, 630 and 641 engines and it flew 444 hours on tests until July 1948, when it was finally dismantled and sent in sections by road to 9 M.U., Cosford, for disposal.

From the test flying with the Lancaster VI some 6,000 running hours experience of Merlin 85/87 engines was gained which considerably reduced engine teething troubles in the Lincoln.

Mamba fitted in Lancaster to basic Mk. VI standard.

Mamba Lancaster

During 1947, Lancaster VI ND784/G was prepared by

Air Service Training as a flying test-bed for the Armstrong Siddeley Mamba. This aircraft had previously tested an Armstrong Siddeley A.S.X. jet-turbine, installed in the bomb-bay; in the case of the Mamba turbo-jet, the original nose was completely removed and the Mamba fitted and faired into a new nose. Testing necessitated a special flight observer's compartment " boffin's cell " in the rear fuselage. Thus rigged, the aircraft first flew from Hamble on October 21st, 1947, in the hands of Wg. Cdr. H. P. Powell, A.F.C., and was delivered to Bitteswell the same month.

Prototype Lancaster Mk. VII NN801 with Martin turret, May 1945.

Lancaster B.VII (Interim)
The designation Lancaster VII (Interim) was not adopted; it was suggested for the 50 Lancaster B.Is ordered from Austin Motors with Martin mid-upper turrets over the bomb bay, which were in fact fitted with normal Fraser Nash turrets in this position, due to delays in delivery of the American turrets. They went into service from February to April 1945 as B.I Lancasters, NX548-589 and NX603-610.

Lancaster B.VII/B.VII(F.E.)
Martin turrets with two .50 machine-guns became available in April 1945 from orders outstanding for nearly two years. The prototype, NN801, a Lancaster B.I, was converted by A. V. Roe but the 180 production B.VIIs were built only by Austin Motors. Basically this was a B.1 incorporating earlier B.I/III modifications, with a Martin mid-upper turret placed further forward (38 ft. 5½ in. from tip of nose to centre of turret) and in lieu of the F.N. mid-upper turret. Apart from the increase in the calibre of the armament, the turret was operated electrically whereas all other turrets had been hydraulically operated.

From August 1945 all Mk. VIIs were required to be tropicalised and the designation B.VII(F.E.) applied to all post-war production models until the earlier models had been retrospectively converted to the same standard.

Detail Data
Power Units and Airscrews: 4 x Rolls-Royce Merlin 24 engines (tropicalised from August 1945) driving Hamilton A5/148 or A5/149 constant speed, hydromatic airscrews.
Crew: As B.1.

Lancaster B.VII of No. 617 Squadron post-war.

Armament: 2 x .303 Browning machine-guns in Fraser Nash F.N.5. nose turret, 2 x .5 Browning No. 2 Mk. II machine-guns in Martin 250CE 23A mid-upper turret and 2 x .50 machine-guns in Fraser Nash F.N.82 rear turret with provision for A.G.L.T. No under-turret was fitted as an H2S ventral housing was a standard fitting.

Dimensions: As B.1 except new type perspex nose and A.G.L.T. in rear turret affecting overall length as 70 ft. 5½ in. tail up, 69 ft. 9½ in. tail down.
Weights: All-up 72,000 lb., Tare 37,974 lb. Limitation take-off/landing 72,000/60,000 lb. Other details as B.1.
Performance: As Mk. I.
Special Installations: Mk. VII(F.E.)s were withdrawn from units to No. 32 Maintenance Unit at the rate of 6 a month for the fitment of Rebecca Mk.II, Loran Mk.I, GEE and AYF Radio Altimeter.

Lancaster VII (Western Union)
Of the 54 Lancasters supplied to the French Naval Air Arm *Aeronavale* under Western Union arrangements, detailed in chapter seventeen, 22 were converted from Mk. VII to full A.S.R. standard. The aircraft concerned are detailed in the Lancaster Log in the NX and RT series.

French civil Lancaster FCL-05 ex-RT679.

One Lancaster has been used for drop tests of a Latécoère-built postal rocket on behalf of the French *Centre National d'Etudes des Telecommunications*.

Five were ordered by the French Government to A.S.R. standard for civil use, fitted with rescue equipment, Decca navigation and Instrument Landing System. Provisional registrations were issued to FCL-01 to 05 as follows: RT693 (G-11-72), NX738 (G-11-70), RT689 (G-11-71), RT673 (G-11-73) and RT679 (G-11-74) respectively.

Lancaster VIII and IX
Mark numbers reserved for development of Lancasters built in Britain.

Lancaster B.X
The story behind the Mk. X Lancaster, built exclusively in Canada, is detailed in chapters seven and fourteen and under KB and FM in the Log.

Detail Data
Power Units and Airscrews: 4 x Rolls-Royce Merlin 38 (KB700-774), Merlin 224 (from KB775), each fitted with Hamilton A5/138 (KB700-774), A5/148 (KB775-796), A5/159 (from KB797) variable pitch, hydromatic airscrews.
Crew: 7. As per Mk. I.
Armament: As per Mk. I except that two Browning machine-guns were initially fitted in the ventral turret and bomb bay doors were larger than the original Mk. I to accommodate 8,000 lb. bombs.
Dimensions: As per Mk. I. The official Victory Aircraft drawings gave Span 102 ft., Length (guns removed from rear turret) 69.55 ft.

Weights: All-up 61,500 lb., Tare 35,415 lb. Maximum permissible take-off/landing 61,500/55,000 lb.
Performance: As Mk. III.
Fuel Capacity: As Mk. I.
Construction: As B.III except that American-made bearings were used due to short supply of U.K. bearings. Parts were interchangeable B.I/B.III/B.VII/B.X with the proviso that when Canadian-built control surfaces were fitted they must be paired. On check testing A. V. Roe engineers found the wing sections to be slightly thicker than standard and comparative test flying showed it to be slightly heavier on controls than the B.I.
Special Equipment: FM201 was used by Handling Squadron of the A. & A.E.E. from April 1946 for Mk. VIII/IX and German Siemens K-12 auto pilot tests; by September 1947 it was fitted with a radar altimeter and in the following March it was used on night photography.
The B.X was declared obsolete for all R.A.F. purposes in January 1947.

Lancaster 10-SR

Eight Lancasters originally produced as B.X were converted to 10-SR in 1949 for air-sea rescue duties with the R.C.A.F. The order called for twelve, but the last four were further modified and winterised to part 10-BR standard and became the 10-BR (Interim).

Lancaster 10-P with modified canopy and turret positions.

Lancaster 10-P

The first of the post-war Lancaster B.X conversions concerned the 10-P version for photo-reconnaissance in 1948. Nine were initially converted for No. 408 Squadron and in 1949 two more with radar altimeters; they were FM120, FM122, FM199, FM207, FM212, FM214-218, KB729. This type remained in service, on extensive mapping work, until 1962.

Prototype 10-BR on a visit to Cranwell from Trenton.

Lancaster 10-BR

Four 10-ASR Lancasters winterised and with other modifications to part 10-BR standard became 10-BR (Interim). Nine B.X Lancasters were then converted to the 10-BR bomber reconnaissance standard, the first of which, FM221, was delivered to Trenton in June 1949.

Lancaster 10-MR/MP

Following conversions to 10-BR standard came modifications of B.X Lancasters to 10-MR for maritime reconnaissance. The first, KB919, flew on December 29th, 1950. Later the designation was changed to MP for maritime patrol. In all, over 70 were so modified.

Lancaster 10-N

Three Lancaster B.Xs modified for navigational training became 10-N.

Lancaster 10-O

Test-bed for Orenda engine, FM209

Lancaster 10-O with outboard Orenda engines on test.

Lancaster 10-U

Designation to classify original Mk. X held in store by R.C.A.F. for modification as necessary; U stands for unmodified.

Lancaster 10-S

Covering designation for Lancaster (standard) to denote KB944 ex-service at R.C.A.F. Station, Greenwood, restored to original standard for museum purposes in Canada and for unmodified aircraft held for spares, viz. KB781, KB801, KB854.

Lancaster 10-DC

Designation to denote Canadian built Lancasters adapted for drone-carrying, of which KB848 and KB851 are the only examples traced.

Lancaster 10-DC KB851 with Ryan Firebee drones.

Lancaster 10-AR

Specially modified for aerial reconnaissance, as the designation denotes, these were to 10-P standard and then prepared for Arctic photographic reconnaissance with lengthened nose and special Arctic survival " dustbin " in place of rear turret. Aircraft concerned were KB839, KB882, KB976, all with No. 408 Squadron at Rockcliffe in 1964.

Civil Lancaster 10

The conversion of R5727 for airline use as CF-CMS Trans-Canada Airlines No. 100 is detailed in chapter nineteen. T.C.A. Nos. 105-106 CF-CMX/MY ex-FM184-185 were received at Hucknall in early 1946 from

FM187 as Trans-Canada Air Lines mailplane No. 108.

Prestwick with Merlin T.24/1 engines which were exchanged for T.24/4s; T.C.A. Nos. 107-108 CF-CMZ/NA ex-FM186-187 were received at Hucknall from Prestwick in late 1944 for their Merlin 38s to be replaced by T.24/4s.

Lincoln prototype photographed January 1945.

Avro Type 694 Lincoln Prototypes

The evolution of the Lincoln from the Lancaster IV is detailed in chapter eighteen. The first, PW925, was delivered to Boscombe Down on June 13th, 1944, by J. H. Orrell, who completed the manufacturers' final test, the dive, en route. An enlarged rudder trimmer was fitted on A. & A.E.E. recommendations and test flown on November 27th. Later this prototype Mk. I became half a Mk. II by the fitting of two outboard Merlin 68s in place of the Merlin 85s. Before becoming instructional airframe 6141M in December 1945 it flew some 125 hours on engine development. PW929, too, became an instructional airframe, 5942M, a year after its first flight on November 9th, 1944. The third prototype, PW932, did not fly till November 6th, 1945, a year after the first production models. It resided for many years after the war at the College of Aeronautics, Cranfield.

Lincoln B.1 photographed from a naval aircraft.

Lincoln B.I

The Lincoln B.II (B.2 later) became the standard service version and Lincoln B.1 production was limited to 82. Although a number entered squadron service in 1945-46, they were withdrawn in favour of the Mk. II. It was declared obsolete for R.A.F. purposes in February 1949 and therefore detail data below are given in full for the B.2 squadron service version, with B.1 details restricted to differences between the two marks.

Detail Data

Power Units and Airscrews: 4 x 1,680 h.p. Rolls-Royce Merlin 85 (or 85A up to February 1949) engines each driving 4-blade Rotol airscrews or, from December 1946, 4-blade D.H. airscrews as an alternative.

Crew: 7. Captain (first pilot), Second pilot, Air Observer (Navigator/Air bomber), 2 Wireless Operator/Air Gunners, 2 Air Gunners.

Armament: To facilitate production, turrets were fitted as per late Lancaster production and not as planned for Lincoln standard. Nose armament was as the B.2, but a Martin mid-upper turret with 2 x .5 machine-guns was an interim measure and F.N.121 tail turrets with 4 x .303 machine-guns were interim for the F.N.82 with 2 x 0.5 machine-guns. Provision was made for an F.N.88 mid-lower turret, but this was not a standard fitting.

Dimensions: As B.2.

Weights: As per B.2. Tested up to 82,000 lb. all-up weight at A. & A.E.E. in April 1945.

Performance: Basically as B.2.

Tankage: As per B.2.

Construction: Basically as the Lancaster B.I, with larger fuselage and wings, revised bomb bay and fuel system. Projects to fit Tudor type wings and a larger tailplane were cancelled. Provision for the carriage of Tallboy " M " bombs was a special modification to limited numbers. Equipment included Mk. VII automatic controls, Beam Approach, F.24 Camera, " Q " or " J " type flotation dinghy, " K " type dinghy, pigeon container, Elsan sanitary closet, etc.

Special Versions. RE228 had its Merlin 85 engines exchanged for Merlin T.85s in early 1945. RE230 was converted to a B.II at Hucknall in March 1945. RE235 was used by Rolls-Royce for general Merlin engine development work from March 1945 to April 1946. RE258 under winterisation tests in Canada 1946-47 had two Merlin 102 engines inboard, a Merlin 85A engine in the starboard outer position and a Merlin 68 in the port outer position. All engines started successfully on 100 octane fuel at minimum temperature range of −35° to −40° centigrade. RE284 had a rig to test the Brabazon undercarriage.

Phoebus engine tested in bomb-bay of Lincoln B.1.

Phoebus Lincoln

The Bristol Aeroplane Company arranged with Napiers at Luton to equip Lincoln B.1 RA643 as a flying test bed for a pure jet version of their original Proteus—the Phoebus, which was installed in the bomb bay. Altogether it was test-flown for 23½ hours.

Lincoln B.II

The Lincoln B.IIs service history is described in chapter eighteen. All were tropicalised by June 1948.

Detail Data

Power Units and Airscrews: 4 x 1,750 h.p. Packard-built Merlin 68A (68 or 300 limited use alternatives) engines driving Hamilton A5/148 or 4-blade D.H. hydromatic,

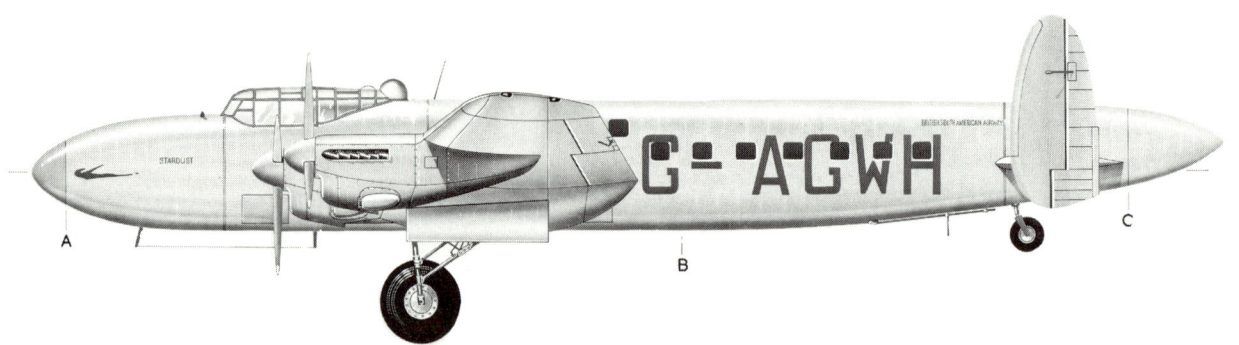

 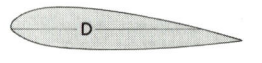

136

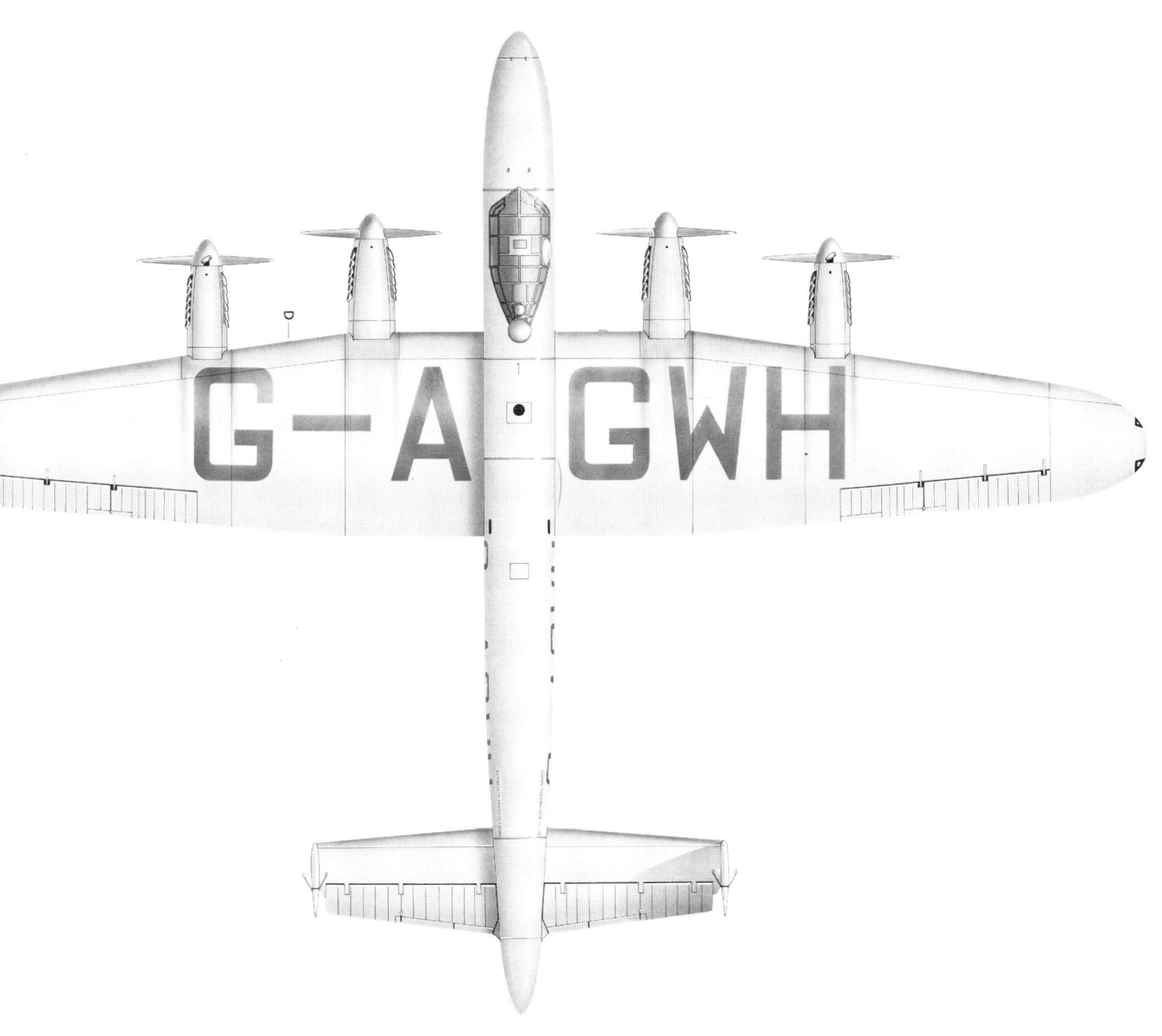

Lancastrian " Star Dust " of British South American Airways Corporation recorded during 1946.

both constant speed, fully-feathering airscrews of 15 ft. diameter.

Crew: 7. As B.1.

Armament: 2 x 0.5 Browning guns in Boulton Paul " F " nose turret, 2 x 20 mm. Hispano No. 4 Mk. 5 cannon in Bristol 17 mid-upper turret, 2 x 0.5 Browning guns in Boulton Paul " D " tail turret became standard for Lincoln B.2/3G and B.2/4A. Early models had interim types of turret as listed under B.I.

Dimensions: Span 120 ft., Length 78 ft. 3 in.; Height 17 ft. on ground, 20 ft. 6 in. tail up; Dihedral 7 deg., Incidence 4 deg., Track 23 ft. 9 in., Gross wing area 1,421 sq. ft., Tailplane span 33 ft. 9 in.

Weights: All up (normal) 75,000 lb., Tare 44,188 lb., Military load other than bombs including crew 5,228 lb., Fuel 3,580 galls. maximum 25,776 lb., Oil 150 gall. 1,350 lb., Wing loading 52.77 lb./sq.ft.; Limitations 82,000/65,000 lb. maximum permissible for take-off/landing, Maximum bomb load 22,500 lb. with 2,275 gall. of fuel.

Performance: Speed with full load, 305 m.p.h. at 19,000 ft., 236 m.p.h. at sea level. Cruising speed 244 m.p.h. at 22,500 ft. Rate of climb from sea level 820 ft./min. to 20,000 ft. in 30 mins.; Range 4,450 miles with 3,000 lb. load, 2,800 miles with 14,000 lb. load, 1,350 miles with 22,000 lb. load. Stalling speed (flap and undercarriage down) 75 m.p.h.

Fuel capacity: 2 x 580 gall. metal tanks in wing centre section, 2 x 780 + 2 x 430 gall. flexible Marston tanks in mainplanes, making a total of 3,580 galls. of fuel; Oil 4 x 37½ gall. tanks totalling 150 gall. Special arrangements were made for Lincolns, e.g. RA657, used in probe and drogue flight refuelling experiments.

Construction: As B.1. Airfoil section NACA 23018.

Special Versions: Apart from those listed below, RF533 was modified by the Portsmouth Aviation Co. for weather radar tests which involved a five-foot extension to the nose. It was used by the R.A.E. as a flying laboratory for the development of fire control systems. The fuselage of SX975 had a cut-away bomb-bay and was faired nose and tail.

RF523 *Thor II* and RF498 *Crusader* were armament and signals demonstration aircraft respectively.

Lincoln of the Argentine Air Force.

Twelve B.2s were prepared by A. V. Roe for the Argentine Air Force as B.001 to B.012 ex-RE343, RE349-356, RE408-410 respectively of which B.003 was to a special standard comparable to *Aries II*. Additionally eighteen B.2s were built for the Argentine as B.013 to B.030 by Armstrong Whitworth.

Lincoln B.2/3G and B.2/4A

In February 1947 Lincoln B.IIs in service were prepared to the different standards and the suffixes to the mark numbers denoted equipment as follows: B.2/3G with H2S Mk. IIIG, Gee Mk. II, Rebecca Mk. II; B.2/4A with H2S Mk. IVA, G-H Mk. II. Rebecca Mk. II or IV.

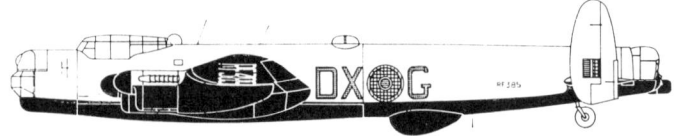

Standard Lincoln B.2/3G as with No. 57 Squadron.

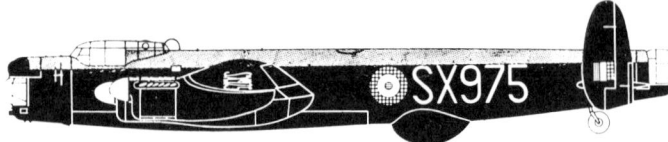

Lincoln B.2/4A, No. 148 Squadron, Upwood, April 1955.

Lincoln B.2 with bulged bomb-bay, February 1948.

Theseus Lincoln

The Theseus turbo-prop unit, developed by the Bristol Aeroplane Company, was flight tested for 165 flying hours in Lincoln B.1 RA716/G, which had two 2,400 h.p. Theseus II units fitted at Filton in place of the two outboard Merlins. Piloted by A. J. Pegg, this Lincoln, so modified, first flew on February 17th, 1947. A second Lincoln B.2, RE418, was similarly modified with Theseus 21 units and flew over 800 hours and RE339/G, which had Pythons at one time, also flew with Theseus engines outboard in 1948.

Avon Lincoln

Lincoln B.II RA716/G, fitted with two Rolls-Royce Avon engines in place of the outboard Merlins, was capable of operating up to 40,000 feet, but as it was unpressurised and unheated it was restricted to 35,000 feet. With 2,200 gall. of kerosene and 600 gall. of petrol the range at 20,000 feet was 1,300 miles. It was used by the Armament and Instrument Experimental Unit as " N " for several years.

Python Lincoln

With Armstrong Siddeley Python axial-flow turbo-props replacing the outboard Merlins, Lincoln RE339/G could reach 40,000 feet at an all-up weight of 61,000 lb. With a fuel capacity of 2,250 gall. of kerosene and 600 gall. of petrol it could fly for 30 minutes at maximum ceiling with a 10,000 lb. bomb load. This Lincoln, with turrets renewed, flew with a crew of three—pilot, engineer and navigator bomber. RF403 similarly modified and painted all-white, except for a black anti-glare panel, was ferried out to Australia with faired turret positions for high altitude bombing trials at Woomera. It was scrapped at R.A.A.F. Base, Tocumwal, N.S.W., in 1958.

Proteus Lincoln

After a trial installation in RF368, Lincoln SX972 had Proteus engines fitted outboard and flew for 958 hours on test following the initial flight on December 12th, 1950.

Derwent Lincoln

A Rolls-Royce Derwent was installed by Air Service Training in a pod under the belly of SX971 for reheat development on behalf of the National Gas Turbine establishment in the early 'fifties.

Last Lincolns in service, B.2/4A.

RA716/G Lincoln B.2 Theseus test-bed.

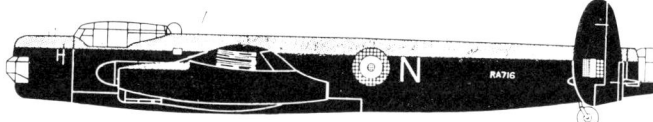

Lincoln of B.T.U. with Avon engines outboard.

Proteus Lincoln B.2 SX972.

Derwent test-pod fitted on SX971 by Air Service Training.

Tyne Lincoln

The Rolls-Royce Tyne engine first flew mounted in the nose of Lincoln B.II RF530, which bore the provisional registration G-37-1. This aircraft arrived from Farnborough on August 27th, 1954, and flew from Hucknall for several years on Tyne trials.

Tyne engine test-rig on Lincoln B.2.

RF402 Lincoln B.2 used by Napiers for various tests.

Naiad Lincoln

Napier's first gas turbine, the 1,500 e.h.p. Naiad turbo-prop, was installed in Lincoln B.2 RF530 in 1946 at Luton. A Double Naiad was also being installed in the nose of the Lincoln, but before flying commenced the aircraft for which this power plant was intended, the Blackburn Y.B.1, was abandoned. In 1948 another Lincoln, RF402, had a Naiad installed in the nose with a rig in connection with de-icing research. This machine was subsequently used in various experiments as detailed below.

RF402's replacement at Farnborough S.B.A.C. show 1959.

Napier Lincoln

After the Naiad de-icing installation, RF402 was used for the development, at high altitudes, of combustion heaters for the Ministry of Supply. Later it was used to evaluate the "hot gas" anti-icing installation on the Beverley by carrying a section of this aircraft's wing on the top of the fuselage in front of which a nozzle mast was erected, together with droplet sampler probes and an auto-camera housing. Similar work was carried out for the Britannia and Comet. With further work in this sphere envisaged, Lincoln RF342 was acquired and RF402 was cannibalised to keep it running. On the new acquisition, registered G-APRJ, de-icing experimentation was carried out on sections of the wing and tail of the Argosy, Avro 748, Buccaneer and Caravelle. Refurbished in R.A.F. colours at the College of Aeronautics, it is to replace Lancaster PA474 on laminar flow wing tests.

Argentine Air Force Lincoln B.003 for polar research.

Nomad Lincoln

The Napier Nomad, weighing over 4,000 lb., was fitted to the nose of Lincoln SX973 in 1953 for test purposes and proved that it could power the aircraft with the four normal engines stopped.

Lincoln Freighters and Tankers

RE290 was modified mid-1949 by Airflight at Langley for freight carrying by fitting Lancastrian type nose and tail cones and an Airtech pannier under the bomb bay. Registered G-ALPF it was flown by Surrey Flying Services on the Berlin Air Lift and ended up at Southend, where it was broken up in 1952.

Freight-carrying Lincolns, planned to convey meat, were modified and sold to Paraguay as ZP-CBG-96, ZP-CBR-97 and ZP-CBR-98, being ex-RF419, RE376 and RF419 respectively.

Lincoln B.2 as a tanker for flight refuelling.

SX993 and RE293 experimental flight refuelling Lincolns were test flown September 1951 and February 1952 respectively.

Lincoln RE364, Aries *II of the Central Navigation School.*

Lincolnians

Lincolnian was an unofficial name for Lincolns converted in a manner similar to Lancastrians with faired nose and tail portions. This applied to Lincolns RE364 *Aries II* (see chapter eighteen) and RE367 *Aries III* which replaced it; *Aries IV*, incidentally, was a Canberra.

Lincoln III

In the summer of 1945 a long-range version of the Lincoln was projected with a saddle-back tank stretching from behind the cockpit to the mid-upper turret. This was

Provisionally Mk. VI, Lincoln with outboard Theseus engines.

tentatively given the designation Lincoln III, later applied to a project for a general reconnaissance aircraft which became the Shackleton.

Lincoln B.IV

Designation covering B.II Lincolns temporarily fitted with Merlin 85 engines.

Lincoln U.5

The policy for drone Lincolns changed after two had been converted by A. V. Roe from the initial ten modification sets supplied by Flight Refuelling Ltd. RF395 was first flown as a drone, but with a check pilot aboard; RF366, the other Lincoln converted, was not flown as a drone.

Special armament demonstration Lincoln.

Lincoln B.XV

Lincoln production in Canada was not pressed until the early summer of 1945 when tooling commenced. By September, when it was evident that bombers were not going to be required in the Far East, contracts were cancelled, but negotiations continued on the completion of a few airframes to keep the factory going until taken over from the government-controlled Victory Aircraft. The B.XVs were planned to B.II standard with Merlin 68A engines, but with a Glenn Martin 23A mid-upper turret.

Lincoln B.30 of the R.A.A.F., completely built in Australia.

Lincoln B.30

B.30 was the designation given to the Lincoln produced by the Beaufort Division, Australian Department of Aircraft Production. The first five were erected from components supplied from Britain and the first of these, A73-1, first flew on March 17th, 1946. From A73-6 onwards, the airframes were completely built in Australia. By May 1947 a dozen had been produced and the output was $1\frac{1}{2}$ per month. Orders were for 85, but this was cut back to 73. The first fifty were initially fitted with Merlin 85 engines but a number in service had Merlin 102s substituted and all built subsequently had the latter engine as initial installation.

Special modifications included a nose probe on A73-29 associated with special gear in the bomb bay for rain-making trials at Richmond, N.S.W.

Of the 54 built, numbered A73-1 to A73-54, nine were lost in service as follows: No. 11 stalled from 300 feet at Amberley, February 19th, 1948; Nos. 16 and 51 were lost together in a landing accident at Cloncurry, June 14th, 1953; No. 31 crashed at Amberley, May 7th, 1953; Nos. 35 and 39 crashed, but while the former became Instructional Airframe No. 1, the latter was scrapped; No. 40 was ditched off Johore, Malaya, February 1st, 1951; No. 44 crashed eleven miles south-west of Amberley, March 7th, 1950; and No. 46 burnt after crashing at Townsville, April 23rd, 1957. Additionally, Nos. 2, 39, 47 and 54 were reduced to spares, mainly through gale damage at Amberley, February 3rd, 1957.

The remaining Lincoln B.30s have either been sold as scrap or are awaiting sale with the exception of those allotted for fire-fighting practice, a role in which they are not likely to last long; this concerns Nos. 10 and 13 (Point Cook), 25 (Amberley), 27 and 45 (Mascot), 36 (Richmond) and 50 (Eagle Farm).

Lincoln M.R.31 of the R.A.A.F., built in Australia.

Lincoln M.R.31

The last 19 Lincolns produced, A73-55 to A73-73, were B.31s with a 6 ft. 6 in. extension on the nose to house radar equipment and two operators, additional to the normal crew. Mid-upper, nose and rear turrets were fitted to most on delivery, but were, in the main, removed in service.

Of the 19 built, two were written off in crashes, Nos. 63 and 69, on March 12th, 1953, and January 18th, 1956, respectively. Nos. 61, 62, 66, 67 and 68 were sold as scrap by 1963 and No. 59 had been reduced to spares, while the remainder awaited disposal, except for No. 58 temporarily reprieved at East Sale, Victoria, for fire fighting practice.

Avro Type 691 Lancastrian

The Lancastrian allotted the Avro Works Type No. 691 evolved as detailed in chapter nineteen.

Lancastrian I

The Lancastrian Is are described in chapter nineteen and production records will be found under the VB673-VF167 range of the Log. Fourteen in B.O.A.C. service were named and disposed as follows: G-AGLS *Nelson*, G-AGLT *Newcastle*, G-AGMP *Newport*, G-AGME *Newhaven*, G-AGMG *Nicosia*, G-AGLW *Northampton*, G-AGLY *Norfolk*, G-AGMJ *Naseby* and G-AGMK *Newbury* survived until scrapped at Hurn, 1950-51; G-AGMD *Nairn*, G-AGLZ *Nottingham*, G-AGML *Nicobar* were sold to QUANTAS as VH-EAS/U/T respectively, G-AGMB

Norwich crashed at Singapore August 27th, 1948, and G-AGMM was written off at Castel Benito, November 7th, 1949.

G-AGLV *Sky Lane* of Skyways as VP-KGT operated the Nairobi to Reunion shuttle service for B.O.A.C.

Detail Data

Power Units and Airscrews: 4 x 1,620 h.p. Rolls-Royce Merlin 24 engines each driving a D.H. hydromatic three-blade, constant speed, fully-feathering airscrew of 13 ft. diameter.

Crew and Accommodation: Crew of five—pilot (port-side) with co-pilot in side-by-side seating with dual control; navigator and wireless operator immediately behind; steward in cabin. Nine passenger seats convertible into six bunks. Main baggage hatch of 228 cub. ft. in nose, compartment in cabin of 63 cub. ft. and rear compartment of 41 cub. ft. for baggage. Windows on starboard side only.

Dimensions: Span 102 ft., Length 76 ft., Height (tail down) 17 ft. 10 in., Track 23 ft. 9 in., Tailplane Span 33 ft. 9 in., Gross Wing Area 1,297 sq. ft.

Weights: Loaded 65,000 lb., Empty 30,220 lb., Equipment and furnishings 5,970 lb., Wing loading 50.1 lb./sq. ft. at 65,000 lb. gross weight.

Performance: At 54,000 lb. weight, maximum speed 315 m.p.h. at 12,000 ft., 285 m.p.h. at sea level; Cruising speed 290 m.p.h. at 12,500 ft., maximum rate of climb 970 ft./min., Service ceiling 24,300 ft., Take-off distance to 50 ft. 1,200 yds.; Range 4,100 miles at 230 m.p.h. at 20,000 ft. with 2,190 lb. payload, 3,600 miles at 280 m.p.h. at 20,000 ft. with 4,850 lb. payload; Take-off run at 58,000 lb.—750 yds.

Fuel capacity: Fuel tanks as per Lancaster in wings giving 2,154 galls., with additional 1,020 galls. in former bomb bay of basic Lancaster structure.

First of the service versions of the Lancastrian, the C.2.

Lancastrian C.II

This service version of the Lancastrian met the requirements of Air Ministry Specification C.16/44 for an interim long range transport. Its service is recorded in chapter nineteen and production details are between VD281 and VM738 of the Log.

Four (VL967, VL977, VL978 and VM738) were sold to B.S.A.C. early in 1948 to become G-AKFF *Star Flight*, G-AKFG *Star Traveller*, G-AKMW *Star Bright* and G-AKTB *Star Glory;* three to B.O.A.C. (VL971-972, VM737) became G-AKPY *Natal*, G-AKPZ *Nile* and G-AKRB *Nyanza*. Two (VL973 and VL974) were disposed to International Air Freight in February 1948 and one (VL979) to Skyways in August 1947. Apart from those used as test beds and VL975 which was written off in a flying accident in August 1947, the bulk left in service were scrapped in February 1949 when the type was declared obsolete for R.A.F. purposes.

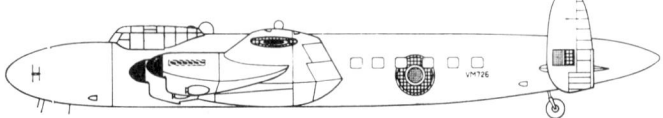

Lancastrian, No. 24 Squadron, Bassingbourn, September 9th, 1946.

Detail Data

As for Mk. I except for service crew, apart from VM728 which was non-standard with Rolls-Royce at Hucknall from April 1947 until October 1949 on Merlin engine development, having Merlin 620, 623, 641 engines successively installed.

Lancastrian C.2 as Avon engine test bed.

Avon Lancastrian

The Rolls-Royce Avon engine first flew in VM732, which was at Hucknall on noise abatement tests with Merlins. Avons were fitted outboard and the aircraft was used up until September 1950, when it was discarded at Shoeburyness after over 350 hours of test flying. Another Lancastrian, C.II, VL970, had its Merlin T.24 engines replaced by Merlin 623s inboard and Avons outboard; this aircraft crashed at Hucknall on March 29th, 1955, after 666 hours of test flying.

Avon-engined Lancastrian fitted with test-rig.

Clyde and Sapphire Lancastrian

The Clyde Lancastrian was a project that did not materialise. In June 1947 VM704 and VM733 were allotted to Rolls-Royce at Hucknall with Merlin 24 engines for installation of Clydes. Due to a policy change this was not effected and Rolls-Royce used VM704 for Griffon development work and VM733, with a Merlin T.24/2 engine in the starboard outer position, flew nearly 40 hours on comparison checks between Rotol and D.H. paddle-blade propellers and was also used for Sapphire engine development.

Griffon Lancastrian

To develop the Rolls-Royce Griffon engine for the Shackleton, VM704, after being earmarked for Clyde development and flown on Merlin T.24 evaluation, was

Lancastrian C.2 modified at Bitteswell for Sapphire engines.

modified as a Griffon test bed The Griffons were fitted inboard and 600, 623 and 625 series Merlins were fitted in succession outboard. Altogether, this Lancastrian flew over 500 hours as a test-bed.

Lancastrian C.2 used for Griffon engine development.

Ghost Lancastrian

VM703 was modified in 1947 to take De Havilland Ghost engines in the outer nacelles and VM749 was similarly modified as an engine test-bed for the Comet 1.

Lancastrian C.2 modified as De Havilland Ghost test-bed.

Lancastrian Mk. III

The Mk. III was a civil version seating 13 passengers, to the 9 of the earlier marks. Details are in chapter nineteen. The initial deliveries were: G-AGWG-L, as *Starlight*, *Star Dust*, *Star Land*, *Star Glow*, *Star Trial* and *Star Guide* of B.S.A.A.C.; G-AHBT/V/W *City of New York*, *City of Canberra* and *City of London* of Silver City Airways; G-AHBU *Sky Path*, G-AHBZ *Sky Ambassador*, G-AHCA, which burnt out in a hangar at Dunsfield, December 7th, 1946, and G-AHCC *Sky Chieftain*, of Skyways; G-AHBX/BY/CB/CD became *Maestrale*, *Libeccio*, *Grecale* and *Scirocco* of Alitalia with " I " replacing " G " as the registration index letter and another *Borea* became I-DALR.

Lancastrian C.2 used by Rolls-Royce for engine development.

Detail Data

Details as for Mk. I except as follows :

Crew and Accommodation: Crew as Mk. I; accommodation for 13 passengers with six seats starboard side and seven port side.

Weights: Loaded 61,860 lb., maximum permissible 65,000 lb.; Empty (but equipped and furnished) 36,190 lb.; Wing loading at normal loaded weight 47.6 lb./sq. ft.

Performance: Range 2,820 miles at 230 m.p.h. at 20,000 ft. with 7,500 lb. payload.

Construction: As Mk. I but with windows both sides.

Lancastrian C.IV

Built as the military 13-seat version for the R.A.F. the eight C.IVs (TX283-290) were disposed to civil operators early in 1947, and declared obsolete for R.A.F. purposes in April that year. TX287-289 went to British Aviation Services and the remainder to Skyways, but some of these changed hands later.

Lancastrian C.2 used as Rolls-Royce Nene test bed.

Nene Lancastrian

Two Lancastrian IVs, VH737 and VH742, were fitted with 5,000 lb. static thrust Rolls-Royce Nene RB41 turbojet engines outboard and had fuselages modified to accommodate extra fuel to a total of 2,385 gall. of kerosene and 740 gall. of petrol, which raised the gross weight to 62,570 lb. Alterations were made to main spar, ailerons, flap and the engine control system.

The first to fly with Nenes was VH742 on August 14th, 1946; the following October it went to Hucknall, where it remained for exactly five years on test flying, during which

time it flew over 600 hours. VH737, with its inboard T.24s replaced by Merlin 621s, flew over 400 hours on engine and icing tests from Church Broughton, Hucknall and Farnborough from late 1945 until dismantled at Woodford at the end of 1955.

Long Range Lancastrian

In 1951 a special long-range Lancastrian was projected to the requirement of the Royal Egyptian Air Force with 2 x 504 gall. auxiliary fuel tanks in the fuselage below the cabin.

Avro 696 Prototypes to A.M. Spec. R.5/46

The Shackleton evolved from the Lincoln (see chapter nineteen) and superseded the Lancaster G.R.3 in service. Three prototypes, VW126, VW131 and VW135, were built.

VW135, the third of the Shackleton prototypes.

Shackleton G.R.1/M.R.1, M.R.2, M.R.3, T.4

The Shackleton's history is briefed in chapter nineteen. An initial production order for a general reconnaissance version of the Lincoln was ordered on March 21st, 1946, before the final form was set, which accounts for the first production batch serial numbers, VP254-268, 281-294, preceding in order those of the prototypes.

Inflatable dinghies later replaced lifeboats on Shackletons.

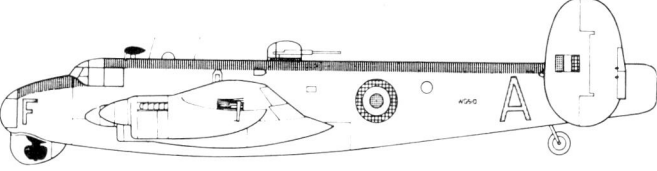

Shackleton M.R.1 of No. 42 Squadron, August 1953.

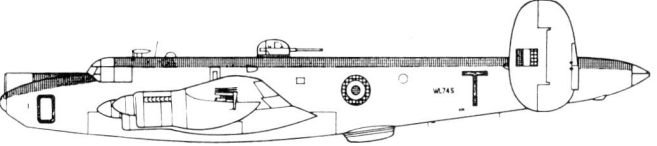

Shackleton M.R.2 of No. 220 Squadron, 1953.

White-topped, glossy sea-grey, Shackleton M.R.2 WR966, **1962.**

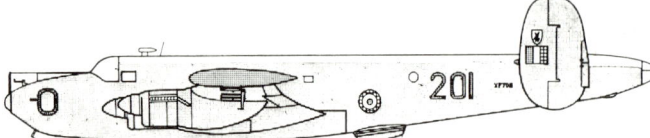

Shackleton M.R.3 WF708 as at St. Mawgan, April 1959.

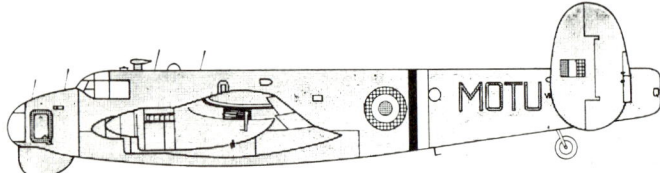

Overall sea-grey Shackleton T.4 ex-M.R.1 VP259, Kinloss, 1957.

Detail Data

Power Units and Airscrews: 4 x 2,450 Rolls-Royce Griffon 67 or 57A engines driving De Havilland 8-blade, contra-rotating airscrews of 13 ft. diameter.

Crew: (M.R.1) 10. Pilot (captain) in side-by-side seating with second pilot, flight engineer, navigator/air bomber, radio operator and air gunners.

Armament: 2 x 20 mm. guns in nose (except G.R.1) 2 x 20 mm. cannon in remotely controlled Bristol B.17 turret initially, but later removed.

Dimensions: Span 120 ft. 0 in. (M.R.1/2), 119 ft. 10 in. (M.R.3); Length 77 ft. 6 in. (M.R.1), 87 ft. 4 in. (M.R.2), 92 ft. 9 in. (M.R.3); Height 17ft. 6 in. (M.R.1), 16 ft. 9 in. (M.R.2), 23 ft. 4 in. (M.R.3); Wing Area (total) 1,421 sq. ft., Dihedral 4 deg., Incidence 4 deg., Track 23 ft. 9 in.

Weights: Loaded 100,000 lb. approx., Tare 57,800 lb.

Performance: Maximum speed 302 m.p.h. at 12,000 ft. loaded to 85,000 lb. Range at cruising speed of 200 m.p.h. at 1,500 ft.—4,215 miles. Service ceiling 19,200 ft. Rate of climb from sea level 850 ft./min., Take-off distance

to 50 ft., 4,4750 ft. (M.R.3). The M.R.2 had a 3,660 miles range and speed of 300 m.p.h. at 12,000 ft.

Fuel Capacity: Varied according to version.

Construction: Of a light alloy, stressed skin, structure, following the basic constructional principles of the Lancaster, the Shackleton wings and fuselage are both built in five sections. The wings, of NACA 23018 section at root, and the undercarriage are substantially the same as for the Lincoln, but the fuselage and tail unit were of completely new design.

Shackleton M.R.2 WR958 with " dust-bin " extended.

The M.R.2 had the chin radome deleted and re-positioned in retractable " dust-bin " aft of the bomb-bay and single fixed tail-wheel replaced by retractable two-wheel assembly; the tail position was fitted with a transparent cone as illustrated.

The M.R.3 had a revised cockpit canopy, tricycle undercarriage and wing-tip tanks.

The T.4 was a maritime trainer conversion of the M.R.1.

Prototype M.R.3 Shackleton prior to service testing.

A Shackleton M.R.3 of No. 120 Squadron, 1962.

MANCHESTER/LANCASTER LOG
* All crew survived   † All crew killed

The production orders and details of contracts are listed below in alphabetical/numerical sequence of serial numbers which is the chronological order of the placing of the contracts.

To record the most information in the minimum of space, shortened abbreviations have been used; the full explanation is given in the Glossary. Where two consecutively numbered aircraft had similar histories, the facts have been integrated in one line and the details, e.g. R5562-3 Missing 1Jul/20Aug42, may be taken as respective dates in 1942. Abbreviations 1654/62 CUs may be taken as service in both Nos. 1654 and 1662 CUs. All entries are in chronological sequence. Letters in brackets are the code letters the aircraft bore in service with the particular unit or squadron given. The place names given in brackets are the targets for the operation on which the aircraft was reported

lost. All aircraft given as lost or missing may be taken as on operations unless otherwise stated. All dates for units are the dates that the aircraft was allotted to the unit. Where total flying hours are known these have been given as a final entry, but apart from that the final entry normally records the final fate of the aircraft. Where a crash is given as the last entry it may be assumed that it was sufficiently serious to warrant the aircraft being struck off charge (SOC). The official dates for aircraft struck off charge have not been given, since this is a purely administrative date when the decision was taken to delete the aircraft from records; the final date in this record is the date of the cause of its deletion, i.e. date of crash or date first reported over-due. In many cases where bombers were lost on night raids it cannot be ascertained if the loss occurred late one night or early next morning, hence the entries, e.g. 7/8Sep44, which infer that the aircraft set out on the night of September 7th, but did not return from operations in the morning of September 8th.

Serials L7246 and L7247
Manchester Prototypes

Two prototypes ordered from A. V. Roe (Manchester) September 8th, 1936, to Air Ministry Specification P.13/36. L7246 first flew from Ringway on July 25th, 1939, and L7247 on May 26th, 1940; they became 3422M and 2738M respectively.

The second prototype and first armed Manchester, L7247.

Serial Range L7276-L7584
Manchester I/Lancaster I

200 Manchesters ordered from A. V. Roe (Manchester) in August 1936 to Air Ministry Specification 19/37 and built as 157 Manchester I/IA from July 31, 1940, and 43 Lancaster I from October 1941 to March 1942.

Manchesters

L7276 AAEE 5Aug40; 61Sq;25 OTU,TDU Dec42,Wrecked 31Oct43
L7277 AAEE 25Oct40; 1654CU, Crashed N.Scarle 2Mar43
L7278 207Sq(EM.A) 10Nov40, Hit trees and burnt out 21Mar41
L7279 6MU 21Oct40,207Sq 6Nov40, RAE, SOC 11Oct43
L7280 207Sq Dec.40,44 ConFlt,83Sq,1654,1660CUs,SOC15Aug43
L7281 AAEE 7Dec40,1654Flt,49Sq, 1661CU,SOC14Sep43. 327hrs
L7282 207Sq Dec40,97Sq Feb41, Grounded at 12STT Jan43
L7283 207Sq,25 OTU,97Sq,1660CU,10AGS Jun43, Became 3743M

The fifth production Manchester, L7280, being assembled.

L7284 207Sq(EM ·D)Nov40,61Sq Apr41,39MU, SOC 18Jun43
L7285 37MU Jul41,83Sq Apr42,RAE, 39MU, SOC Oct42
L7286 207Sq,61Con Flt,83Sq,1660CU,SOC Mar43, 218hrs

Early production Manchester I, L7287.

L7287 86Sq Apr42, 49Sq, Missing(Emden) 6Jun42. 55hrs
L7288 207(EM ·H),97,61Sqs,1654Con Flt, Waddington May43
L7289 83Sq,50Sq Jun42, Lost raiding Bremen 25/26Jun42
L7290 207,97Sqs; 1654Con Flt,49Sq, Lost 30/31May42
L7291 207,97,106,50Sqs; 1654CU, Burnt in crash 4Apr43
L7292 207,97,61Sqs; 39MU,TDU Dec42,SOC 6Nov43
L7293 37MU,R-R; 83,49,61,207Sqs; 1660CU, Became 3773M
L7294 207,97,61Sqs; 1654CU, Stalled and burnt Wigsley 15Apr43
L7295 R-R 4Dec40 for engine tests. Undershot Ternhill 26May41
L7296 49Sq(Y)Con Flt,1661 CU, Benson, SOC 18Apr43
L7297 R-R Derby,83Sq,1661CU, Overshot Winthorpe 19May43
L7298 207,97Sqs, 1654CU, Undershot Wigsley 1Sep42
L7299 207Sq Jan41, 97Sq Feb41, 39MU, SOC 31Oct43
L7300 207Sq(EM ·S), Crashed in lake near Waddington 23Nov41
L7301 50Sq, VC's aircraft see chap 2. Lost 30/31May42
L7302 207Sq(EM ·R), Missing with squadron C.O. 8Apr41
L7303 207Sq(EM ·P), AFDU trials Mar41, Shot down 27Mar41
L7304 207Sq Feb41, 61Sq Apr41, Missing 26Jun41
L7305 Trials a/c, 25 OTU, 106Sq, 3SofTT Sep43, Became 4279M
L7306 97Sq, crash-landed, burnt out, 13Sep41. Crew saved.

L7307 61,97Sqs; 25 OTU;1654/60/68CUs; 5LFS, Became 4118M
L7308 97,49Sqs; 1656CU; Crashed May43
L7309 207Sq(EM ·J), 97Sq,207Sq(EM ·S), Lost 15Jan42
L7310 207Sq(EM ·H), Crashed after take-off 21Jan41
L7311-2 207Sq(EM ·F/L) 22Feb41, Missing 16Aug/13Nov41
L7313 207Sq 27Feb41, Burnt out 13Mar41
L7314 207Sq(EM ·Y), Shot down by Beaufighter 21Jun41
L7315 46MU; 97,61Sqs; Burnt in crash 29Jun41
L7316 27MU,207Sq(EM ·U) 13Apr41. Lost (Essen) 31Aug41
L7317 207,106Sqs; Forced down near Lee-on-Solent 14Apr42
L7318 207Sq(EM ·K) 6Mar41, Burnt out Sep41
L7319 207Sq(EM ·X), Shot down near base by intruder 13Mar42

Early production Manchester 1A, L7320, November 1941.

L7320 AAEE 23Mar41, Crashed on test 12Dec41, 118hrs
L7321 207Sq(EM ·D) 17Mar41, Lost (Nuremburg) 14Oct41
L7322 207Sq(EM ·B) (EM ·Q), Missing from Brest raid 8Jan42
L7323-4 97Sq 4Apr41, Missing 12Aug/16May41. 32/31hrs
L7325 97Sq, 25 OTU, 9Sq, 12SofTT Jun43, Became 3751M
L7373 AAEE 13Apr41, 207Sq(EM ·T) Aug41, Missing 14Oct41
L7374 97Sq 17Apr41, Missing 27Jun41. 82hrs
L7375 97Sq(OF ·B), Crashed 28Sep41 4 miles N. of Boston
L7376 25 OTU Dec41, 106Sq,1654CU,3AGS, Became 3747M
L7377 207Sq(EM ·G) 13Apr41, Missing 13Aug41
L7378 207,106,50Sqs; 1654CU,12SofTT Jun43. Became 3752M
L7379-80 207Sq(EM ·T/EM ·W) Apr41, Missing 23May/8Sep41
L7381 207Sq(EM ·R) 15Apr41, Missing 13Aug41
L7382 97,83,44,83Sqs; 6AGS, Became 3753M
L7383 61Sq 16Apr41, SOC 26Sep41
L7384 97Sq 23Apr41, Accident 13May41, Missing 14/15Aug41
L7385 83(OL ·C),44,207Sqs. Collided with R5550 6Aug42
L7386 49,9,57Sqs; Crashed on fire at Scampton Oct42
L7387 61,97,83(OL ·A),49Sqs; Crashed 21Jun42. 221hrs
L7388 61Sq 24Apr41, Missing 2Sep41
L7389 61,207,83,49,106Sqs; 1660CU 1SofTT, Became 3763M
L7390 106Sq, Crashed in Holland after Essen raid 25Mar42
L7391 207,106Sqs; 1485 Con Flt, Crashed 11Feb43. 160hrs
L7392 AFEE Ringway 9Feb42, 39MU Sep42, SOC Oct43
L7393 207Sq(EM ·V) Apr41, Crashed and became 2600M Aug41
L7394 83,106Sqs; Lost mining 29Mar42
L7395 61Sq, Abandoned over Wittering after raid 13Mar42
L7396 Avro 3Jan42, 61Sq 21Jan42, Missing 31Jan42
L7397 83,49,207Sqs; 1660CU, Became 3762M
L7398 97,106,49,97Sqs; 1661,1660CUs; Scrap 30Apr43. 286hrs
L7399 106Sq 28Apr42,Lost mining 3/4May42
L7400 RAE,1654CU, Scrap May43. 367hrs
L7401 408Sq,1654CU,1485TT Flt,1654/61CUs, Wrecked 15Oct43
L7402 420 Con Flt, 1661CU, SOC Mar43
L7415 50,61,408Sqs,1654/60/61CUs; SOC Oct43. 267hrs
L7416 1654CU, Crashed into trees landing 30Aug42. Crew saved
L7417 106Sq, Missing 19May42 on cross-country flight
L7418 Woodford Feb42; 83,106Sqs; Missing 20May42
L7419 207,50,408Sqs; 1654CU(UG ·B),4AGS, Became 3748M
L7420 25 OTU,49Sq,1660/61CUs, Used by USAAF for ditching
       training 1945 and RAF later. Dumped sandpit, Lincs, 1956
L7421 25 OTU Jan41; 49,97Sqs; 1660CU, Wrecked 16Nov43
L7422 207Sq(EM ·V) 20May41, Crashed 1Sep41, 70hrs
L7423 97Sq(OF ·S), 83Sq Jan42, Missing 13Mar42
L7424 97Sq 1Jun41, Missing 12Aug41
L7425 97,207,50,408Sqs; 1661CU, 8AGS. Became 3741M
L7426 61Sq Jun41, 83Sq Dec41, Down off Holland 9Mar42
L7427 97Sq Jun41, 83Sq(OL ·Q) (OL ·J), Missing 8/9Apr42
L7428 25 OTU Jul41. Crashed Scaftworth 18Nov41. 50hrs

L7429 25 OTU; 97,49Sqs; Missing (Cologne) 30/31May42
L7430 25 OTU Jul41, 44 Con Flt, 1661/54CUs; SOC Sep43
L7431 25 OTU 4Jul41, 1654CU, Became 3772M
L7432 207Sq(EM ·Z),50Sq, Missing (Bremen) 3/4Jun42. 246hrs
L7433 6MU Jul41, 61Sq Dec41, Missing 16Feb42
L7434 25 OTU, 106Sq, 1656CU, 39MU, Became 4221M
L7453 97(OF ·X),83,49,44Sqs; 1661CU, Wrecked 1May43
L7454 207Sq(EM ·M),61Sq Feb42, Missing 29Mar42. 81hrs
L7455 207(EM ·G),50,9Sqs; 1661CU, 8AGS. Became 3742M
L7456 25 OTU, 50Sq, 106Sq, Missing Cologne raid 30May42
L7457 97Sq(OF ·Y), 1654CU, Crashed W. Bank Saxilby 24Jan43
L7458 83,61(QR ·E)Sqs; 1660CU, 3SofTT. Became 4280M
L7459 97Sq; Crashed after practise bomb exploded 8Jan42
L7460 97,83,50,57Sqs; 1656Con Flt Oct42, SOC Jul43
L7461 97,106Sqs; 1661/54/60CUs; 3SofTT. Became 4278M
L7462 97Sq 26Sep41, Missing (Hamburg) 26Oct41
L7463 97Sq,106Sq Jan42. Missing 23/24Apr42
L7464 61,50,57Sqs; 460Sq, 1AAS Mar43, Became 3624M
L7465 Avro Jul41, 83Sq(OL ·H) Dec41, Lost 25/26Mar42
L7466 97Sq(OF ·N) 26Sep41, Missing 8Nov41
L7467 25 OTU,97Sq Con Flt, 1661OCU, Wrecked 25Sep43
L7468 207,50,9Sqs; 1660CU, 12SofTT Jun43. Became 3732M
L7469 25 OTU,49Sq, Missing Emden raid 6Jun42
L7470 61Sq 11Oct41, Missing 8Apr42
L7471 61(QR ·V),50Sqs; Lost in Emden harbour raid 6/7Jun42
L7472 61Sq, Missing on Brest raid 31Jan/1Feb42
L7473 97(OF ·H),61Sqs; 1485B&GFlt, Crash Dunholm 6Oct42
L7474 97,106Sqs, Abandoned over Winceby 12Mar43
L7475 97Sq Oct41, 61Sq,50Sq Apr42, Burnt in crash 16Aug42
L7476 97(OF ·K),207,50Sqs; 1654CU, SOC Apr43
L7477 61Sq Oct41, 1661CU,1485Flt,1654CU, SOC 1943
L7478 38MU,25 OTU Dec42, Wrecked in crash 16Feb43
L7479 25 OTU,48Sq, Missing (Cologne) 30/31May42
L7480 207,61,50,44Sqs; 1661CU, Scrap 30Apr43, 261hrs
L7481 25 OTU. 44 Con Flt,1661CU, SOC Sep43. 323hrs
L7482 25 OTU. 97 Con Flt, 1660CU, Abandoned due to icing and
       fell at Highfield Farm, Metheringham 2Jan43
L7483 207Sq(EM ·H)(EM ·O);10AGS,12STT Jun43,Became 3749M
L7484 49,408,9Sqs; 1458Flt, 1AGS, Became 3776M
L7485 207Sq(EM ·G) Sep41, 106Sq Mar42, Missing 16/17Apr42
L7486 207Sq(EM ·P),50Sq, Stalled Skellingthorpe 14Jan42
L7487 207Sq(EM ·N), Lost in sea 10 miles N. of Yarmouth 21Oct41
L7488 97,207,106,50Sqs; 1654CU, 12SofTT Jun43, Became 3750M
L7489 97Sq(OF ·T),50Sq, Abandoned (Warnemunde) 9May42
L7490 25 OTU,97Sq(OF ·U) Sep41, Wrecked 18Dec41. 89hrs
L7491 97Sq,1654CU, Swung on take-off, Wigsley 17May43
L7492 97,61,50Sqs; 1485Flt,1654CU,4AOS. Became 3985M
L7493 25 OTU,49Sq Aug43,1661CU,SOC Oct43. 392hrs
L7494 61Sq, Lost attacking Bologne docks 7/8Dec41
L7495 61Sq, Abandoned 16Jan42. Fell at Grimoldby
L7496 61Sq,1654CU, Crashed and burnt at Wigsby 5Jul42
L7497 61Sq 10Oct41, Missing 27Mar42
L7515 207Sq Oct41; 106,49Sqs; 1656CU, SOC Nov43
L7516 61Sq,50Sq Apr42, Lost mining 29/30Apr42
L7517 Damaged by fire before delivery. Scrap Dec41
L7518 61Sq 15Oct41, Lost off Bergen-am-Zee 25Mar42
L7519 61,50Sqs, Burnt out at Thorlby, Lincs 13May42
L7520 61Sq 21Oct41, Crashed 2Nov41
L7521 61,50Sqs, Crashed Waddington 5Sep42. 347hrs
L7522 97Sq(OF ·V), 83Sq Jan42, Missing 22Feb42
L7523 207Sq, Crashed Cliff Farm near Withernsea 14Jan42
L7524 25 OTU,49Sq,1485Flt,1661/68CUs, SOC Oct43. 276hrs
L7525 97,106,83,50Sqs; 1485Flt,1661CU, SOC Aug43. 423hrs
L7526 25 OTU Nov41; 49,207Sqs; 1656CU Oct42, SOC Jul43

Lancasters

L7527 AAEE Oct41 AvroApr42,1654CU,15Sq Mar44,Lost27Mar44
L7528 TFU Hurn 11Nov41, Woodford 24Dec41, AFEE, SOC Jul44
L7529 AAEE 15Nov41, Modified by Avro Mar42, Crashed 1May42
L7530 44Sq 28Dec41, 207 Con Flt 25Feb42, SOC 12Feb43
L7531 44Sq 6Jan42; Crashed on take-off, Coningsby 23Apr42
L7532 44,97,61,207Sqs; 1654CU, 3LFS (A5 ·P), 90Sq, Scrap Oct46
L7533 44Sq(KM ·K), Missing 8/9May42
L7534 44Sq(KM ·F),50Sq Jul42, Crashed 14Aug42. 70hrs

L7535 AAEE Dec41, Became 3107M at 4STT and 12STT
L7536 44Sq(KM ·H), Shot down near Bernay 17Apr42
L7537 44Sq(KM ·L) 24Dec41, Missing 3Jul42. 65hrs
L7538 44Sq(KM ·B) 24Dec41, 97Sq Jan42, Crashed 20Feb42
L7539 44Sq(KM ·G)Dec41,50Sq,1654CU,463Sq,10MU,SOCDec46
L7540 44Sq Jan42; 83,207ConFlts, 1654CU, 5LFS SOC Apr44
L7541 44Sq, 1654/60CUs,300Sq,1LFS,1667/2/8CUs, SOC Jun45
L7542 44Sq Jan42, Crashed 7Feb42, 6hrs
L7543 44Sq Jan42, 207Sq Apr42, Missing 12Jul42. 133hrs
L7544 44,207Sqs; 1667/62/51/54CUs, 3LFS; SOC May45
L7545 44Sq. 1654CU, Collided with Oxford AB665 over Barton
    Lodge, Melton Mowbray 8Apr43
L7546 44Sq 17Jan42, Avro wing tests 207Sq, Lost 8Nov42
L7547 44Sq, 207Sq(EM ·M) Sep42, Lost (Milan) 15Feb43. 208hrs

Early production Lancaster I, L7548, January 1942.

L7548 44Sq(KM ·T) Shot down by fighters (Augsburg) 17Apr42
L7549 44Sq(KM ·Q) Jan42, Crashed 23Apr42
L7565 44Sq(KM ·V) Shot down by fighters (Augsburg) 17Apr42
L7566 44Sq First Lancaster to operate. Became 5792M
L7567 44Sq Jan42, 49Sq, Missing 9Jul42. 76hrs
L7568 Avro 1Mar41, 83Sq Apr42, Crashed 10Jul42. 131hrs
L7569 44Sq. 61,106Sqs, Became 4166M at 4STT
L7570 97Sq(OF ·B), Missing 20Mar43
L7571 97Sq 16Feb42, 61Sq May42, Lost with 207Sq 17Sep42
L7572 97Sq(OF ·L) 13Mar42, Lost at Trondheim 27/28Apr42
L7573 97Sq(OF ·K) Feb42, Shot down at Augsburg 17Apr42
L7574 97Sq 17Feb42, 61Sq Nov43, Lost 22Nov43. 334hrs
L7575 97Sq(OF ·Y), 1654CU, Broke up in the air over Warren
    Farm, Colney Hatch, 22Oct43
L7576 97Sq, 622Sq(GI ·K), Jul44, Lost (Stuttgart) 29Jul44. 538hrs
L7577 97Sq(OF ·T) 25Feb42; 1660, 1654CUs. Became 3610M
L7578 207Sq 8Mar42, 83Sq,1654/68CUs,5LFS, Burnt May44
L7579 106Sq, 1654CU, ECFS Dec43, SOC Oct45
L7580 207Sq(EM ·O) 17Mar42,(EM ·C)May42, 5LFS, SOC Nov45
L7581 44Sq(KM ·R) Mar42, Crashed and burnt at base 20May42
L7582 207,106,100Sqs; 1667CU, 1LFS, Became 5453M
L7583 207Sq(EM ·A), 1661CU(GP ·X), 5LFS, Scrap Nov46
L7584 44Sq(KM ·S) Mar42, Crashed 22Aug42. 173hrs

Serial Range R4525—R4744
Manchester
150 Manchester ordered from Fairey Aviation in September 1939 and cancelled. R4525-4554, R4572-4611, R4630-4649, R4670-4694, R4710-4744.

Serial Range R5273—R5477
Manchester
150 Manchesters ordered from Armstrong Whitworth Aircraft in September 1939 and cancelled. R5273-5320, R5339-5380, R5397-5426, R5448-5477.

Serial Range R5482—R5763
Lancaster I
200 Manchesters ordered from A. V. Roe (Manchester) September 1939 and built as Lancaster I delivered from February to July 1942 with Merlin 20 engines. Those remaining operational in early 1943 had Merlin 22s substituted.

R5482 97Sq(OF ·C) Feb42, 101Sq Oct42, Crashed 10Dec42. 84hrs
R5483 97Sq Feb42, 1654CU Apr43, 622Sq, Lost 24Jan44. 450hrs
R5484 44Sq Mar42, 83Sq(OL ·V)Mar43, Lost 17Apr43. 67hrs
R5485 102Sq, TFU, 1657CU, 467Sq, Lost 19Jul44. 542hrs
R5486 97Sq Coningsby 24Feb42, Crashed 24Feb42
R5487 97Sq(OF ·V) 28Feb42, Missing 27Jul42. 174hrs
R5488 97Sq(OF ·F), 61Sq(QR ·F), Mar42, Missing 4Jul42. 123hrs

R5489 Named GEORGE by King George VI, 44Sq, Crashed at
    Branston 16Aug42. 115hrs
R5490 97Sq Feb42-43, 1654CU; 622,15Sqs; 5MU, Scrap Jan48
R5491 61Sq, 24MU, 1656CU Oct42, Wrecked 28May43
R5492 44,106Sqs; 1661CU; Dived into ground, Exeter, 3Sep43
R5493 44Sq, First Lancaster lost on operations, 24Mar42. 6hrs
R5494 44Sq(KM ·O) Mar43, Burst into flames 7Jul42. 97hrs
R5495 97Sq Coningsby 10Mar42, Missing 8/9Jun42. 119hrs
R5496-7 97Sq(OF ·U/Z) Mar42, Lost 5Sep/18Dec42, 155/38hrs
R5498 207Sq, Crashed on road at Bottesford 8Apr42
R5499 207 Con Flt Bottesford, Lost 11Aug42. 176hrs
R5500 207,460Sqs; 1656,1667CUs; 1LFS, Became 4902M 4STT
R5501 207Sq, Struck by Master DK973 and crashed 28Mar42
R5502 97Sq(OF ·M) 15Mar42, Missing 29Aug42. 192hrs
R5503 207Sq,1660CU,50Sq,1664/1651CUs. Became 5452M
R5504 207Sq(EM ·P) Mar42, 1660CU Feb43, Became 3881M 4STT
R5505 207,61Sqs, ECFS Jan43, MUs, Broken up Jan47
R5506 44Sq(KM ·P), Shot down 17Apr42 in Augsburg raid
R5507 207Sq Apr-Nov42, 101Sq,ILFS,VariousCUs. SOC Nov45
R5508 44Sq(KM ·B) Aircraft in which W/C Nettleton won his V.C.
    17Apr42, 1660CU Oct42, 38MU,15Sq(LS ·C), SOC Jan47
R5509 207Sq Bottesford 12Apr42, Missing 17Aug42. 108hrs
R5510 44Sq(KM ·A), Shot down 17Apr42 over Augsburg
R5511 61Sq Apr42; 1654,1656CUs. Became 3606M
R5512 97Sq(OF ·C) Mar42, Crashed in Holland 21Dec42 359hrs
R5513 97Sq(OF ·P), Missing on Augsburg raid 17Apr42
R5514 44,156Sqs; 1654CU,622Sq,3LFS,90Sq, Scrap Nov46
R5515 44Sq(KM ·A) 17Apr42, Fell in N. Sea 6Jun42. 81hrs
R5516 44Sq(KM ·F) 4Apr42, Missing 5/6Jun42. 82hrs
R5517 AAFE,61Sq 2May42, Missing 23Jun42. 67hrs
R5537 97Sq(OF ·B) Coningsby 4Apr42, Lost 25Aug42. 120hrs
R5538 97Sq Apr42, 1660CU Dec42, Became 3481M
R5539 AAEE, Dived into ground on test 18Apr42. 15hrs
R5540 61Sq,44 Con Flt, 1661CU, Crashed 28Jan43
R5541 97Sq 24Apr42, Crashed near Wragsby 30Apr42
R5542 44Sq,106 Con Flt,24MU,46MU,83Sq,1667CU,3LFS,54MU,
    3LFS; 1660,1661CUs; SOC Oct45 after five crashes
R5543 61Sq N. Luffenham Apr42, Damaged 20Aug42. 177hrs
R5544 61Sq N. Luffenham Apr42, Missing 1/2Jun42. 18hrs
R5545 61Sq N. Luffenham Apr42, Crashed 1May42
R5546 Handling Sq AAEE Apr42,50Sq, Lost 31Mar44. 502hrs
R5547 44Sq,1661CU, Crashed 8Sep43 at Balderton. 506hrs
R5548 Named ELIZABETH, 97Sq(OF ·A), Crash 28Dec42. 261hrs
R5549 207Sq,1661CU,12Sq,1667CU,1LFS,1656CU, SOC Nov44
R5550 207Sq(EM ·B), Burnt on Bottesford flarepath. See L7385
R5551 97Sq, 106Sq May42, Missing 15Jun43. 365hrs
R5552 97Sq(OF ·P), 20MU, 166Sq, Missing 20/21Dec43
R5553 97Sq May42, Damaged on operations 6May42
R5454-5 44Sq Apr42, Missing 20Sep42 and 8/9May42

Lancaster I R5482 in February 1942.

R5556 44Sq(KM ·C) Apr42, 1661CU, Crashed 13Mar43. 304hrs
R5557 44Sq Waddington 24Apr42, Missing 9May42
R5558 97Sq Coningsby Apr42, Missing 14Jul42. 61hrs.
R5559 97Sq Apr42, 1662CU Feb43, Became 3605M
R5560 61Sq Apr42, 1654CU Oct42, Became 3471M
R5561 61Sq 27Apr42, Missing 30/31May42. 37hrs
R5562-3 61Sq 26Apr42, Missing 1Jul/20Aug42. 64/45hrs
R5564 83Sq Apr42, Missing 2Jun42. 47 hrs
R5565 83Sq,46MU,83Sq,NTU,61Sq, Missing 22Jan44. 308hrs
R5566 83 Con Flt Apr42, 83Sq Sep42, Lost 7Nov42. 149hrs
R5567 83 Con Flt, 83Sq Sep42, Crashed 26Sep42. 171hrs
R5568 44Sq 30Apr42, Missing 8/9May42
R5569 97Sq 1May42, Crashed on operations 14Nov42, 134hrs
R5570 207Sq(EM ·F) May42, Missing 9Dec42. 230hrs

R5571 97Sq 15May42, Missing 3Jun42, 12hrs
R5572 97Sq 15May, 106Sq Apr43, Missing 26Jun43. 424hrs
R5573-4 106Sq May42, Lost 9Jul43/22Dec42. 477/121hrs
R5575 97Sq, 106 Con Flt, 97Sq, Missing 17Jan43. 100hrs
R5576 106Sq May42, Destroyed by fire 21Jul42. 58hrs
R5603 44Sq(KM ·D) 7May42, Missing 4/5Aug42. 116hrs
R5604 97Sq 15May42, Missing 1Aug42. 25hrs
R5605 61Sq Jun42, Missing over Atlantic 21Aug42. 105hrs
R5606 AFEE May42-May43, Became 4130M at 4STT
R5607 97Sq (RAE in Jun42), Missing 12Mar43. 251hrs
R5608 106Sq 10May42, Missing 26Jul42. 72hrs
R5609 97Sq,TFU,AAEE;97,106Sqs;1LFS,1662CU, Became 5288M
22 R5610 83Sq(OL ·G) May42, Missing 25Aug42. 141hrs
R5611 RAE May42, 106Sq Oct42, Missing 14May43. 239hrs
R5612 97Sq,RAE,97Sq,106Sq,ETPS,38MU, Scrap 22May47
R5613 61Sq 16May42, Missing 2/3Jun42. 24hrs
R5614 97,106Sqs Apr43, Crashed and burnt 1Aug43. 440hrs
R5615 61Sq 16May42, Missing 28Jun42. 79hrs
R5616 207Sq 19May42, Missing 17Aug42. 147hrs
R5617 44Sq 19May42, Crashed and burnt 25May42
R5618 61Sq,20MU,1654CU,54MU,5MU, Scrap May47
R5619 83Sq May42, Accident 4Jun42, Missing 26Jul42. 85hrs
R5620 83Sq 19May42, SOC 26Jun42. 46hrs
R5621 83Sq 20May42, Damaged 11Jun42 and SOC. 29hrs
R5622-3 83Sq 23May43, Missing 18Apr/25Aug43. 247/82hrs
R5624 44Sq May42, 1661CU Nov42; 24,46,5MUs; Scrap May47
R5625 83,50,83Sqs; 38MU,622Sq, Missing 9/10Jul44. 535hrs
R5626 83Sq except for 50Sq in Jul42, Lost 4Apr43. 273hrs
R5627 61Sq 27May42, Missing 3/4Jun42. 13hrs
R5628 207Sq May42, Missing 10Sep42. 105hrs
R5629 83Sq(OL ·J) 25May42, Missing 6May43. 342hrs.
R5630 83Sq(OL ·T) 24May42, Missing 17Jan43. 221hrs
R5631 44Sq,106 Con Flt, 1660CU,3LFS,90Sq, Became 5052M
R5632-3 207Sq 2May42, Lost 24Jul/13Aug42. 103/139hrs
R5634 97Sq,38MU,1667CU,24MU,5MU, Scrap May47
R5635 207Sq 1Jun42, 1661CU Feb43, Became 3508M
R5636 83Sq 1Jun42, Damaged beyond repair 11Jun42.16hrs
R5637 106Sq Jun42, Damaged 28Jan43, Missing 30Jan43
R5638 106Sq 7Jun42, Missing 11Sep42, 118hrs
R5639 50Sq 5Jun42, Lost (Osnabruck) 17/18Aug42. 99hrs
R5640 83Sq 2Jun42, SOC 30Jun42. 9hrs
R5658 49Sq,1654CU,38MU,1668CU,5LFS. SOC May47
R5659 83Sq 2Jun42, SOC 8Jun42. 16hrs
R5660 AFEE, 50 Con Flt, 1654CU, Crashed 30Oct42
R5661 61Sq 7Jun42, Lost 19Aug42 over Atlantic. 152hrs.
R5662 61Sq 8Jun42, Missing 25Aug42. 127hrs
R5663 61Sq 7Jun42, Missing 4Jul42 over Atlantic. 41hrs
R5664 44Sq, Middle East 7Jul42, Damaged 28Aug42. 78hrs
R5665 44Sq Jun-Oct42, 106Sq(ZN ·D) Nov42, Lost 31Jul43. 487hrs
R5666 44Sq(KM ·F) 9Jun42, Lost (Nuremburg) 18Dec42. 289hrs
R5667 83Sq,1656CU Oct42, 1657CU, Crashed 19Aug43. 341hrs
R5668 106,207Sqs; DBU,1661CU,5LFS, Became 4901M 4STT
R5669 83Sq(OL ·E), 44Sq(KM ·Z) Sep43, Lost (Berlin) 24Dec43
R5670 83Sq 11Jun42, Burnt in accident 7Nov42. 168hrs
R5671 83Sq(OL ·F),NTU,1656CU,LFS,MUs,EANS, Scrap Jan47
R5672 97Sq Jun42, 39MU,1656CU,1LFS, Crash 9Apr44. 695hrs
R5673 83Sq(OL ·L) 15Jun42, Missing 7Nov42. 135hrs
R5674 207,103Sqs; 1662CU,54MU,3LFS, Hit R5846 18Dec44
R5675 97Sq 16Jun42, Missing 27/28Jun42. 10hrs
R5676 106Sq & Con Flt, 1660CU, Spun in 12Feb43. 208hrs
R5677 106Sq(ZN ·B) ex-39MU Jun42, Lost 30May43. 512hrs. 67ops
R5678 106Sq ex-39MU Jun42, Missing 16Aug42. 87hrs
R5679 61Sq 20Jun42, Missing 25Sep42. 16hrs
R5680 106Sq ex-39MU Jun42, Missing 15Jan43
R5681 106Sq 19Jun42, Lost on Essen raid 17Sep42. 123hrs
R5682 61Sq 20Jun42, Lost 4/5Sep42 over Bremen. 131hrs
R5683-4 106Sq Jun42, Missing 26Jul/25Aug42. 52/196hrs
R5685 50,44,460Sqs; 1667CU Jul43, Crash 30Sep43, 316hrs
R5686 207Sq,38MU Dec42, 83Sq Mar43, Lost 12Jun43. 176hrs
R5687 44,50Sqs Mar43, Lost (Hamburg) 27/28Jul43. 518hrs
R5688 50Sq,46MU,12Sq Apr43, Ditched 13/14May43. 69hrs*
R5689 50Sq(VN ·N) Jun42, Burnt returning on 19Sep42. 138hrs
R5690 50Sq,50 Con Flt,1654CU,3LFS(A5 ·S),46MU, SOC 28Oct46
R5691 50Sq 29Jun42, Missing (Milan) 4Oct42 213hrs

R5692 RAE,39MU,1667CU; 15,75,90Sqs; 3/5LFS, SOC May47
R5693 39MU Jun42, 207Sq Aug 42, 46MU,5MU, SOC May47
R5694 Middle East Jul42, 207Sq Sep42, Crash 25Nov42. 99hrs
R5695 39MU Jun42, 207Sq Sep42, Missing 26Nov42. 128hrs
R5696 97Sq 29Jun42, Missing 12Jul42. 11hrs
R5697 44Sq; Twice damaged, Missing 21Dec42. 248hrs
R5698 1654CU 4Aug42, Wrecked 1Sep43
R5699 61Sq 2Jul42, Crashed on operations 21Dec42. 346hrs
R5700 106Sq,5MU,9Sq(WS ·N) 29Jun43, Missing 22Sep43. 397hrs
R5701 97Sq 2Jul42, Missing 6Oct42. 137hrs
R5702 106,50,460,100,625Sqs, Lost 15/16Feb44. 147hrs
R5703 61Sq, Crashed after dinghy had inflated 1Oct42
20 R5724 61Sq, Damaged at Viborg, crashed Wittering 25Sep42
R5725 50Sq(VN ·F) 16Jul42, Lost (Dusseldorf) 10/11Sep42
R5726 50,44,100Sqs; 1662CU, 5MU, 5LFS, Crashed 4Apr44
R5727 44Sq, To Canada as pattern. Became CF-CMS
R5728 50Sq 7Jul42, Missing (Saarbrucken) 30Jul42. 30hrs
R5729 44Sq(KM ·A), Twice damaged, Missing 15Jan44
R5730 1654CU,5LFS,1656CU, Crash 15Mar45,MUs,SOC 29Jan4
R5731 106Sq, Crash 8Jan43, Missing (Hamburg) 4Mar43. 183hrs
R5732 44Sq 11Jul42, Crashed 11/12Aug42. 57hrs
R5733 50,44Sqs; 1654CU,5MU,3LFS,6LFS, Scrapped May47
R5734 1654CU,61Sq(QR ·V) Jan44, Missing 31Mar44. 529hrs
R5735 50Sq 12Jul42, Missing 15Aug42. 47hrs
R5736 1654CU,207Sq,1660CU, Crashed 6Jul43. 513hrs
R5737 61Sq 15Jul42, Missing 30Jul42. 12hrs
R5738 97Sq 13Jul42, Damaged on operations 10Jan43. 217hrs
R5739 1654CU,15Sq Dec 43, Missing 20Feb44. 810hrs
R5740 44Sq(KM ·O) Jul42, Missing 26Jun43. 416hrs
R5741 97Sq 15Jul42, Missing 2Sep42. 89hrs
R5742 61Sq 19Jul42, Missing 29Aug42. 32hrs
R5743 83Sq(OL ·H) Crash 18Nov42, Lost 19Feb43. 164hrs
R5744 49Sq Jul42, 9Sq(WS ·E) Dec42, Lost 5/6Sep43. 526hrs
R5745 207,460Sqs; Blown up at Binbrook 3Jul43
R5746 50Sq(VN ·Q) 23Jul42, Missing 12Aug42. 27hrs
R5747 50Sq,1654CU, Crash 21Jul43, Became 4371M
R5748 106Sq 23Jul42, Missing four days later. 8hrs
R5749-50 106Sq Jul42, Missing 13Mar/19Feb43. 88/320hrs
R5751 49,57Sqs; 1661CU,1LFS,1656/62/68CUs then 5257M
R5752 49Sq 21Jul42, Damaged operations 7Sep42. 63hrs
R5753 50Sq 23Jul42, Crashed 17Nov42. 186hrs
R5754 83Sq 25Jul42, Lost (Berlin) 29/30Mar43. 258hrs
R5755 207Sq Jul42, Wrecked Sep42
R5756 207Sq,46MU; 1667,1651,1660,1661CUs; SOC Oct45
R5757 49,156,61Sqs; 1661CU,5LFS,46MU, Scrap Jan47
R5758 207Sq,1660CU(YW ·J), Crash 3May43. 323hrs
R5759 61Sq 1Sep42, Missing Wismar raid 1/2Oct42. 51hrs
R5760-1 207Sq 26Jul42, Missing 13Aug/6Aug42. 43/27hrs
R5762 49Sq Jul42, Damaged 6Oct42, Missing 21Dec42. 201hrs
R5763 49Sq, 28Jul42, Missing 3Sep42.72hrs

Serial Range R5768—R5917 Manchester I/Lancaster I

100 Manchesters were ordered from Metropolitan Vickers in 1939 and built as 43 Manchester I and 57 Lancaster I delivered from March 1941 to August 1942 to A. V. Roe for assembly and testing.

Manchester I
R5768 Avro Mar41, 83Sq Apr42, 1660CU(TV ·A), SOC Nov43

The fourth Metrovick production Manchester I, R5771.

R5769 25OTU Mar42; 106,50,98Sqs; 1661CUs, SOC Dep43. 285hrs
R5770 106Sq, Flown by W/C Guy Gibson, Crash 1660CU 4Jul43

148

Crew of R5724 of No. 61 Squadron.

R5771 25OTU;48,420,57Sqs;1654CU,2AGS Aug43,Became 3746M
R5772 49Sq,25OTU,1654CU, Crashed near Wigsley 26Jan43
R5773 RAE,TDU Gosport May42, Became 3892M
R5774 TDU Apr42, 11 SofTT, Became 3890M
R5775 49,83Sqs; 1654/60CUs,3STT, Became 4281M
R5776 Avro Aug41, 1654 Con Flt, 1654CU, Became 3745M
R5777 Avro Jul41, 1654CU Jun42, 39MU,1654CU, SOC Oct43
R5778 Avro Sep41, 50Sq 25Jan42, Missing 9May42
R5779 Avro Sep41, 83Sq(OL·G) Dec41, Missing 9Mar42
R5780 8,106,49,57Sqs; 1656 Con Flt. Crashed Lichfield 19Oct42
R5781 Avro Aug41, 83Sq Jan42, Missing 28/29Mar42

R5784 of No. 50 Squadron, Hinton-in-the-Hedges, July 1942.

R5782 207,50Sqs Mar42, Missing (Hamburg) 17/18Apr42
R5783 Avro Sep41, 97Sq Sep41, Crashed, Frisking 21Oct41
R5784 61,50,9,57Sqs; 1485Flt,1660CU,9AFU, Became 3984M
R5785 Avro Sep41, 61Sq Oct41, Missing 11Apr42. 140hrs
R5786 61Sq Oct41, 50Sq Apr42, 1654CU, SOC 28Jan43
R5787 61Sq Oct41, Missing on Brest raid 31Jan/1Feb42
R5788 83,49Sqs; 1660CU,1AFU Jul43, Became 3983M
R5789 61Sq 20Oct41, Crashed 9Jan41. 6 of crew baled out
R5790 207,83,49,44Sqs; 1661CU, Became 3774M
R5791 207Sq(EM·V); 1457/85Flts,1654CU, Became 4001M
R5792 97Sq 29Oct41, Burnt in crash 24Nov41
R5793 25 OTU; 49,83Sqs; 1656CU,39MU, SOC May43
R5794 25 OTU,49Sq, Missing (Essen) 2Jun42. 137hrs
R5795 97Sq Nov41, Lost on Brest day raid 18Dec41
R5796 207(EM·W),106,57,50Sqs; 1654/60CUs, SOC Nov43
R5797 Ringway Feb42, Became 3778M
R5829 25 OTU Dec41, 1654 Con Flt, 3AGS, SOC Jul43
R5830 AAEE Jan42, 83Sq Feb42, 1656CU, SOC Nov43
R5831 83Sq(OL·I) 9Jan42, Missing 25/26Mar42. 82hrs
R5832 61Sq Jan42, 1660CU Oct42, Became 3744M. 410hrs
R5833 207,50Sqs; Lost mining near Ile de Quiberon 5/6Jun42
R5834 61Sq 28Jan42, SOC May42
R5835 207,83,49,408Sqs; 1654/61CUs; SOC Oct43. 471hrs
R5836 83,49Sqs; 1661CU, Wrecked landing Scampton 1Dec42
R5837 83Sq(OL·R) 13Feb42, In sea off Frisian Isles 8/9Oct42
R5838 83,9Sqs; 1661CU, Overshot Wickenby 12Mar42. Crew O.K.
R5839 106Sq Mar42, 49Sq,1661CU, SOC Oct43. 299hrs
R5840 106Sq 28Mar42, Lost mining on 3/4May42
R5841 106Sq,1660CU, Crashed at Swinderby on fire 11Apr43

Lancaster I

R5842 Avro 5Jan42, 61Sq Mar42, 44/49 Con Flts,1661CU,5LFS, 46MU,AAEE(ETPS), Crashed 27Mar46
R5843 61Sq,50 Con Flt,1654CU, Missing 18Jan43
R5844 61Sq,97Sq Con Flt,106Sq Con Flt, Missing 2Jun42
R5845 97Sq,1660CU,3LFS,90Sq,1656/67CUs, SOC Sep45
R5846 61,44Sqs; 1661/68/54CUs; 15,622,75Sqs; 5LFS, 3LFS; Collided mid-air with R5674, Hockwold, Norfolk, 18Dec44
R5847 Woodford 19Mar45, 207Sq 3May42, SOC 6Jun42
R5848 106Sq May42, 1660CU Oct42, SOC 11Apr43. 292hrs
R5849 R-R 24Apr42, Caught fire near Hucknall 11Jun43. 422hrs
R5850 83,44Sqs; 1661CU, Burnt Winthorpe 19Feb43. 229hrs
R5851 50 Con Flt,1654CU,46MU,1668CU,1LFS, Crash 14Mar44
R5852 207Sq(EM·R),83Sq(OL·Y), Overshot Condover 10Sep42
R5853 Con Flts,1660CU,576Sq,1LFS,1667/51CUs, SOC Oct45
R5854 97Sq Con Flt,1660CU,1668CU(CE·C), Became 4864M
R5855 49Sq Con Flt,1661CU,5/6LFS,231Sq,SSMar49
R5856 83Sq,1660CU,61Sq(QR·Q), Lost (St. Leu) 8Jul44. 559hrs
R5857 83Sq(OL·F) 1Jun42, Burnt in crash 7Nov42. 179hrs
R5858 44Sq, Ditched 200 miles W. of Ireland 14Jun42. 18hrs
R5859 61Sq 3Jun42, Damaged on operations 7Dec42. 197hrs
R5860 207Sq 8Jun42, Down in North Sea 21Jun42
R5861 106Sq Jun42, Missing 8/9Jul42. 19hrs
R5862 44Sq,1660CU,166Sq, Missing (Berlin) 21Jan44. 328hrs
R5863 207Sq, Crashed at Normanton on night flight 19Aug42
R5864 106,61Sqs, Blown up at Syerston 8Dec42
R5865 207,57Sqs; 1661CU,46MU,1668CU, Became 4950M
R5866 61Sq,1654/67CUs,1LFS, Crashed 25Sep44. 1140hrs
R5867 207Sq Missing 24Jul42. 37hrs
R5868 83Sq(OL·Q), 467Sq(PO·S), 144ops, Now at Scampton
R5888 61Sq 6Jul42, Missing 11Sep42. 127hrs
R5889 49,97Sqs; 1661CU, Burnt in crash 9Jul43. 519hrs
R5890 49Sq 7Jul42, Missing 17Sep42. 137hrs
R5891 1654CU Jul42, Crashed 23Jul42
R5892 49Sq 13Jul42, 1661CU Feb43, SOC Feb43. 86hrs
R5893 1654CU,46MU,1667MU,1LFS, Crash Jan44, SOC May47
R5894 49,9,57Sqs; Hit H.T. cable, Riseholme, 2Mar43
R5895 97 Con Flt,1660CU,38MU,207Sq, Lost 22Jan44. 381hrs
R5896 97Sq,1660CU Apr43, 15Sq Dec43, SOC 7Apr44
R5897 49Sq 28Jul42, Missing 29Aug42. 42hrs
R5898 49Sq Jul42, 44Sq Jan43, Missing 9Apr43. 308hrs
R5899 106Sq 29Jul42, Lost mining 18Sep42. 78hrs.
R5900 106Sq 4Aug42, Crashed 18Jan43
R5901 49Sq Aug42, 39MU,44Sq Apr43, Missing 19Oct43. 418hrs
R5902 50Sq(VN·T) 5Aug42, Missing 13Oct42. 88hrs
R5903 44Sq(KM·R) 8Aug42, Lost (Osnabruck) 6/7Oct42. 123hrs
R5904 9Sq,1661CU Nov42, 15Sq, Missing 21Jul44. 504hrs
R5905 44Sq(KM·R) Sep42, Missing (Wismar) 23/24Sep42. 43hrs
R5906 106,15,622Sqs; 1660CU,3LFS,38MU, Scrap May47
R5907 83 Con Flt, 9Sq Aug42. Hit by flak 23/24Sep42. 71hrs
R5908 207Sq Aug42, 49 Con Flt,1661CU, Crash 28Nov42
R5909 50Sq 2Sep42, Missing (Wismar) 23/24Sep42. 41hrs
R5910 61,106Sqs; 1654CU,5LFS, Became 4948M at 1660CU
R5911 83Sq(OL·C) 4Sep42, Missing 14Oct42. 38hrs
R5912 49,156Sqs; NTU,1668CU, Became 4949M at 1654CU
R5913 83Sq(OL·G) 6Sep42, Lost (St. Nazaire) 1Mar43. 176hrs
R5914 106Sq Sep42, Damaged 24Sep42, Lost 22Dec42. 88hrs
R5915 9,97Sqs; 1660CU,622Sq, Missing 21Jan44. 693hrs
R5916 9Sq(WS·R) 8Sep42, Crashed and burnt 7Nov42
R5917 9,97Sqs; 1660CU Apr43, Crashed 18May43. 300hrs

Serial Range W1280—W1498   Manchester I

150 Manchesters ordered from Armstrong Whitworth Aircraft in December 1939 and cancelled. W1280-1299, W1319-1350, W1374-1410, W1426-1475, W1488-1498

Serial Range W4102—4700   Lancaster I

450 Manchesters ordered from A. V. Roe (Chadderton) in January 1940 of which 207 were built as Lancaster I, delivered from July to November 1942 initially fitted with Merlin 20 engines.

W4102 106Sq 28Jul42. Burnt after wheels up landing 5Oct42
W4103 83Sq(OL·S), 1668CU, 5LFS, Crashed 14Apr44
W4104 83Sq 2Aug42, Missing 11Sep42. 68hrs

W4105 44Sq(KM ·K), Missing 24Aug42. 50hrs
W4106 44Sq(KM ·T), Missing (Cologne) 2Feb43. 368hrs
W4107 49Sq 26Jul42, Missing 23Nov42. 132hrs
W4108 97Sq Jul42, 1654CU Aug42, Missing 14Sep42. 103hrs
W4109 106Sq 31Jul42, Missing 12Aug42. 17hrs
W4110 44Sq(KM ·K), Missing (Pilsen) 13/14May43. 524hrs
W4111 61Sq, Missing 10/11Sep42. 65hrs
W4112 50Sq, Blown up at Scampton 15Mar43
W4113 49,156Sqs; 1661CU(GP ·J), 5LFS, Became 4969M
W4114 Avro Aug42, Mk.III prototype, AAEE Oct42-Nov43 for
Stromberg carburretor tests, 1654,1660(YW ·T)CUs.
W4115 At AAEE with FN79 turret. MUs, Crash 1651CU 29May45
W4116 49Sq 4Aug42, Missing 13Oct42. 95hrs
W4117 50Sq Aug42, 44Sq Nov44, Crashed 24Dec42. 178hrs
18 W4118 106Sq 6Aug42, *Admiral Prune*, Lost 5Feb43. 340hrs
W4119 50Sq, Abandoned on fire near E. Kirkby 12Feb44. 358hrs
W4120 39MU,207Sq(EM ·L) Oct42, Missing 31Aug43. 343hrs
W4121 39MU,207Sq Oct42, Missing 25Oct42. 8hrs
W4122 9Sq(WS ·U) Sep42,1661CU Nov42,5LFS, Scrap Nov46
W4123 83Sq Aug42,NTU,576Sq, Lost (Berlin) 2/3Dec43. 318hrs
W4124 44Sq(KM ·D), Missing 27Aug42. 33hrs
W4125 44Sq Aug42, Missing 22Dec42. 140hrs
W4126 44Sq(KM ·B), Missing (Nuremburg) 17Dec42. 59hrs
W4127 97Sq,1660CU,619Sq(PG ·D), Lost (La Chapelle) 20Apr44
W4128 1660CU Aug42, Crash 24Dec42. Became 3609M 10STT
W4129-30 207Sq Aug/Sep42, Missing 29Aug/16Oct42. 11/54hrs
W4131 50Sq Aug42,1660CU Nov42, Crashed 1Jun43. 267hrs
W4132 9Sq 1661CU,1667CU,1LFS, Crashed 3Feb44. 388hrs
W4133 9Sq, Crashed Bardney and burnt 7Aug43. Crew killed
W4134 207Sq(EM ·U) Aug42, Lost (Essen) 3/4Jan43. 174hrs
W4135 50Sq Aug42, 44Sq Nov42, 97Sq Jan43, Lost 28Jan43
W4136 61Sq 21Aug42, Missing 2/3Sep42. 35hrs
W4137 44Sq 13Aug42, Damaged in action 1Mar43. 326hrs
W4138 83Sq Con Flt, 1654CU, Missing 17Sep42. 42hrs
W4139 97Sq 18Aug42, Missing 28Aug42. 9hrs
W4140 9 Con Flt,156Sq, Lost (Duisberg) 26/27Apr43. 64hrs
W4154 50,44,100Sqs; 1662CU,1LFS,1667CU, Crash 20Jan45
W4155 9Sq(WS ·A) Sep42, Lost (Diepholz) 17Dec42. 135hrs
W4156 106Sq Aug42, Missing (Duisburg) 9Apr43. 211hrs
W4157 9Sq(WS ·V), Missing (Berlin) 17Jan43, 30 operations. 258hrs
W4158 9Sq(WS ·O) (WS ·S) Aug43,622Sq(GI ·U),3LFS,SOC.Dec45
W4159 9Sq(WS ·Y) Sep42, Lost 8Jan43 after 15 ops. 231hrs
W4160 39MU 20Aug42, SOC 5Sep42
W4161 50,44,50Sqs; Became 4451M after 587hrs. 75 ops
W4162 44,83Sqs; NTU,460Sq, Lost (Berlin) 23Nov43. 399hrs
W4163 50Sq Sep42, 20MU,1667CU,622Sq, Lost 15Jan44. 335hrs
W4164 207,9Sqs; 1661CU. Became 4443M
W4165 57Sq 24Sep42, Missing 9/10Nov42. 95hrs
W4166 61Sq 31Aug42, Missing 20Sep42. 23 hrs
W4167 39MU, 207Sq Dec42, Crashed 14Feb43. 83hrs
W4168 61Sq 21Aug42, Crashed 10Dec42. 185hrs
W4169 44Sq(KM ·S) Sep42, Missing (Bremen) 13Sep42. 19hrs
W4170 97Sq Sep42, Missing 16Oct42. 87hrs
W4171-2 207Sq Nov/Dec42, Lost 27Apr/10Feb43. 266/75hrs
W4173 61Sq Sep42, Missing 16/17Sep42 Essen raid. 28hrs
W4174 207Sq,1660CU; 15,75Sqs; 1654CU, Scrap Sep46
W4175 97Sq, Crashed Coningsby village 30Aug43. 287hrs
W4176 44Sq(KM ·X), Lost mining 8Jan43. 169hrs
W4177 44Sq(KM ·W), Missing 18Sep42. 23hrs
W4178-9 106Sq, Missing Essen raid 16Sep42. 17/15hrs
W4180 44Sq(KM ·D), Missing (Hamburg) 9Nov42. 124hrs
W4181 49Sq,1660CU,15Sq,3LFS, Became 4915M. 1052hrs
W4182 9Sq(WS ·B), Collided with W4259 on operations 20Dec42
W4183 49Sq,1661CU Nov42, Crashed 11Jan43. 71hrs
W4184 9Sq(WS ·A) Sep42, Missing on first operation, 19Sep42
W4185 9Sq(WS ·G) Sep42, Missing (Munich) 21Dec42. 163hrs
W4186 9Sq 10Sep42, Missing 17Sep42. 8hrs
W4187 44Sq(KM ·S) Sep42, Lost (Flensburg) 1Oct42. 50hrs
W4188 44Sq(KM ·G), Missing (Osnabruck) 6Oct42. 57hrs
W4189 57Sq Sep42, Missing 31Jan43. 195hrs
W4190 57Sq Sep42, 1661CU Feb43, Crash 24Aug43. 579hrs
W4191 207Sq Sep42, Missing 22Dec42. 166hrs
W4192 61Sq, Lost in Krupp Works attack 12/13Jan43
W4193 83Sq(OL ·A),1662CU,R-R,1668CU, Scrap Jan47

W4194 50Sq 13Sep42, Missing 9Nov42. 107hrs
W4195 106Sq 13Sep42, Missing 17Oct42. 61hrs
W4196 49,50Sqs; Blown up at Scampton 15Mar43

Lancaster 1, W4232, coming in to land.

W4197 9Sq(WS ·J) Sep42, 1667CU,1LFS,SOC Jan47
W4198 61Sq(QR ·H), Lost (Berlin) 75th op. 26/27Nov43. 653hrs
W4199 44Sq(KM ·H), Missing (Berlin) 29/30Mar43. 343hrs
W4200 9Sq(WS ·U) Sep42,97Sq Jan43,1656CU, Crash 28Jul43
W4201 57Sq Sep42, Missing 14Mar43. 239hrs
W4230 9Sq(WS ·P), Lost on first operation 23Sep42. 5hrs
W4231 83Sq,1662/67CUs,1LFS,1651CU. Became 5451M
W4232 57Sq,5LFS, Broke up in air, Syerston, 17Apr44
W4233 61Sq, Crashed near Bilsdale, Yorks 13Apr42. 47hrs
W4234 57Sq 18Sep42, Missing 22Dec42. 115hrs
W4235 49Sq,NTU,9Sq(WS ·C) Dec43-Mar44, Scrap Jan47
36 W4236 61Sq(QR ·K) Sep42, Lost (Mannheim) 9/10Aug43. 640hrs
W4237 9Sq(WS ·W) Sep42, Lost on first operation, 29Sep42
W4238 106Sq, Overshot at Newton and burnt 2Oct42
W4239 9Sq(WS ·T) Sep42, 97Sq Oct42, Crash 21Oct42
W4240 57,467Sqs, Missing (Hanover) 18/19Oct43
W4241 1662CU(Q), 1LFS, 300Sq, B.C.I.S. Became 5287M
W4242 106Sq(ZN ·A) Sep42, Missing 9Oct43. 674hrs. 65 operations
W4243 Ringway,29MU,5MU Apr45, Scrap Jan47
W4244 61Sq, Crashed at Exeter after Adour mining 10Nov42†
W4245 49,576Sqs; Missing (Berlin) 31Jan44. 411hrs
W4246 57Sq 24Sep42, Burnt in crash 7Nov42. 60hrs
W4247 57Sq 26Sep42, Missing 9Nov42. 65hrs
W4248 9Sq(WS ·A),1667CU,622Sq(GI ·H),3LFS,5LFS,SOC Nov45
W4249 9,97Sqs; 1661CU,3LFS,46MU, Scrap Jan47
W4250 57Sq, Stalled 1 mile N. of Woodhall Spa 10Dec42
W4251-2 50Sq. Missing 25Oct42/6Apr43, 46/248hrs
W4253 9,106Sqs; 3LFS, CUs, Became 4914M. 1260hrs
W4254 9Sq(WS ·P), 57Sq Feb43, Missing 21Apr43. 282hrs
W4255 97Sq Sep42, 1654CU Oct42, Crash 12Dec42
W4256 106Sq(ZN ·V) Oct42, Lost 26Jun43. 324hrs. 53 ops
W4257 57Sq 30Sep42, Missing (Essen) 3Apr43. 329hrs
W4258 49Sq, 1661CU,5LFS, W4383 landed on top 27May44
22 W4259 44Sq(KM ·P), Hit W4182 over Bracebridge 20Dec42
W4260 1654CU, Crashed 31Aug43
W4261 106Sq 6Oct42, Missing (Essen) 14Jan43
W4262 57Sq Oct42, Missing 11Nov42. 57hrs
W4263 1656CU; 460,625Sqs; 1LFS,1667CU, SOC Jan47
W4264 1656CU,1LFS; 1662,1668CUs. Became 5289M
W4265 9Sq(WS ·L) Oct42, Crashed 7Nov42. 131hrs. 4 ops.
W4266 50Sq, Missing (Soltan) 17/18Dec42
W4267 50Sq Oct42, 44Sq Nov42, Burnt in crash 27Jan43
W4268 44Sq(KM ·Q), 622Sq, Lost (Munich) 21Dec42. 590hrs
W4269 61Sq Oct42, Lost (Duisburg) 12/13May43. 430hrs
W4270 61Sq Oct42, Burnt in crash 19Feb43. 196hrs
W4271 1661CU,3LFS, Swung landing at Swannington 13Aug44
W4272 61 Con Flt,1654CU; 15,622Sqs; Lost 16Feb44. 280hrs
W4273 460Sq Oct42, Missing 23Nov42. 12hrs
W4274 460Sq(AR ·B), Missing (Essen) 4Jan43. 67hrs
W4275 101Sq(SR ·C) Oct42, Missing 9Jul43. 362hrs
W4276 101Sq Oct42, 207Sq Sep43, Lost (Hanover) 19Oct43
W4277 44Sq(KM ·S) Oct42, Lost mining 8Jan43. 145hrs
W4278 97Sq 11Oct42, Missing 23Oct42. 30hrs
W4279 61Sq(QR ·Z) 11Oct42, Lost (Kassel) 3/4Oct43. 593hrs. 65ops
W4301 61Sq,460Sq May43, Missing (Munich) 2Oct43. 232hrs

W4302 106Sq Oct42, Missing 16Oct42. 16hrs
W4303 1654CU, Broke up in air 24May43
W4304 44Sq(KM ·C) Oct42, Lost (Stuttgart) 22Nov42. 55hrs
W4305 44Sq(KM ·J/G) Oct42, Lost (Pilsen) 13/14May43. 272hrs
W4306 49Sq 12Oct42, Burnt out in action 25Oct42
W4307 57Sq 12Oct42, Missing 10Nov42. 44hrs
W4308 460Sq(AR ·C), Lost (Dusseldorf) 23Jan43. 69hrs
W4309 101Sq,1667CU,1LFS,1664CU, Became 4904M
W4310 460Sq Oct42, Missing (Kiel) 4Apr43. 99hrs
W4311-12 101Sq, Lost 25Jun43/Crash 23Dec42. 98/57hrs
W4313 101Sq Oct42, Missing 12Feb43. 42hrs
W4314 49,156Sqs; 1662CU, Crashed and burnt, Laughton, 1Sep43
W4315 50Sq,NTU,61Sq, Missing 29Jan44. 223hrs
W4316 460Sq(AR ·Q), Missing (Bochum) 12Jun43
W4317 61Sq Oct42, Missing (Pilsen) 17Apr43. 365hrs
W4318 103Sq Oct42, Ditched 15Apr43. 244hrs
W4319 101Sq Oct42, Burnt out 18Dec42. 17hrs
W4320 460Sq, Missing (Wuppertal) 24Jun43
W4321-2 101Sq, Wrecked 17Jan43/Lost 28Mar43. 90/142hrs
W4323 103Sq Oct42, Burnt in crash 24Aug43. 215hrs
W4324 101Sq, Blew up in air over Wales 16Nov42
W4325 9Sq(WS ·C),460Sq, Missing (Stettin) 20Apr43. 182hrs
W4326 101Sq Oct42, Crashed 16Nov42. 28hrs
W4327 460Sq(AR ·S), Shot down in Holland 29Mar43. 150hrs
W4328 103,12Sqs;1656CU,5LFS(CE ·T), Scrap Jan47
W4329-30 460Sq, Lost (Bochum) 12Jun/(Stettin) 20Apr43
W4331 460Sq Oct42, Missing (Pilsen) 16Apr43. 218hrs
W4332 460Sq Oct42, Missing (Cologne) 16Jun43. 218hrs
W4333 103Sq, Crashed near Yaxley 4Mar43. 160hrs
W4334 103Sq Oct42, Missing 21Dec42. 49hrs
W4335-6 103Sq 25Oct42, Missing 21Jan43/27Feb43. 106/103hrs
W4337 103Sq Oct42, 576Sq Nov43, Missing 3Dec43. 512hrs
W4338-9 103Sq Oct42, Missing 14Jan/1Jan43. 67/39hrs
W4340 103Sq Oct42, Missing (Essen) 21Jan43. 95hrs
W4355 97Sq,1661CU,15Sq, Missing 23Feb44. 795hrs
W4356 97Sq 22Nov42, Crashed 6Dec42. 9hrs
W4357 61Sq, Missing (Kassel) 22/23Oct43. 446hrs
W4358 49,57Sqs; 1661CU,9Sq,5LFS,1653CU, Became 4968M
W4359 57Sq 6Nov42, Burnt in crash 18Dec42. 50hrs
W4360 57Sq 6Nov42, Missing 23Nov42. 29hrs
W4361-2 103Sq Nov42, Missing 2Mar/15Feb43. 194/100hrs
W4363-4 103Sq Oct42, Missing 6/7Jul/27Aug43. 346/457hrs
W4365 207Sq(EM ·B) 8Nov42, Lost (Essen) 21/22Jan43. 126hrs
W4366 12Sq Jan43, Missing 13May43. 24ops. 237hrs
W4367 50Sq Nov42, 106Sq Jan43, Missing 26Jan43. 328hrs
W4368-9 12Sq Nov42, Missing 17/18 & 11/12Jan43
W4370-1 12Sq Nov42, Missing 5Sep/2Jan43. 402/?hrs
W4372-3 12Sq 2Nov42, Missing 17/18Jan & 12Jun43
W4374 12Sq, Crashed in wood at Apley 18Jun43
W4375 57Sq 14Nov42, Missing 19Feb43. 154hrs
W4376 57,103,166,300(BH ·O)Sqs; 1LFS,CUs, Crashed 3Jan45
W4377 57Sq, Twice damaged, Missing 22Jun43. 174hrs
W4378 467Sq, Missing (Berlin) 17/18Jan43. 55hrs
W4379 9Sq 23Dec42, Missing 18Jan43. 33hrs
W4380 50,12,9Sqs; 4STT Sep44, Became 4886M
W4381 67,61Sqs, 1661CU Mar43, Crashed 24Aug43. 516hrs
W4382 40Sq Nov42, Missing (Soltan) 17/18Dec42. 24hrs
W4383 50,207Sqs; 1654/68CUs,5LFS, Crashed 27May44
W4384 467Sq,57Sq Jan43, Missing 12Feb43. 74hrs
W4385-4400, W4414-4463, W4481-4524, W4537-4586, W4600-4641,
    W4655-4700 cancelled.

Serial Range W4761—W5012   **Lancaster I/III**

200 Lancasters ordered from Metropolitan Vickers in 1940 and
built as 170 Mk.I (W4761-4982 range) with Merlin 20 engines and
30 Mk.III (W4983-5012 range) with Merlin 28 engines from September 1942 to May 1943. They were delivered to Woodford for
assembly and testing.

W4761 49Sq,9Sq(WS ·P) Jan43, Missing 18Jan43. 17hrs
W4762 61Sq Sep42, 50Sq 1May43, Missing 13May43. 6hrs
W4763 61Sq, Shot down in Holland (Gelsenkirchen) 9/10Jul43
W4764 9Sq(WS ·K) Sep42, Missing (Turin) 9Dec42. 142hrs
W4765 Avro 3Sep42, 9Sq 10Sep42, Missing 17Sep42. 10hrs

W4766 57,61Sqs; Missing Peenemunde raid 17/18Aug43. 289hrs
W4767 Avro 11Sep42, 61Sq 23Sep42, Crashed 18Jan43
W4768 106Sq 20Sep42, Missing 3Oct42. 19hrs
W4769 61Sq, Missing Essen raid 3/4Jan43
W4770-1 106Sq Sep42, Missing 4Feb44/16Oct43. 141/19hrs
W4772 50Sq Con Flt, 1654CU Oct43, Missing 18Jan43
W4773 49,156Sqs; 1662CU, Hit house landing at Blyton 8Sep43
W4774 61Sq, Shot down near Montchanin 17Oct42. 24hrs

W4783, coded AR·G, the famous 'George,' in England.

W4775 57Sq Oct42, 1661CU Apr43, Crashed 6May43

W4783, the famous George, in Australia.

W4776 1656CU Oct42, SOC after 3rd crash 28Oct43. 495hrs
W4777 1656CU, Crashed Thorganby, Yorks, 11/12Jul43, 281hrs
W4778 106 Con Flt, 44Sq, Crashed in Waddensea 2/3Aug43
W4779 1656CU, 1LFS, 4STT Oct44, Became 4903M
W4780 1656CU,166Sq Dec43, Missing (Berlin) 2Jan44. 34hrs
W4781 1656CU 18Oct42. Crashed 3Aug43. 329hrs
W4782 101Sq 21Oct42, Missing 9Dec42. 40hrs
W4783 460Sq(AR ·G) 22Oct42. Became A66-2 R.A.A.F
W4784 101Sq 22Oct42, Crashed 12Nov42, Missing 5May43. 12hrs
W4785 460Sq Oct42, Missing (Duisberg) 8Apr43. 171hrs
W4786-7 103Sq 29Oct/22Dec42, Lost 18/22Dec42. 92/49hrs
W4788 103Sq 16Nov42, Missing (Hamburg) 4Mar43. 126hrs
W4789 12Sq Nov42, Lost on Cologne raid 17/18Jan43
W4790 12Sq,CUs,1LFS, Overshot Hemswell 28Aug44. 837hrs
W4791 12Sq Nov42, Shot down over Holland 11Jun43

Close-up of factory-stencilled serial number.

W4792 12Sq Nov42, Missing 26Feb43
W4793 12Sq,1656CU,1LFS, Crashed nr. Sturgate 6May44. 616hrs
W4794 12Sq,1667CU,5LFS, Crashed, tyre burst, Carnaby, 1May44
W4795 467,207,61Sqs; Missing (Stettin) 21Apr43. 240hrs

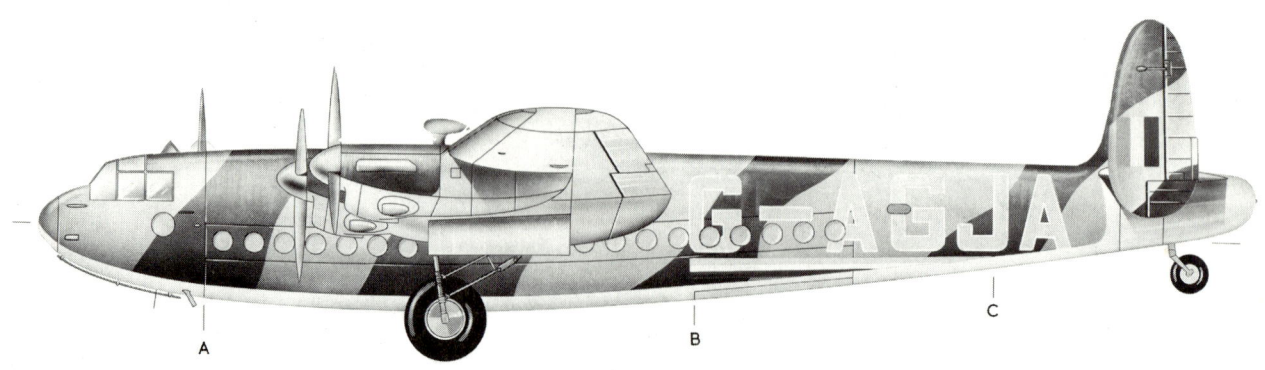

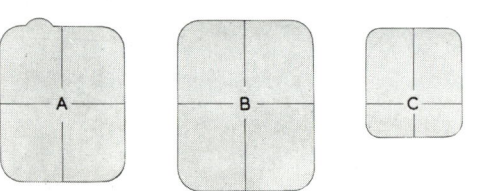

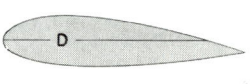

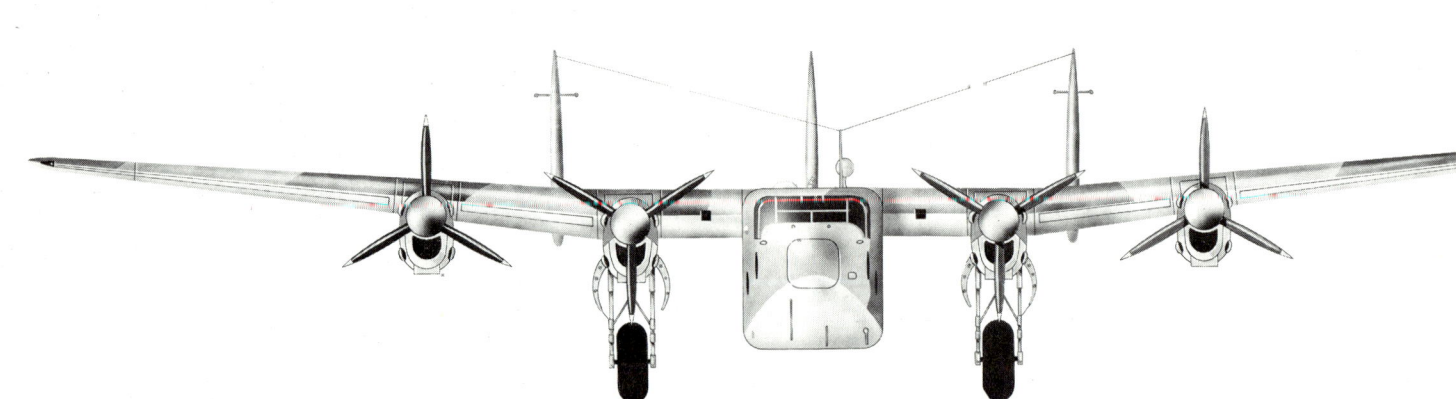

The first of B.O.A.C.'s Yorks ex-C.I MW103 and R.A.F. examples in Nos. 51 (top) and 246 (bottom) Squadrons in 1946.

W4796 101Sq Nov42, Missing 5Jan43. 47hrs
W4797 467,57Sqs; 1668CU,5LFS, Crashed 29Apr44
W4798 467Sq, 61Sq Feb43, Missing 1Apr43. 270hrs
W4799 83Sq Nov42, Missing 1Jan43. 58hrs
W4800 50Sq 22Nov42, Missing (Duisburg) 8/9Jan43. 51hrs
W4815 207Sq, Crashed at Spilsby (Augsberg) a.m. 26Feb44. 406hrs
W4816 460Sq(AR ·K), Abandoned in air 17Jan43
W4817 460Sq(AR ·K), Missing (Dusseldorf) 27Jan43. 63hrs
W4818 460Sq Nov42, Missing (Dortmund) 4May43. 107hrs
W4819 9Sq(WS ·O) Dec42, 44Sq Jan43, Missing 3Feb43
W4820 103Sq 1Dec42, Missing 22Dec42. 8hrs
W4821 103Sq,1656/62CUs,1LFS,300SQ,6LFS, Scrap Mar47
W4822 467,49,57Sqs; Missing (Dusseldorf) 4Nov43. 397hrs
W4823 467,50Sqs; Blown up at Scampton 15Mar43
W4824 467,50Sqs; Lost in day raid 6Aug44. 619hrs
W4825 467,97Sqs; (Merlin 20 to 22Feb43). Lost 2Mar43
W4826 467Sq Dec42, 106Sq Jan43, Missing 31Jan43. 36hrs
W4827·8 103Sq Dec42, Lost 6Mar/14Apr43, 226/160hrs
W4829 9Sq(WS ·T) Dec42, 44Sq(KM ·V), Lost (Berlin) 1/2Mar43
W4830 61Sq, Hit by flak, crashed near Boston 26Jan43
W4831 9Sq(WS ·K) Jan43, 44Sq(KM ·C), Lost (Berlin) 2Jan44
W4832 44Sq(KM ·U), Missing (Lorient) 7/8Feb43. 566hrs
W4833 101,625Sqs(CF ·J), Lost (Stuttgart) 15Mar44. 963hrs
W4834 1656CU,57Sq, Blown up at Scampton 15Mar43
W4835 97Sq 31Dec42, Missing (Hamburg) 31Jan43. 48hrs
W4836 100,12Sqs, Flew into ground Newhall, Lincs 13Feb43
W4837 460Sq 21Dec42, Lost (Dusseldorf) 27Jan43. 26hrs
W4838 44Sq(KM ·B) 21Dec42, Missing 30May42
W4839 44Sq(KM ·B/F), Missing (Berlin) 27/28Mar43. 125hrs
W4840 9Sq(WS ·B) Jan43, Lost on first operation. 16hrs
W4841 44Sq(KM ·W) Dec42, Missing 10/11Mar43. 134hrs
W4842 106Sq Dec42, Lost (Essen) 28May43. 296hrs
W4843 9Sq(WS ·K) Jan43, Lost on first operation. 12hrs
W4844 460Sq, Damaged 5May43, Lost 3Jun43
W4845 103Sq; 1656/62CU; 1LFS, Became 5291M
W4846-7 83Sq Jan43, Lost 27Feb43/SOC 12Mar43. Both 67hrs
W4848 103Sq Jan43, Missing (Pilsen) 17Apr43. 56hrs
W4849 156Sq; 1662CU, Hit barn near Blyton Rly. Sta. 12Dec44
W4850 156Sq Jan43, Missing (Kiel) 5Apr43. 32hrs
W4851 156Sq; 1656CU; 3LFS, Burnt in crash 17Jun44. 744hrs
W4852 103Sq, 1654CU, 15Sq Dec43, Lost 22Jan44. 136hrs
W4853 156Sq Jan43, Damaged on operations 31Jan43. 15hrs
W4854 156Sq Jan43, Missing (Pilsen) 16/17Apr43. 145hrs
W4855 12Sq Jan43, Missing (Hamburg) 3/4Mar43
W4856 156Sq Jan43, Missing (Munich) 10Mar43. 69hrs
W4857 103Sq, Crashed approaching Elsham Wolds 27Feb43
W4858 12Sq Jan43, Lost (Berlin) 29/30Mar43
W4859 1662CU, 1LFS, 1662CU, Wrecked in second crash 12Dec44
W4860-1 103/12Sqs Jan43, Lost 10Mar/13Feb43. 93/190hrs
W4862 101Sq(SR ·E) 2Feb43, Lost (Essen) 13Mar43. 71hrs
W4863 101Sq, Hit trees after airfield diversion 4/5May43
W4864 460Sq, Hit ground at Acton Reynold 2/3Mar43. 7hrs
W4879 460Sq(AR ·D), Shot at by Ju88, crashed S.Cerney 22Mar43
W4880 103Sq Feb43, Missing (Berlin) 2Mar43. 35hrs
W4881 12Sq Feb-Oct43, 460Sq, Lost (Berlin) 2Dec43. 352hrs
W4882 156Sq, 1662CU(1), 5LFS, SOC Sep45
W4883 1656CU, 3 crashes, 231Sq, Dec45, SOC Apr46
W4884 1655CU, 5LFS, 61Sq Feb44; 5,46MUs; Scrap Jan47
W4885 1662CU, 622Sq Dec43, 5LFS, 90Sq, 10MU, Scrap Jan47
W4886 106Sq Feb43, Missing 26Feb43. 44hrs
W4887 97Sq Feb43, 1660CU, Became 4352M at 10STT Mar43
W4888 101Sq 13Feb43, Missing (Essen) 5May43. 102hrs
W4889 1662CU, 1LFS, 1656CU, Burnt out Lindholme 12Jan45
W4890 1662CU, 1LFS, 1667CU, Crash Thorney Island 10Feb45
W4891 156Sq,405Sq Aug43, 5MU, 1LFS, 1667CU, 58MU, SOC Sep45
W4892 1662CU Feb43, 207Sq Nov43, Lost 2Jan44. 70hrs
W4893 1662CU, Crashed 28Mar43 and 7Jun43, Lost 20Jul43
W4894 156Sq Feb43, Missing (Essen) 3/4Apr43. 73hrs
W4895 156Sq Feb43, Missing 28Feb43. 12hrs
W4896 156Sq Feb43, Missing (Nuremburg) 8/9Mar43. 36hrs
W4897 156Sq,NTU Jul43; 106,463Sqs; Lost 2Jan44. 255hrs
W4898 61Sq, Damaged 27Feb43, Lost 29Apr43. 106hrs
W4899 61Sq, 1668CU, Became 4945M at 1662CU

W4900 61Sq(QR ·Q) 56ops, 1669CU Dec44, 1660CU Mar45, SOC Oct45
W4901 103Sq 24Feb43, Missing 17Jun43. 203hrs
W4902 156Sq, 1661/54CUs; Hit ground, Hackthorn, 19Nov43
W4903 61Sq Feb43, Missing (Munich) 9Mar43. 36hrs
W4904 83Sq, 1667CU, Dived into ground Marston Moor 28Sep43
W4905 83Sq,50Sq Aug43, Missing (Frankfurt) 4/5Oct43. 22hrs
W4918 106Sq 28Feb43, Missing (Essen) 6Mar43. 8hrs
W4919 207Sq ex-5MU Feb43, Missing 25May43. 39hrs
W4920 61Sq Feb43, Missing (Berlin) 1/2Mar43. 8hrs
W4921 106,617,619Sqs; 1654CU Jun43, Burnt 18Sep43
W4922 156Sq Apr43, 106Sq Sep43, Lost 6Sep43. 223hrs
W4923 460Sq, Missing (Pilsen) 16Apr43
W4924 156Sq Mar43, 1656CU Aug43, Crashed 11Nov43. 357hrs
W4925 12Sq Mar43, Shot down over Holland 26Mar43. 97hrs
W4926 Conv.Mk.III 617Sq, 1654/64CUs,5MU,6LFS.SSMay47
W4927 460Sq(AR ·C), SOC 23Oct43 after third time damaged
W4928 83Sq 7Mar43, Missing on first operation 13Mar43
W4929 617,619Sqs; 166TCU, Crashed, crew killed 5Sep43. 471hrs
W4930 156Sq Mar43, Missing (Pilsen) 16/17Apr43. 47hrs
W4931 207Sq 14Mar43, Missing (Berlin) 30Mar43. 32hrs
W4932 97Sq Mar43, 50Sq Apr43, Crashed 16Jun43. 156hrs
W4933 156,44,50Sqs, Crashed Skellingthorpe, 30Mar44. 516hrs
W4934 61Sq, Lost on Peenemunde raid 17/18Aug43. 238hrs
W4935 44Sq(KM ·M) Mar43, Lost (Duisburg) 9/10Apr44. 259hrs
W4936 44Sq Mar43, Missing 15Jun43, 141hrs
W4937 156Sq Mar43; 1661/60CUs; Crashed 26Sep43. 456hrs
W4938 207Sq(EM ·A)18Mar43,Lost(Duisburg)12/13May43. 104hrs
W4939 460Sq Mar43, Missing (Krefeld) 21/22Jun43
W4940 617Sq, 1660CU, 5LFS, Became 4874M at 4STT
W4941 460Sq, 38MU, 5LFS, Crashed 1Oct44, Became 4971M
W4942 460Sq 25Mar43, Missing (Pilsen) 17Apr43. 21hrs
W4943 156Sq Mar43, Missing (Essen) 27/28May43. 107hrs
W4944 57Sq 25Mar43, Missing 14May43. 88hrs
W4945 207Sq(EM ·Z) 29Mar43, Lost mining 29Apr43. 79hrs
W4946 467Sq, Missing (Hamburg) 27/28Jul43. 138hrs
W4947 156Sq Mar43, 1661CU May43, Missing 17Jul43. 258hrs
W4948 57Sq 30Mar43, Shot down by intruder 22Sep43. 135hrs
W4949 44Sq Mar43, Missing 15Jun43. 165hrs
W4950 156,61Sqs(QR ·L), 6LFS, Crash Jul45. MUs, Scrap Mar48
W4951 101Sq 31Mar43, Lost (Stuttgart) 14Apr43. 31hrs
W4952 207Sq 31Mar43, SOC after second crash 12Aug43. 201hrs
W4953 83Sq Mar43, 1656CU Aug43, Crashed 24Nov43. 439hrs
W4954 100Sq Missing on first operation with No 12Sq, 28Apr43
W4955 83Sq Apr43, Crashed nr. Eemnes, Holland 13May43. 53hrs
W4956 460Sq, Missing (Stettin) 20/21Apr43. 13hrs
W4957 83Sq,NTU,61Sq,24MU Oct43, 46MU, Scrap Dec46
W4958 12Sq Apr43, Missing (Cologne) 3/4Jul43
W4959 83Sq Apr43, 207Sq Sep43, Missing 24Nov43. 335hrs
W4960 460Sq 14Apr43, Missing (Bochum) 12Jun43
W4961 44Sq 13Apr43, Missing (Berlin) 4Sep43. 288hrs
W4962 207Sq 16Apr43, Lost (Hamburg) 27Jul43. 179hrs
W4963 AAEE, Middle East Nov44, 10MU Jul45, Scrap Nov46
W4964 9Sq(WS ·J)Apr43-Oct44, 106ops, Became4922M SOCNov49
W4965 1656-62CUs, 1LFS; Crashed Sturgate, 16May44. 566hrs
W4966 101Sq Apr43, 166Sq Oct43, Damaged 23Nov43. 334hrs
W4967 460Sq,626Sq, Nov43, 101Sq Jun44, Lost 21Jul44, 458hrs
W4980 1656CU,15Sq,3LFS,90Sq,1662CU,MUs, SOC 9Jul45
W4981-2 83Sq Apr43, Missing 14May/23Jun43. 17/93hrs
W4983 1st MkIII, 467Sq, Lost (Dusseldorf) 11/12Jun43
W4984 460Sq, Shot down in Holland (Dortmund) 23May43. 23hrs
W4985 460Sq Apr43, Lost (Wuppertal) 29May43. 32hrs
W4986 460Sq Apr43, Missing (Dortmund) 23May43. 20hrs
W4987 460Sq Apr43, Missing (Cologne) 3Jul43
W4988 460Sq Apr43, Missing (Berlin) 3Sep43. 202hrs
W4989 100Sq May43, Missing (Bochum) 13Jun43
W4990 12,626Sqs(UM ·V2),1LFS,1656CU,5MU, Scrap Jul47
W4991 12Sq May43, Missing 23Sep43. 250hrs
W4992 12Sq(GZ ·A) May43, Lost (Oberhausen) 14Jun43
W4993 101Sq,625Sq Oct43, 38MU,BDU Sep44, 5MU, ScrapMar47
W4994 12,166Sqs; 1656HCU(EK ·N), Crashed 13Jul45
W4995 101,625Sqs; 1LFS, CU, Crash Lindholme 16May45, SOC Mar48
W4996 101Sq,166Sq Oct43, Missing (Berlin) 27Jan44

154

W4997 101Sq May43, Crashed 5Oct43, 5MU May44, Scrap Jul47
W4998 100Sq 15May43, Missing (Dusseldorf) 26May43
W4999 100Sq May43, 625Sq Oct43, Missing 3Dec43. 264hrs
W5000 61Sq May43, Missing (Hamburg) 2/3Aug43. 142hrs
W5001 207Sq(EM ·J) 17May43, Lost (Dusseldorf) 26May43
W5002 61Sq(QR ·L) May43, Lost (Milan) 15/16Aug43. 201hrs
W5003 467Sq May43, Lost (Hamburg) 27/28Jul43. 99hrs
W5004 50Sq May43, 38MU,5LFS May44, 46MU, Scrap Jan47
W5005 460,550Sqs; Crashed in Humber 27Aug44. 606hrs. 94ops
W5006 207Sq(EM ·G), 9Sq(WS ·X) Jan44, Missing 30/31Mar44
W5007 460Sq, Crashed Elsham Wolds after AA hit 16Jun43†
W5008 57Sq May43, Missing 28Aug43. 91hrs
W5009 101,625Sqs(CF ·Z), Lost (Nuremburg) 30Mar44. 458hrs
W5010 BDU; 49Sq,9Sq(WS ·L) Oct43, Lost (Leipzig) 19Feb44
W5011 9Sq May43, Belly landing 18Nov43, 5MU, Scrap Feb47
W5012 103Sq (PM ·O) 18May43, Lost (Cologne) 3/4Jul43. 64hrs

Serial BT308 — Lancaster Prototype

Built up from Manchester fuselage. First flew January 9th, 1941, with Merlin X engines fitted. See under Type-by-Type Review for details.

Serial DG595 — Lancaster Second Prototype

Ordered from A. V. Roe (Chadderton) in 1940. First flew May 13th, 1941. Delivered to A.A.E.E. August 16th, 1941, with Merlin 20 engines. Wrecked at T.D.U. February 17th, 1944.

Serial Range DS601—DS852 — Lancaster B.II

200 Lancasters ordered from Armstrong Whitworth Aircraft in 1941 and built as B.II from September 1942 to October 1943 with up to DS627 having Hercules VI engines and the remainder Hercules XVI engines.

DS603 on B.2 comparison tests, Syerston, late 1942.

DS601 AAEE Sep42,1657/79CUs,408Sq,1668CU,SOCOct44.439hrs
DS602 AAEE Sep42; 20MU Feb44, 15MU, SOC 11Sep46
DS603 61,115Sqs; 1657CU, Stalled at E. Wretham 16Apr43
28 DS604 61(QR ·W), 115Sq, Missing (Frankfurt) 11Apr43. 49hrs
DS605 61,415Sqs; 1657 Con Flt(V),RAE, SOC 20Mar45
DS606 AAEE Nov42,TDU Jan43,4STT, Became 3995M Nov45
DS607 61,115Sqs; 1666CU, Overshot Topcliffe 7Apr44
DS608 61,115Sqs; 1657CU, Crashed 3Sep43. 229hrs
DS609 61,115Sqs, Missing (Duisburg) 27Apr43. 54hrs
DS610 61,115Sqs; 1657CU, 38MU Oct44. Scrap 22May45
DS611 Used for ballistic trials. Became 4947M at 1STT
DS612 61Sq Jan43, 115Sq,426Sq,1678/68CUs, Became 4865M
DS613 61,115Sqs; 1668CU, Wrecked 8Feb45
DS614 115Sq,1668CU,408Sq,1668CU, Wrecked Carnaby 9Nov44
DS615 115Sq,1697CU, Ran into Halifax DT548, Topcliffe 11Dec43
DS616 115Sq, Damaged beyond repair 30May43. 117hrs
DS617 115Sq,1657/68CUs,54MU,1678CU, SOC 7Feb45
DS618 115Sq 17Apr43, Wrecked 30May43. 82hrs
DS619 115Sq,1657/78/68CUs,6LFS 12Jan45. Became 4990M
DS620 115Sq, 1668CU Aug44, Wrecked 14Nov44. 554hrs
DS621 115,408Sqs, Crashed nr. Pilmoor Junct. 2Jul44. 411hrs
DS622 115Sq Feb43, 1668CU Aug44, Wrecked 28Nov44. 598hrs
DS623 115Sq,1678CU(SW ·T) Jan43. SOC 29Aug44
DS624 115,514(JI ·K),426Sqs, Crashed 24Dec43

DS625 115Sq Mar43, First Mk.II lost (Berlin) 30Mar43. 26hrs
DS626 115,426,408Sqs; 1668CU, SOC 20Mar45
DS627 115Sq(A4 ·R) Apr43, Missing 30May43. 85hrs
DS628 TFU Apr43, 5MU Apr44, SOC Dec44
DS629 115Sq Apr43, Damaged beyond repair 19Mar44
DS630 115Sq Apr43, Lost (Peenemunde) 17/18Aug44. 137hrs
DS631 115Sq,1678/68CUs,408Sq(EQ ·I), SOC 4Nov44. 472hrs
DS632 408Sq, Missing 20Feb44
DS633 426,115,514Sqs; Believed lost in Wash 21/22May44
DS634 115,408(EQ ·A)Sqs; Lost (Hamburg) 28/29Jul44. 424hrs
DS635 115Sq Apr43, 1679CU Jan43, Crashed 3Sep43
DS647 115Sq May43, Missing (Dusseldorf) 11Jan43. 28hrs
DS648 1679CU, Crashed 21Sep43, MUs, Scrap Jan47
DS649 426Sq,1679CU, Hit trees on farm near Torrington 6Nov43
DS650 426Sq,1679/60/66CUs, Crash, Northumberland 3Mar44
DS651 1679CU,408Sq(EQ ·I) Apr44, Wrecked 16Aug44
DS652 115Sq Apr43, Crashed near Udem 12Jun43. 43hrs
DS653 115Sq,1678CU, Fell at Sturminster Newton 25Nov43
DS654 1657/78/68CUs, SOC after second crash 24Oct44. 495hrs
DS655 115Sq Apr43, Missing (Essen) 27/28May43. 23hrs
DS656 115Sq May43,426Sq Jun43,408Sq May44, Crashed 10Jun44
DS657 115Sq,1679CU Jun43, 408Sq(EQ ·L) Mar44. SOC Mar45
DS658 115Sq May43, Wrecked 4Sep43, 128hrs
DS659-60 115Sq May43, Missing 27Aug/13Jul43. 86/45hrs
DS661 115Sq May43, Crashed 20Mar44. 260hrs
DS662-3 115Sq May43, Missing 3Jul/25Jun43. 34/33hrs
DS664 115Sq May43, Missing 25Mar44. 238hrs
DS665 115Sq. Dived into ground near Maidstone 11Aug43. 50hrs
DS666-7 115Sq, Missing 25Jun/2Jan44. 17/117hrs
DS668 115Sq, Lost mining off French coast 19Jun43. 3hrs
DS669 115Sq(KO ·L), 514Sq(JI ·C), Lost (Dusseldorf) 22/23Apr44
DS670 115Sq Jun43, 1678CU Aug43, Wrecked 7Sep43. 55hrs
DS671 BDU Jun43-Jan45, SOC Oct45
DS672 BDU; Became 4958M at School of Aero. Engineering
DS673 115Sq Jun43, Lost (Hamburg) 2/3Aug43. 58hrs
DS674 426Sq Jun43, Lost (Peenemunde) 17Aug43. 15hrs
DS675 115Sq 13Jul43, Lost (Hanover) 22Sep43. 39hrs
DS676-7 426Sq Jun43, Missing (Berlin) 23 & 31Aug43
DS678 115Sq Jun43, Missing (Berlin) 25Mar44
DS679 426Sq 30Jun43, Missing (Berlin) 26Nov43

Lancaster B.II DS708 of No. 426 (R.C.A.F.) Squadron.

DS680 115Sq Jul43, Missing (Berlin) 26Nov43. 146hrs
DS681 426Sq, Lost with C.O. at Peenemunde 17Aug43. 25hrs
DS682 115Sq, Landed Ford, hit by Ju88 5/6Sep43. 246hrs
DS683-4 115Sq Jun43, SOC Oct43/Lost (Turin) 16Aug43
DS685 115Sq Jun43, Lost (Hamburg) 2/3Aug43. 44hrs
DS686 426Sq(OW ·F) Jun43, Missing (Berlin) 27Jan44
DS687 TDU Gosport Jan43-Jul44. SOC Oct45
DS688 426Sq,1679CU,408Sq(EQ ·R), Lost (Cambrai) 12/13Jun44
DS689 426Sq(OW ·S), Missing (Stuttgart) 7Oct43
DS690 115Sq Jan43, Missing 13Jul43. 14hrs
DS691 115Sq Jul43, Missing 9Oct43. 109hrs
DS692 408Sq(EQ ·S), 426Sq, Burnt out 24Jul44
DS704 408Sq(EQ ·W), Missing (Frankfurt) 20/21Dec43
DS705 408Sq(EQ ·K), Overshot at Dalton 23Jul44. 316hrs
DS706 514Sq(JI ·G) Sep43, Missing (Berlin) 30/31Jan44
DS707 426Sq Oct43, 1668CU Aug44, SOC Mar45
DS708 426,408Sqs; Short Bros, Rochester, Feb45; RAE. Tests with servo spring tab controls. Derelict at Foulness Island
DS709 408Sq(EQ ·P), Missing (Berlin) 28Jan44
DS710 514Sq(JI ·J), 408Sq(EQ II/A), Lost (Berlin) 27Jan44

DS711 426Sq Aug43, 38MU Dec44, Scrap May47
DS712 408Sq(EQ ·G), landed in sewage near Lincoln 26/27Nov43
DS713 426Sq Jul43, Missing (Dusseldorf) 3Nov43
DS714 426Sq(OW ·L) Jul43, Damaged Sep43, MUs, SOC Sep46
DS715 115Sq Jul43, Missing (Hamburg) 2/3Aug43. 20hrs
DS716 426Sq(OW ·U), 514Sq(JI ·L), Lost (Frankfurt) 20Dec43
DS717 426Sq, Ditched 3 miles E. of Aldeburgh 18/19Oct43
DS718 408Sq(EQ ·R), Missing (Berlin) 29/30Dec43
DS719 426,408(EQ ·U)Sqs, Missing (Essen) 26/27Apr44
DS720-1 115Sq Jul43, Missing 15Jan44/4Oct43. 115/82hrs
DS722 426,408Sqs, Missing 23Aug43
DS723 498Sq(EQ ·D/B), Missing (Berlin) 26/27Nov43
DS724 408Sq(EQ ·X), Abandoned in air over Yorks. 7Oct43
DS725 408Sq(EQ ·B),1158CU, Missing (Leipzig) 20Oct43
DS726 408Sq(EQ ·Y), Missing (Cambrai) 12/13Jun44
DS727 408Sq(EQ ·X), 1668CU, Became 4972M
DS728 115Sq Aug43, Missing (Cologne) 21Apr44
DS729 408Sq(EQ ·D/H), Ground looped after action 7Jan44
DS730 408Sq(EQ ·E),1668CU, Became 4973M at 1666CU
DS731 408Sq(EQ ·O), Missing (Schweinfurt) 24/25Feb44
DS732 408Sq(EQ ·F), Engines failed over base 7Sep43
DS733 426Sq Sep43, Missing (Leipzig) 4Dec43
DS734 115Sq 4Sep43, Missing 24Apr44. 257hrs
DS735 514Sq(JI ·A) Sep43, Missing (Berlin) 30Jan44
DS736 514Sq(JI ·L) Sep43, Missing (Leipzig) 20Feb44. 84hrs
DS737 408Sq(EQ ·C), Crashed, Yorks, ex-Berlin raid 16/17Dec43
DS738 514Sq(JI ·J) Sep43, Missing (Berlin) 2Dec43. 54hrs
DS739-40 432Sq, Missing 3Jan/15Jan44
DS741 426Sq(OW ·T), Missing (Frankfurt) 22Mar44. 181hrs
DS757 426Sq(OW ·D), hit sea off Bridlington 5Mar44
DS758 408Sq(EQ ·H) Aug43, Missing (Frankfurt) 21Dec43
DS759 426,408Sqs(EQ ·A), Missing (Dortmund) 22/23May44
DS760 426Sq Aug43, Missing (Berlin) 2/3Jan44
DS761 408Sq(EQ ·V) Aug43, 46MU Sep44, Scrap Nov46
DS762 426Sq(OW ·V) Aug43, Missing (Frankfurt) 20Dec43
DS763 426Sq(OW ·O), 1668CU Aug44, Crashed 10Oct44. 551hrs
DS764 115Sq Aug43, Missing (Berlin) 22Nov43. 89hrs
DS765 115Sq(KO.A) Aug43, Lost (Liepzig) 4/5Dec43. 113hrs
DS766 115Sq Aug43, SOC after third time damaged 23Aug44
DS767 426Sq(OW ·P), 408Sq(EQ ·Q), Missing 14/15Jan44
DS768 408Sq(EQ ·J), Overshot landing, Honeybourne 6/7Jun44
DS769 408Sq(EQ ·J), 115Sq(KO ·H), Lost (Hanover) 18Oct43
DS770 426Sq Aug43, Missing (Berlin) 3Dec43
DS771 426Sq, Missing (Stuttgart) 15/16Mar44. 114hrs
DS772 408Sq(EQ ·T), Missing (Cambrai) 12/13Jun44. 362hrs
DS773 115Sq Aug43, Missing (Berlin) 23/24Dec43
DS774 408Sq(EQ ·F) Sep43, Missing 3/4Nov43
DS775-6 426Sq Sep43, Lost (Berlin) 27Jan/(Leipzig) 19Feb44
DS777 115Sq Sep43, Missing (Magdeburg) 22Jan44. 115hrs
DS778 408Sq(EQ ·U) Sep43, Missing (Kassel) 22/23Oct43
DS779 426Sq, Crashed Hunsinggore, breaking cloud 16Dec43
DS780 115Sq, Crashed on rly. embankment Magdalan 14Sep43
DS781 514Sq, Missing (Duisburg) 21/22May44
DS782 115Sq(K), Missing (Berlin) 23Nov43. 194hrs
DS783 514Sq(JI ·J/B) Sep43, Damaged 3Dec43, 5MU, SOC Sep46
DS784 1153q(JI ·C) Sep43, Lost (Mannheim) 18Nov43. 85hrs
DS785 514Sq(JI ·D) 12 Sep43, Lost (Schweinfurt) 24/25Feb44
DS786 514Sq(JI ·E), 1668/61CUs, Became 4976M at 1661CU
DS787 514Sq(JI ·F) Sep43, Missing (Kamen) 11Sep44. 451hrs
DS788 432Sq Oct43, 408Sq Feb44, Missing 20Feb44
DS789 432Sq, 426Sq(OW ·A) Feb44, Lost (Nuremburg) 30Mar44
DS790 408Sq(EQ ·B) Nov43, Missing (Magdeburg) 21/22Jan44
DS791 408(EQ ·F) Nov43, Missing (Augsburg) 25/26Feb44
DS792 432Sq(QO ·U) Nov43, Damaged 3Jan44, 46MU, SOC Jan47
DS793 115Sq 5Nov43, Missing (Berlin) 27Nov43. 6hrs
DS794 432Sq Nov43, 426Sq Feb44, Lost (Berlin) 15Feb44
DS795 115Sq Nov43, Crashed 10Jan44, 24MU,38MU, SOC Aug47
DS796 514Sq(JI ·E) Nov43, 115Sq, Damaged 1Jan44. 80hrs
DS797 408Sq(EQ ·M) Dec43, Lost (Frankfurt) 22/23Mar44. 17hrs
DS813 514Sq(JI ·H) Sep43, Missing 29Jul44. 372hrs
DS814 514Sq(JI ·M) Sep43, Missing (Berlin) 26Nov43. 57hrs
DS815 514Sq(JI ·N) Sep43, Missing 23Mar43. 200hrs
DS816 514Sq(JI ·O) Sep43, Lost (Valenciennes) 15Jun44. 282hrs
DS817 514Sq(JI ·P), Lost (Frankfurt-am-Main) 20Dec43. 39hrs

DS818 514Sq(JI ·Q), Lost (Gelsenkirchen) 12/13Jun44. 305hrs
DS819 AFEE Sep43, Crashed on Continent 29Jun45
DS820 514Sq(JI ·A), (JI ·R) Sep43, Crashed 17May44
DS821 514Sq(JI ·S) Sep43, Ditched 29/30Dec43. 86hrs
DS822 514Sq(JI ·T), Lost (Massy Palaiseau) 7/8Jun44. 309hrs
DS823 514Sq(JI ·M/K) Oct43, Lost (Leipzig) 19/20Feb44. 87hrs
DS824 514Sq(JI ·K), Down in Zuyder Zee 21/22Jan44. 76hrs
DS825 115Sq, Burnt after operation 8Nov43. 6hrs
DS826 514Sq, 1678CU, 514Sq, 1668CU, SOC Mar45
DS827 115Sq(A4 ·D) Oct43, Crashed Gt. Dunmow 5Feb44
DS828 514Sq Oct43, Missing (Dusseldorf) 22/23Apr44
DS829 426Sq(OW ·U), Missing (Stuttgart) 15Mar44. 152hrs
DS830 432Sq,408Sq(EQ ·H), 1668CU, SOC Mar45
DS831 432Sq Oct43, Missing (Berlin) 17Dec43
DS832 432Sq Oct43, Crashed and burnt 18Dec43
DS833-4 115Sq Nov43, Missing 28Jan44/30Dec43. 62/9hrs
DS835 115Sq 24Nov43, Missing (Berlin) 16Dec43. 4hrs
DS836 115Sq, 514Sq(JI ·L), Lost (Nuremburg) 30/31Mar44. 82hrs
DS837 426Sq, Hit ground at Yearsley in cloud 16Dec43
DS838 408Sq(EQ ·A), 426Sq(OW ·J), 1668CU, Crashed 26Feb45
DS389 1679CU, Crashed at Ridgemont, Beds. 23Jan44
DS840 426Sq(OW ·C) Dec43, Missing (Nuremburg) 30Mar44. 86hrs
DS841 426Sq(OW ·Q), 1668CU Oct44, SOC Mar45
DS842 514Sq Dec43-Jul44, 1668CU, SOC Mar45
DS843 432Sq Oct43, Missing 22Jan44
DS844 426,432,408Sqs; Missing 25Feb44
DS845 408Sq(EQ ·T), Forced down in enemy territory 25Feb44
DS846 408Sq 18Oct43, Missing (Berlin) 27Dec43
DS847 432Sq, Crashed 1 mile W. of Ingham, Lincs. 16Nov43
DS848 432,426,408Sqs; 1668CU, Wrecked 26Mar45
DS849 408Sq(EQ ·K), Missing (Berlin) 28/29Jan44
DS850-1 432Sq Oct43, Missing 15Jan44/Wrecked 3Dec43
DS852 432(QO ·C), 426Sq(OW ·P), Missing 30Mar44. 114hrs

Serials DT810 and DT812   **Lancaster II Prototypes**
2 prototypes ordered from A. V. Roe (Chadderton) of which only DT810 was built and was first flown November 26th, 1941, with Hercules VI engines.

Serial Range DV155—DV407   **Lancaster B.I/B.III**
200 Lancasters order from Metropolitan-Vickers in 1941, built as 91 B.I (Merlin 22 engines) and 109 B.III (Merlin 28 engines) as indicated from May to November 1943.

DV155 III 617Sq 31May43, 44Sq Jun43, Lost 3/4Sep43. 194hrs
DV156 III 617Sq May43, 50Sq Jul 43, Lost (Turin) 12/13Jul43
DV157 III 12Sq 31May43, Down in North Sea 11/12Jun43
DV158 III 12Sq(GZ ·A), Lost (Berlin) 23/24Aug43
DV159 III 100Sq, Missing (Hanover) 19Oct43. 275hrs
DV160 III 460Sq, Missing (Oberhausen) 14/15Jun43
DV161 III 12Sq,1667CU; 460,57,9,50Sqs; 1653CU, Crash Jan45
DV162 III 1667CU, 100Sq Jul43, Missing 4Oct43
DV163 III Used by Flt. Refuelling, Staverton, SOC 2Jan46
DV164 III 1667CU May43, 12Sq Jun43, Missing 9/10Jul43
DV165 III 1667CU,300Sq,1LFS,1662,1667CUs, Burnt 9Apr45
DV166 III 49,619,49,44Sqs; 1669/54/60CUs; Crash 27/28Apr45
DV167 III 50Sq 11Jun43, Lost raiding Italy 15/16Jul43. 62hrs
DV168 III 12Sq 14Jun43, Lost (Peenemunde) 17/18Aug43
DV169 III 1662CU 14Jun43, Crashed and SOC 7Jul45. 72hrs
DV170 III R-R 16Jun43, converted Mk. VI SOC 16Dec47
DV171 III 12,626,463Sqs; Lost (Calais) 24/25Sep44. 507hrs
DV172 III 460Sq, Burnt out 3Jul43 by own incendiaries
DV173 III 460Sq Jun43, Crashed Normandy 16/17Dec43. 307hrs
DV174 III 460Sq 21Jun43, Missing 23Sep43. 180hrs
DV175 III 460Sq Jun-Sep43, 5LFS, Scrapped at 46MU Oct46
DV176 III 100Sq 23Jun43, Damaged 23Oct43, Scrap Jul47
DV177 III 12Sq(GZ ·K), 626Sq, Crashed at Boxted 24/25Apr44
DV178 III 49,50Sqs Oct43, Lost (Berlin) 26/27Nov43. 283hrs
DV179 III A. V. Roe tests Jun43, AAEE Nov43, Scrap Oct45
DV180 III 103Sq, 166Sq Sep43, Lost (Berlin) 28/29Jan44
DV181-2 III 106Sq Jan43, Lost 13Jul/6Sep43. 27/164hrs
DV183 III 207Sq Jan43, Missing 16Jul43. 30hrs
DV184 III 207Sq Jan43, Stalled at Langar 2Oct43. 212hrs

DV185 III 12Sq 20Jun43, Missing 1Sep43. 133hrs
DV186 III 61Sq 20Jun43, Missing (Milan) 16Aug43. 132hrs
DV187 III 12Sq(PH ·A) 7Jul43, Missing 27/28Aug43
DV188 III 207Sq 6Jul43, Lost (Berlin) 23/24Dec43. 309hrs
DV189 III RAE,100Sq Jul-Dec43, Missing from 550Sq 2Jan44
DV190 III 12Sq Jul-Dec43, 626Sq, Lost (Berlin) 2Jan44
DV191 III 207Sq(EM ·O)Jul43,Lost(Brunswick)14/15Jan44. 377hrs
DV192 III 100,550,100Sqs; Missing 29Apr44. 430hrs
DV193 III 460Sq, 1LFS, 103Sq. Became 4959M 4STT Dec44
DV194 III 101Sq Jul43, 625Sq(CF ·F), Lost 15/16Mar44. 383hrs
DV195-6 III 106Sq Jul43, Lost 11Aug/8Aug43. 52/59hrs
DV197 III 50Sq 13Jul43, Damaged 31Jul43 and SOC
DV198 III 9Sq(WS ·U) 12Jul43, Lost (Tours) 10/11Apr44. 52ops
DV199 III R-R 6Jul43, converted Mk. VI, SOC 8Jun47
DV200 III 12Sq, 1LFS, 550Sq, 1662CU, BCIS(WB ·S), Scrap 1946
DV201 III 57Sq 17Jul43, Missing 24Sep43. 242hrs
DV202 III 44Sq 17Jul43, Missing 18Aug43. 78hrs
DV217 III 50Sq 18Jul43, Missing 21Dec43. 358hrs
DV218 III 12Sq 22Jul43, Damaged Oct43, Lost 4Nov43
DV219 III 12Sq 22Jul43, Damaged Jul43, Lost 22Sep43. 23hrs
DV220 III 103Sq Jul-Sep43, 166Sq, Lost 30Oct43. 318hrs
DV221 III 103Sq 25Jul43, Missing 27/28Sep43. 138hrs
DV222 III 12Sq 26Jul43, Crashed 26Aug43, Lost 2/3Oct43
DV223 III 50Sq, Crashed at Maison Blanche 8Aug43
DV224 III 12Sq 25Jul43, Missing 2/3Aug43
DV225 III 12Sq 25Jul43, Missing 23/24Sep43. 146hrs
DV226 III 467Sq 29Jul43, Missing (Kassel) 22/23Oct43
DV227 III 50Sq Aug43, Lost (St. Leu d'Esserent) 7/8Jul44
DV228 III 61Sq 31Jul43, Shot down in Holland 22/23Aug43
DV229 III 106Sq Aug43, 463Sq, Lost (Orleans) 10/11Jun44. 541hrs
DV230 III 101Sq(SR ·T) 4Sep43, Missing 19Oct43. 39hrs
DV231 III 101Sq(SR ·R) Sep43, Lost (Berlin) 27/28Jan44. 149hrs
DV232 III 61Sq 15Aug43, Crashed 6Sep43. 72hrs
DV233 III 427,467,207,467Sqs; Missing 24Sep43. 61hrs
DV234-5 III 50/57Sqs Aug43, Lost 9/3Oct43. 172/77hrs
DV236 III 32MU, 101Sq(SR ·G) 19Sep43, Lost 15Feb44, 195hrs
DV237 III 467Sq 20Aug43, Missing 4Sep43. 13hrs
DV238 III 619,49(EA ·O),44Sqs; Lost 17Dec43. 135hrs
DV239 III 61Sq(QR ·V) Aug43, Lost (Hanover) 8/9Oct43. 118hrs
DV240 III 467Sq 22Aug43, Lost (Nuremberg) 30/31Mar44. 388hrs
DV241 III 12Sq 24Aug43, Missing (Berlin) 1Sep43. 16hrs
DV242 III 100,625Sqs; 3LFS, 1656CU, 5MU, Scrap Dec46
DV243 III 207Sq Aug 43, Ditched near Yarmouth 23Oct43. 131hrs
DV244 III 12Sq(PH ·E) Aug43, 626Sq, Lost 26Feb44. 205hrs
DV245 III 101Sq(SR ·S), Lost (Bremen) 23Mar45. 119 operations
DV246 III 617Sq(AJ ·U) Aug43-Jul44; 1661/54CUs; 5MU, SOC Aug47
DV247 III 460Sq Aug43, 166Sq, Lost (Berlin) 26/27Nov43. 146hrs
DV263 III 44Sq(KM ·M) Sep43, Damaged 27Nov43, Missing (Magdeburg) 22Jan44
DV264 III 101Sq 21Sep43, Missing 31Mar44. 276hrs
DV265-6 III 101Sq 2Oct43, Lost 5Nov/19Oct43. 38/6hrs
DV267 III 101Sq(SR ·K) Oct43, Missing 19/20Feb44. 209hrs
DV268 III 101Sq 20Sep43, Missing 27Nov43. 63hrs
DV269 III 101Sq(SR.M) 22Sep43, Missing 3Jan44. 134hrs
DV270 III 101Sq, Hit trees at Binbrook Hall 5Dec43
DV271-2 III 106Sq Sep43, Missing 23Sep/10Oct43. 26/87hrs
DV273 III 106Sq 9Oct43, BDU Jan45, Scrapped Nov46
DV274 III 106,463Sqs; Lost (Augsburg) 26Feb44. 253hrs
DV275 III 32MU; 101,463,101(SR ·X2)Sqs; Lost 4May44
DV276 III Crashed in transit Sep43, 101Sq, Lost 31Mar44
DV277 I A.V. Roe 6Sep43, 467Sq, 5LFS, 46MU, Scrap Nov46
DV278 I 625Sq(CF ·V), 300Sq(BH ·A), Lost 14Aug44. 159hrs
DV279 I 550Sq(BQ.M), Crashed at Seething 19Jul44. 299hrs
DV280 I 463Sq 29Jan44, Missing 26Jun44. 237hrs
DV281 I 626Sq(UM ·D2) Feb44, Lost (Mailly) 3/4May44
DV282 I 300Sq 11Mar44, Missing 28Apr44
DV283 III 32MU,20MU,101Sq, Damaged & SOC 17Dec43. 14hrs
DV284 III 9Sq(WS ·G) 14Sep43, Missing 18Nov43. 14ops
DV285 III 101Sq 9Oct43, Missing 27Nov43. 53hrs
DV286 III 44Sq Sep43, 38MU, 300Sq. Lost 13Jan44
DV287 III 101Sq Oct43, Shot down over Holland 14Jan44
DV288-9 III 101Sq Oct43, Lost 11Apr44/27Nov43. 148/41hrs
DV290 III 101Sq, Dived into USAAF Stn, Welford 31Mar44

DV291 I SIU,32MU,101Sq Oct43, Damaged 23Nov43. 32hrs
DV292 I SIU,32MU,101Sq(SR ·Y), Lost 13Aug44. 269hrs
DV293 I 9Sq(WS ·Y) Sep43, Missing 16Dec43. 18ops
DV294 I 61Sq(QR ·K) Sep43, Lost (Augsburg) 25/26Feb44. 263hrs
DV295 I 626Sq, Crashed near Marham on return 26/27Nov43
DV296 I 460Sq Sep43, Missing (Berlin) 2Dec43. 136hrs
DV297 I 106,61Sqs, Lost on Berlin raid 26/27Nov43. 86hrs
DV298 III 101Sq Oct43, Gale damage 18Jan45, Lost 13/14Mar45
DV299-300 I 32MU Sep43, 101Sq Nov43, Lost 17Dec43. 41/68hrs
DV301 I 32MU Sep43, 101Sq Nov43, Missing 1Jul44
DV302 I 32MU,101Sq(SR ·H) Nov43, 46MU, Scrap Jan47. 121ops
DV303 I 101Sq(SR ·U) Nov43, Lost (Berlin) 30Jan44, 107hrs
DV304 I 101Sq, Conv. Mk.III at 24MU, 61Sq, Lost 18/19Jul44
DV305 I 100Sq Oct43, 550Sq Nov43, Wrecked 31Jan44
DV306 I 100Sq Oct43, 550Sq Nov43, Lost 15Jan44. 141hrs
DV307-8 I 32MU Sep43, 101Sq Nov43, Lost 2Jan44. 73/52hrs
DV309 I 166Sq Oct43, 550Sq Feb44, Missing 22May44. 210hrs
DV310 III 166Sq,5LFS,189Sq,1659CU(RV ·L). Became 5930M
DV311 I 61Sq(QR ·P) Oct43,Lost(Nuremberg)30/31Mar44. 291hrs
DV312 I conv. to III. 61(QR ·Z), 207,50Sqs; Lost 18/19Jul44
DV324 I 50Sq Oct43, Missing (Hanover) 8/9Oct43
DV325 I 50Sq 5Oct44, Missing (Berlin) 2/3Dec43. 80hrs
DV326 I 619Sq Oct43, 5LFS Sep44, Temporary 5055M Lindholme
DV327 I 9Sq(WS ·N) Oct43, Crash landed 23Nov43. 7ops
DV328 I 619Sq(PG ·L) Oct43, Lost (Berlin) 24Mar44. 262hrs
DV329 I 44Sq 7Oct43, Missing 24Nov43. 64hrs
DV330 I 619Sq(PG ·O) Oct43, Missing 15Feb44. 159hrs
DV331 I 44Sq(KM ·Z/T) Oct43, Lost (Turin) 12/13Jul43. 114hrs
DV332 I 9Sq(WS ·D) Oct43, Lost 3Dec44. 9ops
DV333 I 460Sq,576Sq(UL ·K2) Nov43, Lost (Stettin) 5/6Jan44
DV334 I 9Sq, Crashed Markham Clayton, operation 2/3Dec43
DV335 I 619Sq Oct43, Crashed 26Nov43, 46MU, Scrap Jan47
DV336 I 619Sq, Crashed, burnt, landing at Elvington 27Nov43
DV337 I Lost on 463Sq's first raid (Berlin) 26/27Nov43
DV338 I 467Sq Oct43, 463Sq, Lost (Liepzig) 19/20Feb44. 186hrs
DV339 I 61Sq Nov43, Lost Berlin raid 26/27Nov43. 45hrs
DV340 I conv. to III. 460,9Sqs; 1651CU, SOC Apr46
DV341 I 460Sq Oct43, Missing (Berlin) 18Nov43. 26hrs
DV342 I 103Sq Oct43, 467Sq Dec43, Missing 17Dec43. 79hrs
DV343 I 100Sq,550Sq Nov43, Missing 23/24Dec43. 78hrs
DV344 I 106Sq,61Sq Nov43, Lost (Berlin) 1/2Jan44. 91hrs
DV345 I 100Sq,550Sq, Caught fire in air 2Jan44. 103hrs
DV359 I 460Sq, Crashed at Fletton 1Apr44. 212hrs
DV360 I 207Sq Oct45, Lost (Wesseling) 21/22Jun44. 375hrs
DV361 I 207Sq, Caught fire in air, England 22Dec43
DV362 I conv. III. 625Sq(CF ·B), 46MU,5LFS,R-R, SOC Sep46
DV363 I 50Sq Nov43, Lost (St. Leu) 7/8Jul44. 415hrs
DV364 I 625Sq(CF ·D) Nov43, Lost (Berlin) 28Jan44. 100hrs
DV365 I 166Sq(AS ·Z2); Landed, damaged, Ford 26Nov43. 150hrs
DV366 I 50Sq Nov43, Missing (Berlin) 23Nov43. 26hrs
DV367 I 166Sq, Lost (Versailles rly. yds) 7Jun44. 362hrs
DV368 I 50Sq,5LFS, Crash (tyre burst) Syerston 19May44
DV369 I 207Sq(EM ·D) Nov43, Lost (Brunswick) 14Jan44. 140hrs
DV370-1 I 207Sq Nov43, Missing 2/30Jan44. 95/149hrs
DV372 I 467Sq Nov43, 1651CU Nov44, Wrecked 4Oct45
DV373 I 467Sq, Ditched in daylight 5Oct44. 595hrs
DV374 I 463Sq Nov43, Lost (Revigny) 18/19Jul44. 417hrs
DV375 I 50Sq, Lost (Berlin) 29/30Dec43 (rear gunner rescued)
DV376 I 50Sq Nov43, Lost (Berlin) 15/16Feb44. 139hrs
DV377 I 50Sq Nov43, Burnt 27Nov43
DV378 I 467Sq 7Nov43, Missing 31Jan44. 115hrs
DV379 I To BAOC Nov43, Became G-AGJI BOAC test-bed
DV380 I 617Sq Nov43, Damaged 16Mar and 24Apr45. SOC Mar46
DV381 I 619Sq(PG ·B) Nov43, Lost (Berlin) 26Nov43. 30hrs
DV382 I 617Sq, Flew into hill 10 miles N.E. Chichester 13Feb44
DV383 III 207Sq(EM ·G) Nov43, 46MU, SOC Nov47
DV384 III 44Sq Nov43, 50Sq, Lost (Frankfurt) 22/23Mar44
DV385 I 617Sq Nov43, Damaged 4 times, 46MU Apr45, Scrap Nov46
DV386 I 166,576Sqs(UL ·E2), Lost (Leipzig) 19/20Feb44. 120hrs
DV387 I 166Sq Nov43, Missing (Berlin) 26/27Nov43. 4hrs
DV388 I 626Sq(UM ·S2) Nov43, Lost (Berlin) 26Nov43
DV389 I 101Sq(SR ·P) ex-32MU Dec 43, Lost 25May44. 229hrs
DV390 I 626Sq, Damaged beyond repair 29Nov43

DV391 I 617Sq(Y) Nov43, Damaged 4 times 46MU Scrap Oct46
DV392 I 625Sq Nov43, Missing (Berlin) 23Dec43. 13hrs
DV393 I 617Sq(T) Nov43, 9Sq Mar45,38MU Feb46, Scrap May47
DV394 I 617Sq 25Nov43, Missing 25Apr44. 165hrs
DV395 III 156,9(WS ·T),15Sqs; 1660,1654HCUs; SOC 25Aug47
DV396 I 9Sq Nov43, 467Sq Oct44, Lost 2Nov44, 442hrs
DV397 I 61Sq(QR ·N) 30Nov43, Lost (Berlin) 24/25Mar44. 227hrs
DV398 I 617Sq 30Nov43, Missing (Liege) 21Dec43. 12hrs
DV399 I 61Sq, Missing (Berlin) 29/30Dec43
DV400-1 I 61Sq, Lost (Berlin) 27/28 & 2/3Jan44. 99/64hrs
DV402 I 617Sq(X) Dec43, SOC after 4th time damaged Nov45
DV403-4 I 617/166Sqs Dec44, Lost 25Jun/15Jan44. 217/64hrs
DV405 I 617Sq(J) except AAEE Jun44, 46MU, Scrap Jan47
DV406 I 166Sq Dec44, Missing (Berlin) 30Jan44. 52hrs
DV407 I 101Sq(SR ·R2) ex-32MU,46MU May45, SOC Feb46

Serial Range ED303—EE202   **Lancaster B.I/B.III**

620 Lancasters ordered from A. V. Roe (Chadderton) in 1941 and
built from November 1942 to June 1943 as 129 B.I and 491 B.III as
indicated up to ED782 and all as Mk.III from ED783 onwards.
Mk.Is were initially fitted with Merlin 20 and Mk.IIIs with Merlin
28 engines.

ED303 I 467Sq Nov42, 106Sq, Merlin 22s Feb43, Lost 28Jul43
ED304 I 467Sq Nov42, Lost (Dusseldorf) 11/12Jun43. 167hrs
ED305 I 44Sq(KM ·S) Nov42, Lost mining 10/11Mar43. 129hrs
ED306 I 57Sq Nov42, Blown up at Scampton 15Mar43. 140hrs
ED307 I 9Sq,44Sq(KM ·R) Feb43, Lost mining 28/29Jun43. 302hrs
ED308 I 9(WS ·R),57Sqs; 1661CU,50Sq, Lost 18/19Mar43. 423hrs
ED309 I 50Sq,44Sq(KM ·S), Lost mining 7/8Feb43. 139hrs
ED310 I 97Sq,1654CU; 15,75Sqs; 1LFS,CUs, Crashed 24Apr45
ED311 I 83Sq(OL ·X) Nov42, Missing 23Nov42. 6hrs
ED312-3 I 83Sq Nov42, Lost 21Apr/12Mar43. 225/1131hrs
ED314 I 44Sq, 61Sq(QR ·Y), Lost (Hanover) 27/28Sep43. 574hrs.
ED315 I 460Sq Dec42, Crashed 28Jun43   [63ops
ED316 I 1656CU Nov42, Missing 18Jan43. 42hrs
ED317 I 1656CU; 101,625(CF ·W)Sqs; Lost (Berlin) 24Mar44
ED318 I 44Sq(KM ·X) Nov42, Lost (Kiel) 17Jan43. 48hrs
ED319 I 57Sq 28Nov42, Missing 9Jan43. 53hrs
ED320 I 101Sq Dec42, Crashed 13Aug43. 365hrs
ED321 I 101Sq,625Sq(CF ·U), Lost (Dusseldorf) 4Nov43. 371hrs
ED322 I 101Sq Nov42, Missing 7Dec42 on first operation
ED323 I 97Sq,1661CU May43, 15Sq Dec43, Lost 28Jan44. 745hrs
ED324 I 1656/62CUs, 5MU, 1LFS, 1662CU, Became 5290M
ED325-6 I 12Sq Nov42, Lost 28Apr/20Apr43
ED327 I 101,166,300Sqs; Lost (Stettin) 28/29Aug44. 593hrs
ED328 I 101Sq Nov42, Damaged 16Dec42, Lost 24Aug43, 396hrs
ED329 I 207Sq(EM ·T),617Sq Mar43,57Sq 9May43, Lost 13May43
ED330-1 I 207/44Sqs Dec42, Lost 19Feb/13Jul43. 99/309hrs
ED332 I 61Sq Dec42, Wrecked 17Jan43
ED333-4 I 97/83Sqs Dec42, Lost 18Dec42/4Apr43. 7/140hrs
ED347 I 9Sq(WS ·N) Nov42, Lost (Duisburg) 20/21Dec42. 30hrs
ED348 I 49Sq Nov42, 57Sq,5MU,44Sq, Lost 20Oct43. 232hrs
ED349 I 9Sq(WS ·S)Nov42, Lost (Cloppenburg) 17Dec42. 27hrs
ED350 I TFU, Defford Jan43, with H2SMk.III. SOC 1Oct44
ED351 I 44Sq(KM ·Y) Dec42, Lost (Duisburg) 8/9Apr43. 176hrs
ED352-3 I 49/83Sqs Dec42, Lost 5Feb43/21Dec42 54/11hrs
ED354 I 460(AR ·O) Dec42, Lost (Duisberg) 26Mar43. 89hrs
ED355 I 44Sq(KM ·D) Dec42, Lost (Nienburg) 17Dec42. 4hrs
ED356-7 I 207/12Sqs Dec42, Lost 26Feb/12Jun43. 83/?hrs
ED358 I 106Sq, Lost 21Oct43 after three major repairs. 300hrs
ED359 I 61Sq Dec42, Missing (Lorient) 7/8Feb43. 82hrs
ED360 I 467Sq,106Sq Feb43, Burnt in crash 9Jul43. 354hrs
ED361 I 207Sq, Hit JA844, fell in sea, 13Aug43. 315hrs
ED362 III 100Sq from 39MU 12Mar43, Missing 28Jun43
ED363 I 467Sq Dec42, Lost (Cologne) 28/29Jun43. 174hrs
ED364 I 467,207Sqs; 1654CU,622Sq; Lost 31Jan44. 398hrs
ED365 I 207Sq(EM ·U) Jan43, Lost (Hamburg) 4Mar43. 82hrs
ED366 I 100Sq,46MU,166Sq, Lost (Kassel) 22Oct43. 19hrs
ED367 I First Lancaster lost by 467Sq (Essen) 8/9Jan43
ED368 I 83Sq,NTU,1668CU,5LFS,MUs,BCIS, Crashed 11Jun45
ED369 I 460Sq 8Dec42, Missing 9Jul43
ED370 I 101,460Sqs, Missing (Berlin) 26Nov43. 250hrs
ED371/G III RAE Lincoln nose fitted, 207,57Sqs; Scrap Sep46

ED372 I 83,101,166Sqs; Lost 27Sep43 with cine unit. 307hrs
ED373-4 I 101Sq Dec42, Lost 26Jun43/Wrecked 17Feb43
ED375 I 101Sq 9Dec42, Missing (St. Nazaire) 23Mar43. 129hrs
ED376 I 100Sq, 1662CU, 15Sq,3LFS, Crashed 17Jan44. 660hrs
ED377 I 101Sq Dec42, Crashed 15Feb43, Lost 27/28Jun43. 186hrs
ED378 III 1662CU 5Apr43, Missing from training 20Aug43
ED379 I 101Sq Dec42, Accident 24Jan43, Lost 17Apr43. 165hrs
ED380 I 100Sq Dec42, 103Sq 4Feb43, Lost 17Feb43. 38hrs.
ED381 I 1656CU, Collided with Wellington BJ845 over Brize
        Norton 17Jun43. Fell at Wigstead Farm near Highworth
ED382 I 101,625Sqs; 5MU,300Sq,1LFS,CU,BCIS, Became 5296M
ED383 III 1656CU; 622,15Sqs; Crash Lakenheath 26Feb44. 628hrs
ED384 I 103Sq 15Dec42, Missing (Essen) 9Jan43. 9hrs
ED385 I 57Sq Dec42, 20MU,106Sq Aug43, Lost 4Sep43. 99hrs
ED386 I 12Sq Dec42, Missing 23/24Jan43
ED387 III 49,50Sqs; Lost (Nuremburg) 25/26Feb43. 48hrs
ED388 III Converted to Mk.I; 100,12Sqs; Lost 17/18Jan43
ED389 I 100Sq Dec42, 103Sq Feb43, Lost 24Jul43. 336hrs
ED390 III 57Sq Apr43, Stalled at Coltishall 11May43. 49hrs
ED391 I 100,460Sqs, Shot down in Holland 30Mar43. 139hrs
ED392 I 50Sq, 12Sq(GZ ·D) Jun43, Lost 6Sep43. 135hrs
ED393 III 50Sq Apr43, Crashed on houses, Hayton 26/27Nov43

Lancaster III ED413 of No. 207 Squadron.

ED394 I 50Sq, Crashed night landing at Crosby 9Jan43
ED395 I 156,9,15Sqs; 3LFS; 1660/1654CUs; SOC Aug47
ED396 III 103Sq 7Apr43, Missing 15Jun43. 50hrs
ED408 III 12Sq 2Apr43, Missing mining 28/29Apr43
ED409 I 50Sq, 106Sq Jan43, Missing 31Aug43. 433hrs
ED410 III 101Sq 23Apr43, Missing 4Sep43. 220hrs
ED411 I 57,166Sqs; Missing (Berlin) 16Dec43. 7hrs
ED412 I 57Sq Dec42, 207Sq May43, Lost 14Jul43. 108hrs
ED413 III 57,630,207(EM ·P)Sqs; 1651CU Nov44, SOC 27Jan45
ED414 I 100Sq Dec42, 1662CU Feb43, Crashed 7Jul43. 268hrs
ED415 III 50Sq, Damaged May43, Lost (Mannheim) 23/24Sep43
ED416 III 49Sq 9Jan43, Missing (Mannheim) 5/6Sep43
ED417 III 103Sq, Mid-air crash, Halifax JN966, 27Nov43
ED418 I 207Sq 29Dec42, Missing 13May43. 230hrs
ED419 III 103Sq ex-39MU 26Mar43, Missing 16Mar43. 5hrs
ED420 I 83,9,106,463Sqs; Lost (Berlin) 23/24Dec43. 194hrs
ED421 III 460Sq ex-38MU 27Apr43, Lost (Berlin) 23/24Aug43
ED422 I 101,166Sqs; Hit trees 17Nov43. 411hrs
ED423 III 50Sq ex-46MU 20Dec42, Lost (Berlin) 1/2Mar43
ED424 III 12Sq(GZ ·E),626Sq(UM ·E2) 7Nov43, Missing 25Apr44
ED425 I 97Sq,1660/54CUs; 622,75Sqs; 5LFS, 1651CU, SOC Sep47
ED426-7 III 49Sq Dec42, Lost (Stuttgart) 8Oct43/20Apr43
ED428 III 49Sq, Crashed at Reepham Crossing 30/31Jan43
ED429 III 50Sq ex-46MU 27Jan43, Missing (Bochum) 13Jun43
ED430 I 97,50,622(GI ·A)Sqs; 3LFS, MUs, Scrap Feb47
ED431 III 49Sq direct from A. V. Roe 24Dec42, Lost 9Feb43
ED432 III 49Sq 24Dec42, Missing (Oberhausen) 14/15Jan43
ED433 III 44Sq ex-39MU 12Mar43, Twice damaged, Lost 4Oct43
ED434-5 III 49Sq, Lost (Oberhausen) 14Jun/30Mar43. 156/75hrs
ED436 I 9Sq 23Dec42, Missing 18Jan43. 25hrs. 2ops
ED437 III 50,617Sqs; 1661HCU,622Sq; 3,5LFS; Became 5060M
ED438 III 49Sq 28Dec42, Damaged 3/4Jul43, Lost 17Jul43
ED439 I 83Sq, Dived from cloud into Scredington 18Jun43
ED440 III 49Sq 24Dec42, Missing (Koln) 3Feb43. 25hrs
ED441 III 49Sq 29Dec42, Missing (Pilsen) 17Apr43
ED442 III 50Sq damaged Feb43, 5MU,207Sq, Lost 22Sep43
ED443 I 101Sq 30Dec42. Crashed 21/22Jan43. 28hrs
ED444 III 49Sq 31Dec42, Missing 18Jan43. 11hrs
ED445 III 49Sq Jan43, 50Sq Oct43, Lost (Berlin) 23/24Dec43

158

ED446 I 101Sq, Crashed on beach near Hornsea 20Mar43. 93hrs
ED447 I 101Sq 29Dec42, SOC 30Jan43. 14hrs
ED448 III 49Sq Dec42, Damaged Feb and Jun, Crashed 16Sep43
ED449 III 50Sq Skellingthorpe 9Jan43, Lost (Essen) 12/13Mar43
ED450 III 49Sq, Hit balloon cable, Devon, fell in sea 13Feb43
ED451 I 106Sq 8Jan43, Missing (Essen) 1May43. 240hrs
ED452 III 49Sq Scampton Jan43. Damaged in action 14May43
ED453 III 49Sq Jan43, Missing (Oberhausen) 14/15Jan43
ED467 III 49Sq 5Jan43, Missing 1Mar43. 87hrs
ED468 III 50Sq Jan43, Burnt out after operations 30Jul43
ED469 III 49Sq 8Jan43, Missing (Berlin) 30Mar43. 100hrs
ED470 III 50,61Sqs; Missing (canal raid) 23Sep44. 214hrs
ED471-2 III 50Sq, Lost 17/18Jan & 12/13Jun43. 5/151hrs
ED473 III 50Sq, 1667CU, 15Sq(LS·H), Missing 8May44
ED474 III Converted to Mk.I. 156Sq, NTU,1667CU,622Sq,3LFS,
      1653CU, 1651CU, Temporarily 5454M
ED475 III 50Sq Jan43, Ditched off Hastings 9/10Jul43.* 260hrs
ED476 III 9Sq(WS·M),39MU,12Sq May 43, Lost 13May43. 30hrs
ED477 III 9Sq(WS·O) 15Jan43, Missing 30/31Jan43. 14hrs. 2ops
ED478 III 50Sq, Lost jettisoning bombs off Skegness 10/11Apr43
      143hrs
ED479 III 9Sq(WS·Z) 14Jan43, Missing 4Apr43. 102hrs. 15ops
ED480 III 9Sq 21Jan43, Missing 10Jul43. 250hrs. 32ops
ED481 III 9Sq(WS·N) 15Jan43, Damaged 30/31Jan43. 19hrs
ED482 III 50Sq 12Jan43, Missing 2/3Apr43. 99hrs
ED483 III 50Sq(VN·R) 12Jan43, Lost (Kassel) 22/23Oct43. 456hrs
ED484 III 50Sq 12Jan43, Lost (Lorient) 13/14Feb43. 39hrs
ED485 III Conv.I. 156Sq, Lost (Wilhelmshaven) 19Feb43. 53hrs
ED486 III 50Sq Jan43, Crashed, bombs exploded, 27Jan43. 14hrs
ED487 III 9Sq(WS·D) 14Jan43, Missing 16/17Jun43. 261hrs
ED488 III 50Sq 12Jan43, Lost (Cologne) 2/3Feb43. 18hrs
ED489 III 9Sq(WS·B) Jan43, Crashed near base 21May43, 188hrs
ED490 III 9Sq 21Jan43, Crashed 1/2Mar43. 42hrs. 7ops
ED491 III 50Sq, 46MU, 5MU, 115Sq, AAEE, SOC Oct45

ED499 WS.X of No. 9 Squadron, mid-1943.

ED492 III 9Sq(WS·W) 21Jan43, Missing 16Feb43. 47hrs. 6ops
ED493 III 9Sq(WS·A) 15Jan43, Missing 2/3Aug43. 37ops
ED494 III 9Sq(WS·G) 15Jan43, Missing 13Mar43. 87hrs. 12ops
ED495 III 9Sq(WS·Y) 21Jan43, Missing 25/26Feb43. 46hrs
ED496 III 9Sq, Dived to earth Young's Fm. Scopwick, 4Feb43
ED497 III 49Sq 21Jan43, Lost (Cologne) 16/17Jun43. 280hrs
ED498 I 207Sq(EM·D) Feb43, Lost (Milan) 15/16Aug43. 309hrs
ED499 III 9Sq(WS·X) 21Jan43, Lost 18/19Oct43. 442hrs
ED500 III 467Sq 29Jan43, Salvaged 7Aug43 but SOC. 213hrs
ED501 III 9Sq 21Jan43, Lost 11Apr43 (W/C K. B. T. Smith) 111hrs
ED502 III 9Sq(WS·V) 21Jan43, Missing 9/10Apr43. 142hrs
ED503 III 9Sq 23Jan43, Crash 29Feb43. 85mins total flying
ED504 III 467Sq 23Jan43, Lost (Essen) 27/28May43. 204hrs
ED520 III 9Sq(WS·T) 26Jan43, Missing 2Feb43. 44hrs. 7ops
ED521 I 460Sq, Missing (Duisburg) 9Apr43. 15hrs
ED522 I 12Sq Jan43, Missing (Dusseldorf) 11Jun43
ED523 III 467Sq 23Jan43, Lost (Stuttgart) 12Mar43. 69hrs
ED524 III 467Sq 23Jan43, Lost (Essen) 3/4Apr43. 111hrs
ED525 I 460,467Sqs; Lost (Wilhelmshaven) 19/20Feb43

ED526 III 467Sq 23Jan43, Lost (Nuremberg) 25/26Feb43. 40hrs
ED527 III 50Sq 26Jan43, Missing (Turin) 5Feb43. 5hrs
ED528 I 103Sq Jan43, Accident 5May43, Lost 26Jun43. 206hrs
ED529 III 467Sq 23Jan43, Lost (Wilhelmshaven) 19/20Feb43. 8hrs
ED530 III 467Sq 26Jan43, Missing 2Oct43
ED531 III 467Sq 26Jan43, Lost (Turin) 12/13Jul43. 230hrs
ED532 III 467Sq Lost (Gelsenkirchen) 21/22Jan44. 671hrs
ED533 I 207Sq(EM·N) Feb43, Lost mining 3Mar43. 34hrs
ED534-5 III 467Sq Jan43, Lost 30Jul/SOC Feb43. 230/11hrs
ED536 III 100Sq Jan-Oct43, 550Sq, 1LFS, 1667CU, Scrap 47
ED537 I 207Sq(EM·O) 7Feb43, Lost (Dusseldorf) 12Jun43. 208hrs
ED538 III 467Sq, Burnt out 8Aug43. 214hrs
ED539 III 467Sq 23Jan43, Lost (Berlin) 27/28Feb43. 484hrs
ED540 III 100Sq 3Feb43, Crashed and burnt 15Feb43
ED541 III 467Sq 26Jan43, Missing 4Sep43. 383hrs
ED542 III 106Sq from 46MU 11Mar43, Lost 4Sep43. 44hrs
ED543 III 467Sq 28Jan43, Lost (Pilsen) 13/14May43. 164hrs
ED544 III 100Sq 30Jan43, Missing (Essen) 13Mar43
ED545 III 467Sq 28Jan43, Missing 14May43. 456hrs
ED546 III 467Sq 29Jan43, Crashed 15Oct43
ED547 III 467Sq 28Jan43, Lost (Berlin) 29/30Dec43. 511hrs
ED548 I 12Sq Feb43, Dived into Firth of Forth, 7Jul43
ED549 III 100Sq Feb43, Overshot Langer and burnt 5Mar43
ED550 I 207Sq(EM·K) Feb43, Lost (Berlin) 24Aug43
ED551 III 9Sq(WS·M) 4Feb43, Missing 14Mar43. 46ops
ED552 I 101Sq, Hit trees near S. Cliff, Yorks 28/29Mar43. 113hrs
ED553 III 100Sq 30Jan43, Missing 17Jun43
ED554 I 207Sq(EM·Q) 12Feb43, Lost (Duisburg) 19Apr43. 97hrs
ED555 III 100Sq 29Jan43, Missing 21Oct43. 367hrs
ED556-7 III 9/100Sqs Feb/Jan43, Lost 22Jan/20Apr43
ED558 III 9Sq(WS·N) 5Feb43, Missing 12/13Jun43. 272hrs
ED559 III 100Sq 8Feb43, Missing 5Mar43 after mining
ED560-1 III 100Sq Feb43, Crashed 17Feb43/Lost 13Jul43
ED562 III 100,576,550Sqs; Abandoned Needham Mkt, 18Jul44
ED563-4 III 100Sq Feb43, Both missing (Pilsen) 17Apr43
ED565 III Ringway Feb43, A.V. Roe, Austin, 39MU, Scrap Mar49
ED566 III 9Sq(WS·P) 6Feb43 (WS·J), Missing 9/10Apr43. 85hrs
ED567 I 1656CU Feb43, 1LFS, Crashed 17May44
ED568 III 100Sq 4Feb43, Missing (Duisburg) 9Apr43
ED569 I 207Sq(EM·B) 20Feb43, Lost (Cologne) 28Jun43. 219hrs
ED583 III 100Sq, Broke up in air over N. Thoresby, 4Oct43
ED584 III 49Sq 7Feb43, Missing 13Jun43
ED585 III 1656CU 11Feb43, 1LFS, 50Sq(VN·G), SOC 10Apr45
ED586 I 207Sq(EM·F) Feb43, Lost (Stettin) 5/6Jan44. 443hrs
ED587 III 100Sq 6Feb43, Missing (Munich) 10Mar43
ED588 I 97Sq,50Sq Mar43, Lost 29/30Aug44. 116ops. 1052hrs
ED589 III 9Sq(WS·P) 5Feb43(WS·O), Lost 13/14May43. 125hrs
ED590 III 9Sq 6Feb43, Missing 9Apr43, 70hrs
ED591 I 97Sq Feb43, 1654CU Apr43, Crashed 26Jul43
ED592 III 50Sq 7Feb43, Crashed in Zoelen 1/2Mar43. 38hrs
ED593 III 106Sq Feb43-May44, 5LFS, Became 4944M 1656CU
ED594 I 83,57Sqs; Blown up at Scampton 15Mar43. 77hrs
ED595 III A. V. Roe Ringway Feb43, 7Sq, Missing 25Jan43
ED596 III 106Sq 7Feb43, Missing 30Mar43. 92hrs
ED597 III 49Sq Feb43, 619Sq, Lost Jan44, Crashed 3Mar44. 46hrs
ED598 III Ringway Feb43, 156Sq May43, Lost 29/30Aug43
ED599 III 83Sq,156Sq; Crashed near Maarn, Holland, 23Jan43
ED600 I 207Sq(EM·P) Feb43, Lost (Dusseldorf) 26May43. 164hrs
ED601 I 83Sq Feb43, 207Sq Sep43, Lost 3Dec43. 467hrs
ED602 III Ringway Feb43; 467,83,49,619Sqs; Lost 26/27Sep44
ED603 III Ringway Feb43, 83Sq May43, Lost 13Jun43. 20hrs
ED604 I 207Sq 6Mar43, Lost 13Mar43 on first operation
ED605 III Ringway Feb43, SIU, America, BDU, SOC 8 Nov45
ED606 III 467Sq(PO·X) Apr43, 463Sq(JO·E) Nov43, Collided in
      mid-air with ND637 over Branston 15/16Mar44.†
ED607 III 1656CU Feb-Jul44,1LFS; 1662,1654CUs;RWE,SOC 47
ED608-9 III 101Sq Feb43, Lost 10Apr/28Jun43
ED610 I 1662CU, 15Sq Dec43, Missing 29Jan44. 463hrs
ED611 III 44Sq Apr43, 463Sq Feb44, BTU, SOC Jan47
ED612 III 103Sq 11Feb43, Missing 15Jun43
ED613 III 61Sq ex-20MU Feb43, Missing (Essen) 25/26Jul43
ED614 III 103Sq ex-46MU 19Feb43, Lost (Essen) 21Apr43. 72hrs
ED615 I 156Sq Feb43, Missing (Kiel) 4/5Apr43. 81hrs
ED616 III 57Sq 19Apr43, Missing 30Jul43. 107hrs

ED617 III 50Sq May43, Lost (Gelsenkirchen) 9/10Jul43. 134hrs
ED618 III 101Sq from 5MU 23Mar43, Lost 10Apr43. 19hrs
ED619 III Ringway Feb43, 622Sq Dec43, Lost 31Mar44. 557hrs
ED620 III 49Sq from 5MU 4Apr43, Lost 20/21Apr43. 29hrs
ED621 III 467Sq from 39MU 22Mar43, Missing 3Oct43
ED622 I 156Sq Feb43, Lost (Duisburg) 8/9Apr43. 38hrs
ED623 III 207,626,101Sqs; 1LFS; 1667,1656CUs; Scrap Oct46
ED624 III 1660CU Apr-Dec43, 622Sq, Lost 28Jan44. 623hrs
ED625 III 49Sq ex-20MU 29Apr43, Lost (Nuremburg) 11Aug43
ED626 III 103Sq 11Mar43, Crashed near Hulshurst 1Apr43. 39hrs
ED627 III 207Sq ex-20MU 19Apr43, Lost 28Aug43. 280hrs
ED628 III 1662CU Mar43, 15Sq Dec43, Lost 16Feb44. 502hrs
ED629 III 12Sq ex-38MU, 23Apr43, Missing 16/17Jun43
ED630 III 61Sq Mar43, Lost (Kassel) 22/23Oct43. 307hrs
ED631 I 38MU,1662CU,622Sq,115Sq,38MU,1651CU, Destroyed
      in belly-landing at Woolfox Lodge 10May45
22 ED645-6 III 103Sq 20Feb43, Lost 2/31Aug43, 189/248hrs
ED647 III 100Sq 28Feb43, Missing 18Aug43
ED648 III 20MU,9Sq(WS·D) Aug43, Ditched 29/30Sep43. 90hrs
ED649 III 106Sq 22Feb43, Missing 15Jun43. 217hrs
ED650 I 101Sq 20Feb43, Missing 26Jun43. 172hrs
ED651 III 467Sq 21Feb43, Lost (Pilsen) 16/17Apr43. 97hrs
ED652 III 100Sq 23Feb43, Damaged 24Aug43 and SOC
ED653 III 100Sq 23Feb43, Missing (Stuttgart) 15Apr43
ED654 III 9Sq(WS·W) Feb43, Lost (Stuttgart) 20/21Feb44
ED655 III 59,630Sqs; Hit hut, Old Bolingbroke, 16Feb44
ED656 III 20MU,9Sq(WS·V) 19Apr43, Crashed Lincs 23Nov43
ED657 III 467Sq 4Mar43, Lost (Duisburg) 21/22May44. 408hrs
ED658 III 100Sq,38MU,460Sq, Lost (Hanover) 8/9Oct43. 59hrs
ED659-60 III 101Sq ex-46MU, Lost 4Sep/26May43. 213/85hrs
ED661 I 61Sq, Lost 17/18Aug43 on pilot's last trip of tour
ED662 III 9Sq 26Mar43, Crashed near Mildenhall 7Apr43. 21hrs
ED663 III 49Sq ex-5MU Apr43, Lost (Cologne) 8/9Jul43. 108hrs
ED664 III 460Sq ex-39MU Mar43, Lost (Berlin) 24Nov43. 356hrs
ED665 III 44Sq ex-5MU 20Apr43, Missing 31Aug43. 172hrs
ED666 III 20MU,9Sq(WS·G) 29Apr43, Lost 5/6Sep43. 236hrs
ED667-8 III 57Sq 4Mar43, Both lost 14May43. 84/89hrs
ED688 III 100Sq ex-20MU 6Apr43, Lost 3Aug43
35 ED689 III 9Sq(WS·K) 12Apr43, Lost 3/4Jul43. 146hrs
ED690 III 50Sq Feb43, BDU Mar43, SOC Oct45
ED691 III 50Sq 28Feb43, Missing 17Apr43. 98hrs
ED692 I 5MU Feb43, 207Sq Mar43, Lost 22Jun43. 176hrs
ED693 III 50Sq 28Feb43, Lost (Pilsen) 13/14Aug43. 149hrs
ED694 III 9Sq(WS·G) Mar43, Crashed near Stevensbeek 3Apr43
ED695 III 467Sq 28Feb43, Lost (Dusseldorf) 26Apr43. 148hrs
ED696 III 9Sq(WS·T) 2Mar43, Missing 5Apr43. 47hrs. 3ops
ED697 III 101Sq ex-20MU Apr43, Missing 8/9Jul43. 94hrs
ED698 III 57,630,207Sqs; Damaged, SOC 20Feb44. 418hrs
ED699 III 20MU,9Sq(WS·L), Missing 22/23Jun43. 89hrs
ED700 III 20MU,9Sq(WS·O), Ditched 20/21Dec43
ED701-2 III 103/49Sq Mar43, Lost 23Aug & 23/24Sep43
ED703 I 61Sq, Ditched S.W. of Scilly Isles 13/14Apr43. 14hrs
ED704 III 1660CU Apr43, 1654CU Jan43, Became 4370M
ED705 III 100Sq 14Mar43, Missing 3Aug3
ED706-7 III 57Sq 8Mar43, Lost 1Jun43/24May43. 91/91hrs
ED708 III 106Sq 9Mar43, Missing 28Jul43. 177hrs
ED709-10 III 100Sq Mar43, Lost 20Apr/Burnt out 14May43
ED711 III 460Sq 10Mar43, Lost (Pilsen) 16/17Apr43. 53hrs
ED712 III 50Sq 12Mar43, Lost (Wuppertal) 25Jun43. 117hrs
ED713 III 103Sq(PM·N), 567Sq(UL·W2) Nov43, Lost 24Dec43.
      485hrs. 69+ops
ED714 III 103Sq(OF·L) Mar43, 12Sq Apr43, Lost 13/14Apr43
ED715 I 156Sq 12Mar43, Accident 27Mar43, Wrecked 5May43
ED716 III 44Sq Mar-Dec43; 550,166Sqs; 1667CU, Scrap Jun47
ED717 III 61Sq 14Mar43, Missing 14Apr43. 57hrs
ED718 III 61Sq 14Mar43, Missing (Munich) 2/3Oct43. 386hrs
ED719 III 49Sq 12Mar43, Lost (Mannheim) 9/10Aug43
ED720 III 106Sq 12Mar43, Lost (Mannheim) 9Jul43. 249hrs
ED721 III 49Sq Mar-Oct43, 9Sq Oct43, Missing 14/15Jan44
ED722 III 61Sq(QR·B) 14Mar43, Lost (Milan) 15/16Aug43. 334hrs
ED723 III 44Sq(KM·U) Mar43, Lost (Dortmund) 23/24May43.
      133hrs
ED724 III 103Sq(PM·M) 14Mar43, Damaged 10Apr43 and SOC
ED725 III 103Sq 14Mar43, Missing 18Aug43. 286hrs

ED726 III 49Sq 28Mar43, Lost (Turin) 12/13Jul43. 163hrs
ED727 III 1662CU; 15,622Sqs; 5LFS; Scrapped at 46MU Nov46
ED728 III 101Sq 14Mar43, Missing 28Apr43. 74hrs
ED729 III 1662CU Mar43, Crash 2Apr43 after 5 flying hours
ED730 III 460,550Sqs; Collided with ND327 23/24Dec43
ED731 III 103Sq Mar43. 166Sq, Lost (Berlin) 24/25Mar44. 576hrs
ED732 I 100Sq 14Mar43, Wrecked in collision 21/22Aug43
ED733 III 103Sq 13Mar43, Missing 29Apr43. 77hrs
ED734 III 156Sq Mar43, Lost (Essen) 25/26Jul43. 91hrs
ED735 I 617Sq(R) 27Mar43, Missing 19Nov43. 338hrs
ED736 III 101Sq 16Mar43, Missing 4Apr43. 21hrs
ED737 III 467Sq(PO·F) Mar43, Lost (Cologne) 16/17Jan43. 194hrs
ED749 I 100Sq(HW·J), 300Sq, 1LFS, CUs, SOC Sep45
ED750 100 Sq Mar-Jan44, 460Sq, Lost 31Mar44. 496hrs
ED751 III 103Sq Mar43, Missing 6Sep43. 288hrs
ED752 III 106Sq 15Mar43, Missing 16Apr43. 52hrs
ED753 III 50Sq 17Mar43, Lost (Essen) 25/26Jul43. 255hrs
ED754 I 97Sq Mar43, Missing 29Mar43. 20hrs
ED755 I 50Sq Mar43, Lost (Berlin) 3/4Sep43. 366hrs
ED756 III 49,617,619Sqs; 1654CU; 5LFS; Became 4946M at
      1667CU
ED757 I 57Sq, Crash Morrison's Farm, near Charlton 10Jul43*
ED758 I 57,630,207(EM·V)Sqs; Lost (Berlin) 30Jan44. 452hrs
ED759-60 III 460,100Sqs; Missing 31May/11Apr43
ED761 I 57Sq 21Mar43, Lost (Berlin) 30Mar43 on first operation
ED762 I 57Sq 17Mar43, Damaged 3May43, Became 4011M 4STT
ED763 I 617Sq(AJ·D) Apr43, (AJ·Z) Dec43, SOC 14May45
ED764 III 467Sq Mar43, Missing (Peenemunde) 18Aug43
ED765/G III RAE 8Apr43, 617Sq Jul43, Crashed 6Aug43. 32hrs
ED766 I 57Sq 25Mar43, Missing 10Apr43. 41hrs
ED767 III 103,576(UL·A2)Sqs; 1651CU, 22MU, Scrap Aug47
      50 + ops
ED768 III 467Sq Mar43, Missing (Dusseldorf) 25/26May43
ED769-70 I 103/57Sqs Mar43, Lost 13Jul/21Apr43. 110/60hrs
ED771 III 467Sq 25Mar43, Missing (Essen) 1May43. 64hrs
ED772 III 467Sq Mar43, 463Sq Nov43, Lost (Berlin) 30/31Jan44
ED773 I 103Sq Mar43, Damaged 27Apr43, Lost 23Jun43. 109hrs
ED774 I 460Sq Mar43, Burnt at Binbrook 3Jul43, Repaired and
      returned 460Sq Aug43, 100Sq Aug43, Lost 24Aug43
ED775 III 101Sq, Force-landed 2 miles N.E. Coltishall 24May43
ED776 III 101Sq Mar43, Crashed 3Aug43. 68hrs
ED777 I 57Sq Mar43, 630Sq Nov43, Missing 3Dec43. 396hrs
ED778 I 57Sq Mar43, Damaged 17Apr43, Lost 13May43. 41hrs
ED779 III 57,300Sqs; 1LFS; 1662,1656CUs; SOC Aug47
ED780 I 467Sq. 29Mar43, Missing 17Apr43. 9hrs
ED781 I 97Sq Mar43, 57Sq Apr43, Missing Jun43, 148hrs
ED782 I 61Sq Mar43, Lost (Hamburg) 29/30Jul43. 250hrs
      N.B.   All Lancaster B.III from ED783 onwards.
ED783 44Sq(KM·F) Mar43, Lost (Essen) 30Apr/May43. 58hrs
ED784 50Sq Mar43, Missing (Pilsen) 17Apr43. 66hrs
ED785 49Sq, Missing (Cologne) 16/17Jun43
ED786 100Sq Apr43, Missing (Dusseldorf) 12Jun43
ED799 9Sq(WS·G) Mar43, Lost 22Apr43. 71hrs. 9ops
ED800 50Sq Mar43, Lost Skoda Works raid 16/17Apr43. 41hrs
ED801 106Sq,1661CU,207Sq,1653CU, Crash Mar45, 46MU, SS
      Nov47
ED802 207,44Sqs; 5LFS, 39MU, 2MPRD Jun47
ED803 467Sq, Repaired three times, lost (Magdeburg) 21/22Jan44
ED804 460Sq 31Mar43, Missing 28May43. 70hrs
ED805 49Sq Mar43, Lost (Peenemunde) 17/18Aug43
ED806 9Sq(WS·L) Apr43, Lost on first operation 9Apr43. 9hrs
ED807 101Sq; Crashed landing at Holme 13/14Apr43. 2hrs
ED808 1660CU, Repaired three times, 622Sq, Lost 11Apr44. 509hrs
ED809 101Sq,625Sq(CF·T) Oct43, Lost (Berlin) 26Nov43. 318hrs
ED810 50Sq(VN·Z) Mar43, Lost (Oberhausen) 14/15Jun43. 145hrs
ED811 1660CU Mar43, Wrecked on third accident 10Dec43. 574hrs
ED812 1660CU, Tail broke off over Dunholme Lodge 10Nov43
ED813 49Sq Mar43, Lost (Dortmund) 23/24May43. 63hrs
ED814 97,625(CF·K),300Sqs; Lost 1Jul44. 614hrs
ED815 100Sq(P) Apr43, Lost (Schweinfurt) 24/25Feb44. 388hrs
ED816 97Sq 4Apr43, Lost 13Jun43. 53hrs
ED817/G 617Sq(AJ·C), See Chap 6, Scrapped from 46MU Jan45
ED818-9 12/106Sqs Apr43, Lost 20Apr/7Sep43. ??/355hrs
ED820-1 12(PH·E)/100Sqs Apr43, Lost 3Jul/27May43

ED822-3 156Sq/1661CU Apr43, Lost 30Jul43/Crashed 10Apr43
ED824 100Sq 13Apr43, Damaged beyond repair 21May43

ED817 modified for the Dams raid, Spring 1943.

ED825/G AAEE,617Sq Jun43, Lost over France 10Dec43 180hrs
ED826 CUs,15Sq, Fell in Wash after mining 13Jan44. 737hrs
ED827 57Sq Apr43, Accident 1Jul43, Burnt out 28Aug43
ED828 50Sq Apr43, Lost (Bochum) 12/13Jan43. 117hrs
ED829/G SIU Defford, 156Sq, Lost (Berlin) 23/24Aug43
ED830 101Sq, Crashed at dawn 5May43. 20hrs. 1 injured
ED831 9Sq(WS·Y) (WS·H), Lost 25Jun43. 120hrs. 14ops
ED832-3 207Sq/1654CU Apr43, Lost 4Sep43/Crashed 11Jun43
ED834 9Sq(WS·Z) Apr43, Lost 18Apr43. 35hrs
ED835 101Sq Apr43, Crashed 5May43. 49hrs
ED836 9Sq(WS·T) Apr43, (WS·C) Jun43; Lost 1Oct43. 338hrs
ED837 156Sq Apr43, Missing (Duisberg) 12/13May43. 45hrs
ED838 9Sq(WS·R) Apr43, Missing 30Apr43. 19hrs. 2ops
ED839 97Sq Apr43, 619Sq Sep43, Damaged 9Oct43, 275hrs
ED840 156Sq Apr43, Lost (Cologne) 16/17Jun43. 61hrs
ED841 156,101,166Sqs; Lost (Berlin) 15Feb44. 270hrs
ED842 156,405Sqs; NTU,RAE, Dorsal turret removed, SOC Mar51

ED866 with Flight Refuelling Ltd. post-war.

ED856 156,50Sqs; Abandoned over Le Mans, 25/26Aug44. 664hrs
ED857-8 156Sq, Lost 13May43/24Jun43 (Elberfeld) 26/64hrs
ED859 619Sq(PG·V), Lost on 71st operation 21Jun44. 630hrs
ED860 156Sq Apr43, 61Sq(QR·N), SOC Skellingthorpe 28/29Oct44 1,032hrs. 130ops
ED861-2 57/97Sqs Apr43, Lost 13Jul/30Jul43.142/146hrs
ED863 156Sq Apr43, Missing (Cologne) 16/17Jun43. 671hrs.
ED864/G Tested 16Apr43, 617Sq(AJ·B). Lost 17May43. 23hrs
ED865/G 617Sq(AJ·S) 19Apr43, Lost Gilze Rigen. 17hrs
ED866 97Sq Apr43, 61Sq Sep43, 5LFS May44, To Flt-Refuelling (Tanker No. 28) G-AHJW, Crashed near Andover 22Nov48
ED867 97,467(PO·T)Sqs: Missing (Berlin) 28/29Jan44. 364hrs
ED868 AFEE,97Sq(OF·A) May43, Damaged 23/24Sep43. 235hrs
ED869 97,44Sqs(KM·G); 5LFS, Became 4967M at 1651CU
ED870 97,50Sqs(VN·I) Sep43, Lost3/4May44. 538hrs. 59ops.
ED871 9Sq(WS·Z) Nov43, Lost 18Nov43. 156hrs. 2ops
ED872 RAE Apr43, 37MU Sep47, SS Feb49
ED873-4 97,106Sqs; Wrecked 27Nov43/Lost 3Dec43. 215/294hrs
ED875 97Sq(OF·R), 166Sq, Crashed near Caistor 27/28Sep43.
ED876 SIU Apr43, 83Sq(OL·V) May43, Lost 28Aug43. 229hrs
ED877 156Sq Apr43, Missing (Dortmund) 4/5May43. 11hrs
ED878-9 103Sq Apr43, Lost 24Jul43/Burnt 9Jun43. 121/86hrs
ED880 97Sq(OF·D), Hit Stirling BF393 at Waterbeach 5May43

ED881 103Sq Apr43, Damaged three times, Lost 21Oct43. 188hrs
ED882 97Sq Apr43, 103Sq 1Aug43, Lost 10Aug43. 182hrs

B.I(Spec) ED906 of Station Flight, Scampton, postwar.

ED883 156Sq Apr43, 100Sq Aug43, Lost 23Sep43
ED884-5 103/156Sqs Apr43; Lost 26Jul43/21Jun43. 156/89hrs
ED886/G 617Sq 23Apr43, Missing (France) 10Dec43. 139hrs

Dam-buster ED909 depicted subsequent to the raid.

ED887/G 617Sq(AJ·A) 17Apr43, Lost on dam raid. 25hrs
ED888 103Sq Apr43, 576Sq Nov43, 103Sq Oct44, Damaged 20Feb45, 10MU Aug45, Scrap Jan47. 135ops. 941+hrs
ED904 103Sq Apr43, 166Sq Sep43, Lost (Bochum) 29/30Sep43
ED905 103,166,550Sqs; 1LFS,1656CU, Crash 20Aug45, 628+hrs
ED906/G 617Sq(AJ·J) Apr43, 46MU, 61Sq Aug46, Scrap Jul47
ED907 SIU Apr43, 83Sq May43, Lost 17Jun43. 59hrs
ED908 SIU, 83Sq May43, NTU Nov43, Lost 21Jul44
ED909/G 617Sq(AJ·P) 23Apr43, Became 6242M, Scrap Jul47
ED910/G 617Sq(AJ·C) 28Apr43, Lost in dam raid. 20hrs
ED911 97Sq(OF·E) Apr43, 405Sq Aug43, Crashed 3Sep43
ED912/G 617Sq 3May43-Dec43 46MU Feb45, Scrap Sep46
ED913 103SqApr43,576Sq(UL·U2)Nov43,Lost23/24Dec43.409hrs
ED914 Tested 19Apr43, 103Sq Apr43, Lost 12Jun43. 44hrs
ED915/G 617Sq 28Apr43, 46MU Feb45, Scrap Oct46
ED916-7 103/97Sqs Apr43, Lost 13Jun/4Jul43. 44/56hrs
ED918/G 617Sq(AJ·F), Damaged 17May43, Burnt 21Jan44. 112hrs
ED919 156Sq Apr43, Missing (Turin) 12/13Jul43. 74hrs
ED920 630Sq Nov43, Missing 4Dec43. 364hrs
ED921/G 617Sq(AJ·W) 30Apr43, Damaged 17Aug43, 46MU Jan45
ED922 103Sq Apr43, Missing 3Aug43. 152hrs
ED923 617Sq(AJ·T) May43, Missing 8/9Jul43. 76hrs
ED924/G 617Sq 30Apr43, Damaged 2Jul44, 46MU, Scrap Sep46
ED925/G 617Sq(AJ·M), Lost on dam raid 17/18May43. 16hrs
ED926 SIU, 156Sq, Wrecked 21Sep43
ED927/G 617Sq(AJ·E) 3May43, Lost 17May43. 21hrs
ED928 97Sq 2May43, Missing 23Jul43. 54hrs
ED929/G 617Sq(AJ·L) 30Apr43, 46MU Jan45, Broken up Oct46
ED930 39MU May43 for Australia, Became A66-1 of RAAF
ED931 57Sq May43, Missing 30Jul43, 160hrs
ED932/G 617Sq 30Apr43, W/C Gibson's a/c, Scrap Jul47
ED933/G 617Sq, Damaged 12May43, 46MU Feb45. Scrap Oct46
ED934/G Tested 29Apr43, 617Sq 3May43, Lost 17May43. 13hrs
ED935 SIU, 156Sq May43, Lost (Munster) 11/12Jun43. 21hrs
ED936/G 39MU, 617Sq(AJ·H) 12May43, Crashed 21Jul44. 65hrs
ED937/G 39MU,617Sq(AJ·Z) 14May43, Lost 17May43. 7hrs
ED938 97,635(CF·C)Sqs; Shot down near Alkmaar 13Jun44. 580hrs
ED939 97Sq 7May43, Missing 10Aug43. 112hrs
ED940 97,625Sqs; 38MU,5LFS,RWE,CSE,9MU,2MPRD Nov47
ED941 57Sq May43, Damaged Jul43, Crashed, burnt 28Sep43
ED942 103,460,550(BQ·Q)Sqs; Lost 25/26Feb44. 365hrs
ED943 57Sq 11May43, Missing 28Jan43. 91hrs

ED944 57,630Sqs; Nov43, 5LFS Apr44, 1661CU, Became 5455M
ED945 103Sq 9Jun43, Missing 17Jun43. 48hrs
ED946-7 57Sq 9May43, Crashed 28Aug43/Lost 9Jul43
ED948 97Sq May43; Crashes, minor 23Jun43, major 9Aug43
ED949 467Sq, 463Sq Nov43, Lost (Berlin) 30/31Jan44. 399hrs
ED950 97Sq(OF·X) May43, Missing 23/24Aug43. 177hrs
ED951 101,625Sqs; Hit hillside, Gayton-le-Wold 16/17Dec43
ED952 SIU,156Sq,NTU Nov43, Crashed 5Oct44, MUs,ScrapJan47
ED953 97(OF·H),467Sqs; Crash-landed Waddington 2Jun44
ED967 12Sq 11May43, Missing 26May43. 22hrs
ED968 12Sq(GZ·G) May43, Dived into ground 25Jun43
ED969-70 156/57Sqs May43, Lost 9Oct/25May43
ED971 9Sq,NTU Nov43, 1659CU Jan45, 22MU, Scrap Jun47
ED972 12Sq Mar43, Lost (Munchen Gladbach) 30Aug43
ED973 460,100Sqs, Lost 15Jun43
ED974 SIU, 83Sq May43, two minor crashes, Lost 21Jan44. 265hrs
ED975 9Sq(WS·Y) May43, Crashed 6Sep43. 176hrs. 21ops
ED976 460Sq 15May43, Missing (Dusseldorf) 12Jun43
ED977 619Sq(PG·A) May43, Lost (Stettin) 5Jan44. 440hrs
ED978-80 619Sq May43, Lost 12/28/6Jun43. 26/71/32hrs
ED981-2 619Sq May43, Lost 24/17Aug43. 186/180hrs
ED983 619Sq, Crashed 4½mls W. of Mablethorpe 29Sep43. 199hrs
ED984 SIU, 83Sq May43, Missing 24Aug43. 195hrs
ED985 460Sq, Crash 19Aug43, Lost (Hanover) 18Oct43. 252hrs
ED986 460Sq(AR·J) May43, Lost (Berlin) 31Aug43. 194hrs
ED987-8 101/100Sqs May43, Lost 13/26Jun43. 31/?hrs
ED989-90 57/156Sqs May43, Lost 18Aug43/7Sep43. 119/?hrs
ED991-2 100/57Sqs May43, Lost 19Nov/11Aug43. 267/110hrs
ED993 12Sq May43, SOC after third crash 9Oct43. 140hrs
ED994 57Sq, 467Sq Oct43, Lost (Stettin) 5/6Jan44. 359hrs
ED995-6 12Sq May43, Lost 9Oct/30May43. ?/14hrs
ED997 SIU May43, 83Sq 4Jun43, Lost 22Jun43. 20hrs
ED998 467Sq May43, Lost (Milan) 15/16Aug43 (W/C C. L. Gomm)
ED999 49Sq Jun43, 44Sq(KM·X) Nov43, Lost 23Dec43. 333hrs
EE105 97Sq 22May43, Shot down over Marham 23/24Aug43
EE106 617Sq 20May43, 619Sq, Lost in sea 30Sep43
EE107 97,100,550Sqs; Missing (Magdeburg) 22Jan44
EE108 156Sq(GT·Z) Jun43-Apr44, ETPS 1945, Scrap 2MPRD1947
EE109 619Sq 23May43, Lost (Hanover) 18Sep43. 282hrs
EE110 619Sq 22May43, Burnt out after Hagen raid 1/2Oct43
EE111 619Sq May43; Abandoned, crashed in Humber 27Nov43
EE112-3 619Sq May43, Lost 11Aug/10Jun43. 163/4hrs
EE114 619Sq May43, Damaged 16Jun43, Lost (Liepzig) 21Oct43
EE115-6 619,61Sqs May43, Lost 3Sep43/14Apr44. 179/560hrs
EE117 619Sq May43, Missing (Peenemunde) 17Aug43. 159hrs
EE118 32MU to 156Sq 22Jun43, Crashed 29Sep43, SOC 19Oct43
EE119 7Sq Jan43, Damaged Aug43, Missing 23Nov43
EE120 83Sq Apr43, 97Sq Feb44, 1655HCU(QF·P), Crash 23Mar44
EE121 83Sq ex-32MU Jun43, Lost on first operation 22Jun43
EE122 156Sq 2Jun43, Missing 17Jun43. 9hrs

EE131 crash-landed near Molotovsk, Russia.

EE123 44Sq 27May43, Lost from first operation 30Aug43. 2½hrs
EE124 50Sq 27Aug43, 5MU,300Sq Apr44, Lost 24Jun44
EE125 106Sq 27May43, Missing 26Jun43. 56hrs
EE126 207Sq 28May43, Lost (Liepzig) 19/20Feb44
EE127 32MU to No. 156Sq Jun43, Missing 25Jun43. 6hrs

EE134 ended as a Rolls-Royce static test-rig.
It was used on fire-prevention tests after a service life
of 99 operations.

EE128 156Sq 9 Jun43, NTU, 1661CU(KB·H), Became 5295M
EE129 7Sq(MG·V), Missing (Berlin) 1/2Jan44. 311hrs
EE130 617Sq May43, Lost (Dortmund-Ems canal) 16Sep43. 178hrs
EE131 617Sq(B) 28Aug43, Crash-landed N. Russia 18Sep44
EE132 460Sq May43, Shot down near Benschop 3/4Sep43. 71hrs
EE133 12,626Sqs; 1LFS; 1662,1653CUs; Scrapped 23Oct46
EE134 49Sq May43, 619Sq Sep43, 5LFS(CE·O) Nov44, SOC 31Mar45
EE135 467Sq 31May43, Missing 23/24Sep43. 94hrs
EE136 9Sq(WS·R) May43-Oct44, Named "Spirit of Russia" 189Sq Oct44, 1659HCU, Became 5918M at No. 1RS. 109ops
EE137 101Sq Aug43, 166Sq Oct43, Lost (Brunswick) 14/15Jan44
EE138 460Sq 31May43, Missing (Berlin) 3/4Sep43. 174½hrs
EE139 100,550Sqs; Named "Phantom of the Ruhr", 1656,1660 HCUs; 121 + operations, SOC 12Jan46. 830 + hrs
EE140 100Sq 31Jun43. SOC 27Jun43
EE141 207Sq 31May43, Missing (Berlin) 16/17Dec43. 385hrs
EE142 12Sq 31May43, Missing 8Aug43
EE143 467Sq 31May43, Missing (Lille) 10/11May44
EE144 617Sq 31May43, Lost (Dortmund-Ems canal) 15/16Sep43
EE145 617Sq 31May43, Crashed 7Jun43 and SOC. 4hrs
EE146 Conv. to Mk.I. 617Sq(D) Jun43, Damaged 6Apr45
EE147 617Sq,619Sq May43, Missing (Peenemunde) 17/18Aug43
EE148 617Sq 4Jun43, 626Sq(UM·S2), Lost (Mailly) 3/4May44
EE149 617Sq 4Jun43, Lost in March 1945
EE150 617Sq(Z) 6Jun43, 619Sq Dec43, Damaged, SOC 17Dec43
EE166 460Sq 6Jun43, Missing (Mulheim) 22/23Jan43
EE167 460Sq 8Jun43, Missing (Oberhausen) 14/15Jun43
EE168 97Sq 11Jun43, 619Sq 6Oct43, Burnt out 27Nov43
EE169 100Sq 8Jun43, Missing 28Jul43
EE170-1 619/100Sqs Jun43, Lost 3Dec/24Aug43
EE172 97Sq Jun43, Missing 30Jul43
EE173 156Sq Jun-Sep43, 207Sq(EM·K), Lost (Berlin) 15Jan44

162

EE174 97Sq,39MU,50Sq 17Mar44, Lost (Nuremburg) 30/31Mar44
EE175 83Sq,207Sq Oct43, Lost (Berlin) 30/31Jan44
EE176 7,97,61(QR ·M)Sqs; Did 120 operations, 1653CU (H4 ·X), Became 5260M at BOAC Whitchurch
EE177 156Sq, Missing (Nurnberg) 28Aug43
EE178 7Sq,156Sq(GT ·R), Missing 28Jul43. 47hrs
EE179 7Sq Jun43 only, 97Sq,44Sq, Lost 2/3Dec43. 215hrs
EE180-1 100Sq 11Jun43, Lost 24/31Aug43
EE182 101,103Sqs; USA Jul53; Winter tests in Canada 1944/5
EE183 100Sq Jun43, Missing 13Jul43
EE184-5 44Sq Jun43, Lost 21Oct43/4May44. 323/469hrs
EE186 49,106,61Sqs; Lost (St. Leu) 4/5Jul44. 434hrs. 52ops
EE187 Defford and Farnborough, Decca trials Aug46. Became 6747M at Cosford. Oct47
EE188 9Sq(WS ·B) 14Jun43, Missing 16/17Dec43. 45ops
EE189 50Sq 13Jun43, Lost (Hanover) 27/27Sep43. 276hrs
EE190 61Sq 13Jun43, Missing 23Jul43. 87hrs
EE191 106Sq (six months), 463Sq(JO ·S), Lost 19Mar44. 115ops.
EE192 101Sq 13Jun43, Missing 24Aug43. 128hrs
EE193 57Sq 13Jun43; 166,550Sqs; Lost 30Aug43. 300hrs
EE194 467Sq, Missing (Nurnburg) 27/28Aug43
EE195 12Sq 16Jan43, Lost 28/29Jun43. (S/L F. V. Knight)
EE196 103Sq Jun43, 166Sq Sep43, Lost (Kassel) 22/23Oct43
EE197 57Sq(DX ·Y) Apr43, 207Sq 1944, Damaged SOC 15Jan44
EE198 619Sq 13Jun43, Missing (Krefeld) 22Jun43. 11hrs
EE199 12Sq 16Jun43, Scrapped after operations 29Jun43
EE200 156,7,166Sqs; Swung on take-off, burnt 10Apr44
EE201 83Sq Jun43-Mar44; NTU: 1667CU, SOC 8Nov45
EE202 12Sq 16Jun43, Missing (Hanover) 8/9Oct43. 156hrs

Serial Range FM100—FM299   Lancaster B.X

200 Lancaster B.X ordered from Victory Aircraft of Canada as FM100—299 of which 130 were built as indicated. Deliveries were from April to August 1945. Production of this FM series followed the KB series recorded later. Normally delivery was direct to 20 M.U. on arrival in United Kingdom in each case. Subsequent R.C.A.F. instructional numbers, e.g. A552, are given as applicable.

FM100 20MU 10Apr45, 32MU Jun45, 22MU Oct45. Scrap Jan47
FM101 Arr.UK Apr45, 32MU Jun45, Canada 19Aug45
FM102 32MU Jun45, Canada Aug45. Mod 10MR,404Sq, Crash 15Aug42
FM103 32MU Jan45, To Canada Aug45, Disposed Jan. 1947
FM104 428Sq To Canada Jun45, Mod 10MR, 10 Rescue Unit Torbay (CX ·104)1962
FM105 Arr.UK 19Apr45, To Canada 27Jul45, Disposed Jan48
FM106 Arr.UK 26Apr45, 32MU Jun45, Crashed 11Aug45
FM107-8 Arr.UK Apr45, Held in various MUs. Scrap Jun47
FM109 Arr. UK Apr45, 32MU Jun45, 20MU Oct45,SS(CC) May47

Lancasters 10-P FM120 and FM122, No. 408 Squadron, R.C.A.F.

FM110 Arr.UK May45,405Sq Jun45, Mod 10MR, Scrap Jun45
FM111 Arr. UK Apr45, 32MU Jun45, Canada Aug45, Scrap Apr48
FM112-4 Arr.UK Apr45, Held in 20MU, SS(CC) May47
FM115 405Sq, Canada Jun45, Mod 10MR,404Sq, Crash 6Nov53
FM116 Arr.UK 2May45, 32MU Jul45, 22MU Oct45. Scrap Jun47
FM117 Arr.UK 30Apr45, Held at 20MU, SS(CC) May47
FM118 UK Apr45, 32MU, Canada Aug45. Canadian Army Mar48
FM119 Arr.UK Apr45,32MU Jun45, Canada Dec45, SS(CC) May47
FM120 408Sq, Flown back Jun45. Mod 10P,408Sq(MN120) SOC Sep62 in Canada
FM121 Arr.UK 24Apr45, 218MU 9Aug45, 39MU Oct45, Scrap Jun47
FM122 UK May45, 405Sq Jun45, Canada Jun45,10P,408Sq, SOC Sep62
FM123 UK25Apr45, 32MU23Jun45, Canada11Aug45, Scrap Jan47
FM124 UK May45, 32MU Jun45, Canada Aug45, Became A552 Mar47
FM125 Arr.UK 5May45, 32MU Jul45, 39MU Oct45, Scrap Jun47
FM126 UK May45, 32MU, Canada in 1945. Became 551B Mar47
FM127 UK May45, 32MU Jun45, Canada Aug45, Scrap Jan47
FM128 32MU, Canada Aug45, Mod 10MR,404Sq, Scrap May56
FM129 Arr.UK May45, 218MU Jul45, 39MU Oct45, Scrap Jul47
FM130 Dishforth May45, 408Sq, Canada Jun45, Scrap Jan47
FM131 Arr.UK 11May45,218MUJul45,20MUSep45,SS(CC)May47
FM132 Arr.UK 5Jun45, 218MU Aug45, 39MU Sep45, Scrap Jun47
FM133-4 5MU on arrival in UK,20MU Sep45, SS(CC) Aug47
FM135 Arr.UK 17May45; 5,32,22MUs May-Oct45; Scrap Jun47
FM136 32MU, Canada Aug45, Mod 10MP,407Sq(RX136), Pres'vd
FM137 Arr.UK May45; 20,218,20MUs in succession; SS May47
FM138-9 Arr.UK May45, Held in various MUs, Scrap Jun47
FM140 5,218MUs;Canada23Aug45,Mod10MP,404Sq, ScrapSep55
FM141-2 Arr.UK May45, Held in various MUs, Scrap Jun47
FM143 Arr. May45, Crashed flying from 32MU,20MU,SS May47
FM144-7 Arr.UK Jun45, Held in various MUs, Scrap Jun47
FM148 UK MUs. Winterisation trials Canada 1946/47, (FC ·D), Scrap Jan58
FM149 Sold
FM150-1 Arr.UK May45, Held in various MUs, Scrap Jun47
FM152 Arr.UK 3Jun45, 32MU Jul45, 39MU Sep45, Scrap Jun47
FM153 Arr.UK 3Jun45, 218MU, To Canada Aug45, SS Jan48
FM154 Arr.UK May45, 32MU Jul45, 39MU Sep45, Scrap Jun47
FM155 32M: Jul45, Flown to Canada 27Aug45. SSJan48
FM156 Arr.UK 6Jun45, 32MU Jul45, 39MU Sep45, Scrap Jun47
FM157 Arr.UK 5Jun45,218MU Aug45,20MU Sep45,SS Aug47
FM158 Arr.UK 30May45,32MU Jul45,29MU Oct45. Scrap Jun47
FM159 UK May45,32MU, Canada 1Sep45, mod 10MP(RX159) Sold Oct60
FM160-1 20,32,20MUs in succession in UK, SS(CC) May47
FM162-3 20MU Jun45, Held in other MUs, Scrap Jun47
FM164 Arr.UK Jun45; 20,218,20MUs; SS(CC) May47
FM165-7 Arr.UK Jun45, 39MU from Aug45 until scrap Jun47
FM168 Arr.UK 13Jun45, Held in 20MU until scrapped May47
FM169 Arr.UK 12Jun45, 1668CU(ZK ·J), MUs, Scrap Jun47
FM170-1 Arr.UK 7Jun45; 20,32,39,218,20MUs; Scrap Jun47
FM172-3 313FTU 21Jun45,Canada Nov45,mod10MP,Scrap Sep55
FM174-183 Arr.UK Jun45. Held in MUs until scrapped May47
FM184 Became CF-CMX
FM185 Became G-AKDP and CF-CMY ⎫ Used by Trans-
FM186 Became G-AKDR and CF-CMZ ⎬ Canada Air Lines
FM187 Became G-AKDS and CF-CNA ⎭
FM188-9 Arr.UK Jun45; 218,20MUs; SS May47
FM190 Arr.UK 27Jun45, Crashed leaving 5MU 3Aug45
FM191-8 Arr.UK Jun45, Held in MUs, SS at Hounslow May47
FM199 313 FTU Jul45, Canad Nov45, Mod 10P, 408Sq, Scrap Jun60
FM200 Arr.UK 3Aug45, 20MU, Sold as scrap
FM201 Arr.UK 5Aug45, RAE Sep45, Sold May50
FM202-3 Arr.UK Aug45, Held in 20MU, Sold as scrap May47
FM204 Arr.UK 11Aug45, 20MU, EANS, SS May47
FM205 Arr.UK Aug45, Test-bed for Orenda 1951
FM206 UK,To Canada Aug45, Mod 10-N *Northern Star,*Sold May57
FM207 Last Canadian Lancaster to RAF 22Aug45, Returned Nov45, 408Sq, Used for spares 28Sep62
FM208 Mod. 10-N *Polaris,* Based at Trenton, Became CF-KHH
FM209 Held by Avro (Canada), Orenda tests, Burnt out 24Jul56

The Orenda test-bed Lancaster 10-0 FM209.

FM210 Stored, Mod 10MR,407Sq Comox, Spares and scrap Jun55
FM211 Stored, Mod 10N Jun49, CFS RCAF *Zenith* (VC-GSX) Scrap May56
FM212 Stored, Mod 10P; 9,408Sqs; Held in reserve.
FM213 Stored, Mod 10MR,107RU (CX ·213), Held in store
FM214 Stored, Mod 10P; 413,408Sqs; Crashed and SOC 23May50
FM215 Mod 10P; 9,413,408Sqs; SOC 28Sep62
FM216 Mod 10P; 408Sq(VC-APD) (AP ·D), SOC 17Aug50
FM217 Mod 10P; 9,408Sqs; Crashed 2Jun60
FM218 Mod 10P; 9,408,413(AP ·U)Sqs; Crashed 5Mar52
FM219 Mod 10MR, 407Sq Aug59, Held at Dunnville
FM220 Mod 10MP, 404Sq(AF·K) 405Sq, Scrap Jan55
FM221 Prototype 10BR 1948 (DD ·R), Crash 23Sep50
FM222 Mod 10SR,103 Rescue Unit, Sold to Spartan Air Service Apr56
FM223 Mod 10MR, 404Sq(N ·223),405Sq, Scrap Sep60
FM224 Mod 10MR; 405,407Sqs; Held in reserve at Dunnville
FM225-6 Accepted 21Aug46, Mod 10MP, Spares and scrap 1955
FM227-8 Accepted 21Aug46, Mod 10MP, Based Greenwood, Scrap 1954/55
FM229 Last Mk.X produced. 405Sq, Scrap 13Sep55

Serial Number FM300   **Lincoln B.XV**

One Lincoln prototype completed by Victory Aircraft of Canada.

Serial Range HK535—HK806.   **Lancaster B.I**

200 Lancasters ordered from Vickers Armstrong (Castle Bromwich) as Mk.II in September 1941 and changed to B.III in February 1943, but built as B.I from October 1943 to February 1945. Up to HK773 had Merlin 22 engines initially installed, and all subsequent Merlin 24 engines.

HK535 First flew 22Oct43, 463Sq, Lost (Lille) 10/11May44
HK536 463Sq, Missing (St. Leu) 4/5Jul44
HK537 463Sq, Missing (Berlin) 31Jan44. 18hrs
HK538 61Sq, Missing (Leipzig) 19/20Jul44. 14hrs
HK539 626Sq(UM ·A2), Missing 28Mar44
HK540 9Sq(WS ·H) Mar44, Missing (Stuttgart) 15Mar44. 2ops
HK541 115Sq(KO ·P), 3LFS, 1651CU, AAEE, 10MU, SOC Jan47
HK542 115Sq, Missing (Kjeller) 27Apr44. 21hrs
HK543 AAEE Mar44, 10MU Jul46, Scrap 31Dec46
HK544-5 115Sq Apr44, Lost 18Oct/13Jun44. 290/90hrs
HK546 115Sq,149Sq(TK ·K), 10MU Jan46, Scrap Jan47
HK547-8 115Sq, Missing 20May/8Jun44. 50/57hrs
HK549 115Sq(KO ·Q), 1653CU(H4-V), 15MU, Scrap May47
HK550 115Sq, Missing 16Jun44. 44hrs
HK551 75Sq Apr44; 115,149Sqs; 10MU, Scrap 11Nov46
HK552-3 115/75Sq May44, Lost 8Jun/10Jun44. 43/41hrs
HK554 75Sq May44-Apr45, 44Sq, 20MU, SOC 31Mar46
HK555 115Sq, Crashed out of control with RA533, 3Apr45
HK556 115Sq May44, Missing (Kiel) 27Aug44. 126hrs

HK557 75Sq, 5MU Sep44, Sold Flt. Refuelling, Became G-AKAJ
HK558 75Sq 2Jun44. Missing 30/31 Aug44 on Caen day raid
HK559-60 115Sq 2Jun44, Lost 18Jun/27Aug44 (Kiel). 15/118hrs
HK561 75Sq Jun44, 44Sq Jul45, 20MU, SS(CC) May47
HK562 75Sq, 44Sq(KM ·C), 39MU Sep45, 2MPRD Jun47
HK563 75Sq Jun44, 44Sq Jul45, 20MU Sep45, Scrap Jul46
HK564 115Sq May44, 75Sq 2Aug44, Lost 12/13Aug44. 74hrs
HK565 75,115Sqs; 1659CU(RV ·A), 39MU, Scrap Jul46
HK566 115Sq, 1654/65/61CUs; 279Sq Aug45, 5MU, Scrap Nov46
HK567-9 75Sq Jun44, Lost 8Aug/25Jul/21Jul44. 68/41/26hrs
HK570 514Sq(P), Missing (Hamburg) 20/21Jul44. 31hrs
HK571 514Sq 1Jul44, Missing 21Jul44. 22hrs.
HK572 115(KO ·Y),149,115Sqs; 1661/54CUs; Scrap Aug46
HK573 75Sq 1Jul44, 46MU Jun45, Scrap Oct46
HK574 75Sq Jul44, Damaged in action 7Dec44
HK575 75Sq 18Jul44, Missing (Stuttgart) 25Jul44. 5hrs
HK576 75Sq Jul44, 44Sq Jul45, 20MU, Scrap Apr46
HK577 149Sq(TK ·H) Aug44-Jun45, 10MU, Scrap Jan47
HK578 115(KO ·C),149Sqs; 46MU, Jun45, Scrap Sep46
HK579 115Sq 22Jul44, Lost (Le Havre) 8Sep44. 90hrs
HK593 75Sq(JN ·X) Jul44, 46MU Jun45, Scrap Jan47
HK594-5 75/115Sqs Jul44, Lost 30Aug/15Nov44. 65/143hrs
HK596 75Sq 29Jul44, Lost (Flushing) 21Oct44. 155hrs
HK597 75Sq 1Aug44, 46MU, Jun45, Scrap Oct46
HK598 115,149Sqs; G-H Flt, 1654/60CUs, Burnt out, Claypole 20Apr45
HK599 115Sq 1Aug44, Lost (Duisburg) 14Oct44. 128hrs
HK600 75Sq(AA ·K) Aug44-Apr45, 44Sq, 39MU, SOC Dec46
HK601 75Sq(JN ·D) Aug44-May45, 10MU, Jun45, Scrap Oct46
HK602 90Sq 5Aug44, Damaged 29Oct44. 138hrs
HK603 90Sq Aug44, Missing (Lugwigshafen) 5Jan45
HK604-5 90Sq Aug44, Lost 26Aug (Kiel)/13Sep44
HK606 90(WP ·Y),186,138Sqs; 46MU Aug45, Scrap Nov46
HK607 90Sq, 1660CU Feb45, 20MU Aug45, SOC Apr46
HK608 90Sq Aug44, Lost (Gelsenkirchen) 19Mar45
HK609 90Sq 18Aug44, 10MU 9Jan45, Broken up Nov46
HK610 90Sq, Collided with PD336 Bury St. Edmunds 2Feb45
HK611 90Sq 21Aug44, 10MU, 10Jun45, SOC Mar46
HK612 15Sq 25Aug44, Burnt out, operations 2Nov44. 133hrs
HK613 90,186(XY ·Y),195Sqs; 38MU Aug45, Scrap May47
HK614 622Sq, Crashed 14Jan45, 46MU, Scrap Jan47
HK615 622Sq/138CU Mar45, 15MU, Scrap May47
HK616 460Sq(AR ·D),622Sq(GI ·W),44Sq, Scrap Oct46
HK617 622Sq(GI ·Q), Crew baled out near Arras 1/2Feb45
HK618 15Sq 2Sep44, Missing (Kassel) 29Jan45
HK619 15Sq 31Aug44, Damaged 1Jan45. SOC Oct45
HK620 15Sq Aug44, Burnt out on operations 9Feb45
HK621 622(GI ·O), Landed damaged in France 20Apr45. 115hrs
HK622 90,186Sqs(XY ·Z), Lost (Hamburg) 20Nov44. 116hrs
HK623 622Sq(GI ·F) Sep44-Feb45, 44 Sq, 38MU, Scrap May47
HK624 149Sq Sep44, 115Sq Nov44, Missing 27Nov44
HK625 90Sq Oct44, 10MU 9Jun45, Scrap Jan47
HK626-7 15Sq Oct44, Missing 4Dec/14Dec44
HK628 622Sq(GI ·X), 15Sq Aug45, 5MU, Scrap Dec46
HK644 622Sq(GI ·D) 27Sep44, Missing 6Nov44. 71hrs
HK645 149Sq(TK ·D) Oct44, 186Sq Jun45, Scrap Oct45
HK646 622Sq(GI ·M),44Sq Aug45, 38MU Oct45, Scrap May47
HK647 15Sq(LS ·K), CGS Oct45, Became 5713M
HK648 15Sq Sep44, SOC Oct45
HK649 149Sq(OJ ·S/F) Sep44, 20MU Oct45, Scrap Nov46
HK650 186Sq(XY ·T), Lost (Hohenbudberg) 8/9Feb45
HK651 622Sq(GI ·B) Sep44, 44Sq Aug45, SOC Oct45
HK652 149Sq Sep44-Feb45, 186Sq Jun45, Scrap Oct45
HK653 149Sq Oct44, Damaged 5Nov44, Lost (Essen) 12Dec44
HK654 149Sq(TK ·G) Oct44, 186Sq Jun45, Scrap Oct45
HK655 149Sq, 1651CU(BS ·F), Stalled Fiskerton 2Apr45
HK656 115Sq(KO ·Q), 20MU Sep45, SS(CC) May47
HK657 149Sq 7Oct44, Damaged 15Jan45, 46MU, Scrap Jan47
HK658 195Sq(A4 ·C), Exploded over Solingen 4Nov44. 11hrs
HK659 186Sq Oct44, 195Sq May45, 38MU Aug45, Scrap May47
HK660 195Sq(A4 ·J), 550Sq Aug45, SOC Nov45
HK661 186Sq Oct44, 138Sq Mar45, 10MU Apr45, Scrap Nov46
HK662 186Sq, Damaged 19Feb45; 24, 5MUs; Scrap May47
HK663-4 195/90Sqs Oct44, Lost 2Nov44. 18/?hrs

HK679 195Sq(A4·A), 39MU Jan46 after damage, Scrap Mar47
HK680 186Sq, Abandoned over Le Mans in storm, 6/7Dec44 when struck by lightning. 6 baled out
HK681 195(A4·K)Sq, Damaged Mar45, 38MU Aug45, Scrap May47
HK682 186,138,218Sqs; 10MU Aug45, Scrap Oct46
HK683 195Sq 26Oct44, Missing (Nordstern) 23Nov44
HK684 186Sq, 195Sq, 38MU Aug45, Scrap May47
HK685 90Sq Oct44, Damaged 3/4Feb45, 10MU Jan45, Scrap Oct46
HK686 195Sq(A4·E), Abandoned in air 13Jan45, Crew baled
HK687 195Sq(A4·D), 50Sq, 39MU Jan46, 2MPRD Jan47
HK688 186Sq(XY·W) 27Oct44, Lost (Dortmund) 3/4Feb45
HK689 195Sq(A4·B) Lost Solingen day raid 4Nov44. 6hrs
HK690 195Sq(A4·X) Oct44, 22MU 21Sep45, Scrap Jun47
HK691 115Sq(KO·R) 27Oct44, 39MU 6Sep45, Scrap Jan47
HK692 90,186,138,115(KO·T)Sqs; 39MU Sep45, 2MPRD Jun47
HK693 15Sq, 1659CU May45, 22MU, SOC Nov45
HK694 90,186,138,218Sqs; 10MU 4Aug45, Scrap Oct46
HK695 15Sq; G-H Flt Methwold Jan45, 46MU, Scrap Jan47
HK696 90Sq, 115Sq Jan45, 20MU Sep45, Scrap Nov46
HK697 195Sq(A4·C), Lost in day raid (Witten) 12Dec44
HK698 115Sq(IL·K) 7Nov44, 20MU 25Sep45, Scrap Nov45
HK699 149Sq(OJ·H), 54MU, 149Sq, 20MU, Scrap Nov46
HK700 622Sq(GI·Y), 1659CU Jun45, 22MU Sep45, SOC Nov45
HK701 195Sq, Twice damaged, 38MU Aug45, Scrap May47
HK702 1653CU, Crashed 23May45, 46MU, Scrap Jan47
HK703 44Sq, 1653CU, Belly-landed near N. Luffenham 18Sep45
HK704 1653CU, 1656CU Oct45, 22MU Nov45, Scrap May47
HK705 1669CU, 1668CU, Mar45, 1660CU Oct45, SOC Nov45
HK706 1653CU(A3·J), Crash 19Mar43, Repaired, SOC Jan46
HK707 1653CU until crash 19Jan45, 46MU, Scrap Oct46
HK708 1653CU(A3·A) 25Nov44, 1656CU 24Oct45, SOC 13Nov35
HK709 1653CU, Crashed N. Luffenham 7May45, 38MU, Scrap May47
HK710 1653/56CUs, Conv. B.III, AAEE, Became 6234M 10STT
HK728 1653CU(A3·K) Nov45, Deteriorated beyond repair Aug46
HK729 1669CU, Crash Barnston Railway Station 20Feb45
HK730 1666CU,1659CU Aug45, 22MU, Sold as scrap Aug46
HK731 1669,1668CU Mar45, Crashed 2Jun45, Condemned Feb46
HK732 1669CU Dec44, 1668CU Mar45, Scrapped Dec45
HK733 1669,1653,1651CUs; 24MU Jul45, SOC Oct45
HK734 1667CU(GC·K) Dec44, 20MU Oct45, Scrap Dec46
HK735 1666CU(ND·T) Dec44, 5MU Aug45, Scrap May47
HK736 CU Dec44, 279Sq Aug45, 5MU Sep45, Scrap May47
HK737 1661CU, 58MU, 1661CU, 5MU Aug45, Scrap May47
HK738 1661CU(KB·D), Crash near Langford, Notts, 24/25Mar45
HK739 1669,1668CUs; Swung, take-off, Bottesford 18May45
HK740 1662CU Dec44, 1667CU Mar45, 20MU Oct45, SS(CC) May47
HK741 1669,1668CUs; SOC after third mishap 4Sep45
HK742 1666CU,1659CU(RV·D),39MU Sep45, Scrap Aug46
HK743 1662CU Dec44, 1667CU Mar45, 20MU Oct45, Scrap Oct46
HK744-5 1666CU,1659CU Aug45, MUs Sep45, Scrap Jun47/Dec46
HK746 1654CU Jan45, Crashed at Wigsley 19Jul45
HK747 1666CU Jan45, 1659CU Aug45, 38MU Sep45, Scrap May47
HK748 1654CU Jan45, 15MU Aug45, Scrap Oct46
HK749 1662CU, Burnt in crash landing, Blyton, 16Mar45
HK750 1651CU Dec44, 24MU Jul45, Scrap Oct45
HK751 1667CU Jan45, 75Sq Feb45, Crashed 7May45
HK752 1662,1667,1656CUs; 32,38MUs; Scrap May47
HK753 1662,1656,1660CUs; 22MU Apr46. Scrap Jun47
HK754 1667CU Jan45, 22MU Oct45, Scrap Jun47
HK755 1667/56CUs, 10MU after crash 1Apr45, Scrap Feb47
HK756 1666CU 4Jan45, Missing 15Jan45
HK757 1654CU 19Jan45, 15MU 14Aug45, Scrap Oct46
HK758 1666/59CUs, 22MU Sep45, SS Hight Duty Alloys Mar46
HK759 195Sq Mar45, 576Sq Aug45, 15MU Sep45, Scrap May47
HK760 1654CU Jan45, 15MU Aug45, Middle East, Scrap Sep45
HK761 BCIS(WB·E) Jan45-May46, 15MU May47, Scrap Aug47
HK762 BCIS(WB·F) Crash landed 23Oct46, Condemned Nov46
HK763 BCIS(WB·G) Jan45-Jun46, 15MU Mar46, Scrap Mar47
HK764 195Sq Feb-Jul45, 38MU Aug45, Scrap May47
HK765 15Sq(DJ·Z) Feb45, 20MU, Near East, Scrap Jul46
HK766 115Sq until crash 3Sep45, 20MU Mar46, SS(CC) May47

Lancaster B.1 built by Vickers Armstrong.

HK767 186Sq Feb45, Crash landed Stradishall 4/5Apr45
HK768 115Sq Feb45, 20MU Sep45, Scrap Sep46
HK769 622Sq(GI·D), Direct AA hit over Germany 2Mar45
HK770 622Sq 10Feb45, Shot down (Bremen) 22Apr45
HK771 195Sq, Damaged 19Mar45, Lindholme, 46MU, Scrap Jan47
HK772 15Sq Feb45, 44Sq Sep45, 20MU, Near East, Scrap Sep46
HK773 15Sq Feb45, Crashed in Norfolk 22Mar45
HK787 622Sq(GI·F), 44Sq Aug45, 39MU Jan46, SOC Mar47
HK788 9Sq(WS·E), Crashed at Langford 7/8Apr45. Crew killed
HK789 15Sq Feb45, 20MU Oct45, Near East, Scrap Sep46
HK790 115Sq(KO·Y) Feb45, 20MU Sep45, SS(CC) May47
HK791 9Sq(WS·M) Mar-Nov45, 22MU Mar46, Scrap Jun47
HK792 149,138,15,44Sqs; 20MU Sep45, SS(CC) Mar47
HK793 149Sq(OJ·B) 2Feb45, 20MU 30Oct45, Scrap Aug46
HK794 186,195Sqs; 38MU Aug45, Scrap May47
HK795 149Sq(OJ·O) 14Feb45, 20MU 1Nov45, Scrap Nov46
HK796 186,195,550Sqs; 38MU Nov45, Scrap May47
HK797 195Sq Feb45, 625Sq Aug45, 22MU Nov45, Scrap May47
HK798 115Sq(KO·H/L) 18Feb45. Wrecked 17Aug45
HK799 15Sq(LS·D) 13Feb45, 20MU 3Oct45, Scrap Nov46
HK800 195Sq, 550Sq(BQ.O), 39MU, 2MPRD Jun47
HK801 195,186,195,550Sqs; 20MU, Near East, Scrap Oct46
HK802 186,195,100Sqs; 38MU Nov45, Scrap May47
HK803 9(WS·Q),619,463Sqs; 22MU Oct45, Scrap Jun47
HK804 195Sq Feb45, TFU Apr45, SOC May46
HK805 622Sq(GI·H), 44Sq(KM·F), 20MU, Scrap Nov46
HK806 75Sq Feb45, 44Sq Jul45, 39MU Sep45, Scrap Dec46

Serial Range JA672—JB748   **Lancaster B.III**

550 Lancasters ordered from A. V. Roe (Chadderton) late in 1941 and delivered as B.III from June to December 1943 with Merlin 28 engines initially installed in early production, Merlin 28 or 38 engines at mid-production, and Merlin 38 engines only on late production.

JA672 103Sq 17Jun43, Lost (Cologne) 3/4Jul43. 38hrs
JA673 156Sq, 582 Apr44, 1669/56CUs, 22MU, SS(HDA) Aug46
JA674 156Sq ex-32MU Jul43, Lost (Frankfurt) 20/21Dec43
JA675-6 462Sq, Lost (Milan/Turin) 15/16Aug & 12/13Jul43
JA677 83,7Sqs(MG·S) Mar44, NTU,CUs, Became 5294M
JA678 32MU,7Sq Jul43, Missing (Berlin) 24Aug43. 91hrs
JA679 9Sq(WS·P) 20Jun43, Missing 15Jul43. 71hrs. 8ops
JA680 460Sq 19Jun43, Wrecked after action 28Sep43. 204hrs
JA681 156Sq ex-32MU Jul43, Lost (Berlin) 3/4Sep43
JA682 7Sq ex-32MU Jul43, Lost 13Aug43. 50hrs
JA683 460Sq, Accident 27Jun43, 300Sq May44, Lost 13Jun43
JA684 44Sq, 5LFS, 1668CU, Crashed at Bottesford 7/8Feb45
JA685 7Sq ex-32MU Jul43, Lost (Leipzig) 4Dec43. 215hrs
JA686 83Sq, Blew up at Wyton 26Nov43. 291hrs
JA687 460Sq, Accident 5Sep43, Wrecked 7Mar44. 368hrs
JA688 460Sq, Abandoned, hit by incendiaries, 25Jul43
JA689 460Sq, 20Jun43, Missing 30Jul43
JA690 49Sq Jun43, 9Sq(WS·M) Sep43, Missing 7/8Jul44
JA691 49Sq 22Jun43, Missing (Peenemunde) 17/18Aug43
JA692 9Sq(WS·D) Jun43, Lost (Remscheid) 29Jul43. 85hrs

165

JA693 7Sq(MG ·J) Jun43; 1667,1656CUs; Became 5293M
JA694 156Sq ex-32MU Jul43, Lost (Berlin) 23Nov43
JA695 57Sq Jun43, 5MU,61Sq Mar44, Lost 12Apr44. 23hrs
JA696 57Sq, Damaged 29Jun43, Missing 3Aug43, 47hrs
JA697 156Sq Jul43, Missing (Berlin) 3Dec43
JA698 156Sq ex-32MU, Missing (Brunswick) 15Jan44
JA699 460,100Sqs Aug43, Became 4313M at Woodford Nov43
JA700 44Sq(KM ·P) Jun43, Damaged 19Oct43, Lost 2/3Dec43
JA701-2 32MU, 83/156Sqs Jun43, Lost 21Oct43/31Jan44
JA703 44Sq(KM ·W) 28Jun43, Lost (Munich) 6Sep43. 194hrs
JA704 103,166Sqs Sep43, Lost (Hanover) 27/28Sep43. 180hrs
JA705 83Sq(OL ·M Sugar Plum), 617Sq, 38MU, Scrap May47
JA706-7 7/9Sqs Jul/May45, Lost 9Oct/28Aug43. 159/92hrs
JA708 97Sq(OF ·Z) Jun43, Lost (Mannheim) 23/24Sep43. 103hrs
JA709 156Sq ex-32MU Jul43, Lost (Hamburg) 27/28Jul43. 20hrs
JA710 7Sq ex-32MU Jul43, Lost (Berlin) 31Aug43. 80hrs
JA711 97Sq(OF ·Y), 9Sq(WS ·A), Lost (Berlin) 1/2Jan44
JA712 83,166,550(BQ ·H)Sqs; Lost 27/28May44. 385hrs
JA713 7Sq 29Jun43, Missing 4Sep43, 111hrs
JA714 156,625Sqs(CF ·R), Lost (Leipzig) 20Oct43. 189hrs
JA715 97Sq Jul43, 576Sq Dec43, 101Sq(SR ·C) Jun44, Crashed
    and repaired six times, Wrecked by bomb explosion Feb45
JA716-7 97/7Sqs, Lost 1Aug/23Oct43. 52/122hrs
JA718 7Sq(MG ·T) ex-32MU Jul43, Scrap Jun47
JA843 44Sq(KM ·O) 7Jul43, Missing (Berlin) 31Jan44
JA844 619Sq; Hit ED361, fell at Plaistow, 13Aug43. 91hrs
JA845 32MU,SIU,106Sq,TFU,1667CU,ECFS,10MU, Scrap Oct47
JA846 97Sq(OF ·M) Jul43, 5LFS Feb45, 5MU, Scrap Sep47
JA847 619Sq(PG ·C) Jul43, Lost (Berlin) 2/3Dec43. 298hrs
JA848 619Sq 7Jul43, Missing 31Aug43. 131hrs
JA849-50 7Sq ex-32MU, Lost 28Sep/15Aug43, 94/33hrs
JA851 49Sq 7Jul43, Lost (Peenemunde) 17/18Aug43
JA852 9Sq(WS ·L), Accident 28Jul44, Lost 23/24Sep43. 81hrs
JA853 7Sq(MG ·R) ex-32MU Jul43, Lost 17Dec43. 239hrs
JA854-5 7/103Sqs Jul43, Lost 4Sep/26Jul43, 50/37hrs
JA856 460Sq Jul43, Lost (Munich) 20Oct43. 160hrs
JA857 32MU; 97(OF ·G),635,103Sqs; Lost (Dessau) 7/8Mar45
JA858 156Sq ex-32MU Jul43, Missing (Mannheim) 6Sep43
JA859-60 460Sq, Lost (Hanover/Berlin) 22Sep43/27Jan44
JA861 460Sq 10Jul43, Missing 29Sep43. 161hrs
JA862 460,625Sqs(CF ·T), Lost (Leipzig) 19/20Feb44. 382hrs
JA863 101Sq 7Jul43, Missing 28Jul43. 32hrs
JA864 12Sq Jul43, 626Sq, Missing (Berlin) 3Dec43
JA865 12,166Sqs Nov43, Lost (Berlin) 23/24Nov43. 212hrs
JA866 103Sq 7Jul43, Missing 24Jul43. 23hrs
JA867 619Sq(PG ·X) Jul43, Lost (Berlin) 16/17Dec43. 265hrs
JA868 103,576Sqs, 1656CU Nov44; 46,45MUs; Scrap Aug47
JA869 9Sq(WS ·H) Jul43, Missing 7/8Oct43. 236hrs. 28ops
JA870 AAEE Jul43, BDU Apr44, 46MU Mar45, Scrap Jan47
JA871 106Sq 11Jul43, Missing 23Aug43. 104hrs
JA872 57,630Sqs Nov43, 61Sq(QR ·K) Jun44, 46MU, Scrap
    Jan47
JA873 61Sq Jul43, Lost (Hamburg) 2/3Aug43. 52hrs
JA874 61Sq Jul43, 617Sq Sep43, Lost 16/17Sep43. 159hrs
JA875 57Sq Jul43, Missing 23Sep43, 142hrs
JA876 106Sq,1661CU,622Sq,46MU,RAE,20MU,2MPRD Nov47
JA892 49Sq 11Jul43, Missing (Peenemunde) 17/18Aug43
JA893 106Sq 14Jul43, Wrecked 4Sep43, 146hrs
JA894 49Sq Jul43, 617Sq Sep43, AAEE, Hit Oxford EB981 of
    7FTS near High Post on 10Sep43
JA895 44Sq(KM ·H) Jul43, Lost (Remscheid) 30/31Jul43. 41hrs
JA896 57Sq, Crashed in night landing at Scampton 16Aug43
JA897 44Sq 13Jul44, Missing 18Aug43. 93hrs
JA898 619Sq Jul43, 617Sq Sep43, Lost 16/17Sep43. 26hrs
JA899 50Sq(VN ·D), Damaged three times, Lost (Prouville) 24Jun44.
    545hrs
JA900 61Sq Jul43, Lost (Peenemunde) raid 17/18Aug43. 95hrs
JA901 467Sq, Middle East Oct43, Lost (Mailly) 3/4May44
JA902 463Sq, Shot down in Ijssellake (Berlin) 2/3Jan44. 241hrs
JA903 1577Flt, Flown to India 5Oct43; 44,75Sqs. SOC Nov46
JA904 1577Flt, India Oct43-Nov44, Wrecked 4Oct45
JA905 7Sq(MG ·V) Jul43, Lost (Brunswick) 14/15Jan44. 221hrs
JA906 467Sq,427Sq Sep43, Lost (Kassel) 3/4Oct43
JA907 7Sq 18Jul43, Missing (Kassel) 21Oct43. 151hrs

JA908 97Sq(OF ·W), 15MU, 1668CU, Crash landed E. Kirkby
    12Dec44
JA909 156(GT ·B),405,467Sqs; Crashed near Winthorpe 4Jun45
JA910 57Sq 17Jul43, Missing 29Sep43. 135hrs
JA911 7Sq(MG ·A) (MG ·N), 1653CU Nov44, SOC Oct45
JA912 156Sq ex-32MU Jul43, Missing 21/22Jan44
JA913-4 83/57Sqs Jul43, Lost 29Nov/4Sep43. 200/84hrs
JA915 156Sq, Crashed Kenninghall near Thetford 3/4Sep43
JA916-7 32MU; 97/7Sqs; Lost 31Aug/19Oct43. 64/162hrs
JA918 AAEE Jul43, 550Sq Mar44, Lost 9/10May44. 154hrs
JA919-20 32MU, 156/83Sqs, Lost 27Sep43/Crashed 11Aug43
JA921 156Sq 23Jul43, Missing 20Feb44.
JA922 12(UM ·J2),626,300Sqs; 1LFS, CUs, MUs, Scrap May47
JA923 97Sq(OF ·H) ex-32MU Jul43, Lost 5Oct43. 103hrs
JA924 32MU, 405Sq, Repaired Nov43, Lost 30Jan44. 234hrs
JA925-6 156/101Sqs Jul43, Lost 2Jan44/6Sep43. ?/116hrs
JA927-8 83Sq Jul43, Lost 24Aug43/27Apr44
JA929-30 7/100Sqs Jul43, Both lost 4Sep43. 11/?hrs
JA931-2 7Sq Jul43, Wrecked 11Aug43/Lost 24Nov43. 10/191hrs
JA933 7Sq(MG ·R) Jul43, 582Sq Mar44, Lost 23Apr44. 352hrs
JA934 100Sq Jul43, 550Sq Oct43, Lost 16Feb44
JA935 7Sq(MG ·O) Jul43, Lost (Brunswick) 14/15Jan44. 230hrs
JA936-7 7Sq Jul43, Both missing 31Aug43. 64/21hrs
JA938 RAE Jul43, Temporarily 5603M Cranwell, Scrap Feb47
JA939 97Sq Jul43, Missing 11Aug43
JA940 83Sq, Crashed at Hinchingbroke Castle 19Feb44*
JA941 156Sq 30Jul43, Missing 23Feb44
JA957 103,576(UL ·X2),9(WS ·D)Sqs; Lost 7/8Jul44
JA958 97Sq 26Jul43, Missing 23Aug43. 24hrs
JA959 32MU,BDU Oct43, 49Sq Jan45, Became 5925M at 4STT
JA960 97Sq(OF ·E) Jul43, Missing 2Jan44. 231hrs
JA961 50Sq Aug43, Wrecked 27Nov43
JA962 7(MG ·Q),582,103Sqs; 1668CU,ECFS Sep45, Scrap Aug48
JA963 97Sq(OF ·Q) Aug43, Lost (Berlin) 16/17Dec43. 101hrs
JA964 7Sq(MG ·P) Jul43, Lost (Frankfurt) 22/23Mar44. 254hrs
JA965 SIU Aug43, 101Sq Sep43, Wrecked 28Sep43. 20hrs
JA966-7 97/83Sqs Aug43, Wrecked 4Sep43/Lost 29Jan44
JA968 75Sq,576Sq(UL ·Y2) Mar44, Lost 3/4May44. 392hrs
JA969-70 100/7Sqs Aug43, Lost 4Sep/19Nov43. ?/96hrs
JA971-2 7/83Sqs Aug43, Lost 4Oct43/Wrecked 1Dec43
JA973 106Sq,463Sq Dec43, Lost (Berlin) 30/31Jan44. 317hrs
JA974-5 405/156Sqs, Aug43; Both lost 15Jan44. 233/?hrs
JA976 405Sq Aug43, Lost 28Apr44. 315hrs
JA977 101Sq ex-SIU Aug43, Missing 23/24Sep43. 27hrs
JA978 7Sq 15Aug43, Wrecked 11Sep43. 45hrs
JA979 405Sq; Dived into ground, Gransden Lodge, 5Nov43
JA980 405Sq ex-32MU Aug43, Lost 9Oct43. 75hrs
JA981 617Sq, Missing in sea 15Sep43 after recall. 41hrs
JB113 156Sq 18Aug43, Missing (Frankfurt) 20/21Dec43
JB114-5 83/7Sq Aug43, Lost 3Jan44/23Nov43. 230/100hrs
JB116 61Sq(QR ·R) Aug43, 9Sq Jun44, Missing 7/8Jul44
JB117 97Sq(OF ·C) Aug43, Crashed ex-Berlin raid 16/17Dec43
JB118 97 or 83Sqs, Missing 6Sep43. 32hrs
JB119 97Sq Aug43, Crashed trying to locate Bourn 17Dec43. 158hrs
JB120 405Sq 27Aug43, Missing 27/28Sep43
JB121 467Sq 20Aug43, Missing (Dusseldorf) 3/4Nov43
JB122 100Sq Aug43, Missing (Berlin) 30/31Jan44
JB123 619Sq(PG ·D) 20Aug43, 625Sq Oct43, Lost (Berlin) 3Jan44
JB124 467Sq, Missing (Berlin) 23/24Aug43
JB125 619Sq, 5MU, 5LFS, Crashed in flames Syerston 12Jan45
JB126 49Sq 22Aug43, Down in sea operations 4Sep43
JB127 Conv. Mk.I AAEE, R-R Jan-Sep44
JB128 101Sq ex-32MU 19Sep43, Missing 3Dec43. 45hrs
JB129 61Sq(QR ·G) 20Aug43, Lost (Berlin) 25Mar44. 217hrs
JB130 467Sq Aug43, MUs, 1668CU Aug44, 20MU, SS May47
JB131 619Sq Aug-Dec44, 5LFS, 46MU, SOC Jan47
JB132 61Sq Aug43, Collided and burnt near Bleasby 1Sep43
JB133 619Sq 21Aug43, Missing 6Sep43. 31hrs
JB134 619Sq(PG ·G) 22Aug43, Missing 3/4May44. 354hrs
JB135 57Sq Aug43, 630Sq Nov43, Lost (Berlin) 23/24Nov43
JB136 44Sq 22Aug43, Lost (Berlin) 3Oct43, 76hrs
JB137 61Sq Aug43, 5MU, 5LFS, 15MU, SOC Oct46
JB138 61Sq(QR ·J) Aug43, 113 operations, 5LFS Feb45, Became
    5224M at 4STT

166

JB139 49Sq Aug43, 617Sq Sep43, Missing 5Aug44. 364hrs
JB140 467Sq 23Aug43; Crashed, operations, 4Dec43. 169hrs
JB141 100Sq Aug43, 626Sq Nov43, Lost (Brunswick) 14/15Jan44
JB142 101,166Sqs(AS ·P), Crashed New Barnetby 25May44
JB143 50Sq Aug43; Ditched and lost, mining 29/30Sep43
JB144 49Sq, 617Sq Sep43, Lost (Canal raid) 16Sep43. 37hrs
JB145 12Sq Aug43, 166Sq Sep43, Lost (Berlin) 2/3Dec43. 177hrs
JB146 106Sq 24Aug43, Crashed on operations 31Aug43. 23hrs
JB147 103Sq 26Aug43, Missing 19Oct43. 107hrs
JB148 100Sq, Crashed into hill near N. Elkington 23Oct43
JB149-50 101Sq Aug43, Missing 4Sep/1Sep43. 3/8hrs
JB151 166Sq Sep43, Missing (Frankfurt) 22/23Mar44. 164hrs
JB152 103Sq 26Jul43, Missing 23/24Sep43. 56hrs
JB153 103Sq 28Aug43; Burnt out, Wymeswold 8Sep43. 35hrs
JB154 83Sq 26Aug43, Missing 21Oct43. 68hrs
JB155 7Sq(MG ·S) Sep43, NTU Jun44, Crashed 4Oct44. 513hrs
JB174 97Sq 28Aug43, Missing 9Oct43. 68hrs
JB175 7Sq ex-32MU 30Aug43, Missing 21Oct43. 72hrs
JB176 97Sq(OF ·K) Sep43, Wrecked near Bourn 17Dec43. 138hrs
JB177 156Sq 29Aug43, Missing 7Sep43
JB178 49Sq 4Sep43, Lost (Revigny) 18/19Jul44
JB179 156Sq 30Aug43, Missing (Berlin) 3Dec43
JB180 405Sq 2Sep43, 83Sq Mar44, Lost 22Jun44. 426hrs
JB181 7Sq ex-32MU 18Sep43, Missing 9Oct43. 17hrs
JB182 405Sq 17Sep43, Missing 24Nov43
JB183 405Sq 11Sep43, NTU, 22MU, Oct45, Scrap May47
JB184 7Sq 4Sep43, Missing 22/23Sep43. 27hrs
JB185 7Sq(MG ·Y) Sep43, 1651CU Nov44, Scrap Oct45
JB186 156Sq,619Sq(PG ·O) Jan44, Lost 18/19Jul44. 405hrs
JB187 83Sq Sep43, Abandoned by crew 29Sep43
JB188-9 405/97Sqs, Lost 22Jan44/Crashed 9Oct45
JB190 97Sq Sep43, Missing 3Dec43. 154hrs
JB191 97Sq 2Sep43, Damaged beyond repair 6Jan44. 122hrs
JB216-7 156Sq Sep43, Lost 17Dec43/Crashed 23May44
JB218 97Sq ex-32MU 9Sep43, Lost (Berlin) 24Nov43. 89hrs
JB219 97Sq ex-32MU 11Sep43, Damaged beyond repair 17Dec43
JB220 97Sq ex-32MU 9Sep43, Missing 19Oct43. 55hrs
JB221 97Sq 4Sep43, Lost (Frankfurt) 25/26Nov43. 77hrs
JB222-3 405/156Sqs Sep43, Lost 4Dec43/24Nov43
JB224 7Sq(MG ·W) 10Sep43, Lost (Berlin) 15/16Feb44. 215hrs
JB225 7Sq ex-32MU 10Sep43, Crashed 29Sep43. 17hrs
JB226 405Sq 20Sep43, Missing (Mannheim) 18Nov43
JB227 97Sq(OF ·J) ex-32MU, Missing (Berlin) 23Nov43. 84hrs
JB228 156,514Sqs; 1668CU; Crashed at Fiskerton 10Mar45
JB229 49Sq 7Nov43, Damaged and SOC 24Nov43
JB230 405Sq 11Sep43, 156Sq Mar44, Missing 24Jun44
JB231 49Sq 6Sep43, Missing (Berlin) 3Jan44
JB232 97Sq(U) 16Sep43, Lost (Heilbronn) 4Dec44. 141hrs
JB233-4 57Sq 6/18Sep43, Missing 24Dec/21Oct44. 136/50hrs
JB235 49Sq, Crashed on approach Fiskerton 26/27Nov43
JB236 57,630Sqs, Missing (Berlin) 23/24Nov43. 127hrs
JB237 57Sq 7Sep43, Missing 23Oct43. 57hrs
JB238 97Sq(OF ·A) ex-32MU, Missing (Berlin) 23Jan44. 114hrs
JB239 97Sq,NTU; 156,35,635Sqs; Missing 12Jun44
JB240 Crashed in transit from 32MU 15Sep43 and SOC
JB241 405Sq ex-32MU 15Sep43, Missing 25Feb44. 137hrs
JB242 156Sq ex-32MU 16Sep43, Missing 5Oct43
JB243 97Sq, Crashed in bad visibility near Graveley 17Dec43
JB275 97Sq ex-32MU 20Sep43, Missing 21Oct43. 33hrs
JB276-7 103Sq 9/11Sep43, Lost 23Oct43/28Jan44. 91/161hrs
JB278-9 103Sq Sep43, Lost 25Apr44/19Oct43. 322/77hrs
JB280 405Sq ex-32MU 16Sep43, Lost 2Jan44. 180hrs
JB281 12Sq Sep43, 38MU, 5LFS, 1660CU, Scrap Jun46
JB282 156Sq ex-32MU 18Sep43, Burnt out 17Dec43
JB283 12Sq 16Sep43, Missing 27/28Jan44 (S/L Goule)
JB284 83Sq 19Sep43, Missing 24Nov43. 84hrs
JB285 12Sq 17Sep43, Lost (Berlin) 2/3Dec43
JB286 405Sq(LQ ·O), 467Sq, Aug44, Crashed near Eye 7Jan45
JB287 12Sq 15Sep43, Lost (Kassel) 20/21Oct43
JB288 1660CU Sep43, 630Sq Jan44, Lost 30/31Mar44. 327hrs
JB289 1656CU Sep43, 100Sq Nov43, Lost 30Jun44. 452hrs.
JB290 1660CU Sep43, 630Sq(LE ·C) Jan44, 39MU, SOC Jul46
JB291 1656CU Sep43, 100Sq Nov43, Lost 4Dec43. 124hrs

JB292 1660CU Sep43, 106Sq Jan44, Missing 8May44
JB293 156Sq ex-32MU 30Sep43, Burnt out 24Nov43
JB294 1660CU 14Sep43, 630Sq 4Jan44, Lost 22Jan44. 146hrs
JB295 49Sq 17Sep43, Missing 28Sep43
JB296 1656CU Sep43, 460Sq Dec43, Lost (Berlin) 27/28Jan44
JB297 405Sq Sep43, 166Sq Jun44, 153Sq, Lost 14Oct44. 430hrs
JB298 1656CU Sep43, 460Sq Nov43, Lost (Berlin) 29/30Dec43
JB299 97Sq(OF ·W) ex-32MU 17Sep43, Lost 22Jan44. 193hrs
JB300 97Sq ex-38MU 19Sep43, Missing 19Mar44
JB301 49Sq 16Sep43, Missing (Mannheim) 23/24Sep43
JB302 83Sq Oct43, 156Sq Dec43, Missing 31Jan44
JB303 7Sq 29Sep43, Missing 27Nov43. 75hrs
JB304-5 156/49Sqs Sep43, Lost 23Nov & 3/4Nov43 (Dusseldorf)
JB306 NTU 7Oct43, 1667CU 5Dec44, Crashed 19Jun45
JB307 156Sq 30Sep43, Missing 27Apr44
JB308 7Sq(MG ·B) Sep43. Overshot Oakington 24Feb44. 123hrs
JB309 83Sq Oct43, 207Sq Jul44, 1668CU, 5MU, SOC 1Jul47
JB310-1 156/57Sqs Sep43, Lost 3Jan/29Jan44. ?/238hrs
JB312 97Sq Oct43, Damaged on delivery 97Sq, Lost 29Jan44
JB313 7Sq(MG ·H) 9Oct43, Lost (Aachen) 24/25May44. 352hrs
JB314 49Sq 12Sep43, Lost (Nuremburg) 30Mar44. 351hrs
JB315 57Sq 21Sep43, Wrecked in crash 18Nov43. 100hrs
JB316 NTU Oct43, 1667CU Jan44, Crashed 25Aug45
JB317 156Sq 8Oct43, Missing (Berlin) 3Jan44
JB318 57Sq 21Sep43, Missing 19Jul44. 483hrs
JB319 103Sq,5LFS,3LFS,1654CU,15MU, Scrap Oct46
JB320 57Sq 21Sep43, Missing 23Oct43. 49hrs
JB344 83Sq 27Nov43, Burnt out, operations, 17Dec43. 62hrs
JB345 7,582,550Sqs; 5MU, Scrap Jul47
JB346 103Sq Sep43, Crashed after take-off 4Oct43. 9hrs
JB347-8 7/405Sqs 4Oct43, Lost 19/21Oct43. 9/17hrs
JB349-50 103Sq Sep43, Lost 19Oct/27Nov43. 16/100hrs
JB351 83Sq Oct43, Missing 22Jun44. 43hrs
JB352 SIU Defford Sep43, 83Sq Nov43, Lost 31Jan44. 137hrs
JB353 97Sq 13Oct43, Missing 28Jan44. 152hrs
JB354 12Sq 22Sep43, Crashed 27Nov43
JB355 83Sq 13Nov43 ex-SIU Defford, Lost 3Jan44. 80hrs
JB356 97Sq(OF ·X),635Sq Mar44, Lost 31Mar44. 234hrs
JB357-8 12Sq 26Sep43, Missing 5/6 & 27/28Jan44
JB359 12Sq 26Sep43, Missing (Berlin) 24/25Mar44
JB360 49Sq 27Sep43, Missing (Berlin) 28Jan44
JB361 97Sq(OF ·B) ex-32MU 3Oct43, Missing 16Mar44
JB362 49Sq 29Sep43, Missing (Berlin) 26/27Nov43
JB363 156Sq ex-32MU 3Oct43. Lost (Leverkusen) 19Nov43
JB364 57Sq 5Oct43, Missing 3Jan44, 126hrs
JB365 Avro Sep-Oct43, 83Sq Nov43, Lost 26Jan44. 111hrs
JB366 57Sq 27Sep43, Missing 28Jan44. 142hrs
JB367 97Sq(OF ·S) 3Oct43, Missing 19Nov43. 38hrs
JB368 49Sq 27Sep43, Missing (Berlin) 22/23Nov43
JB369 405Sq Oct43, Burnt out, Graveley, operations, 16/17Dec43
JB370-1 57/9Sqs Oct43, Lost 7Jul44/30Dec44. 338/?hrs
JB372-3 57Sq Oct43, Missing 3/17Dec43. 75/16hrs
JB374 405Sq Oct43, 46MU, NTU, 1667CU, Scrap Sep45
JB375 Defford Oct43, 1BDU Aug44; 54,38MUs; SOC May47
JB376 103Sq 1Oct43, Missing 23Oct43. 38hrs
JB398 7Sq(MG ·C) 17Oct43, Lost (Brunswick) 14/15Jan44, 126hrs
JB399 49Sq Oct43, 1653CU(H4 ·Q) Nov44, 39MU, SOC Jun47
JB400-1 103Sq 2Oct43, Both missing 3Dec43. 71/93hrs
JB402 83Sq ex-SIU Defford Nov43, Missing 3/4May44
JB403 103Sq 2Oct43, Missing 3Dec43. 93hrs
JB404 NTU ex-32MU Oct43, 12Sq, Became 5292M at 1660CU
JB405-6 12Sq Oct43, Lost 3/4May44 & 9Oct43
JB407 12Sq(PH ·A) 17Oct43, Missing (Berlin) 29/30Dec43
JB408 7Sq(MG ·A) 21Oct43, Lost (Magdeburg) 21/22 Jan44. 113hrs
JB409 12Sq 7Oct43, 626Sq Dec43, Lost (Hasselt) 11/12May44
JB410 405Sq Oct43, 12Sq,576Sq Sep44, 20MU, SS(CC) May47
JB411 49Sq 5Oct43, Crashed 18Oct43
JB412 83Sq ex-SIU Defford Nov43, Lost 29Jan44. 62hrs
JB413 49Sq 7Oct43, Lost (Kassel) 22/23Oct43
JB414 83Sq Oct43, 7Sq Dec43, Missing 15/16Feb44. 150hrs
JB415 RAE Farnborough 6Oct43, 38MU Apr44, SOC May47
JB416 49Sq 4Oct43, Missing (Kassel) 22/23Oct43
JB417 7Sq(MG ·F),582Sq Mar44, Crashed Radlett 24Jul44
JB418 57Sq 18Oct43, Missing 19Nov43. 25hrs

167

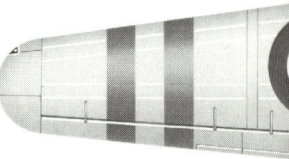

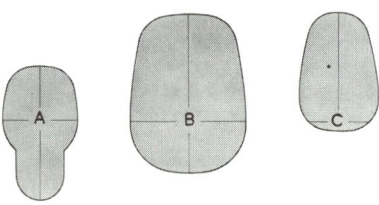

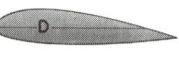

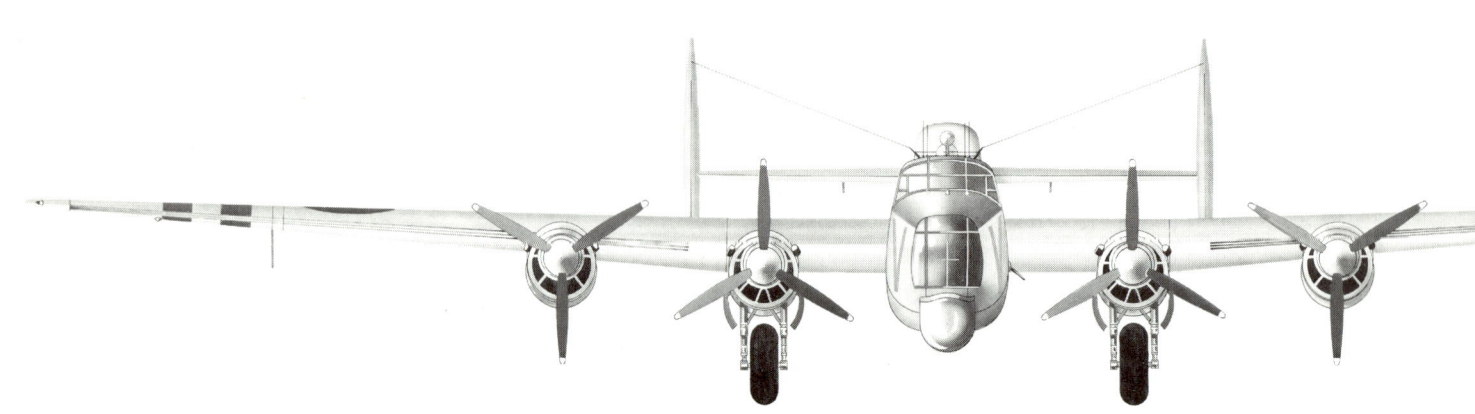

168

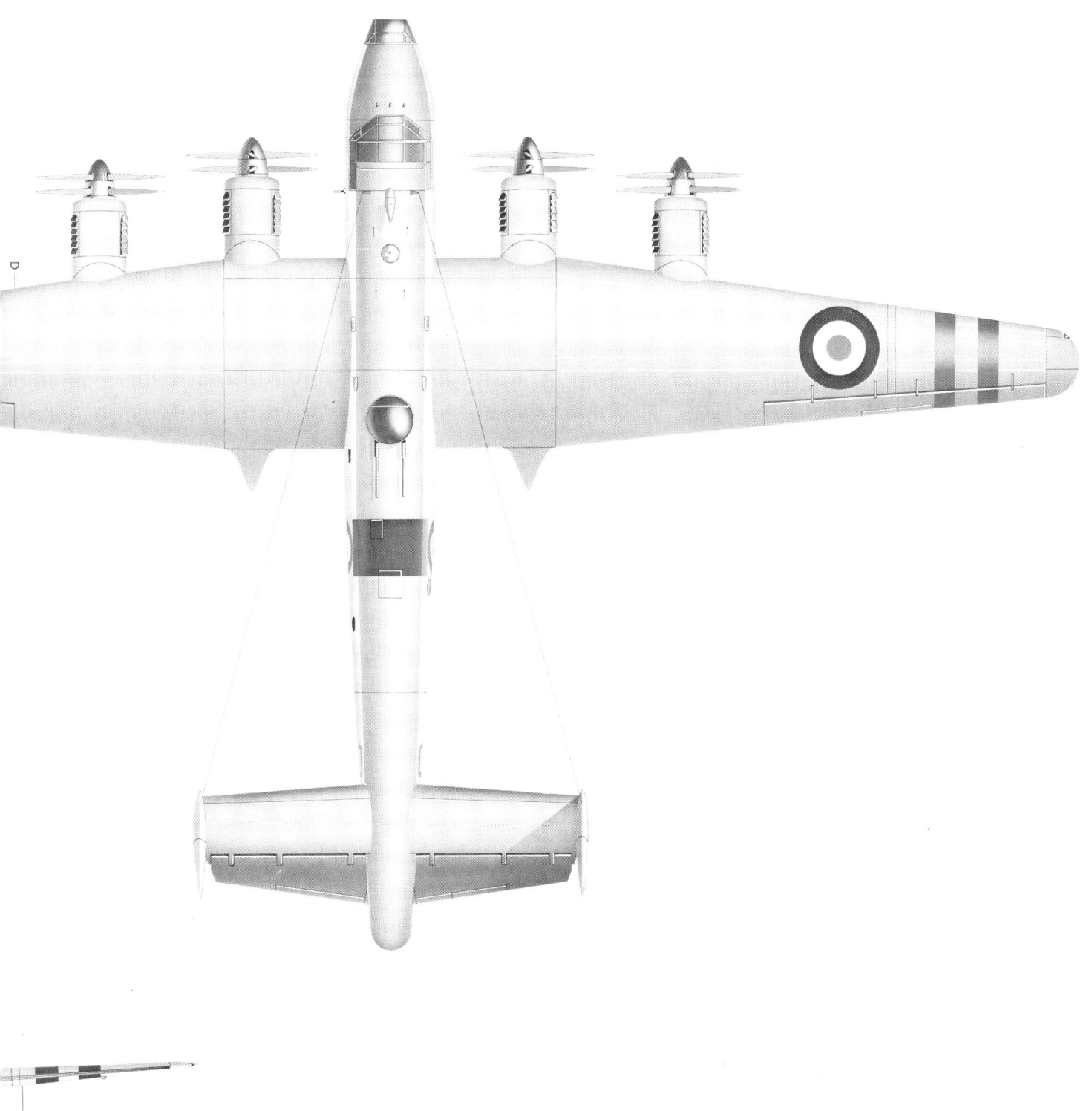

The Shackleton M.R.1 which superseded the Lancaster G.R.3. The fuselage and
wingtip bands are exercise markings.

JB419-20 57Sq 7Oct43, Lost 21Jan/16Feb44. 115/142hrs
JB421 49Sq 7Oct43, Missing (Salbris) 7/8May44. 399hrs
JB422 97,653,582Sqs; BCIS Jan45, Scrap Sep46
JB423 103Sq Oct43, 427Sq, Damaged & SOC 4Dec43. 77hrs
JB424 83Sq ex-32MU 16Oct43, Missing 23Nov43. 38hrs
JB453-4 83/103Sqs Oct43, Lost 3Jan44/21Dec43. 109/46hrs
JB455 83Sq Oct43, 7Sq(MG ·P) Dec43, Lost (Lens) 15/16Jun44
JB456 AAEE & Filton, various turrets. Became 5338M Snailwell
JB457 AAEE 9Oct43; Became 5533M at 1RS, Cranwell
JB458-9 103/83Sqs 9Oct43, Both lost 27Nov43, 68/33hrs
JB460 103Sq 20Oct43, 576Sq Mar44, Lost 25Jun44. 228hrs
JB461 83Sq(OL ·N) (OL ·L) ex-SIU Nov43, Lost 21Jan44. 94hrs
JB462-3 12Sq 21Oct43, Lost 30Jun44/3Dec43. 305/?hrs
JB464-5 12Sq 18Oct43, Crashed 26/27 and 24Nov43
JB466-7 49Sq Oct44, Missing 31Mar44/21Dec43. 353/?hrs
JB468 7Sq(MG ·G) ex-32MU 24Oct43, Lost 19/20Feb44. 159hrs
JB469 49Sq 18Oct43, Missing (Leipzig) 20Feb44
JB470 97Sq Oct43, 635Sq Mar44, Missing 12Apr44. 157hrs
JB471 156Sq Oct43, NTU Nov34, Burnt after crash 11Apr44
JB472 83Sq Oct43, 156Sq Nov43, Lost (Berlin) 3Dec43
JB473-4 49/57Sqs Oct43, Lost 19Jul/16Mar44. 473/154hrs
JB475 7,514,15,195(JE ·G),186Sqs; 1659CU, SOC Sep45
JB476 83Sq 3Nov43, 156Sq 23Nov43, Missing 2Jan44
JB477 405Sq 25Oct43, Burnt near Graveley 17Dec43. 131hrs
JB478 12Sq 25Oct43, Missing (Berlin) 3Dec43
JB479-80 156/7Sqs ex-32MU Oct43, Lost 25Feb44/24Nov43
JB481 405Sq 27Oct43, Flew into ground 17Dec43. 53hrs
JB482 405Sq,97Sq, Abandoned 17Dec43, Wreck not located
JB483 156Sq 23Nov43, Missing (Brunswick) 15Jan44
JB484 405Sq NTU, 1666CU, Damaged gale 19Jan45. SOC47
JB485 57Sq 21Oct43, Missing 27Nov43. 50hrs
JB486 57Sq(DX ·F) 21Oct43, Missing 5Jul44, 397hrs
JB487 103Sq 24Oct43, Missing 20Dec43. 108hrs
JB488 83Sq(OL ·X) 6Nov43, Missing 21Jan44. 119hrs
JB526 57Sq(DX ·D) 10Nov43, Missing 22Jun44. 424hrs
JB527-8 103Sq Oct43, Lost 27 and 24Nov43. 57/27hrs
JB529 57Sq 21Oct43, Missing 3Dec43. 62hrs
JB530 103Sq, Hit ND334 over Elsham Wolds 20Feb44
JB531 97Sq ex-32MU 25Oct43, Abandoned 17Dec43. 28hrs
JB532 61Sq(QR ·A) Oct43, 630Sq Nov43, Lost 2Jan44. 74hrs
JB533 49Sq 27Oct43, Burnt out on operations 11Nov43
JB534 61Sq Oct43, 106Sq Nov43, Burnt out 16Feb44. 150hrs
JB535 97Sq ex-32MU 6Nov43, Missing 31Jan44. 97hrs
JB536-7 12Sq Oct43, SOC 21Jun47/Lost 4Nov43
JB538 83Sq Nov43, 7Sq, Missing 27Nov43. 5hrs
JB539 57Sq 25Oct43, Missing 25Mar44. 236hrs
JB540 12Sq(UM ·L) 5Nov43, Missing (Schweinfurt) 24Feb44
JB541-2 57/12Sqs Nov43, Lost 6 & 14/15Jan44
JB543 405Sq 6Nov43, 7Sq 24Nov43, Lost 17Dec43. 24hrs
JB544 12Sq,24MU,TFU Aug44, NBC-1 trials Nov47, SOC Jan48
JB545 49Sq 30Oct43, Missing (Berlin) 17Dec43
JB546 630Sq 17Nov43, Lost (Brunswick) 22/23May44. 311hrs
JB547 460Sq Nov43, Hit ME641 mid-air 25Feb44. Crew baled

JB558 with Mk. IIIF H2S, Defford, September 1944.

JB548 57Sq 10Nov43, Missing 2Jan44. 48hrs
JB549 100Sq ex-32MU, Missing 24Dec43. 106hrs
JB550 103Sq 3Nov43, 567Sq, Missing 4Dec43. 55hrs
JB551 103Sq, 38MU, 5LFS, 1668CU. Beyond repair Nov45
JB552 7Sq ex-32MU 6Nov43, Missing 17Dec43. 28hrs
JB553 156Sq 24Nov43, Missing (Berlin) 3Jan44
JB554 100Sq ex-32MU 7Nov43, Damaged 27Nov43. 4hrs
JB555 103,567Sqs; 1668CU, NTU Dec44. Became 4970M
JB556 12Sq,630Sq Nov43, Belly-landing E. Kirkby 25Apr44
JB557 100Sq Nov43-44; 1667,1662,1653CUs; 15MU, SOC Aug47
JB558/G TFU Nov43, H2S Mk.IIIF with 6ft scanner. SOC Sep45
JB559 12,626,300,12Sqs; 1LFS; 1662/7CUs; SOC Aug47
JB560 100Sq 27Nov43, Burnt on operations 17Dec43. 19hrs
JB561 61,630Sqs; 5MU; 12,300Sqs; Lost 26Aug44. 112hrs
JB562 106Sq ex-32MU 10Nov43, Missing 27Apr44.
JB563-4 100Sq Nov43, Lost 22/23Mar44/24Nov43. 199/18hrs
JB565 61Sq Oct43, 57Sq Nov43, Lost 25Feb44. 136hrs
JB566-7 106Sq Nov43, Lost 31Mar/23Apr44
JB592-3 106Sq Nov43, Lost (Berlin) 26/27Nov43/30Aug44
JB594 100Sq ex-32MU 10Nov43, Missing 23Dec43. 72hrs
JB595 626Sq(UM ·O2) 12Nov43, Lost (Berlin) 15/16Feb44. 23hrs
JB596 100Sq ex-32MU 16Nov43, Burnt out 17Dec43. 40hrs
JB597 630Sq 17Nov45, Damaged and SOC 27Nov43. 16hrs
JB598 460Sq ex-32MU, Missing (Essen) 23Mar44. 235hrs
JB599 626Sq(UM ·Q2) 12Nov43, Missing 23Mar44
JB600 460Sq Nov43, Lost (Villeneuve St. Georges) 10Apr44
JB601 106Sq 6Nov43, Missing (Schweinfurt) 27Apr44
JB602 100Sq 30Nov43, SOC damaged 15Jan44
JB603-4 100Sq 3Nov43, Missing 5Jan45/24Feb44
JB605 100Sq, Abandoned, crashed Broadstone Farm, 19Nov43
JB606-7 460Sq 3Nov43, Lost (Berlin) 2/3Jan44/30Dec43
JB608 460Sq 5Nov43, Missing (Berlin) 2/3Dec43. 49hrs
JB609 12Sq(PH ·F),626Sq Feb44, 12Sq, Lost (Leipzig) 20Feb44
JB610 460Sq 5Nov43, Lost (Leipzig) 19/20Feb44. 60hrs
JB611 460Sq ex-32MU 16Nov43, Lost (Berlin) 2/3Dec43. 19hrs
JB612 106Sq 17Nov43, Missing (Salbris ammo dump) 7May44
JB613 460Sq Nov43-May44, 38MU; 625,150Sqs; SOC Dec45
JB614 100Sq ex-32MU Nov43, Lost (Essen) 26/27Apr44. 270hrs
JB637 460Sq ex-32MU Nov43, Lost (Berlin) 27/28Jan44. 111hrs
JB638 106Sq 17Nov43, Missing 18Dec43. 49hrs
JB639 626Sq,166Sq, Crashed near Barton on Humber 17Dec43
JB640 156Sq ex-32MU 25Nov43, Missing (Berlin) 3Jan44
JB641-2 106Sq Nov43, Missing 8Jul/2Jan44. 403/87hrs
JB643 7Sq(MG ·M) Nov43, 46MU, 12Sq, 46MU, Became 5945M
JB644 405Sq Nov43, 166Sq Jun44, Lost 12/13Jul44. 335hrs
JB645 106Sq 17Nov43, Missing 3Jan44. 84hrs
JB646 626Sq Nov43, 300Sq,1656CU,46MU,45MU, SOC Aug47
JB647 460Sq, Hit high ground Kelstern, H2S training, 24Nov43
JB648 106Sq 17Nov43, Missing (Frankfurt) 23Mar44. 252hrs
JB649 626Sq Nov43, 166Sq Jan44, Missing 28Jul44. 393hrs
JB650 12Sq 11Nov43, Missing (Berlin) 28Jan44
JB651 7Sq(MG ·K) ex-32MU 29Nov43, Lost (Stettin) 5/6Jan44
JB652 7Sq ex-32MU 25Nov43, Crashed 22Dec43. 31hrs
JB653 97Sq 2Nov43, later 7Sq, Lost (Le Mans) 19/20May44. 271hrs
JB654 630Sq 17Nov43, Lost (Berlin) 28/29Jan44. 136hrs
JB655 103Sq Nov43, 165CU Nov44, 1660CU Nov45, SOC Jan46
JB656 7Sq ex-32MU 24Nov43, Missing 17Dec43 25hrs
JB657 460Sq, Stalled into wood at Market Stanton 16Dec43†
JB658 103Sq 13Nov43, Missing 17Dec43. 59hrs
JB659 97Sq(OF ·J) ex-32MU 23Nov43, Missing 31Jan44. 119hrs
JB660 12Sq Nov43-Oct44, BCIS Mar45, 15MU, SOC Aug46
JB661 7Sq(MG ·Z) Nov43, 300Sq Aug44, 626Sq, Missing 7Jan45
JB662 460Sq 24Nov43; Swung on take-off, blew up, 19Apr44
JB663 106Sq, 24MU Mar45, 15MU, SOC Oct46, 1000+hrs, 111ops
JB664 106Sq 15Mar43, Missing 28Jun44. 433hrs
JB665-6 630Sq 17Nov43, Lost 16Feb/(Berlin) 29Jan44
JB667-8 156/460Sqs Nov43, Lost 25Mar44/Crash 25Feb44
JB669 TRE 24Nov44, 405Sq Dec44, SOC Dec45
JB670 103Sq; Crashed, hit LM332 over Lincs 16Dec43†
JB671 97Sq 4Dec43, Missing (Berlin) 25Mar44
JB672 630Sq 17Nov43, Lost (Duisburg) 21/22May44. 335hrs
JB673 100Sq(P) 22Nov43, Lost (Berlin) 30/31Jan44. 109hrs
JB674 100Sq, Hit JB678 over Waithe 16/17Dec43. 16hrs
JB675 Conv Mk. VI. R-R Nov43, 635Sq, Scrapped Jul48

JB676 Wyton ex-32MU Nov43, 7Sq 1Jan44, Lost 27/28Apr44
JB677 32MU, 7Sq(MG ·U), Lost (Berlin) 2Jan44. 5hrs
JB678 100Sq Nov43, Hit JB674 in low cloud 16/17Dec43. 13hrs
JB679-80 49Sq Nov43, Lost 27Apr/27Mar44. 263/95hrs
JB681 57Sq Nov43, Missing 3Jan44, 65hrs
JB682 7Sq(MG ·A) ex-32MU Dec43, Lost (Berlin) 1/2Jan44. 22hrs
JB683/G 97Sq(OF ·C),12Sq; 1668,1653CUs; 5MU, Scrap Sep47
JB684 405Sq 11Dec43, Missing 23Apr44. 263hrs
JB699 405Sq 13Dec43, 156Sq, 1651CU, Burnt 3/4Mar45
JB700 460Sq 24Nov43, Missing (Vire) 6/7Jun44. 316hrs
JB701 49Sq 29Nov43, Lost (Stuttgart) 28/29Jul44. 468hrs
JB702 460Sq 24Nov43, Lost (Magdeburg) 21/22Jan44. 79hrs
JB703 156Sq 23Dec43, Missing (Berlin) 2Jan44
JB704 460Sq Nov43, Landed in field near Breighton 17Dec43*
JB705 TFU Defford ex-32MU 12Dec43, SOC Jul47
JB706 97Sq(OF ·F/H) Dec43, 635Sq Mar44, Lost 31Mar44. 194hrs
JB707 405Sq ex-32MU 4Jan44, Missing 29Jul44. 400hrs
JB708-9 97/12Sqs 14Dec43, Lost 10/11May & 9/10Apr44
JB710 630Sq 27Dec43, Lost (Leipzig) 19/20Feb44. 114hrs
JB711 156Sq 11Dec43, Missing (Berlin) 23/24Dec43
JB712 12,97Sqs(OF ·U), Missing 29Jan44. 82hrs
JB713 Conv Mk. VI, R-R; 7,405,635Sqs; Lost (Ghent) 18Aug44
JB714 49Sq 29Nov43, Lost (Etampes) 10Jun44, 279hrs
JB715 12Sq 30Nov43, Damaged 16/17Dec43
JB716 12Sq 30Nov43, Crashed (burnt) 10/11Aug44. 340hrs
JB717 SIU Dec43, 7Sq Jan44, Lost (Berlin) 28/29Jan44. 18hrs
JB718 12Sq Nov43, 101Sq(SR ·Q) Oct44, 38MU, Scrap May47
JB719 SIU Dec43, 7Sq Jan44, Lost (Karlsruhe) 24/25 Apr44
JB720/G 32MU Nov43, 97Sq(OF ·S) Dec43, Lost 6Jan44. 13hrs
JB721 156Sq ex-32MU 4Dec43, Missing 25Feb44
JB722 Defford Dec43, 7Sq(MG ·U) Jan44, Lost 31Mar44.144hrs
JB723 57Sq 30Nov43, Missing 5Jul44
JB724 Defford Dec43, 83Sq Jan44, Missing 28Jan44. 6hrs
JB725-6 57/97Sqs Dec43, Lost 10Apr/15Jan44. 227/61hrs
JB727 49Sq 30Nov43, Missing (Berlin) 3Jan44
JB728 97Sq(OF ·P) Dec43, 635Sq Mar44, Lost 16Jun44
JB729 405Sq ex-32MU, Missing 16Jun44. 299hrs
JB730 103Sq 10Dec43, Missing 24Dec43. 26hrs
JB731 97Sq Dec43, Missing 23Mar44. 146hrs
JB732-3 103Sq Dec43, Lost 11Apr & 11/12May44. 232/268hrs
JB734 460Sq Dec43, Lost (Villeneuve St. Georges) 9/10Apr44
JB735 7Sq ex-32MU 1Dec43, Damaged 24Dec43. 6hrs
JB736 103Sq 10Dec43, Missing 31Mar44. 199hrs
JB737 405Sq ex-32MU 11Dec43, Missing 2Jan44, 29hrs
JB738 460Sq, Crashed after take-off, Binbrook Village, 2Jan44
JB739 460Sq 11Dec43, Lost (Berlin) 20/21Jan44. 68hrs
JB740 100Sq Dec43, Missing 2Jan44. 38hrs
JB741 460Sq 11Dec43, Lost (Mailly le Camp) 3May44, 263hrs
JB742 460Sq 11Dec43, Missing 26Feb44. 118hrs
JB743 460Sq 11Dec43, 625Sq 13Jun44, Lost 1Jul44. 304hrs
JB744 103 and 576Sqs; Burnt, operations, 19Mar44. 116hrs
JB745 103Sq 11Dec43, Lost (Leipzig) 19/20Feb44. 96hrs
JB746-7 103Sq Dec43, Lost 1Aug44/3Jan44. 407/34hrs
JB748 12Sq(PH ·Z) Dec43, Lost (Mailly le Camp) 3/4May44

Serial Range KB700—KB999   Lancaster B.X

300 Lancaster B.X ordered from Victory Aircraft of Canada delivered from September 1943 to March 1945 for ferrying to the United Kingdom. Up to KB774 initially fitted with Merlin 38 engines and all subsequent with Merlin 224 engines. R.C.A.F. instructional airframe numbers, e.g. A448, given where appropriate.

KB700 405Sq(LQ ·Q) 5Oct43, 419Sq(VR ·Z); Overshot, Middleton 2Jan45*
KB701 419Sq, Crashed near Wombleton 16/17May44. 122hrs†
KB702-3 Retained in Canada
KB704 419Sq,428Sq(NA ·X), Crashed 11May44
KB705 R-R Jan44, 428Sq(NA ·F),1664/66CUs,20MU, SOC Mar46
KB706 419Sq Dec43, Missing (Aachen) 24/25May44
KB707 419Sq May44, Wrecked 20Sep44
KB708 R-R,419Sq, Overshot Boscombe Down 25/26Aug44
KB709 428Sq(NA ·G) Aug44, Lost (Stettin) 29/30Aug44. 107hrs
KB710 419Sq(W) Mar44, Lost (Louvain) 13/14May44. 107hrs

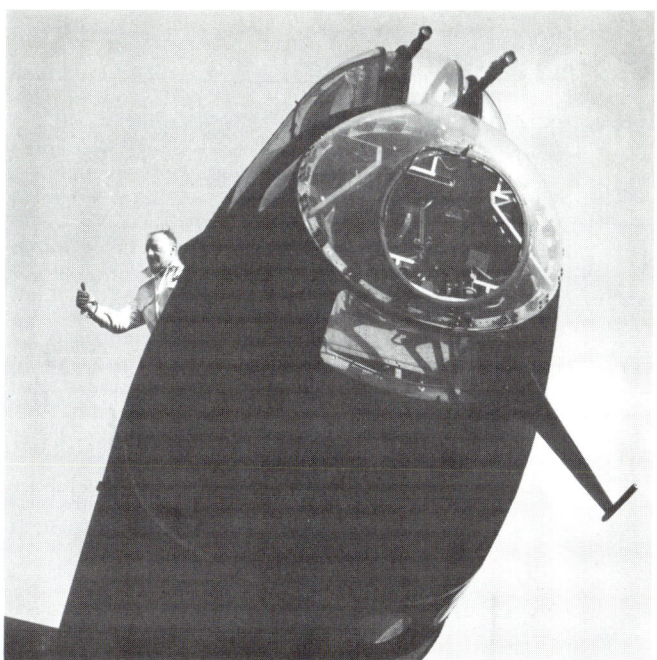

Lancaster being passed out at the works.

KB711 70MU, 419Sq(NA ·U), Lost (St. Ghislain) 1/2May44. 92hrs
KB712 419Sq (VR ·L) Apr44, Lost (Cologne) 28Oct44. 409hrs
KB713 419Sq(X) Apr44, Lost (Louvain) 12/13May44. 80hrs
KB714 419Sq 13May44, Missing 13Jun44. 87hrs
KB715 419Sq(T), Missing (Lehausen airfield) 24Dec44. 60 ops
KB716 419Sq(D) 21Apr44, Crashed 7May44
KB717 419Sq(E) 10Apr44, Lost (Dortmund) 22/23May44. 94hrs
KB718 419Sq(J) Apr44, Lost (Villeneuve St. Georges) 4/5Jul44
KB719 419Sq(T) Apr44, Lost (Stuttgart) 24/25Jul44. 225hrs
KB720 419Sq(P),1664CU Aug44,1666CU Nov44,20MU,SS May47
KB721 AAEE Apr44, 419Sq Aug44, Canada Jun45, Became A448
KB722 419Sq; Crash landed near St. Quentin, France 5/6Jan45*
KB723 419Sq(U), Lost (Villeneuve St. Georges) 4/5Jul44. 181hrs
KB724 419Sq(VR ·K) 1May44, Wrecked 28Aug44. 298hrs
KB725 428Sq(NA ·L), Crashed at Elton Hall 3Feb45
KB726 419Sq(A) 27May44, Lost (Cambrai) 12/13Jun44. 46hrs
KB727 419Sq(H), Lost (Villeneuve St. Georges) 4/5Jul45. 158hrs
KB728 419Sq(V) 13Apr44, Missing 17Jun44. 159hrs
KB729 Became G-AKDO Modified 10-P R.C.A.F.
KB730 Retained in Canada
KB731 419Sq(VR ·S) 30Apr44, Missing 13Jun44. 118hrs
KB732 419Sq(VR ·X) 16May44, Canada Jun45, Disposed Apr48
KB733 419Sq(VR ·G) Apr44, Canada Jun45, Became A450 Mar48
KB734 419Sq May44, Crashed near Zeist 17Jun44. 85hrs
KB735 419Sq(O), Overshot Eastmoor 18/19Sep44. 314hrs
KB736 419Sq(A), Missing (Cambrai rly yds) 12Jun44
KB737 428Sq(NA ·R) 25May44, Lost (Essen) 25Oct44. 359hrs
KB738 419Sq(VR ·D) 16May44, Missing (Opladen) 28Dec44
KB739 428Sq(NA ·W), Winter trials Canada 1945/46, SS 1948
KB740 428Sq(NA ·V) Jul44, Damaged in action 25Jul44
KB741 431Sq(SE ·Y) Nov44, 434Sq, Lost (Chemnitz) 14/15Feb45
KB742 428Sq; Overshot runway, Middleton, 4Nov44. 314hrs
KB743 428Sq(NA ·I) Jun44, Lost (Bremen) 18/19Aug44. 159hrs
KB744 428Sq(NA ·J) 11Jun44, Canada 31May45, Disposed May47
KB745 419Sq, Flew into high ground near Hope, 4Oct44. 207hrs
KB746 419Sq, Flown back to Canada Jan45, Scrap Jan48
KB747 428Sq Jun44, Canada Jun45, Scrap Jan48
KB748 419Sq Sep44, Canada Jun45, Became A449 Aug45
KB749 428Sq(NA ·A) Jun44, Missing(Soesterberg)15Aug44. 145hrs
KB750 419Sq(N) 15Jun44, Missing (Wiesbaden) 2/3Feb45
KB751 428Sq(NA ·Q) Jul44, Lost (Stettin) 16/17Aug44. 138hrs
KB752 419Sq(S/V) 13Jun44, Abandoned in air 8Apr45
KB753 419Sq(L), Lost (Schloven Oil Refinery) 29Dec44
KB754 419Sq(C) Jun44, Missing(Bochum) 9Oct44. 226hrs

Lancaster fuselages under repair at Bracebridge Heath

KB755 419Sq(F) Jun44, Missing (Caen) 7/8Aug44. 122hrs
KB756 428Sq(NA ·Q) Jun44, Missing 5Jul44. 62hrs
KB757 428Sq(NA ·C) Jul44, Canada 31May45, Scrap Jan47
KB758 428Sq(NA ·Z) Jun44, Lost (Brunswick) 12/13Aug44. 163hrs
KB759 428Sq(NA ·K) Jul44, Lost (Hamburg) 28/29Jul44. 85hrs
KB760 428Sq(NA ·P) Jul44, Canada Jun45, Scrap Jan47
KB761 419Sq(VR ·H) Jul44, Missing (Hamburg) 31Mar45
KB762 419Sq(VR ·J) Jul44, Crashed 23Apr45
KB763 428,419Sqs; Wrecked, u/c collapsed 23Apr45
KB764 428Sq, Ditched in Atlantic off Azores 4Jun45
KB765 419Sq(VR ·M/Q), Lost (Schloven Oil Refinery) 29Dec44
KB766 428Sq 27Jun44, Crash-landed France 2/3Dec44
KB767 419Sq(VR ·U) 26Jul44, Damaged 1Nov44. 224hrs
KB768 428Sq, Collided with a 426Sq a/c near Rugby 5Dec44
KB769 419Sq Jul44, Lost (Merseburg Refinery) 14Jan45
KB770 428Sq(NA ·D) Jul44, Missing 28/29Jan45
KB771 428Sq Jul44, Canada Jun46, Scrap May47
KB772 419Sq Nov44, Canada Jun46, Scrap May47
KB773 431Sq(SE ·A), Flown to Canada Jun46. Scrap Mar48
KB774 419Sq(VR ·P),413Sq(SE ·D), Canada Jun46, Scrap Jan47
KB775 419Sq(Y) Aug44, Lost (Russelsheim) 25Aug45. 64hrs
KB776 419Sq Aug44, Missing 23Oct44. 164hrs
KB777 428Sq, Shot down by Ju88 near Hildersheim 22Mar45
KB778 428Sq(NA ·Y), Crashed from 2,000ft, Baraque, 5/6Mar45
KB779 419Sq(B) Aug44, Missing (Osnabruck) 6Dec44
KB780 428Sq(NA ·T) Jul44, Lost (Duisberg) 14Oct44. 186hrs
KB781 428Sq(NA ·U), Canada 31May45. Mod 10S, Scrap Jan56
KB782 428Sq(NA ·H) Aug44, Missing 2Nov44. 233hrs
KB783 AAEE Oct44, trials of Martin turret, 419Sq Mar45, Canada
Jun45, Scrap Jan46
KB784 428Sq(K) Aug44, Lost (Kiel) 13/14Apr45
KB785 419Sq, Crashed near Bradbury Range, Durham, 24Nov44
KB786 419Sq, Believed in sea returning from Heide 21Mar45
KB787 419Sq, Collided over Ardennes en route Bonn 4Feb45
KB788 419,431Sqs; Damaged in action 1Dec44
KB789 434Sq(V) Dec44, Canada Jun45, Scrap Mar48
KB790 Arr.UK 15Mar45, Held in MUs, Scrap May47
KB791 428Sq(W) Aug44, Canada Jun45, Scrap May47
KB792 428Sq(I) Sep44, Missing (Wiesbaden) 2/3Feb45
KB793 428Sq, Crashed in Durham after fire in air 13Jan45
KB794 428Sq Sep44, Canada Jun45, Disposed Jan47
KB795 428Sq, Crash landed Middleton St. George 7Apr45
KB796 431Sq(SE ·R), Damaged 8Jan45, Canada Jun45, ScrapJan47
KB797 419Sq(K) Sep44, Missing (Dessau) 7Mar45
KB798 428Sq Sep44, Missing (Opladen) 28Dec44
KB799 419Sq(W), Missing (Merseburg Refinery) 14Jan45
KB800 419Sq(C), Missing (Duisberg) 14Oct44. 29hrs
KB801 431Sq(SE ·S) Nov44, Canada Sep44, Mod 10S, Scrap May56
KB802 431Sq(SE ·V) Nov44, Canada Sep44, Disposed Jan47

KB803 431Sq(SE ·N), Crashed at Yafforth 26Jan45
KB804 419Sq(E) Nov44, Missing (Dortmund) 20Feb45
KB805 5MU, TFU, American remote gun control, Scrap Jul47
KB806 431Sq(SE ·X) Nov44, Missing (Leuna) 15Jan45
KB807 431Sq(SE ·B), Canada Jun45, Disposed Jan47
KB808 431Sq(SE ·U), Missing in day raid 22Mar45
KB809 431Sq(SE ·Q) Nov44, Missing (Dortmund) 21Feb45
KB810 431Sq(SE ·H), Canada Jun45, Disposed Mar48
KB811 431Sq(SE ·T), Canada Jun45, SOC 24Aug50
KB812 431Sq(SE ·F) Jun44, Canada Oct44, SOC 6Apr50
KB813 431Sq Dived into ground near Tingrith, Beds, 25Oct44
KB814 419Sq(N), Shot down by fighter (Hagen) 15/16Mar45
KB815 431Sq(SE ·K) Oct44, Missing 15/16Mar45
KB816 434Sq Dec44, 428Sq Feb45, Crashed 14Apr45
KB817 431Sq(SE ·P) Oct44, Missing 1Nov44. 76hrs
KB818 431Sq(SE ·G), Crashed at Ford 7Feb45
KB819 431Sq(SE ·J) Nov44, Canada Jun45, Disposed Apr48
KB820 428Sq Nov44, Crashed 3Dec44, Canada Jun45, SOC Apr50
KB821 431Sq 9Nov44, Missing 6/7Jan45
KB822 431Sq, Collided over sea with KB831 25Apr45
KB823 431Sq(SE ·E) Oct44, 419Sq Jan45, Canada Jun45, SS Jan48
KB824 434Sq Dec44,Damaged 23/24Feb45,CanadaJun45, SSJan47
KB825 434Sq(A) Dec44, Canada Jun45, Disposed Jan47
KB826 434Sq, Canada Jun45, Conv 10N *Orion* SS May57
KB827 431Sq(SE ·M)Nov44, Crashed twice,CanadaJun45,SS Jan47
KB828 Crashed in transit 25Sep44
KB829-30 434Sq(C/D) Dec44, Canada Jun45, Disposed Mar48
KB831 431Sq(SE ·E), Collided over sea with KB822, 25Apr45
KB832 434Sq(F), Collided and exploded at Croft 22Mar45
KB833 434Sq(B) Dec44, Canada Jun45, Disposed Mar48
KB834 434Sq(Y), Missing on day attack, Essen, 11Mar45
KB835 434Sq(J), Shot down by Ju88 near Landen 15/16Mar45
KB836 434Sq(H) Dec44, Canada Jun46, Disposed Mar48
KB837 431Sq(SE ·X), Canada Jul45, SOC 24Aug50
KB838 428Sq(O) Dec44, Canada 31May45, Disposed Apr48
KB839 419Sq Jan45, Canada Jun45, Mod 10AR, 408Sq
KB840 434Sq(N) Dec44, Canada Jun45, Disposed Jan47
KB841 419Sq Jan45, Canada Jun45, Disposed Apr48
KB842 434Sq(L), crash landed after collision 5/6Mar45
KB843 434Sq Dec44, 428Sq Feb45, Canada Jun45, SS May47
KB844 434Sq(W) Dec44, Canada Jun45, Disposed Mar48
KB845 419Sq, Crashed Drayton Parsloe 5/6Mar45
KB846 428Sq, Crashed in Allied lines 15/16Mar45
KB847 431Sq(SE ·R) Jan45, Canada Jun45, SOC 24Aug50
KB848 428Sq Jan45, Canada Jun45, Mod 10DC (PX848)
KB849 434Sq(T) Dec44, Canada Jun45,SOC 6Apr50
KB850 434Sq, Lost after oil plant raid, Zeitz, 17Jan45
KB851 419Sq Jan45, Canada Jun45, Mod 10DC, Scrap Aug61
KB852 434Sq(R) Dec44, Canada Jun45, Disposed Mar48
KB853 Arr.UK 16Nov44, 431Sq, Missing 11Mar45
KB854 419Sq Jan45, Canada Jun45, Mod 10S, Scrap Oct55
KB855 428Sq(NA ·F), Crash landed Middleton St. G. 20Feb45
KB856 431Sq(SE ·K) Mar45, Canada Jun45, Disposed Jan47
KB857 419Sq, Conv. 10MR; 404(MN857),407Sqs; Scrap Sep58
KB858-9 431Sq Feb45, Missing 5Mar/31Mar45
KB860 UK Nov44, 419Sq Feb45, Canada Jun45, Disposed Jan48
KB861 431Sq(SE ·Q) Feb45, Canada Jun45, SOC 24Aug50
KB862 434Sq Feb45, Canada Jun45, Disposed Jan47
KB863 434Sq(P) Feb45, Canada Jun45, Disposed Jan47
KB864 428Sq(S) Feb45, Canada Jun45, Disposed Jan47
KB865 419Sq Feb45,Canada Jun45, Mod 10MP,407Sq, Scrap Jan60
KB866 419Sq(M) Feb45, Missing (Kiel) 13Apr45
KB867 Arr.UK 21Nov44, 428Sq Feb45, Canada Jun45, SS Apr48
KB868 431Sq(SE ·E)Mar45, CanadaJun45, Mod10MP, Scrap Jun55
KB869 419Sq(Q) Feb45, Missing (Hamburg) 31Mar45
KB870 419Sq(K), Blew up after fighter attack 15/16Mar45
KB871 431,420Sqs, Canada Jun45, Mod 10MP,407Sq, Scrap Sep60
KB872-3 431/434Sqs Feb45, Canada Jun45, Disposed 1947
KB874 Defford Jan45, 431Sq, Damaged in action 25Mar45
KB875 419Sq, Canada Jun45, Mod. 10MP, 407Sq, Scrap Jun50
KB876 Arr.UK 5Jan45, 425Sq May45, Canada Jun45, SS Jan47
KB877 408Sq(S), Canada Jun45, Disposed Jun45
KB878 419Sq Mar45, Canada Jun45, Became A538 Jul48
KB879 428Sq, Dived to earth from 16,000ft. near Hixon 30Apr45

172

KB880 434Sq, Crashed 18Apr45, Canada Jun45, SOC 6Apr50
KB881 419Sq Mar45, Canada Jun45, Disposed Jan47
KB882 428Sq Mar45, Canada Jun45, Mod 10AR, 408Sq(MN882)
KB883 434Sq, Crashed Mar45, 20MU, 434Sq, Canada Jun45, Mod 10MP (RX883), Scrap Jun60
KB844 419Sq Mar45, Canada Jun45, Became A526
KB885 434Sq(Q) Mar45, 420Sq Apr45, To Canada Jun45, Became CF-IMF of Spartan Air Services
KB886 420Sq Apr45, Canada Jun45, Disposed Jan48
KB887 Arr.UK 1Apr45, 5MU 7Apr45, Scrap Dec46
KB888 431Sq(SE ·O) Mar45, Canada Jun46, SOC 6Apr450
KB889 428Sq Apr45, Canada Jun46, Mod 10MP, 107RU
KB890 434Sq Apr45, Canada Jun45,Mod 10MP,404Sq,SOC Oct61
KB891 428Sq(F) Mar45, Canada 31May45, Disposed Jan47
KB892 419Sq 29Mar45, Canada 4Jun45, Mod 10MP, 407Sq, SOC Jun60
KB893 Tested Woodford 23Feb45; 431,434Sqs; Canada Jun45 Mod 10MP, Based at Trenton, SOC after crash 8May52
KB894 425Sq 1May45, Flown back to Canada Jun45. Modified 10MR, 407Sq, SS Apr61
KB895 434Sq(O) Mar45, Canada Jun45, Disposed Jan47
KB896 419,420Sqs; Canada Jun45, Disposed Jan47
KB897 Arr.UK Mar45; 218,39MUs; Scrap Jun47
KB898 Arr.UK Jan45,420Sq Apr45,CanadaJun45,Disposed Jan47
KB899 428Sq Apr45, 425Sq May45, Canada Jun45, Disposed Jan48
KB900 431Sq(SE ·C) Canada, Jun45, SOC 24Aug50
KB901 420Sq, Canada Jun45, Mod 10MR, 2MOTU, Scrap Jun60
KB902 434,420Sqs; Canada Jun45, Became 606C
KB903 420,425Sqs; Modified 10MR, 2MOTU, Scrap Jan57
KB904 408Sq, Canada Jun45, Mod. 10MP, Scrap Jun60
KB905 408Sq, Canada Jun45, Disposed Jan47
KB906 UK 12Apr45; 20,32MUs; Canada 9Aug45, Disposed May47
KB907 408Sq(U), Canada Jun45, Mod 10SR, Sold (Spartan) Apr56
KB908 UK 24Feb45, 420Sq, Canada Jun45, Disposed Apr48
KB909 419,420Sqs; Canada Jun45, Sold (Spartan) Apr46
KB910 428Sq Mar45, 420Sq Apr45, Canada Jun45, Disposed Jan47
KB911 Arr.UK Jan45, 434Sq 18Mar45, Lost 31Mar45
KB912 5MU, 425Sq, Canada Jun45, Disposed 1948
KB913 5MU, 408Sq, To Canada Jun45, Disposed Jan47
KB914 434,420Sqs; Canada Jun45, Mod 10MP, Missing 19Mar53
KB915 419,425Sqs; Canada Jun45, Disposed 27Jan48
KB916 420,425Sqs; Canada Jun45, Burnt at Trenton Jan52
KB917 420,425Sqs; Canada Jun45, SOC 2Jan47
KB918 420,425Sqs; Canada Jan45, Disposed Jan47
KB919 408Sq, Canada Jun45, 1st 10MR, 2MOTU, Scrap Aug55
KB920 434,428Sqs; Canada 31May45, Mod 10MP, Scrap Jan60
KB921 419Sq Apr45, Canada Jul45, Disposed Apr48
KB922 431Sq 8Apr45, Canada 6Jun45, Disposed Jan47
KB923 420Sq 21Apr45, Canada 12Jun45, Became 542C
KB924 425Sq 6May45, Canada 14Jan45, Disposed Apr48
KB925 408Sq(E), Canada Jun45, Mod 10MP, 407Sq, Scrap Jun60
KB926 425Sq, Canada 13Jun45, Disposed Jan48
KB927 420Sq, Canada Jun45, Mod. 10MP, 2MOTU, Scrap Aug55
KB928 420Sq Apr45, Canada Jun45, Disposed Jan47
KB929 408Sq(O), Canada Jun45, Mod 10MP, 20TU, Scrap Sep55
KB930-1 UK Mar45, 425Sq May45, Canada Jun45, Scrap 1947/48
KB932 UK 3Mar45, 425Sq May45, Canada Jun45, Disposed Jan47
KB933 UK 6Mar45, 420Sq May45, Canada Jun45, Disposed Jan47
KB934 425Sq May45, Canada Jun45, Mod 10MP, Burnt Jan52
KB935 Arr.UK May45; 20,32,20MUs; Scrap May47
KB936 425Sq, Crashed 15Jun45, Canada later, Scrap Jan48
KB937 420Sq Apr45, Canada Jun45, Mod 10MP, 2MOTU, SOC 2Jan60
KB938 420Sq, Apr45, Canada Jan45, Mod 10MP, Crashed 25Jun55
KB939 408Sq(W), Canada Jun45, Disposed Jan48
KB940 32MU, Canada Aug45, Mod 10MP, Crashed Dec52
KB941-2 420Sq Apr45, Canada Jun45, Disposed Jan47/48
KB943 32MU, Canada Aug45, Mod 10MP, 107RU
KB944 UK 8Mar45,425Sq May45,Canada Jan45,Mod10S, Museum
KB945 405Sq May45, Canada Jun45, Mod 10MP, SOC (Crash) 19May54
KB946 420Sq May45, Canada Jun45, Mod 10MP, Scrap Jan60
KB947 408Sq, Canada Jun45, Disposed Jan48
KB948 408Sq, Canada Jan45, Mod 10MP, 2MOTU, Scrap Aug55

KB949 405Sq May45, Canada Jun45, Mod 10MP, Scrap Apr61
KB950 405Sq May45, Canada Jun45, Mod 10MP, 2MOTU, Scrap Aug45
KB951 408Sq(A), Flown back to Canada Jun45, Disposed Jan48
KB952 UK Mar-Jun45, 405Sq, Disposed Jan48
KB953 Arr.UK 23Mar45,32MU,Canada 22Aug45, Disposed Apr48
KB954 425Sq 15May45,Canada 13Jun45,Mod10MR,SOC20May55
KB955-6 405Sq May45, Canada 16Jan45, Mod 10MP, Scrap 1955
KB957 UK Mar45, 405Sq May45, Canada Jun45, Scrap Jan60
KB958 UK Mar45, 32MU Jul45, Canada 23Jul45, Scrap Jan60
KB959 405Sq 30May45, Canada Jun45, Mod 10MP, 404Sq(AF ·A)
KB960 408Sq(F), Canada Jun45, 2MOTU, Scrap Sep55
KB961 405Sq, Canada Jun45,Mod10MP;408,404Sqs;Scrap Sep55
KB962 Arr.UK Mar45, 405Sq, Canada 14Jun45, Disposed Jan48
KB963 408Sq(H), Canada Jun45, Disposed Jan48
KB964 405Sq May45, Canada Jun45,Mod 10MP,405Sq,ScrapJan55
KB965 405Sq, Canada Jun45, Mod 10BR, 405Sq, SOC(Crash) 10Aug50
KB966 32MU, Canada Jul45, Mod 10MR, 405Sq, SOC (Crash) 4May53
KB967 405Sq, Canada Jun45, Mod 10MR, 103RU, 2OTU, Scrap Jun53
KB968 405Sq 29May45, Canada Jun45, Disposed 15Apr48
KB969 5MU Apr45, 32MU Jun45, Canada Aug45, Scrap Jan47
KB970 Arr.UK Mar45,32MU Jun45,Canada Jul45,Disposed Jan47
KB971 To RCAF 14Mar45, Crashed during flight testing
KB972 408Sq(C), Canada Jun45, Mod10MR, SOC(Burnt) 30Jan52
KB973 405Sq May45,Canada Jun45,Mod10MP,407Sq,Scrap Sep60
KB974 Held in 20,5,32MUs; Canada Aug45, Mod 10MP, Scrap Jun55
KB975 32MU Jun45, Flown to Canada 14Jul45, Disposed Jan47
KB976 405Sq May45, Canada Jun45, Mod 10AR, 408Sq(MN976) Scrap Sep55
KB977 405Sq May45, Canada Jun45, Mod 10MP, 2MOTU, Scrap Sep55
KB978 UK Mar45, 32MU Jun45, Canada Sep45, Disposed Jan47
KB979 408Sq(L), Canada Jun45, Disposed Jan48
KB980 Arr.UK 7Apr45, 5,32,20MUs; Scrap May47
KB981 UK 1Apr45; 5,32,MUs; Canada Aug45, Disposed Jan48
KB982 UK15Apr45, 32MU Jun45, Canada Aug45, Disposed Jan47
KB983-4 UK Apr45, 32MU Jun45, Canada Aug45, Disposed Jan47
KB985 Arr.UK 15Apr45, 405Sq May45, Crashed and SOC 3Jun45
KB986 32MU Jun45, Canada Aug45, Mod 10N, Sold May57
KB987 Arr.UK 9Apr45; 5,32,29,22MUs; Scrap Jun47
KB988 UK 17Apr45, 32MU Jun45, Canada Jul45, Disposed Jan47
KB989 Arr.UK 7Apr45; 20,32,20MUs; Scrap May47
KB990 Arr.UK 8Apr45, 32MU Jun42, Canada Jul45, Became A527
KB991 405Sq May45, Canada Jun45, Mod 10BR, SOC(Crash) 29Jul48
KB992 32MU Jun45, Canada Jul45, Mod 10MR,407Sq,Scrap Jan55
KB993 408Sq(U), Hit hill on Shelf Moor 18May45
KB994 408Sq(K), Canada Jun45, Disposed Jan47
KB995 408Sq(OW ·B), Canada Jun45, Mod 10MR, SOC(Crash) 16Jan53
KB996 408Sq(P), Canada Jun45, Mod 10MP, 407Sq, Scrap Jun60
KB997 405Sq, Canada Jun45, Conv. 10MP, Scrap Jun55
KB998 408Sq(G), Canada Jun45, Disposed Jan48
KB999 Victory Aircraft Gift *Malton Mike*, 419,405Sqs; To Canada Jun45, Mod 10MR, 405Sq, SOC(Crash) 22Oct45

Serial Range LL617—LM296   **Lancaster B.I/II**
   450 Lancasters ordered from Armstrong Whitworth Aircraft in April 1942 and delivered as 100 Mk.II with Hercules XVI engines and 350 Mk.I with Merlin 24 engines initially installed.

Lancaster B.II (Delivered October 1943 to March 1944)
LL617 432,426Sqs; 1678, 1668CUs; Became 4957M at 1654CU
LL618 432Sq 24Oct43, Missing (Berlin) 3Dec43
LL619 RAE Oct43, AAEE Mar45, SOC Feb46
LL620 514Sq, Tail broke off over Villers Bocage 30Jun44
LL621 426,408Sqs; 1668CU, Wrecked 23Jan45
LL622-3 115/405Sqs Nov43, Missing 30Mar44/24Nov43

LL624 514Sq(JI·B), SOC after fourth crash 28Sep44
LL625 514Sq(JI·C) Nov43, Lost over Berlin 25Mar44
LL626 115Sq Nov43, Crash 1Feb44, 5MU, SOC Sep46

LL735 at the R.A.E., March 1944, as jet test-bed.

LL627 514Sq(JI·U), Shot down in Ijssellake 21/22Jan44
LL628 426Sq 7Nov43. Missing (Berlin) 21Jan44. 33hrs
LL629 426Sq; Flew into hill, Mowthorpe, Yorks, 23/24Nov43
LL630 426Sq 7Nov43, Missing (Frankfurt) 20Dec43
LL631 408Sq(EQ·G), Missing (Berlin) 2/3Jan44
LL632 432Sq(QO·G),408Sq(EQ·G), Lost (Leipzig) 19/20Feb44
LL633 115Sq,408Sq(EQ·L), Lost (Nuremberg) 30/31Mar43
LL634 426Sq Nov43, 1668CU Aug44, SOC Mar45
LL635 AFEE,514Sq, Apr44; Damaged, operations, 14Sep44
LL636 432Sq(QO·B),408Sq, 1668CU, Crash 7Jan45
LL637 432Sq Jan44, 408Sq Mar44, Lost 16Mar44. 122hrs
LL638 432Sq 9Jan44, Missing (Berlin) 28Jan44
LL639 115Sq Jan44, 514Sq Mar44, Missing 4Apr44. 44hrs
LL640 115Sq 24Jan44, Missing 19Mar44. 87hrs
LL641 514Sq(JI·K), Crashed near Newmarket (Le Mans) May44
LL642 408Sq(EQ·B), 1668CU Sep44, SOC Mar45
LL643 408Sq(EQ·Q), Missing (Acheres) 7/8Jun44. 162hrs
LL644 115Sq, Missing 25Feb44, 37hrs
LL645 514Sq, Port wing hit ground near Waterbeach30/31Mar44
LL646 115Sq(KO·G) Feb44, Crash Mar44, 46MU, Scrap Jan47
LL647 426Sq(OW·R), Lost (Frankfurt) 22/23Mar44. 155hrs
LL648-9 115Sq Nov43, Missing 31/29Jan44. 54/26hrs
LL650-1 115Sq Nov43, Missing 21Jan/16Feb44. 32/110hrs

A standard production Lancaster B.2, LL678.

LL652 115,514Sqs, Missing (Aachen) 27/28May44. 181hrs
LL653 514Sq, Missing (Stuttgart) 15/16Mar44. 134hrs
LL666 514Sq, 1668CU, RAE, Became 5423M
LL667 514Sq Nov43, 115Sq, Burnt after operation 19Apr44
LL668 514,115Sqs, Missing 28Jan44. 16hrs
LL669 514Sq(JI·S); Crashed, overshot 17Mar44. 53hrs
LL670 115,514Sqs(JI·K2); 1668CU, Wrecked 23Jan43
LL671 115Sq(JI·B2),514Sq(A2·B), Lost (Berlin) 24Dec43
LL672 115Sq(A2·C), Missing (Magdeburg) 21Jan44, 50hrs
LL673-4 115/514Sqs, Dec43, Lost 18Jan44/Crashed 28Mar44
LL675 408Sq, Caught fire in air and crashed 11Jul44
LL676 408Sq(EQ·E) Dec43, Missing (Berlin) 16/17Dec43
LL677 115,514Sqs; SOC after third crash 8Sep44
LL678 514Sq(JI·L2), Lost (Gelsenkirchen) 12/13Jun44. 192hrs
LL679 115Sq 2Dec43, Lost (Brunswick) 14Jan44. 6hrs
LL680 115,514Sqs, Missing 22Jan44. 19hrs
LL681 115Sq Dec43, 514Sq, Lost (Leipzig) 19/20Feb44. 40hrs
LL682 115,514Sqs, Missing (Dusseldorf) 22/23Apr44
LL683 115Sq Dec43, Crashed 30/31Mar44. 128hrs
LL684 115Sq Dec43, 514Sq, Lost (Frankfurt) 22/23Mar44. 101hrs

LL685 115Sq, Missing (Brunswick) 14Jan44. 32hrs
LL686 432Sq, Dived into ground from 1,000ft. near Ripon 2Feb44
LL687 408Sq(EQ·M), Missing (Hamburg) 28/29Jul44
LL688 514,426Sqs, Missing (Berlin) 27Jan44
LL689-90 115/514(JI·J)Sqs, Lost 16Feb/16Jun44. 7/186hrs
LL691 115,514Sqs, Missing 30Apr44. 108hrs
LL692 115,514Sqs, Missing (Stuttgart) 28/29Jul44
LL693-4 115Sq Feb44, Missing 16/25Mar44. 26/35hrs
LL695 115,514Sqs(JI·A), Lost (Duisburg) 21/22May44. 76hrs
LL696 514Sq(JI·A), Missing (Nuremburg) 30/31Mar44. 29hrs
LL697 514Sq(JI·E/A2·B) Mar44, Damaged, operations, 12Aug44
LL698 514Sq(JI·J2), Lost (Nuremburg), 30/31Mar44. 37 hrs
LL699 408Sq(EQ·C), Missing (Brunswick) 14/15Jan44
LL700 408Sq(EQ·J), 426Sq, 1668CU Aug44, SOC Mar45
LL701-2 115Sq Dec43, Lost 25Feb/Wrecked 15Jan44. 80/8hrs
LL703 514Sq(JI·L) Dec43, Crashed 20May44
LL704 115Sq, Missing 31Mar44. 44hrs
LL716 115,514Sqs, Lost (Bois de Casson) 3Aug44. 256hrs
LL717 408Sq(EQ·W) Dec43, Lost (Schweinfurt) 24/25Feb44
LL718 432,408Sqs(EQ·E), Lost (Stuttgart) 15/16Mar44. 88hrs
LL719-20 408Sq(EQ·V/R), Both lost (Leipzig) 19/20Feb44
LL721 426Sq(OW·U), Missing (Berlin) 27Jan44
LL722 408Sq(EQ·N), 1668CU Sep44, Became 4974M at 1660CU
LL723 408Sq(EQ·H), Missing (Dortmund) 22/23May44
LL724 408Sq, Missing 22Jan44
LL725 408Sq(EQ·C) Jan44, Lost (Hamburg) 28/29Jul44. 321hrs
LL726 115,514Sqs; 1668CU Sep44, SOC Deteriorated 22Mar45
LL727 514Sq(JI·C2), Missing (Massy Palaiseau) 7/8Jun44. 184hrs
LL728 514Sq(JI·B), Missing (Kiel) 26Aug44. 295hrs
LL729 115Sq, Crashed at Skellington, Beds. 21Feb44. 18hrs
LL730 514,115Sqs; Missing 25Mar44, 59hrs
LL731 514Sq(JI·U) Feb44, Missing 13Sep44. 302hrs
LL732 514Sq(JI·H2) Feb44, Lost (Chambly) 1/2May44. 115hrs
LL733 115Sq,514Sq(JI·G), Missing (Caen) 30Jul44. 263hrs
LL734 514Sq(JI·S), 1668CU, Wrecked 23Jan43
LL735 Used as jet engine test bed, Scrapped in 1950
LL736 TFU 1945-48, AGLT fitted, 9MU, SS Mar50
LL737 TFU & RAE armament experiments, Scrap Jan47
LL738 514Sq(JI·D), Reported lost 30/31Mar44, Scrap Jun47
LL739 514Sq Mar44, Missing 11/12May44. 69hrs

Lancaster B.I (Delivered from November 1943 to August 1944)
LL740 463Sq Nov43, Lost (Schweinfurt) 24/25Feb44. 132hrs
LL741 50Sq Nov43, Burnt after 92nd operation 21/22Feb45
LL742 9Sq(WS·D), 38MU, 5LFS, 1660/8CUs, Became 6541M
LL743 166Sq Dec43, Lost (Mailly le Camp) 3/4May44. 252hrs
LL744 50Sq, Missing (Brunswick) 22/23May44. 303hrs
LL745 9Sq 22Dec43, Missing (Berlin) 27/28Jan44. 9ops
LL746 467Sq 1Jan44, Missing 26Feb44. 87hrs
LL747 550Sq(BQ·P) Jan44, Missing 16/17Jun44. 291hrs
LL748 476,550Sqs; 1LFS, 1656/62/56CUs, Accidents 21Nov45
LL749 166Sq Jan44, Missing (Essen) 26/27Mar44. 59hrs
LL750-1 101Sq ex-32MU Mar44, Missing 28/8Apr44. 35/?hrs
LL752 15Sq ex-32MU Mar44, Missing 12May44. 69hrs
LL753/G 626Sq, Lost (Mailly le Camp) 3/4May44
LL754 15Sq 26Mar44, Missing 21Apr44. 19hrs
LL755 101Sq(SR·U) Apr44, Missing (Bremen) 23Mar45
LL756 101,467Sqs, Missing (Augsburg) 25/26Feb44. 261hrs
LL757-8 101Sq ex-32MU Apr44, Lost 30Aug/5Oct44. 214/311hrs
LL771 101Sq May44, Crash 22Jun44, Lost 11Oct44. 282hrs
LL772 626,101Sqs(SR·R2), 46MU May45, Scrap Jan47
LL773 101Sq(SR·U) Feb44, SOC after 2nd crash 7Jun44
LL774 101Sq, Minor crashes Apr & May 1944, Lost 14/15Oct44
LL775 61Sq(QR·O) Jan44, Lost (Augsburg) 25/26Feb44. 72hrs
LL776 207Sq Jan44, Lost (Brunswick) 22/23May44. 206hrs
LL777 61Sq(QR·S) landed in Belgium 6Dec44 (Giessen). 592hrs
LL778 619Sq Jan44, 5LFS Sep44, Crashed 5Nov44
LL779 101Sq ex-32MU Feb44, Lost 21Jul44. 193hrs
LL780/G RAE Jan44, held for BP Sep46, MUs 47, ventral and
    dorsal barbettes at CBE(DF·N) 1946-7 SS(JD) Jun48
LL781 15Sq Jan44, Wrecked on operations 8Jun44. 248hrs
LL782 622Sq 21Jan44, Missing 1Jun44. 191hrs
LL783 619Sq(PG·C), Lost in D-Day attack on Caen, 257hrs
LL784 619Sq(PG·M) Jan44, Lost (Dachen) 11Apr44. 127hrs

174

LL785 9Sq(WS ·F) Feb44, Missing 4/5Jul44. 46ops
LL786 576,50Sqs; 5LFS; 1668/60CUs, SOC Nov45
LL787 9Sq(WS ·Y), Missing (Mailly le Camp) 3/4May44. 22ops
LL788-9 467Sq Jan44, Lost 10May/13Sep44. 202/503hrs
LL790 463Sq, Missing (Konigsberg) 29/30Aug44. 477hrs
LL791 50Sq, Missing (Augsburg) 25/26Feb44. 37hrs
LL792 467Sq, Lost (Bourg Leopold) 11/12May44. 145hrs
LL793 622Sq(GI ·Q) Jan44, Missing 22May44. 159hrs
LL794 576Sq, 5MU, 1651CU Nov44, 24MU, SOC Oct45
LL795 463Sq; 1660(TV ·Q),1668CUs; 9MU, SS(JD) Feb49
LL796 576,550Sqs(BQ ·O), Missing 12Jul44. 296hrs
LL797 626Sq(UM ·B2) 8Feb44, Lost (Schweinfurt) 24/25Feb44
LL798 626,300(BH ·V)Sqs; 1LFS, 1667/56CUs, SOC Nov45
LL799 576Sq(UL ·N2), Missing (Stuttgart) 28Jul44. 346hrs
LL800 576,550Sqs; 1660CU Feb45, 20MU Aug45, SOC May46
LL801 15Sq 11Feb44, Missing 28Apr44. 124hrs
LL802 622Sq, Hit LM167 in cloud over Essex 20Sep44. 329hrs
LL803 622Sq(GI ·G/S), Missing (Homberg) 2Nov44. 331hrs
LL804 115,300Sqs(BH ·F), 1656/60CUs, SOC 28Mar46
LL805 15Sq 21Apr44, Missing 28Apr44. 11hrs
LL806 15Sq(LS ·J) Apr44. SOC 5Dec44 after 134 operations
LL807 300Sq 26Apr44, Missing 13Jun44
LL808 619Sq(PG ·D), Missing (Wesseling), 21Jun44, 98hrs.
LL809 To Staverton May44 for Flight Refuelling Ltd. Became G-AHJT, Scrap 1950
LL810 550Sq 1May44, Missing 28May44. 43hrs
LL811 550Sq, 1LFS, 1662/56CUs, Crashed 20Jun45
LL812 622Sq 11Feb44, Missing 13Jun44. 135hrs
LL813 AAEE Aug45, Was operated by De Havilland's Dec44 and Aug45, 15MU, SOC 26Nov46
LL826-7 550/15Sqs Feb44, Lost 4May/16Jun44. 144/248hrs
LL828 622Sq 19Feb44, Missing 16Mar44. 18hrs
LL829 626,101Sqs(SR ·J), 46MU, Scrap Jan47
LL830 576Sq 17Feb44, Missing 11Apr44. 87hrs
LL831 550Sq, 1LFS, 1667/56CUs, 20MU, SOC 17Dec45
LL832 101Sq ex-32MU Feb44, Missing 31Mar44
LL833 101Sq, Ditched in Channel, operations, 6Jun44
LL834 550Sq, Ditched and sunk off Donna Nook 23Apr44
LL835 626Sq(UM ·C2), 38MU Oct44, Scrap May47
LL836 550Sq(BQ ·E), Missing (Aulnoye) 10/11Apr44. 40hrs
LL837 550Sq(BQ ·Q) Feb44, Missing 14/15Jul44. 268hrs
LL838 576,550Sqs; Wrecked, burnt, 22Jun44. 207hrs
LL839 626Sq Feb44, Missing 27Mar44
LL840 50Sq Feb44, Lost (Gelsenkirchen) 21/22Jun44. 265hrs
LL841 50Sq Feb44, Missing (Rennes) 8/9Jun44. 223hrs
LL842 50Sq Feb44, Missing (Stuttgart) 24/25Jul44. 378hrs
LL843 467,61Sqs; 1659CU, 279Sq, 20MU, SS(CC) May47. 118ops
LL844 463Sq Feb44, 46MU Mar45, Scrap Jan47. 464hrs
LL845 9Sq(WS ·L) Mar44-Aug45, 97ops, 15MU, Scrap Jan47
LL846 467Sq Feb44, Lost (Stuttgart) 28/29Jul44. 205hrs
LL847-8 463Sq, Lost Munich raids 17/18Dec & 24/25Apr44
LL849 626,101Sqs, Hit tree Lichfield, Staffs 1Aug44
LL850 550Sq Mar44, Wrecked 8Jul44. 219hrs
LL851 550Sq(BQ ·V) Mar44, Missing 21/22May44. 126hrs
LL852 550Sq, Missing 15/16Mar44. 220hrs
LL853 9Sq(WS ·W) Mar44, Missing 25Jun44. 36ops
LL854 15Sq 4Mar44, 186Sq Mar45, 44Sq, 10MU, Scrap Oct46
LL855 300Sq 5Mar44, Missing 25Apr44
LL856 300Sq, 5MU, 6LFS, Dec44, 231Sq, SOC 25Feb46
LL857 300Sq, Hit butts landing at Faldingworth 23May44
LL858 15Sq, Swung on take-off, Mildenhall, 10.30 p.m., 1May44
LL859 622Sq(GI ·Q) 12Mar44, Missing 23Jul44, 225hrs
LL860-1 101Sq ex-32MU Mar44, Lost 27Apr/31Mar44
LL862-3 101Sq ex-32MU Mar44, Lost 21/7Jul44. 122/112hrs
LL864 115Sq Mar44, Missing 8Jun44. 107hrs
LL865 Conv.Mk.III; 75,463Sqs; Crash 15Jan45, 20MU, SS May47
LL866 75Sq 16Mar44, Missing (Russelsheim) 26Aug44. 252hrs
LL867 115Sq 28Mar44, Wrecked 19Apr44. 31hrs
LL880 75Sq Mar44, 115Sq Apr44, Missing 7Oct44. 251hrs
LL881-2 463Sq Mar44, Both lost (Lille) 10/11May44. 92/115hrs
LL883 9Sq(WS ·C), Swung on take-off Bardney 2May44 5ops
LL884 9Sq, Landed in bog, N. Russia, 12Sep44. 60ops. 402hrs.
LL885 622Sq(GI ·J) Jul44, 44Sq, 39MU, SOC Mar47. 600+hrs. 100ops

LL886 630Sq Mar44, Missing (Berlin) 24/25Mar44. 8hrs
LL887 100Sq, Missing 22/23Apr44 (P/O W.J. Shaw), 25hrs
LL888 75Sq 26Mar44, Missing (Valenciennes) 16Jun44
LL889-90 15Sq 29Mar44, Lost 15Jul/6Jul44. 144/197hrs
LL891 106Sq(ZN ·S) 26Mar44, Missing 7May44
LL892 463Sq, Shot down in Holland 23Apr44. 49hrs
LL893 57Sq 27Mar44, Missing 21Apr44. 44hrs
LL894 625Sq 26Mar44, Lost mining 15/16May44. 110hrs.
LL895 626Sq(UM ·Y2) Mar44, Lost (Stuttgart) 28/29Jul44. 203hrs
LL896-7 106/625Sqs Mar44, Lost 18Jul/16Jun44. 216/142hrs
LL898 100Sq Mar44, Dived into sea 2Jan45
LL899-900 49Sq 30Mar44, Lost 12Apr/22Jun44. 15/187hrs
LL901 9Sq(WS ·V) Apr44, Lost (Munster) 23/24Sep44. 368hrs
LL902 207Sq(EM ·A), Crash, Lt. Rissington, 02.50hrs 15Mar45
LL903 166Sq Mar44, Lost (Friedrichshafen) 27/28Apr44. 42hrs
LL904 619Sq Apr44, Missing (Schweinfurt) 27Apr44. 22hrs
LL905 576Sq(UL ·H2), Lost (Stuttgart) 28/29Jul44. 249hrs
LL906 460Sq Apr44, Lost (Friedrichshafen) 27/28Apr44. 31hrs
LL907 460Sq, 38MU, 1653HCU(H4 ·Q), Accident 28Nov45
LL908 49Sq 7Apr44, Lost (Schweinfurt) 27Apr44. 37hrs
LL909-10 12Sq Apr44, Lost 14Oct/29Jun44. 307/150hrs
LL911 61Sq(QR ·X) Apr44, Lost (Politz) 8/9Feb45 on 99th op.
LL912 49Sq, Wrecked 8May45, taxiing at Fiskerton, 75hrs
LL913 103Sq Apr44, Lost (Dusseldorf) 23Apr44. 20hrs.
LL914 9Sq(WS ·U) Apr44, Lost (Munster) 23/24Sep44. 373hrs
LL915 100Sq Apr44, Missing 25/26Jul44. 219hrs
LL916 166Sq Apr44, Lost (Aachen) 27/28May44. 49hrs
LL917 12Sq, Belly landing at Wickenby 22/23Jun44. 131hrs
LL918 626,625,460(AR ·S),61Sqs; 9MU Jun46, Scrap Feb47
LL919-20 619/44Sqs Apr44, Both lost (Schweinfurt) 27Apr44
LL921 115,75Sqs, Missing 19Jul44. 158hrs
LL922 50Sq Apr44, Lost (Secqueville) 7/8Aug44. 321hrs
LL923 15Sq May44, Missing 5Jan45
LL935 115Sq(KO ·N),57Sqs, 3/5LFS, 57Sq, SOC Oct45
LL936 115Sq 20Apr44, Missing 1Jun44. 42hrs
LL937 RAE 20Apr44, 20MU Jun46, SS(CC) Jan47
LL938 44Sq(KM ·S), Missing (Wesseling) 21/22Jun44
LL939 57Sq(DX ·H) Apr44, Lost 11Nov44. 345hrs
LL940 57Sq(DX ·S) Apr44, Crash 15Jan45. SOC Mar46
LL941 103Sq Apr44, Accident 9May44, Lost 25Jul44, 179hrs
LL942 75Sq, Blown up at dispersal, Mepal, 30Jul44. 95hrs
LL943-4 115Sq Apr44, Lost 19Jul/16Dec44. 104/?hrs
LL945-6 15/103Sqs May44, Lost 8Jun/23May44. 58/39hrs
LL947 300Sq(BH ·W) Aug44, Missing 29/30Aug44. 271hrs
LL948 Conv.B.III. 106Sq Apr44, Lost 14/15Mar45
LL949 630Sq(LE ·E), Crashed by the Humber 22/23Nov44
LL950 630Sq Apr44, Lost mining 21/22May44. 43hrs
LL951 460Sq Apr44, Missing (Duisberg) 21May44. 34hrs
LL952 460,100Sqs(HW ·W2), Crashed in sea 21May45
LL953-4 106/166Sqs May44, Lost 6Nov44/22Jun44. 375/44hrs
LL955 106Sq Apr44, Missing 22Jun44. 116hrs
LL956 625Sq, Crashed in flames at Bradley's Farm, Little Grimsby 14Oct44. 366hrs
LL957 460Sq May44, Lost (Geilsenkirchen) 18Jul44. 155hrs
LL958 100Sq May44, Missing 1Jul44
LL959 300Sq, 625Sq(UM ·A2), Lost (Merseburg) 14/15Jan45
LL960 100Sq May44, Missing 21/22Mar44. 21hrs
LL961 626Sq(UM ·S2), Collided in dark near Laon 7Jan45
LL962 625Sq May44, Lost (Stuttgart) 28/29Jul44. 189hrs
LL963 103Sq May44, Lost mining (Kiel Bay) 16May44. 11hrs
LL964 460Sq May44, 103Sq Aug44, Lost 31Oct44. 389hrs
LL965 44Sq(KM ·C/V) May44, Lost (Darmstadt) 11Sep44. 236hrs
LL966 630Sq(LE ·P), Lost (Rositz oil plant raid) 14/15Feb45
LL967 57Sq,46MU,1651CU Nov44, Wrecked in late 1945
LL968 207Sq May44, Lost (Heilbronn) 4Dec44
LL969 619Sq(PG ·G) May44, Lost (Revigny) 12Jul44. 134hrs
LL970-1 9Sq May44, Lost 24/25Jun & 22Jun44
LL972 630Sq(LE ·T) May44, Lost (Stettin) 16/17Aug44. 178hrs
LL973-4 207/106Sqs May44, Lost 22Jun/28Jun44. 82/116hrs
LL975-6 106/49Sqs May44, Lost 25Jun/8Jul44. 98/96hrs
LL977 619Sq(PG ·H) May44, Lost (Wesseling) 21/22Jun44. 68hrs
LM100 467Sq; Crashed, France, on way to Karlsruhe 2Feb45
LM101 467Sq May44, Lost (Courtrai) 24Jul44. 134hrs
LM102 626Sq(UM ·Z2) May44, Lost (Rheims) 22/23Jun44. 59hrs

LM103-4 625/75Sqs May44, Lost 13Sep/6Oct44. 276/158hrs
LM105 625Sq May44, Accident 29Jul44, Lost 21/22Feb45
LM106-7 12Sq, May44, Lost 20Jul/28Jul44. 135/159hrs
LM108-9 622/15Sqs May44, Lost 29May/25Sep. 11/259hrs
LM110-1 15/90Sqs May44, Lost 13Sep/7Aug44. 244/?hrs
LM112 626Sq(UM ·A2), Abandoned in air (Caen) 7Jul44. 100hrs
LM113 626Sq(UM ·F2),15Sq(LS ·K) Oct45, 38MU, Scrap May47
LM114 57Sq(DX ·O) May44-Nov45, 38MU, Scrap Sep47
LM115-6 57/103Sqs May44, Lost 22Jun/30Aug44. 67/283hrs
LM117 630Sq(LE ·J) May44, Lost (Revigny) 18Jul44. 90hrs
LM118 630Sq May44, Lost (Wesseling) 21Jun44. 60hrs
LM119 467Sq May44, Lost (Courtrai) 27Jul44. 137hrs
LM120-1 576/15Sqs, Lost 25May/1Jun44. 18/10hrs
LM122 576Sq 23May44, Lost 2Nov44. 419hrs
LM123 207Sq May44, SOC at Spilsby after third crash Nov45
LM124 103Sq,24MU,46MU,6LFS,32MU,6LFS,231Sq, SOC Feb46
LM125 207Sq Jun44, Lost (St Leu d'Esserent) 5Jul44. 42hrs
LM126 166Sq, Lost Versailles railway yards raid 7Jun44. 12hrs
LM127 115Sq Jun44, Lost (Kiel) 27Aug44. 129hrs
LM128 90Sq Jun44; Flew into ground, Freckenham, 30Aug44
LM129 207Sq, Missing (St. Leu d'Esserent) 7/8Jul44. 51hrs
LM130 463Sq May44, Crashed at Metheringham 11Mar45
LM131 103Sq(PM ·V); Abandoned, hit by 250lb bomb, 12Mar45
LM132 103Sq(PM ·I) May44, 57Sq Apr45, SOC Mar46
LM133 576Sq, 3 times damaged, Crashed in Sweden 16/17Aug44
LM134 550Sq(BQ ·H) May44, Missing 16/17Jun44. 38hrs
LM135 166Sq May44, Missing (Acheres) 10Jun44. 28hrs
LM136 626Sq(UM ·D2) May44, Lost (Courtrai) 20Jul44. 113hrs
LM137 12Sq May44, 626Sq Jun44, Missing 13Sep44. 181hrs
LM138-9 622(GI ·N)/625Sqs, Lost 24/16Jun44. 33/11hrs
LM140 626Sq(UM ·O2), Lost (Russelsheim) 25/26Aug44. 199hrs
LM141-2 460/15Sqs Jun44, Lost 6Nov/25Jul44. 29/86hrs
LM156 15Sq 3Jun44, Missing 13Jun44. 7hrs
LM157 90Sq; Crash-landed Chippenham, near Newmarket 6Feb45
LM158 90Sq Jun44, Missing 13Jun44. 3hrs
LM159 90Sq(WP ·H), 207Sq May46, 15MU, SOC Dec46
LM160 90,186(XY ·W),626(UM ·F2),15(LS ·D)Sqs; 2MPRD Oct47
LM161 101Sq(SR ·F) Jun44, 46MU May45, Wrecked 4Oct45
LM162 50Sq, Crashed 12/13Sep44 when fin was struck. 253hrs
LM163 625Sq Jun44, Lost(Trossy St. Maximin) 3Aug44. 133hrs
LM164-5 90Sq Jun44, Lost 8Aug44/Damaged 15Oct44
LM166 115Sq 10Jun44, Damaged 18Jul44, Lost 9Aug44. 71hrs
LM167 622Sq, Collided with LL802 over Wormington 20Sep44
LM168 625Sq(CF ·K) 15Jun44, Lost (Kiel) 26Aug44. 186hrs
LM169 90Sq 11Jun44, Lost 16/17Sep44. 186hrs
LM170 44Sq(KM ·E) Jun44, 1668CU(2K ·D) Oct44, Crashed 13Apr45
LM171 103Sq(PM ·Z), 44Sq(KM ·R). Lost (Stuttgart) 28/29Jul44
LM172 300Sq(BH ·Q) Jun44, Lost (Russelsheim) 25/26Aug44. 43hrs
LM173 103Sq 8Jun44, Missing 17Jun44. 7hrs.
LM174 625Sq(CF ·P) Jun44, Missing (Kiel) 23/24Jul44. 66hrs
LM175 100Sq Jun44, 1656CU Nov44, Disappeared 6Feb45
LM176 166Sq; Crashed Brocklesby Park, crew killed, 4Dec44
LM177 103Sq(PM ·Z), Accident 2Jul44, Lost mining 4/5Apr45
LM178-9 300/90Sqs Jun44, Lost 27Jul/25Jun. 78/2hrs
LM180-1 514Sq Jun44, Lost (Russelsheim) 12/13Aug & 21Jul44
LM182 550Sq Jun44, 20MU 12Nov45, Scrap Nov46
LM183-5 90Sq Jun44, Lost 21Jul/30Aug/21Jul44
LM186 57Sq(DX ·D), Lindholme Jan46, Became 5846M at 12STT
LM187 90Sq Jun44, 218Sq Dec44, Damaged 6Jan45
LM188 90,186Sqs(XY ·S), G-H Flt, 1656/68CUs, Became 5724M
LM189 90Sq Jun44, Missing (Homburg) 21Jul44
LM190 49Sq Jun44, 38MU Jan45, 1654CU, 15MU, Scrap Oct46
LM191 49,619Sqs(PG ·O) Aug44, Lost (Darmstadt) 11Sep44
LM192 44Sq, 46MU, BCIS (WB ·A) Dec44-Jan47, 15MU, Scrap Mar48
LM205 467Sq Jun44, Lost (Beauvoir) 29Jun44. 32hrs
LM206 514Sq Jun44, Missing (Stuttgart) 28/29Jul44. 60hrs
LM207 49,619Sqs; Crash-landed Brussels 11Mar45
LM208 207Sq Jun44, Lost mining 15/16Oct44. 122hrs†
LM209-10 619 50Sq Jun44, Lost 12Sep/29Jul44. 189/83hrs
LM211 106Sq,7Sq Jun45, 15MU Sep45, Shoeburyness Feb49
LM212 50Sq, Lost raiding canal at Munster 23/24Sep44
LM213 12Sq Jul44, Missing 16/17Jan45. 64 operations

LM214 57Sq Jun44, 38MU Oct44; 1653/56CUs; SOC Mar46
LM215 106Sq Jun44, Crashed 5Feb45, SOC Jun47
LM216 630Sq(LE ·K),186,189Sqs; Lindholme Feb46, SOC Mar46
LM217 463Sq Jun44,9Sq(WS ·O) Oct44, 15MU Jan45, Scrap Dec46
LM218-9 207/467Sqs Jun44, Lost (St. Leu d'Esserent) 7/8Jul44
LM220 9Sq(WS ·Y) Jun44, Damaged 16Mar45, 5MU, Scrap Nov46
LM221-2 9(WS ·K)/50Sqs, Lost 13Jul/30Aug44
LM223 467,463Sqs; Lost (Dortmund-Ems canal raid) 24Sep44
LM224 12Sq Jun44, EANS Jul45, Crash 22Oct46, SOC Nov46
LM225-6 12/467Sqs Jun44, Lost 26Aug44 (Kiel)/13Sep44
LM227 576Sq Jun44, Damaged 23Feb45, Wrecked 16Oct45
LM228 550Sq(BQ ·G2) Jul44, Crashed 19Nov45, SOC Mar46
LM229 550Sq(BQ ·S), Swung on take-off N. Killingholme 4Jul44
LM230 12Sq Jul44, Lost (Kiel) 26Aug44. 168hrs
LM231 57Sq(DX ·T) Jul44, Damaged 1/2Feb45, SOC Nov45
LM232 57Sq Jul44, Lost (Konigsberg) 26Aug44. 79hrs
LM233 467,635,35,15Sqs; 38MU Feb46, Scrap May47
LM234 50Sq Jul44, Missing (Merseburg) 14Jan45
LM235 622Sq(GI ·B/G) Jul44-45, 44Sq Aug45, 15MU, SOC Feb47
LM236 50Sq, CUs, Crash-landed Oakley 24Sep44
LM237 467Sq Jul44, Lost (Konigsberg) 29/30Aug44. 148hrs
LM238 15Sq Jul44, 44Sq Jul46, 37MU Dec46, 2MPRD Oct47
LM239 467Sq Jul44, Lost (Karlsruhe) 26/27Sep44. 125hrs
LM240 15Sq Jul44, Damaged 2/3Feb45, 149Sq,15MU, SOC Mar48
LM241 622Sq(GI ·Q) Jul44, Lost (Russelsheim) 25/26Aug44
LM242-3 463/103Sqs Jul44, Lost 12Sep/31Aug44. 171/136hrs
LM257 218Sq(HA ·P) Jul44, 10MU Aug45, SOC Sep47
LM258 514,218Sqs, Lost (Vincley) 26Aug44. 34hrs
LM259 227Sq(9J ·U) Oct44, Lost (Heilbronn) 4Dec44
LM260 630Sq(LE.S) Jul44, Lost (Wurzburg) 16/17Mar45
LM261 207Sq Jul44, Lost 12Sep44. 143hrs
LM262 630Sq(LE ·G) Jul44, Lost (Secqueville) 7/8Aug44. 30hrs
LM263 207Sq Jul44, Lost (Deelen) 15Aug44. 71hrs
LM264 50Sq, Lost in day raid on Calais 24Sep44. 231hrs
LM265 514Sq Jul44, Lost (Russelsheim) 12/13Aug44. 39hrs
LM266 75Sq, Damaged three times, 46MU Oct45, Scrap Jan47
LM267 467Sq Jul44, Lost (Konigsberg) 29/30Aug44. 139hrs
LM268-9 75/630Sqs Jul44, Lost 12Sep/19Aug44. 102/64hrs
LM270 626Sq Jun44, Wrecked 9Sep44. 95hrs
LM271 207Sq(EM ·L) Jul44, Lost (Bergen) 28/29Sep44. 207hrs
LM272 103Sq Aug44, Damaged 6Dec44, 5MU Jan45, Scrap Mar48
LM273 550Sq Aug44, Lost (Pforzheim) 23Feb45
LM274 61Sq(QR ·F) Aug44. SOC Lindholme Apr46. 695hrs. 69ops
LM275 514Sq(JI ·B), 138Sq Mar45, 15MU, Shoeburyness Aug49
LM276 75Sq(AA ·S) Aug44, 44Sq Jul45, 20MU, SOC Mar46
LM277 514Sq Jul44, Lost 21Sep44. 93hrs
LM278 57Sq Jul44, Lost (Konigsberg) 26Aug44. 190hrs
LM279 57Sq(DX.T), Crashed out of control near Crick 2Sep44
LM280 90Sq(WP.F)Jul44, Damaged 29Jan45, Wrecked 10Jul45
LM281 218Sq(HA ·E), Lost in day raid (Gremberg) 28Jan45
LM282 622Sq, 218Sq Dec44, 138Sq Jun45, Crashed 20Sep45
LM283 622Sq(GI.O) Jul44, Lost (Stuttgart) 19Oct44. 201hrs
LM284 57Sq, Believed down in Wash 30Jul44. 2hrs
LM285 514Sq(JI ·A), Crash-landed at Venlo 19.30hrs 22Apr44
LM286 514Sq(JI ·F?) Jul44, Lost (Hamburg) 20Nov44
LM287 630Sq(LE ·O); 1651/68/60CUs; Became 5759M, Swinderby
LM288 514Sq Jul44, Damaged 15Nov44, BCIS Mar45, SOC Mar46
LM289 166Sq Jul44, Crashed at Barnetby-le-Wold 4/5Apr45
LM290 626Sq(UM ·W2) Jul44, Lost (Bochum) 4Nov44. 193hrs
LM291 622Sq(GI ·F) Jul44, Lost (Frankfurt) 12Sep44. 139hrs
LM292-3 103Sq, Fire in air/Wrecked, 8 & 9Aug44
LM294 576Sq, Damaged 14Oct & 17Dec44, 22MU, Scrap Jun47
LM295 103Sq(PM ·Z) Aug44, 57Sq Nov45, SOC Scampton Apr46
LM296 50Sq(VN ·T), Damaged 16Nov44, Wrecked 27Mar45. 561hrs. 54ops

Serial Range LM301—LM756   **Lancaster B.III/B.I**
350 Lancasters ordered from A. V. Roe (Yeadon) as B.III except for first 10 as B.I (LM301-310), delivered from October 1942 to October 1944. Mk.Is had Merlin 20 engines and Mk.IIIs Merlin 38 engines initially installed.

LM301 12Sq Nov42, 100Sq Sep43, 580Sq Nov43, Lost 3Dec43
LM302 83Sq(OL ·H) Nov42, Missing (Essen) 3/4Apr43. 49hrs

LM303-4 106/156Sqs Jan43, Lost 12Feb43/6Mar43 (Essen)
LM305 165CU 3Feb43, Missing on exercise 23May43. 210hrs
LM306 Conv.III 49,44Sqs ; Lost (Frankfurt) 18/19Mar44. 493hrs
LM307 1661CU, Hit ground near S. Muscombe 16Dec43. 443hrs
LM308 Conv. Mk.III, 1661CU, 5LFS, Crashed Syerston 29Jan45
LM309 CUs, 463Sq, Lost (Dortmund-Ems Canal) 23Sep44. 927hrs
LM310 467,106,61Sqs; Lost (Schweinfurt) 24/25Feb44. 267hrs
LM311 467Sq, Broke up landing, Bottesford (Milan), 13Jul43
LM312 101Sq Apr-Sep43, 166Sq, Lost (Leipzig) 20/21Oct43
LM313 12Sq 5Apr43, Missing 28/29Apr43 (S/L E. F. Tyler)
LM314 156,97,103Sqs; Missing 23Oct43. 259hrs
LM315 460Sq 15Apr43, Lost (Schweinfurt) 24/25Feb44. 383hrs
LM316 406Sq 16Apr43, Missing (Berlin) 2/3Dec43. 357hrs
LM317 100,625Sqs(CF·U) Oct43, Lost (Mailly) 4May44. 483hrs
LM318 101Sq 26Apr43, Missing 26Jun43. 77hrs
LM319 100Sq May-Jul43, 550Sq, Lost 22May44. 494hrs
LM320 100Sq 8May43, Missing 26May43
LM321 12(GZ·Y), 460,550,100Sqs; Lost 10/11Jan44. 549hrs
LM322 57Sq; Crashed on take-off, Scampton. 3Aug43. 120hrs
LM323 97Sq 22May43, Missing 28/29Jun43. 27hrs
LM324 460Sq 25May43, Missing (Oberhausen) 14/15Jun43
LM325 101Sq 31May43, Missing 23Jun43. 21hrs
LM326 207Sq(EM·Z) 31May43, Lost (Hanover) 19Oct43. 267hrs
LM327-8 97/12(GZ·F)Sqs Jun43, Lost 25Jun/12Jan43
LM329-30 9/44Sqs Jun43, Lost 14Jun/22Jun44. 7/4hrs
LM331 460Sq 22Jun43, Crashed 12Jul43
LM332 103Sq,576Sq Nov43, Hit JB670 17Dec43. 224hrs
LM333-4 100/207Sqs Jul43, Lost 24Aug/28Aug43. ?/83hrs
LM335 103,12,166Sqs; Crashed, take-off, 25Feb44. 341hrs
LM336-7 57/44Sqs Jul43, Lost (Milan) 23Sep43/15Aug43
LM338 467Sq 16Jul43, Missing 8Jul44, 519hrs
LM339 61Sq 21Jul43, Missing (Milan) 7/8Aug43. 31hrs
LM340 467,405,635,405,57Sqs; 1668CU, SOC Oct45
LM341 101Sq Jul-Sep43, 166Sq, Lost (Leipzig) 20/21Oct43
LM342 467Sq 29Jul43, Lost (Peenemunde) 17/18Aug43. 42hrs
LM343 103Sq 4Aug43, Missing 6Sep43. 92hrs
LM344 156Sq 10Sep43, Missing 15Jan44
LM345 32MU 3Sep43; 156,405Sqs; Missing 27/28Sep43
LM346 NTU; 97(OF·O),35,635,97,100Sqs; 22MU, Scrap May47
LM359 61Sq(QR·B) 27Aug43, Lost (Munich) 24/25Apr44. 261hrs
LM360 61Sq,50Sq Aug44, 9Sq, SOC 11Nov44
LM361 9Sq(WS·T), Missing (Juvissy) 19Apr44
LM362 100,12Sqs; 626Sq(UM·A2), Crash-landed 26/27Nov43
LM363-4 101Sq ex-32MU Oct43, Both lost 3Dec43
LM365 SIU Defford, 101Sq Sep43, Missing 4Nov43. 26hrs
LM366 207Sq(EM·H) 15Sep43, Lost (Berlin) 28/29Jan44. 145hrs
LM367 SIU Defford, 101Sq(SR·C) Oct43, Lost 14/15Jan44. 113hrs
LM368 101,467,50Sqs; 1653,1660,1668CUs; Scrap Jan47
LM369 101Sq Oct43-Oct44; 1656,1653CUs; SOC Jan47
LM370 101Sq ex-32MU 27Oct43, Missing 19Nov43, 18hrs
LM371 32MU,20MU,101Sq Nov43, Missing 30Dec43. 16hrs
LM372 467Sq 2Oct43, Missing (Berlin) 1/2Jan44. 134hrs
LM373-4 44Sq Oct43, Both lost (Berlin) 24Nov43. 72/56hrs
LM375 460,103,463Sqs; Missing 15Oct44. 272hrs
LM376 467Sq 14Oct43, Lost (Nuremburg) 30/31Mar44. 265hrs
LM377 106Sq, 61Sq(QR·F) Nov43, Lost (Berlin) 1/2Jan44. 104hrs
LM378 619Sq(PG·J) 18Oct43, Lost (Revigny) 19Jan44. 448hrs
LM379 100Sq 20Oct43, 550Sq, Missing 27Nov43. 39hrs
LM380 460Sq Oct43, 626Sq Nov43, Missing 28Jan44
LM381 460,103,576Sqs; Lost (Brunswick) 14/15Jan44. 121hrs
LM382 166Sq, Crashed at Manston after combat 19/20Feb44
LM383 207Sq Nov43, Lost (Brunswick) 14/15Jan44. 126hrs
LM384 625Sq(CF·X) 11Nov43, Lost (Leipzig) 20Feb44. 161hrs
LM385 166Sq Nov43, Crashed high ground near Caister 17Dec43
LM386 166Sq 15Nov43, Lost (Stuttgart) 24Jul44. 413hrs
LM387 101Sq(SR·O) ex-32MU 19Dec43, Lost 21Jan44. 50hrs
LM388 166Sq 15Nov43, Lost (Revigny) 12/13Jul44. 335hrs
LM389-90 101/166Sqs Nov43, Lost 17Dec43/22Jan44. 28/96hrs
LM391 626Sq,1664CU,1LFS; 1664,1666,1659CUs; Scrap 47
LM392 166Sq Nov43, 550Sq Feb44, Lost 15/16Feb44. 155hrs
LM393 626Sq(UM·W2) 26Nov43, Missing (Berlin) 24/25Mar44
LM394 50Sq(VN·R) Nov43, Lost (Nuremburg) 30/31Mar44. 250hrs
LM395 RAE Dec43, 101Sq Jan44, Missing 23May44
LM417 101Sq ex-32MU 22Dec43, Missing 4May44. 86hrs

LM418-9 619Sq(PG·S/N) Dec43, Wrecked 31Mar44/Lost 24Feb44
LM420 619Sq Dec43-Nov44, 5LFS,231Sq, Sold Scrap May47
LM421 625Sq(CF·Q) 4Dec43, Lost (Berlin) 23/24Dec43. 17hrs
LM422 9Sq(WS·N) 29Nov43, Missing (Frankfurt) 22/23Mar44
LM423-4 619(PG·H)625Sqs, Lost (Berlin) 2Jan44/16Dec43
LM425 550Sq(BQ·N), Lost 30/31Mar44. 110hrs
LM426 R-R 20Dec43, 10MU 17Aug45 as Mk.I. SOC Feb47
LM427 625Sq 11Dec43, Missing (Tersnier) 1Jun44. 289hrs
LM428-9 50Sq Dec43, Lost (Berlin) 28Jan/22Feb44. 82/270hrs
LM430 9Sq(WS·B) 20Dec43, Lost (Frankfurt) 22/23Mar44
LM431 467Sq 29Dec43, Lost 6Jan44. 5hrs
LM432 9Sq(WS·O), Flew into ground near Pooley 29Mar44
LM433 9Sq(WS·H) Jan44, Missing (Schweinfurt) 24/25Feb44
LM434 44Sq(KM·F) 28Dec43, Lost (Wesseling) 26Jun44. 256hrs
LM435 50Sq 31Dec43, Lost (Chatellerault) 9/10Aug44. 460hrs
LM436 207Sq 13Jan44, Lost (Nuremburg) 30/31Mar44, 123hrs
LM437 50Sq 4Jan44, Missing (Mailly) 3/4May44. 266hrs
LM438 576Sq, 3LFS; 1660, 1668CUs; SOC 5Mar46
LM439 576Sq(UL·T2) 8Jan44, Lost (Aachen) 24May44. 408hrs
LM440 467Sq, Struck tree near Catfoss 8/9Jun44. Six killed

A No. 622 Squadron ground and air crew.

LM441-2 15/622Sqs Jan44, Lost 25Mar/25Feb44. 83/52hrs
LM443 622Sq(GI·T) Jan44,1653CU Nov44-Jun45. Became 5358M
LM444 463Sq 21Jan44, Missing 25Feb44. 61hrs
LM445 9Sq(WS·Z) 24Jan44, Missing (Munich) 24/25Apr44
LM446 619Sq(PG·H) 31Jan44, Missing 9/10May44. 215hrs
LM447 98Sq(WS·K) 28Jan44, Lost (Stuttgart) 20/21Feb44
LM448 Conv.B.I.,467,9(WS·M)Sqs, Landed in Sweden 12Nov44
LM450 467Sq 27Jan44, Lost (Prouville) 24/25Jun44. 291hrs.
LM451 AFEE Jan44, EAAS Jan45, Scrapped Jan47
LM452 61Sq(QR·T) Jan44, Lost (Stuttgart) 28/29Jul44. 366hrs
LM453 9Sq(WS·E) 25Jan44, Missing 1Aug44
LM454 61Sq(QR·Z) Feb44, Lost 26Feb 169hrs
LM455 550Sq(BQ·T) Feb44, Lost 29Jul44. 318hrs
LM456 15Sq 4Feb44, Missing 21Feb44. 6hrs
LM457 101Sq(SR·V2) 16Feb44, SOC 2Jan45
LM458-9 463/101Sqs Feb44, Lost 4May44/28May44.
LM460 550Sq(BQ·R), 38MU, 1666CU, 5MU, SOC Mid47
LM461-2 550/101Sqs Feb44, Lost 20Feb/29Jul44. ?/248hrs
LM463-4 101Sq 12Mar44, Lost 31Mar/19Mar44. 43/22hrs
LM465 15Sq 16Feb44, Missing 13Jun44. 169hrs
LM466 622Sq(GI·P) Feb44,Lost (Russelsheim) 12/13Aug44. 303hrs
LM467 101Sq ex-32MU 29Feb44, Missing 4May44. 82hrs
LM468-9 15/576Sqs Feb44, Lost 11Jun/25Mar44. 163/50hrs
LM470 476Sq(UL·U2)Feb44,Lost (Nuremburg) 30/31Mar44. 63hrs
LM471 576(UL·J2)Sq, Lost (Berlin) 24/25Mar44. 10hrs
LM472 626Sq Feb44, 100Sq May44, SOC Jan45
LM473 15Sq(LS·P) 21Feb44, 3LFS, G-H.Flt. SOC 46MU Mar46
LM474 101Sq ex-32MU 5Mar44, Missing 17Jun44
LM475 467Sq 28Feb44, Lost (Lille) 10/11May44. 149hrs
LM476 61Sq 1Mar44, Missing 27May44. 115hrs
LM477 622Sq(GI·L) Feb44, Lost (Stuttgart) 24/25Jul44. 226hrs
LM478 61Sq, Hit ditch landing Skellingthorpe 12May44
LM479 101Sq ex-32MU 3Mar44, Missing 30Aug44. 307hrs
LM480 50Sq ex-32MU 2Mar44, Lost (Mailly) 3/4May44. 118hrs

LM481 61Sq Mar-Oct44, 1653CU from Nov44 SOC Jan46
LM482 617Sq Mar44, Missing 8Oct44, 202hrs
LM483 61Sq(QR ·Y) Mar44, Crashed after 28hrs, Became 4767M
LM484 619Sq(PG ·M) 6Mar44, Lost (Givors) 26/27Jul44. 476hrs
LM485 15Sq(LS ·U),617Sq, Conv.B.I. Wrecked 6Apr45
LM486-8 300Sq Mar44, Lost 25Apr/23May/24Aug44
LM489 61Sq(QR ·U), Conv.BI 617Sq
LM490-1 15/622Sqs 13Mar44, Lost 25Mar/8Jun44. 11/153hrs
LM492 Conv.B.I., 617Sq(AJ ·W), Broken up Nov46
LM493 101Sq ex-32MU 26Mar44, Missing 30Apr44. 50hrs
LM508 101Sq ex-32MU 25Mar44, Missing 22Jun44
LM509 12Sq,1LFS; 1667,1662,1667CUs; SOC May47
LM510 75Sq Mar44, Damaged on 115Sq operation 22Jul44
LM511 622Sq(GI ·C) Mar44, Lost (Rostock) 11/12Sep44. 390hrs
LM512 625Sq(CF ·H) 29Mar44, Lost (Frankfurt) 12/13Sep44.
    371hrs
LM513 625Sq, Lost (Duisburg) 22May44 with U.S. officer
LM514-6 12/625/12Sqs Apr44, All lost (Mailly) 3/4May44
LM517 57Sq(DX ·C) Mar44-Oct45, RAE(HV ·C) Broken up Dec46
LM518 61Sq 7Apr44, Missing 25Jun44. 211hrs
LM519 9Sq(WS ·N) 9Apr44, Lost (Brunswick) 22/23May44
LM520 9Sq(WS ·X) 8Apr44, Missing 10/11May44
LM521 166Sq(AS ·F) 10Apr44, Damaged 28May44. 74hrs
LM522 1st prod. with H2S,57Sq(DX ·G) Mar43, Lost 8Jul44
LM523 460Sq Apr44, Lost (Friedrichshafen) 27/28Apr44. 23hrs
LM524 635Sq(F2 ·G) Apr44-Jun45; 1656,1653CUs; Crash 15Aug46
LM525 460Sq 14Apr44, Missing (Dusseldorf) 23Apr44. 6hrs
LM526 207Sq(EM ·R) Apr44,Lost (Schweinfurt) 26/27Apr44. 24hrs
LM527 576Sq, Abandoned, headed to sea 30May44. Crew baled
LM528 9Sq(WS ·D) 16Apr44, Missing (Lille) 10/11May44
LM529 166Sq 1Apr44, Missing (Karlsruhe) 24/25Apr44
LM530 460Sq Apr-Jul44, 626Sq(UM ·J2) Jul44-Jul45. SOC Mar48
LM531 460Sq 18Apr44, Lost (Mailly-le-Camp) 3May44. 27hrs
LM532 576Sq(UL ·A2) Apr44, Lost (Orleans) 4/5Jul44. 189hrs
LM533-4 15/115Sqs May44, Lost 7Jun/8Jun44. 35/21hrs
LM535 207Sq Apr44-Sep45, scrapped at Hounslow May47
LM536 619Sq 25Apr44, Missing 29Jul44. 195hrs
LM537 630Sq(LE ·X) 25Apr44, Lost (Revigny) 18Jul44. 175hrs
LM538-9 103/49Sqs Apr44, Lost 1Aug44/22May44. 159/64hrs
LM540 207Sq 28Apr44, Lost (Brunswick) 22/23May44. 26hrs
LM541 49Sq 1May44, Missing 8Aug44. 122hrs
LM542 100Sq 3May44, Missing (Dortmund) 23May44. 32hrs
LM543 186Sq Apr-May44, 115Sq Jul45. Scrap May47
LM544 115,75,138,75,514(JI ·A)Sqs; SOC Aug47
LM545 460Sq 6May44, Lost (Merville) 27/28Aug44. 19hrs
LM546 625Sq(CF ·O) 12May44, Lost (Stuttgart) 29Jul44. 103hrs
LM547 460Sq 6May44, Missing 23Jun44. 83hrs
LM548 9Sq(WS ·C) 23Apr44, 463Sq Oct44, Burnt Feb45
LM549 106Sq 9May45, Damaged operations 28May44. 44hrs
LM550 166Sq Apr44, 153Sq Oct44, Scrapped May47
LM551 463Sq 9May44, Missing (Revigny) 18/19Jul44. 161hrs
LM552 467Sq, Believed crashed 12Jun44. 53hrs
LM569 100Sq 2May44, Missing (Scholven) 18/19Jul44. 74hrs
LM570 106Sq 13May44, Lost 22Jun44. 90hrs
LM571-2 463/49Sqs May44, Both lost 24/25Jun44. 100/93hrs
LM573 57Sq 14May44, Missing 22Jun44. 84hrs.
LM574 463Sq 15May44, Lost (Prouville) 24/25Jun44. 82hrs
LM575 90Sq May44, 15Sq Jun44, Lost 8Jun44. 10hrs
LM576 90Sq May44, 15Sq Jun44, Burnt in accident 21Jun44
LM577 622Sq(GI ·E) Jan-Dec44, 218Sq Dec44. SOC May47
LM578 207Sq 9May44, Lost (Wesseling) 21/22Jun44. 94hrs
LM579-80 57Sq May44, Lost 26Aug/22Jun44. 189/103hrs
LM581 166Sq May44, Shot down near Epe, Holland 13Jun44. 83hrs
LM582 57Sq(DX ·B) May44-mid45, 5MU, Scrap Jul47
LM583 467Sq May-Jul44, Lost (Konigsberg) 29/30Jul44. 226hrs
LM584 100Sq(HW ·F2) 26May44, To 5MU Aug45 for scrap
LM585 100Sq 26May44, Missing 1Aug44. 239hrs
LM586 166Sq 17May44, Lost (Chalon Bernapre) 27/28Jun44
LM587 463Sq May44, Equipped for filming, Lost 27Sep44
LM588 90Sq 19Aug44, Lost 26Aug44
LM589 463Sq May44; Lost on day raid, St. Cyr, 25Jul44. 89hrs
LM590 61Sq May44, 1669CU Dec44, 1668CU, Scrap 48
LM591 50Sq,BCIS(WB ·O),1653HCU 1947, Became 6260M
LM592 44Sq(KM ·Q) May44, Lost (Wesseling) 21/22Jun44. 49hrs

LM593 75Sq 2Jun44, Lost on 622Sq operation 21Jul44
LM594 576Sq May44-Mar45, 1651CU, 10MU, SOC Feb47
LM595 622Sq(GI ·O) Jun44, Lost (Hamburg) 20/21Jul44. 73hrs
LM596 101,626Sqs, Lost (Duisburg) 14/15Oct44. 163hrs
LM597-8 463/101Sqs May44, Lost 24Jun/13Aug44. 59/119hrs
LM599 626Sq(UM ·A2) May44, Lost (Brunswick) 12/13May44
LM615 90Sq(WP ·B)Jun44,1653CU(A3 ·N)Nov44,38MU, SOC
    22May47
LM616 115Sq, Hit tree Gt. Offley, Herts, 18Jul44. 45hrs
LM617 90Sq(WP ·X) 58ops, 186Sq; 1653, 1656CUs; Scrap 47
LM618 90,186Sqs(XY ·U) Oct44, Crash landed Holland 2Nov44
LM619 460,100Sqs Jul44, 1668CU, Crashed Westborough 15Jan45
LM620 100Sq 12Jun44, Missing (Scholven) 8/9Jul44. 72hrs
LM621 100Sq 14Jun44, Lost (Vierzen Rly yds.)1Jul44
LM622 460Sq 15Jun44, Missing (Kiel) 26/27Aug44. 175hrs
LM623 460Sq Jun-Jul44, 100Sq Aug44, Missing 14Feb45
LM624 57Sq(DX ·A) 23Jun44, Missing 6Nov44. 326hrs
LM625 44Sq Jun44-mid45, 75Sq, 39MU, Scrap Oct45
LM626 57Sq(DX ·M) 23Jun44, Missing 18Dec44
LM627 514Sq Jun44; 1664,1668(ZK ·E)CUs; Crashed 30May45
LM628 50Sq 26Jun44, Lost (Gravenhorst) 6/7Nov44. 352hrs
LM629 50Sq 26Jun44, 5LFS Dec44, Crashed 4Feb45
LM630 619Sq Jun44-Jun45, 20MU, Scrapped Mar47
LM631 44Sq(KM ·W) 18Jun44, Missing 8Jul44. 31hrs
LM632 626Sq Jun-Sep44, 300Sq Oct44, Missing 9/10Apr45
LM633 626Sq(UM ·T2) Jun44, Lost (Courtrai) 20/21Jul44. 27hrs
LM634 100Sq Jul44; Swung on take-off, Grimsby, 17/18Jul44
LM635 626Sq(UM ·12) Jul44 to early 45, 10MU, Scrapped Oct46
LM636 467Sq 4Jul44, Lost (Calais) 24/25Sep44. 239hrs
LM637 630Sq, Hit PD319 over target in day raid 9Dec44
LM638 44Sq(KM ·P) 8Jul44, Missing 1Aug44. 17hrs
LM639 44Sq Jun44, Flt Refuelling, Became G-AHJV, Scrap Jul51
LM640-1 619/106Sqs Jul44, Lost 19Jul/8Aug44. 26/81hrs
LM642 467Sq Jul44, 35Sq Jun45, 39MU, Scrap Oct46
LM643 619Sq 11Jul44, Missing 25Jul44. 29hrs
LM644 100Sq(HW ·B2) 2Jul44, 22MU, Scrapped mid-May47
LM645 44Sq(KM ·P), Lost (Flushing gun positions) 23Oct44
LM646 467,156,35Sqs; 39MU, Scrap 2MPRD Jun47
LM647 550Sq(BQ ·S) 5Jul44, Missing eight days later. 18hrs
LM648 49Sq Jul44, 44Sq Aug44, Hit PB428 11Nov44
LM649 49,169,630,75Sqs; 39MU Oct45, Scrap Jan47
LM650 44Sq 9Jul44, Crashed 2Nov44 after 309hrs
LM651 576Sq Jul44-Sep45; 427,166Sqs; 22MU, Scrap 47

Ex-ED866 refuelling ex-LM681 over the Atlantic, 1947.

LM652 166Sq 28Jul44, Missing 27Aug44. 89hrs
LM653 49Sq Jul-Aug44, 57Sq, Lost 20/21Mar45
LM654 44Sq(KM ·L) 28Jul44, Missing (Bohlen) 5/6Mar45
LM655 44Sq Jul44-mid45, 75Sq(AA ·U), SOC 7Sep45
LM656 619Sq(PG ·M) 1Aug44, Lost (Konigsberg) 29/30Aug44
LM657 619Sq(PG ·Q) 1Aug44, Damaged 26May45. Became 5602M
LM658 100Sq 3Aug44, Missing 13Aug44. 12hrs.
LM671 207Sq 17Jul44, Missing (Gdynia) 18/19Dec44
LM672 100Sq(HW ·Y) Aug44-May45, 5MU, Believed SOCJul45
LM673 57Sq Jul44, Blown up by PB360 17Apr45
LM674 625Sq 5Aug44, Missing 17Aug44. 34hrs

LM675 463Sq, Landed in France after Boulogne raid 17Sep44*
LM676 50Sq 10Aug44, Missing (Munich) 17/18Dec44
LM677 467Sq, Repaired 4 times, Lost (Ladbergen) 3/4Mar44
LM678 57Sq(DX ·V) Aug44, 227Sq Mar45. Scrap Sep46
LM679 626Sq Aug44, 576Sq Apr45, 20MU, Scrap May47
LM680 50Sq Aug44, 630Sq(LE ·Z) Mar45, ME Jan46, Scrap Oct46
LM681 619Sq, Flt. Refuelling, G-AHJU Tanker No. 18, Scrap 50
LM682-3 103/463Sqs Aug44, Lost 13Feb45/Wrecked 19Sep44
LM684-5 514Sq Aug44, Lost 21Nov44/14Feb45. 161/?hrs
LM686 467Sq Aug44,156Sq Jan45,35Sq(TL ·K),22MU,SOC May47
LM687 166Sq 16Aug43, Abandoned in air 2Jan45
LM688 100Sq Aug44, To ME 16Jan46 where it was SOC Oct46
LM689 626Sq Aug44, 166Sq Mar45, 22MU, Scrap May47
LM690 106Sq Aug44, 106Sq May45, 7Sq, 15MU, Scrap May47
LM691 625Sq(CF ·O) 21Aug44, Lost (Essen) 23/24Oct44. 149hrs
LM692 149,90,186Sqs; 1659CU(FD ·A), 38MU, SOC May47
LM693 115Sq(KO ·T) 14Aug44, Missing 17Sep44. 62hrs
LM694 166Sq 22Aug44, Lost mining in Danzig Bay 26Aug44
LM695 Conv.Mk.I 617Sq Aug44, Lindholme Jan46. SOC Mar46
LM696 115Sq(KO ·U) Aug44, Crash Jun45, MUs, SOC May47
LM697 149(OJ ·E), 186(XY ·A)Sqs; 1659CU, 38MU, SOC May47
LM713 630,9,189Sqs; To ME 3Nov45, Scrapped UK Jun47
LM714 12Sq 29Aug44, Lost (Leuna) 14/15Jan45
LM715 9Sq(WS ·O) Aug44, Lost (Nuremburg) 19/20Oct44
LM716 100Sq Aug44, Wrecked, tyre burst, take-off, 13Apr45
LM717 514Sq,G-H Flt; 1656,1668,1660CUs; SOC 2Nov45
LM718 61Sq 21Aug44, Lost (Munster) 23/24Sep44. 45hrs
LM719 514Sq, 1653CU, Nov44, Crashed snowstorm 27/28Apr45
LM720 61Sq, Crashed Bard Hill near Langham 15/16Jan45
LM721 149Sq(OJ ·O) Aug44, 150Sq Mar45, 38MU, SOC May47
LM722 166Sq 2Sep44, Missing (Neuss) 24Sep44. 46hrs
LM723 100Sq 28Aug44, Crash-landed nr. Ghent 2Mar45. Crew OK
LM724 514Sq Sep44, 1661CU & 1668CU early 45, Crash 13Aug45

A Lancaster B.III at Hucknall.

LM725 115Sq(KO ·X) 5Sep44, Missing (Chemnitz) 14/15Feb45
LM726 626Sq 9Sep44, Missing (Dortmund) 20/21Feb45
LM727 514,550Sqs; ME Dec45, Scrap UK Jun47
LM728 514Sq Sep44, 75Sq(AA ·R) Mar45, Crashed 14Apr45
LM729 61Sq 12Sep44, Missing (Gydnia) 19Dec44
LM730 AAEE 14Sep44 for mining project, SOC 18Apr46
LM731 625Sq 16Sep44, Missing 9Nov44. 92hrs
LM732 625Sq 9Sep44, 170Sq(TC ·B) Oct44, 5MU, SOC Aug47
LM733 514Sq Sep44, 75Sq(AA ·R) Dec44, Missing 21Mar45
LM734 514,115(IL ·J)Sqs; ME Jan46 where it was SOC Oct46
LM735 514Sq 12Sep44, Missing 7Oct44. 43hrs
LM736 9Sq Sep44, 189Sq, 1654CU, 39MU, SOC Jul46
LM737-8 619/115Sqs Sep44, SOC Oct45/Lost 27Sep44
LM739 100Sq 24Sep44, 5MU May45, 24MU, Scrap Oct45
LM740 75Sq 23Sep44, Missing (Kamen) 25Feb45
LM741 100Sq Sep44, 1656CU Nov44, 1653CU Nov45, SOC Mar46
LM742 619Sq 29Sep44, Missing 6Nov44. 64hrs
LM743 195Sq(A ·4R) Oct44, Lost (Hamburg) 2Nov44. 23hrs
LM744 115,195Sqs; G-H Flt; 1656,1668,1660CUs; SOC Mar45
LM745 9Sq Sep44, 189Sq,1654CU,MUs, Scrap Jun47
LM746 467Sq, Collided near Swinderby, landed Carnaby 29Oct44
LM747 625Sq Sep44 (loaned G-H Flt, Methwold), Scrap May47
LM748 467Sq Sep44, 1654CU, Burnt out 3/4Mar45
LM749 625Sq Sep44, 170Sq Oct44, Missing 16/17Mar45
LM750 166Sq Sep44, 153Sq Oct44, Shot down in sea 3/4Mar45
LM751 619Sq(PG ·X) Sep44, Lost (Heilbronn) 4/5Dec44
LM752 166Sq,153Sq Oct44-mid45, 20MU, Scrap Aug46
LM753 195Sq Oct44-Mar45, 218Sq, 1659CU(FD ·B), SOC May47

LM754-5 153/101Sqs Oct44, SOC Oct45/Lost 29Oct44
LM756 227Sq Oct44 only, 619Sq(PG ·F), Lost 25Apr45

Serial Range ME295—ME551   Lancaster B.I/B.III

200 Lancasters ordered from A. V. Roe (Yeadon) in May 1942 and built as 44 B.I. and 156 B.III as indicated, from October 1944 to March 1945. Merlin 22 engines were fitted in Mk.Is, and in Mk.IIIs, Merlin 38 engines up to ME376 and Merlin 224 engines thereafter.

ME295 III 50Sq Oct44, 463Sq Jan45, 38MU, Scrap May47
ME296 III 166Sq Oct44, Lost (Zeitz/Troglitz) 16Jan45
ME297 III 166Sq Oct44, 22MU Dec45, Scrap May47
ME298 III 463Sq Oct44, Lost (Karlsruhe) 2/3Feb45
ME299 III 44Sq(KM ·E) Oct44, Lost (Politz) 8/9Feb45
ME300 III 189Sq, Collided with ND473 over Cognac 5Jan45
ME301 III 550Sq(BQ ·X) Oct44, Lost 4/5Apr45
ME302 III 170Sq, Wrecked on take-off Hemswell 1Feb45
ME303 III 218Sq Oct44, 22MU Jul45, Scrap May47
ME304 III 32MU; 405,467,207Sqs; 20MU Apr46, SS Aug47
ME305 III 32MU,101Sq(SR ·N) Oct44, 22MU Nov45, Scrap May47
ME306 III 170Sq(TC ·S),576Sq Apr45, 15MU, Scrap May47
ME307 III 170Sq(TC ·O) 4Oct44, Lost (Nuremburg) 16/17Mar45
ME308 III 32,8MUs, 49Sq Nov44, Lost (Nordhausen) 4Apr45
ME309 III 32MU,227Sq(9J ·Y), 1654CU Jan45, Crashed 4May45
ME310 III 32MU,101Sq(SR ·Z) Oct45,22MU Nov45, Scrap May47
ME311 III 32MU, 83Sq Oct44, 9MU Jul46, 2MPRD Apr47
ME312 III 630Sq, 1661CU Dec44, 20MU Mar46, Scrap Aug46
ME313 III 32MU, 582Sq, NTU Dec44; 106,189Sqs; Scrap Apr46
ME314 III 32MU, 619Sq Oct44, Lost (Politz) 8/9Feb45
ME315 III 405Sq; 1667/68/53CUs; 230OCU, 9MU, Scrap Nov47
ME316 III 12Sq Nov44, Lost on benzol plant raid 3/4Feb45
ME317 III 32MU, 576Sq Oct44, Lost (Nuremburg) 16/17Mar45
ME318 III 32MU, 166Sq Nov44, Lost (Karlsruhe) 4Dec44
ME319 III 32MU,50Sq,1651CU,10MU Jun45, Scrap Nov46
ME320 III 32MU, 170Sq(TC ·L), Lost (Chemitz) 5Mar45
ME321 III 32MU, 75Sq Nov44, Lost (Vohwinkel) 1Jan45
ME322 III 32MU,49Sq Nov44,115Sq(KO ·U) Sep45, SOC 22Feb46
ME323 III 32MU, 12Sq Nov44, Burnt 4/5Mar45
ME324 III 32MU,106Sq,1661CU,20MU, Became 5794M at1RS
ME325/G III 463Sq,1651CU(BS ·P), Crash, Woolfox Lodge 7Feb45
ME326 III 460Sq, Collided at 19,000ft. with PD286 2/3Feb45
ME327 III 463,467(PO ·G)Sqs; 1660CU, 20MU, Scrap May46
ME328 I 150Sq Nov44, SOC 30Nov45
ME329 III 467Sq,463Sq 7Nov44; 1669/68CUs,22MU, Scrap May47
ME330 I 12Sq Nov44, 5MU, Scrap May47
ME331 III 35Sq; 1656CU,1653CU(A3 ·K); Became 6497M
ME332 III 32MU,625Sq Nov44, 153Sq Sep45, SOC 22Oct45
ME333-4 III 32MU, 35Sq Nov44, Lost 5/6Mar45 and 4/5Feb45
ME335 III 32MU, 35Sq Nov44, Lost 21/22Feb45
ME336 III 32MU; 514,106,50Sqs; 15MU Sep46, Scrap May47
ME337 III 32MU; 35,156,467Sqs; Crashed 14Dec45
ME350 I 218Sq(HA ·L) Nov44; 138,149(OJ ·W/G)Sqs; SOC Feb46
ME351/G III 32MU,514Sq(JI ·P),207Sq,39MU, Scrap Jun47
ME352 I 218,149(OJ ·K)207Sqs; 15MU Mar46, SOC Mar48
ME353 III 32MU, 49Sq Nov44, Lost (Politz) 8/9Feb45
ME354/G III 32MU; 514(JI ·M),83,12,101,300Sqs; Scrap Mar47
ME355 III 514,106(ZN ·S),50Sqs; 20MU May46, SS May47
ME356 III 7(MG ·P),106,617,106,50Sqs; 15MU, Scrap May47
ME357 III 460,49Sqs; Hit sea off Skegness 19Apr45
ME358/G III 514(JI ·O),83,50Sqs; 20MU May46, SS May47
ME359 III 32MU; 514Sq,106,50Sqs; 15MU Oct46, Scrap May47
ME360 III 32MU; 7,106,189,106Sqs; SOC Apr46
ME361 III 32MU Nov44, 35Sq Dec44, Lost 7/8Mar45
ME362 III 32MU; 35,467,83,97Sqs; 9MU Jul46, Scrap Feb47
ME363 III 32MU; 514,83,61Sqs; 9MU Jun46, Scrap Feb47
ME364/G III 32MU, 514Sq(JI ·P),83Sq, 9MU Jul46, Scrap Oct47
ME365 III 32MU,514Sq, Exploded over Salzbergen 6Mar45
ME366-7 III 32MU, 35Sq Jan45, Lost 3Feb/21Feb45
ME368 III 32MU;156Sq;1654,1660CUs;15MU Aug46,Scrap Jan47
ME369 III 32MU; 35,7,106Sqs; Crashed 7Feb46
ME370 III 7,405,467,97Sqs; Became 5852M at 12STT

ME371 I 1661CU Dec44, 279Sq Aug45, MU Sep45, SOC May47
ME372 I 227Sq(9J·U) Dec44, Lost (Hamburg) 21/22Mar45
ME373 I 61Sq 18Dec44, 39MU May46, SOC 2MPRD Oct47
ME374 I 189Sq Dec44, RWE Mar46, SS(IA)Mar49
ME375/G I 433Sq Jan45, 38MU Mar45, SOC Sep47
ME376 III 582,156Sqs; 1660(TV·H),1663(A3·H)CUs, Later6496M
ME377 III 32MU,156Sq; 1656/53CUs; 45MU, Scrap Nov47
ME378 III 32MU,156Sq, Crashed 24Mar45, 38MU, Scrap Mar48
ME379 III 32MU; 405,467Sqs; 207Sq(EM·B),20MU, Scrap Sep51
ME380 III 32MU,514 Mar45,Conv.ASRIII,218MU,6OTU, Middle
      East 1946, 38Sq Dec47, 38MU, Scrap Sep51
ME381 III 32MU,582Sq,BDU,CBE,15MU Nov46, SOC Mar48
ME382 III 32MU,97Sq,50Sq(VN·A),15MU Oct46, SOC May48
ME383 I 622Sq Jan45, 44Sq Aug45, RWE Jan46, SOC Sep47
ME384 I 153Sq Jan45, 12Sq Sep45, SOC Apr46
ME385 III 61Sq Feb45, Lost (Lutzkendorf) 8/9Apr45
ME386 III 207Sq Feb45, Missing (Bohlen) 5/6Mar45
ME387/G III 32MU; 514,82,9(WS·N)Sqs; 10MU, Scrap Nov46
ME388 III 170Sq(TC·H) Feb45, Lost (Dessau) 7/8Mar45
ME389 III 32MU,207Sq Feb45, 20MU Nov45, Scrap Jul46
ME390 III 32MU, 550Sq Feb45, 20MU Aug45, Scrap May47
ME391 III 32MU, RAE Mar45, SOC 5Oct45
ME392 III 32MU, 103Sq, Missing (Chemnitz) 5/6Mar45
ME393 III 427Sq(ZL·D),429Sq,15MU Jun46, Scrap May47
ME394 III 44Sq; Swung taking off, Spilsby, 28Jun45
ME395 III 463Sq(JO·S) Feb45, 20MU Aug 45, Scrap Jun46
ME417 III 32MU,83Sq Feb45, 5MU Jun46, Scrap Jul47
ME418 III 153Sq,170Sq(TC·V), Lost (Dessau) 7/8Mar45
ME419 I 101Sq 21Jan45, 38MU 27Feb46, SOC May47
ME420-1 I 1654CU Jan45, Held in MUs, Scrap Oct/Nov46
ME422/G III 32MU; 514(JI·Q),106,50,101Sqs; 37MU Nov46
ME423 III 32MU, 83Sq Feb45, Lost (Leipzig) 10/11Apr45
ME424 III 153Sq Feb45, Shot down over Bremen 22Apr45
ME425/G III 514(JI·L), 106,50,617Sqs; 9MU,2MPRD, Sep47
ME426 III 427Sq(ZL·C) Feb45, 15MU, Scrap May47
ME427 III 32MU, 463Sq Feb45, 20MU Aug45, Scrap Jul46
ME428 III 32MU, 166Sq Feb45, Lost 7/8Mar45
ME429 III 50Sq, Crashed Sturgate, 22MU Feb46, Scrap May47
ME430 III 61Sq Feb45, SOC Feb46
ME431 I 1661CU Jan45, 279Sq Aug45, 5MU, Scrap Jan48
ME432 I 467Sq 3Jan45; 635,35Sqs; 39MU, Scrap Oct46
ME433 I 50Sq or 1661CU Jan45, 10MU Aug45, Scrap Jan47
ME434 I 15Sq 11Jan45, Missing 7Feb45
ME435 I 1661CU(KB·M) Jan-Aug45, 5MU, SOC May47
ME436 I 1654CU ex-32MU Jan45, 10MU, Scrap Dec46
ME437 I 170Sq Jan-Nov45, 1LFS, Struck hill 14Nov45
ME438 I 218Sq Jan-Jul45, 7Sq, 22MU, Scrap Jun47
ME439 I 61Sq ex-32MU Jan45, Crashed 14Nov45
ME440 I 1654CU Jan45, Missing in storm 5Feb45
ME441 III 50Sq Feb45, Lost 20/21Mar45
ME442 III 44Sq(KM·V), Shot down by intruder 3/4Mar45
ME443 III 61Sq Feb45, Lost (Bohlen) 19Feb45
ME444 III 189Sq(CA·F) Feb45, Pershore, 20MU, Scrap May47
ME445 I 582,405,467,83,50,101Sqs; SOC Nov46
ME446 I 166Sq Jan45, 5MU Dec45, Scrap Dec46
ME447 I 166Sq 17Jan45, Missing 1Mar45
ME448 I 101Sq 17Jan45, 38MU Jun46, SOC May47
ME449 I 103Sq 23Jan45, Lost mining 12/13Mar45
ME450 I 75Sq Jan45, Crashed 1 mile N of Chatteris 26Feb45
ME451 I 150Sq 19Jan45, Missing (Hildesheim) 22Mar45
ME452 I 189Sq Feb45, Lost (Hamburg) 7/8Mar45
ME453 III 467Sq Feb45, Missing (Ladbergen) 3/4Mar45
ME454 III 227Sq, 49Sq Mar45, Lost (Wurzburg) 16/17Mar45
ME455 I 15Sq Jan45, 1659CU Apr45, 38MU, SOC Sep47
ME456 I 424Sq(OB·K) 17Jan45, Lost (Dortmund) 20/21Feb45
ME457 I 433Sq 17Jan45, 38MU Nov45, SOC Sep47
ME458 I 424Sq(QB·T) 1Feb45, 39MU Apr45, SOC Nov46
ME470 I 300Sq(BH·F) Feb45, 15MU Aug46, Scrap Dec46
ME471 III 49Sq, Crash 7/8Mar45; 106,7Sqs; 22MU, Scrap May47
ME472 III 619,207Sqs; Crashed Brohl, near Coblenz, 10/11Apr45
ME473 III 207Sq, Hit Lancaster on fighter affiliation 2Mar45
ME474 III 61Sq Feb45, Missing (Hamburg) 7/8Mar45
ME475 I 103Sq Feb45, 57Sq Nov45, 60MU, SOC Mar45
ME476 I 1660CU or 550Sq Feb45, 5MU, SOC Feb46

ME477 I 1660CU 4Feb45, 20MU Aug45, SOC Mar46
ME478 III 463Sq, Abandoned in air S of Kassel 8/9Apr45
ME479 I 1660CU 3Feb45, 5MU Aug45, SOC Jan47
ME480 I 1661CU 15Feb45, 20MU Aug45, Scrap May46
ME481 III 61Sq Feb45, SOC 19Feb46
ME482 I 1651CU Feb45; 24,38MUs; SOC Sep47
ME483 III 50Sq Feb45, SOC 19Feb46
ME484 III 467,35Sqs; Ground crash 15Sep45, 39MU, SOC Oct46
ME485 III 153,12,427(ZL·A)Sqs; 10MU May46, SOC Sep47
ME486 III 150Sq Feb45, Wrecked 17Dec45
ME487 III 153Sq Feb45, 156Sq Jun45, Crashed 30Nov45
ME488 III 467Sq, 35Sq Jun45, 39MU Feb46, 2MPRD Jun47
ME489 III 463Sq(JO·P) Feb45, 20MU Aug45, Scrap May47
ME490 I 1660CU 9Feb45, Crashed 25Feb45
ME491 III 49,61Sqs; Tyre burst, take-off, Carnaby 29Jun45

Lancaster G.R.3 ME525 of 210 Squadron at St. Eval.

ME492 III 576Sq Feb45, 20MU Sep45, Scrap Sep46
ME493 III 61Sq Feb45, Damaged 7/8Mar45, SOC Feb46
ME494 III 101Sq,Damaged 23Mar&20Apr45,22MU,Scrap May47
ME495 I 1661CU 15Feb45, 5MU Aug45, Scrap May47
ME496 III 170 or 300Sq, Lost (Nuremburg) 16/17Mar45
ME497 III 100Sq(HW·E) Feb45, 39MU Feb46, Scrap Jun47
ME498 III 427Sq(ZL·K) Feb45, 39MU, Scrap May47
ME499 III 550 or 166Sq Feb45, Crashed 18Dec45
ME500 III 166Sq Mar45, 22MU Dec45, Scrap May47
ME501 III 427Sq(ZL·T) Feb45, 5MU Feb46, Scrap Aug47
ME502 III 626Sq,576Sq Apr45, 20MU Aug45, SOC Jun46
ME503 III 550Sq(BQ·R) Mar45, Lost (Dessau) 7/8Mar45
ME517-8 III 101Sq(SR·M/P), 15MU Jul46, Scrap 1947
ME519 III 550Sq Feb45, 22MU Sep45, Scrap May47
ME520 III 32MU,97Sq(OF·V) Mar45, 5MU Jul46, Scrap Aug47
ME521 III 166Sq, Missing (Hanover) 25Mar45

Close-up of the Boulton Paul test-rig on ME540.

ME522 III 207Sq Feb45, Lost (Hamburg) 21/22Mar45
ME523 III 514Sq(A2·G), Force-landed near Topcliffe 23Apr45
ME524 III 625Sq Feb45, RAE Sep45, 1MPRD Dec46
ME525 III 32MU, 83Sq Mar45, Conv.ASRIII,39MU, Conv.
      GRIII,SMR(H·T),210Sq; 15MU Sep53
ME526 III 12Sq Mar45, Missing 16/17Mar45
ME527 III 32MU,83Sq,Conv.ASRIII; 218,5MUs; Scrap Jul47
ME528 III 32MU,83Sq,Conv.ASRIII, 218MU,6OTU, Became
      6610M at Yatesbury
ME529 III 514Sq, 5MU, Middle East Jan-Jun46, Scrap Jun47

ME530/G III 514Sq(JI ·C), 97Sq(OF ·T) Aug45, 20MU, Scrap
　May47
ME531 III 75,44Sqs; 15MU,38MU, Became 6334M at Henlow
ME532 III 207Sq, Crash 14May45, 22MU Jan46, Scrap May47
ME533 III 32MU,97Sq(OF ·O)Mar45,20MU May46, Scrap May47
ME534 III 429Sq(AL ·O), SOC at Lindholme 8Apr46
ME535 III 514Sq(JI ·G), RWE,CSE,20MU,2MPRD, Scrap Nov47
ME536 III 429Sq(AL ·Q) Mar45, 10MU May45, SOC Sep47
ME537 III 429Sq(AL ·N), Crashed 10Jul45, 15MU, Scrap Aug47
ME538-9 III 429Sq(AL ·E/A) Mar45, 38/5MUs 1946, Scrap 1947

ME559 crash-landed at Kegostrov, Russia.

ME540 III 429Sq(AL ·P),5MU, Boulton Paul Exp. SOC Oct53
ME541 III 153Sq 9Mar45, Damaged 24Mar45 and SOC Mar46
ME542-3 III 550/429(AL ·B)Sqs 1945, 22/5MUs 1946, Scrap 47
ME544 III 153Sq,12Sq Sep45, Lindholme Mar46, SOC Apr46
ME545 III 218Sq; 22,15,38MUs; RWE Watton May46, Damaged
　in gale 16Mar47, 60MU,CSE, Became 6295M at Upwood
ME546 III 300Sq, Crashed 23Aug46, 15MU Dec46, Scrap May47
ME547 III 189Sq Mar45,106Sq Nov45,22MU Mar46, Scrap May 47
ME548 III 550Sq(BQ ·Q), Lost 18Mar44
ME549 III 300Sq Mar45, 20MU Aug45, Scrap Sep46
ME550 III 44,75,207Sqs; 20MU Nov45, SOC Jun46
ME551 III 103Sq(PM ·Y) Mar45, 5MU Aug45, Scrap Aug47

Serial Range ME554—ME868　　　　　　　　　**Lancaster I**

　250 Lancaster B.1 ordered from Metropolitan-Vickers in May
1942 and delivered from November 1943 to January 1944 with
Merlin 22 engines initially installed up to ME639 and Merlin 24
engines from ME640 except for ME668-9 with Merlin 22 engines.

ME554 617Sq 16Dec43, Damaged 6Apr44 and SOC
ME555 617Sq(C) 16Dec43, 9Sq(WS ·Z) Mar-Nov45, SOC May47
ME556-7 550/617Sqs Dec43, Lost 7Jun/1Aug44. 167/247hrs
ME558 101Sq ex-32MU 4Jan44, Missing 16Mar44
ME559 617Sq Dec43, Crash-landed in N. Russia 18Sep44
ME560 617Sq 16Dec43, Burnt out in accident 15Jul44. 231hrs
ME561 617Sq(T) Dec43, Struck ground in fog 22Dec44
ME562 617Sq(K) 20Dcc43, 46MU Apr45, SOC Jan47
ME563 463Sq 29Dec43, Missing (Koln) 27/28Jan44. 47hrs
ME564 101Sq ex-32MU 6Jan44, Missing 3/4May44
ME565 101Sq ex-32MU 19Dec43, Missing 8Jun44
ME566 101Sq from 32MU 6Jan44, Missing 15Jan44. 4hrs
ME567 50Sq, Conv. Mk. III, 1664/66CUs; 15MU; Scrap May47
ME568 619Sq(PG ·F) 23Dec43, Lost (France) 3/4Aug44. 448hrs
ME569 619Sq Dec43; 1668,1660CUs; SOC Nov45
ME570 ATDU Gosport 20Jan44, SOC Jan47
ME571 44Sq Dec43, 463Sq Feb44, Lost (Duisburg) 21/22May44
ME572 50Sq Dec43, Lost Aachen bridge raid 11/12Apr44
ME573 44Sq Dec43, 463Sq Feb44, Lost (Stuttgart) 15/16Mar44
ME574 44Sq 24Dec43, Burnt out in accident 7Jan44
ME575 467Sq 24Dec43, Missing (Berlin) 27/28Jan44. 59hrs
ME576 626Sq(UM ·A2) 1Jan44, Lost (Brunswick) 14/15Jan44
ME577 626Sq 1Jan44, Ditched North Sea 6Jan44
ME578 50Sq 2Jan44, Missing (Frankfurt) 22/23Mar44
ME579 9Sq(WS ·A), Crashed at Belvoir Castle 6/7Jan44
ME580 463Sq 5Jan44, Lost (Duisburg) 21/22May44. 260hrs
ME581-2 550Sq 4Jan44, Lost 23Apr/26Feb44. 125/62hrs
ME583 576,550Sqs; 1LFS, 1656CU(BL ·O), SS(HDA)46
ME584 626Sq,ECFS May45, Crashed near Hullavington 7Sep45
ME585 576Sq(UL ·H2) Jan44, Lost (Brunswick) 14/15Jan44. 7hrs
ME586 576Sq 8Jan44, Missing 3/4May44. 191hrs

ME587 626Sq(UM ·X2) 8Jan44, Lost (Berlin) 30/31Jan44
ME588-9 625Sq Jan44, Lost (Leipzig) 19/20Feb44. 50hrs
ME590 32MU,101Sq, Conv. B.III,1651CU,5MU, Scrap Apr47
ME591 61Sq 14Jan44, Lost (Leipzig) 19/20Feb44. 56hrs
ME592 101Sq ex-32MU 31Jan44, Missing 30Aug44. 256hrs
ME593 576Sq 8Jan44, Missing 28Jan44, 17hrs
ME594 625Sq Jan44, 300Sq Jun44, Crashed 23Jul44
ME595 61Sq(QR ·R) 14Jan44, Crashed 14/15Oct44. 528hrs
ME596 61Sq(QR ·H) 14Jan44, Lost (Russelsheim) 12/13Aug44
ME613 101Sq ex-32MU 20Jan44, Missing 22Jun44
ME614 463Sq Jan44, Lost (St. Leu d'Esserent) 5Jul44. 268hrs
ME615 463Sq 21Jan44, Lost (Stuttgart) 28/29Jul44. 364hrs
ME616-7 101Sq 31Jan44, Lost 1Jul/13Aug44. 242/321hrs
ME618-9 101Sq ex-32MU Feb44, Lost 31Mar/23Apr44
ME620 Conv.Mk.III, 32MU,SIU;83,35Sqs; Lost 9May44. 100hrs
ME621 Conv.Mk.III, 32MU; 83,35,635Sqs; Lost 5Jul44. 135hrs
ME622 Conv.Mk.III, 32MU,SIU,405Sq Feb44, Lost 15Mar44
ME623 Conv.Mk.III, 32MU,SIU;75,582, 97Sqs; Crashed 9May45
ME624 166Sq 8Feb44, Missing (Nurnberg) 30/31Mar44. 83hrs
ME625 Conv.Mk.III, 97Sq, Feb44, Burnt in crash 24Jun44
ME626 57Sq(DX ·J) Jun-Oct44,1653CU Nov44-Aug45, SOC Dec45
ME627 166Sq 9Feb44, Missing (Leipzig) 19/20Feb44. 11hrs.
ME628 44Sq(KM ·V) Feb44, Lost (Pommerval) 24/25Jun44. 236hrs
ME629-30 44/?Sq Jan44, Lost 3Mar44/20Feb44
ME631 207Sq(EM ·K) Feb44, Lost (Schweinfurt) 26/27Apr44
ME632 12Sq 2Feb44, Missing 25/26Feb44
ME633 207Sq Feb44, Lost (Leipzig) 19/20Feb44. 10hrs
ME634 44Sq(KM ·P), Lost (St. Leu d'Esserent) 7/8Jun44
ME635-6 166Sq 5Feb44, Lost (Berlin) 24/25Mar & 15/16Feb44
ME637 166Sq 5Feb44, Lost (Leipzig) 19/20Feb44. 8hrs
ME638 166Sq 10Feb44, Missing (Nurnberg) 30/31Mar44. 77hrs
ME639 166Sq 10Feb44, Missing (Augsburg) 24/25Feb44. 40hrs
ME640 460Sq 12Feb44, Missing (Berlin) 24/25Mar44. 53hrs
ME641 166Sq 12Feb44, Hit JB547 over Lincs 10 p.m., 24Feb44
ME642 12Sq 20Feb44, Ditched 23/24Jun44, 125hrs.*
ME643 166Sq 10Feb44, Missing (Mailly) 3/4May44. 136hrs
ME644 12Sq 20Feb44, 1651CU,1653CU, SOC Oct45
ME645 12Sq Feb-Oct44, 1LFS,1656CU,20MU, Scrap Aug46
ME646 460Sq 20Feb44, Crashed on 1st operation 7Mar44
ME647 166Sq 21Feb44, Missing (Osterfeld) 31Dec44
ME648 100Sq,300Sq Apr44, 166Sq Aug48, Lost 1/2Feb45
ME649 460Sq Feb44, 103Sq Sep44, Missing 12Dec44
ME650 630Sq(LE ·B) Feb44, Lost (Konigsberg) 26/27Aug44
ME663 460Sq Feb44, Lost (Villeneuve St. Georges) 9/10Apr44
ME664 630Sq 24Feb44, Missing (Nuremburg) 30/31Mar64. 67hrs
ME665 103Sq 21Feb44, Missing 25Mar44. 51hrs
ME666 207Sq 28Feb44, Lost (Frankfurt) 22/23Mar44. 26hrs
ME667 207Sq 28Feb44, Missing (Bremen) 6Oct44. 480hrs
ME668-9 106Sq Feb44, Lost 8Jul/27Apr44. 204/?hrs
ME670 100Sq 1Mar44, Lost (Dortmund) 22/23May44. 150hrs
ME671 103Sq Mar44,300Sq Apr44,576Sq Aug44, Lost 3/4Apr45
ME672-3 44/103Sqs Mar44, Lost 25Mar/3May44. 31/124hrs
ME674-5 103/49Sqs Mar44, Lost 13Jul/21Jun44. 245/258hrs
ME676 460Sq,625Sq Jun44, Abandoned in air 31Aug44. 255hrs*
ME677 100Sq Mar44, Lost 75 miles N. of Duisburg 21/22May44
ME678 207Sq Mar44, Lost (Etampes) 9/10Jun44. 212hrs
ME679 57Sq 3Mar44, Lost 27Apr44. 125hrs
ME680-1 207Sq Mar44, Lost (Berlin) 23Mar/(Revigny) 18Jul44
ME682 625,75Sqs; 1662,1667CUs; 20MU; SOC 31Mar46
ME683 207Sq 7Mar44, Lost (Wesseling) 21/22Jun44. 225hrs
ME684 625Sq 3Mar44, Lost (Berlin) 24/25Mar44. 12hrs
ME685 207Sq 11Mar44, Lost (Toulouse) 5/6Apr44. 39hrs
ME686 166Sq 11Mar44, Lost (Nuremburg) 30/31Mar44. 12hrs
ME687 550Sq Mar44, 576Sq Apr44, Lost 22/23May44. 126hrs
ME688 207Sq 11Mar44, Lost mining 9/10Apr44. 32hrs
ME689-90 75Sq 13Mar44, Lost 1May/23May44. 66/193hrs
ME691-2 75/115Sqs Mar44, Lost 20Jul/15Oct44. 214/334hrs
ME693-4 626/44(KM ·L)Sqs Mar44, Lost 25Apr/26Jul44
ME695 15Sq Mar44, 1653CU(HA ·Y) Nov44, 15MU, SOC Aug46
ME696 460Sq 19Mar44, Missing 10Jun44. 91hrs
ME697 625Sq Mar44, Lost (Mailly le Camp) 3May44. 66hrs
ME698 AAEE Mar44, 460Sq Jun44, 103Sq Jan45, SOC 47
ME699 44Sq(KM ·T) 15Mar44, Missing (Crcil) 4/5Jul44
ME700 50Sq Mar44, Lost (Munster) 23/24Sep44. 446hrs

ME701 463Sq(JO ·F) Mar44, Damaged beyond repair 2Jul44
ME702 75Sq 25Mar44, Missing 10Jun44. 58hrs
ME703 576Sq 26Mar44, Damaged 3/4May44 and SOC. 99hrs
ME704 9Sq(WS ·B) 25Mar44, Missing 21/22Jun44 25ops
ME717 630Sq Mar44, Damaged operations 27Apr44. 55hrs
ME718 115Sq 24Mar44, Missing 30Aug44. 244hrs
ME719 61Sq Mar44, 5MU, 1666CU Dec44, 20MU, SS Mar47
ME720 166Sq Mar44, Lost (Friedrichshafen) 27/28Apr44. 59hrs
ME721-2 103Sq Mar44, Lost 31Mar/22May44. 11/111hrs
ME723 619(PG ·X), Shot down over Kelstern 18Apr44. 34hrs
ME724 9Sq(WS ·O), Missing (Brunswick) 22/23Apr44
ME725 61Sq(QR ·G) Mar44, Lost (Giessen) 6Dec44. 49ops
ME726 576Sq(UL ·X2) Mar44, Lost (Kiel Harbour) 15/16May44
ME727 460Sq, Crashed after take-off from Binbrook 7Apr44
ME728 460Sq 31Mar44, Lost (Mailly le Camp) 3/4May44. 46hrs
ME729 630Sq Mar44, Damaged 8May44, Crashed 19Jul44. 216hrs
ME730 44Sq(KM ·R) 1Apr44, Lost (Schweinfurt) 27Apr44. 48hrs
ME731 625Sq 6Apr44, Missing (Cologne) 20/21Apr44. 10hrs
ME732 61Sq 31Mar44, Missing (Munster) 23/24Sep44. 304hrs
ME733 625Sq 8Apr44, Missing (Brunswick) 12Aug44. 264hrs
ME734 625Sq Apr44, Burnt out, operations, 19Apr44. 6hrs
ME735 576Sq Apr44, Repaired 3 times, Lost 22Feb45
ME736 622Sq(GI ·J) Mar44, Damaged beyond repair 27Apr44
ME737-8 630/103Sqs Apr44, Lost 11May/28Apr44. 114/34hrs
ME739 630Sq(LE ·F/T) 10Apr44, Lost (Leipzig) 10/11Apr45
ME740 460Sq Apr44, Lost (Mailly le Camp) 3May44. 46hrs
ME741 103Sq Apr44, Lost (Dusseldorf) 23Apr44. 31hrs
ME742 12Sq Apr44, 626Sq Jun44, Lost 29/30Aug44. 246hrs
ME743 44Sq(KM ·G) Apr44, Lost (Marquise) 27/28Jun44. 181hrs
ME744 460Sq 10Apr44, 300 Sq, Missing (Wiesbaden) 3Feb45
ME745 619Sq(PG ·L) Apr44, Lost (St. Leu d'Esserent) 7Jul44
ME746 166Sq Apr44, 116ops, 103Sq Nov45, 57Sq, Scrap Feb46
ME747 619Sq 14Apr44, Missing 24Apr44. 12hrs
ME748-9 166Sq Apr44, Lost (Duisburg) 4Oct44/(Mailly) 3May44
ME750 626Sq Apr44,1666CU, Nov44,1660CU, Wrecked 10Feb45
ME751 115Sq Apr-Jun44; 75,138Sqs; 37MU, Scrap Oct47
ME752 115Sq Apr44, 75Sq, Missing 21Jul44. 139hrs
ME753 115,75Sqs; 1651CU Nov44, 22MU, Scrap May47
ME754 75(AA ·A),166,100Sqs; 38MU, SOC Sep47
ME755 460Sq Apr44, Lost (Revigny) 14/15Jul44. 174hrs
ME756 115Sq,1651CU Nov44, 1668CU,279Sq, SS(CC) May47
ME757 9Sq(WS ·O) 23Apr44, Missing 13Aug44. 35ops
ME758 12Sq(PH ·N) 28Apr44, SOC 19Oct45, 108 operations
ME759 9Sq Apr-May44, 46MU,1661CU,227Sq, Lost 2/3Feb45
ME773 103Sq 26Apr44, Missing 15Jul44. 175hrs
ME774 626Sq(UM ·L2) Apr44, Lost (Vierzan Junction) 30Jun44
ME775 166Sq 20May44, Missing 30Jun44. 49hrs
ME776 460Sq Apr-Jul44, 550Sq, 24MU, SOC Oct45
ME777 166Sq 29Apr44, Shot down in Holland 13Jun44. 53hrs
ME778-9 106/166Sqs 30Apr44, Lost 29Jul/11May44. 207/203hrs
ME780 300Sq May44, 625Sq Nov44, Crashed 1Jul45, SOC May48
ME781 460Sq,1651CU Nov44, Crashed Woolfox Lodge 2/3Mar45
ME782 630Sq(LE ·N) 1May44, Lost (Wesseling) 21/22Jun44
ME783 61Sq May44, Lost (Chatellerault) 15/16Jun44. 120hrs
ME784 460Sq 4May44; Crashed, operations, 29Jun44. 94hrs
ME785 100Sq May44, 460Sq, Missing 13Jun44. 69hrs
ME786 12Sq May44, Repaired 3 times, 5MU, SOC 15May47
ME787 49Sq May44, 619Sq Aug44; 617,106,189Sqs; SOC47
ME788 12Sq May44, Ditched near Skegness 14Oct44, Crew saved
ME789-90 106Sq 9May44, Lost 8Jul/23May44. 114/?hrs
ME791 44Sq; Crashed UK, hit by flash bomb, 11Jun44*
ME792 576Sq May44, Lost mine-laying Gydnia 27Aug44. 320hrs
ME793 460Sq 12May44, Missing 27/28Jun44. 77hrs
ME794 44Sq, Crashed and blew up at Westcott, 1Jun44
ME795 630Sq 14May44, Burnt out in crash 22Jun44. 83hrs
ME796 630Sq(LE ·S) 14May44, Lost (Revigny) 18Jul44. 127hrs
ME797 50Sq 15May44, Missing 7 days later (Duisberg)
ME798 50Sq 15May44, Lost (Prouville) 24/25Jun44. 137hrs
ME799 103Sq 16May44, Lost (Stuttgart) 28/29Jun44. 167hrs
ME800 576Sq(UL ·W2), Lost (Stettin) 29/30Aug44. 307hrs
ME801 576Sq(UL ·W2), Crashed 16Oct45
ME802 90Sq 19May44, Missing (Russelsheim) 25/26Aug44
ME803 115Sq May44, 1659CU May45, 39MU, SOC Nov46
ME804 44Sq(KM ·O) May44, Lost (Wesseling) 21/22Jun44. 67hrs

ME805 207Sq 24May44, Missing 8Jul44. 74hrs
ME806 166Sq May44; Hit PD227, fell in sea 5/6Aug44
ME807-8 207/49Sqs May44, Lost (Nevers) 15Jul/22Jun44
ME809 9Sq(WS ·X) May44, 38MU 1945, SOC 1947
ME810 576Sq(UL ·K2) 27May44, Lost (Sterkgrade) 16Jun44. 43hrs
ME811 75Sq 26May44, Lost 7Jun44. 21hrs
ME812 166Sq May44, 153 Oct44, 20MU Oct45, Scrap Oct46
ME813 50Sq May44, Damaged operations, SOC 8Aug44. 210hrs
ME814 207Sq 29May44, Missing (Revigny) 18/19Jul44. 86hrs
ME827 207Sq 29May44, Missing (Wesseling) 21/22Jun44. 43hrs
ME828-9 100/166Sqs 30May44, Lost 13Sep/24Sep44. 244/?hrs
ME830 626Sq(UM ·K2) May44, AAEE Feb45, 5MU, Scrap May48
ME831-2 106Sq Jun44, Lost 8Jul/5Jul44. 57/61hrs
ME833 9Sq 6Jun44, Missing 18/19Jun44. 14ops
ME834 75Sq Jun-Sep44, 115Sq, Swung at Bari 17Aug45
ME835 166Sq 7Jan44, Missing (Bochum) 4Nov44. 389hrs
ME836 75Sq Jun44, 115Sq(KO ·S), 99 ops, Scrap 2MPRD 47
ME837 101Sq Jun44-Mar45, 46MU, SOC Oct45
ME838-9 90/116Sq Jun44, Lost 12Sep/3Aug44. 153/138hrs
ME840 550Sq 11Jun44, Lost 17Jun44. 11hrs
ME841 514Sq Jun-Sep44, 3LFS,90Sq; 1654,1660CUs; SOC 46
ME842 514,218(HA ·R),115Sqs; SOC on HAA trials 1949
ME843 630Sq 11Jun44, Lost (Wesseling) 22Jun44. 16hrs
ME844 15Sq(LS ·C) 16Jun44,44Sq Sep45,39MU Nov45, SOC Jun47
ME845 630Sq(LE ·Q) Jan44; 57(DX ·F),630,617Sqs; SOC 47
ME846 619Sq 11Jun44, Missing (Wesseling) 22Jun44
ME847 101,300,15,103,57(DX ·R)Sqs; SOC at 10MU Feb47
ME848 15Sq Jun44, 103Sq Feb45, Missing 16/17Mar45
ME849 15Sq(LS ·C) Jun44, 44Sq Jul46, 15MU Nov46, Scrap 1947
ME850 15Sq Jun44, Damaged beyond repair, 1Jan45
ME851 467Sq 17Jun44, Lost (Nevers) 15/16Jul44
ME852 90Sq 16Jun44, Missing (Brunswick) 12Aug44
ME853 467Sq Jun44, Believed collided 3Aug44
ME854 576Sq 18Jun44, Missing 13Sep44. 246hrs
ME855 619Sq(PG ·X) Jun44, Lost (Brunswick) 12/13Aug44. 155hrs
ME856 476Sq 17Jun44, Lost (Stuttgart) 28/29Jul44. 98hrs
ME857 101Sq 18Jun44, Lost over Russelsheim 20Aug44. 127hrs
ME858 514Sq 17Jun44, Lost 21Jul44. 48hrs
ME859 44Sq(KM ·S), Lost (St. Leu D'Esserent) 7/8Jul44. 14hrs
ME860 90Sq Jun44, 218Sq Dec44, 10MU Aug45, SOC Jan47
ME861 RAE 20Jun44, 10MU Mar47, SOC Sep47
ME862 90Sq Jun44, 625Sq Feb45, 576Sq Apr45, Scrap47
ME863 101Sq Jun44, Wrecked in bomb explosion 1/2Feb45
ME864 57Sq(DX ·E) 23Jun44, Missing 29Jul44. 66hrs
ME865 101Sq 24Jun44, Missing (Bochum) 4Nov44
ME866 619Sq(PG ·W) 24Jun44, Missing 9/10Aug44. 120hrs
ME867-8 630/57Sqs Jun44, Lost 5Jul/8Jul44. 9/12hrs

Serial Range ND324—NE181   **Lancaster B.III**
   600 Lancasters ordered from A. V. Roe (Chadderton) and
delivered from December 1943 to May 1944 with Merlin 38 engines.

ND324 12Sq Jan44, 626Sq(UM ·D2), Missing 5/6Jan44
ND325 12Sq 11Dec43, Missing (Berlin) 2Jan44
ND326 100Sq Dec43, 463Sq Apr45, 20MU Aug45, SS May47
ND327 100Sq, Hit ED730 at 12,000 ft. over Fulstow 23/24Dec43
ND328-9 100/103Sqs Dec43, Lost 24Apr/24Mar44. 225/97hrs
ND330-1 83/106Sqs Dec43, Lost 3Jan/30Aug44, 4/551hrs
ND332 106Sq Dec43, Wrecked 31Mar44
ND333 83Sq Jan44, 106Sq(ZN ·S) Sep44, 10MU, Scrap Nov46
ND334 103Sq, Crashed into JB530 at dawn 20Feb44. 111hrs
ND335 630Sq,1668CU Jan45, 20MU, Became 5793M at 1RS
ND336-7 106/630Sqs Dec43, Lost 31Jan/5Apr44. 90/240hrs
ND338-9 630/106Sqs Dec43, Lost 20Feb/5Jul45. 144/340hrs
ND340 32MU,156Sq(GT ·J),R-R May45, SOC Dec48 1,000+hrs
ND341 32MU, 405Sq Dec43, Lost 15Jan44. 26hrs
ND342 32MU,156Sq Nov43, 12Sq Sep44, Lost 12Dec44
ND343-4 32MU,405Sq Jan44, Lost 16Jun/12Jun44. 289/260hrs
ND345 32MU,115Sq Jan44, Missing (Stuttgart) 21Feb44
ND346 97Sq(OF ·N) Dec43, 467Sq Jul44, Lost 3Aug44. 341hrs
ND347 32MU Dec43, 405Sq Jan44, Lost 8/9May44
ND348 32MU,156Sq,1668CU(ZK ·C), Crash 14May45. Became
   5727M
ND349 32MU, 156Sq Dec43, Missing (Dusseldorf) 23Apr44

182

ND350 SIU,7Sq, Overshot and burnt, Feltwell, 31Mar44
ND351-2 32MU, 97/405Sqs Jan44, Lost 21Jan/10Jun44
ND353 32MU,SIU,7Sq(MG ·N), Lost (Dusseldorf) 23/24Apr44
ND354 32MU Dec43, 7 or 83Sqs. Lost 2Jan44. 7hrs
ND355 97Sq Dec43, 635Sq(F2 ·W) Mar44, Lost 26Aug44. 365hrs
ND356 32MU Dec43, 100Sq Jan44, 5MU Aug45. Scrap Aug47
ND357-8 156Sq Dec43/Jan44, Lost 15Jan/20Feb44
ND359 97Sq,635Sq(F2 ·H)Mar44, 1651CU, 24MU, Wrecked 4Oct45
ND360-1 100/460Sqs Dec43, Lost 31Jan/30Mar44. 72/159hrs
ND362 576Sq Dec43, 103Sq May44, Lost 28May44. 221hrs
ND363-4 103/460Sqs, Lost 16Feb/27Apr44 (Friedrichshafen)
ND365 7Sq Dec43, Lost 16Feb44. 110hrs
ND366 460Sq Jan44, Hit Whitegate Hill, Caistor, 22Jan44
ND367-8 97/7(MG ·U)Sqs Dec43, Lost (Berlin) 20/21Jan44
ND380 156Sq Dec43, Missing (Berlin) 3Jan44
ND381 103Sq,1LFS,Nov44,1662CU,1668CU,22MU, Scrap May47
ND382 32MU,166Sq Dec43, Lost (Berlin) 28/29Jan44. 63hrs
ND383 49Sq Dec43, 1668CU 29Aug44. SOC 10Sep45
ND384 156Sq 20Dec43, Missing (Berlin) 2Jan44
ND385 576Sq(UL ·N2),170Sq,58MU,9MU, Scrap Oct47
ND386 576Sq(UL ·P2) Jan44, Lost (Berlin) 28/29Jan44. 68hrs
ND387 7Sq(MG ·O)Jan44,90Sq Sep44,1651CU, Crashed 3/4Mar45
ND388-9 100/83Sqs Dec43, Lost 24Dec44/12Apr44
ND390 32MU,83Sq(OL ·U)Jan44,97Sq Mar44,SOC 3Apr44. 149hrs
ND391 100Sq Dec43, Missing 16Feb44
ND392 460Sq Dec43, 1656CU Nov44, 1660CU Nov45, SOC 26Mar46
ND393 460Sq Dec43, Lost (Stuttgart) 15Mar44 50hrs
ND394 460Sq Dec43, Lost (Schweinfurt) 24/25Feb44 117hrs
ND395 32MU,7Sq Dec43, 83Sq, Missing 12Apr44 165hrs
ND396-7 550/103Sqs Jan44, Lost 31Jan/6Jan44. 40/11hrs
ND398 100Sq, Lost jettisoning bombs, pilot ill, 30/31Mar44
ND399 166Sq, Shot down near Apeldoorn 18Jun44. 300hrs
ND400-1 83(OL ·Q)/166Sqs, Lost 29Apr44/24Apr44 (Berlin)
ND402 576,103Sqs: Crashed and burnt Elsham Wolds 27Mar44
ND403 550Sq Dec43, 576Sq 6May44, Lost 12/13May44. 198hrs
ND404 12Sq Dec43, Lost (Berlin) 15Feb44
ND405 57Sq Jan44, 166Sq Oct44, 5MU Dec45, SOC Sep47
ND406 57/156Sqs, Lost 31Mar44
ND407 625Sq, Crash landed and burnt Kelstern 10Apr44
ND408-9 103/156Sqs Jan44, Lost (Leipzig) 20Feb/28Apr44
ND410-11 12/103Sqs Jan44, Lost 20Feb/3May44 (Mailly)
ND412 405Sq(LO ·M), 630Sq(LE ·H), 22MU, Sep45, Scrap May47
ND413 100Sq, Hit ground, low flying, Laceby, 21Jul44. 388hrs
ND414-5 83/97(OF ·B)Sqs Jan44, Lost 21Jan44/Wrecked 23May44
ND416-7 576/103Sqs Jan44, Wrecked 31Jan44/Lost 26Feb44
ND418 Conv.VI R-R Jan44:83,7,635,582Sqs:RAE, Dumped Oct47
ND419 460Sq, Hit trees at N. Witham in snowstorm 21Feb44†
ND420-1 103/97Sqs Jan44, Lost 10Apr/15Jan44. 153/6hrs
ND422 156Sq Jan44, NTU Oct44, BCIS Dec44, Wrecked Sep45
ND423-4 405/12(PH ·G)Sqs Jan44, Lost 15Jan/28Jun. 8/196hrs
ND425 550Sq(BO ·C) Jan44, Lost 30/31Mar44. 131hrs
ND438 156,582Sqs Jun44, 1667CU Dec44, 38MU, Scrap May47
ND439-40 12/97Sqs Jan44, Both lost 24Mar44
ND441 12Sq Jan44, Missing 30Mar44
ND442 83Sq(OL ·O),1666CU Jan45, 1659CU,38MU, Scrap May47
ND443-4 7/156Sqs Jan44, Lost 31Mar/12Aug44 44/272hrs
ND445 32MU,SIU,7Sq(MG ·L)Jan44, Lost(Nurnberg)30/31Mar44
ND446-7 156/12Sqs Jan44, Lost 31Mar/16Mar44
ND448/G & ND449 97/156Sqs Jan44, Lost 20Feb/7May44
ND450 97,635Sqs(F2 ·Y),NTU,1669/61CUs,20MU, Scrap May46
ND451 32MU, 97Sq Jan44, Missing 22Jun44. 270hrs
ND452 97Sq(OF ·E) Jan44, 170Sq(TC ·D) Oct44. SOC Dec45
ND453 156Sq, 635Sq(F2 ·K/D), Crashed 6Oct44. 338hrs
ND454 156Sq Jan44, Lost 25Feb44
ND455 97Sq, 635Sq Mar44, 83Sq Apr44, Lost 26Aug44. 396hrs
ND456 100Sq, hit barn on take-off at Woodbridge 2/3Jun44
ND457 7Sq(MG ·F2) Jan44, Lost 25Mar44 140hrs
ND458 100Sq Jan44, BCIS,5MU, Scrap Aug47. 834+hrs 123ops
ND459-60 625/7(MG ·S)Sqs, Lost 1Jul/7Aug44. 371/355hrs
ND461 625Sq(CF ·W) Jan44, Lost (Berlin) 27Jan44. 6hrs
ND462 32MU, 405Sq 20Jan44, Lost 31Jan44. 15hrs.
ND463 460Sq Jan44, Lost (Berlin) 24Mar44. 121hrs
ND464 32MU, 405Sq(LQ ·V), 83Sq, Crashed and burnt 16Jul44

ND465 32MU, SIU, 83Sq(UL ·L) Jan44, Wrecked 12Aug44. 348hrs
ND466-7 32MU,156/83Sqs Jan44, Lost 2Mar/7Jun44
ND468-9 57/83Sqs Jan44, Lost 3May/25Apr44. 225/?hrs
ND470 32MU,SIU,7Sq(MG ·S) Jan44, Lost (Leipzig) 19/20Feb44
ND471 57Sq(DX ·A) Jan44, Lost 22Jun44. 315hrs
ND472 57Sq(DX ·I) Jan44, Blown up by PB360 at E. Kirkby
ND473 49,467Sqs; Collided with ME300, Cognac, 4/5Jan45
ND474-5 49/57Sqs Jan44, Wrecked 16Mar/19Apr44. 97/174hrs
ND476 32MU, 156Sq Feb44, Lost 31Mar44
ND477 156Sq Jan44, NTU Oct44, 1667CU Dec44, Scrap Apr46
ND478 32MU, 97Sq Feb44, Lost 16Feb44. 13hrs
ND479 Conv. Mk.VI R-R Jan44, Avro. AAEE. Wrecked 26Apr44
ND492-3 32MU, 156/405Sqs Jan44, Lost 31Mar/31Jan44
ND494 32MU, 83Sq Jan44, Missing 10May44
ND495 32MU, 97Sq Jan44, 9Sq Aug45, 22MU, Scrap May47
ND496 32MU, 7Sq(MG ·T), 44Sq(KM ·A), 75Sq Jul45. SOC Oct45
ND497 32MU, 97Sq Jan44, Missing 25Feb44. 31hrs
ND498 49Sq, Swung at Fiskerton, bomb exploded 20/21Feb44
ND499-500 83/97(OF ·G)Sqs Jan44, Lost 27Apr/25Apr44
ND501 97Sq Jan44, 106Sq Nov44, Crashed 2/3Apr45
ND502 156Sq Jan44, 582Sq Apr44, Lost 16Jun44. 274hrs
ND503-4 57/156Sqs Jan44, Lost 20Feb/16Feb44. 39/?hrs
ND505 32MU, 83Sq Jan44, Lost 20Feb44. 27hrs
ND506 57Sq, 166Sq Oct44, Lost (Pforzheim) 23/24Feb45
ND507 32MU, SIU Jan44, 405Sq Feb44, Lost 3Jun44. 187hrs
ND508 32MU, 97Sq Jan44, 635Sq Mar44, SOC 1May44. 136hrs
ND509 57Sq(DX ·C/I),61Sq,625Sq Jun45, 39MU, Scrap 1946
ND510-11 207/106Sqs Jan44, Lost 16Feb/9May44. 31/?hrs
ND512 49Sq,1653CU(HA ·R) Nov44, 1656CU,22MU, Scrap Jun47
ND513 207Sq Jan44, Lost (Clarmont Ferrand) 10/11Mar44. 62hrs
ND514 44Sq(KM ·C) 21Jan44, Wrecked on operations 31Jan44
ND515 44Sq(KM ·Z) Jan44, 207Sq, Lost (Mailly) 3May44. 150hrs
ND516 49Sq 21Jan44, Missing (Leipzig) 19/20Feb44
ND517 44Sq(KM ·U); Lost, day raid, Caen steel works, 18Jul44
ND518-20 44Sq Jan44, Lost 26Feb/23Mar/7Jun44.
ND521 207Sq Jan44, 460Sq(AR ·F2),57Sq(DX ·F), SOC 20Feb46
ND522 207Sq 22Jan44, Lost mining 21/22Aug44. 227hrs
ND523 32MU, SIU, 7Sq(MG ·X) Feb44, Lost (Frankfurt) 22/23Mar44
ND524 SIU, 405Sq(LO ·G) Feb44, 635Sq Dec44, Lost 24Dec44
ND525-6 44/405Sqs Feb44, Both lost (Schweinfurt) 24Feb44
ND527-8 630(LE ·O)/12Sqs, Lost 27Jul/24Jun44. 378/218hrs
ND529 32MU, 83Sq(OL ·D) Feb44, Lindholme Jan46, Scrap Feb46
ND530 630Sq Jan44, Lost (Stuttgart) 1Mar44. 85hrs
ND531 550Sq Jan44, Lost (Wesseling) 21/22Jun44. 266hrs
ND532 630Sq Jan44, Missing (Leipzig) 19/20Feb44. 42hrs
ND533-4 49/156Sqs Feb44, Lost 9Jun/11Sep44. 112/388hrs
ND535-6 106/49Sqs Jan44, Lost 31Mar/23Mar44. 104/87hrs
ND537-8 49/44Sqs Feb44, Lost 25Apr/23Mar44. 126/70hrs
ND551 32MU Jan44, SIU,83Sq Feb44, Lost 22Jun44. 268hrs
ND552 44Sq(KM ·X) Jan44, Lost (Wesseling) 21/22Jun44. 289hrs
ND553 460Sq, BDU, Dinghy release caused crash 30Apr44
ND554 630Sq(LE ·A) Jan44, Lost (Politz) 8/9Feb44
ND555 207Sq, Lost canal raid, Gravenhorst, 6Nov44. 593hrs
ND556 207Sq(FM ·F) Jan44, Lost (Mailly) 3/4May44. 192hrs
ND557 32MU,SIU,7Sq(MG ·F), Lost (Stuttgart) 15/16Mar44
ND558 Conv. Mk.VI, R-R Jan44, AAEE, 635Sq, R-R 1944-46
ND559 32MU Jan44, 156Sq Feb44, Lost 22May44
ND560 57Sq(DX ·N) Jan44, 100Sq, Missing (Berlin) 30/31Jan44
ND561-2 630/12Sqs Feb44, Lost 2Mar/30Mar44. 52/?hrs
ND563 630Sq, Crashed with bombs E. Kirkby 20/21Feb44. 21hrs
ND564 207Sq(EM ·H), Lost (La Chapelle) 20/21Apr44. 123hrs
ND565-6 44Sq 1Feb44, Lost 25Mar/2Mar44. 106/?hrs
ND567-8 207Sq Feb44, Lost 8Jul/31Mar44. 316/84hrs
ND569 460Sq Feb44, Lost (Leipzig) 19Feb44. 11hrs
ND570 207Sq, Lost (St. Leu d'Esserent) 4/5Jul44. 306hrs
ND571 100Sq 1Feb44, Lost 20Feb44. 11hrs
ND572 103,57Sqs; Written off after crash 24Mar44
ND573 44Sq, 49Sq, Lost (Munich) 24/25Apr44
ND574 44Sq, Flight Refuelling, 1BDU, 22MU, Scrap Nov48
ND575 Not delivered to the RAF
ND576-7 44/156Sqs Feb44, Lost 17Mar/8Jun44. 80/?hrs
ND578 44Sq(KM ·Y) Feb44, 75Sq Jul45, SOC Spilsby 27Oct45
ND579 166Sq, Down in N. Sea off Hook of Holland 21/22May44

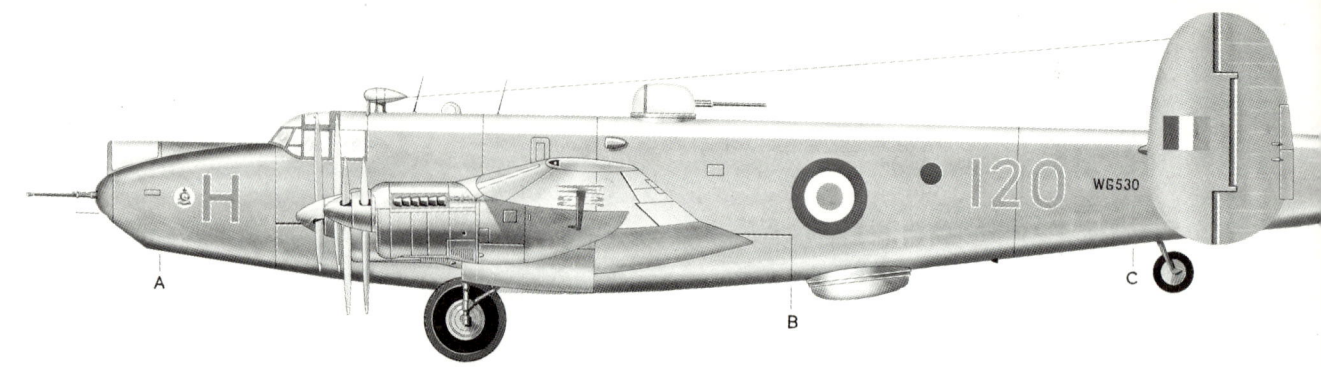

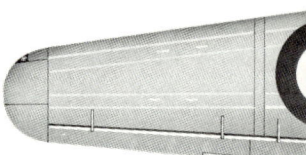

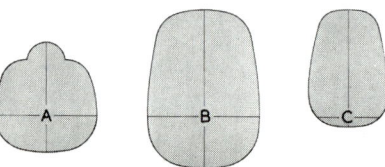

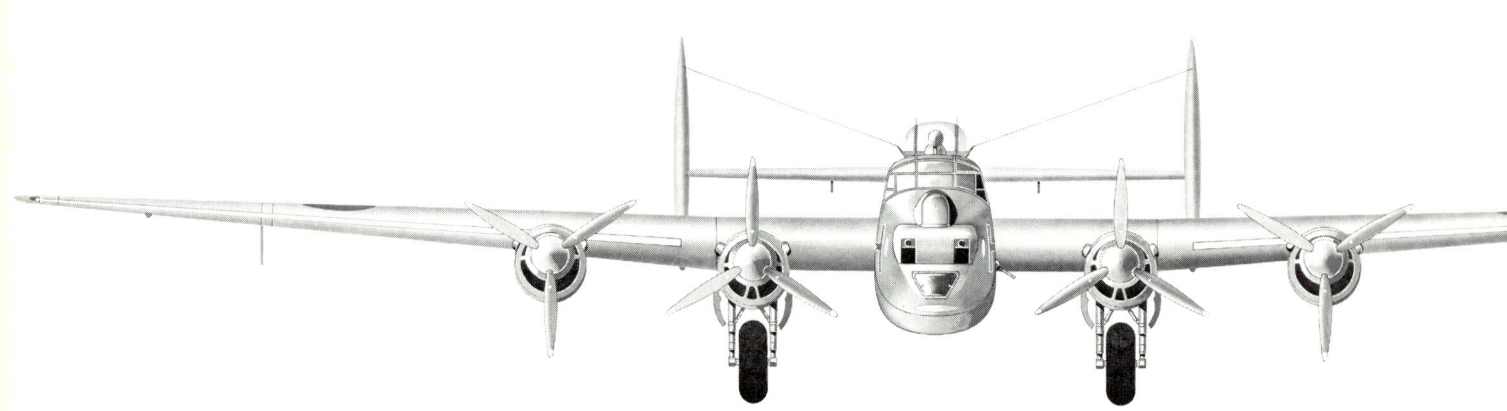

184

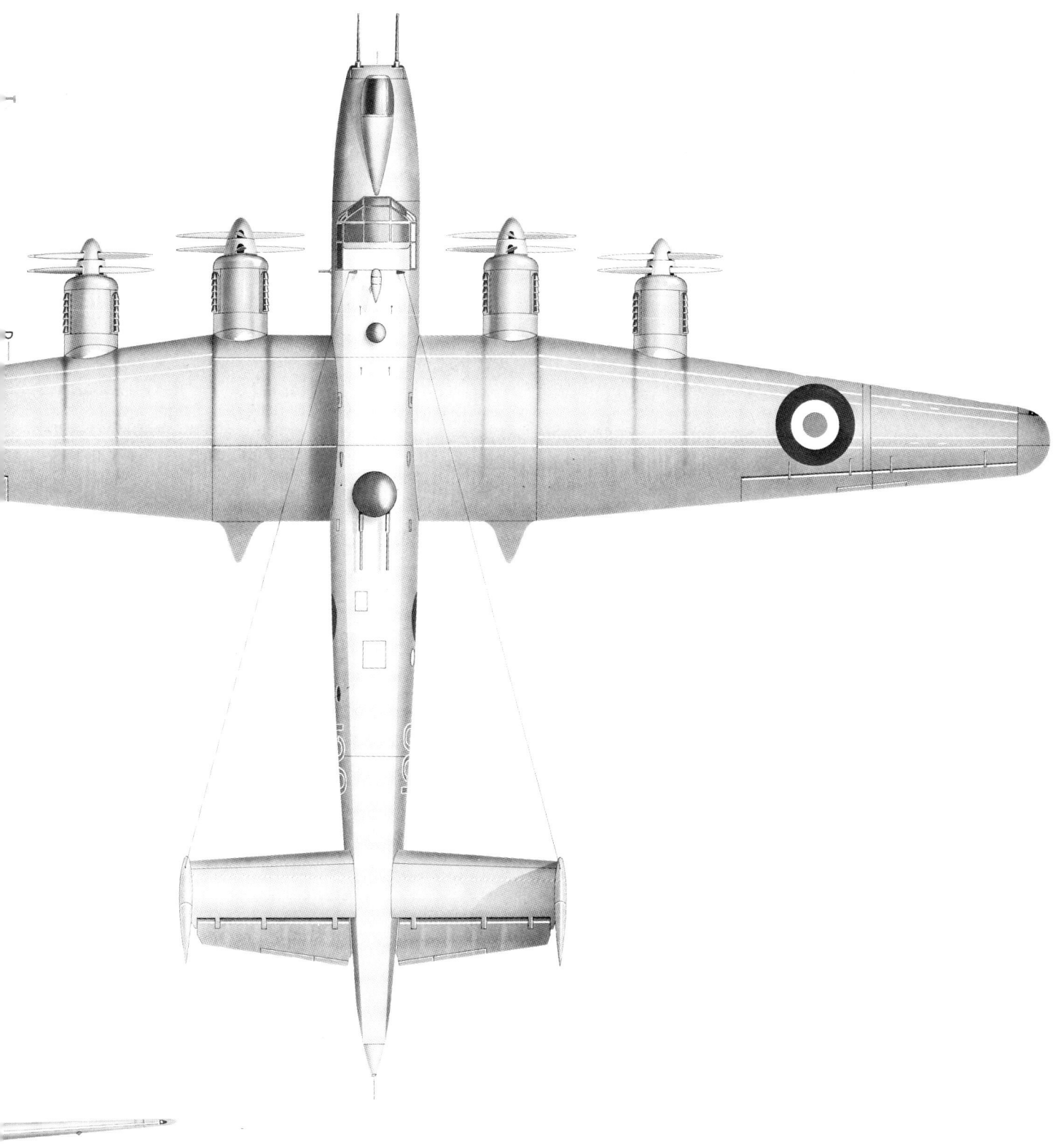

A Shackleton M.R.2 of No. 120 Squadron as its markings indicate. Later the mid-upper turret was removed.

185

ND580 630Sq, Lost raiding Bourg Leopold Camp 11/12May44
ND581 32MU,SIU,7Sq(MC·M) Feb44, Lost (Berlin) 24/25Mar44
ND582-3 57(DX·S)/630Sqs, Wrecked 21Apr44/Lost 16Mar44
ND584 32MU, SIU, 460Sq,BDU,CBE,54MU, Became 5865M
ND585-6 106/460Sqs Feb44, Lost 31Mar/11Apr44. 105/107hrs
ND587 32MU, 405Sq Feb44, Lost 8/9May44
ND588 7Sq(MG·Q) Feb44, Lost (Duisberg) 21/22May44. 168hrs
ND589 SIU, 97Sq(OF·D), R-R Oct44, Conv. ASRIII, MUs SOC Oct46
ND590 7Sq(MG·B) Lost (Wks. at Coubronne) 23/24Jun44. 203hrs
ND591 32MU,156Sq,83Sq(OL·A)May45,20MU May46, SS May47
ND592 7Sq Feb44, Lost raiding rly. yards, 22/23Apr44. 126hrs
ND593 100Sq, Lost at sea, operations, 24/25Feb44. 4hrs
ND594-5 100Sq Feb44, Lost 10/11Jun & 25/26Feb44. 228/23hrs
ND596 625Sq Feb44, Lost (Frankfurt) 18Mar44. 54hrs
ND597 32MU Feb44, 35Sq Mar44, Lost 25Mar44. 43hrs
ND613 625Sq Feb44, 103Sq Jul44, Lost 15Aug44. 337hrs
ND614 166Sq(AS·A), Crashed on return (Kiel) 23Jul44. 304hrs
ND615 32MU,460Sq Feb44, 1656CU Dec44, 20MU, SOC Apr46
ND616 405Sq, NTU, 106Sq, Crashed 17Jul45. Became 5532M
ND617 32MU, 405Sq Feb44, Missing 6/7May44
ND618 156Sq; Wrecked when ND978 blew up, Upwood, 9Sep44
ND619 625Sq; 1662,1668CUs: 20MU, Became 5795M at 1RS
ND620-1 166Sq Feb44, Lost (Berlin) 24Mar/(Revigny) 6Jul44
ND622 32MU, 57Sq Feb44, Lost 31Mar44. 64hrs
ND623/G 32MU, 166Sq(AS·F), Flt. Refuelling, Crashed 11Oct45
ND624 103Sq Feb44, Damaged 27Mar44, Lost 25May45. 159hrs
ND625 166Sq Feb44, Lost mining (Danzig Bay) 9Apr44. 78hrs
ND626 166Sq, Lost mining (Frisian Islands) 26Oct44. 519hrs
ND627-8 12/166Sqs Feb44, Lost 4Jul/24Jul44. 235/256hrs
ND629-30 103/460Sqs Feb44, Lost 23May/3May44. 136/120hrs
ND631 44Sq(KM·B) Feb44, Missing (Leipzig) 10/11Apr45
ND632 103Sq, Hit aircraft at Ford and burnt 26Aug44. 319hrs
ND633 5LFS Feb44, Repaired twice, 46MU May45, Scrap Jan47
ND634 460Sq Feb44, 166Sq 15Jul44, Lost 25Jul44
ND635 166Sq 21Feb44, Lost (Nuremburg) 25Jun45
ND636 625Sq Feb44, Missing (Aulnoye) 10Apr44. 83hrs
ND637 625Sq(CF·L), Hit ED606 over Branston 16Mar44
ND638 103Sq 20Feb44, Damaged 25Apr44 and SOC. 96hrs
ND639 625,100Sqs; 1656/67CUs: Burnt out, Crawle, 5Apr45
ND640 32MU,97Sq 29Feb44, Lost 31Mar44. 42hrs
ND641 625Sq, Shot down in Holland (Berlin) 24Mar44. 45hrs
ND642-3 100/35Sqs Mar44, Lost 25Mar/3May44. 58/105hrs
ND644 100Sq Feb44(HW·N), Lost 16/17Mar45. 115ops 800hrs
ND645 32MU Feb44, 35Sq 7Mar44, Lost 23Mar44. 38hrs
ND646 35Sq Mar44,NTU Nov44,106Sq Jun45,10MU,SOC Jan45
ND647 49Sq,1653CU, Crashed at Scraptoft on fighter affiliation 8Apr45
ND648 35Sq, 32MU, Became G-33-1 with Flt. Refuelling
ND649-50 32MU, 35/12Sqs Mar44, Lost 23 & 25Mar44. 32/?hrs
ND651 166Sq, Lost raiding railway gun at Calais 2Jun44
ND652 32MU, 460Sq Feb44, Lost (Essen) 26Apr44. 78hrs
ND653 35,635Sqs; Overshot Downham Market 14Sep44. 324hrs
ND654 32MU,SIU,460Sq Mar44, Lost (Courtrai) 20Jul44. 90hrs
ND655 32MU,630Sq Feb44, Lost (Brunswick) 22/23May44 189hrs
ND656 460Sq,103Sq Jul44, 38MU, 1666CU, Crashed 24/25Mar45
ND657 32MU, 630Sq Feb44, Lost (Berlin) 24/25Mar44. 45hrs
ND658 32MU, 460Sq, 46MU, 170Sq(TC·P), SOC 12Dec45
ND671-2 32MU, 57/49Sqs Mar44, Lost 25 & 23Mar44. 28/17hrs
ND673 Conv. VI, R-R Mar44; 7,653Sq(F2·V): RAE
ND674 32MU, 460Sq Feb44, Lost (Hasselt) 11May44. 116hrs
ND675-6 32MU,100/49Sqs Feb44,Lost 10Apr44/Wrecked 27Mar44
ND677/G 460Sq Feb44, Damaged 15Aug44, 49Sq Apr45, 115Sq (KO·X) 1Sep45, First Lanc. with Monica radar. Scrap Jul46
ND678 32MU,166Sq(AS·Q), Last seen over Caen 7Jul44. 219hrs
ND679-80 32MU, 12/106Sqs Mar44, Lost 27May/7Jun44
ND681-2 100/106Sqs Mar44, Lost 16Mar/16Dec44
ND683-4 49Sq Mar44, Lost 22Jun/19Jul44. 117/341hrs
ND685-6 630Sq Feb44, Lost (Caen) 7Jun44/19Mar44. 233/34hrs
ND687-8 49/630Sqs Mar44, Lost 27Apr44/8Jul44 (Creil)
ND689 32MU Feb44, 44Sq Mar44, Wrecked 1Jun44. 165hrs
ND690 32MU, 35Sq, NTU Nov44; 106,83Sqs: SOC 16Nov45
ND691 32MU Feb44, 35Sq Mar44, Lost 12Sep44. 335hrs
ND692 32MU,83Sq Aug44, 9Sq Aug45, SOC Tollerton 27Nov45

ND693 32MU, NTU, 635Sq, Missing 26Aug44. 314hrs
ND694 35,635Sqs: Missing (Russelsheim) 12Aug44. 132hrs
ND695 32MU, 49Sq Mar44, Lost (Wesseling) 21/22Jun44
ND696 35Sq March44, Crashed 30Apr44
ND697 35Sq, Crashed, take-off, Graveley, 29Apr44, Crew saved
ND698 44Sq, Overshot landing at Oakley 1Jun44. 214hrs
ND699-700 12/103Sqs Mar44, Lost 28Jul/11May44. 292/122hrs
ND701-2 32MU,35Sq Mar44, Lost 10Apr/12Sep44. 47/281hrs
ND703 35Sq, 635Sq(F2·F) Jun44, Lost (Merseburg) 6Dec44
ND704-5 635/166Sqs Mar44, Lost 25Mar/18Mar44
ND706 32MU, 97Sq(OF·H) Mar44, Lost 3/4May44
ND707 166Sq, Damaged 3 times, Lost (Lutzkendorf) 4/5Apr45
ND708 32MU, 35Sq Mar44, Lost 16Mar44. 5hrs
ND709 635(F2·J),405,35Sqs; 1667/53/60/53CUs; SOC Aug47
ND710-11 12/635Sqs Mar44, Lost 25Mar/31Mar44
ND712 32MU, TFU Defford Mar44, 15MU Jul44, Scrap May47
ND713 SIU,5MU,460Sq,1LFS,460Sq,1323Flt. SOC Oct45
ND714-5 12/582Sqs Mar44, Lost 15Jun/28Apr44
ND727-8 61/619Sqs Mar44, Lost (Frankfurt) 18Mar/7Sep44
ND729-30 467/619Sqs, Lost (Prouville) 24Jun/7Aug44
ND731-2 35/467Sqs, Lost 5Jul44/(La Chappelle) 20Apr44
ND733 550,463Sqs: Abandoned in air near Juvincourt 17Apr45
ND734 32MU, 35Sq Mar44, Lost 24Jun44. 77hrs
ND735 635Sq(F2·F/P/L) from Mar44, Lost (Dessau) 7Mar45
ND736 7Sq, Lost raiding Mt. Couple radar jammer 19/20May44
ND737 582Sq: Hit houses, take-off, Little Staughton 22Apr44
ND738-9 460/97Sqs Mar44, Lost (Nuremburg) 30Mar/6Jun44
ND740/G 32MU, 97Sq(OF·F), 83Sq, Lost 12Sep44. 358hrs
ND741-2 44/625Sqs Mar44, Lost 7May/10Jun44. 118/182hrs
ND743 RAE except for repairs after 3 crashes, SOC Jan47
ND744 7Sq(MG·F), Lost in raid on French railways, 15/16Jun44
ND745 115Sq 29Mar44, Missing 23May44. 87hrs
ND746 32MU, 97Sq(OF·N) Mar44, 15MU Jul46, Scrap Nov46
ND747 75Sq Mar44, 3LFS,G-H Flt, 1656/68CUs, Crashed 13Oct45
ND748 32MU, 97Sq Mar44, Lost 21Apr44. 49hrs
ND749 12Sq Mar44,1668CU(ZK·H)Aug44,1660CU,SOC 2Nov45
ND750 582Sq Mar44, 1654CU Jun45, 10MU, SOC Apr46
ND751 44Sq(KM·J)Mar44, Lost(Pommereval)24/25Jun44. 252hrs
ND752-3 75/115Sqs Mar44, Lost 21Jul/23Apr44. 199/40hrs
ND754-5 115/35Sqs Mar44, Lost 22May/19Oct44. 74/357hrs
ND756 75Sq 13Mar44, Missing 29Jul44. 229hrs
ND757 166,153Sqs; 1656CU, Overshot Lindholme 15Jan45
ND758 115Sq, 3LFS Nov44, 1653CU Feb45, 15MU, Scrap May47
ND759-60 35/115Sqs Mar44, Lost 29Apr/8Jun44. 52/125hrs
ND761-2 115/35Sqs Mar44, Lost 8Jun/23May44. 103/111hrs
ND763-4 15/79Sqs Mar44, Wrecked 23Apr44/Lost 9Jun44
ND765-6 622/7(MG·P)Sqs, Lost 8 & 25Jun44. 111/144hrs
ND767-8 622/75Sqs Mar44, Lost 31Mar/23May44. 6/113hrs
ND781 32MU, 622Sq 23Mar44, Lost 28Apr44. 64hrs
ND782 32MU,75Sq,3LFS,1651CU,1653CU,5MU, Scrap Jul47
ND783 576Sq, Lost 6May44 with A/Cdre Ivelaw-Chapman (p.o.w.)
ND784/G Conv. VI. R-R Mar44, AWA, 11Oct44 to Power Jets, Mamba in nose. Scrapped 1951
ND785 100Sq, Lost (marshalling yards, Cologne), 20/21Apr44
ND786 32MU, 57Sq Mar44, Lost 27Apr44. 80hrs
ND787 32MU,49Sq,1668CU Sep44, 22MU Sep45, Scrap May47
ND788 630Sq Mar44, Missing (Berlin) 24/25Mar44. 12hrs
ND789 630Sq Mar44, Missing (Schweinfurt) 26/27Apr44. 82hrs
ND790 115Sq 24Mar44, Missing 8Jun44. 98hrs
ND791 32MU,SIU,5MU,460Sq,49Sq,115Sq Sep45, SOC 31May46
ND792 49Sq Mar44, 619Sq Sep44, Crashed 4Feb45
ND793 630Sq, Flt. Refuelling and BDU 1945-6, Scrap Aug49
ND794/G SIU Mar44, AAEE test of FN150. Scrap Oct45
ND795 32MU, 44Sq 25Mar44. Lost (Nuremburg) 31Mar44. 9hrs
ND796 75Sq Mar44, Lost (Friedrichshafen) 27Apr44. 40hrs
ND797 32MU, 630Sq Mar44, Lost 29Jul44. 205hrs
ND798 166Sq Mar44, Lost (Nuremburg) 30Mar44. 5hrs
ND799 12Sq Mar44, Crashed near Faldingworth 6Jul44. 222hrs
ND800 115Sq, Crashed 25Apr44, 75Sq, Lost 21Jul44. 53hrs
ND801 75Sq(JN·X), Crashed at Sutton village 3Feb45
ND802-3 75/115Sqs Mar44, Lost 28May/28Apr44. 106/22hrs
ND804-5 75/115Sqs Mar44, Lost 22May/14Oct44
ND806 166Sq, Crashed at Woodbridge after combat 27Apr44
ND807 32MU, 97Sq, shot down in sea 26Aug44. 255hrs

ND808 156Sq, BCIS Dec44; Swung landing, Finningley, 31Mar45
ND809 635Sq(F2 ·C) Apr44, 1661CU Dec44, 20MU, SOC May46
ND810 32MU, 582Sq Apr44, Missing 29Jul44. 192hrs
ND811 635Sq(F2 ·T) Mar44, Lost (Trossy St. Maximin) 4Aug44
ND812 582,635Sqs; Overshot Downham Market 23Oct44. 250hrs
ND813 32MU, 582Sq Apr44, 97Sq, Lost 10/11May44
ND814-5 582/97Sqs Apr44, Lost 28May/6Jun44. 111/32hrs
ND816-7 32MU, 582Sq Apr44, Lost 25May/7Aug44. 121/246hrs
ND818-9 32MU, 83/635Sqs Apr44, Lost 8May/22May44
ND820 635Sq, Dived in flames, morning of 10Apr44. 6hrs
ND821 635Sq(F2 ·X), 1662CU Dec44, 20MU Aug45, Scrap Nov46
ND822 SIU, 460Sq, Crashed at Ludford Magna 14Jan45
ND823 32MU,SIU,TFU,1317Flt Jun44,5MU Mar46, Scrap Sep47
ND824 32MU, 83Sq Apr44, 15MU Jul46, SOC 28Nov46
ND825 166Sq Mar44, Lost (Friedrichshafen) 27Apr44. 68hrs
ND826 32MU, 635Sq Apr44, Lost 21Apr44. 9hrs
ND839 32MU,NTU Apr44,1669CU Dec44,22MU Sep45, Scrap May47
ND840 32MU, 83Sq Apr44, 97Sq Jun44, Lost 6Aug44. 239hrs
ND841 635Sq; Hit hangar, blew up, Downham Market 4Jun44
ND842 12Sq Mar44, Lost 30Jun44. 192hrs
ND843 44Sq, Flt. Refuelling, BDU,22MU, SS(ERM) Feb49
ND844 12Sq Mar44, Lost (Aulnoye Rly Yds) 10Apr44
ND845 7Sq(MG ·C), Lost (Le Mans Rly. Yds.) 19/20May44. 58hrs
ND846 35Sq(TL ·J), Shot down near Réau, France, 4Jul44. 124hrs
ND847-8 103/635Sqs Apr44, Lost 27Apr/25Apr44. 56/8hrs
ND849 32MU, 7Sq Apr44, 582Sq Jan45, Lost 15/16Mar45
ND850-1 106Sq Apr44, Lost 27Apr/10May44
ND852 7Sq(MG ·D), Lost (Russelsheim) 25Aug44. 262hrs
ND853-4 106/83Sqs Apr44, Lost 27Apr44/15Aug44
ND855 405Sq(LQ ·V) Apr44, 1667CU Dec44, 46MU May45, SOC Aug47
ND856 32MU, 83Sq Apr44, Lost 27Jul44. 188hrs
ND857 166Sq Apr44,Damaged 7Oct44,15MU Aug45,Scrap May47
ND858 32MU,83Sq Apr44,5LFS Feb45,46MU Apr45, Scrap Jan47
ND859 576Sq(UL ·L2) Apr44, Lost (Revigny) 12Jul44. 216hrs
ND860 32MU, 460Sq Apr44, Lost 3/4May44. 20hrs
ND861 300Sq, 103Sq Aug44, Crashed near Hull 4Jan45
ND862 582,207Sqs; 1661CU, 20MU, SOC in Middle East Oct46
ND863 32MU, 300Sq,625Sq,170Sq(TC ·E),38MU, Scrap May47
ND864 32MU,460,626Sqs Aug44, 15MU Aug45, Scrap May47
ND865 61Sq Apr44, 5LFS Feb45, 46MU Apr45, Scrap Nov46
ND866 32MU, 207Sq, Lost (St. Leu d'Esserent) 7/8Jul44. 189hrs
ND867-8 61/106Sqs Apr44, Lost 8Jul/24Sep44
ND869 44Sq(KM ·M), Down in sea off Skegness 16Mar45
ND870 106Sq 5Apr44, Missing (Salbris ammo dump) 7May44
ND871 207Sq 7Apr44, Lost (Brunswick) 22/23May44. 94hrs
ND872-3 207/12Sqs Apr44, Lost 29Jul/27Apr44. 176/24hrs
ND874 50Sq, Lost early on D-Day raiding coastal battery. 176hrs
ND875 32MU, 16Sq; 1668/60/53CUs; 15MU, SOC Aug47
ND876 50Sq 8Apr44, Missing 25Apr44. 26hrs
ND877 32MU; 635,156Sqs; 1660/56/68/53CUs; 9MU, 2MPRD Nov47
ND878-9 57Sq Apr44, Both lost 23May44. 116/103hrs
ND880-1 582/405Sqs Apr44, Lost 12Oct/3May44
ND882 32MU, 156Sq Apr44, 46MU,1661CU Feb45, 5MU, Scrap Sep47
ND895 32MU, 635Sq(F2 ·N) Apr44, Lost 6Jul44. 133hrs
ND896 61Sq Apr44, 5LFS Dec44, 46MU Apr45, Scrap Oct46
ND897 7Sq(MG ·C), Lost with Master Bomber attacking Siracourt rocket sites 29Jun44
ND898 32MU, 635Sq(F2 ·W), 1656/53CUs, Crashed 15Oct45
ND899 582Sq(6O ·J),156Sq(GT ·L),AAEE Sep45, Scrap Mar47
ND900 32MU,115Sq(KO ·S)Apr44; 1651,1667,1656CUs; SOC 4Dec45
ND901 32MU, 7Sq(MG ·B) Apr44, Lost 2May44. 22hrs
ND902 61Sq Apr44, SOC on 3rd time damaged 31Oct44. 272hrs
ND903 103Sq, Lost (Stuttgart) 26Jul44. 221hrs
ND904 115Sq Apr44, 75Sq, Missing 5Oct44. 282hrs
ND905 103Sq 14Apr44, Lost (Mailly le Camp) 3/4May44. 44hrs
ND906 7Sq(MG ·N), Crashed at Church Lawford 5May44. 10hrs
ND907 32MU,35Sq,NTU Nov44; 106,83,12Sqs;15MU, Scrap Jul46
ND908 75Sq, Missing 28May44. 71hrs
ND909 32MU,582Sq,38MU,1669CUNov44,1668CU, Became5726M

ND910-11 582/75Sqs; Lost 3May/20Nov44
ND912 32MU, 7Sq Apr44, 405Sq Jan45, Lost 8/9Feb45
ND913 115Sq 20Apr44, Missing 21Jul44. 103hrs
ND914 75Sq, Swung on landing at Mepal 28May44. 43hrs
ND915 75Sq, Missing 21Jul44. 168hrs
ND916 32MU, 35Sq Apr44, 405Sq Jan45, 12Sq, Crashed 16Feb46
ND917 115Sq, Crashed 12May44, Lost 4Nov44. 358hrs
ND918 32MU,75Sq,38MU,1660CU(TV ·N) Feb45, 15MU, Scrap Dec46
ND919-20 75/115Sq, Lost 11May/23Jun44, 13/115hrs
ND921-2 582/83Sqs May44, Lost 6Jun/25Jul44. 75/136hrs
ND923-4 115/635Sqs, Lost 11May/12May44. 20/21hrs
ND925 32MU, 103Sq Apr44, Missing (Aachen) 27May44
ND926-7 622/115Sqs Apr44, Lost 1Jun/12Aug44. 56/183hrs
ND928 32MU, 35Sq, NTU Nov44, Crashed at Warboys 28Apr45
ND929 35Sq Apr44, 146,582Sqs;1654CU,39MU,2MPRD Jun47
ND930-1 83/582Sqs May44, Lost 6Aug/24Jul44. 209/158hrs
ND932 619Sq(PG ·U) Apr44, Missing (Heilbronn) 4Dec44
ND933 35Sq,NTU,106Sq,97Sq(OF ·P) Aug45,15MU, Scrap Jan47
ND934 32MU, 35Sq, 5MU, 1660CU, 20MU, SS May47
ND935 619Sq Apr44, Damaged 22Jun44, Lost 26Jul44. 168hrs
ND936 32MU, 35Sq, NTU; 1660CU(YW ·O), 1653CU, Wrecked 14Mar46
ND948 9Sq(WS ·H) Apr44, Lost 24Jun44. 24ops
ND949 630Sq, Crashed Foxton near Market Harboro', 9/10Apr45
ND950 635Sq(F2 ·M) May44, Lost 27Aug44. 231hrs
ND951 9Sq(WS ·Z) Apr44, Missing (Bourg Leopold) 11/12May44
ND952 626Sq(UM ·E2) Apr44, Lost (Vierzan Junction) 30/31Jun44
ND953 50Sq Apr44, Lost (Mailly le Camp) 3/4May44
ND954-5 57(DX ·Q)/15Sqs Apr44, Lost 1Aug/25May44. 246/71hrs
ND956 166Sq Apr44, Shot down S.W. of Utrecht 21/22May44
ND957 32MU, 49Sq Apr44, 619Sq Sep44, Lost 7Jan45
ND958 15Sq, 3LFS Nov44, Wrecked near Barnham 29Jan45
ND959 460Sq, Crash 11Jan45, 1661CU, 1323Flt, Scrap Feb47
ND960-1 32MU, 57/97Sqs May44, Lost 22May44/9Feb45
ND962-3 156/83Sqs, Wrecked 2Jul44/Lost 23May44
ND964 626Sq(UM ·K2) Apr44, Lost (Duisburg) 21/22May44
ND965 635Sq(F2 ·K), 46MU,1660CU(TV ·L)15MU, Scrap May47
ND966 32MU Apr44, 83Sq May44, Lost 8Jul44. 88hrs
ND967 460Sq,429Sq(AL ·O/L) Apr45, 20MU May46, Scrap Sep47
ND968 32MU, 460Sq, Damaged 8Jan45, Scrapped Oct45
ND969 582Sq(6O ·F), Lost (Russelsheim) 12/13Aug44. 222hrs
ND970 460Sq(AR ·S) Jun44, Lost (Laffen-Hausen) 28Jan45
ND971 460Sq Jun44, Missing (Merseburg) 6Dec44
ND972 32MU,100Sq,550Sq Jul44, 15MU Aug45, Scrap May47
ND973 44Sq(KM ·A) May44, Lost (Wesseling) 21/22Jun44. 107hrs
ND974 83,44Sqs Nov44, 75Sq Jul45, 39MU, Scrap Oct46
ND975-6 300/44Sqs May44, Lost 1Jul/12May44
ND977 57Sq(DX ·R) Apr44, 5MU Oct45, Scrap Dec46
ND978 156Sq, Blown up by bombs at Upwood 9Sep44. 229hrs
ND979 32MU, 83Sq, Crash 14Aug45, 22MU, Scrap Feb46
ND980 405Sq(LQ ·W) May44, 1668CU Dec44, Crash 16/17Apr45
ND981 32MU Apr44, 97Sq May44, Wrecked 24Jun44. 65hrs
ND982 405Sq(LO ·E),630Sq(LE ·Y),Lost (Königsberg)29/30Aug44
ND983-4 101/300Sqs, Wrecked 7Sep44/Lost 25Jul44
ND985 626Sq(UM ·W2) May44, Lost (Aachen) 27/28May44
ND986 619Sq(PG ·S) Jun44, Lost (Wesseling) 21Jun44. 97hrs
ND987-8 61Sq, Lost (Prouville)/(Munster) 24Jun/23Sep44
ND989 50Sq, Hit house at Crowmarsh 20May44. 42hrs
ND990 103Sq; Abandoned over Carnaby, operations, 13Sep44
ND991 50Sq, Flt. Refuelling, BDU, 22MU, Scrap Aug47
ND992 625Sq,170Sq(TC ·A)Oct44,207Sq Mar45,Wrecked 24Aug45
ND993-4 103/576Sqs May44, Lost 13Jul/15Jul44. 154/167hrs
ND995 625Sq May44, 100Sq Jul44, Lost 26Aug44. 195hrs
ND996 166Sq May44, Lost (Aachen) 27May44. 19hrs
NE112 166Sq May44, Twice damaged, Lost 31Aug44. 208hrs
NE113 166Sq May-Sep44, 153Sq Oct44-Mar45. Scrap Oct46
NE114 116Sq 6May44, Missing (Dortmund) 22/23May44. 29hrs
NE115-6 576/460Sqs May44, Lost 2Nov/22Jun44. (Rheims)
NE117-8 103/626Sqs May44, Lost 29Jul/23Apr44. 207/?hrs
NE119 156Sq May-Oct44, 405Sq Jan45, Missing 15/16Mar45
NE120 156Sq May44-Jun45; 1656,1668,1653CUs; SOC Aug46
NE121 97Sq 13May44, Missing 30Jul44. 158hrs
NE122 7Sq May-Nov44,1669/61CUs;20MU,Became 5895M at 1RS

NE123 7Sq(MG ·J) 7May44, Missing (Brest) 25/26Aug44. 244hrs
NE124 97Sq 10May44, Missing 25Jun44. 101hrs
NE125 49Sq ex-32MU 13May44, Lost (Brunswick) 23May44
NE126 7Sq(MG ·R) ex-32MU 14May44, Missing (Frankfurt) 13Sep44
NE127 57Sq 16May44, Missing 23May44. 7hrs
NE128 49Sq ex-32MU May44, Lost (Wesseling) 1Jun44. 80hrs
NE129 7Sq 22May44, Lost (Dreux rly. yds.) 10/11Jun44. 52hrs
NE130 582Sq, Abandoned after Zeitz raid 16/17Jan45. 1 killed
NE131 635Sq 4Jun44, Missing 30Aug44. 208hrs
NE132 156Sq, 1653CU Nov44; Down in sea, Llanbedr, 6Feb45
NE133 463Sq 10May44, Lost (Dortmund-Ems canal) 4Nov44

NE165, 83 Squadron, after 25 operations, circa October 1944.

NE134 12Sq 11May44, Missing 22/23May44
NE135-6 50/103Sqs May44, Lost (Russelsheim) 12Aug/15Jul44
NE137 625Sq May44, 1667CU Nov44, 38MU, SOC May47
NE138 44Sq(KM ·Z) 11May44, Lost mining 26/27Aug44. 261hrs
NE139 460Sq ex-32MU 14Jun44. Crashed 5Jul44
NE140 582Sq May-Oct44, 405Sq,1656CU,12Sq, Crash 1Feb46
NE141 460Sq(AR ·P) Jun44, Missing (Aschaffenburg) 27Nov44
NE142 460Sq 1Jun44-Apr45, 49Sq,1323Flt,39MU, Scrap47
NE143 156Sq 22May44, Missing 1Jun44
NE144 460Sq ex-RAE 12Jul44, Lost (Stettin) 29/30Aug44 74hrs
NE145 90Sq May44, Burnt after operations 28Jun44. 54hrs
NE146 622Sq(GI ·F) May44, Lost (Stuttgart) 24/25Jul44. 110hrs
NE147/G BDU May44-45,Flt.Refuelling mods.15MU, SOC May47
NE148 115Sq 20May44, Lost from 75Sq on 29Jul44. 118hrs
NE149-50 90/100Sqs May44, Lost 10Jun/7Jun44. 31/40hrs
NE151 619Sq(PG ·W) May44, Lost (Wesseling) 21Jun44. 77hrs
NE163 460Sq May-June44, 626Sq, Lost (Duisburg) 14Oct44. 242hrs
NE164 460Sq May-Jun44, Lost from 550Sq 29Jul44. 163hrs
NE165 83Sq except for R-R Sep-Dec44, Missing 21/22Feb45
NE166-7 582/97Sqs May44, Lost 6Jun/17Aug44. 20/120hrs
NE168 207Sq May44, Missing (Houffalize) 6Jan45
NE169 582Sq 27May44, Missing 6Jul44. 75hrs
NE170 166Sq ex-32MU 21May44, Missing 21Aug44. 266hrs
NE171 576Sq(UL ·Y2) 17May44, Lost (Aachen) 24/25May44. 17hrs
NE172 582Sq ex-32MU 29May44, Crashed returning 8Jun44
NE173 103Sq 17May44, Missing (Vire) 7Jun44. 38hrs
NE174-5 460/35Sqs May44, Lost 4/5Jul44/25Jul44. 30/115hrs
NE176 460Sq,1LFS; 460,49Sqs; 1323Flt, SOC Oct45
NE177 90Sq 19May44, Lost on training 10Jun44. 23hrs
NE178 90Sq May44, 1651CU Nov44, 5MU, Scrap May47
NE179 635Sq(FL ·Y), 1669CU, Crashed near Drem 19Feb45
NE180 405,635Sqs; NTU; 106,218,166Sqs; Became 6150M
NE181 75Sq(AA ·M) May44, 514Sq Jul44, 5MU, 101ops. Ear-marked to fly to New Zealand but was scrapped, Sep47

Serial Range NF906—NG503   **Lancaster B.I**
    400 Lancasters ordered from Armstrong Whitworth Aircraft (Baginton) and delivered from July 1944 to February 1945 mainly with Merlin 24 engines from Baginton and Bitteswell.

NF906 218Sq(AA ·B) Jul44, Lost (Frankfurt) 12/13Sep44. 40hrs
NF907 626Sq(UM ·K2) 4Aug44, Lost mining 18/19Feb45
NF908 467Sq Aug44; Crashed and burnt, Leck, 3Jan45
NF909 103Sq 6Aug44, Missing (Pforzheim) 23/24Feb45
NF910 467Sq, MUs, Hatfield Aug46, 4-blade props, SOC Aug50
NF911 218Sq(HA ·F) 4Aug44, Lost (Frankfurt) 12/13Sep44. 52hrs
NF912 61Sq, Crashed on take-off, Skellingthorpe, 1Feb45
NF913-4 103/61Sqs. Lost (Dessau) 7Mar45/25Sep44
NF915 622Sq(GI ·U) 18Aug44, Missing (Bonn) 24/25Dec44
NF916 218Sq Aug44, 15Sq Oct44, Missing 5Nov44. 104hrs
NF917 467Sq Aug44, Missing (Hamburg) 11Nov44. 207hrs

NF918-9 50Sq, Lost (Bohlen)/(Darmstadt) 5/6Mar45/11Sep44
NF920 617Sq, Landed in Sweden after *Turpitz* raid 29Oct44
NF921 50Sq 13Aug44, Lost (Königsberg) 29/30Aug44. 33hrs
NF922 50Sq, Damaged 20Feb and 14/15Mar45, SOC Dec45
NF923 617Sq 13Aug44, Missing 24Sep44
NF924 101Sq, Crash-landed L. Magna 4Jan45, 5MU, SOC May47
NF925 12Sq Sep44, Crashed and burnt 7/8Feb45
NF926 218Sq(HA ·X), Missing (Vohwinkel) 31Dec44
NF927 149Sq(OJ ·D), Damaged three times, Scrapped Apr46
NF928 12Sq 3Sep44, Missing 14Oct44. 48hrs
NF929 9(WS ·P),619,463Sqs; 22MU Oct45, Scrap Jun47
NF930 50Sq,533Sq Apr45 only, 39MU, Scrap Oct46
NF931 550Sq Sep44, 100Sq Oct45, 38MU May46, SOC May47
NF932 550Sq(BQ ·B2) 13Sep44, Blown up 13Feb45†
NF933 101Sq, Damaged 19/20Oct44, 46MU, SOC Nov46
NF934 218Sq Sep44, 149Sq Dec44. SOC Jun47
NF935 75Sq, 514Sq 20Jul45, 22MU Sep45, Scrap May47
NF936 101Sq 16Aug44, Missing 4Nov44. 142hrs
NF937 9Sq(WS ·L) 16Aug44, Missing 14/15Feb45. 17ops
NF938 9Sq, Crash landed N. Russia 18Sep44. 33hrs
NF939 622Sq(GI ·D), Lost mining Gulf of Danzig 6Jan45
NF952 15Sq 18Aug44, Lost over Kiel 27Aug44. 3hrs
NF953 15Sq Aug44, 149Sq Mar45, 10MU Jun45, SOC Feb47
NF954 101Sq Damaged 11Nov44, Overshot 20/21Feb45
NF955 218Sq(HA ·H); Crashed, take-off, Chedburgh 24Apr45
NF956 218Sq(HA ·E), Crash Feb45, RWE 1945, SOC Feb46
NF957 15Sq Aug44, 38MU Sep45, SOC Sep47
NF958-9 15/300Sqs 21Aug44, Lost 13Sep44/14Oct44. 39/58hrs
NF960 115Sq(KO ·R), Damaged 14Oct44, Lost 28Oct44. 99hrs
NF961 218,630Sqs Aug44, Wrecked in crash 18Oct44. 68hrs
NF962-3 550Sq Aug44, Lost 31Aug44/Crashed 4Oct44. 23/99hrs
NF964 622Sq(GI ·L) 25Aug44, Exploded over Dortmund 3Jan45
NF965 622Sq(GI ·S) Aug44, Lost (Frankfurt) 13Sep44. 36hrs
NF966 514Sq(JI ·R),138Sq, Crashed burnt, Norway, 7Nov44
NF967 12Sq 31Aug44, Missing 29Nov44 after 25 operations
NF968 514Sq, 1668CU Apr45, Sold Scrap Feb46
NF969 149Sq(OJ ·F) Aug44-Jan45, 10MU Jun45, SOC Jun46
NF970 149Sq(OJ ·R),207Sq Jan46, 20MU Apr46, Scrap Jun47
NF971 149Sq up to Apr45, 207Sq, 15MU, SS(IA) Mar49
NF972 149Sq(OJ ·H) 26Aug44; Shot down, Gelsenkirchen, 5Mar45
NF973 149Sq up to end of 1945, 207Sq, 15MU, SOC Mar48
NF974-5 166/57Sqs Aug44, Lost 12/13Sep44 & 20/21Feb45
NF976 576Sq to Feb45, 15MU, Destroyed at Shoeburyness 1949
NF977 463Sq 6Sep44, Missing 23Oct44. 109hrs
NF978 100Sq(HW ·Q) 3Sep44, 38MU Jun46, SOC Sep47
NF979 207Sq 29Aug44, Lost during day raid 16Nov44. 153hrs
NF980 75Sq, Damaged 30Oct44, Missing (Osterfeld) 30Nov44
NF981 75Sq, Damaged 4 times, 44Sq, 39MU, SOC Aug46
NF982 101Sq, Destroyed in collision over sea 24Sep44
NF983 101Sq(SR ·D) Sep44, 46MU Apr45, SOC Jan47
NF984 50Sq Aug44, Damaged operations 1Jan45, and SOC
NF985 9Sq 2Sep44, Crash landed N. Russia 18Sep44. 15hrs
NF986 166,153Sqs, Burnt out near Croxley 4Nov44. 143hrs
NF987 90Sq(WP ·Q) Sep44, 61Sq Jun46, 15MU, Scrap Dec46
NF988 61Sq 1Oct44, Missing (Hamburg) 7/8Mar45
NF989 467Sq 28Sep44, Lost Flushing raid 23Oct44. 30hrs.
NF990 463Sq 1Oct44, Missing (Ems-Weser Canal) 6/7Nov44
NF991 44Sq(KM ·D) 4Oct44, 75Sq 21Jul45, SOC Oct45
NF992 617Sq 12Oct44, Missing (Bergen) 2Jan45
NF993 625Sq Damaged 21/22Feb45, 39MU Nov45, 2MPRD Jun47
NF994 218Sq(HA ·N) Oct44, Overshot Chedburgh 22/23Apr45
NF995 195,186,138,90(WP ·D)Sqs, 9MU Jul47, Scrap 1948
NF996 625Sq(CF ·J2) 20Oct44, Missing (Chemnitz) 14/15Feb45
NF997 61Sq 30Oct44, 39MU May46, SOC 2MPRD Jun47
NF998 550Sq Sep44; Wrecked, operations, Manston 23/24Feb45
NF999 103Sq, Damaged 24Sep44, Lost (Munich) 7/8Jan45
NG113 75Sq(AA ·D) 2Sep44, Missing (Chemnitz) 14/15Feb45
NG114 166Sq 3Sep44, Missing (Harpenerweg) 24Mar45
NG115 166,57Sqs Nov45, 39MU May46, SOC Jan47
NG116 12Sq 6Sep44, Missing 24Sep44. 22hrs
NG117 12,626Sqs Sep45, 5MU Nov45, Scrap Oct46
NG118 514Sq(A2 ·E), 1653CU, Crashed 25Oct45
NG119 576Sq 8Sep44, Lost (Nuremburg) 2/3Feb45
NG120 550Sq Sep44, SOC Nov45

NG121 514Sq(JI ·N) Sep44, Damaged 21Nov44 and SOC
NG122 115Sq(KO ·W), Damaged 3/4Feb45, 20MU Sep45, SOC May46
NG123 630Sq(LE ·U) Sep44, 39MU Oct45, Scrap Aug46
NG124 115Sq(KO ·U), Twice damaged, 46MU May45, SOC Jan47
NG125 630Sq(LE ·F) Sep44, Lost 38MU Sep45, SOC May47
NG126 57Sq 9Sep44, Lost ten days later (Bremerhaven). 25hrs
NG127 50Sq 10Sep44, Crashed at Skellingthorpe 1Jan45
NG128 101Sq Sep44, 46MU May45, Broken up Jan47
NG129 101Sq, Damaged 20/21Feb45, 46MU Apr45, SOC Sep46
NG130 195(A4 ·V), 218(HA ·N), 138,90Sqs; Became 6174M
NG131 101Sq, Damaged 14Oct44, Missing 17Dec44
NG132 550Sq Sep44, Missing in sea 17/18Mar45
NG133-4 550Sq Sep44, Lost 14Oct44/Wrecked 29Oct45
NG135 550Sq(BQ ·K2) Sep44, Broken up Dec45
NG136 166Sq(AS ·Z),153Sq,100Sq, Broken up on gun trials
NG137 90Sq,186Sq(XY ·D) 7Oct44, 5MU Aug45, SOC May47
NG138 90Sq Sep44, 37MU Nov46, SOC 2MPRD Feb48
NG139 101Sq(SR ·W2) Sep44, 41MU Apr45, SOC Sep46
NG140 90Sq,168Sq Oct44, 149Sq(OJ ·U) Jul45, 38MU, SOC May47
NG141 514Sq, Blown up at Waterbeach by PD325's bombs
NG142 514Sq(JI ·J) Sep44, 1668CU, SOC Dec45
NG143 207Sq 16Sep44, Lost mining 15/16Oct44. 57hrs
NG144 207Sq 16Sep44, Missing (Gdynia) 18/19Dec44
NG145 630Sq Sep44, 57Sq Dec44, Missing 4Dec44
NG146 186Sq Oct44, 170Sq Jul45, 30MU Mar46, SOC May47
NG147 186Sq Oct44; Crashed, exploded, Keddington 16Jan45
NG148 186Sq, 54MU, 149Sq Dec45, 15MU, SOC Mar48
NG149 186Sq Oct44, 300Sq Jul45, 15MU Dec46, SOC May47
NG162 195(A4 ·W), 186,150Sqs; 39MU Dec45, SOC Feb47
NG163 150Sq Nov44, 576Sq Sep45, Wrecked Oct45 and SOC
NG164 625Sq Oct44, 150Sq Nov44, Missing 31Dec44
NG165 550Sq Nov44, 166Sq Jan45, 38MU Dec45, SOC May47
NG166 195Sq(A4.H), 39MU Feb46, SOC Mar47
NG167 153Sq 6Nov44, SOC Oct45
NG168 115Sq Nov44, 15Sq Sep45, 5MU Oct45, SOC May47
NG169 625Sq(CF ·B2) 20Nov44, Missing 16/17Mar45
NG170 227Sq(9J ·S) 23Nov44, Lost (Ladbergen) 3/4Mar45
NG171 50Sq, Wrecked by pothole, Florrenes, 23Mar45
NG172 To Waddington 23Nov44, ASWDU SOC Nov48
NG173 103Sq Sep44, 57Sq Nov45, 60MU, SOC Mar46
NG174 186Sq Oct44, 625Sq Jul45, 39MU SOC Jan47
NG175 186Sq, Shot down in flames, Geilsenkirchen, 27Feb45
NG176 90Sq, 186Sq(XY ·H), Missing 19/20Oct44. 7hrs
NG177 50Sq 27Sep44, Missing (Lutzkendorf) 14/15Mar45
NG178 61Sq, 1659CU May45, 279Sq Sep45, 20MU, SOC May47
NG179 61Sq, Missing (Trondheim) 22Nov44. 242hrs
NG180 617Sq 27Sep44, Missing 8Oct44. 7hrs
NG181 617Sq,195Sq Mar45, 617Sq, SOC Oct45
NG182 61Sq Oct44, Damaged 6Dec44, Missing 7/8Mar45
NG183 166Sq 15Oct44, Missing (Dortmund) 20/21Feb45
NG184 153Sq Oct44, Lost returning from Mannheim 1Mar45
NG185 153Sq 7Oct44, Missing (Duisburg) 21/22Jan45
NG186 195Sq(A4 ·O), Missing (Dessau) 7/8Mar45
NG187 195,218,138Sqs; 541Sq 1946, 15MU, SOC Jan47

Jane graced NG206 of No. 9 Squadron.

NG188 195Sq Oct44, 115Sq(A4 ·U) Feb45, 39MU, SOC Jan47
NG189-90 153Sq Oct44, Wrecked 3Dec44/Lost 14Oct44
NG191 463Sq 1Oct44, Missing (Ems-Weser canal) 6Nov44

NG192 550Sq Oct44, Lost 19/20Oct44 on first operation
NG193 463Sq, Damaged 1Nov44, Missing 15Jan45
NG194 463Sq, 58MU Aug45, 22MU Mar46, Scrap Jun47
NG195 44Sq, Damaged 13Feb45, 46MU Jun45, SOC Jan47
NG196 467Sq, Crash 18Apr45, 46MU Oct45, SOC Jan47
NG197 467Sq 5Oct44, Missing (Siegen) 1/2Feb45
NG198 To 619Sq 6Oct44 and crashed same day.
NG199-200 57/166Sqs 5Oct44, Lost 6Dec/27Nov44. ?/92hrs
NG201 153Sq 18Oct44, Lost on day raid (Essen) 11Mar45
NG202 170Sq 15Oct44, 58MU May45, SOC Dec45
NG203 514Sq 10Oct44, 138Sq 19Mar45, SOC Feb46
NG204 207Sq 18Oct44, Missing (Ladbergen) 3/4Mar45
NG205 115Sq (IL ·D), 54MU Mar45, 39MU Sep45, SOC Jan47
NG206 9Sq(WS ·J) Oct44, To Tollerton for scrap Sep45. 31ops
NG218 153Sq Oct44, Scampton Oct45, 20MU Nov45, SOC Oct46
NG219 195Sq(A4 ·T) 10Oct44, Lost (Solingen) 4Nov44. 32hrs
NG220 9(WS ·B),619,463Sqs; 22MU Oct45, Scrap Jan47
NG221 550Sq Oct44, Damaged 16Nov44, SOC Oct45
NG222 106Sq,1654CU Jan45, Fell in sea 12Apr45
NG223 9,106,9Sqs; Missing (Ladbergen) 1Jan45
NG224 149,138,149Sqs; 15MU 27Jul46, SOC Jan47
NG225 9Sq,57Sq(DX ·K),514Sq(A2 ·J), Scrap Feb46
NG226 189Sq 29Nov44, 5MU 12Jan46, Scrap Feb47
NG227 1656CU 5Dec44, Crashed 2/3Apr45
NG228 617Sq(V), Missing from *Lützow* attack 16/17Apr45
NG229 7Sq(MG ·S) Jan45, Missing (Harburg) 4/5Apr45
NG230 207Sq, Missing (Bohlen) 5/6Mar45
NG231 61Sq Jan45, 46MU Jul45, Broken up Jan47
NG232 433Sq, 20MU, to Royal Navy, 10MU, SOC Mar47
NG233 433Sq 5Jan45, Missing mining 12/13Mar45
NG234 Conv. to Mk.III, 463Sq Oct44, Lost 13/14Feb45
NG235 9Sq(WS ·H) Oct45, Missing 8Apr45. 23ops
NG236 195,514,115(KO ·J)Sqs; Crash Jul45, 39MU, Scrap 46
NG237 625Sq(CF ·S) 21Oct44, Missing (Nordhausen) 3/4Apr45
NG238 625Sq(CF ·E2) 21Oct44, Missing (Duren) 16Nov44
NG239 625Sq, Last seen, wheels down, Wanne Eickel 9Nov44
NG240 625Sq(CF ·F2) 21Oct44, Missing (Chemnitz) 5/6Mar45
NG241 61Sq, Crashes 29Oct/19Dec44, Abandoned Metz 2/3Feb45
NG242 9,619,463Sqs; 22MU Oct45, Scrap Jun47
NG243 550Sq 24Oct44, SOC Nov45
NG244 626Sq 22Oct44, Crashed and blew up at Wickenby 22Dec44
NG245 207Sq Oct44, Crash 3May45, 15MU, SS(IA)Mar49
NG246 550Sq 22Oct45, SOC Nov45
NG247 626Sq Oct44, 39MU Oct45, 2MPRD Jun47
NG248 626,138,149Sq(OJ ·W)Sqs; 10MU Jul47, SOC Feb47
NG249 7Sq, Lindholme 9Jan46, 38MU Feb46, SOC May47
NG250 550Sq Nov44, 100Sq Nov45, SOC Mar46
NG251 550Sq 2Nov44, Missing (Leuna oil plant) 6Dec44
NG252 9Sq(WS ·R) Oct44, Burnt after take-off 7 a.m. 1Jan45
NG253 625Sq Nov44, Crashed 24Jul45, SOC Oct45
NG254 100Sq Nov44, 15MU May46, Destroyed in trials Sep49
NG255 166Sq Oct44-Aug45, Broken up Nov45
NG256 463Sq 2Nov44, Undershot at Seething 6Nov44
NG257 9Sq Oct44, Missing 12Jan45. 10ops
NG258 630Sq, Hit ground at Scanfield Farm, Lincs, 22Dec44
NG259 630Sq(LE ·N), 617Sq Jul45, 300Sq, 46MU, SOC Jan47
NG263 150Sq; Crew baled, crashed at Watlington 13Mar45
NG264 150Sq Nov44-May46 then 10MU, Scrap Mar47
NG265-6 300Sq Nov44, SOC Feb46/Lost 23/24Feb45
NG267 625Sq 27Oct44, Lost (Dortmund) 20/21Feb45
NG268 150Sq 1Nov44, Damaged 25Mar45, SOC Nov45
NG269 300Sq Nov44, Hit tree 8Jun46 in search operation
NG270 1651CU, Crashed in bad weather near Upton 11Dec44
NG271 1651CU, 50Sq Dec44, Burnt Waddington village 6Apr45
NG272 1651CU,1653CU Jul45, 38MU Feb46, Scrap May47
NG273 576Sq Nov44-Sep45, 22MU Oct45, Scrap Jun47
NG274 1651,1668CUs; Overshot Cottesmore, burnt 3Oct45
NG275 1651CU Nov44, 463Sq Jan45, Missing (Siegen) 1/2Feb45
NG276 103Sq 12Nov44, Missing (Leuna oil plant) 6Dec44
NG277 424Sq(QB ·G) 6Jan45, 20MU 14Nov45, Scrap Oct46
NG278 9Sq Jan45, Damaged 23Mar45, 20MU, Scrap Nov46
NG279 424Sq,427Sq Oct45, 15MU Mar46, Scrap Mar48
NG280-1 424Sq(QB ·U/X)Feb45. 22/5MUs Nov45, Scrap May47
NG282 12Sq Feb45, Short's Oct45, 38MU, Scrap May47

189

NG283 300Sq 8Feb45, Crashed 5Oct45
NG284 Defford Feb45; 186,218Sqs; 5MU Aug45, SS Aug48
NG285 626Sq(UM ·O2) 22Feb44, 39MU Nov45, Scrap Feb47
NG286 207Sq Feb45, 619Sq, Missing (Hamburg) 7/8Mar45
NG287 550Sq 1Nov44, Missing 15/16Mar45
NG288 150Sq 13Nov44, 46MU Jun45, Scrap Jan47
NG289 550Sq 3Nov44, SOC Mar45
NG290 550Sq, 166Sq, Missing (Munich) 7/8Jan45
NG291 150Sq Nov44, SOC Nov45
NG292 100Sq Nov44, 15MU May46, Used as target Jan48
NG293 186Sq Nov44, Crash May46, 46MU Sep45, SOC Dec45
NG294 625Sq Nov44, Missing (Ludwigshafen) 15Dec44
NG295 150Sq, 1651CU, 1668CU (ZK ·N) Jul45, SOC Dec45
NG296-7 227/166Sq Nov44, Lost 6Dec44/(Cologne) 24Dec44
NG298 514Sq,75Sq Apr45, 1659CU, 38MU, Scrap Sep47
NG299 622,149,207,90Sqs; 37MU Nov46, Scrap Feb48
NG300 622Sq(GI ·T) 5Nov44, 39MU 17Feb45, SOC Nov46
NG301 622Sq Dec44, 1659CU Jun45, 38MU Sep45, Scrap May47
NG302 50Sq 14Nov44, Hit by Allied A.A. fire 17Dec44
NG303 166Sq 9Nov44, Overshot Leeming 22Dec44
NG304 166Sq, Twice damaged, Overshot Kirmington 8Oct45
NG305 195Sq 9Nov44, Damaged 5Dec44. SOC Jun47
NG306 90Sq(WP ·B), Repaired after crash 8Dec44. SOC Feb46
NG307 189Sq Nov44, Crashed near Jarny, France 2/3Feb45
NG308 189Sq 10Nov44, Missing (Harburg) 7/8Mar45
NG321 189Sq Twice damaged, Missing 21/22Feb45
NG322 75Sq Nov44, 514Sq Jul45, 54MU,5MU, Scrap Feb47
NG323-4 90/625Sqs Nov44, Crashed 21Dec44/Lost 7Mar45
NG325 189Sq Nov44, Crashed at East Rudham 3/4Mar45
NG326 50Sq Nov44, Hemswell Dec45, 39MU, 2MPRD Jan47
NG327 49Sq 28Nov44, Missing (Gravenhorst) 21/22Feb45
NG328 100Sq(HW ·G2) Nov44, 60MU Feb46, SOC Mar48
NG329 463Sq 28Nov44, Missing (Gravenhorst) 21/22Feb45
NG330 218Sq(HA ·M) 19Nov44, Lost (Vohwinkel) 31Dec44
NG331 550Sq 18Nov44, Missing (Hanover) 5/6Jan45
NG332 115Sq Shot down by Allied A.A., Namur 1Jan45
NG333 150Sq(IQ ·S), 39MU Apr46, 2MPRD Jun47
NG334 625Sq, Dam op. 21/22Feb45, 20MU Nov45, Scrap Oct46
NG335-6 153/550(BQ ·B)Sqs Nov44, Lost (Zeitz) 16Jan/16Mar45
NG337 625Sq Nov44, Scampton and 39MU Nov45, Scrap Sep46
NG338 15Sq(LS ·M) Nov44, 5MU Oct45, Broken up May47
NG339 617Sq, Damaged 23Mar45; 15,44Sqs; 37MU, SOC Oct47
NG340 617,15,44Sqs; Became 6421M at Locking
NG341 9Sq,61Sq Jan45, 9MU Jun46, 2MPRD Apr47
NG342 50Sq Jan45, Lost Hamburg day raid 9Apr45
NG343 434Sq Jan45, 429Sq Mar45, 39MU Mar46, 2MPRD Jun47
NG344 434Sq,429Sq(AL ·U), 15MU Feb46, 2MPRD Oct47
NG345 434Sq Feb-Mar1945, 429Sq(AL ·V), Lost (Hamburg) 31Mar45
NG346 424Sq(QB ·N) 22Jun45, Missing (Dessau) 7/8Mar45
NG347 424Sq(QB ·P) Jun45, 22MU Nov45, Scrap May47
NG348 424Sq(QB ·Q) 24Jan45, 5MU Apr45, Scrap Dec46
NG349 170Sq(TC ·A2), 576Sq Sep45, 38MU, Scrap May47
NG350 514Sq(JI ·G) 19Nov44, Lost (Osterfeld) 16Dec44
NG351-2 195/49Sqs Nov44, Lost 12Dec44 & 16/17Mar45
NG353 186Sq(XY ·X) 23Nov44, Missing (Dresden) 13/14Feb45
NG354 186Sq Nov44, 626Sq Jul45, 39MU Oct45, SOC Dec46
NG355-6 149Sq(OJ ·F/O) Dec44, 10MU Apr46, Scrap Sep47
NG357 15Sq Dec44, SOC Mar45
NG358 15Sq(LS ·H)/(DJ ·U) Dec44, A. V. Roe Oct45, SOC Oct45
NG359 150Sq, Damaged 7/8Feb45, 20MU Jun45, SS(CC) May47
NG360 103Sq(PM ·F),100Sq, 15MU, Destroyed on tests Dec48
NG361 149Sq(OJ ·E) 6Dec44, 10MU 23Apr46, SOC Feb47
NG362 149Sq 6Dec44, Crashed and burnt Methwold 2Jan45
NG363 550Sq 5Dec44, Missing (Munich) 8Jan45
NG364 15Sq 25Nov44, A. V. Roe Oct45, SOC Oct45
NG365 15Sq Nov44, 138Sq Mar46, 15MU Dec46, 2MPRD Oct47
NG366 467Sq Nov44, 46MU May45, Scrap Jan47
NG367 61Sq Nov44, 50Sq Feb46, 83Sq Mar46, 9MU, 2MPRD, Apr47
NG379 1656CU Dec44, 20MU Aug45, SOC Aug46
NG380 61Sq Nov44, 5MU Jun46, Scrap Nov46
NG381 50Sq 30Nov44, Missing (Karlsruhe) 2/3Feb45
NG382 1669CU Dec44, Crashed taking off from Langar 25Feb45

NG383 1669CU Dec44, 1668CU(ZK ·G) Mar45, 1660CU, SOC Nov45
NG384 9Sq Dec44, 75Sq Mar45, 38MU Feb46, Scrap Sep47
NG385 1669CU Dec44, 50Sq Jan45, Missing (Politz) 8/9Feb45
NG386 61Sq Jan45, Missing (Bohlen) 20/21Mar45
NG387 149Sq Dec44, 54MU,149Sq,10MU, Scrap Mar47
NG388 195,35,207(EM ·N)Sqs; 20MU Apr46, Scrap Aug47
NG389 1666CU 6Dec44, 5MU 27Mar45, Scrap May47
NG390 550Sq Dec44, 100Sq Nov45, 60MU Feb46, SOC Mar46
NG391 550Sq Dec44, 166Sq Jan45, Missing 1/2Feb45
NG392 1666CU Dec44,1659CU Aug45,38MU Sep45, Scrap May47
NG393 166Sq Dec44, 1659CU Aug45, 38MU Sep45, Scrap May47
NG394 1666CU Dec44, 1659CU Aug45, 38MU Sep45, Scrap Sep47
NG395 57Sq(DX ·J), East Kirkby Nov45, Scrap Feb46
NG396 1661CU Dec44, 44Sq Jan45, Lost (Sassnitz) 6/7Mar45
NG397 1661CU, 44Sq Jun45, 39MU, Scrap Jan47
NG398-9 57/207Sqs Nov/Dec44, Both lost 14/15Mar45
NG400 424Sq(QB ·R) Jan45, 5MU Nov45, Scrap May47
NG401 9Sq, Hit near Bohlen, crashed Juvincourt 5/6Mar45*
NG402 101Sq(SR ·C) Feb45, 39MU Nov45, Scrap 17Jan47
NG403 170Sq Feb45, Lindholme Dec45, Scrap Sep46
NG404 460Sq Feb45, Crashed 14Jul45
NG405 101Sq(SR ·L) Feb45, 39MU Nov45, Scrap Sep46
NG406 Waddington, 1659CU Jul45, 38MU Sep45, Scrap May47
NG407 149,138(AC ·B),149Sqs; 10MU Apr46, Scrap Sep47
NG408 AAEE 16Feb45; 90,106,218Sqs; 5MU, Scrap Aug48
NG409 149,138Sqs; 15MU, Scrap Jan47
NG410 57Sq Dec44, Crashed at Nuneaton 5/6Mar45
NG411-2 625Sq Dec44, 20MU Nov45, Scrap Nov46
NG413 630(LE ·M),106,189Sqs; 22MU Feb46, Scrap Jun47
NG414 106Sq, Swung taking-off at Metherington 16Apr45
NG415 44Sq,207Sq Apr45, Spilsby Oct45, SOC Nov45
NG416-7 1661CU, 189Sq Jan45, Missing (Harburg) 7/8Mar45
NG418 625Sq,576Sq Apr45, 22MU Oct45, Scrap Jun47
NG419 9Sq(WS ·U), 617Sq, 100Sq, 15MU, Target aircraft Jan49
NG420 103Sq(PM ·Q) Dec44, Missing (Cologne) 24Dec44
NG421 150Sq; Collided with PB515 over Lincs, 2Jan45
NG434 35Sq,467Sq Jun45, 38MU Feb46, Scrap May47
NG435 Crashed in transit from A.W.A. Ltd., 18Jan45
NG436 35Sq, 1656CU Aug45, 12Sq, 15MU, Scrap Nov46
NG437 35,405,35Sqs; 1656,1653CUs; stalled 18Mar46
NG438 35,467,207Sqs; 5MU Feb46, Scrap May47
NG439 32MU, 463Sq, Crashed Nocton-Scopwick Rd. 25Mar45
NG440 32MU, 35Sq Jan45, Missing 8/9Apr45
NG441 433Sq Jan45, 424Sq(QB ·L), 20MU Nov45, Scrap Jul46
NG442 9Sq(WS ·F) Jan-Sep45, Lindholme, 38MU, Scrap Sep47
NG443 35,582,15(LS ·B)Sqs; 38MU Jul45, Scrap Sep47
NG444 15Sq(LS ·Y) Jan45, 38MU Feb46, Scrap May47
NG445 617,15(DJ ·E),44(KM ·O)Sqs; 9MU, Scrap Apr48
NG446 424,427Sqs Oct45, 15MU Mar46, Target Apr49

A Merlin 24 of Lancaster NG465.

NG447 622Sq(GI ·U) Jan45, Lost (U-boat yards, Kiel) 9/10Apr45
NG448 75,138,149Sqs; 10MU Jul46, Scrap Jan47
NG449 75Sq(AA ·T), Lost in Munster viaduct raid 21Mar45

NG450 195Sq,218Sq Jan45, Missing 22Feb45
NG451 424Sq,427Sq Oct45, 39MU May46, Scrap Sep46
NG452 195,103,57Sqs; Tollerton for scrap Mar46
NG453 83Sq, Caught fire at Coningsby, exploded, 9Feb45
NG454 83Sq Jun45, 9MU Jul46, Scrap Feb47
NG455 467Sq 3Jun45, Lost Ladbergen raid 7/8Feb45
NG456 424Sq(QB·D) Jan45, 5MU Nov45, Scrap Jan47
NG457-8 424Sq(QB·C/H) Jan45, Lost Mar45 (Chemnitz)
NG459 433Sq Jan45, 39MU Apr45, Scrap Jan47
NG460 433Sq, Crashed in Dishforth village 1Feb45
NG461 189Sq Jan-Dec45, 5MU, 39MU, Scrap Feb47

Lancaster centre sections at the Austin works.

NG462 218,90,207Sqs; 15MU Sep46, Scrap Dec46
NG463 218Sq,7Sq Aug45, 5MU Sep45, Scrap Mar48
NG464 576Sq 7Feb45, Burnt in crash 21/22Feb45
NG465 SIU; 90,186,218Sqs; Marham Aug45, 20MU Mar46, R-R Aug46, Dart fitted in nose Oct47, Disposal Mar54
NG466 460Sq(AR·Y) 1Feb45, Lost (Bruchstrasse) 21/22Mar45
NG467 Defford; 90,186,218Sqs; 1BDU, 15MU, Scrap Oct46
NG468 460Sq(AR·J2) 1Feb45, Lost (Duisberg) 21/22Feb45
NG469 463Sq Feb45, Lost in canal raid, Ladbergen, 3/4Mar45
NG482 97Sq(OF·A), 15MU Jul46, Destroyed HAA trials Dec48
NG483 619Sq,463Sq Aug45, 22MU Oct45, Scrap Jun47
NG484 424Sq Jan45, 5MU Nov45, Scrap Jan48
NG485 467Sq, 35Sq Jun45, 5MU Apr46, Scrap Nov46
NG486 9Sq Jan45, Lindholme Jan46, 38MU Feb46, Scrap Sep47
NG487 9Sq 14Jan45, SOC Apr46. 21ops
NG488 153Sq 1Feb45, Missing (Misburg) 15/16Mar45
NG489 617,15(DJ·M),44Sqs; Became 6501M at Lindholme
NG490 61Sq Jan45, 46MU May45, Broken up Jan47
NG491-2 103Sq Jan45, Missing 18/19 and 16/17Mar45
NG493 433Sq, Damaged 24Mar45, 20MU, Scrap Jul46
NG494 617,15(DJ·B)Sqs; From 44Sq to 2RS as 6449M
NG495 9Sq(WS·R) Jan45, 38MU Feb46, Scrap Sep47
NG496 433Sq(BM·N) Feb45, 20MU Nov45, Scrap Nov46
NG497 434(IP·B),433,427Sqs; 15MU, Scrap Mar48
NG498 433Sq Feb45, 39MU Nov45, SOC Dec46
NG499 9Sq(WS·W) Jan45, 38MU Feb46, Scrap May47
NG500 153Sq Feb45, 12Sq Sep45, Lindholme Mar46 and SOC
NG501 300Sq 3Feb45, Wrecked 8Mar45
NG502 460Sq, Shot down by intruder, Langworth, 3/4Mar45
NG503 619Sq 13Feb45, Missing (Wurzburg) 16/17Mar45

Serial Range NN694—NN816   **Lancaster B.I**

100 Lancaster B.I ordered from Austin Motors (Longbridge) and delivered from March 1944 to February 1945 with Merlin 24 engines except for last ten with Merlin 22 engines.

NN694 Avro 27Mar44, 50Sq Apr44, Lost (Lille) 10Nov44. 20hrs
NN695 619Sq 27Apr44, Crashed 22May44
NN696 576Sq ex-32MU 24May44, Missing 22Jun44
NN697 44Sq(KM·R) 25May44, Missing (Etampes) 9Jun44. 25hrs
NN698-9 90/625Sqs, Wrecked 28Nov44/3Dec44
NN700 15Sq 15Jul44, Missing 8Aug44. 58hrs
NN701 57Sq (DX·K), 429Sq (AL·T) Mar45, 39MU May45, Scrap Jan47
NN702 630Sq(LE·J),617Sq Jul45, 46MU Mar46, Scrap Jan47
NN703 630Sq,467Sq Jul45, 39MU Jan46, 2MPRD Jan47
NN704 15,218(HA·S)514,195Sqs; 10MU Jan46, Scrap Oct46
NN705 101Sq ex-32MU, Lost over Russelsheim 26Aug44. 22hrs
NN706 115Sq 18Aug44, Missing 15Nov44. 168hrs

NN707 166Sq,57Sq 26Nov45, SOC Apr46
NN708 149Sq(OJ·Q) 25Aug44, Missing (Wiesbaden) 2/3Feb45
NN709 622,44(KM·U),15Sqs; 54MU Oct45, Scrap May47
NN710 75Sq, hit by bombs over target (Rheydt) 24Dec44
NN711 576Sq(UL·L2) 29Aug44, Lost (Neuss) 23Sep44. 51hrs
NN712 12Sq(PH·A) 2Sep44, Lost 17Jan45 after 19 ops.
NN713 166,103Sqs; 1660CU Feb45, SOC Mar46
NN714 467Sq Sep44, Lost (Harburg) 11/12Nov44. 112hrs
NN715 550Sq 13Sep44, Missing 21/22Feb45
NN716 218Sq(HA·Y),514,279Sqs; 5MU Sep45, Scrap May47
NN717 514,138(AC·G)Sqs; 15MU, Fairey Aug47, SS Mar49
NN718 12,514(AL·J),300Sqs; Crash 25Apr45, Scrap Jun47
NN719 106,7,100(HW·R)Sqs; 15MU Sep45, Target 1948
NN720 90,186,576Sqs; 15MU, HAA Trials Jun49
NN721 463Sq Sep44, Missing (Rositz) 14/15Feb45
NN722 9Sq Sep44, Damaged 17/18Dec44, Lost 14Jan45
NN723 Conv. Mk.III, 619Sq Oct44, Lost 6Nov44. 16hrs
NN724 207Sq 14Oct44, Missing (Ladbergen) 7/8Feb45
NN725 106Sq Oct44, 7Sq Jan45, 38MU Sep45, Scrap May47
NN726 106Sq 14Oct44, Missing (Gydnia) 18Dec44
NN739 170Sq(TC·Q) Oct44, Missing (Bottrop) 3/4Feb45
NN740 195,218,514,279Sqs; 5MU Sep45, Scrap Dec46
NN741 12Sq 25Oct44, Lost 7/8Mar45 after 31 operations
NN742 150Sq(IQ·U) Nov44, 38MU Feb46, Scrap May47
NN743-4 150/170(TC·W)Sqs, Lost 12Dec44/21Feb45
NN745 75Sq 4Nov44, Lost mining (near Oslo) 21Nov44. 17hrs
NN746 300Sq ex-38MU, Broken-up 20Feb46
NN747 75Sq(JN·O), 44Sq Jul45, 39MU Sep45, Scrap Mar46
NN748 300Sq,625Sq(CF·PL), 20MU Nov45, SS(CC) May47
NN749 576Sq Nov44, Crash 5Jan45, 38MU Jun45, Scrap Sep47
NN750 576Sq 7Nov44, Burnt after operations 28Dec44
NN751 619Sq,617Sq Jul45, 106Sq Sep45, Scrap Feb46
NN752 150Sq Nov44, 5MU Dec45, Scrap May47
NN753 90Sq, 15MU Feb46, Destroyed as target 1948
NN754 115Sq,195Sq(IL·F), 39MU Sep45, Scrap Nov46
NN755 115,195(JE·B),186,153Sqs; SOC Oct45
NN756 149Sq 25Nov44, 15MU 30Apr46, Scrap Mar48
NN757 625Sq,106Sq(ZN·K), 20MU Nov45, Scrap May47
NN758 103Sq, Damaged 20/21Feb45, Lost 16/17Mar45
NN759 227Sq Dec44, 24MU Mar45, 46MU Oct45, Scrap Jan47
NN760 149Sq Nov44, 207Sq Apr46, 15MU Apr46, Scrap May47
NN761 115,90(WP·V),207Sqs; 15MU Sep46, Scrap Dec46
NN762 90Sq(WP·Y), Air Survey Flt, 541Sq, 20MU, Scrap Aug47
NN763 166Sq Dec44, 38MU 13Dec45, SOC Sep47
NN764 1667,1662,1656,1653CUs; 15MU Sep46, Deteriorated
NN765 57Sq Jan45, Blown up by PB360 17Apr45
NN766 103Sq 11Dec44, Missing (Munich) 7Jan45
NN767 1666CU Jan45, 15MU Sep45, Destroyed HAA trials 1949
NN768 619Sq Dec44, 44Sq Jan45, Lost (Harburg) 7/8Mar45
NN769 57Sq Jan45, 20MU Aug45, Scrap Aug46
NN770 166Sq, Damaged 13/14Feb45, 5MU Dec45, Scrap May47
NN771 1662,1656,1653CUs; Scrap Apr46
NN772 514Sq(JI·C2) 3Jan45, Missing (Wiesbaden) 2/3Feb45
NN773 514,75,44Sqs; 39MU Sep45, 2MPRD Jun47
NN774 630(LE·L), 186Sqs Jul45, SOC Feb46
NN775 514Sq(JT·F2) 3Jan45, Missing (Gelsenkirchen) 5Mar45
NN776 514Sq, Damaged 13/14Apr45, 38MU Jun45, Scrap Sep47
NN777 424Sq 5Jan45, Crashed at Dishforth 14/15Mar45
NN778 227Sq Jan45, 115Sq Sep45, 5MU Nov45, Scrap Nov46
NN779 433Sq 14Jan45, 22MU Nov45, Scrap May47
NN780 424Sq(QB·Y) 4Feb45, 38MU Nov45, Scrap Sep47
NN781 514,138(NF·N),149Sqs; 10MU Jul46, Scrap Feb47
NN782 514Sq,138Sq(AC·E),207Sq(EM·E), Wrecked Oct46
NN783 90Sq Feb45, 15MU Nov46, Fairey Aug47, SS(IA) Mar49
NN784 100Sq, Lindholme Dec45, 38MU Feb46, Scrap May47
NN785 153Sq 3Feb45, Missing (Dortmund) 20/21Feb45
NN786 RAE Feb45, 15MU Jul46, New Ranges Shoeburyness
NN798 625Sq Feb45, 20MU Nov45, Scrap Sep46
NN799 460Sq(AR·M) Feb45, 20MU Nov45, SS(CC), May47
NN800 12Sq Feb45, Missing 2Mar45 after 8 operations
NN801 Tested 7Apr45, turret trials as Mk.VII prototype
NN802 227Sq,115Sq Sep45, 39MU Nov45, Scrap Aug46
NN803 153Sq 3Feb45, Missing (Chemnitz) 14/15Feb45
NN804 463Sq Feb45, 22MU Oct35, Scrap Jun47

NN805 467Sq Feb45, 635Sq Jun45, 35Sq Aug45, SOC Feb46
NN806 576Sq 7Feb45; Swung, take-off, Fiskerton, 8May45
NN807 1660CU Feb45, 1668Oct45, Scrap Mar46
NN808-9 1660CU Feb45, Crashed, Swinderby, 20Jun45/2Mar45
NN810 1660CU Feb45, 5MU Aug45, SOC Dec45
NN811 1660CU Feb45, 1668CU Oct45, Scrap Mar46
NN812 1660/8CUs; Crashed 23Oct45, Became 5909M 12STT
NN813 1667,1656,1653CUs; Missing on training, 30Oct45
NN814 1667,1656(EK·O),1660CUs; Crashed, 30Nov45
NN815 1656CU Feb45, Crash-landed Lindholme 25Mar45
NN816 1653CU Feb45, Crashed 26Oct45

Serial Range NX548—NX794   Lancaster B.I/B.VII

200 Lancasters ordered from Austin Motors (Longbridge) in March 1943 and delivered as 50 B.I and 150 B.VII from February to November 1945 with Merlin 24 engines.

Lancaster I (Mk.VII interim)

NX548 427Sq(ZL·J) 24Feb45, 5MU Aug45, Scrap May47
NX549 427Sq Feb45, 433Sq Oct45, 22MU Nov45, Scrap Jun47
NX550 427Sq(ZL·V),433Sq Oct45, 22NU Nov45, Scrap Mar48
NX551 427Sq(ZL·G),424Sq Oct45, 20MU Nov45, Scrap Oct46
NX552 427Sq(ZL·S) Feb45, 10MU May46, Scrap Dec46
NX553 427Sq(ZL·H),424Sq Oct45, 5MU Nov45, Scrap May47
NX554 427Sq(ZL·F),424Sq Oct45, 20MU Nov45, Scrap Oct46
NX555 427Sq Feb45, 433Sq Oct45, 22MU Nov45, Scrap Mar48
NX556 153Sq Mar45, 20MU Oct45, Scrap Nov46
NX557 150Sq, 16 Ferry Unit Jan46, 10MU, Scrap Jan47
NX558 Avro Feb45, Austin Mar45, 46MU Apr45. Scrap Jan50
NX559 115Sq Mar45, 15Sq Sep45, 5MU Oct45, Scrap Mar48
NX560 460,207Sqs, 20MU Mar45, Became 5845M at 1RS
NX561 15Sq(LS·L) 2Mar45, 5MU Oct45, Scrap May47
NX562 576Sq Mar45, 15MU Sep45, SOC Mar48
NX563 153Sq Mar45, Missing 4/5Apr45
NX564-5 12Sq Mar45, 44Sq Apr46, 15MU Jul46, Scrap Dec46
NX566 227,619Sqs; BC Film Unit Aug45, 39MU, Scrap Mar48
NX567 189Sq 10Mar45, Missing 14/15Mar45
NX568 460Sq(AR·U) Mar45, 20MU Apr45, Scrap Nov46
NX569 101Sq Mar45, 44Sq May46, 10MU Apr47, SS(IA) Mar49
NX570 460Sq Mar45, 207Sq Aug45, 20MU Nov45, Scrap Nov46
NX571 138Sq Mar45, 3MU 24Jul47, 2MPRD Feb48
NX572 101Sq(SR·S),617Sq May46, 9MU Jul46, Scrap Jan47
NX573 153Sq Mar45, 20MU 8Oct45, Scrap May47
NX574 619Sq(OL·E) Mar45, 10MU Jul45, Scrap Oct46
NX575 101Sq Mar45, 619Sq May46, 10MU Jul46, Scrap Mar47
NX576 576Sq 19Mar45, 22MU Oct45, Scrap Mar48
NX577 170Sq May45, 50Sq Nov45, 5MU Apr46, Scrap Jun47
NX578 189Sq(CA·N) Mar45, 106Sq Nov45, SOC Feb46
NX579 101,9,101Sqs; BCIS, Became 6305M at Stradishall
NX580 57Sq(DX·V), E. Kirkby Nov45, 39MU Dec45, SOC Nov46
NX581 49,50,429(AL·W),463Sqs; 22MU, Scrap Jun47
NX582 150Sq 29Mar45, 5MU 8Dec45, Scrap Jan46
NX583 150Sq 29Mar45, Crash landed 1Jul45
NX584 463Sq Mar45, Abandoned in air (Lutzkendorf) 8/9Apr45
NX585 460Sq(AR·M) 30Mar45, Lost (Berchtesgaden) 25Apr45
NX586 420Sq Mar45, 38MU Feb46, Scrap Sep47
NX587 424Sq 8Apr45, 20MU 14Nov45, SS(CC) May47
NX588 460Sq(AR·C),57Sq(DX·B), 20MU Oct45, Scrap Aug46
NX589 460Sq(AR·T) Mar45, 20MU Nov45, Scrap Aug46
NX603 460Sq Mar45, 20MU Nov45, Scrap Sep46
NX604 460Sq(AR·D),57Sq(DX·D), 20MU Oct45, Scrap Oct46
NX605-7 460Sq(AR·B/C/N) Mar45, 20MU Nov45, SS Sep46
NX608 460(AR·H),550,12Sqs; 38MU, Scrap Sep47
NX609 101Sq(SR·A) Apr45, 44Sq May46, Crashed 17Sep46
NX610 101Sq(SR·F2) Apr45, 39MU Nov45, Scrap Sep46

Lancaster B.VII delivered to F.E. standard

NX611 38MU 16Apr45, Became WU·15 of *Aéronavale* & G-ASXX
NX612 38,32,20MUs and Austin Motors; SS(CC) Feb50
NX613 38MU, Avro Jun50, Became WU·1 of *Aéronavale*
NX614 Held in 38,32,38,39MUs; 2MPRD Oct47
NX615-16 38MU, Became WU·12 and WU·22 of *Aéronavale*
NX617 Held in 38,32MUs, SS(CC) Dec54
NX618 38MU,SIU, Doppler trials TFU 1949, Sold Avro Nov19

NX611 at Biggin Hill after flying from Australia.

NX619-23 38MU, Became WU·11/20/19/16/14 of *Aéronavale*
NX624-5 Held in 38,32,22MUs; SSMay52
NX626 38,32,39MUs and Austin Motors, 2MPRD Oct47
NX627 38,5MUs; Became WU·09 of *Aéronavale*
NX628 Held in 38, 22MUs; SSMay52
NX629 38,5MUs; CFS May48, Became 6735M at Cosford 1950
NX630 38,32,22MUs; Held for Near East Nov51. SS May52
NX631 40Sq(BL·U) Jan46, 10MU Sep46, Scrap Jun47
NX632 Swinderby Jan46, 5MU Mar46, EAAS Jan48, Scrap Jul50
NX633 32MU, 9Sq(WS·T), EAAS Jun49, Scrap Apr50
NX634 32MU, Middle East 1946, Became 6216M of 12SST
NX635 32MU, Crashed on take-off from St. Athan 22Oct45
NX636 9Sq(WS·A), RAE Oct48, SS Sep55
NX637 32MU, 9MU, Middle East, 2MPRD Oct47
NX638 9Sq(WS·Q) Dec45, 20MU Apr46, SS(BA) Sep53
NX639 32MU, Sold to France Oct53
NX640 32MU, Middle East 1946, 15MU, SS Sep54
NX641 9Sq(WS·U); 20,5MUs; CNCS Feb52, SS Dec54
NX642 Held in No. 32MU, SS Oct54
NX643 32MU Oct45, Near and Middle East Service, SS (BA) Feb55
NX644 30,32MUs; Near East, SS(CC) Dec54
NX645 267MU, EAAS, CGS, 5MU, SS Nov50
NX646 32MU, 40Sq in Near East, SS(BA) Feb45
NX647 32MU, Near East, 22MU, SS Oct54
NX648 32,109,22MUs; CNCS, 5MU
NX661 32MU, 2MPRD Nov47 after gale damage 16Mar47
NX662 32,5MUs; EAAS, CGS, 5MU, SS Nov50
NX663-5 38MU, Became WU·10/WU·21/WU·13 of *Aéronavale*,
    WU·13 is being preserved in New Zealand
NX666-9 38MU, Became WU·05/WU·23/WU·24/WU·18
    Aéronavale
NX670 38,32,39MUs; Ground damage Mar47, MUs, SS(IA) Apr51
NX671 Held in 38,32,39,5MUs; SS Nov50
NX672 Held in 38,32,39,15MUs; Near East, SS Dec54
NX673 9Sq; Film work, 1952 Upwood, 1954 Hemswell, SS Jul56
NX674 617Sq, Crashed end of Waddington runway 15Dec45
NX675 Held in 32,15MUs; SS Dec54
NX676 32,9,32MUs; EANS(CNS), RAE Oct51, Scrap
NX677 32,5MUs; EANS(CNS), 1689Flt, SS(BA) Feb55
NX678 9Sq(WS·A) (WS·S), 20MU, SS(BA) Feb55
NX679 617Sq Dec45, Filming Upwood and Hemswell, SS Jul56
NX680 32MU, 9Sq(WS·P), 20MU, SS(BA) Feb55
NX681 Held in 32,5MUs; SS(CC) Aug45
NX682 32MU, 40Sq(BL·S) 1945, 20MU, SS Jul47
NX683 32MU, 16AFU, 40Sq (BL·A) (BL·G), 20MU, SS Feb55
NX684-5 32MU, 40Sq(BL·O/B), 20MU, Scrap Dec49/Nov47
NX686 32MU, Middle East 1945-46, 5MU, Scrap May47
NX687 15Sq,5MU,EFS,EAAS, Crash France, Became 6816M
    Halton
NX688 Wyton 16Jul45, 22MU, SS(MOS) May52
NX689 Mildenhall 25Aug45, 15MU, SS Dec54
NX690 7Sq,40Sq(BL·W), Crashed N. Africa 19Sep46. 25 killed
NX691 32MU, Near East, 7Sq Dec47, SS Aug50
NX692 32MU, Near East, 20MU, 2MPRD Nov47
NX693 32MU, 40Sq(BL·H), 9MU, 2MPRD Apr47
NX694 32MU, Middle East, 20MU, 2MPRD Nov47
NX695 32MU, 40Sq(BL·P), 70MU, SS(W. F. Lamant) Aug49
NX696 32MU, Near East Feb46, 9MU, CFS, Scrap Mar50
NX697 32,20MUs; EANS(CNS), 5MU, SS(CC) Sep54
NX698-9 Held in MUs, SS(MOS) Apr52/SS(CC) Feb50

The end of NX732, Abu Sueir 1946.

NX700 32,20MUs; Empire Air Armament School Feb49, CGS Jul49, Scrap Mar50
NX701 32MU, Middle East 1946-7, 22MU, SS Sep54
NX702 Held in 32 and 15MUs, SS Dec45
NX703 32,38MUs; Became WU·O8 of *Aéronavale*
NX715-6 EANS(CNS) Jul47 until 1949, MUs, SS Jan51
NX717-8 32MU, 22/39MU, SS Oct54/2MPRD Oct47

Mk. VII used for official photography post-war.

NX719 32MU, EANS Shawbury Aug47, Crashed 18Dec47
NX720 32MU, EANS Jul47, 15MU Mar50, Shoeburyness Jul51
NX721 MUs, EANS Jun47, Scrap after ground mishap May49
NX722 32MU Dec45, 15MU Sep50, SS Dec54
NX723 32MU Dec45, 22MU Mar46, Sold to France Sep53
NX724 32MU,40Sq(BL·S) Middle East 1946-7, SS Mar48
NX725 32MU, Middle East Dec45-May46, 15MU, SS Dec54
NX726 Middle East, Became G-ALVC of Eagle Aviation
NX727 32MU, Middle East 1946-7, 20MU, 2MPRD Nov47
NX728 32MU, Middle East Dec45-Sep46, 9MU, 2MPRD Sep47
NX729 32MU, 40Sq(BL·F), 10MU, Scrap Sep47
NX730-1 32MU, Middle East 1946-7, MUs, Scrap Nov47/Jun52
NX732 32MU, 104Sq Crashed in Middle East 11Apr46
NX733-4 32MU, Middle East 1946-7, SS Oct45/2MPRD Nov47
NX735 32MU, Middle East 1946, CFS, Became 6713M of 12STT
NX736 32MU, 104Sq(EP·E), 10MU, SOC Sep47
NX737 40Sq(BL·Q), CFS(FDI·B) Jun47, Became 6736M
NX738 32MU, 40Sq(BL·C), To France as FCL·O2
NX739 English Electric Oct45, 617Sq Dec45, India, 20MU, loaned Silver City Airways, 15MU, SS(CC) Jul57
NX740 32MU, Middle East 1946, 20MU, 2MPRD Nov47
NX741-2 22MU 40Sq(BL·R/BL·T), 10/20MUs, Scrap 1947
NX743 32MU, Middle East 1946-8; 22,9MUs; Sold Avro May51
NX744 9Sq,617Sq(KC·J), Far East, 20MU, CNCS, Scrap Dec52
NX745 32MU, 617Sq, Far East 1946, Crash 24Jul46, SS Aug48
NX746-7 32MU, Middle East 1946, 5/20MUs, 2MPRD 1947
NX748 9Sq(WS·F) Nov45, Far East Jan-Apr46, 20MU, SS(BA) Feb55

NX749 MUs, EANS Shawbury Sep47, Scrap Apr51
NX750 9Sq(WS·V), 1689Flt Jun49, 20MU, SS Mar52
NX751 32MU, 22MU, SS Aug54
NX752-3 9Sq(WS·H/WS·R), 20MU May46, SS(BA) Feb55
NX754 32MU,ME 1946,15MU,CFS Jun47-50,5MU,SS(CC)Aug54
NX755 617Sq Dec45, 20MU May46, SS(BA) Feb55
NX756 9Sq,20MU Apr46, EFS May48, EAAS Jun49, Scrap Sep50
NX757 617Sq Nov45, 1689Flt Oct48, SS(MOS) Mar52
NX758 9Sq(WS·O) Nov45; 20,5MUs; Sold to France Oct53
NX770 9Sq(WS·D) Nov45, 15MU Aug46, SS Dec45
NX771 Damaged 24Oct45, EAAS Jan48, Crashed 15Mar48
NX772 32MU, Damaged 24Oct45, 58MU, SS(CC) Sep54
NX773 9Sq(WS·M)Nov45;20,5MUs;CNCS Feb51,5MU,SS Jun54
NX774 Damaged 24Oct45; 32,5MUs; EANS May47, Scrap Apr51
NX775 Damaged 24Oct45, F.E. Mar-Apr46, Sold France Aug53
NX776 617Sq Dec45, 20MU,EAAS Jan48, CGS Jul48, SS Nov50
NX777 617Sq Dec45, EFS Sep48, EAAS Jan49, Scrap Jul50
NX778 9Sq(WS·B), EAAS(FG·AD) Sep48, CGS Jul49, SS May50
NX779 Damaged 24Oct45, EAAS(FG·AB) Jan48, Scrap Sep50
NX780 617Sq Dec45,20MU,Lindholme Jan50,5MU,SS(CC)Dec54
NX781 Damaged 24Oct45, EANS May47, 15MU, Shoeburyness Aug51
NX782 Damaged 24Oct45, Film work Upwood & Hemswell, SS Jul56
NX783 617Sq(KC·G) Dec45, 20MU Apr46, SS(BA) Feb58
NX784 9Sq(WS·X), 20MU Apr46, EAAS Aug48, CGS Jul49, SS Mar50
NX785 617Sq Dec45, 20MU May46, SS(JD) Dec49
NX786 617Sq(KC·H) 20Apr46,EAAS Feb48,CGS Jul49,SS Nov50
NX787 617Sq Dec45, 20MU May46, SS Jun54
NX788 32MU 19Oct45, Crashed 30Nov45
NX789 617Sq Dec45, 20MU, EAAS Jul48, Crashed 23May49
NX790 617Sq Dec45, Temporarily instructional as 6786M
NX791 617Sq, Flying College Oct49, Exhibitions, SOC Nov53
NX792 32MU, Middle East 1946-7, SS(BA) Sep55
NX793 32MU, Middle East 1946, Became 6424M at EANS
NX794 32MU, Middle East Feb46-Nov47, 22MU, SS Oct54

Serial Range PA158—PA835　　　　　　　　**Lancaster I**

500 Lancaster B.Is ordered from Vickers-Armstrong (Chester) on April 5th, 1943, of which 235 were delivered from June 1944 to September 1945 with Merlin 24 engines. Many, as indicated, were modified to Far East (FE) standard.

PA158 90Sq 18Jun44, Missing (Dortmund) 3/4Feb45
PA159 90Sq 28Jun44, 1651CU Nov44, 22MU, SOC Jun47
PA160 300Sq(BH·E) 5Jul44, Crashed Goltho Hall 15Jan45
PA161 300Sq(BH·X) 6Jul44, Missing (Pforzheim) 23/24Feb45
PA162 61Sq Jul44, Lost (Trossy St. Maximin) 3/4Aug44. 51hrs
PA163 300Sq(BH·M) Aug44, Missing 29/30Aug44. 30hrs
PA164 622Sq(GI·P) Aug44, 44Sq Aug45, 38MU, SOC May47
PA165-6 61/149Sqs Aug44, Lost 5Jan45/Crashed 19Jul45
PA167 90Sq(WP·K) 10Sep44, 39MU Nov46, SOC Feb48
PA168 153Sq 7Oct44, 20MU Oct45, Scrap Sep46
PA169 467Sq 16Sep44, Abandoned (Ladbergen) raid 1Jan45*
PA170-1 15/227(9J·D)Sqs Oct44, Lost 4Dec44/SOC Jan47
PA172 9Sq(WS·G) 9Oct44, 38MU Nov45, SOC May47
PA173 576Sq 17Oct44, Missing (Munich) 7Jan45
PA174 626Sq(CF·G); Burnt out Wesley Lodge, Clacton, 23Oct44
PA175 576Sq(UL·K2) 5Nov44, 22MU Oct45, SOC Mar48
PA176 625Sq Oct44, 576Sq Apr45, 39MU Oct45, Scrap Sep46
PA177 100Sq 28Oct44, SOC Dec45
PA178 1651CU Nov44, 24MU Jul45, 10MU, SOC Jan47
PA179 166Sq 7Nov44, Missing 20/21Feb45
PA180 619Sq(PG·G) Nov44, 9Sq Jul45, 38MU, SOC May47
PA181 115Sq(KO·A) Nov44, 44Sq(KM·M) Sep45, 15MU, Scrap Nov46
PA182-3 189/207Sqs Nov44, SOC 21Dec45/Scrap Jan47
PA184 1656CU 2Dec44, Crashed 5Sep45
PA185 300Sq(BH·W) Nov44, Crashed Apley near Wragby 2Mar45
PA186 514Sq Nov44, 149Sq Mar45, 10MU, Scrap Dec46
PA187 467Sq(PO·F) Dec44; 635,35Sqs; TDU Gosport, SOC Jan47
PA188-9 1656CU/100Sq Dec44, SOC 28Dec45/Lost 16Jan45
PA190 12Sq 6Dec44, 626Sq Jan45, Missing (Nordhausen) 3Apr45

PA191 1666CU Dec44, 1659CU Aug45, 22MU, SOC Nov45
PA192 1667CU Dec44, 1656CU Oct45, Broken up Dec45
PA193 90Sq Jan45, 138Sq(AC·D) Mar45, 15MU, Scrap Feb47
PA194 1661CU Dec44; 106,7Sqs; SOC as target 1949
PA195 44Sq 30Dec44, Missing (Karlsruhe) 2/3Feb45
PA196 189Sq Dec44, 207Sq, Missing (Bohlen) 20/21Mar45
PA197 189Sq 31Dec44, Missing (Ladbergen) 3/4Mar45
PA198 619Sq Jan45, 9Sq Jul45, 15MU, SOC as target 49
PA214 227Sq(9J·P) Dec44, Lost (Lutzkendorf) 14/15Mar45
PA215 1662CU Jan45, 1665CU Apr45, 20MU, Scrap
PA216 626Sq(UM·C2) 31Dec44, Lost mining 18/19Feb45
PA217 103Sq Jan45, 100Sq May45, 22MU, Scrap Jun47
PA218 622Sq(GI·K) Jan45, 44Sq Aug45, 38MU, SOC Sep47
PA219 433Sq 6Jan45, Missing 4/5Feb45
PA220 300Sq(BH·P) 9Jan45, 15MU Oct46, SOC Mar48
PA221 100Sq(HW·V2) 12Jan45, 22MU Jan46, Scrap Jan47
PA222 50Sq Jan45, 61Sq Feb46, 5MU Jun46, Scrap Feb47
PA223 50Sq 12Jan45, Missing (Karlsruhe) 2/3Feb45
PA224 115Sq Jan45, 115Sq,R.Navy Nov45, SOC 780Sq Apr47
PA225 434,429(AL·H/G),433Sqs; 22MU, Scrap May47
PA226 434Sq(X) Jan44, 429Sq(AL·H) Apr45, 20MU,SS(CC)Mar47
PA227 BCIS Jan45, Wrecked Nov45
PA228 BCIS 21Jan45, 5MU Nov45, Scrap Mar48
PA229 625Sq 1Feb45, 22MU 8Nov45, SOC Mar48
PA230 460Sq 3Feb45, 207Sq Oct45, 20MU, Scrap Aug46
PA231 166Sq Feb45, Lindholme Dec45, SOC Feb46
PA232 106Sq Feb45, RWE Jan46, Scrap Nov50
PA233 300Sq(BH·J) 23Feb45, 15MU Aug46, SOC Jan47
PA234 166Sq 6Feb45, Missing (Nuremberg) 16/17Mar45
PA235 15Sq 19Feb45, 15MU Jul46, Scrap Nov46
PA236 166Sq; Crashed on approach, Kirmington, 30Jul45
PA237 101Sq 10Feb45, Missing (Pforzheim) 23/24Feb45
PA238 101Sq(SR·Z) 14Feb45, 38MU Feb46, SOC Sep47
PA239 90Sq(WP·S) 10Feb45, 15MU Sep46, SOC Nov46
PA252 90Sq Feb45, Became 6169M at 10STT Kirkham Nov46
PA253 90Sq Feb45, 207Sq May46, 90Sq Jun46, Scrap Oct47
PA254 90Sq Feb45, Shot down over Datteln, day raid, 9Mar45
PA255 619Sq(PG·V) Feb45, 9Sq Jul45, 617Sq Jan46, SOC Aug47
PA256 44Sq Feb45, 75Sq Jul45, 39MU, Scrap Sep46
PA257 460Sq Feb45, 433Sq, 15MU, Scrap Oct47
PA258 49 or 227Sqs, 115Sq, 22MU, Scrap May47
PA259 227Sq(QJ·Z), Missing (Bohlen) 20/21Mar45
PA260 427Sq(ZL·Q) 21Feb45, 39MU May46, Scrap Jun47
PA261-2 300Sq(BH·L/X) 20Feb45, 15MU, Scrap Dec46/May47
PA263 427Sq(ZL·E) Feb45, 5MU Mar46, Scrap Mar48
PA264 153Sq 1Mar45, 12Sq 29Sep45, SOC Apr46
PA265 576Sq 26Feb45, Missing 16/17Mar45
PA266 630(LE·P), 44,75,207Sqs; 5MU, Scrap May48
PA267 106Sq Mar45, 7Sq Jun45, 20MU, Scrap Nov46
PA268 550Sq 5Mar45, 39MU Nov45, Scrap Sep46
PA269 300Sq 12Mar45, Crashed at Wigston Magna 4Feb46
PA270 100Sq(HW·H) 2Mar45, 22MU 21May46, Scrap Jun47
PA271 427Sq(ZL·W) 6Mar45, 20MU May46, SS(CC)47
PA272 429Sq(AL·C) 6Mar45, 39MU May46, SOC Sep46
PA273 429Sq(AL·R) 8Mar45, 39MU May46, SOC Jan47
PA274 429Sq(AL·F) 10Mar45, 20MU May46, SS(CC) May47
PA275 207,460(AR·A),207Sqs; SOC Nov45
PA276 619Sq Mar45, 617Sq Jul45, 15MU, SS(IA) Mar49
PA277 619Sq 18Mar45, Crashed 11May45
PA278 103Sq 10Mar45, Lost Operation DODGE 4Oct45
PA279-80 227Sq Mar45, 115Sq Sep45, 22MU, Scrap 1947-8
PA281 101Sq(SR·J) 16Mar45, Crashed 12Dec45
PA282 576Sq Mar45, 150Sq Sep45, 39MU, Scrap Sep46
PA283 227Sq(9J·J) 15Mar45, 5MU Sep45, Scrap Jan47
PA284 189Sq 17Mar45, 106Sq 15Nov45, SOC Feb46
PA285 622Sq 20Mar45, Missing on day raid 20Apr45
PA286 424Sq 20Mar45, 39MU 14Nov45, SOC Jan47
PA287 227Sq(9J·N), Stretton Mar46, Scrap Jan47
PA288 550Sq(BQ·R) 22Mar45, 5MU Nov45, Scrapped later
PA303 103Sq(PM·E), 57Sq(DX·E) Nov45, 39MU, Scrap 47
PA304 460Sq(AR·K) Mar45, 207Sq Oct45, Crashed 29Jan46
PA305 166Sq Mar45, 15MU, Scrap May47
PA306 12Sq Mar45, 300Sq Jan46, 15MU, Scrap 47
PA307 576,170,50,83Sqs; 20MU, SS(CC) May57

PA308 166Sq(AS·W) 29Mar45, Crashed 4Sep45
PA309 550Sq Mar45, 39MU Nov45, Scrap Sep46
PA310 106Sq Mar45, 7Sq Jun45, 20MU, Scrap Nov46
PA311 170Sq Mar45, Lindholme Nov45, 20MU, SS(CC) May47
PA312 170Sq Mar45, 50Sq Nov45, 61Sq Feb46, Scrap Aug47
PA313 153Sq Mar45, 12Sq Sep45, SOC Apr46
PA314 463Sq Mar45, 15MU Oct45, Scrap Mar47
PA315 189Sq 30Mar45, 38MU Jan46, Became B·O36 Argentine
PA316 189Sq 30Mar45, 15MU Mar46, Scrap May48

Two views of PA474 in the seventies, marked to represent the aircraft flown by Sqn Ldr Nettleton V.C.; and missile testing by the French using PA389.

PA317 100 or 460Sqs, 10MU Aug45, Scrap Nov46
PA318 576Sq Mar45, 150Sq Sep45, 10MU, Scrap Dec46
PA319 103Sq Mar45, 57Sq Nov45, 39MU Aug46, Scrap Oct47
PA320 166Sq Apr45, 100Sq(HW·S), 22MU Mar46, Scrap 47
PA321 166Sq 31Mar45, 38MU Dec45, SOC Sep47
PA322 57(DX·P),630(LE·V),460,57(DX·P)Sqs; Scrap 47
PA323 427 or 433Sqs Apr45; 22MU Nov45, SOC Mar48
PA324 429 or 424Sqs Apr45, 39MU Nov45, SOC Dec46
PA325 103 or 530Sqs Apr45, 39MU Nov45, SOC Feb47
PA326 427 or 424Sq Apr45, 5MU Nov45, Scrap Mar47
PA327 427Sq(ZL·U) Oct45, 10MU Apr46, SOC Sep47
PA328 424Sq Apr45, 5MU Nov45, SS(CC)Aug48
PA329 61Sq 13Apr45, 9MU 20Jan46, Broken up 2MPRD Sep47
PA330 463Sq 17Apr45, 15MU 3Oct45, Scrap May47
PA331 106Sq Apr45, 7Sq, 20MU, SS(CC) May47
PA332 57Sq Apr45, E. Kirkby Nov45, 300Sq, 15MU, SOC 48
PA333 46MU 21Apr45, 45MU Oct46, SS 13Jun50
PA334 Ringway Apr45, ATDU Gosport Jan46, 15MU, SOC 48
PA335-6 46MU Apr45, 45MU Oct46, SS Jun50
PA337-8 46,45MUs; Royal Navy Dec46, Scrap Jun50
PA339 46MU Apr46, 45MU Oct46, Sold Avro Feb48
PA340 46MU Apr46, Mod.FE Jul46, SS(JD) 55
PA341 46MU Apr46, Airspeed Ltd Sep46, SS(JD)49
PA342 46MU May46, Broken up Jan47

194

PA343 46MU Apr46, Miles Aircraft Ltd Mar48, RAE 1948
PA344 46MU May45, 10MU Sep46, Became B ·037 Argentine
PA345 46MU Apr45, 45MU Nov46, SS Jun50
PA346 46MU Apr45, 10MU Sep46, Became B ·039 Argentine
PA347 46MU May45, Modified FE, SS(JD) Feb49
PA348-50 Held in MUs, Became B ·035/36/34 Argentine
PA351 46MU May45, Broken up 15Jan47
PA365 46MU May45, 10MU Sep46, Became B ·040 Argentine
PA366 46MU May45, AWA May48, 5MU, Scrap Sep51
PA367 46MU, Night photo trials RAE 1947, Scrap Aug50
PA368 46MU May45, 45MU Oct46, Scrap Feb48
PA369 46MU, May45, 10MU Sep46, Became B ·038 Argentine
PA370-1 46MU May45, 9MU Oct45, SS(JD)Mar49
PA372-4 46MU May45, 45MU Oct46, Scrap Feb48
PA375-8 10MU May45, Became B.031/32/32/45 Argentine
PA379 Mod.FE/P.R.1 ME Oct50, 683Sq, Crashed 10May51
PA380 15MU, Mod.FE, Gale damage Mar47, CSE, Scrap Apr50
PA381 38MU Mod.FE, CSE Watton 28Feb47, Scrap Jul50
PA382 Mod.FE; 22,32,9MUs; Became 6505M at Yatesbury
PA383 38MU Mod.FE, 115Sq(KO·D) (KO·K), Crashed 26Apr49
PA384 Mod.FE, 7Sq Apr46, 148Sq Oct46, Scrap Apr48
PA385 Mod.FE, 35Sq(TL·S) Feb46, 148Sq Oct46, SS(JD) Feb55
PA386 Mod.FE, 7Sq May46, 214Sq Dec46, Scrap Oct48
PA387 Mod.FE, 35MU May46, Became WU ·25 of *Aéronavale*
PA388 Mod.FE; 38,32,9MUs; SS Apr48

PA429 in French service at Dakar, 1959.

PA389 Mod.FE, Held at 38MU, Became WU ·24 of *Aéronavale*
PA390 38MU Jun45, Mod FE/PR, 15MU Jan47, SS Nov54
PA391 Mod.FE, MUs, 230OCU, No. 1806 Egypt AF, Sep50
PA392 Mod.FE, Held at 38MU, Became WU ·36 of *Aéronavale*
PA393 Mod.FE, 32MU, SS(Enfield Rolling Mills) Jan55
PA394 Mod.FE/PR, Middle East, 683Sq Jul51, SS Nov54
PA395 Mod.FE, Held 38MU, Became WU ·32 of *Aéronavale*
PA396 Mod.FE, Held at MUs, SS(CC) Jul45
PA410 Mod.FE, 115Sq(KO·A),149Sq(OJ·X), Crashed 14Feb49
PA411 Mod.FE, 35Sq(TL·P), 230OCU Mar47, Burnt crash 21Dec48
PA412 Mod.FE,115Sq(KO·J),15MU,Became WU ·38 of *Aéronavale*
PA413 Not traced.
PA414 Mod.FE, 35Sq(TL·Q) Feb46, 7Sq(MG·G) Oct46, Scrap Oct48
PA415 Mod.FE, 115Sq(KO·B) Jun46, 138Sq Oct46, SS(CC) Feb50·
PA416 Mod.FE, 7Sq 1946, 15MU Nov46, Became WU ·39 of *Aéronavale*
PA417 15MU Jan45, TFU Defford 46-49, Sold Avro Nov49
PA418 Mod.FE, 207Sq Jul46, 138Sq Sep46, SS(CC)Jun54
PA419 38MU Jan45, Mod P.R. 1 by AWA Jul50, SS(CC) Jun54
PA420 Mod.FE, Held in MUs, SS Jan51
PA421 Mod.FE, MUs, CSE(V7·F) Watton, Apr47, 58MU Aug50
PA422-3 Held in MUs until scrapped 1948/1949
PA424 Mod.FE, Kept 58MU for exhibitions 1950, Scrap Jan51
PA425-6 Mod.FE, Held in MUs, Became WU ·29/WU ·34

PA474 flying on airflow research from Cranfield.

PA427 Mod.FE, 230OCU,49Sq,Mod.P.R.1,82Sq,SS(JD)Sep55
PA428 Mod.FE, 49Sq(EA·H) (EA·K) Jun46, SOC May48
PA429 Mod.FE, 49Sq May46, Became WU ·46 of *Aéronavale*
PA430 Mod.FE, 49Sq(EA·U), Crashed Jun46, SOC May48
PA431-2 Mod.FE, MUs, Avro early 52, Became WU ·43/WU ·40
PA433 Mod.FE, 115Sq(KO·E) (KO·J) (KO·L), Target May51
PA434 Mod.FE, Mod. P.R.1; 541,82Sqs; Became 6493M
PA435 Mod.FE, 115Sq(KO·L), 2300CU, Became No. 1805 Eygptian Air Force
PA436 Mod.FE, 115Sq(KO·H) May46, 35Sq(TL·G) Jul46
PA437-8 Mod.FE, 7(MG·C)/49Sqs, Scrap Dec48/Feb49
PA439 Mod.FE,Mod.PR1; 541,82Sqs; Scrap Nov50
PA440 Mod.FE, 49Sq(EA·J) Jan46, 35Sq Jan48, SS May50
PA441 Mod.FE, 115Sq(KO·K), 230OCU, No. 1802 Egypt A.F.
PA442 Mod.FE; 207,90(WP·W)Sqs; 230OCU, Scrap Jul48
PA443 Mod.FE, Held at 20MU from Mar46,SS(IA)Apr51
PA444 Mod.FE, CSE(4S·A) Feb47, Bomb trials Dec52
PA445 Mod.FE, 15Sq, 230OCU ex-1653 HCU, Scrap May49
PA446 Mod.FE, 115Sq(KO·J), MUs, SS Nov45
PA447 Mod.FE, MUs, CSE Watton Mar47, Scrap Jul50
PA448 Mod.FE; 38,32,15MUs; Became WU ·45 of *Aéronavale*
PA449 Mod.FE; 149Sq(OJ·S) Jul46, 214Sq, SS Aug50
PA450 Mod.FE, 49Sq(EA·H), Crashed 5Oct48
PA451 Mod.FE, Wyton Jul46, BCIS, 230OCU, Crashed 10Nov48
PA452 Mod.FE, 115Sq(KO·G), Became WU ·35 of *Aéronavale*
PA473 Mod.FE; 22,32,15MUs; SS Nov54
PA474 Mod.FE, PR1, 82Sq Sep48, Flt. Refuelling Aug52
PA475 Mod.FE Mod.PR1, 82Sq(H) Oct50
PA476 Mod.FE, 44Sq Feb47, 230OCU, No.1801 Egypt A.F. 1950
PA477 Mod.FE, Held at 38MU, Became WU ·33 of *Aéronavale*
PA478 Mod.FE, CSE(4S·B), 6811M at School of Fire Fighting
PA509 Mod.FE; 38,32,5MUs; SS(CC) Dec54

Cancelled numbers were PA479-508, PA510-512, PA526-563, PA579-625, PA646-687, PA701-737, PA752-799 and PA816-835.

Serial Range PA964—PD196   Lancaster B.III/B.I

800 Lancasters ordered from A. V. Roe (Chadderton) in April 1943 of which 756 were delivered as 255 Mk.I and 500 Mk.III and one Lancastrian between May 1944 and March 1945 mainly from Chadderton with 87 from Yeadon. The following are all B.IIIs unless otherwise stated with Merlin 38 engines initially installed except for late production models which had Merlin 224 engines.

PA964 32MU 20May44, 7Sq 24May44, Lost 6/7Oct44. 244hrs
PA965 405Sq Jun44-Mar45; 1660,1656CUs; 12Sq, Scrap 15Nov46
PA966 35,156Sqs; 1661,1660HCUs; Accident 2Sep46 and SOC
PA967 115Sq 20May44, Later 75Sq, Lost 21Jul44. 109hrs
PA968 50Sq 21May44, Missing (Donges) 24/25Jul44. 169hrs
PA969 100Sq May44, Lost (Gelsenkirchen) 12/13Jun44. 39hrs

"VULTURE Strikes." PA995 poses after its 100th operation.

PA970 460Sq 2Jun44, re-allotted later to 405Sq, Lost 8Sep44
PA971 35Sq from 32MU 2Jul44, Missing (Kiel) 26Aug44
PA972 35Sq 3Jun44, 405Sq(LQ·D), Damaged 26Jul44
PA973-4 97Sq, Lost in sea 21Mar45/24Sep44
PA975 635,7Sqs; 1660CU, Cunliffe Owen May46, Scrap Oct47

PA976 35,7Sqs,TFU with H2S Mk.VI,213Sq,15MU, SOC 25Mar48
PA977 635Sq May44, 405Sq(LQ·T) Jun44, Missing 23Dec44
PA978-9 7/97Sqs Jun44, Lost 22Feb45/21Jul44
PA980 405Sq from 32MU 14Jun44, Missing 1Jul44. 16hrs
PA981 582Sq 2Jun44, 405Sq(LQ·K) 7Jun44, Lost 12Sep44. 196hrs
PA982 156,405,7Sqs; 1660CU, Modified ASR/GR; 203,179,224, 210Sqs; Crash May47
PA983-4 635/156Sqs Jun44, Lost 4Aug/15Jul44. 91/52hrs
PA985 103Sq 28May44, Damaged on operations 29Jul44. 167hrs
PA986 12Sq 28May44, Shot down over Holland 13Jun44. 6ops
PA987 Allotted 405Sq Jun44, transferred to 625Sq, Lost 16Jun44
PA988 582,35,405Sqs; Missing 17Aug44. 97hrs
PA989 626Sq(UM·U2) 27May44, Lost (Russelsheim) 25/26Aug44 207hrs
PA990 626Sq(UM·R), 5MU, Scrap Aug47
PA991 550Sq 29May44, Missing 29Aug44. 207hrs
PA992 630Sq May44, Missing (Stuttgart) 24/25Jul44. 106hrs
PA993 626Sq; Crashed, Stainton Crossing, Lincs. 20Oct44
PA994 50Sq 30May44, Missing (Königsberg) 30Aug44. 265hrs
PA995 550Sq(BQ·V), Missing (Dessau) Mar45, 100+ops. 600+hrs
PA996 50Sq May44, Lost (St. Leu d'Esserent) 7/8Jul44. 94hrs
PA997 576Sq 5Jun44, Missing (Sterkgrade) 16/17Jun44. 34hrs
PA998 61Sq 30May44, Missing (Darmstadt) 25/26Aug44. 102hrs
PA999 103Sq 29May44, Missing (Darmstadt) 13Jul44. 115hrs
PB112 15,195(JE·H)Sqs; Lost day raid (Witten) 12Dec44
PB113 405Sq(LQ·L), Crashed in fog near Downham Market 27Dec44
PB114-5 156/15Sqs, Wrecked 29Aug44/Lost 2Nov44. 103/350hrs
PB116 1661CU, 1323Flt Jul45, 39MU Oct45, SOC Nov46
PB117 460Sq(AR·T), 100Sq Dec44, Lost 16/17Mar45
PB118 7Sq ex-32MU,46MU,1654CU; Wrecked, burnt 3/4Mar45
PB119 582Sq Jul44, 1654CU Jan45, 10MU Aug45, Scrap Sep47
PB120 582Sq(6O·P), Lost Gremburg railway yards, 23Dec44
PB121 630Sq, Missing (Etampes) 9/10Jun44. 4hrs
PB122 106Sq Jul44, Crash landed in France 14Jun45
PB123 35Sq, 582Sq(6O·O), Lost (Le Havre) 8Sep44
PB124 7Sq(MG·H),106Sq Jun45; 50,617Sqs; 15MU, Scrap Nov46
PB125 460Sq Jul44, Missing 4Aug44. 9hrs
PB126-7 625/115Sqs Jun44, Lost 1Jul/13Aug44. 46/125hrs
PB128 576Sq(UL·S2) Jun44, Lost (Stuttgart) 28/29Jul44. 141hrs
PB129 405Sq(LQ·K) ex-32MU Jun44, Missing 26Sep44. 141hrs
PB130-1 115Sq Jun44, Lost 30Jul/30Aug44. 63/161hrs
PB132 75Sq Jan44, 514Sq Jul45, 5MU Sep45, Scrap Mar48
PB133 32MU, 97Sq Jan44, Overshot landing 13Jul45
PB134 83Sq ex-32MU Jun44, Lost 4Jan45
PB135 83Sq Jun44, 20MU,ASWDU Jan46, 34MU, Scrap Apr49
PB136 582Sq, 5MU, EAAS Jan45, Became 6261M at 10STT
PB137-8 15/156Sqs Jun44, Lost 16Nov/13Aug44. ?/92hrs
PB139 15Sq,195Sq(JE·F),186Sq, SOC in Middle East 31Oct46
PB140 83Sq ex-32MU, Wrecked 6Aug44. 81hrs
PB141 582Sq(6O·F) Lost after Cologne attack 23Dec44
PB142 514Sq(JI·A), Crashed 6Dec44, Became 5725M at 16STT
PB143 514Sq Jun44, Lost (Stettin) 29/30Aug44. 143hrs
PB144 106Sq 11Jun44, Missing 8Jul44. 52hrs
PB145 106Sq, Accident 6Apr45, 20MU Aug45, SS(CC) May47
PB146 9(WS·A),189(CA·A)Sqs; 1659CU(RV·K), Scrap Jul46
PB147 103Sq 12Jun44, Missing 29Jul44. 132hrs
PB148 7Sq(MG·C) Jun44, Lost (Sterkrade) 18/19Aug44. 102hrs
PB149 582,156Sqs; 1654,1656,1653CUs; Crashed 31Oct45
PB150 625Sq Jun44, 38MU Aug45, Scrap May47
PB151 TFU Defford 13Jun44, 15MU Mar47, Scrap May47
PB152 460Sq ex-32MU, Lost (Stuttgart) 19Oct44. 135hrs
PB153 166Sq Jun44, Missing (Nuremburg) 16Mar45
PB154 625Sq 12Jun44, Missing 4Nov44. 319hrs
PB155 460Sq(AR·K), Crashed near Kelstern village 19Mar45
PB156 97Sq(OF·R) ex-32MU Jun44, 20MU May46, SS(CC) May47
PB157 97Sq Jan44 until crash Mar46, 83Sq,20MU,SS(CC) May47
PB158 625Sq 15Jun44, Missing 2Mar45
PB171-2 300/100Sqs Jun44, Lost 19Jul/29Jul44. 68/102hrs
PB173-4 32MU, 635(F2·C)/405(LQ·P)Sqs, Lost 8Jan45/21Jul44
PB175 460Sq 7Jul44, Missing 19Oct44. 225hrs
PB176 460Sq, Down in N. Sea off Flushing (Ruibert) 1Sep44
PB177 32MU, 156Sq Jun44, Lost 25Sep44. 216hrs
PB178 514Sq, Collided over Pittsham Farm, Midhurst, 30Jun44

PB179 32MU; 582,7Sqs; Converted to ASRIII Dec45, 6OTU Jun46 236 OCU, Crashed 29Jan48
PB180 7Sq(MG·F) Jul44, Lost (Kiel) 26/27Aug44. 131hrs
PB181 97,83Sqs; Collided over France, abandoned, 8Feb45
PB182 32MU, 582Sq(60·D) Jul44, Crashed 20Jan45
PB183 32MU, 405Sq Jul45, Missing 13/14Feb45
PB184 582Sq(60·N) Jul44, Lost (Castrop Rauxel) 12Sep44
PB185-6 514/165Sqs Jun44, Lost 25Jul44/29Jan45. 56/?hrs
PB187 32MU, 460Sq(AR·E), Hit by own defence 2Jan45, Damaged in gale 18Jan45, Lost (Dortmund) 12Mar45
PB188 83Sq ex-32MU Jul44, Lost 11Nov44. 273hrs
PB189/G 44Sq(KM·A), Lost (Stuttgart) 12/13Sep44. 246hrs
PB190/G 44Sq(KM·J), 75Sq Jul45, SOC Oct45
PB191 106Sq, Crash 1Jan45, 24MU, ECFS, 10MU, Scrap Sep47
PB192/G 44Sq(KM·F), Missing (Ladbergen) 4Nov44. 379hrs
PB193 90Sq Jul44, Accident 29Jul44, Missing 13Sep44. 139hrs
PB194 12Sq ex-32MU Jun44, 1651CU, 5MU, Scrap Sep47
PB195 49Sq ex-32MU Jun44, Lost (Creil) 4Jul44. 9hrs
PB196 195Sq(JE·D), Lost in day raid (Witten) 12Dec44
PB197 35Sq, Crashed returning from operations 18Nov44. 165hrs
PB198-9 90/35Sqs Jul44, Lost 29Jul/30Nov44. ?/270hrs
PB200 35,582,97Sqs; Wrecked in France 10Nov44. 285hrs
PB201 12Sq ex-32MU Jul44, Wrecked 26Aug44. 142hrs
PB202 582Sq(60·E) ex-32MU Jul44, Lost 29/30Aug44. 121hrs
PB203 106Sq ex-32MU Jul44, Lost 12Sep44. 207hrs
PB204 90Sq Jul44, 1653CU(A3·E), Wrecked 19Oct44
PB205 44Sq, 619Sq Sep44, 1661CU Jan45, 20MU Aug45, SS(CC) May47
PB206 44Sq(KM·Q) Jun44, Lost mining 15/16Jul44. 43hrs
PB207 49Sq Jul44, Wrecked 8Jul44. 22hrs
PB208 619Sq(PG·S) Jun44, Missing 23/24Jul44. 49hrs
PB209 156Sq ex-32MU Jul44, Missing 12Aug44. 83hrs
PB210 619Sq(PG·V) Jun44, Lost (Karlsruhe) 2/3Feb45
PB211 630Sq; Hit sea in low cloud, mining, 24Jul44. 44hrs
PB212 7Sq(MG·S); Crashed in flames, Bungay, 28Jul44. 46hrs
PB213 460Sq, 1661CU, Crashed Hall Farm, Oxton 15/16Apr45
PB226 460(AR·G),49,115Sqs; 50 operations, 10MU, Scrap Sep47
PB227 460Sq, 1661CU, Swung landing at Winthorpe 25May45
PB228 635Sq(GI·A) Jul44, Missing (Hanau) 6Jan45
PB229 405Sq Jul44, Missing 2Jan45
PB230-1 83/49Sqs Jul44, Lost 13Aug/19Jul44. 55/44hrs
PB232 106Sq, Twice damaged; 46,45MUs; BTU, Scrap May48
PB233 405,7Sqs; 1660CU, 10MU, Scrap Sep47
PB234 467Sq Jul44, Lost (Revigny) 18/19Jul44. 39hrs
PB235 44Sq(KM·C) Jun44, Lost mining 4/5Oct44. 209hrs
PB236 630Sq(LE·F) Jun44, Missing (Revigny) 18Jul44. 42hrs
PB237 Jun44, Landed on fire in France 26Dec44
PB238 582Sq(60·K), 1654CU Jun45; 10,39MUs; Scrap Mar48
PB239 405Sq(LQ·D) ex-32MU Jul44, Lost 16/17Aug44. 56hrs
PB240 83Sq ex-32MU Jul44, Missing 13Aug44. 41hrs
PB241 7Sq(MG·X) Jul44, Lost (Scholven Buer) 6Oct44. 159hrs
PB242 166Sq 29Jun44, Wrecked 26Sep44. 271hrs
PB243 12Sq, Wrecked at Stainton-le-Vale 26Feb45
PB244 630Sq ex-32MU Jul44, Lost 18Aug44. 170hrs
PB245 619Sq(PG·L) Jul44, Lost 9Jul44. 41hrs
PB246 463,582Sqs; NTU, 1659CU, 39MU, SOC Nov46
PB247 12Sq ex-32MU Jul44, Lost 12Aug44. 85hrs
PB248 106Sq, 5LFS,115Sq Sep45, 22MU, Nov45, Scrap May47
PB249-50 32MU, 83/49Sqs, Lost 30Aug/26Jul44. 75/40hrs
PB251/G 44Sq(KM·O) ex-32MU Jul44, Lost 21/22Mar45
PB252 300Sq(BH·M) 4Jul44. Missing 25/26Jul44. 50hrs
PB253 576Sq(UL·A2) Jul44, Lost (Stuttgart) 28Jul44. 67hrs
PB254 460Sq(AR·K),156Sq Mar45; 58,39MUs; Scrap Feb45
PB255 460Sq(AR·X), Lost raiding Nippes railway yards 24Dec45
PB256 101Sq(SR·P) Jul44, Missing (Ludwigshafen) 1Feb45
PB257 32MU, 35Sq; 1667,1656,1660CUs; Wrecked 17Nov45
PB258 101Sq ex-32MU Jul44, Missing 13Aug44. 55hrs
PB259 514,218(HA·A)Sqs; 1659CU(FD·G), 39MU, SOC Aug46
PB260 626(UM·Z),463Sqs; SOC in Middle East Oct46
PB261 SIU, 619Sq,57Sq(DX·L) Nov45, 20MU, Scrap Oct46
PB262 405Sq ex-32MU Jul44, Wrecked 12Sep44. 65hrs
PB263 463Sq Jul44, Missing 29Sep44. 226hrs
PB264 463Sq Jul44, 20MU Aug45, Scrap Jul46
PB265 576Sq(UL·V2), Crashed in France 24Jul45. 54hrs

PB266/G 44Sq(KM ·S) Jul44, Lost (Stuttgart) 28/29Jul44. 75hrs
PB267 582,405(LQ ·X)Sqs; 1656,1653CUs, Scrap Aug47
PB280 57Sq(DX ·W) Jul47, SOC Oct45
PB281 106Sq Jul44, Missing 4Dec44
PB282 405Sq ex-32MU, 1665CU, 39MU; 12,9Sqs; Scrap Dec46
PB283/G 44Sq(KM ·K) Jul44, 1661CU Jan44, Scrap Dec46

The men flown home in PB341 with Nazi souvenirs.

PB284 106Sq Jul44, ' S ' mine experiments, RAE, SOC Mar51
PB285 460Sq, 1661CU Apr45, 1323Flt. Jun45, Crashed 11Sep45
PB286 207Sq Jul44, Spilsby Oct45, 20MU Nov45, Scrap Nov46
PB287 635Sq(F2 ·T) ex-32MU, Missing 14/15Feb45
PB288 35Sp,405Sq Apr45, 1653CU Sep45, Crashed 19Oct45
PB289 9Sq(WS ·B), 189Sq Oct44, Lost 21/22Dec44
PB290 463Sq Jul44, Missing (Giessen) 6/7Dec44
PB291 514,218Sqs(HA ·O), Damaged 8Feb45, MUs, Scrap Aug47
PB292 83Sq ex-32MU Aug44, Missing 26/27Aug44. 46hrs
PB293 207Sq Jul44, Spilsby Oct45, 20MU Nov45, SOC Nov46
PB294 207Sq; Down in sea on fire, operations, 28Jul44†
PB295 207Sq Aug44, Missing (Gravenhorst) 21/22Feb45
PB296 106Sq Jul44, Damaged 23/24Feb45, 5MU, Scrap Sep47
PB297 619Sq,57Sq(DX ·H) Apr45, Became 5849M of 12STT
PB298 106Sq; Belly landing, hit trees near Brandon, 19Sep44
PB299 467Sq Aug44, Missing (Rheydt) 19/20Sep44. 171hrs
PB300-1 49/460Sqs Jul44, Lost 21Nov44 & 3/4Feb45
PB302-3 156/106Sqs Jul44, Lost 27Aug/17Nov44. 56/291hrs
PB304 106Sq, Dived into ground at Pendleton 30Jul44. 47hrs
PB305 7Sq (MG ·K), 106Sq, Conv. ASRIII, 38Sq, Scrap 25Jul49
PB306 467Sq Aug44, Missing (Karlsruhe) 2/3Feb45
PB307 35Sq, 1667CU Feb45, 20MU Sep45, Scrap May46. 108hrs
PB308 35Sq ex-32MU, Missing 12Sep44. 79hrs
PB341 83Sq ex-32MU, 10MU Aug45, Scrap Sep47
PB342 61Sq,617Sq Apr45, 1653CU, Became 5914M
PB343 35Sq ex-32MU Aug44, Missing 5Jan45
PB344 630Sq(LE ·R), Lost on bomb disposal flight 15Jun45
PB345 83Sq ex-32MU Aug44, Missing 26Aug44. 31hrs
PB346 32MU, 619 and/or 44Sq, Missing 27Jul44
PB347 106Sq ex-32MU Sep44, Missing 20Sep44
PB348 57Sq ex-32MU Aug44; Crashed, burnt, 5Jan45
PB349 35Sq Aug44, 115Sq Sep45, 10MU Jun46, Scrap Nov46
PB350 101Sq(SR ·G), Damaged 2Oct44 & 15Aug45, Scrap Aug46
PB351 460Sq, Hit high tree, Houghton Hall, Norfolk 23Oct44
PB352 460,218,149Sqs; 1661CU, 1323Flt, 39MU, Scrap Jan47

PB353-4 49Sq ex-32MU Aug44, Lost 6Oct/21Nov44
PB355 49Sq, Crashed and exploded, Worthing beach, 17Dec44
PB356 619Sq 27Jul44, Missing 17Nov44. 257hrs
PB357 7Sq ex-32MU, Crashed 16Sep44, Lost 14/15Oct44. 80hrs
PB358 97Sq ex-32MU Aug44, Down in sea 15Aug44. 21hrs
PB359 49Sq Jul44, 106Sq Aug44, Missing 20Sep44
PB360 49,44,57Sqs; Blown up by own bombs E. Kirkby 17Apr45
PB361 35Sq,49Sq(EA ·R) Nov44, 38MU Sep45, Scrap May47
PB362-3 83/103Sqs ex-32MU, Lost 18Aug/19Aug44. 9/78hrs
PB364 35Sq ex-32MU Aug44, 1656CU, 12Sq Nov45, SOC Jan46
PB365 103Sq Jul44, Missing 30Aug44. 92hrs
PB366 35Sq ex-32MU Aug44; Damaged, burnt, 24Dec44
PB367 35Sq Nov44, 5MU Nov45, Scrap Feb47
PB368 83Sq Sep44, 50Sq Mar46, 20MU May46, SS(CC) May47
PB369-70 49Sq Jul/Aug44, Lost 11/12 & 4Nov44. 169/?hrs
PB371 9Sq Aug44, 582Sq Nov44, Lost (Cologne) 23Dec44
PB372 SIU,582,35,97Sqs; Damaged 27Sep45, 5MU, Scrap Aug47
PB373 32MU, 49Sq, 115Sq Sep45, Exploded mid-air 21Feb46
PB374 32MU, 49Sq Aug44, Damaged 1Nov44, Missing 8/9Apr45
PB375 156Sq; 1668,1660(TV ·P),1653CUs; 15MU, Scrap Aug48
PB376 97,83(OL ·F)Sqs; 15MU Jul46, Scrap Nov46
PB377 582,35Sqs; Abandoned in air 14/15Apr45
PB378 582(6O ·T)Sq, Lost 16Sep44. 91hrs
PB379 460Sq, Crashed in Sweden, 30Aug44. 24hrs
PB380 44Sq(KM ·S),75Sq Jul45, 39MU Nov45, Scrap Aug46
PB381 635(F2 ·S),582Sqs; Various CUs, 15MU, Scrap Aug46
PB382 57Sq(DX ·N) Aug44, Missing (Politz) 8/9Feb45
PB383 460,49,115Sqs; 20MU May46, SS(CC) May47
PB384-5 57/49Sqs Aug44, Lost 17Aug/2Nov44. 49/85hrs
PB397 625Sq, 170Sq(TC ·X) Oct44, Lost (Munich) 7/8Jan45
PB398 97Sq ex-32MU Aug44, Lost 26Aug44. 17hrs
PB399 101Sq(SR ·T) ex-32MU Aug44, 46MU Apr45, Scrap Jan47
PB400 576Sq(UL ·J2) Aug44, Lost (Kiel) 26/27Aug44. 52hrs
PB401-2 32MU, 635/405Sqs Aug44, Lost 12Sep/17Aug44
PB403 156Sq ex-32MU Aug44, Lost 16/17Apr45
PB404 619,227(9J ·X), 115Sqs; 39MU Nov45, Scrap Dec46
PB405 619Sq(PG ·S) Aug44, Lost 19/20Sep44. 116hrs
PB406 32MU, 460Sq,49Sq Apr45, 1323Flt Jul45. SOC Oct45
PB407 460Sq ex-32MU Aug44, Lost 7Oct44. 80hrs
PB408 32MU,97Sq,5MU,Cunliffe Owen Dec45,15MU, SOC Oct46
PB409 97Sq ex-32MU Aug44, Lost 24Sep44
PB410 97Sq ex-32MU Aug44, 12Sq Feb46, 15MU, Scrap Jan47
PB411 626Sq(UM ·Y2) Aug44, Lost (Lutzkendorf) 4/5Apr45
PB412 626Sq(UM ·Z2) Aug44, Lost mining 4/5Oct44. 127hrs
PB413 405Sq ex-32MU Aug44, Damaged beyond repair 2Nov44
PB414 No record of delivery to service: on exhibition
PB415 Conv. Mk.I, 617Sq Aug44, Overshot Lossiemouth 5Apr45
PB416 617Sq Aug44, Missing over Norway 17Sep44
PB417 44Sq(KM ·R) Aug44, Lost (Hamburg) 7/8Mar45
PB418 75Sq(AA ·C),514Sq Jul45, 20MU Aug45, Scrap Sep46
PB419 514Sq Aug44, BCIS Apr45, 15MU, Scrap May47
PB420 7Sq(MG ·O), 1660CU, Temporarily 6259M, Scrap Sep47
PB421 75Sq Aug44, 1653CU (H4 ·J), 15MU Oct45, Scrap May47
PB422 97Sq Aug44, Crash take-off Coningsby 13Jul45
PB423 32MU, 514Sq Aug44, BCIS Apr45, 15MU Aug46, Scrap Nov46
PB424 44Sq(KM ·X), 75Sq, Near East Dec45-May46, Scrap May47
PB425 57Sq ex-32MU Aug44, Lost 19Oct44. 70hrs
PB426 32MU, 514Sq, 1666CU Apr45, 5MU, Scrap Jul47
PB427 32MU, 75Sq, 1653CU May45, 1656CU, 39MU, Scrap Feb47
PB428 32MU, 207Sq, Collided on circuit 11Nov44. 145hrs
PB429 32MU 13Aug44, 49Sq 29Aug44, Lost (Bremen) 6Oct44
PB430 75Sq ex-32MU Aug44, Wrecked landing 17Sep44. 70hrs
PB431 7Sq(MG ·D),279Sq, Down in sea night training 7Nov45
PB432 49Sq Aug44, Crashed at Dry Doddington 26Nov44
PB433 49Sq, 115Sq Sep45, Crashed twice, SOC Apr46
PB434 61Sq 13Aug44, Wrecked 22Sep44. 64hrs
PB435 635,7(MG ·R),12(PH ·G)Sqs, 9MU Aug46, Scrap Apr47
PB436 61Sq Aug44, Missing (Königsberg) 29/30Aug44. 40hrs
PB437 7Sq(MG ·W); 1660,1668,1653(A3 ·P)CUs; 10MU, Scrap Oct47
PB438 115Sq(KO ·A), 97Sq, Crashed 10May45
PB450 97Sq Aug44, Missing on training 10Nov44. 146hrs
PB451 405Sq(LQ ·C) Sep44, Missing 18/19Mar45

PB452 83Sq Aug44, 12Sq Mar46, 9Sq, 15MU, Scrap Jan47
PB453 32MU, 635Sq(F2 ·S) Aug44, Missing (Essen) 12Dec44
PB454 7Sq(MG·J) Aug44, 46MU, Middle East 1946, Scrap May47
PB455 49Sq Aug44, 115Sq Sep45, 38MU Mar46, Scrap May47
PB456 101Sq Aug44, Crashed in flames Stirling 13/14Sep44
PB457 101Sq(SR ·V) Aug44, Missing (Pforzheim) 23Feb45
PB458 83Sq, Damaged Nov44, 46MU May45, 38MU, Scrap May47
PB459 460Sq(AR ·V) Sep44, Missing (Dortmund) 29Nov44
PB460 49Sq Aug44, 46MU May45, 5MU,BTU,9MU,SS(JD) Aug48
PB461 97Sq Aug44, Missing 21/22Dec44
PB462 100Sq(HW·P2), 1653CU(A3·D), Became 5815M
PB463 460,49Sqs; Dived into ground Fulbeck 22Apr45
PB464 625Sq Aug44, 5MU, Middle East 1945-6, 2MPRD Jun47
PB465 103Sq Aug44, Missing 29Nov44. 236hrs
PB466 7Sq, Lost (Emden) with Deputy Master Bomber 6Sep44
PB467 576Sq Aug44, Missing 23Oct44. 156hrs
PB468 156Sq ex-32MU Aug44, Missing 31Mar45
PB469 460Sq ex-32MU, Lost (Aschaffenburg) 21Nov44
PB470 83Sq, 9Sq Aug45, Became 5850M at12STT
PB471 460Sq(AR ·F2), Crashed in Belgium, 20Feb45
PB472 576Sq Aug44, 153Sq Oct44; 15,22MUs; Scrap May47
PB473 97Sq Sep44, Conv ASRIII Apr46, 39MU, 2MPRD May47
PB474 7Sq ex-32MU Sep44, Missing 12Oct44. 71hrs
PB475 582Sq, Crashed after operating at Bellingdon 6Mar45
PB476-7 12/405Sqs, Burnt 3/4Mar45/Lost 2Jan45
PB478 83Sq, Wrecked by an explosion at Coningsby 7Feb45
PB479 32MU Aug44, 460Sq Sep44, 49Sq Apr45, Wrecked 27Sep45
PB480 625Sq,170Sq(TC ·G), 37MU, Became 6710M at Padgate
PB481 7Sq Sep44, 5LFS Feb45, 619Sq Apr45, SOC May45
PB482 514Sq, 1653CU Apr45, Became 5723M, Scrap Oct47
PB483 149,186Sqs; Hit PB488 circling Stradishall, 14Apr45
PB484 49Sq ex-32MU Aug44, 38MU Sep45, Scrap May47
PB485 405Sq ex-32MU, 582Sq Oct44, Wrecked 17Oct44. 23hrs
PB486 156Sq; Crash, premature u/c retraction, Upwood 2Nov44
PB487 149Sq(OJ·V) Aug44, 1668CU Jul45, SOC Dec45
PB488 149,186Sqs; Hit PB483 on return, burnt 14Apr45†
PB489 7Sq(MG ·F), 1660CU(TV ·S),1653CU, Became 6241M 10STT
PB490 7Sq(MG ·B), 12Sq Nov45, 10MU Jul46, SOC Jan47
PB504 49Sq(EA ·U), Repaired after crash 7Nov44, Scrap May47
PB505 156Sq Sep44, Damaged beyond repair 3/4Feb45
PB506 149Sq(OJ ·B) Aug44; 1656,1668,1660CUs; SOC Nov45
PB507 32MU, 156Sq, NTU, 1656CU, 1653CU, Crashed 8Nov45
PB508 149Sq, G-H Flt, 1656/68/60CUs, 39MU Nov45, 2MPRD Jun47
PB509 149Sq(OJ ·C) Aug44, 186Sq Apr45, 1659CU, 22MU, SOC Dec45
PB510-1 97/582Sqs, Lost 12Sep44/Wrecked 7Oct44. 4/17hrs
PB512 582Sq, Crashed 4 miles E. of N. Weald 23Sep44. 30hrs
PB513 405Sq,467Sq Jun45, Lindholme Jan46, Scrap Feb46
PB514 550Sq Aug44, Crashed 3Jul45 and scrapped at 24MU
PB515 166,153Sqs; Collided in mid-air with NG421 2Jan45
PB516 32MU, 405Sq, Damaged 8Jan45, Lost 15/16Mar45
PB517-8 156/100Sqs Sep44, Lost 31Mar/2Jan45
PB519 49Sq, Crashed on road Marston Moor, 29Oct44, Crew saved
PB520-1 75/97Sqs Sep44, Lost 20Nov44/21Mar45
PB522 32MU; 460,49,115Sqs; 15MU Mar46, Scrap May47
PB523 32MU, 35Sq Sep44, 582Sq 18Dec44, Lost 23Dec44
PB524 115Sq(KO·C), Damaged 4Nov44, 1659CU, 39MU, Scrap Dec46
PB525 405Sq ex-32MU Sep44, Lost 29Dec44
PB526 7Sq(MG ·N) Sep44, Lost (Hanover) 6Jan45
PB527-8 405/103Sqs Sep44, Lost 16Sep44/5Jan45. 4/?hrs
PB529 32MU,35Sq,NTU Dec44, 106Sq Jun45, 5MU, Conv.ASRIII then GRIII, 218MU, 6OTU, 224Sq May46, 120Sq Nov47, 220Sq, Flight Refuelling 1951, SMR, Scrap Jul53
PB530 405Sq ex-32MU Sep44, Missing 20/21Feb45
PB531 625Sq ex-32MU Sep44, Lost (Essen) 23Oct44. 75hrs
PB532 550,100(HW·S2)Sqs; TFU, 15MU, SS Jul51
PB533 83Sq, Crashed landing by FIDO, Metheringham, 22Dec44
PB534 44Sq Sep44, 75Sq Oct45, 39MU Nov45, Scrap Jan47
PB535 44Sq(KM·Z) Sep44, Lost (Darmstadt) 11/12Sep44. 16hrs
PB536 625Sq ex-32MU Sep44, 39MU Nov45, Scrap Sep46
PB537 49Sq ex-32MU Sep44, Lost 7/8Mar45
PB538 582Sq(60 ·M), Abandoned in air 23/24Feb45

PB539 BBU Sep44, 10MU Mar47, Scrap Oct47
PB540 619Sq(PG ·Z) Sep44, Crashed Woodbridge 1Nov44. 123hrs
PB541 460Sq ex-32MU Sep44, Missing 18Nov44
PB542 460Sq(AR ·D2) Sep44, Missing (Essen) 12Dec44
PB554 582Sq(60 ·M), Missing (Essen) 12Dec44
PB555 35,635,405,467,207(EM ·T)Sqs; 20MU May46, SS Aug47
PB556 625Sq, Disappeared night training flight 8Nov44
PB557 460Sq(AR ·B2/A2) Sep44, Missing (Chemnitz) 5Mar45
PB558 582Sq, Damaged 6Oct44, Lost 23Dec44
PB559 460Sq,49Sq Apr45, 115Sq(KO·T) Sep45, Scrap Aug47
PB560 156Sq Sep44, 1660CU Mar46, 15MU Sep46, Scrap May47
PB561-2 626/550Sqs Sep44, Damaged 31Dec44/Lost 6Nov44
PB563-4 103/635Sqs, Lost 5/6Mar45 & 5Jan45
PB565 156Sq, 1667CU, Crashed at Owston Ferry 15Apr45
PB566 35Sq, 1653CU Sep45, 1660CU, 15MU, Scrap Dec46
PB567 460Sq(AR ·U), Missing (Cologne) 31Oct44. 40hrs
PB568-9 49/100Sqs, Lost 21/22 & 3/4Feb45
PB570 7Sq, 1669CU Nov44, Crashed 5Feb45
PB571 49Sq, Damaged 14/15Mar45, 115Sq Sep45, Wrecked 7Aug46
PB572 100Sq 10Sep44, Missing 1/2Feb45
PB573 170Sq(TC ·H) Oct44, Missing (Duisberg) 21Feb45
PB574 625Sq Sep44, 576Sq Apr45, 15MU Sep45, Scrap Mar48
PB575 582Sq Sep44, 1661CU(KB ·G) Dec44, 20MU, SS(CC) May47
PB576 7Sq ex-32MU Sep44, 1667CU Dec44, 38MU, Scrap May47
PB577 115Sq, G-H Training Flt. 1668CU, SOC Dec45
PB578 156Sq, NTU Oct44, 1666CU, 5MU, Scrap Sep47
PB579 Crashed on initial test flight from Woodford 11Sep44
PB580 625Sq, Crashed 29Nov44, 625Sq,39MU, Nov45, SOC Nov46
PB581 625, 170Sqs; BCIS, 10MU Jan46, Scrap Dec46
PB582 7Sq(MG ·T); 1661,1660,1653CUs; 10MU, Scrap Oct47
PB583 405(LQ ·P),35,635,106,189,106,50Sqs; SS (CC) May47
PB584 7Sq(MG ·M); 1660(TV ·M), 1653CUs; 45MU, Scrap Nov47
PB585 635,405(LQ ·P),467,617,106,50Sqs; Became 6167M
PB586 49Sq ex-32MU Sep44, Missing (Munich) 7Jan45
PB587 7Sq, Damaged 6Oct & 24Dec44; 106,50Sqs; Scrap May47
PB588 97Sq ex-32MU Oct44, Shot down by Ju88 23/24Feb45
PB589 35Sq Sep44, 635Sq Dec44, 75Sq, 1660/53CUs, Scrap May47
PB590 619Sq(PG ·V) (PG ·O) Sep44, Wrecked 5Sep45
PB591 582Sq, Damaged 7/8Mar45, 1653CU,9MU,SS Apr48
PB592/G I (Spec.) AAEE 15Oct44, 46MU May45, Scrap Jan47
PB593 156Sq ex-32MU, 1653CU(A3 ·C), 10MU, Scrap Oct47
PB594 9Sq(WS ·D),189Sq(CA ·D) Oct44,22MU Feb46, Scrap Jan47
PB595 170Sq(TC ·J) Oct44, Lost (Pforzheim) 23/24Feb45
PB596 9,61,227(9J ·O)Sqs; 1668CU, Crashed Bottesford 6Sep45, Repaired, BTU Feb46, Crashed 12Aug47
PB609 106Sq(ZN ·U),156Sq, Undershot Upwood 16Nov44
PB610 227Sq(9J ·O), Swung on runway Balderton 7Mar45
PB611 32MU, 156Sq; 1660/68/53CUs; Crashed 18Nov46, SS Apr48
PB612 32MU Sep44, 35Sq Oct44, Lost 28Oct44. 11hrs
PB613 32MU, 35Sq,156Sq Apr44, 467Sq Jun44, Scrap Feb46
PB614 35,405,467,207Sqs; Crashed 21Nov45, Scrap May47
PB615 32MU,35Sq Oct44, 7Sq Nov44, 46MU Apr45, Scrap Jan47
PB616 83Sq, Crashed on take-off, Rheine, " EXODUS " 9May45
PB617-8 106Sq Sep44, Lost 5Jan45/Wrecked 5Jun45
PB619 BBU Woodbridge Sep44, 39MU, SOC Mar48
PB620-1 463/156Sqs, Lost (Flushing) 23Apr44/30Dec44
PB622 32MU; 7(MG ·C),106,189,106Sqs; Crashed 7Feb46
PB623 7Sq(MG ·L), 1660CU(TV ·B), 230 OCU, 9MU, 2MPRD Nov47
PB624 32MU, 97Sq Oct44, Crashed, 15MU, Scrap Jan47
PB625 32MU; 582,156,467,207Sqs; 39MU Jun46, 2MPRD Jan47
PB626 7Sq(MG ·E); 106,189,106Sqs; Wrecked 24Jan46
PB627 635Sq,405Sq (LQ ·T), 1660CU (TV ·T), 1653CU (A3 ·T) SS May47
PB628 635Sq(F2 ·D), 405Sq(LQ ·W), 467Sq, Scrap Feb46
PB629 582Sq(60 ·J) Nov44, Missing (Heimbach) 3Dec44
PB630 582Sq(60 ·A) Oct44, Missing (Walcheren) 29Oct44. 40hrs
PB631 32MU,635Sq,156Sq Mar45, 83Sq Jun45, 20MU, Scrap May47
PB632 166Sq Sep44, Damaged 7Oct44, 38MU Feb45, Scrap May47
PB633 153Sq Oct44, Mid-air collision over Ham 17Dec44
PB634 32MU, 101Sq(SR ·U) Oct44, Missing 28Dec44
PB635 576,166Sqs; Lost (Nuremburg) 2Jan45
PB636-7 153/103Sqs, Missing (Duisberg) 22Jan45/7Jan45
PB638-9 153Sq, Lost (Stuttgart/Dusseldorf) 28Jan45/2Nov44

PB640 AAEE Sep44, Avro Nov44, 46MU May45, Scrap Jan47
PB641 TFU, 38MU, Conv.ASRIII/GRIII, 120Sq, Flt. Refuelling, SMR, 210Sq, 15MU, SS(ERM) Sep54
PB642 153Sq Oct44, Lost 16/17Mar45
PB643-4 I 227Sq Oct44, Lost 12Nov44/5Mar45
PB645 I 227Sq(9J ·A) Oct44, Crash 3Sep45, 5MU, Scrap Nov46
PB646 I 227Sq Oct44, Lost 6Dec44
PB647 I 227Sq(9J ·Q) Oct44, 115Sq Sep45, SOC Tollerton 1Nov45
PB648 166Sq Oct44, Missing (Duren) 16Nov44. 67hrs
PB649 227Sq(9J ·K) Oct44, Damaged 22Dec44 beyond repair
PB650 32MU, 405Sq Oct44, Missing 28/29Jan44
PB651 227Sq Oct44, 1654CU Jan45, 20MU, Scrap Oct46
PB652 32MU, 582Sq Oct44, Damaged 21/22Feb45
PB653 32MU; 405,467,207Sqs; Crashed 30Oct45
PB666-7 227/7Sqs Oct44, Lost 21Feb45/Crashed 20Mar45
PB668 32MU, 635Sq Oct44, Damaged 21/22Feb45
PB669 Pathfinder NTU Nov44, Crashed in Hunts. 11Mar45
PB670 32MU,NTU Nov44, 1653CU Sep45, 15MU, Scrap Aug46
PB671 I 101Sq(SR ·M), Crash 21Nov44, Lost (Dortmund) 20Feb45
PB672 I 32MU Oct44, 227Sq Oct44, Missing 4Dec44
PB673 I 101Sq Oct44, BCIS Jun45, SOC Nov45
PB674 I 218Sq(HA ·Q), Damaged 2Nov44, Lost 12Dec44
PB675 32MU, 156Sq Oct44, SOC 28Dec44
PB676 32MU, 35Sq Oct44, 106Sq Jun44, SOC Apr46
PB677 7Sq(MG ·N) Nov44; 106,617,106,50Sqs; SS Aug47
PB678 35Sq Oct44, Collided mid-air with PD683 23Dec44
PB679 7Sq(MG ·O) Nov44,10MU,ECFS Sep45,49MU,Scrap Sep48
PB680 32MU; 635,156Sqs; 1656CU, 12Sq, 9Sq(WS ·B), 2MPRD Apr47
PB681 635,582,405(LQ ·M)Sqs;1667/56/68/53CUs; Crash 20Jun46
PB682 405Sq, NTU Apr45, 106Sq Jun45, Crashed 3Oct45
PB683 35Sq, Collided with PB678 in mid-air 23Dec44
PB684 35Sq Nov44, Twice damaged, Crashed and SOC 18May45
PB685 35Sq Oct44, Twice damaged, 44Sq, 10MU, Scrap Sep47
PB686 I 115Sq(KO ·D), Dived into Jancourt, France 13/14Feb45
PB687 I 626Sq(UM ·Q2), Shot down 31Dec44
PB688 I 463Sq, Crash, bad weather, near Waddington 21/22Dec44
PB689-90 I 75/227Sqs Oct44, Lost 20Nov44/21Feb45
PB691-2 I 189/101Sqs Oct44, Missing (Politz) 21Dec/6Nov44
PB693 170Sq(TC ·W) Oct44, Damaged 21Mar45, SOC 12Dec45
PB694 32MU, 83Sq Oct44, Lindholme Jan46, Became 5851M 12STT
PB695 I 463Sq 15Oct44, Missing 5Jan45
PB696 I 9Sq(WS ·V) Oct44, 619Sq Jul45, 463Sq, MU, SS Jun47
PB697 32MU;83,149,83,12,9(WS ·O),12Sqs;12MU,2MPRD Apr47
PB698 32MU, NTU Nov44; 35,12Sqs; 15MU, Scrap Jan47
PB699/G 32MU, 619Sq(PG ·Z) Nov44, Lost (Harburg) 7/8Mar45
PB700 32MU, 97Sq Nov44, 15MU Jul46, Scrap Feb47
PB701 32MU, 156Sq Oct44, Missing 20/21Feb45
PB702 83Sq, Crashed in sea off Skegness 14Nov44. 34hrs
PB703 I 625,195,100(HW ·O)Sqs; 22MU Feb46, Scrap Jun47
PB704 I 170Sq(TC ·R), Missing (Kiel) 9/10Apr45
PB705 I 300Sq Oct45, 15MU Dec46, Scrap May47
PB706 32MU, 97Sq Nov44, 9MU Jul46, Scrap Feb47
PB707 32MU, 550Sq Nov44, 15MU Aug45, Scrap May47
PB708 I 625Sq, 1654CU Feb45, 5MU Sep45, Scrap May47
PB721 I 218Sq(HA ·D),115Sq(KO ·U),39MU Sep45, SOC Dec46
PB722 I 300Sq(BH ·J) Oct44, Missing 20/21Feb45
PB723 I 227Sq Oct44, Missing 28Dec44
PB724 I 106Sq, Crashed into trees Maligny-le-Grand 7Aug45
PB725 I 61Sq, Lost in canal raid on Gravenhorst 6/7Nov44
PB726 I 467,635,35,207(EM ·G)Sqs; 20MU Apr46, SS Aug47
PB727 I 61Sq Oct44, 39MU Aug46
PB728 32MU, 170Sq(TC ·W) Oct44, SOC 12Dec45
PB729/G 32MU,227Sq,1660CU(YW ·N)Feb45,20MU,Scrap May46
PB730 I 300Sq(BH ·R), Swung landing at Wing, Operation EXODUS, 10May45
PB731 I 227Sq Oct44, 5MU Sep45, Scrap Mar47
PB732 I 189Sq,106Sq(ZN ·K) Nov45, Lindholme, SOC 21Feb48
PB733 32MU, 44Sq, 1661CU Dec44, Crashed 2May45
PB734 I 106Sq(ZN ·E) Oct44,Crashed 1/2Feb45,MUs,Scrap May47
PB735-6 I 625Sq Oct44, 20MU Sep45, SS(CC) May47
PB737 I 61Sq 23Oct44, Missing 8/9Feb45
PB738 150Sq Nov44, 576Sq Sep45, SOC Oct45

PB739 I 12Sq Nov44, 50Sq Mar45, 39MU, 2MPRD Jun47
PB740 I 467Sq Nov44, Missing (Heilbronn) 4/5Dec44
PB741 I 75Sq(AA ·E), Hit by flak Heinrich Hutte 14Mar45
PB742 I 189Sq 5Nov44, Missing 4Dec44
PB743 I 189Sq 5Nov44, Missing (Karlsruhe) 2/3Feb45
PB744 I 189Sq(CA ·U), 106Sq Nov45, 22MU, Mar46, Scrap Jun47
PB745 I 189Sq Nov44, Burnt after operation 27Nov44
PB746 I 150Sq Oct44, Crashed Feb46, 38MU, Scrap May47
PB747 I 150Sq, 151Repair Unit Apr45, 5MU Dec45, Scrap May47
PB748 I 101Sq Nov44, 44Sq, Damaged 4th time 17Jul46
PB749 I 1651CU Nov44, Exploded in air, Langtoft, 7Dec44
PB750 I 12Sq Nov44, Crashed 29Sep45 and SOC Dec45
PB751 I 44Sq(KM ·G) Nov44, Missing (Heilbronn) 4Dec44
PB752 I 170Sq(TC ·M), Dunlop Flt, Compacta tyres, RAE, Scrap
PB753 I 576Sq Nov44, Damaged 2nd time 13Oct45 and SOC
PB754 I 467Sq,35Sq Jan45, Damaged on ground 17Aug45
PB755 I 50Sq, Abandoned in air POST MORTEM 25Jun45
PB756 I 115Sq(IL ·A) (IL ·H),44Sq Sep45, 10MU, Scrap Nov46
PB757 I 115Sq(IL ·E), 55 operations, 20MU Sep45, Scrap Mar46
PB758 619Sq,1661CU,BTU, SOC after 2nd crash 1Feb46
PB759 I 61Sq Nov44, Missing (Politz) 8/9Feb45
PB760 I 195Sq(A4 ·L)Nov44, Crashed 31Dec44,MUs,Scrap Feb47
PB761 I 75Sq, Returning low, hit ground, Wood Ditton, 17Jan45
PB762 I 467,35Sqs; Crashed 17Oct45, Scrap Jun47
PB763 I 75Sq Nov44, 49Sq Jul45, 39MU Sep45, Scrap Jan47
PB764-5 I 207Sq Nov44, SOC Nov45/Lost (Heilbronn) 4Dec44
PB766 I 218Sq 15Nov44, Down in sea off Felixstowe 19Dec44
PB767 I 514,115(KO ·T), 138Sqs; Crashed 5Feb46
PB768 I 218Sq, Shot down by American AA Namur 2Jan45
PB780 I 150Sq(T) Nov44, Missing (Pforzheim) 23/34Feb45
PB781 I 150Sq(IQ ·V) Nov44, Lindholme Jan46, SOC Mar46
PB782 I 207Sq 23Nov44, Spilsby 19Oct45, SOC Nov45
PB783 I 153Sq Nov44, 625Sq Sep45, 22MU Mar46, Scrap Mar48
PB784 I 57Sq Nov44, Damaged in action 19/20Mar45
PB785 I 576Sq Nov44, Missing 16/17Mar45
PB786 I 153Sq(P4 ·D) Nov44, 20MU Oct45, Scrap Nov45
PB787 I 1669,1663CUs; 38MU Jan45, Scrap May47
PB788 I 101Sq(SR ·E) Nov44-Dec45, CBE, 39MU, Scrap 1947
PB789 I 115Sq(KO ·B), 44Sq(KM ·B), Crash Sep45, Scrap Dec46
PB790 I 195Sq,186Sq(XY ·B),100Sq, 22MU Jan46, Scrap Jan47
PB791 I 49Sq Nov44, 1654CU Jan45, 22MU Sep45, Scrap Jun45
PB792 I 463Sq, Hit hill returning from Heilbronn 4/5Dec44
PB793 I 189Sq(CA ·X) Nov44, 106Sq, Lindholme Mar46, SOC Mar46
PB794 I 195Sq(JE ·A) Nov44, 186Sq May, 550Sq Aug, SOC Nov45
PB795 I 622Sq(GI ·V) Nov44, 44Sq Aug45, 15MU, Scrap Oct46
PB796 I 1669CU Nov44, 1651CU Mar45, 24MU, Wrecked 4Oct45
PB797 I 49Sq Nov44, 50Sq Mar45, 61Sq Jul45, 9MU, Scrap Apr47
PB798 I 115Sq(IL ·G) Dec44, 44Sq Sep45, 15MU, Scrap Sep46
PB799 I 49Sq, Believed in sea off Gt. Ormes Head, 11Dec44
PB800 I 101Sq(SR ·N) 18Nov44, SOC 19Oct45
PB801 I Coningsby Nov44, 1659CU Jul45, 22MU, Scrap Mar48
PB802 I 15Sq; Crashed, disintegrated, Harling, 17Jan45
PB803 I Coningsby Nov44, 1659CU Jul45, 22MU, Scrap Mar48
PB804 I 463Sq, Abandoned in air (Gravenhorst) 21/22Feb45
PB805 I 227Sq Dec44, Crashed 3Sep45, 5MU Sep45, Scrap Nov46
PB806 I 467Sq Nov44, Missing (Ladbergen) 3/4Mar45
PB807 I 460Sq(AR ·H) Dec44, Missing (Weisbaden) 2/3Feb45
PB808 I 1323Flt Dec44, 635Sq Jul45, 39MU Dec45, SOC Nov46
PB809 I Coningsby Nov44, ASWDU Jun45, 15MU Apr47, SOC Mar48
PB810 I Coningsby Nov44, 1659CU(RV ·P) Jul45, 22MU, Scrap Mar48
PB811 I 1669CU Nov44, 1654CU Mar45, 10MU Aug45, Scrap Dec46
PB812 I 460Sq Dec44, Crashed, burnt 10Feb45
PB813 I 1669CU Nov44, 1654CU Mar45, 15MU Aug45, Scrap Oct46
PB814 I 207Sq Nov44, Lost (Gravenhorst) 21/22Feb45
PB815 I 625Sq, Hit by incendiaries, abandoned, France, 23Feb43
PB816 I 460Sq(AR ·E2) Dec44, Lost (Nuremburg) 16/17Mar45
PB817 I 150Sq Dec44,Lindholme Dec45,22MU Feb46,Scrap Jun47
PB818 I 195(JE ·J),115(KO ·X),44(KM ·C)Sqs;22MU;Scrap Jun47
PB819 I 622Sq Nov44, 44Sq(KM ·K) Aug45, 38MU, Scrap Sep47

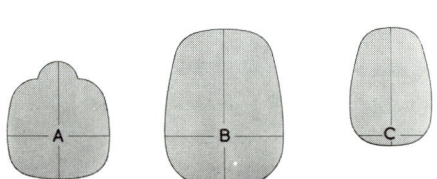

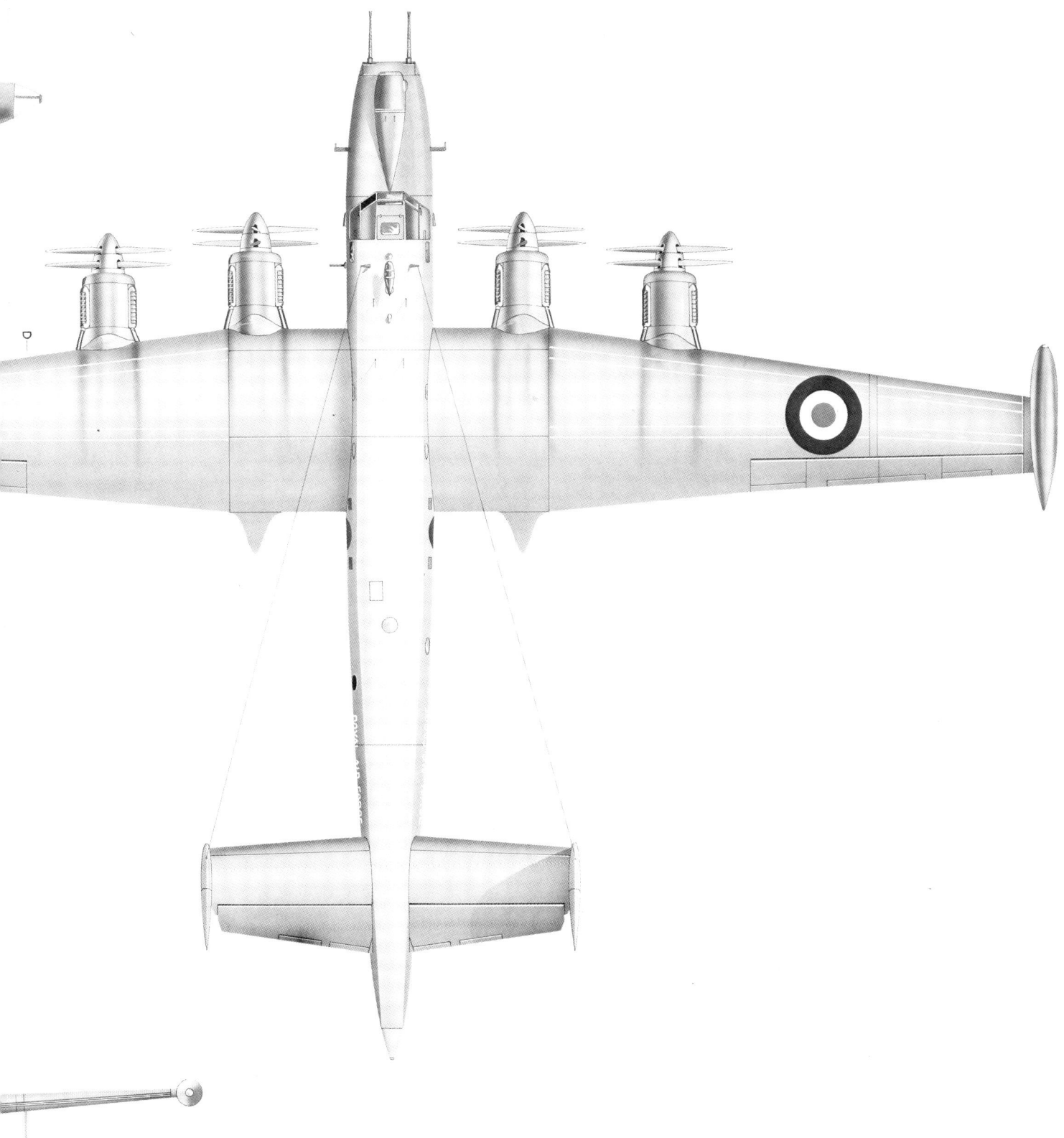

A late production Shackleton M.R.3, which served in No. 201 Squadron from delivery in March 1959.

PB820 I 75Sq Nov44, 514Sq(JI·M) Jul45, 20MU, SS(CC) May47
PB821 I 50Sq(VN·E) Nov44, SOC Apr46
PB822 I 1666CU Dec44, 15MU Sep45, Shoeburyness Mar49
PB823 I 300Sq 28Nov44, Missing 2Jan45
PB836 I 626Sq Nov44, 1654CU Feb45, 20MU Oct45, Scrap Nov46
PB837/G I 195Sq(A4·T) Dec44; 103,57Sqs; 5MU, Scrap Feb47
PB838 I 149Sq,138Sq(AC·T) Apr45, 149Sq, Scrap Oct46
PB839 I 100Sq Nov44, 460Sq Apr45, 10MU Jun45, Scrap Oct46
PB440 I 189Sq Nov44, Missing (Karlsruhe) 2/3Feb45
PB841 I 32MU, 1666CU, Belly landing near Skipton 17Dec44
PB842 I 619Sq(PG·Y), Crashed in Sweden (Politz) 13Jan45
PB843 I 550Sq Dec44, 1660CU Feb45, Scrap Mar46
PB844 I 49,57Sqs(DX·N); Swung on take-off, Italy, 7Nov45
PB845 I 463Sq Dec44, Missing (Bohlen) 20/21Mar45
PB846 I 300Sq 3Jan45, Missing 29Jan45
PB847 I 227Sq Dec44, 38MU, May45, 10MU Jan47, Scrap Sep47
PB848 I 189Sq Nov44, Missing (Karlsruhe) 2/3Feb45
PB849 I 12Sq Jan-Apr45, Wickenby Oct45, 5MU, Scrap Nov46
PB850 I 625Sq Dec44, 1654CU, Feb45, 10MU Aug45, Scrap Dec46
PB851 I 156Sq(GT·G), 12Sq Dec44, Missing 7Jan45
PB852 I 57Sq Dec44, Missing (Harburg) 7/8Mar45
PB853 I 150Sq Dec44, Missing on oil refinery raid 24Mar45

PB873 " THOR " armament demonstration aircraft 1949.

PB854 I 300Sq Dec44, Missing 2Mar45
PB855 I 1656CU(EK·J) Dec44, Became 5847M of 12STT
PB856 I 195Sq(JE·D/N),35Sq(TL·A),22MU Mar46, Scrap Jun47
PB857 I 1656CU Dec44, Crashed near Lindholme Lake 9Oct45
PB858 I 195Sq(JE·C); 186,550,100Sqs; 38MU, Scrap Sep47
PB859 I 1656CU 2Dec44, Crashed 30Dec44, MUs, Scrap Mar48
PB860 I 1656CU 2Dec44, SOC 20Dec45
PB861 I 1669CU Dec44, 1651CU Mar45, 24MU, Wrecked 4Oct45
PB862 I 619Sq Dec44, 1660CU Feb45, 22MU Sep45, SS(HDA) Aug46
PB863 I 1667Sq Dec44, Crashed 29Jun45, 58MU, SOC Oct45
PB864 I 550Sq, 1660CU, Crashed St. Pierre Eglise 31May45
PB865 I 1661CU Jan45, 10MU 3Aug45, Scrap Oct46
PB866 I 1667Sq Dec44, 22MU Sep45, Scrap Jun47
PB867-8 I Served in various CUs only, Both SOC Nov45
PB869 I 1661CU(KB·L) Jan45, 5MU Sep45, Scrap Jan47
PB870 I 1667Sq Dec44, 20MU Oct45, Scrap Oct46
PB871 I 1669CU, 1651CU, Crashed at Woolfox Lodge 24Mar45
PB872 I 1535Sq Dec44, Missing (Chemnitz) 5Mar45
PB873 I 460,49Sqs; EAAS Oct45 *Thor*, 5MU Jan49, SS Nov49
PB874 I 207Sq Dec44, SOC at Spilsby Nov45 after 2 crashes
PB875 I 460,49,115(KO·G)Sqs; 9MU Jul46, 2MPRD Apr47
PB876 I 1669CU Dec44,1660CU Mar45,5MU Aug45,Scrap May47
PB877 I 195Sq(A4·Z) Dec45; 186,100Sqs; 38MU May46, Scrap Sep47
PB878 I 207Sq, 460Sq Aug45, 57Sq Oct45, SOC Feb46
PB879 I 189Sq Dec44, Lindholme Dec45, 5MU, Scrap Mar48
PB880 I 630Sq, Crashed in Sweden 13/14Jan45. 1 killed
PB881 I 32MU, 97Sq Dec44, 9MU Jul46, Scrap Feb47
PB893 I 32MU, 433Sq Jun45, 38MU Nov45, SOC Sep47
PB894 I 630Sq Dec44, Lost mining 31Dec44
PB895 I 97Sq(OF·M)Dec44,83Sq Mar46,9MU Jul46, Scrap Feb47
PB896/G I 195Sq(A4·Y),186Sq Apr46, 166Sq, Wrecked 1Dec46
PB897 I 424Sq(QB·B) Jan45, 32MU Nov45, Scrap Jan47
PB898/G I 103Sq, 1660/54CUs, Fuselage to Cranfield Jul46
PB899 I 424Sq(QB·A), Lost mining (Pomerania Bay) 14/15Feb45
PB900 I 97Sq Dec44, 1660CU Feb45, Crashed 28Feb46
PB901 I 1661CU Jan45, 5MU Sep45, Scrap Nov46

PB902 I 514Sq,149Sq Mar45, Crashed in Norway 13Aug45
PB903 I 433Sq ex-32MU Jan45, Shot down in day raid by predicted flak over Leipzig Mockau 10Apr45
PB904 I 1669CU Dec44, 1660CU Feb45, SOC Mar46
PB905 I 97,9,207Sqs; Lindholme Feb46, 38MU, Scrap Sep47
PB906 I 514Sq ex-32MU Jan45, Missing 17Jan45
PB907 I 49Sq,115Sq(KO·O) Sep45, Wrecked 12Jun46
PB908 I 433Sq ex-32MU Jan45, 38MU Nov45, Scrap Sep47
PB909 I 635Sq ex-32MU Jan45, 39MU Sep45, Scrap Jan47
PB910 I 582Sq(60·B), 7Sq(MG·B) Sep45, 10MU, Scrap Mar47
PB911 I 635Sq, Crashed and burnt 30Mar45
PB912 I Cunliffe Owen Mar45, TFU Oct45, Scrap May47
PB913-4 I 635Sq(F2·D/?) Feb45, 15MU Sep45, Scrap May47
PB915 I 635Sq(F2·M), Damaged 22Apr46, 20MU, SS(CC) May47
PB916 I 635Sq(F2·C) ex-32MU, 5MU Sep45, Scrap Nov46
PB917 I 635Sq,156Sq Jun45, 49Sq Sep45, 10MU, SOC Jul46
PB918 I 635,35,582,7Sqs; BCIS Jun46, 15MU, Scrap Aug47
PB919 I 582Sq(60·S),635Sq Jun45, 15MU Sep45, SS Mar49
PB920 I 635Sq, BDU Aug45, Became 6386M at 2RS
PB921 I 635Sq ex-32MU Feb45, Missing 5/6Apr45
PB922 I 635Sq(F2·U) Feb45, 39MU Jan46, 2MPRD Jun47
PB923 635Sq,146Sq Jun45, 49Sq, 10MU, Scrap Nov46
PB924-5 I 1323Flt; 635,115(KO·N)Sqs; 15MU, SS May49/Aug49
PB926 I 166,156,49Sqs; Became 5966M Empire Radio School
PB927 I 635(F2·X),156,49Sqs; CBE, 19MU, Scrap Feb47
PB928 I 635Sq(F2·J) Feb45, Valley May46, 15MU, Scrap Oct46
PB929 I 635Sq(F2·Y) ex-32MU, 20MU Nov45, Sold May47
PB930 I TFU Defford 21Jan45, 5MU 8Mar46, Scrap Jan47
PB931 I 635Sq(F2·W),Valley Mar46,15MU Jun46, Scrap Oct46
PB932 I 1323Flt, 635Sq Aug45, 115Sq Sep45, 15MU, Scrap Mar48
PB933 I 635Sq(F2·N), Croydon Victory Week Sep45, SOC Dec45
PB934 I 582Sq(60·O), Damaged 15Apr45, 15MU, Scrap Mar48
PB935 I 635Sq(F2·Z),582Sq Jul45, 7Sq Sep45, 39MU, SOC Dec46
PB936 I 635Sq,156Sq(GT·B), 49Sq Oct45, Scrap at 10MU Jan46
PB949 I 635Sq(F2·T) ex-32MU Feb45, Missing 4/5Apr45
PB950 I 635Sq(F2·A) Mar45, 39MU Oct45, Scrap Jan47
PB951 I 32MU Dec44; 35,156,49Sqs; 15MU Jan46, Shoeburyness
PB952 I 635Sq Feb45, Crashed 1Aug45; 54,22MUs; Scrap May47
PB953 I 635(F2·K),156(GT·R),49Sqs; 5MU Mar46, SOC Dec46
PB954 I 582Sq(60·P), Swung on take-off at Bari 4Sep45
PB955 I 582Sq(60·F) Mar45, 7Sq Sep45, 39MU, SOC Jan47
PB956 I 582Sq(60·N),7Sq,CBE, Feb46, 9MU, 2MPRD Nov47
PB957 I 1323Flt, 635Sq Aug45, 115Sq, 20MU, Scrap Jun46,
PB958 I 32MU, 635Sq, Missing (Hamburg day raid) 31Mar45
PB959 I 1323Flt,635Sq,115Sq(KO·M),32MU,15MU,SS(IA)Mar49
PB960 1323Flt,635Sq Aug45,115Sq Sep45, Scrap Mar48
PB961 I 582Sq(60·R) Mar45, 49Sq Oct45, 7Sq, Scrap Nov46
PB962 582(60·G) Mar45, 7Sq Sep45, 5MU Jun46, SOC Aug47
PB963 582Sq(60·J),7Sq(MG·O), 10MU May46, SOC Jan47
PB964 582Sq(60·Q), 7Sq Sep45, 15MU, Scrap Jan47
PB965 582Sq(60·E/L), 7Sq, 5MU Jan46, Scrap Jun47
PB966 35,582(60·H), 7(MG·H)Sqs, 39MU, SOC Dec46
PB967 156,49Sqs(EA·Q), 10MU Jun46, Dumped Dec46
PB968 582,7Sqs;Conv.ASR/GRIII,236OCU,SMR, Crash 5Feb54
PB969 582Sq(60·Z) Mar45, 7Sq Sep45, 399MU May46, SS Jan47
PB970 32MU,582Sq(60·C),7Sq Sep45, CBE,10MU, Scrap Mar47
PB971 32MU; 35,156,49(EA·T)Sqs; 10MU Jun46, Scrap Dec46
PB972 Refuelling Flight, Staverton Mar45, Became G-33-2
PB973 32MU; 35,156,49(EA·L)Sqs; 10MU Jun46, SOC Jul46
PB974 32,38,5MUs; On loan to RAAF, 38MU, Scrap May47
PB975 582,635Sq(F2·S),7Sqs; Crash 25Oct45, 7Sq, Scrap Sep47
PB976 582Sq(60·T/D),7Sq(MG·Z), 10MU May46, Scrap Sep47
PB977 582Sq, 7Sq(MG·A/U), CBE, 39MU, 2MPRD Jun47
PB978 635(F2·F),35,156,49Sqs; 10MU Jun46, Scrap Jan47
PB979 635,582,7Sqs; 10MU May46, Scrap Sep47
PB980 32MU; 35,156,49(EA·M)Sqs; 10MU Jun46, SOC Jul46
PB981 I 35,156,49Sqs; CBE Apr46, 10MU, Scrap Feb47
PB982 I 35,156,49Sqs; 10MU, Scrap Dec46
PB983 I 582Sq(60·A); Crashed, Deenthorpe, in storm 28Apr45
PB984 I 582Sq Apr45, 7Sq Sep45, 39MU May46, Scrap Nov46
PB985 I 32MU; 35,156,49Sqs; Wrecked 30May47
PB986 I 582,7Sqs; BCIS, Became 6304M at Marham
PB987 I 35Sq Apr45, 156Sq, 49Sq Oct45, Wrecked 30May46
PB988 I 32MU; 35,156,49Sqs; CBE Feb46, 39MU, Scrap Mar48

202

PB989 I 32MU; 35,156,49Sqs; 49Sq Oct46, 10MU, Scrap Nov46
PB990 I 32MU, 635Sq Apr45, 15MU Sep45, Scrap Mar48
PB991 32MU, 35Sq,156Sq(GT·H),49Sq,38MU, Scrap May47
PB992 MUs; Middle East Oct45-Jun46, 5MU, Scrap Oct47
PB993 32,38,5MUs; Middle East Nov45-Jan46, SS Feb49
PB994 32,46,38,5MUs; Middle East Nov45-Jul46, Scrap Jan47
PB995 B.I(Spec),AAEE 21Feb45, 617Sq, MUs, Scrap Mar48
PB996 B.I(Spec),617Sq, Damaged 10Apr45, MUs, Scrap Nov47
PB997 B.I(Spec),617Sq 24Feb45, Lindholme Dec45, SOC Mar46
PB998 B.I(Spec),617Sq Feb45, Damaged Apr45,MU, Scrap Nov47

PD133 Lancaster B.1 (Special), Woodhall Spa, Spring 1945.

PD112 B.I(Spec),617Sq, Dropped 1st 'Grand Slam' MUs, SS Mar48
PD113 B.I(Spec),617Sq Feb45, Damaged Apr45,MU,Scrap Nov47
PD114-5 B.I(Spec),617Sq 1Mar45,Lindholme Dec46,Scrap May47
PD116 B.I(Spec),617Sq 1Mar45, 46MU Sep45, Scrap Mar48

Lancaster B.1 (Special) PD137 at Farnborough.

PD117 B.I(Spec),617Sq 1Mar45, Missing 21Mar45
PD118 B.I(Spec),617Sq Mar45,Lindholme,38MU, Scrap May47
PD119 B.I(Spec),617,156,15Sqs; RAE, Shoeburyness May51
PD120 B.I(Spec),46MU Mar45, 45MU, Scrap Mar48
PD121 B.I(Spec),617Sq,15Sq Jun45, MU Oct46, Scrap May47
PD122 B.I(Spec), 46MU,75Sq, Damaged 16Mar47, MU, Scrap Mar48
PD123 B.I(Spec), 46MU Mar45, 45MU Dec46, Scrap Mar48
PD124 B.I(Spec),BBU Woodbridge Dec45, 5MU Mar49, SS Aug50
PD125-6 B.I(Spec), 46MU,15Sq Jun46, 15MU, Scrap Mar48
PD127 B.I(Spec),617Sq,15Sq(LS·S),15MU Nov46, 2MPRD Oct47
PD128 B.I(Spec),617,15,44(KM·A)Sqs; 15MU, Scrap Mar48
PD129 B.I(Spec),617Sq,15Sq(LS·R), 22MU, Scrap Jan47
PD130 B.I(Spec),617Sq,46MU Aug45, 45MU Oct46, Scrap Mar48
PD131 B.I(Spec),617Sq,Damaged 10Apr45,15Sq,MU,Scrap May47
PD132 B.I(Spec),617Sq Mar45; 46,54MUs; Scrap Mar48
PD133 B.I(Spec),617Sq Mar45, Lindholme, MU Feb46, Scrap May47
PD134 B.I(Spec),617Sq,Damaged Mar45,MUs Sep45,Scrap Nov47
PD135 B.I(Spec),617Sq Mar45, MUs from Sep45, Scrap Mar48
PD136 B.I(Spec),617Sq, Lindholme Jan46, 15MU, Scrap Mar47
PD137 B.I(Spec), BBU Woodbridge, 9MU, RAE, SS(MOS) Apr52
PD138 B.I(Spec), 46MU Mar45, 45MU Oct46, Scrap Mar48
PD139 B.I(Spec),617Sq, Struck ground Brunswick, 16May45
PD140-146 and PD159-171 reserved for B.O.A.C. Lancastrians and later cancelled except PD163; PD174-196 was also allotted. PD167 and PD179 built and renumbered VH737 and VH742.

Serial Range PD198—PD444　　　　**Lancaster B.I**
200 Lancaster B.Is ordered in April 1943 from Metropolitan-

Vickers and delivered from June to December 1944 with Merlin 24 engines.
PD198 9Sq(WS·W), Damaged by FW190 12Jan45 103Sq(PM·W), 57Sq Nov45, 38MU, Scrap May47
PD199 61Sq 27Jun44, Missing (Dusseldorf) 2/3Nov44. 232hrs
PD200 625,97Sqs, Wreckage found in France 10Nov44
PD201 12Sq Jul44, Stalled over Holbeach Drive 15Dec44
PD202 166Sq Jun44, Missing 13Jul44. 22hrs
PD203 463Sq 3Jul44, 22MU Oct45, Scrap Jul47
PD204 625Sq(CF·P2), Abandoned over Belgium 10Apr45*
PD205 9Sq(WS·H) Jun44, Missing 20/21Jul44. 7ops
PD206 625Sq,170Sq(TC·B), Missing (Geilsenkirchen) 29Dec44
PD207 12Sq Jul44, Lost 16/17Mar45 after 50 operations
PD208 550Sq, Dived into ground at Winsford 14Aug44. 113hrs
PD209 207Sq, 429Sq(AL·K) Mar45, 38MU, Scrap Sep47
PD210 207Sq Jul44, Missing (Revigny) 18/19Jul44. 20hrs
PD211 9Sq Jul44, Crash landed N. Russia 18Sep44. 166hrs
PD212 57Sq 11Jul44, Missing 29Jul44. 58hrs
PD213 9Sq(WS·F), Crash landed after operations 22Dec44
PD214 106Sq 14Jul44, Missing 6Oct44, 238hrs
PD215 467Sq Jul44, Abandoned over Chalon 17/18Dec44
PD216 207Sq, Missing (Darmstadt) 25/26Aug44. 128hrs
PD217 207Sq, 1659CU Jun45, 22MU Sep45, Scrap Jun47
PD218 467Sq,46MU, 6LFS, 231Sq, 20MU, SS(CC) May47
PD219 622Sq Jul44, 1654CU Jan45, 15MU Aug45, Scrap Sep46
PD220 207Sq Jul44, Spilsby Oct45, Lost 6Nov45
PD221 550Sq 15Jul44, Wrecked 3/4Feb45
PD222 44Sq(KM·U), Lost on Brest raid 14Aug44. 68hrs
PD223 218Sq(HA·U), Damaged 4 times, 7Sq, 39MU, Scrap Jan47
PD224 166Sq Aug44, Missing (Duisberg) 14Oct44. 89hrs
PD225 622Sq,44Sq Aug45, 15Sq Sep45, 20MU, SS(CC) May47
PD226 166Sq, Lost mining in Stettin Bay 29Aug44. 88hrs
PD227 166Sq Aug44, Crashed 12Oct44. 131hrs
PD228 622Sq(GI·A) Nov44, 44Sq Aug44, 38MU, Scrap May47
PD229 622(GI·K),218(HA·D),514(JI·H)Sqs; 39MU, 2MPRD Jun47
PD230 467Sq Jul44, Lost (Russelsheim) 12/13Aug44. 38hrs
PD231 467Sq Aug44, Lost (Wurzburg) 16/17Mar45
PD232 576Sq 30Jul44, Missing (Dresden) 13/14Feb45
PD233 617Sq 29Jul44, Missing 12Jan45
PD234 218Sq(HA·C) Jul44, 15Sq,138Sq, 15MU, 2MPRD Oct47
PD235 576Sq 30Jul44, Missing 25Sep44. 157hrs
PD236 103Sq(PM·X) Jul44, 57Sq Nov45, Scrap Feb46
PD237 50Sq 30Jul44, Missing 14Aug44. 45hrs
PD238 617Sq Jul44, Wrecked 7Nov45
PD239 166Sq 4Aug44, Missing 7Oct44. 144hrs
PD252 218Sq 4Aug44, Missing 12Aug44. 8hrs
PD253 630Sq(LE·D) Aug44, Twice damaged, SOC Oct45
PD254 630Sq(LE·W)Aug44,467Sq Jul45,5MU Oct45, Scrap May47
PD255 Woodford 29Jul44, 550Sq Aug44, Lost 2Nov44. 175hrs
PD256 218Sq Aug44, 514Sq Jul45, 5MU Sep45, Scrap Mar48
PD257 Woodford 29Jul44, 300Sq 7Aug44, Missing 17Jan45
PD258 463Sq, Missing (Königsberg) 29/30Aug44. 53hrs
PD259 463Sq; Crashed in Scotland, operations, 31Aug44. 57hrs
PD260 166Sq 9Aug44, Missing 13Aug44. 11hrs
PD261 166Sq Aug44, Missing (Stettin) 29Aug44. 47hrs
PD262 218Sq(HA·G), Missing (Frankfurt) 12/13Sep44. 44hrs
PD263-4 57Sq 11Aug44, Missing 11Dec/6Dec44
PD265 514Sq(A2·A) 12Aug44, Missing 21Nov44.' 190hrs
PD266 61Sq 11Aug44, 5MU 19Jun46, Scrap May47
PD267 207Sq 13Aug44, Lost (Stuttgart) 12/13Sep44. 71hrs
PD268 101Sq(SR·O) Aug44, Missing (Dassau) 7/8Mar45
PD269 90Sq 14Aug44, Exploded over Bottrop 31Oct44. 135hrs
PD270 12Sq 16Aug44, 300Sq 23May45, SOC Feb46
PD271 576Sq 17Aug44, Wrecked 10Oct45
PD272-3 103/12Sqs Aug44, Lost 1Mar45/29Aug44
PD274-5 115/12Sqs Aug44, Lost 26Aug44/16Mar45
PD276 115Sq 23Aug44, Missing 25Oct44. 113hrs
PD277 218(HA·A),115(KO·C)Sqs; 20MU, Scrap Dec45
PD278 218Sq(HA·V) Aug44, Missing 7/8Mar45
PD279 218Sq(HA·W) Aug44, 15MU Aug45, SOC Dec45
PD280 207Sq(EM·V) Aug44, Lindholme Jan46, Scrap Sep47
PD281 103Sq; 46,38MUs; Middle East Sep45, Became 5001M
PD282 57Sq(DX·E) Aug44, 57Sq Sep45, 39MU, Scrap Sep46

PD283 630Sq 24Aug44, Missing 12Sep44. 25hrs
PD284 149Sq Aug44, 138Sq Jul46, 15MU, Scrap May47
PD285 622Sq,50Sq Mar45, 83Sq(OL·M) Mar46, Scrap Oct46
PD286 626Sq(UM·O2), Hit ME326 at 19,000ft 2/3Feb45
PD287 626Sq Aug44, Crashed 14Jul45
PD288 218(HA·H),514(A2·F)Sqs; 5MU Sep45, Scrap Nov46
PD289 12Sq Aug44, Wickenby 3Oct45, SOC Oct45
PD290 207Sq, Crashed into Halifax on take-off 1Nov44. 129hrs
PD291 50Sq Aug44, 1656CU Feb45, 1660CU Jan46, Scrap Jul46

PD328 Aries at Malton, Ontario, Canada.

PD292 50Sq Aug44, Missing (Royan) 4Jan45
PD293 115Sq, Down in sea during H2S Training 26Nov44
PD294 50Sq Sep44, Lost (Darmstadt) 11/12Sep44. 18hrs
PD295 626Sq(UM·B2) Sep44, Lost (Lutzkendorf) 4/5Apr45
PD296 218Sq(HA·B), Lost in day raid on Gremberg 28Jan45
PD309 576Sq 2Sep44, Missing 16Jan45
PD310 166Sq Sep44, 100Sq, 22MU May46, Scrap Jun47
PD311 463Sq Sep44, Missing (Ems-Weser canal) 6/7Nov44
PD312 576Sq; Abandoned, crew baled out 2Feb45
PD313 550Sq Sep44, Damaged 29Nov44, SOC 26Oct45
PD314 626Sq, Flew into ground approaching Wragby 12Nov44
PD315 626Sq Sep44, Damaged 16Nov44, 39MU Oct45, SOC Oct46
PD316 50Sq 9Sep44, Missing 7/8Feb45
PD317 630Sq, Crashed at E. Kirkby after colliding 7/8Jan45
PD318 207Sq, Shot down near Apeldoorn 23Nov44. 12hrs
PD319-20 550Sq Sep44, Missing 14Oct44/24Mar45
PD321 550Sq Sep44, 38MU Nov45, Scrap May47
PD322 207Sq 14Sep44, Missing (Giessen) 6Dec44
PD323 218Sq(HA·K)Sep44, 38MU Jun45, Scrap Sep47
PD324 514Sq Sep44, 427Sq Apr45, 38MU May46, Scrap Sep47
PD325 514Sq, Blown up by own bombs at Waterbeach 29Dec44
PD236 50Sq 25Sep44, Missing (Bergen) 28/29Oct44. 64hrs
PD327 630Sq(LE·Y) Sep44, 75Sq Jul45, SOC Oct45
PD328 Avro Sep44,38MU 18Sep44,ECNS 2Oct44,37MU,SS Aug48
PD329 463Sq(JO·Y) Sep44, 39MU Feb46, 2MPRD Jun47
PD330 463Sq Sep44, 5MU Sep45, Scrap May47
PD331 12Sq Sep44, Missing 23/24Oct44. 30hrs
PD332 622Sq(GI·N) Sep44, 44Sq(KM·N) Aug45, 10MU, Scrap Jan47
PD333 514Sq(A2·K),115Sq(KO·V) Dec44, 20MU, Scrap Sep46
PD334 514,149,207(EM·D)Sqs; Damaged 4 times, SS Aug47
PD335 166Sq,103Sq,57Sq(DX·D) Nov45, 39MU, 2MPRD Jun47
PD336 90Sq Sep44, Collided and crashed 2Feb45
PD337 463Sq Sep44, 5 Group Film Unit, 39MU, Scrap Sep46
PD338 463Sq Sep44, Missing 3Nov44
PD339 50Sq; Crashed Lodge Farm, Hardingstone, 26Apr45
PD340 50Sq Sep44, Crashed 21Feb46
PD341 90Sq 28Sep44, Missing 15Oct44. 13hrs
PD342 227Sq(9J·B) Oct44, Crashed 13Jul45 and SOC
PD343 550Sq(BQ·S), Missing Italy-UK flight 29Sep45
PD344 115Sq 28Sep44, Missing 5Oct44. 7hrs
PD345 227Sq(9J·F) Oct44, 115Sq Sep45, 39MU, Scrap Nov46
PD346 50Sq Oct44, Missing 1/2Feb45
PD347 57Sq Oct44, Wrecked in ground accident 17Apr45
PD348 227Sq, Crash 8Feb45, Middle East 1946, Became 5000M
PD349 227Sq(9J·G) Oct44, Damaged 21Mar45, MUs, Scrap Sep47
PD361 12Sq 6Oct44, Crashed 21May45, Scrap Jun47
PD362 467Sq Oct44, Damaged 19/20Feb45, MUs, Scrap Sep47
PD363 576Sq Oct44, Missing 7/8Mar45
PD364 218Sq(HA·R), 7Sq Aug45, 15MU, Shoeburyness Jan49
PD365 166Sq Oct45, Missing (Hildesheim) 22Mar45
PD366 622Sq(GI·E) Oct44, 44Sq Aug45, SOC Oct45
PD367 115Sq Oct44, Missing (Osterfeld) 30Nov44

PD368 9Sq(WS·A); Crashed on take-off, Bardney, 1Jan45
PD369 12Sq Oct44, 5MU Nov45, Scrap Nov46
PD370 115Sq(IL·C),138Sq Jun45, 149Sq May46, Crash 13Jul46
PD371 617Sq, Damaged 6Feb45, 38MU Feb46, Scrap May47
PD372 44Sq Oct44, 75Sq Jul45, 38MU Oct45, Scrap May47
PD373 44Sq(KM·X) Oct44, Lost (Heilbronn) 4Dec44
PD374 218Sq Oct44, Missing 8Nov44. 37hrs
PD375 625Sq(CF·R) Oct44, Lost (Chemnitz) 5Mar45
PD376 625Sq Oct44, 576Sq Apr45, 39MU Nov45, Scrap Dec46
PD377 9Sq Oct 44, V.C's aircraft, Lost (Ladbergen) 1Jan45
PD378 153Sq(P4·L), Shot up by Ju88, 6 baled out. 3Feb45
PD379 300Sq Oct44, 15MU Dec46, SS(IA) Mar49
PD380 153Sq Oct44, Missing 29Nov44. 68hrs
PD381 Conv. Mk.I, 44Sq, 1661CU, RWE, Damaged 16Mar47, 2MPRD Nov47
PD382 550Sq Oct44, Under repair Aug45, SOC Nov45
PD383 300Sq, Lost off Corsica with 26 aboard, 5Nov45
PD384 166Sq, Overshot on Limber-Caistor Rd. 22Mar45, SS Mar48
PD385 166Sq Oct44, Lost (Ludwigshafen) 1Feb45
PD386 38MU; 1651,1653,1656CUs; SOC Nov45 at Tollerton
PD387 300Sq Nov44, Damaged 8Mar45,15MU Aug46, Scrap Jan47
PD388 625Sq Oct44, Missing 14Jan45
PD389 514Sq 4Nov44, 38MU 17Jun45, Scrap May47
PD390 12Sq Nov44, 626Sq Sep45, 39MU Oct45, Scrap Nov46
PD391 626Sq 3Nov44, 39MU 1Dec45, Scrap Feb47
PD392 38MU Oct44, 1651CU Nov44, 1653CU Jul45, SOC Apr46
PD393 626Sq(UM·N) Nov44, Lost (Nuremberg) 16Mar45
PD394 166Sq Nov44, Damaged 26Dec44, Lost (Chemnitz) 14Feb45
PD395 195Sq Nov44-Jun46, Repaired 3 times, Scrap Mar48
PD396 101Sq, Damaged 21/22Feb45, 39MU Nov45, Scrap Sep46
PD397 166Sq Nov44, Missing (Cologne) 24Dec44
PD398 467Sq Nov44, Wrecked after operations 26Nov44. 29hrs
PD399 195Sq(JE·H) Nov44, 39MU 25Oct45, SOC Dec46
PD400 90Sq Dec44, 10MU Aug45, Scrap Dec46
PD401 115Sq, Crash-landed Munster 18May45, MUs, Scrap Jul46
PD402 90Sq(WP·G) Dec45, SOC Jan46
PD403 476Sq Nov44, Missing 5/6Mar45
PD404 626Sq(UM·Q2) Nov44, 15Sq Oct45, 44Sq, 15MU, Scrap May47,
PD417 Waddington Nov44, 1659CU Jul45, 38MU, Scrap Sep47
PD418 467Sq(PO·P) Aug45, Became 5736M at Locking
PD419 15Sq Nov44, Damaged 4Dec44, Lost 3/4Feb45
PD420 100Sq, Abandoned near Kirkham after sortie 24Dec44
PD421 150Sq Nov44, Missing 20/21Feb45
PD422 44Sq(KM·T) Dec44, 75Sq Jul45, Broken up Dec45

PP689 serving British South American Airways.

PD423 1666CU Dec44, 1659CU Aug45, 39MU Sep45, SOC Dec46
PD424 1669CU Dec44,1668CU Mar45,1660CU Oct45, SOC Nov45
PD425 619Sq(PG·T) Dec44, Missing (Bohlen) 20Mar45
PD426 195,186,626,149(OJ·H)Sqs; 15MU Apr46, Scrap Mar48
PD427 57Sq Nov45, Lindholme Jan46, 22MU Feb46, Scrap Jun47
PD428 BDU, Crashed 2Jul45 and 1Oct45, Scrap Sep46
PD429 106Sq, Crashed 14Feb45; 186,626Sqs; 39MU, Scrap Nov46
PD430 90Sq(WP·A) Nov44, Scrapped 30Apr46
PD431 1653CU Nov44, Crashed 4Mar44. Named *Edith Weston*
PD432 Avro 18Nov44, 626Sq 5Dec44, Crashed 25May45
PD433 90Sq(WP·P) Nov44, 39MU Apr46, 2MPRD Jun47
PD434 1666CU, Ground accident 11Feb45, 38MU, Scrap Sep47
PD435 AAEE Boscombe Down Dec44, 46MU May45, SOC Jan47
PD436 1666CU Nov44, 1659CU Aug45, 39MU Sep45, Scrap Jan47
PD437 1667CU,1662CU, Crashed near Woodbeck Valley 5/6Mar45
PD438 Blind Landing Experimental Unit, 10MU, SS(CC) Feb49
PD439 218Sq(HA·J),514Sq(A2·C), 22MU Sep44, Scrap May47

PD440 218(HA ·C),138,149Sqs; 10MU 26Jul46, Scrap Jan47
PD441 619Sq Dec44, 463Sq Aug45, 22MU Oct45, Scrap Jun47
PD442 1662CU Dec44, 1667CU Apr45, 5MU Sep45, SOC Dec45
PD443 1662,1656CUs; Fired by flashbomb at Lindholme 9Jun45
PD444 1662CU,115Sq, Accident 20Feb45, MU Oct45, Scrap May47

Serial Range PP663—PP918   Lancaster B.I

200 Lancaster B.Is ordered from Vickers Armstrong (Castle Bromwich) of which 100 were delivered from February 21st to August 22nd, 1945, with Merlin 24 engines.

PP663 75Sq Feb45, 44Sq Jul45, 20MU Sep45, Scrap Jul46
PP664 15Sq Feb45, 20MU Oct45, Scrap Oct46
PP665 195Sq Feb45, 100Sq Aug45, 38MU Feb46, Scrap Sep47
PP666 115Sq(KO·W) Feb45, 24MU Apr45, 20MU Sep45, SS(CC) May47
PP667 195Sq Mar45, 153Sq Aug45, SOC Oct45
PP668 195Sq Apr45, 626Sq(UM ·N) Aug45, 20MU Oct45, Scrap Oct46
PP669 195Sq Apr45, 550Sq Aug45, 5MU Dec45, Scrap Mar47
PP670 115,622,44(KM ·G)Sqs; 20MU Nov45, Scrap Oct46
PP671 195,625,50Sqs; 39MU Jan46, Scrap Feb47
PP672 15Sq; EXODUS, Swung taking off in France 13May45
PP673 149Sq, Dived from 2,000ft over Arras 5Jun45
PP674 1666CU Mar45, 1659CU Aug45, 22MU Sep45, Scrap Jun47
PP675 138Sq Mar45, 115Sq Jun45, 39MU Sep45, Scrap Dec46
PP676 1666CU,1659CU(RV ·M) Aug45, 39MU Sep45, 2MPRD Jun47
PP677 149Sq Mar45, 44Sq Oct45, 5MU Jul46, Scrap May47
PP678 138Sq, 75Sq Jun45, 44Sq Jul45, 39MU, Scrap Jan47
PP679 138Sq Apr45, 218Sq Jun45, 10MU Aug45, Scrap Jan47
PP680 90Sq(WP ·D)Mar45,218Sq Jun45,10MU Aug45,Scrap Oct46
PP681 149Sq Mar45,44Sq(KM ·G)Oct45,15MU Sep46,Scrap Mar48
PP682 90Sq(WP ·J)Mar45,218Sq Jun45,10MU Aug45,Scrap Oct46
PP683 46MU 17Mar45, Scrap Jan47
PP684 149Sq Mar45, 20MU Oct45, Scrap Jul46
PP685 149Sq(OJ·G) Mar45,44Sq Oct45,10MU Jul46, Scrap Jan47
PP686 149Sq Mar45,44Sq(KM ·U)Oct45,15MU Sep46, Scrap Feb47
PP687 149Sq Mar45,44Sq(KM ·W)Oct45,15MU Apr46, SOC Dec46
PP688 5MU, Became G-AGUK Star Gold of BSAAC, Scrap 1947
PP689 5MU, Became G-AGUJ Star Pilot of BSAAC, Scrap 1947
PP690 Became G-AGUL Star Watch of BSAAC, Crash 23Oct47
PP691 46MU 30Mar45, Scrap Jan47
PP692 46MU 29Mar45, Crashed 9Apr45, Kemble, Scrap May47
PP693-5 and PP713 46MU Apr45, Scrapped Jun47
PP714 Avro 13Apr45, 9Sq 24Apr45, 5MU Sep45, Scrap Jan47
PP715-33 46MU Apr-May45, Scrapped Jan47
PP734 5MU May45, Became G-AKAM of Flight Refuelling
PP735-8 46MU May45, Scrapped late 1946-early 1947
PP739 Became G-AKAB Sky Trainer of Skyways, Scrap Nov48
PP740 15MU May45, Scrap May47
PP741 5MU, Became G-AJMW, Sold to Italy for Alitalia 1948
PP742-3 5MU, Became G-AKAL/AKAK of Flight Refuelling
PP744 20MU, Became G-AGUN Star Belle of BSAAC/BOAC and later G-AHVN of Flight Refuelling, Scrap 1950
PP745 10MU 31May45, Scrap Jan47
PP746 20MU, Became G-AGUO Star Bright of BSAA SS(CC) May47
PP747-50 10/10/15/46MUs respectively, Jun45, Scrap 1947
PP751 20MU, Became G-AGUM Star Ward BSAAC, Scrap 1949
PP752-4 46/38/38MUs; Scrapped between Jan & May 1947
PP755 RAE Jan45, Tested elevator control for Brabazom
PP756 10MU 26Apr45, Scrap Feb47
PP757 Finningley Jul45, BCIS 5Dec45, Flew into ground 22Jul46
PP758 10MU 26Jan45, Scrap Feb47
PP772-7 46MU Jun45, Scrap late 1946 or early 1947
PP778 ATDU Gosport 27Jul45, SOC Jan46
PP779 Rolls-Royce 18Jul45, BTU 1948, 34MU Scrap Oct48
PP780 511Sq 18Jul45, Wrecked 13Jun46
PP781-5 38/38/30/10/46MUs; Scrap late 1946/early 1947
PP786-7 ATDU Gosport Aug45, SOC Jan46
PP788 22MU 8Aug45, Scrap May47
PP789 22MU, EPTS Cranfield May46, 15MU, 2MPRD Oct46
PP790 39MU 23Aug45, 2MPRD Jun47

PP791 15MU, Rolls-Royce test bed; 5MU, SS(JD) Jan50
PP792 15MU 22Aug45, Scrap Mar47
PP793-806, PP820-866 and PP880-918 were cancelled.

Serials PW925, PW929, PW932   Lincoln Prototypes

Three prototype Lancaster Mk. 1V/V ordered from A. V. Roe and delivered to R.A.F. October 22nd, November 13th, 1945, and January 15th, 1946, respectively.

Serial Range RA500—RA806   Lancaster B.I/Lincoln B.I/B.II

250 Lancasters ordered from Metropolitan Vickers in August 1943 of which 201 aircraft were built and delivered from December 1944 to April 1945 as 121 Lancaster B.I with Merlin 24 engines initially installed, 28 Lincoln B.I and 52 Lincoln B.II.

RA500 103Sq Jan45, Damaged 29Jan45 and 7/8Mar45
RA501 106Sq 17Jan45, Damaged beyond repair 20/21Feb45
RA502 550Sq, Collided over France and crashed 1/2Feb45
RA503 550Sq Jan45, Damaged 21Mar45, SOC Nov45
RA504 424Sq(QM ·B) Jan45, Crashed 27Nov45
RA505 433Sq Jan45, 20MU Nov45, SS(CC) May47
RA506 433Sq Jan45, 427Sq Oct45,20MU May46,SS(CC) May47
RA507 424Sq(QB ·S), Damaged twice, 10MU, Scrap Feb47
RA508 106Sq 5Feb45, Missing 12Mar45
RA509 433Sq 22Jan45, 39MU 27Nov45, Scrap Mar46
RA510 1000th by Metro-Vickers, 75Sq(AA ·J), MU, SOC Nov46
RA511-2 433Sq Jan45, 20MU Nov45, Scrap May47/Sep46
RA513 433Sq Jan45, Royal Navy Nov45, 10MU, Scrap Jan47
RA514 576 Feb45, Damaged 24Mar45, 15MU, Scrap May47
RA515-6 103/576Sqs Feb45, Lost 23/24 & 21/22Feb45
RA517 189Sq 5Feb45, Lost 14/15Feb45
RA518 227Sq(9J ·C) 20Feb45, 22MU Feb46, Scrap Jun47
RA519 619Sq(PG ·U) Feb45; 617,467Sqs; SOC Nov45
RA520 630Sq(LE ·E),617Sq Jul45, 38MU Feb46, Scrap Sep47
RA521 619Sq(PG ·D),9Sq Jul45, 22MU Feb46, Scrap Jun47
RA522 218Sq(HA ·V) Mar45, 7Sq Aug45, 39MU, Scrap Jan47
RA523 101Sq(SR ·I) Feb45, Lost (Pforzheim) 23Feb45
RA524 Avro Jan45, 460Sq Feb45, Missing 2Mar45
RA525 460Sq, 57Sq Aug45, 15MU, Scrap Mar48
RA526 153Sq 9Feb45, Missing 12/13Mar45
RA527 619Sq(PG ·M) 10Feb45, 15MU 3Oct45, Scrap Mar47
RA528 103Sq Feb45, 57Sq Apr45, 60MU Feb46, SOC Mar46
RA529 170Sq Feb45, Lindholme Dec45, SOC Mar46
RA530 57Sq, Hit house at Stickney after take-off 20Mar45
RA531 49Sq 10Feb45, Missing (Lutzkendorf) 8/9Apr45
RA532 218Sq 21Feb45, Damaged beyond repair 19Mar45
RA533 186Sq, Collided with HK555 over Giesh, 4Apr45
RA534 429Sq Feb46, 20MU Nov45, SS(CC) May47
RA535 626Sq(UM·X2),12Sq Sep45, 101Sq, 38MU, Scrap Sep47
RA536-7 427Sq(ZL ·N/P) Feb45, MUs 1946, Scrap 1947
RA538 427Sq Feb45, 20MU Feb46, Scrap May47
RA539 427Sq(ZL ·O) Feb45, 15MU Feb46, Scrap Mar46
RA540 170Sq Feb45, Pershore Jan46, 20MU, SS(CC) Mar47
RA541 75Sq,514Sq(JI ·D) Jul45, 279Sq Sep45, Scrap Nov46
RA542 463Sq, Force-landed in Sweden (Tonsburg) 25/26Apr45
RA543 626Sq Feb45, 15Sq(LS ·A) Oct45, 5MU, Scrap Jan47
RA544-5 153Sq Mar45, Lost 4/5Apr45/SOC Oct45
RA546 227Sq(9J ·J), Lost (Lutzkendorf) 14/15Mar45
RA547 550Sq Feb45, 32MU Nov45, Scrap 1947
RA560 Avro Feb45, 61Sq 1Mar45, Missing 20/21Mar45
RA561 Avro Feb45, 61Sq 1Mar45, 9MU Jan46, Scrap Jan47
RA562 576Sq 28Feb45, Wrecked 16Oct45, Scrap Oct45
RA563 576Sq 28Feb45, 15MU Sep45, Scrap May47
RA564 75Sq(JN ·P), Lost Munster viaduct raid 21Mar45
RA565 50Sq Mar45, 83Sq Mar46, SS(CC) Mar47
RA566 103Sq Mar45, 57Sq Nov45, 39MU, Scrap Jan47
RA567 106Sq Mar45, 7Sq Jun45, 15MU, Scrap Mar48
RA568 189Sq Mar45, 106Sq Nov45, 15MU Mar46, SS(IA) Mar49
RA569-70 SIU Mar45, 186Sq Apr45, 218Sq, 5MU SS(CC) Aug48
RA571 429Sq(AL ·D), Hit hill at Pullans Farm, Ilkley, 5Nov45
RA572 460Sq Mar45, 57Sq Oct45, SOC Feb46
RA573 463Sq Mar45, 20MU Oct45, Scrap Jun47
RA574 12Sq Mar-Apr45, 44Sq Apr46, 5MU Scrap Dec46
RA575 170Sq Mar45, Lindholme 29Dec45, Scrap Jun47

RA576 Avro Feb45, 463Sq Mar45, 39MU Oct45, Scrap Jan47
RA577 SIU,186Sq,218Sq(HA ·N),BDU Aug45,20MU,SS(CC) May47
RA578 424Sq Mar45, 20MU Nov45, RN Nov45, 10MU, Scrap Mar47
RA579 103Sq Mar45, 57Sq, 39MU, Scrap Nov46
RA580 SIU, 186Sq Apr45, 218Sq Jul45, 5MU, SS(CC) Aug48
RA581 106Sq Mar45, 35Sq Jun45, 22MU Dec45, Scrap May47
RA582 153Sq Mar45, 20MU Oct45, Scrap Nov46
RA583 12Sq Mar-Apr45, Lindholme Apr46, 38MU, Scrap May47
RA584 150Sq Mar45, Crash 24Dec45, 54MU,150Sq, SOC Nov45
RA585 12Sq Mar-Apr45, Lindholme Jan46, 38MU, Scrap May47
RA586 150Sq, 5MU Apr46, Scrap Mar48
RA587 576Sq Mar45, 150Sq Sep45, 15MU Feb46, SS(IA) Mar49
RA588 619Sq(PG ·W) Mar45; 9,207,149Sqs; Scrap Mar48
RA589 166Sq Mar45, 5MU Dec45, Scrap May47
RA590 619Sq(PG ·Y)Mar45, 9Sq Aug45,38MU Feb46, Scrap Sep47
RA591 50Sq(VN ·P) Mar45, 39MU Mar46, 2MPRD Jan47
RA592 100Sq(HW ·M2) Apr45, 22MU May46, Scrap May47
RA593 61Sq Mar45, 9MU Jan46, 2MPRD Oct47
RA594 576Sq Mar45, 170Sq Sep45, 50Sq Dec45, SOC Apr46
RA595 101Sq, Crashed taking off Brussels EXODUS 10Apr45
RA596 57Sq Apr45, 22MU Feb46, Scrap Jun47
RA597 101Sq Mar45, 617Sq May46, 300Sq,15MU, Scrap Mar48
RA598 460,75,207(EM ·R),138,149Sqs; 15MU, Scrap Nov46
RA599 514Sq,54MU; 207,90,207Sqs; 15MU, Scrap Feb47
RA600-1 32MU,514Sq,54MU; 514,97Sqs; 20MU,SS(CC) May47
RA602 32MU, 514Sq, 97Sq(OF ·U), 20MU, SS(CC) May47
RA603 630,617,97Sqs(OF ·W); 5MU, Scrap Jan47
RA604-5 Avro Mar45, 46MU, To Near East Oct46, SS Jun50
RA606-7 To Near East Dec46, Scrap Jun50
RA623 46MU Apr45, To Near East Oct46, Scrap Jun50
RA624 46MU May45, 45MU Nov46, Scrap Feb48
RA625 10MU May45, Became B ·041 Argentine Air Force
RA626 Conv.FE, Conv.PRI May50, 683Sq, Scrap Nov54
RA627 Mod (FE); 15,38MUs; Became of WU ·49 Aéronavale

(RA628-655 produced as Lincoln B.I from January to September 1945 and RA656-658, RA661-693 and RA709-724 as Lincoln B.II from September to December 1945. RA725-749 and RA763-786 were cancelled numbers.)

RA787 Mod FE; 5,38MUs; Became WU ·30 of Aéronavale
RA788-9 10MU Jun45, Became B ·043/4 Argentine Air Force
RA790-1 46MU Jun45, 45MU Oct46 for Near East SS Jun50
RA792 Mod FE by AWA Jan47, 32,39MUs; SS Sep50
RA793 Mod FE by AWA, 38MU Jul45, Scrap Sep47
RA794 Avro Apr45, 38MU Jul45, Scrap Sep47
RA795-6 Mod FE Jan47, Became WU ·50/WU ·51 of Aéronavale
RA797 Mod FE by AWA Dec46, Became WU ·26 of Aéronavale
RA798 10MU, Became B.042 Argentine Air Force
RA799-800 Mod FE Mar47, Became WU ·31/WU ·52 of Aéronavale
RA801 20MU,CSE Sep46, Damaged in gale Mar47, Scrap Mar48

RE131 tested scaled-down controls for the Brabazon.

RA802 20MU,CSE Sep46, Gale damage Mar47, Became 6426M
RA803 ConvFE Jul46 and PR Jun40, 82Sq, Scrap Dec52
RA804/6 46MU Jun45, 45MU Oct46, Scrap Feb48
RA805 46MU, Became G-11-29, and 80001 of Royal Swedish Air Force.

N.B. Last 7 Lancasters and 11 Lincolns were transferred, un-assembled, for completion at Vickers-Armstrong, Chester.

Serial Range RE100—RF119   Lancaster B.III(Lincoln B.I/B.II)
700 Lancasters ordered from A. V. Roe (Yeadon) which were built as 87 Lancaster B.III with Merlin 224 from March to June 1945, 50 Lincoln B.I and 112 Lincoln B.II. RE100-114 cancelled.

RE115/G 32MU,97Sq(OF ·G),ConvASRIII,179,210Sqs; Conv GRIII,210Sq,SMR(H ·P) Apr54, Scrap May57
RE116/G 32MU,541Sq(JI ·F) (A2 ·F), Mod ASRIII, Middle East; 38,37Sqs; Conv GRIII, 15MU, 203Sq, Crashed 25Jan51
RE117 514Sq(JI ·D2), Conv.ASRIII, Middle East, Scrap Jun47
RE118-9 100(HW ·N)/97(OF ·G)Sqs, 39/9MUs 1946, 2MPRD 1947
RE120 32MU,514Sq,ConvASRIII, Middle East, 8MU, SS Aug48
RE121 103Sq(PM ·I),RWE,CSE, Became 6586M at Watton
RE122 12Sq Mar45, 61Sq Sep45, SOC Feb46
RE123 514Sq(JI ·K2), Conv.ASRIII; 38,37Sqs; Scrap Aug51

Flying shots of RE172.

RE124 460Sq, 22MU, Middle East 1946, 2MPRD Jun47
RE125 12Sq Mar45, 626Sq Sep45, 20MU Oct45, Scrap Oct46
RE126 170Sq Mar45, 12Sq Oct45, 427Sq, 10MU, Scrap Sep47
RE127 576Sq, Crash 8/9Apr45, 38MU,CSE,20MU, 2MPRD Nov47
RE128 207Sq Mar45, Spilsby Oct45, 20MU, SOC Jun46
RE129 32MU,97Sq,ConvASRIII, Middle East 1946, SOC Jul49
RE130 106Sq, NTU, 7Sq Jun45, 20MU Aug45, Scrap Aug46
RE131 44,75,207Sqs; 5MU, AWA and Bristol, SOC Apr53
RE132 44,75,207Sqs; Spilsby Oct45, 20MU Nov45, Scrap Aug46
RE133 and RE135 50Sq Mar45, SOC 19Feb46
RE134 467Sq Mar45, 35Sq Jan45, 22MU Feb46, Scrap May47
RE136 467Sq Apr45, 35Sq Jun45, 38MU Mar46, Scrap May47
RE137 514Sq, Air Service Training, NGTE, 10MU, Scrap May50
RE138 101Sq(SR ·W/D2) Apr45, 10MU Jul46, Scrap Jan47
RE139 MUs, Conv ASRIII, 38Sq, Conv GRIII, SS Sep51
RE140 514Sq, Conv ASRIII, Middle East May46, SOC Mar49
RE153-4 429(AL ·V)/101 (SR ·X2)Sqs, MUs 1946, Scrap 1947
RE155 429Sq Apr45, Crashed 15Sep45
RE156 38MU, 514Sq, To Middle East Dec45 where SOC Jan46
RE157 101Sq(SR ·R) Apr45, 39MU Nov45, Scrap Oct46
RE158 514Sq, Conv ASR/GRIII, 120Sq, Crashed 25Oct49
RE159 32MU,514Sq,10MU,Conv ASRIII; 39,218MUs; 37,38Sqs; Conv GRIII, MRS May51, SS Sep56
RE160-1 427(ZL ·G)/101(SR ·L2)Sqs MUs 1946, Scrap 1947
RE162 101Sq Apr45, 39MU Nov45, SOC Jan47

206

RE163 101Sq(SR·T2) Apr45, 617Sq May46, Wrecked 26Jul46
RE164 32MU,46MU,Conv ASRIII,224Sq Oct46, ASWDU Dec46, JASS,Conv GRIII,SMR(H·U),Flt.Refuelling, SOC Aug56
RE165 Conv ASRIII/GRIII, 210Sq, SMR, SS Sep56

RE206 fitted with wingtip rocket rails.

RE166 32,10MUs; Conv ASR3, Middle East, SOC Mar49
RE167 Conv ASR/GRIII, MUs, 37Sq Jun49, SOC Jun53
RE168 Conv ASR/GRIII; 224,203Sqs; SS Dec53
RE169 Conv ASR/GRIII, 203Sq, SS Oct56
RE170 Conv ASR/GRIII, 38Sq Jan49, UK Aug53, SS Jul56
RE171 Conv ASR/GRIII, ASWDU,ML Aviation, RAE, SS Sep56
RE172 38,218MUs; Middle East Nov45-May46, 39MU, 2MPRD Jun47
RE173 Conv ASR/GRIII, 37Sq Oct48, SOC Jun53
RE174 38MU Apr45, 214Sq, Crashed landing at Lydda 5Mar46
RE175 Conv ASR/GRIII, 224Sq, 210Sq Jul48, Scrap Jul50
RE176-7 103Sq/38MU May45, Both scrapped mid-1947
RE178 38,218MUs; To Middle East Jan46 where SOC Oct46
RE179 30MU, Believed Conv ASRIII, Sold as scrap May45
RE180 32MU May45; Crashed Mortehoe, Devon, 16Dec45
RE181 Conv ASR/GRIII, 236OCU(K7·LJ),SMR,SS(ERM) Sep56
RE182 38MU, Middle East Dec45-Aug46,214Sq,5MU,Scrap Jan47
RE183 38MU, Middle East Nov45-Jun45, 5MU, SOC Mar48
RE184 38MU, Conv ASRIII, 39MU, SOC Mar48
RE185 Conv ASR/GRIII, 37Sq Jun49, 38Sq, SS(ERM) Sep56
RE186 Conv ASR/GRIII, 236OCU(K7·C); SMR(L·H), SS May57
RE187 Conv ASR/GRIII; 37,38Sqs; Scrap at 137MU Oct53
RE188 10MU May45, Conv ASRIII, Shoeburyness Apr51
RE200 Conv ASRIII,236OCU,Conv GRIII,203Sq, Crash 22May52
RE201 15,218MUs; Middle East Dec45, MU, Scrap Mar48
RE202 15MU;70,178Sqs; Hit high ground landing, Fazid, 21Jan46
RE203-4 5,16MUs; Middle East Oct45, Scrap Mar48/Jan46
RE205 Conv ASR/GRIII,236OCU(K7·LP),SMR,15MU,SS Sep56
RE206 10MU,ASR/GRIII,ASWDU Aug48, loaned Flt. Refuelling Ltd,AAEE,203Sq,ASWDU, Fitted with RP rails, SS Oct56
RE207 Conv ASRIII,120Sq,Conv GRIII,120Sq, Crashed 2Mar49
RE208 10MU, Believed conv ASRIII,10MU Oct46, SS(IA) Apr51
RE209-10 Middle East 1946, Scrap (ME) Oct46/UK Feb49
RE211 Conv ASR/GRIII, 236OCU(K7·LM),SMR, To Avro Apr46
RE212 46MU Jun46, Middle East Nov45-Jun46, Scrap Mar47
RE213-4 Held in MUs, SS(ERM) Nov49/SS(IA) Apr51
RE215 10,218MUs; Middle East Dec45-May46,38MU,SOC Mar48
RE216 10MU Jul45, Believed Conv ASRIII,SS(IA) Apr51
RE217 Conv ASR/GRIII, 203Sq, 236OCU(K7·LL), Crashed 22Mar49
RE218 46MU, Middle East Dec45-Jul46, 5MU, Scrap Jul47
RE219 46MU, 38MU, Became 6599M at EFS
RE220 46MU, Middle East Dec45-Jan46, 10MU, Scrap Sep47
RE221 Conv ASR/GRIII,120Sq,SMR(H·J), 38Sq, SS May57
RE222 38MU,ASR/GRIII,120Sq,SMR(H·K) Dec55, Scrap May57
RE225 46MU Jan45, 16FU, Crashed take-off, Dunkeswell, 7May46
RE226 46MU, Held in MUs, Scrap Apr51
RE227-268 and RE281-288 Lincoln B.I delivered from March to July 1945; RE289-325, RE338-380, RE393-424 Lincoln B.II delivered from July 1945 to April 1946; RE425-435, RE449-493, RE518-561, RE575-605, RE621-670, RE683-726, RE740-785, RE798-839, RE853-895, RE918-955, RE967-999 and RF111-119 cancelled.

Serial Range RF120-RF599   Lancaster B.I/B.III

370 Lancasters ordered from Armstrong Whitworth Aircraft in October 1943 and delivered as 65 Lancaster B.I and 105 Lancaster B.III, from February to May 1945 and 2 Lincoln B.I and 198 Lincoln B.II from Baginton and Bitteswell.

Lancaster B.I (Merlin 24 engines initially installed)
RF120 576Sq Feb45, Missing 7/8Mar45
RF121-2 61/630Sqs 5Feb45, Lost 9 & 10Apr45
RF123 61Sq 10Feb45, 9MU Jun46, 2MPRD Apr47
RF124 57,630Sqs, Crashed on road, Wednesfield, 17May45
RF125 101Sq, Force-landed France 4/5Apr45, Scrap Oct46
RF126 186Sq Feb45, 576Sq Jul45, 15MU, Shoeburyness Sep49
RF127 75Sq(AA·W) Feb45, 44Sq, Jul45, 20MU, SS(CC) May47
RF128 424Sq(QB·V) Feb45, 22MU Nov45, Scrap Mar48
RF129 75Sq Feb45, 44Sq Jul45, 20MU Sep45, SS(CC) Mar47
RF130 106Sq Feb45, 7Sq Jun45, 39MU Sep45, SOC Oct46
RF131 227Sq(9J·B)Feb45,115Sq Oct45,39MU Nov45,Scrap Sep46
RF132 189Sq 13Feb45, Missing (Bohlen) 20Mar45
RF133 218Sq Feb45, 7Sq Aug45, 20MU Oct45, Scrap Nov46
RF134 12Sq Feb-Apr45, Lindholme, 15MU Feb46, Scrap Mar48
RF135 550Sq, 100Sq(HW·W2) Apr45, Crashed 14Dec45
RF136 550Sq Feb45, Crashed in Italy DODGE 6Oct45
RF137 61Sq(QR·E), Blew up at Skellingthorpe 24Feb45
RF138 50Sq Feb45, Missing (Gravenhorst) 21/22Feb45
RF139 467Sq, 35Sq Jun45, 22MU Feb46, Scrap Jun47
RF140 467,635,35,15,44Sqs; 37MU Nov46, 2MPRD Oct47
RF141 463Sq(JO·U) 20Feb45, 22MU Oct45, Scrap Mar48
RF142 138Sq(AC·A), Air Survey Flt, Jan46, 5MU, Scrap May47
RF143 138Sq Mar45, Missing 15/16Apr45
RF144 207Sq Feb44, 15MU Feb46, Shoeburyness Apr49
RF145 625Sq Feb45, Missing (Nuremberg)) 5Mar45
RF146 625Sq Feb45, 39MU Nov45, Scrap Jan47
RF147 SIU; 186,218(HA·T)Sqs; 5MU,AAEE, SS(JD) Feb49
RF148-9 424/433Sqs Feb45,22/39MU Nov45, Scrap May47/Sep46
RF150 424Sq, Hit hill S.W. of High Wycombe 5Apr45
RF151 189Sq(CA·E), 106Sq(ZN·E), SOC Feb46
RF152 463Sq 26Feb45, SOC Oct45
RF153 50,49Sqs; Missing 14/15Mar45
RF154 166Sq 22Feb45, Missing (Nuremberg) 16/17Mar45
RF155 12Sq Feb-Apr45, 39MU Dec45, Scrap Oct46
RF156 626Sq(UM·P), 20MU Nov45, SS(CC) Mar47
RF157 75Sq(AA·X), 44Sq, 38MU, Scrap Sep47
RF158 166Sq 22Feb45, Kirmington Dec45, Scrap Jun47
RF159 626Sq(UM·C2), Crashed in France 7Aug45
RF160 61Sq 1Mar45, 5MU 19Jan46, Scrap May47
RF161 12Sq Feb45, Lindholme 7Mar46, SOC Mar46
RF175 463Sq Mar45, 15MU Oct45, Scrap May47
RF176 61Sq, Missing (Wurzburg) 16/17Mar45
RF177 463Sq Feb45, 39MU Oct45, Scrap Aug46
RF178 227Sq, 155Sq(KO·V) Sep45, 39MU Dec45, Scrap Sep46
RF179 49,57,460,57Sqs; 38MU Jan46, Scrap Sep47
RF180 467,635,35,207(EM·H)Sqs; 20MU, SS Apr46
RF181-2 12Sq Mar45, Lost 16/17Mar & 4/5Mar45
RF183 32MU; 35,156,49Sqs; 10MU, Scrap Jan47
RF184 90(WP·C),207,138Sqs; 377MU, 2MPRD Oct47
RF185 90Sq(WP·T); 15MU Feb46, Scrap Feb47
RF186 103,57Sqs; 39MU Apr46, 2MPRD Jun47
RF187 12,101,44(KM·P)Sqs; Became 6294M at Wyton
RF188 12Sq Mar45, Missing 16/17Mar45
RF189 625,300Sqs; To Alvis Ltd, Coventry, May47
RF190 75,44Sqs; 19MU Sep45, SOC Nov46
RF191 460(AR·J),57(DX·J)Sqs; MUs, Scrap Jun47
RF192 630(LE·A),617,57Sqs; 39MU, 2MPRD Oct47
RF193 103Sq, 57Sq(DX·G), 39MU May46, 2MPRD Jun47
RF194 207,186,106(ZN·T)Sqs; 22MU Mar46, Scrap Jun47
RF195 57Sq, Blown up by PB360's bombs, E. Kirkby, 17Apr45
RF196 460Sq(AR·E), Crashed at Rothwell Top 4/5Apr45
RF197 576Sq Apr45, Wrecked 10Oct46

Lancaster B.III (Merlin 224 engines initially)
RF198 186Sq Mar45,1659CU(FD·M) May45,39MU, 2MPRD Jun47
RF199 170,Sq,231Sq Dec45, Crashed 27Nov46, Scrap Apr47
RF200 576Sq Mar45, 15MU Aug45, Scrap May47
RF201 61Sq(QR·C), Crashed 21Mar46, Became 5848M at 12STT

RF202 57,630,467Sqs; 20MU Dec45, SS(CC) May47
RF203 44Sq Mar45, Crashed 13May45
RF204 189Sq Mar45, 12Sq Feb46, 5MU Sep46, Scrap Sep47
RF205 153,12,427,300Sqs; 15MU Dec46, Scrap May47
RF206 44Sq Mar45, 75Sq Sep45, Spilsby Oct45, SOC Nov45
RF207 429Sq(AL ·S) Mar45, 22MU 22May46, Scrap Jun47
RF208-9 207Sq Mar43, Spilsby Oct45, Scrap 1947
RF210 44Sq Mar45, Crashed 8May45, Conv ASRIII Aug46, 203Sq,
    Conv GRIII, 203Sq, Lost at sea 23Jan52
RF211 166Sq 19Mar45, 5MU 11Dec45, Scrap Aug47
RF212 460Sq Mar45, 57Sq Oct45, 15MU Jan46, 2MPRD Oct47
RF213-4 576/550Sqs, 20MU Sep45/Scrap Sep46
RF215 106Sq Apr45, 7Sq Jun45, 5MU Aug45, Scrap Mar48
RF216 189Sq Apr45, 5MU Feb46, Scrap Sep47
RF229 103(PM ·O), 57Sq Apr45, 39MU, SOC Nov46
RF230 514Sq, Crashed Roye-Ami 9May45, 31 killed
RF231 514Sq, Conv ASRIII Feb45, 6 OTU, Crashed 25Jun47
RF232 460Sq Mar45, Middle East Dec45-Jul46, 2MPRD Apr47
RF233 460Sq Mar45, 5MU Aug45, Scrap Mar46
RF234 619Sq(PG ·T), Film Unit Aug45, RWE,2MPRD Nov47
RF235 106Sq 26Mar45, Crashed 9May45
RF236 106Sq(ZN ·V), Middle East Dec45 until scrapped Jan47
RF237 550Sq(BQ ·H) Mar45, 20MU Aug45, SS(CC) May47
RF238 44,75,207Sqs; TFU Defford Jan46, 20MU, SS(CC) May47
RF239 619(PG ·K),83,12,9,300Sqs; Scrap Mar48
RF240 44,75,207Sqs; Spilsby Oct45, 5MU Nov45, Scrap Sep47
RF241 626Sq, Accident 13Sep45, 20MU Oct45, Scrap Aug46
RF242 300Sq Apr45, 10MU Dec46, Scrap Sep47
RF243 150Sq Apr45, 231Sq Dec45, 20MU Apr46, SS(CC) May47
RF244 166Sq, ATDU Gosport Jan46, SOC Aug46
RF245 150Sq Apr45; 12,427,300Sqs; 10MU, Scrap Sep47
RF246 460Sq Apr45, BSAAC Oct45, Broken up 1946
RF247 460Sq Apr45, 20MU Aug45, Scrap Jul46
RF248 460Sq Apr45, 22MU Aug45, SOC in Middle East Sep46
RF249 50Sq Apr45, 83Sq Mar46, 20MU, SS(CC) May47
RF250 460Sq, BSAAC Oct45, Broken up later
RF251 460Sq 7Apr45, 5MU Aug45, Scrap Mar48
RF252 429Sq 7Apr45, 38MU May46, Scrap May47
RF253 429Sq, Engine failure on bomb disposal 26Jun45
RF254 460Sq 31Mar45, 5MU Sep45, Scrap Mar48
RF255-6 626Sq(UM ·G2/T2) Apr45, 15/20MU Oct45, Scrap May47
RF257 427Sq 9Apr45, Overshot landing at Leeming 10Jan46
RF258 32MU,BDU(Later CBE)Apr45,Became 6313M Waddington
RF259 429Sq(AL ·H), Crashed on take-off Leeming 14Feb46
RF260 424Sq, 427Sq(ZL ·Z), 10MU, SS(IA) Apr51
RF261 101Sq (SR ·B) Apr45, 15MU Jul46, Scrap Jan47
RF262 101Sq Apr45, 300Sq May41; Crashed, burnt, 7May46
RF263 101Sq Apr45, 9MU Jul46, 2MPRD Oct47
RF264 101Sq(SR ·H) Apr45, 39MU Nov45, Scrap Aug46
RF265 44,75,207Sqs; Spilsby Oct45, 5MU Nov45, Scrap Jul47
RF266 207Sq Apr45, 231Sq Dec45, 20MU May46, SS Aug47
RF267 50Sq(VN ·M) 16Apr45, SOC Feb46
RF268 101Sq,RAE with auto-control guns, Became 6206M St. Eval
RF269 32,46MUs; Conv ASRIII, Near East Jun-Oct47;
    37,38Sqs; Conv GRIII, SMR Jul51, SS(BA) Jul46
RF270 463Sq Apr45, 20MU, BSAAC Oct45, Scrap Aug 46
RF271 MUs,ConvASRIII,230OCU(K7 ·LF)Jan46, Became 6673M
RF272 32MU,514Sq,5MU,279Sq, Mod ASRIII Dec45, Near East,
    37Sq May48, Mod GRIII 1949, 5MU, SMR Jul51, SS(EM)
    Oct56
RF273 MUs, Mod ASRIII then GRIII,38Sq Jan50, SS Jan55
RF286 38MU, Near East 1946, Filton May48, Wrecked 28Jan49
RF287 MUs, Conv ASRIII Nov46; Middle East May47, 37Sq,
    Conv GRIII, 236OCU(K7 ·G) Sep50, SMR, Jul51 SS(ERM)
    Sep56
RF288 38MU,RAE Apr45,Ground accident 4Feb46,1MPRD Jan47
RF289 38MU, Conv ASRIII 1947 and GRIII 1948, 13MU, 120Sq
    Feb49 SMR May51, Scrap Jul55
RF290 38MU,ConvASRIII Dec46,ASWDU May47,38MU, Mod
    GRIII, JASS Flight Eglinton, SMR, Crashed 17Dec54
RF291 32,10MUs; Mod ASRIII 1946, 39MU, Mod GRIII 1948,
    15MU, MEAF 1949, 37Sq, MUs, 38Sq, SOC Oct53
RF292 Mod ASR/GRIII; 279,179,224,210Sqs; Crashed 16Jan50
RF293 UK MUs to Middle East MU Dec46, SOC in M. East Oct46

RF294 Sent for conversion but returned to MU, Scrap May47
RF295 Conv ASR then GRIII, 236OCU, SMR,SS(ERM) Oct56
RF296 38MU, To Middle East Dec45 where SOC Sep46
RF297 38MU, Middle East 1946, 5MU, Scrap 1947 in UK
RF298 38MU, Middle East 1946, 20MU, SS(CC) May47
RF299 38MU Apr45, Middle East Jan46 where SOC Nov46
RF300 Conv ASRIII,20MU,ME Jul-Oct47,38Sq,Scrap Sep50

RF325 the last of the Lancasters in Coastal Command.

RF301 Conv ASRIII, 39MU, Became 6679M at North Coates
RF302 Conv ASRIII,1651CU(BS ·G),120Sq, Crash 23Nov48
RF303 Conv ASR/GRIII, 236OCU(K7 ·T), SMR(H ·F), SS(BA)
    May57
RF304 38MU, Middle East Jan-May46, 10MU, SS(CC) Feb49
RF305 Conv ASRIII/GRIII, JASS, 38MU, SMR, Crash 9Aug54
RF306 Conv ASRIII/GRIII, 37Sq Oct48, Lost at sea 15Aug51
RF307 Conv ASR/GRIII; 179,224,203,210,203Sqs; SS Sep56
RF308 Conv ASRIII/GRIII,MEAF,37Sq May51, Crashed 28Sep53
RF309 Conv ASRIII Mar46, 120Sq Sep46, Conv GRIII, Flt.
    Refuelling Apr51, SMR Oct51, 38MU, SS Dec53
RF310 32,46MUs; Conv ASRIII,279Sq, Crashed Burma 4Mar46
RF311 32,10MUs; Conv ASRIII 1946, GRIII 1949, 203Sq Sep50,
    15MU, SMR(H ·M) Dec55, SS May57
RF312 Conv ASR/GRIII; 179,120,203Sqs; Crashed 21Feb52
RF313 Conv ASRIII,279Sq Dec45,38Sq Dec47,Conv GRIII, Flt.
    Refuelling 1951 2, 38Sq, SMR(H ·N), SS(BA) May57
RF314 15MU Conv ASRIII; 210,224Sqs; 236OCU, Crash Jul48
RF315 15MU, Conv ASRIII; 179,210,120Sqs; 45MU, Scrap Mar48
RF316 15MU,Conv ASRIII,Middle East May46 where SOC May49
RF317 218MU, Crashed after conversion to ASRIII 22Feb46
RF318 Conv ASR/GRIII,236OCU(K7 ·LB),203Sq,SS(ERM) Sep56
RF319 Conv ASR/GRIII,6OTU, 236OCU Jan46, Scrap Jan50
RF320 ConvASRIII,279Sq,38Sq Feb48,Conv GRIII 1949, 236OCU
    (K7 ·U)Feb51,SMR Jul51,38MU Mar55,SS(ERM)Oct56
RF321 Flt. Refuelling and Dowty Equipment Trials SS Mar49
RF322 Conv ASRIII; 279,37,38Sqs; Conv GRIII,5MU,SMR, SS
    Oct56
RF323 Conv ASRIII,38Sq(RL ·C) then (RL ·R), SOC May47
RF324 15MU, Conv ASRIII; 179,224Sqs; Crashed 1May47
RF325 Mod ASRIII, ASWDU, Conv GRIII, ML Aviation, RAE,
    ASWDU, SMR(H ·D), Last Lancaster in RAF service,SS
    Oct56
RF326 218MU, Crashed on take-off after ASRIII conv Mar46
RF333-334 Lincoln B.I delivered on April 4th and May 7th, 1945,

respectively; RF329-332, RF335-370, RF383-427, RF440-485, RF498-539 and RF553-577 Lincoln B.II delivered from March 1945 to May 1947.

Serial Range RS102—RS225   **Lancaster** (not built)

100 Lancaster B.IV/V ordered from Vickers-Armstrong (Castle Bromwich) in December 1943 as RS102-147, RS159-198 and RS203-225 and changed later to B.I, but subsequently cancelled before production commenced.

Serial Range RT140—RT456   **Lancaster** (not built)

240 Lancaster B.VII ordered from Vickers-Armstrong (Chester) as RT140-183, RT197-228, RT245-290, RT315-350, RT362-403 and RT417-456. Cancelled before production commenced.

Serial Range RT670—RT750   **Lancaster B.VII**

68 Lancasters ordered from Austin Motors (Longbridge) of which 30 were built with Merlin 24 engines, November-December 1945.

RT670 32MU 6Nov45,Swinderby Feb46,22MU Mar46,SOC Jun52
RT671 To ME 17Feb46, returned Nov47; Sold Scrap Nov54
RT672 32MU and 39MU, Scrapped by R. J. Coley Feb50
RT673 32,39,5MUs; Sold France Apr53, FCL-04
RT674 Held at Swinderby,Pershore,Newton; Sold France Apr53
RT675 32MU 16Nov45 later 39 and 5MUs, Sold Scrap mid-54
RT676 Far East Feb-Apr46, MUs, Held for Exhibition, SOC Nov53
RT677-8 32MU, Held at Swinderby and Pershore, SS Oct54
RT679 32MU, Swinderby and 5MU, Sold to France as FCL-O5
RT680 32MU Dec45, EFS, EAAS Jan49, Scrapped Mid-50
RT681 MUs, EANS, CNS, CFS, Became 6748M at Cosford
RT682 MUs,Damaged in gale 16Mar47, Became WU ·04 *Aéronavale*
RT683 32MU Dec45, 22MU Mar46, Sold as Scrap Aug54
RT684 32,20,32MUs; EANS Aug47, SOC Feb51

Late production Mk. VIIs at the Austin works.

RT685 32,20,32MUs; EANS Dec47, Sold as Scrap Aug50
RT686 MUs, Hemswell for filming 1954, SS(BAC) Jun56
RT687 MUs, EANS Feb48, 1689Flt Jun51,Scrap Jun44
RT688 MUs, EANS Apr47, To Shoeburyness Jan51
RT689 MUs, EANS Jan47, Sold to French as FCL.03
RT690 Used by Avro, Fitted conical nose, MUs Oct56
RT691-2 Held in MUs, Scrap Dec54/2MPRD Oct47
RT693 32,38MUs; EANS Oct47, 5MU, Sold to France as FCL.O1
RT694 MUs, EANS Apr47, Crashed and SOC Dec48
RT695-6 32MU Dec45, 39MU Mar46, 2MPRD Oct47/SS Nov49
RT697-9 32MU,38MU Mar46, Became WU ·03/06/07 of *Aéronavale*
RT700-701 and RT713-750 cancelled numbers.

Serial Range SR707—SR907   (Not built)

150 Lancaster IV/V ordered from Vickers-Armstrong (Castle Bromwich) in March 1944 as SR707-749, SR766-790, SR814-851, SR864-907. Order cancelled before deliveries.

Serial Range SS341—ST475   **Lincoln B.I/B.II**

800 Lancaster IV/V ordered from A. V. Roe (Yeadon) in March 1944 as SS341-386, SS399-435, SS449-480, SS493-535, SS549-589, SS603-650, SS664-698, SS713-758, SS773-815, SS828-869, SS882-925, SS937-968, SS980-999, ST113-157, ST171-215, ST228-269, ST283-327, ST339-369, ST381-425, ST438-475 of which only six were built as follows: SS713-714 as Lincoln B.I and SS715-718 as Lincoln B.II from August 1945 to April 1946.

Serial Range ST477—ST790   **Lancaster** (not built)

250 Lancasters ordered from Metropolitan Vickers in March 1944 as: ST477-513, ST528-569, ST583-627, ST641-680, ST693-735 and ST748-790. Order cancelled before production commenced.

Serial Range SW243—SW279   **Lancaster B.I**

37 Lancasters built by Metropolitan Vickers and assembled by A. V. Roe from November 24th to December 22nd, 1944, with Merlin 24 engines.

SW243 32MU, 1668CU, Crashed twice, 38MU, Scrap Sep47
SW244 AAEE Apr45, Saddle-tank, 10MU Dec45, Scrap Nov46
SW245 Woodford Nov44, 57Sq 9Dec44, Lost 17Dec44
SW246 1667CU Dec44, 38MU 10Oct45, Scrap Sep47
SW247 227Sq Jan45, 115Sq Sep45, 39MU Mar46, SOC Oct46
SW248 106Sq, NTU, 7Sq Jun45; 44,22MUs; Scrap Jun47
SW249 50Sq Dec42, Lindholme 14Mar46, SOC 26Mar46
SW250 1666CU ex-32MU Dec44, 5MU Sep45, Scrap Jun47
SW251 44Sq(KM ·X) Dec44, Missing 2/3Feb45
SW252 1668CU, Damaged 20/21Mar45, SOC 21Dec45
SW253 50Sq Dec44, RAE Aug45, 5MU Oct45, Scrap Mar48
SW254 619Sq Dec44, Missing 11Apr45
SW255 405,467,617,106Sqs; Lindholme Jan46, SOC Jun46
SW256 1661CU,49Sq,57Sq, Lindholme Jan46, SOC 20Feb46
SW257 1662CU Jan45, 1667CU Mar45, 38MU Oct45, Scrap May47
SW258 1669CU Dec44, 1653CU Mar45, 20MU May46, SS(CC) May47
SW259 156,467,97Sqs; Near East, Scrap Oct46
SW260 582,405(LQ ·E),467,207(EM ·Q)Sqs; Scrap Jun47
SW261 50Sq Jan45, 83Sq Mar46, Scrap Jan47
SW262 50Sq Jan45, 83Sq Mar46, 5MU, Scrap Oct46
SW263 467Sq 4Jan45, 35Sq,207Sq; 5,20MUs; SS Aug47
SW264 50Sq Jan45, Lindholme Mar46, SOC Mar46
SW265 49,106(ZN ·O),7(MG ·D)Sqs; 39MU, Scrap Oct46
SW266 35,156,35,207Sqs; 22MU Mar46, Scrap Jun47
SW267 SIU; 90,186,218Sqs; 1BDU, 22MU, SS(CC) May47
SW268 463Sq Jan45, 22MU Oct45, Scrap May47
SW269 218Sq(HA ·R), 7Sq Aug45; 54,38MUs; Scrap May47
SW270 189Sq(CA·O), Lindholme Jan46, 5MU, Scrap Jan47
SW271 626(UM ·L),101,300Sqs; 15MU, Scrap May47
SW272 SIU; 90,186,218Sqs; 5MU Aug45, Scrap Jan47
SW273 300Sq(BH ·E),433Sq; 38MU, Scrap Aug47
SW274 49,619,9Sqs; Lindholme, 22MU, Scrap Jun47
SW275 SIU; 90,186,218Sqs; 5MU Aug45, Scrap May47
SW276 576Sq Jan-Jun45, 22MU Oct45, SOC Mar47
SW277 9Sq Jan45, 61Sq Feb45, Damaged on ground 24Feb45
SW278 166Sq Jan45, Crashed in Bristol Channel 3Jul45
SW279 626Sq Jan45, 300Sq Feb45, Near East, Scrap Jan47

Serial Range SW283—SW316   **Lancaster B.I/III**

34 Lancasters ordered from Armstrong Whitworth Aircraft and delivered from May 1945 as Mk. I or III as detailed:

SW283 III Conv ASR/GRIII, 210Sq, SMR(H ·Q), Scrap May57
SW284 III Conv ASR/GRIII, 120Sq, 236OCU, SMR, SS Scrap 56
SW285 III Conv ASR/GRIII, 236OCU,SMR(V ·H), Crash 8Mar55
SW286 III Conv ASR/GRIII,236OCU(K7·L),SMR,Crash28Mar53
SW287 III Conv ASR/GRIII, 37Sq Apr50, 38MU, SS Jan57
SW288 III Conv ASR/GRIII, 38Sq(RL ·G) (RL ·P), Sold
SW289 III Conv ASRIII, AAEE, Conv GRIII; 37,39Sqs; SOC Aug53
SW290-1 III Conv ASRIII, 179Sq, ASWDU, Wrecked 20Mar/19 Apr47
SW292 III 5MU, Conv ASRIII, Middle East May46, SOC Jul49
SW293 III Conv ASRIII,37Sq,Conv GRIII,203Sq,SMR,SS May57
SW294 III Conv ASR/GRIII; 224,203Sqs; Scrap Jun50
SW295 III Conv ASR/GRIII; 38,37Sqs; Became 6762M at 12STT
SW296 I MUs,149Sq(OJ ·U), Mod.PRI, 82Sq, SS(JD) Feb55
SW297 I 38MU, Mod PRI, 38MU, Became WU.02
SW298 I (FE); 38,32,15MUs, Near East, Scrap Nov54
SW299 I (FE), MUs, 149Sq(OJ ·U), Near East, Scrap Dec49
SW300 I (FE); 10,22,32,15MUs; Near East, Scrap Nov54
SW301 I (FE); 5,32,15MUs; Near East, Scrap Nov54
SW302 I (FE); 46,32,9,15MUs; 82Sq; Scrap Jul53
SW303 I (FE); 38,32MUs; 207Sq Jul46, Scrap Sep48
SW304 I (FE), Mod.PRI, 82Sq, Crash Eastleigh burnt 28May47

SW305 I (FE), 38,32MUs; 149Sq(OJ·V), Scrap 13Dec49
SW306 I (FE), MUs, BCIS, 230OCU, Wrecked 22Nov48
SW307 I (FE), 46MU Jun45, Scrap 6Feb48
SW308 I (FE), MUs, BCIS, No.1803 Egyptian A.F., Jul50
SW309 I (FE), MUs; 149,90Sqs; 39MU, Scrap Mar48
SW310 I (FE), 15MU Jun45, 38MU May46, SS(JD) Sep51
SW311 I (FE), 46MU, 83Sq(OL·B), 38MU, SS(JD) Sep51
SW312 I (FE); 20,32,15MUs; Near East, Scrap Nov54

Adder engine in rear of SW342, 1952.

SW313 I (FE), 35Sq(TL·B), 230OCU, No.1808 Egypt A.F. Nov50
SW314 I (FE); 46,32,9MUs; SS Apr48
SW315 I (FE), 35Sq(TL·A), 230OCU, 115Sq, Scrap Mar49
SW316 I (FE); 15,32,15MUs; Scrap Oct52

Serial Range SW319—SW377   **Lancaster B.III**
47 Lancasters ordered from A. V. Roe (Yeadon) and delivered from June to September 1945 with Merlin 224 engines

SW319 38MU, Conv ASR/GRIII, 210Sq, Crashed 18Mar50
SW320 MUs, Conv ASR/GRIII, 210Sq,15MUJul53,SS(ERM)Sep56
SW321-2 Held in MUs from July45, Sold as Scrap 1949
SW323 46MU, Middle East Dec45-Jul46, 10MU, SS Feb49
SW324 Conv ASR/GRIII, 210Sq, SMR(H·A) 1957, Scrap May57
SW325 Conv ASR/GRIII, 38Sq, SOC Middle East Nov52
SW326 Conv ASRIII,ASWDU,236OCU(K7·LD) Crashed 17Feb48
SW327 Conv ASR/GRIII, 236OCU,SMR(N·H) Jul51,Scrap Sep56
SW328 38MU 9Jul45, Became 6761M at 10STT Aug50
SW329 46,22MUs; Conv ASRIII,224Sq,203Sq Nov47, Scrap Jul50
SW330 38MU,Conv ASR/GRIII,JASS Mar51, 20MU, Scrap Jul56

Late production Lancaster in the SW range.

SW331-3 46MU Jul45, Sold as Scrap Nov49
SW334 Conv ASR/GRIII, Flt Refuelling,SMR Oct51, Scrap May55
SW335 46MU Jul45, Sold as Scrap Nov49
SW336 Conv ASR/GRIII,37Sq Apr59,38MU Mar52,SS(BA)Jul56
SW337 38MU, Conv ASRIII, 203Sq Jul46, Scrap Nov49
SW338 Conv ASR/GRIII,236OCU Mar51, SMR Sep51, SS Sep56
SW339 15,218MUs; Mid. East Dec45-May46,20MU,SS(CC) May47
SW340 15MU,38MU, ECFS Jun46, 49MU Aug48, Scrap Nov48
SW341 15MU,Middle East Dec45-Jun46, 5MU, Scrap Mar48
SW342 Flight Refuelling Sep45; Air Service Training, Hamble Mar47; Armstrong Siddeley Motors Jan49, Scrap Jun56
SW343 10,218Sqs; Mid. East Dec45-Jun46; 39MU; 2MPRD Jun47
SW344 Conv ASR/GRIII, MEAF, 37Sq, Apr51, Crash 28Jan53
SW345 10,218MUs; Middle East Dec45-Jun46, 10MU, Scrap Sep47
SW358 & SW360 10MU Aug45, Sold to Shoeburyness Apr51
SW359 10MU, Middle East Dec45-Jun46, 38MU, Scrap Mar48
SW361 10MU, Conv ASRIII, 6OTU, 236OCU, Crashed 23Aug48
SW362-3 10MU, Conv ASR/GRIII, 236OCU 1948, Scrap 1949/50
SW364 10MU, Conv ASR/GRIII, 203Sq, Scrap Sep50
SW365 Conv ASR/GRIII, 210Sq, 203Sq Mar52, SMR(H·W), SS May57
SW366 Conv ASR/GRIII,SMR(H·Z) Jun51,22MU,SS(BA) May57
SW367 Conv ASR/GRIII,210Sq Jan50,SMR Aug53,SS May57
SW368 Conv ASR/GRIII; 203,210 Sqs;38Sq May53,38 MU,SS Jul56
SW369 Conv ASR/GRIII,224Sq,JASS Flt,20MU,SS Jul56
SW370 Conv ASR/GRIII,ASWDU,JASS,SMR,210Sq(L),SSMay57
SW371 Conv ASRIII, ASWDU, JASS(C), Crashed 14Aug47
SW372 Conv ASR/GRIII,38Sq 1950,37Sq(C) 1952, Scrap Oct53
SW373 Conv ASRIII, 210Sq, Conv GRIII, 210Sq, Crashed7Feb50
SW374 Conv ASR/GRIII, 38Sq Mar49, SOC Jun53
SW375 38Sq (RL·M), SOC Aug50
SW376 SMR(H·Y), SOC Aug56
SW377 5MU, Conv ASR/GRIII, 203Sq, Scrap May51

Serial Range SX558—SX921   **Lancaster** (not built)
280 Lancasters ordered from Vickers Armstrong (Chester) as: SX558-589, SX605-648, SX663-698, SX713-759, SX772-813, SX828-863 and SX879-921. Cancelled before production commenced.

Serial Range SX923—SZ493   **Lincoln B.II**
350 Lancasters ordered from Armstrong Whitworth Aircraft of which 60 only were delivered as Lincoln B.II SX923-958 and SX970-993 from May 1947 to August 1949. Cancelled numbers were: SX994-999, SZ113-158, SZ172-215, SZ228-259, SZ275-306, SZ319-363, SZ380-415, SZ429-471 and SZ488-493.

Serial Range TG758—TG799   **Lancaster** (not built)
150 Lancasters ordered from Austin Motors in 1944 as TG758-799, TG813-856, TG870-908 and TG921-945 and cancelled before production commenced.

Serial Range TW647—TW911.   **Lancaster B.I (FE)**
75 Lancaster B.I ordered from Armstrong Whitworth Aircraft and delivered from Baginton, Bitteswell and South Marston as ordered with Merlin 24 engines initially installed from June 21st to March 24th, 1946, to MUs, to await conversion by Short & Harland or A.W.A. to F.E. standard, which was effected during 1946-47.

TW647 MUs,35Sq Dec46, Crashed and burnt 11Nov47
TW648 46,48MUs; Converted Aug51, Became WU.28 *Aéronavale*
TW649 46MU, AWA Feb46, 39MU Mar46, Scrap Mar48
TW650 46MU, AWA Feb46, 5MU Apr46, Scrap Dec46
TW651 15MU,38MU, Became WU·27 of *Aéronavale*
TW652 Various MUs, MEAF, 683Sq, SS Nov54
TW653 MUs, Became 6506M at No. 2 Radio School
TW654 MUs, Mod PRI, 82Sq Nov48-Mar50, SS Jan55
TW655 46MU, 38MU, Became WU.17 of *Aéronavale*
TW656 35Sq Nov45, 230OCU, No. 1809 Egyptian A.F. Nov50
TW657 32MU, 35Sq(TL·C), To Shoeburyness Jun51
TW658 MUs, Mod PRI, 82Sq 4May47, Broken up Jan49
TW659 35(TL·M), 7(MG·D),214Sqs; Scrap Aug50
TW660 35(TL·N),7(MG·F),35,49Sqs; Scrap Jun50
TW661 32MU,TFU,G-H Survey Mk.II fitted for 82Sq, Scrap Feb51
TW662 MUs, Conv PRI, 82Sq May50, 5MU Sep52, SS Jan55
TW663 207,149(OJ·X)Sqs; 38MU, Near East, SS Feb55
TW664 5MU for overseas replacement, Sold Avro Aug52
TW665 MUs, Mod PRI Oct50, Near East 1953, Scrap Jan55
TW666 20MU, Short & Harland, 20MU, SS(IA) Apr51

TW667 MUs, 230OCU, Crashed 14Dec48, Broken up Mar49
TW668 38,32,5MUs; 230OCU, 148Sq, 15MU, SS Aug50
TW669 (FE) AWA May46, Benson Jan51, 38MU, Near East 1953,
  Special photography aircraft, SS(JD) Feb55
TW670 15,38,32,9MUs; SS Apr48
TW671 38MU Jul45, Mod PRI, 32Sq, Crashed 12Jan51
TW858 MUs, CSE Watton Dec46, Scrap Nov50
TW859 MUs, Conv PRI Jul50, MEAF Aug52, 683Sq, Scrap Feb55
TW860 MUs, 207Sq Jul46, 214Sq Oct48, 15MU, SS Aug50
TW861 MUs,CSE Watton Jan47, Near East Sep53, SS(JD) Feb55
TW862 MUs, Upwood May52, Near East Sep53, SS(CC) Dec54
TW863 15,38,15MUs; Near East Sep53, SS Nov54
TW864 32MU, CSE Mar47, Near East Sep53, SS(CC) Aug54
TW865 35Sq(TL ·N) (TL ·A), 149Sq Sep49, Scrap Dec49
TW866 MUs, Near East Sep53, SS(JD) Feb55
TW867 15,32MUs; RWE Oct46, Scrap Jun50
TW868 MUs, Conv PRI, 82Sq, SS Oct53
TW869 35(TL ·G),115,138,207,148Sqs; SS Aug50
TW870 35Sq(TL ·R), Crashed at Gander 29Aug46
TW871 49Sq(EA ·K), 214Sq Oct46, Used as target 1951.
TW872 35(TL ·D),214,7Sqs; Wrecked 24Feb48
TW873 7Sq Apr46, 214Sq Oct46, Crashed 23Apr47
TW878 35Sq(TL ·H), 214Sq Feb49, 20MU, SS Jan50
TW879 32MU Nov45, 35Sq Feb46, Crashed 17Apr47
TW880 35Sq(TL ·F); Damaged, Shallufa, Feb49; 15MU, SS Aug50
TW881 149Sq, 90Sq(WP ·Y), 39MU, SS(IA) Nov49
TW882 35Sq(TL ·O), 214Sq Oct46, 5MU, SS Jan51
TW883 49Sq(EA ·N), Loaned Mayflower Film Group 1950 SS Mar55
TW884 541Sq Mod PRI, 82Sq(B), Scrap Jul50
TW885 149Sq(OJ ·Y), 115Sq Nov49, 15MU, Scrap Aug50
TW886 149Sq,115Sq Dec46, Damaged Mar48, Scrap May48
TW887 149Sq(OJ ·T), 230OCU, 207Sq, 5MU, SS Nov50
TW888-9 32MU Mar46, 9MU Jun46, SS Apr48
TW890 35Sq, BCIS, 230OCU, No. 1807 Egyptian A.F. Oct50
TW891 35(TL ·L),207,138(NF ·K),49Sqs; 20MU, SS Jan50
TW892 35Sq(TL ·L), 7Sq(MG ·B), 20MU, SS(JD) Nov50
TW893 115,138Sqs; 230OCU, No. 1804 Egyptian A.F. Aug50
TW894 149Sq(OJ ·Z), 90Sq Oct46, Near East, SS(IA) Nov49
TW895 32MU Nov45, 7Sq May46, 148Sq Oct46, Wrecked 16Feb49
TW896 149Sq(OJ ·V), 230OCU, Became 6638M
TW897 207,138,148Sqs; Damaged by gale Mar47, SS Aug50
TW898 32MU; 7,148,7,148Sqs; 15MU, SS Feb50
TW899 82Sq Jan46, Modified PRI, 82Sq, SOC Nov50
TW900 207Sq, 115Sq (KO ·M), To Shoeburyness Apr51
TW901 541Sq, Mod PRI, 'B' Flt, 82Sq; Became 6899M Spitalgate
TW902 32MU, 115Sq(KO ·G) May46, Burnt 31Jan48
TW903 49Sq(EA ·H), Near East Sep53, SS Nov54
TW904 32MU, 82Sq, Modified PRI, 82Sq(E), Scrap Feb50
TW905 32MU, Modified PRI, 82Sq(G), Scrap Jun50
TW906 149Sq(OJ ·W), To Near East Sep43, SS(JD) Feb55
TW907 32MU, 49Sq(EA ·L), 5MU, Scrap Jan51
TW908 7,148Sqs; Lost on flight 9Nov49
TW909 32MU, 35Sq Nov47, 9MU, SS(JD) Aug48
TW910 32MU Feb46, 207Sq Jul46, 115Sq Aug49, Scrap Mar50
TW911 Delivered 7Mar46, Used as Python test-bed, SOC Jan53

Serial Range TW915—TW929   Lancaster B.I/B.I (FE)
15 Lancasters transferred unassembled from Metropolitan
Vickers to Vickers Armstrong (Chester) for completion which
commenced June 5th, 1945, and was effected August 13th, 1945.
Built as B.Is with Merlin 24 engines initially installed, all except
TW923-6 and TW929 were delivered to Armstrong Whitworth in
the second half of 1946 for conversion to B.I (FE).

TW915 20,38MUs; Became WU.42 of *Aéronavale* in 1952
TW916 20,38,32,9MUs; MEAF Nov50, 683Sq, SS Nov54
TW917 15,32MUs; CSE Feb47, Near East Sep43, SS(CC) Jun54
TW918 15,38MUs; Became WU.45 of *Aéronavale*
TW919 10,38,32MUs; CSE Feb47, Near East Oct52, Scrap Nov52
TW920-2 10,38MUs; Became WU.47/WU.48/WU.37 *Aéronavale*
TW923 39MU, Wigtown Dec47, RAE Jan48, SS Sep50
TW924 39MU, CSE Watton Nov46, 10MU Nov47, Scrap Mar48
TW925-6 Held in MUs, Scrap Mar48/May47
TW927-8 38MU Aug45, Became WU.53/WU.41 of *Aéronavale* 1952
TW929 38MU,CSEJun47,20MUJul47,Became6425M,SS(JD)Dec49

Lancaster G.R.3 TW669 special photography aircraft.

Serial Range TX263—TX290   Lancaster B.III/Lancastrian C.IV
19 Lancasters ordered from A. V. Roe (Yeadon) delivered as
11 Lancaster B.III with Merlin 224 engines from September 8th to
October 31st, 1945, and 8 Lancastrian C.IV delivered from March
8th to April 2nd, 1946.

TX263 38MU, Conv ASRIII, Middle East Jul46, 38Sq, SS Aug50
TX264 Conv ASR/GRIII, 120Sq, Lost at Sea 14Mar51
TX265 Conv ASR/GRIII, 236OCU(K7 ·LF),SMR,Crashed22Dec53
TX266 39MU, Conv ASRIII, 236OCU, JASS May48, Crash 2Jun48
TX267 Conv ASR/GRIII, 5MU, MEAF, 38Sq, 15MU, Scrap Sep56
TX268 Conv ASR/GRIII, 38MU, 236OCU(K7 ·O),SMR, SS Oct46
TX269 Conv ASRIII, 218MU, MEAF, 38Sq, Crashed 4Sep48
TX270 Conv ASR/GRIII. MEAF Jun49, 37Sq,38Sq, Crash 28Jan53
TX271 Conv ASR/GRIII,236OCU(K7 ·LD)Feb48,Crashed 2Nov49
TX272 Conv ASR/GRIII, MEAF Mar51, 38Sq, SOC Feb53
TX273 Conv ASR/GRIII, MEAF Nov49, 38Sq, SS Sep56
TX283-290 8 Lancastrian C.IV delivered from March to April, 1946

A.T.C. cadets awaiting a trip in a Lancastrian.

Serial VB673   Lancastrian C.I
Prototype conversion of Lancaster airframe for B.O.A.C.
Lancastrian for which Certificate of Airworthiness was issued
February 7th, 1945, as G-AGLF.

Serials VD238-VD253   Lancastrian C.I
Lancaster airframes earmarked for completion as Lancastrian I
of which only VD238, VD241 and VD253 were converted as
G-AGLS, G-AGLT and G-AGLU respectively.

Serial Range VF137—VF167   Lancastrian I
28 Lancastrians ordered for B.O.A.C. as VF137-156 and VF160-
167 and became respectively : G-AGMR/MS/MT/MU/MV/MW/
MX/MY/MJ/MK/ML/MM/MO/MP/MA/MB/MC/MD/ME and
G-AGMF/MG/MH/LV/LW/LX/LY/LZ.

Serials VH737 and VH742   Lancastrian
2 Special Lancastrians, of which VH737 was originally airframe
numbered PD176, delivered August 8th and October 31st, 1945.

Serial Range VL967—VL986   Lancastrian C.II
20 Lancastrian C.II ordered from A. V. Roe (Manchester) in
February 1945 and delivered from Woodford January to March
1946 following the VM701-738 batch. Merlin 24 engines initially
installed. VL982-VL986 cancelled.

VM701—VM738   Lancastrian C.II
18 Lancastrian C.II ordered from A. V. Roe (Manchester) in
February 1945 and delivered as VM701-704 and VM725-738 at
Woodford from October 1945 to January 1946 prior to the VL
batch above. Merlin 24 engines initially installed.

WD122—WD149   Lincoln B.2
21 Lincoln B.2 ordered from A.W.A. and delivered from May
1950 to March 1951 as WD122-133 and WD141-149.

Left to right, top to bottom : "The Great Zeke" and Flt. Lt. A. S. MacWilliams, D.F.C., captain of a mixed Scottish/Australian crew. Sgt. F. Hartley, of No. 218 Squadron at Chedburgh, and the symbol on R5565 "Old Dragon" in 1942. FM136, in 1962 with markings based on a photograph of R5689 in 1942, being placed on a plinth at Calgary. A Canadian navigator, Flg. Off. E. N. Hooke, of Toronto (right), Plt. Off. E. T. Jones (left) viewing through their damaged Lancaster.

Left to right, top to bottom : RF389, which commenced service as one of the only two Lincolns in No. 75 Squadron, was coded AA.A on a standard Tiger Force finish. Symbolic of the end of the Lincoln era is this view of a dumped Lincoln. Modifications to Lincolns included a transparent H2S housing which gave the impression of an under-turret, the extended nose of the M.R.31 represented here by R.A.A.F. Lincoln A73-62 and an R.A.F. B.2 with an additional astrodome in place of a mid-upper turret.

Four establishments that were favourite off-duty haunts of thousands of aircrew members. The Saracen's Head at Lincoln in its pre-war setting; the George Hotel, Grantham, patronized by the " Dam-busters "; the White Hart at Newark and Betty's Bar, York. At Betty's, cakes were sold at the corner entrance, and in the bar is the original mirror inscribed with the autographs of hundreds of aircrew.

Glossary

A.A.	Anti-aircraft	Flt.	Flight	Oboe	Ground-controlled Blind-bombing Radar System
A. & A.E.E. (AAEE in Log)	Aircraft and Armament Experimental Establishment.	Flt. Lt.	Flight Lieutenant	Ops (Log)	Operational Sorties
		Flt. Sgt.	Flight Sergeant	O.T.U.	Operational Training Unit
A.C.	Aircraftman	F.N.	Fraser Nash (Turret)	(OTU in Log)	
A.C.M.	Air Chief Marshal	ft.	Feet		
A.F.C.	Air Force Cross	ft./min.	Feet per minute	PEE (Log)	Proof and Experimental Establishment
A.F.E.E. (AFEE in Log)	Airborne Forces Experimental Establishment	gall.	Gallons	P.F.F.	Pathfinder Force
A.G.L.T.	Automatic Gun-laying (Turrets)	gall/hr.	Gallons per hour	Plt. Off.	Pilot Officer
		Gardening	Mining in enemy waters	P.O.W.	Prisoner of War
AGS (Log)	Air Gunnery School	G.C.B.	Knight Grand Cross of the Bath	P.R.	Photographic Reconnaissance
Air Cde.	Air Commodore				
A.M. Spec.	Air Ministry Specification	GEE	Navigating Device	P.R.U.	Photographic Reconnaissance Unit
A.M.W.D.	Air Ministry Works Department	G-H	Radar Blind Bombing System		
		G.P.	General Purpose	R.A.A.F.	Royal Australian Air Force
A.O.C.	Air Officer Commanding	Gp. Capt.	Group Captain	R.A.E. (RAE in Log)	Royal Aircraft Establishment
A.P.	Armour Piercing	G.R. (GR in Log)	General Reconnaissance		
ASWDU (Log)	Anti-submarine Warfare Development Unit			R.A.F.	Royal Air Force
		H2S	Airborne Radar Navigational and Target Location Device	Radar	**R**adio **D**etection **A**nd **R**anging
A.S.R. (ASR in Log)	Air Sea Rescue				
				R.C.A.F.	Royal Canadian Air Force
A.S.V.	Air to surface vessel	H.C.Flt.	Heavy Conversion Flight	R.E.A.F.	Royal Egyptian Air Force
A.T.A.	Air Transport Auxiliary	H.C.U.	Heavy Conversion Unit	Rebecca	Radar Navigational Aid
A.T.C.	Air Training Corps	HDA (Log)	High Duty Alloys	R.N.A.S.	Royal Naval Air Service
A.V.M.	Air Vice-Marshal	H.P.	Handley Page	R.N.Z.A.F.	Royal New Zealand Air Force
A.V.Roe	(Sir) Alliott Verdon-Roe	h.p.	Horse Power		
A.W.A. (AWA in Log)	Armstrong Whitworth Aircraft	IA (Log)	International Alloys	R-R (Log)	Rolls-Royce
				RS (Log)	Radio School
BA (Log)	British Aluminium Ltd.	in.	Inch or Inches	RWE (Log)	Radio Warfare Establishment
B.B.C.	British Broadcasting Corporation	JASS (Log)	Joint Anti-submarine School		
				S.A.A.F.	South African Air Force
BBU (Log)	Blind Bombing Unit	JD (Log)	John Dale Ltd.	S.B.A.C.	Society of British Aircraft Constructors (now Society of British Aerospace Companies)
BCIS (Log)	Bomber Command Instructors' School				
		K.B.E.	Knight Commander of the Order of the British Empire		
BDU (Log)	Bomber Development Unit				
B & G	Bombing and Gunnery				
B.E.A.C.	British European Airways Corporation	K.C.B.	Knight Commander of the Bath	SIU (Log)	Special Installation Unit
				SMR (Log)	School of Maritime Reconnaissance
B.O.A.C.	British Overseas Airways Corporation	L.A.C.	Leading Aircraftman		
		lb.	Pounds (weight)	SOC (Log)	Struck Off Charge
B.S.A.A.C.	British South American Airways Corporation	lb./sq.ft.	Pounds per square foot	(Spec)	Special
		L.F.S. (LFS in Log)	Lancaster Finishing School	Sq (Log)	Squadron
C.	Freighter or Passenger Aircraft			sq. ft.	Square feet
		Loran	**L**ong **R**ange Navigational Aid	Sqn. Ldr.	Squadron Leader
C.B.E.	Commander of the Order of the British Empire			SS (Log)	Sold as Scrap
				STT (Log)	School of Technical Training
CC (Log)	Coley & Co.	M.C.	Medium capacity (bomb)		
CGS (Log)	Central Gunnery School	MEAF (Log)	Middle East Air Force	TDU (Log)	Torpedo Development Unit
C.O.	Commanding Officer	M.I.Mech.E.	Member of the Institute of Mechanical Engineers		
Con.Flt (Log)	Conversion Flight			T.F.U. (TFU in Log)	Telecommunications Flying Unit
Conv (Log)	Converted	min.	Minutes		
CSE (Log)	Central Signals Establishment	Mk.	Mark	T.T.	Target Tug
		mm.	Millimetres	U.	Unmanned
CU (Log)	Conversion Unit	mod.	Modified	U.K.	United Kingdom
cub.ft.	Cubic feet	Monica	Airborne Radar Warning Device	U.S.A.A.F.	United States Army Air Force
D-Day	The Day, June 6th, 1944	M.O.S.	Ministry of Supply		
Deg	Degrees	MOTU (Log)	Marine Operational Training Unit	V.H.F.	Very High Frequency
D.F.C.	Distinguished Flying Cross			V.I.P.	Very Important Person (for use of)
D.F.M.	Distinguished Flying Medal	MPRD (Log)	Metal Produce and Recovery Depot		
D.H.	de Havilland			V-J	Victory, Japan (August 1945)
D.S.O.	Distinguished Service Order	m.p.h.	Miles per hour		
		M.R.	Maritime Reconnaissance	W.A.A.F.	Women's Auxiliary Air Force (now Women's R.A.F.)
E.A.A.S. (EAAS in Log)	Empire Air Armament School	M.U. (MU in Log)	Maintenance Unit		
EANS (Log)	Empire Air Navigational School	N.A.C.A.	National Advisory Council for Aeronautics	W.O.	Warrant Officer
				Wg. Cdr.	Wing Commander
ECFS (Log)	Empire Central Flying School	N.A.T.O.	North Atlantic Treaty Organisation	Wimpy	Slang for Wellington Aircraft
EFS (Log)	Empire Flying School	NGTE (Log)	National Gas Turbine Establishment	Window	Strips of metallised paper dropped to disrupt enemy radar defences
ERM (Log)	Enfield Rolling Mills				
ETPS (Log)	Empire Test Pilots School	NTU (Log)	Night Training Unit, P.F.F.		
F.A.A.	Fleet Air Arm			W/T	Wireless Telegraphy
FE	Far East (standard)	O.B.E.	Order of the British Empire	WU	Western Union
FIDO	Fog Investigation and Dispersal Operation			yds.	Yards

Lancaster Personalities Index

N.B. Rank is given as for the highest rank recorded in the text. Decorations are given in the text where appropriate, but are not included in this index. An asterisk denotes a photograph of the personality.

Pages

ANDERSON, Flt. Sgt., L. T. 32
Astell, Flt. Lt. W. 31
Avis, Wg. Cdr. G. G. 70

BALFOUR, Plt. Off. D. C. 66
Ball, Flg. Off. 15
Barber, Miss Margaret 80
Barlow, Flt. Lt. R. N. G. 32
Barnes, Flg. Off. 13
Baveystock, Sgt. 13
Bazalgette, Sqn. Ldr. I. W. 29, 66, *112
Bazin, Wg. Cdr. 76
Beaverbrook, Lord 10
Beckett, Wt. Off. J. F. 17
Beesley, Flt. Sgt. *87
Bennett, A.V.-M. D. C. T. 107
Bennett, Wg. Cdr. J. S. 60
Bennington, Wg. Cdr. G. W. 83
Bernadotte, Count Folke 98
Birney, L.A.C. J. 67
Boden, Flg. Off. W. 55
Bogarde, Dirk 100
Bottomley, A.V.-M. N. H. 14
Boyd, Sgt. J. 16
Boylan, Sqn. Ldr. T. H. 18-19
Brickhill, Paul 30
Brookes, Wg. Cdr. E. J. 98
Brophy, Flg. Off. G. P. 64-5
Brown, Sgt. C. H. *55
Brown, Capt. H. A. 8, 80, 101, 124
Brown, Plt. Off. J. F. *55
Brown, Flt. Sgt. K. W. 32-*3
Burghley, Lord 45
Burnett, Wg. Cdr. P. 39
Burpee, Plt. Off. L. J. 32
Byams, Mr. Guy 75
Byers, Sgt. V. A. 32

CALDER, Wg. Cdr. C. C. 84, 93
Carpenter, Flt. Lt. 70
Carr, Sqn. Ldr. W. D. 22
Carter, Sgt. G. K. 28
Carter, Gp. Capt. R. A. C. 60
Chadwick, Roy *7, *16, 30, 79, 100
Cheshire, Wg. Cdr. L. 51, 53, 64, 65, *112
Chivers, Flg. Off. M. E. 29
Churchill, Sir Winston 17, 50, 108
Clayton, Wg. Cdr. G. T. B. 119
Clifford, Sgt. C. E. W. 16
Cluff, Sgt. E. B. 16
Coad, Wg. Cdr. R. M. 26
Cochrane, A. M. Sir Ralph A. *33, 75
Cockshott, Sgt. J. B. 23
Cockshott, Sqn. Ldr. J. V. 84
Collins, Sgt. A. D. 38-9
Collins, Capt. N. 45
Connolly, Wg. Cdr. 63
Copley, Flt. Off. E. M. 45
Cowls, J. *42
Cousens, Wg. Cdr. A. G. S. 119
Crabbe, Mr. P. G. 80
Crooks, Wg. Cdr. L. 118
Crum, Wt. Off. H. V. 17
Curtin, Rt. Hon. Mr. *47
Cushing, Sgt. C. 50
Cuthbertson, Sgt. 67

DARLEY, L.A.C. A. (clearing snow off wing) *52
Davidson, Flt. Sgt. J. McN. 16
Davies, S. D. 79
Davis, Sgt. 82
Debreyne, Flg. Off. A. 64
De Baie, L.A.C. F. M. 99
Deering, Flt. Sgt. *33
Delaney, Plt. Off. D. 45
Deveral, Flt. Lt. 17
Dixon, W. A. 80

Dobson, Sir Roy 80
Duncan, Mr. B. A. 80
Dunlop-Mackensie, Flt. Lt. P. J. 73
Dunston, Flg. Off. R. C. *36-7
Durant, Mr. G. A. 81

EAGER, Plt. Off. W. H. *36
Edwards, Gp. Capt. H. I. 37
Elizabeth, H.M. Queen 15, *33
Elliott, Sgt. P. L. 23
Everest, Wg. Cdr. M. H. d'L. 95

FENNELL, Flt. Sgt. 50
Ferguson, Flt. Sgt. L. 23
Fielding, Mr. N. C. E. 80
Field-Richards, Mr. P. J. 67, 127
Finucane, Sqn. Ldr. P. C. 77
Flower, Sgt. W. H. 16
Flynn, Plt. Off. 82
Forbes, Bryan 100
Ford, Messrs. Edsell and Henry 26
Foster, Plt. Off. A. E. 23
Fowler, Flt. Lt. T. R. 127
Fraser, Sgt. G. 85
Fraser, Mr. T. 80

GARWELL, Flg. Off. A. J. 17
Gaunt, 2/Lt. S. 36
George VI, H.M. King 15, *33
Gibson, Wg. Cdr. Guy 13, *19, 21, 33, 30-*3, *115
Gloucester, H.R.H. Duke of 47
Gomm, Wg. Cdr. G. L. 34
Gordon, Flg. Off. W. C. 47
Gossell, Flg. Off. A. R. 99
Gowrie, Sgt. *33
Greenacre, Flt. Lt. E. 39
Greig, Nordhal 51
Grosse, Flt. Sgt. J. 45

HALE, L.A.C. J. *42
Harris, A.C.M. Sir Arthur 29, *33, 50-1, 79, 93, *112
Harris, Sqn. Ldr. J. D. 18
Hartley, Sgt. F. *212
Harvey, Flg. Off. 76
Harvey, Flt. Sgt. D. B. 51
Hatton, Mr. C. L. 81
Haynes, Flt. Sgt. O. 21
Haynes, Wg. Cdr. P. 119
Hazeldon, Sqn. Ldr. H. G. 126
Head, Flt. Lt. D. G. 97
Healy, Plt. Off. F. G. 23
Hearne, Sgt. W. *42
Henshaw, Mr. Alex 80
Hewish, Flt. Lt. *36
Hook, Flg. Off. E. N. *212
Hopgood, Flt. Lt. J. V. 31
Horsley, Flg. Off. 13
Huckford, Wg. Cdr. P. D. W. 115
Hudson, Flt. Lt. E. A. 47
Hudson, Mr. S. G. 47
Hunter, Ian 100
Hutcheson, Flg. Off. J. C. 67
Hyde, Wg. Cdr. N. C. 9

ISAACSON, Flt. Lt. P. S. 45
Ivelaw-Chapman, A.C.M. Sir Ronald 63

JACKSON, Wt. Off. N. C. 53-4, *112
Jarvis, Flt. Sgt. K. W. 86
Jefferies, Flt. Sgt. J. S. 39
Jones, Plt. Off. E. T. *212
Joslin, Sgt. P. C. 21

KAN, Flt. Sgt. A. E. 35
Kay, Mr. J. A. R. 80
Kelsall, Mr. Alan 10
Kerr, Bill 100

King, Sgt. 13
Kingsford-Smith, Wg. Cdr. R. 53
Knight, Sgt. 16
Knight, Plt. Off. L. 86
Knight, Plt. Off. L. G. 31
Kujundzic, Flg. Off. 27

LAWRENCE, Sgt. *36
Learoyd, Wg. Cdr. R.A.B. 14
Lees, Flg. Off. J. S. *55
Lefevre, Mr. 80
Leslie, Mr. A. J. 80
Lever, Wt. Off. R. 23
Levy, Flg. Off. F. 76
Lockwood, Mr. W. S. D. 80
Loginov, Col. 76

MACK, Alderman C. 100
MacWilliam, Flt. Lt. A. S. *212
Maling, Wg. Cdr. J. M. 65
Maltby, Flt. Lt. D. J. H. 31
Manser, Flg. Off. L. T. 13, *112
Marston, Sgt. R. A. 16
Martin, Wg. Cdr. C. E. 35
Martin, Flt. Lt. H. B. 31, *33, 64
Martin, Major R. P. 86
Maudsley, Sqn. Ldr. H. G. 31
McCarthy, Sqn. Ldr. J.C. 32-*3
McCarthy, Flg. Off. T. V. 47
McDonald, Flt. Sgt. *33
McGhie, Wg. Cdr. I. J. 119
McIntosh, Plt. Off. J. 37
McKinley, Wg. Cdr. D. C. 102
McLean, Flt. Sgt. *33
McLeod, Flt. Sgt. E. T. *55
McMullen, Gp. Cpt. C. C. 75
Meagher, Sgt. A. 26
Middleton, Sgt. R. 37
Mills, Sgt. 13
Mullock, Major 34
Munro, Flt. Lt. K. L. 32
Murdoch, Sgt. A. F. 16
Murray, Plt. Off. E. J. 52
Mycock, Wt. Off. 17
Mynarski, Plt. Off. A. C. 65, *112

NAYLOR, Sgt. 13
Neilson, Flt. Lt. R. S. McF. 45
Nettleton, Sqn. Ldr. J. D. 14, 17, 35, *112, 122
Norris, Sgt. J. W. 39
Nutting, Wt Off. S. H. 51

OANCIA, Sgt. *33
O'Brien, Sgt. *33
Ottley, Plt. Off. W. H. T. 32
Overgaauw, Flt. Lt. 66
Ower, Sgt. K. A. 47
Oxland, Gp. Capt. R. D. 7

PAGE, Flt. Sgt. A. F. 45
Palmer, A. C. 20
Palmer, Sqn Ldr. R. A. M. 70, *112
Pangborn, Mr. Clyde 45
Pattison, Wg. Cdr. R. V. L. 60
Pearson, Sgt. R. E. *55
Peate, Flt. Sgt. R. 34
Pegg, Mr. A. J. 138
Petts, Sgt. *36
Picton, Flt. Lt. R. W. 52
Pigeon, Sgt. *33
Powell, Wg. Cdr. H. P. 133
Power, Mrs. C. G. 38
Purnell, Sqn. Ldr. 69

RADCLIFFE, Flt. Sgt. *33
Reid, Flt. Lt. W. 39, *112
Renwick, Sir Robert 9
Rhodes, Sgt. G. T. 15, 17
Rice, Plt. Off. G. 32
Richardson, Sqn. Ldr. 21

Richie, Flt. Lt. A. V. 45
Robinson, L.A.C. J. E. *42
Rogerson, Harold 42
Rose, Plt. Off. B. A. 86
Ross, Air Cdre. and Mrs. A. D. 81
Ross, Plt. Off. H. J. 29
Ross, Wt. Off. N. R. 35
Ruskell, Flt. Lt. K. 97

SAINT-SMITH, Flt. Sgt. J. A. 46
Salmon, P. 7
Salter, Wg. Cdr. P. S. 18
Sandford, Flt. Lt. R. R. 17
Saunders, A. C. 16
Saward, Gp. Capt. D. 50
Searby, Flg. Off. A. L. 21
Searby, Gp. Capt. J. H. 37
Shannon, Flt. Lt. D. J. 33
Sharrard, Sgt. *36
Shaw, A. C. 16
Shearer, Flt. Lt. J. M. 63
Sherriff, Mr. R. C. 100
Sherwood, Sqn. Ldr. 17
Singer, Plt. Off. A. M. *111 (right)
Singer, Plt. Off. P. L. (left) *111
Sinclair, Sqn. Ldr. E. K. 62
Slee, Gp. Cpt. L.C. 19, 20, 22, 34
Slessor, A.V.-M. J. C. 14-15
Smith, Flg. Off. E. P. 47
Smith, Mr. F. V. 81
Smith, Wg. Cdr. M. A. 86
Smith, Wg. Cdr. W. J. *117
Smythe, Sgt. J. 51
Spencer, Cpl. C. 45
Stockton, Mr. N. 51
Stone, Sgt. *36
Strickland, Mr. George 38
Sutherland, Sgt. *33
Swales, Capt. E. 83, *112
Sullivan, Plt. Off. D. J. 62
Sylvester, Mr. William 100

TAERUM, Plt. Off. *33
Tait, Wg. Cdr. J. B. 75, *76, 77
Tayler, L.A.C. R. 67
Thomas, Wt. Off. J. E. 38
Thompson, Flt. Sgt. G. 82, *112
Thorne, Bill 7, *16
Thorne, Sqn. Ldr. G. A. 69, 85
Thrasher, Flt. Sgt. *33
Tickle, Flt. Sgt. H. 46
Tindall, Flg. Off. G. H. 47
Townsend, Flt. Sgt. W. C. 32

VANNER, Sgt. *36
Vernon-Brown, Air Cdre. 44

WAGHORN, Gp. Capt. 90
Wakeford, Flt. Lt. *35
Walker, Flg. Off. *33
Walker, Ronald 66
Wallis, Dr. Barnes 30, 64
Warren-Smith, Flt. Sgt. L. 16
Watts, Flt. Sgt. 76
Weeks, Flt. Sgt. *33
West, Mr. W. E. 75
Whamond, Flt. Lt. W. N. 23
White, Wt. Off. 39
Whittle, Air Cdre. F. 96
Whitworth, Gp. Capt. J. C. 100
Wilkins, Flg. Off. G. A. 15
Williams, Sqn. Ldr. 76
Williams, Sgt. K. T. C. 52
William, Mr. E. 95
Wincott, Gp. Capt. C. V. 45
Withey, Cpl. R. T. *42
Woodhams, Mr. H. M. 80
Wray, Air Cdre. A. M. 60

YOUNG, Flg. Off. 47
Young, Sqn. Ldr. H. M. 31-2

ZAMMITT, Sgt. 70

216